Annual Report of the Board of Regents

of the

SMITHSONIAN

INSTITUTION

PUBLICATION 4478

Showing the Operations, Expenditures, and Condition of the

Institution for the Year Ended June 30

1961

U.S. GOVERNMENT PRINTING OFFICE

WASHINGTON : 1962

LETTER OF TRANSMITTAL

Smithsonian Institution,
Washington, December 29, 1961.

To the Congress of the United States:

In accordance with section 5593 of the Revised Statutes of the United States, I have the honor, on behalf of the Board of Regents, to submit to Congress the annual report of the operations, expenditures, and condition of the Smithsonian Institution for the year ended June 30, 1961.

Respectfully,

Leonard Carmichael, *Secretary.*

II

CONTENTS

GENERAL APPENDIX

LIST OF PLATES

THE SMITHSONIAN INSTITUTION

June 30, 1961

UNITED STATES NATIONAL MUSEUM

Director.—A. Remington Kellogg.
Registrar.—Helena M. Weiss.

MUSEUM OF NATURAL HISTORY

Director.—A. C. Smith.
Administrative Officer.—Mrs. Mabel A. Byrd.

DEPARTMENT OF ANTHROPOLOGY: T. Dale Stewart, head curator; A. J. Andrews, exhibits specialist.

Division of Archeology: W. R. Wedel, curator; Clifford Evans, Jr., G. W. Van Beek, associate curators.

Division of Ethnology: S. H. Riesenberg, curator; G. D. Gibson, E. I. Knez, associate curators; R. A. Elder, Jr., assistant curator.

Division of Physical Anthropology: T. D. Stewart, acting curator; M. T. Newman, associate curator.

DEPARTMENT OF ZOOLOGY: F. A. Chace, Jr., acting head curator.

Division of Mammals: D. H. Johnson, curator; C. O. Handley, Jr., H. W. Setzer, associate curators.

Division of Birds: H. G. Deignan, curator.

Division of Reptiles and Amphibians: Doris M. Cochran, curator.

Division of Fishes: L. P. Schultz, curator; E. A. Lachner, W. R. Taylor, associate curators.

Division of Insects: J. F. G. Clarke, curator; O. L. Cartwright, R. E. Crabill, Jr., W. D. Field, O. S. Flint, Jr., associate curators.

Division of Marine Invertebrates: F. A. Chace, Jr., curator; F. M. Bayer, T. E. Bowman, C. E. Cutress, Jr., associate curators.

Division of Mollusks: H. A. Rehder, curator; J. P. E. Morrison, associate curator.

DEPARTMENT OF BOTANY (NATIONAL HERBARIUM): J. R. Swallen, head curator.

Division of Phanerogams: L. B. Smith, curator; R. S. Cowan, E. C. Leonard, Velva E. Rudd, J. J. Wurdack, associate curators.

Division of Ferns: C. V. Morton, curator.

Division of Grasses: J. R. Swallen, acting curator; T. R. Soderstrom, assistant curator.

Division of Cryptogams: M. E. Hale, Jr., associate curator in charge; P. S. Conger, associate curator; R. R. Ireland, Jr., assistant curator.

Division of Woods: W. L. Stern, curator.

DEPARTMENT OF GEOLOGY: G. A. Cooper, head curator.

Division of Mineralogy and Petrology: G. S. Switzer, curator; P. E. Desautels, E. P. Henderson, associate curators; R. S. Clarke, Jr., chemist.

Division of Invertebrate Paleontology and Paleobotany: R. S. Boardman, associate curator in charge; P. M. Kier, Richard Cifelli, E. G. Kauffman, associate curators.

Division of Vertebrate Paleontology: C. L. Gazin, curator; Nicholas Hotton, III, associate curator; F. L. Pearce, exhibits specialist.

MUSEUM OF HISTORY AND TECHNOLOGY

Director.—F. A. Taylor.
Assistant Director.—J. C. Ewers.
Administrative officer.—W. E. Boyle.
Chief exhibits specialist.—J. E. Anglim.

In charge of Taxidermy.—W. M. Perrygo.
Assistant chief exhibits specialists.—B. S. Bory, R. O. Hower, B. W. Lawless, Jr.
DEPARTMENT OF SCIENCE AND TECHNOLOGY: R. P. Multhauf, head curator.
   Division of Physical Sciences: R. P. Multhauf, acting curator.
   Division of Mechanical and Civil Engineering: R. M. Vogel, curator in
      charge; E. A. Battison, associate curator.
   Division of Transportation: H. I. Chapelle, curator; K. M. Perry, J. H.
      White, Jr., associate curators.
   Division of Electricity: R. P. Multhauf, acting curator.
   Division of Medical Sciences: J. B. Blake, curator; S. K. Hamarneh,
      associate curator.
DEPARTMENT OF ARTS AND MANUFACTURES: P. W. Bishop, head curator.
   Division of Textiles: Grace L. Rogers, associate curator in charge.
   Division of Ceramics and Glass: P. V. Gardner, associate curator in charge.
   Division of Graphic Arts: Jacob Kainen, curator; Eugene Ostroff, F. O.
      Griffith, associate curators.
   Division of Manufactures and Heavy Industries: P. W. Bishop, acting
      curator; C. O. Houston, Jr., associate curator.
   Division of Agriculture and Forest Products: E. C. Kendall, associate
      curator in charge.
DEPARTMENT OF CIVIL HISTORY: R. H. Howland, head curator; P. C. Welsh,
   associate curator; Arlene P. Kringold, assistant curator.
   Division of Political History: W. E. Washburn, curator; Mrs. Margaret
      Brown Klapthor, associate curator; Mrs. Anne W. Murray, H. R. Collins,
      assistant curators.
   Division of Cultural History: C. Malcolm Watkins, curator; Rodris C. Roth,
      associate curator; Cynthia L. Adams, J. N. Pearce, assistant curators;
      Anthony Hathaway, junior curator.
   Division of Philately and Postal History: G. T. Turner, associate curator
      in charge; F. J. McCall, associate curator; C. H. Scheele, assistant
      curator.
   Division of Numismatics: Vladimir Clain-Stefanelli, associate curator in
      charge; Mrs. Elvira Clain-Stefanelli, associate curator.
DEPARTMENT OF ARMED FORCES HISTORY: M. L. Peterson, head curator.
   Division of Military History: E. M. Howell, curator; C. R. Goins, Jr.,
      associate curator.
   Division of Naval History: P. K. Lundeberg, associate curator in charge.

BUREAU OF AMERICAN ETHNOLOGY

Director.—F. H. H. Roberts, Jr.
Anthropologist.—H. B. Collins, Jr.
Ethnologists.—W. C. Sturtevant, W. L. Chafe.
RIVER BASIN SURVEYS.—F. H. H. Roberts, Jr., *Director;* R. L. Stephenson,
   Chief, Missouri Basin Project.

ASTROPHYSICAL OBSERVATORY

Director.—F. L. Whipple.
Assistant Director.—C. W. Tillinghast.
Astronomers.—G. A. Bakos, G. Colombo, G. H. Conant, Jr., L. Goldberg, I. G.
   Izsak, Y. Kozai, K. Lassovszky, J. Slowey, P. E. Zadunaisky.
Mathematicians.—R. E. Briggs, D. A. Lautman.
Physicists.—R. J. Davis, E. L. Fireman, F. Franklin, O. Gingerich, M. Grossi,
   P. W. Hodge, L. G. Jacchia, M. Krook, R. E. McCrosky, R. B. Riggs, Jr.,
   O. Rustgi, A. Skalafuris, R. B. Southworth, D. Tilles, C. A. Whitney.

Geodesists.—J. Rolff, G. Veis.
Geologist.—J. Wood.
TABLE MOUNTAIN, CALIF., FIELD STATION.—A. G. Froiland, *physicist.*
DIVISION OF RADIATION AND ORGANISMS:
    Chief.—W. H. Klein.
    Plant physiologists.—J. L. Edwards, V. B. Elstad, L. Loercher, L. Price.
    Biophysicist.—W. Shropshire.
    Biochemist.—M. Margulies.
    Cytogeneticist.—R. L. Latterell.
    Electronic Engineer.—J. H. Harrison.
    Instrument maker.—D. G. Talbert.

NATIONAL COLLECTION OF FINE ARTS

Director.—T. M. Beggs.
Associate curator.—Rowland Lyon.
SMITHSONIAN TRAVELING EXHIBITION SERVICE.—Mrs. Annemarie H. Pope, *Chief.*

FREER GALLERY OF ART

Director.— A. G. Wenley.
Assistant Director.—J. A. Pope.
Head curator, Near Eastern Art.—Richard Ettinghausen.
Curator, Japanese Art.—H. P. Stern.
Associate curator, Chinese Art.—J. F. Cahill.
Head curator, Laboratory.—R. J. Gettens.

NATIONAL AIR MUSEUM

Advisory Board:
    Leonard Carmichael, *Chairman.*
    Maj. Gen. Brooke Allen, U.S. Air Force.
    Rear Adm. P. D. Stroop, U.S. Navy.
    Lt. Gen. James H. Doolittle.
    Grover Loening.
Director.—P. S. Hopkins.
Head curator and historian.—P. E. Garber.
Associate curators.—L. S. Casey, W. M. Male, K. E. Newland.
Junior curator.—R. B. Meyer.

NATIONAL ZOOLOGICAL PARK

Director.—T. H. Reed.
Associate Director.— J. L. Grimmer.
Veterinarian.—James F. Wright.

CANAL ZONE BIOLOGICAL AREA

Resident Naturalist.—M. H. Moynihan.

INTERNATIONAL EXCHANGE SERVICE

Chief.—J. A. Collins.

NATIONAL GALLERY OF ART

Trustees:
    EARL WARREN, Chief Justice of the United States, *Chairman.*
    DEAN RUSK, Secretary of State.
    DOUGLAS DILLON, Secretary of the Treasury.
    LEONARD CARMICHAEL, Secretary of the Smithsonian Institution.
    F. LAMMOT BELIN.

Trustees—Continued
    JOHN HAY WHITNEY.
    CHESTER DALE.
    PAUL MELLON.
    RUSH H. KRESS.
President.—CHESTER DALE.
Vice President,—PAUL MELLON.
Secretary-Treasurer.—HUNTINGTON CAIRNS.
Director.— JOHN WALKER.
Administrator.—ERNEST R. FEIDLER.
General Counsel.—HUNTINGTON CAIRNS.
Chief Curator.—PERRY B. COTT.

* * * *

Honorary Research Associates, Collaborators, and Fellows

OFFICE OF THE SECRETARY

John E. Graf

UNITED STATES NATIONAL MUSEUM

MUSEUM OF NATURAL HISTORY

Anthropology

J. M. Campbell, Archeology.
N. M. Judd, Archeology.
H. W. Krieger, Ethnology.
Betty J. Meggers, Archeology.

F. M. Setzler, Anthropology.
H. Morgan Smith, Archeology.
W. W. Taylor, Jr., Archeology.
W. J. Tobin, Physical Anthropology.

Zoology

Doris H. Blake, Insects.
J. Bruce Bredin, Biology.
M. A. Carriker, Insects.
Ailsa M. Clark, Marine Invertebrates.
C. J. Drake, Insects.
Herbert Friedmann, Birds.
D. C. Graham, Biology.
H. H. Hobbs, Jr., Marine Invertebrates.
A. B. Howell, Mammals.
F. M. Hull, Insects.
Laurence Irving, Birds.

W. L. Jellison, Insects.
Allen McIntosh, Mollusks.
J. P. Moore, Marine Invertebrates.
C. F. W. Muesebeck, Insects.
W. L. Schmitt, Marine Invertebrates.
Benjamin Schwartz, Helminthology.
R. E. Snodgrass, Insects.
T. E. Snyder, Insects.
H. K. Townes, Insects.
Alexander Wetmore, Birds.
Mildred S. Wilson, Copepod Crustacea.

Botany

C. R. Benjamin, Fungi.
Agnes Chase, Grasses.
E. P. Killip, Phanerogams.
F. A. McClure, Grasses.

Kittie F. Parker, Phanerogams.
J. A. Stevenson, Fungi.
W. N. Watkins, Woods.

Geology

R. S. Bassler, Paleontology.
R. W. Brown, Paleobotany.
P. E. Cloud, Invertebrate Paleontology.

C. W. Cooke, Invertebrate Paleontology.
W. T. Schaller, Mineralogy.

MUSEUM OF HISTORY AND TECHNOLOGY

Exhibits

W. L. Brown.

History

Mrs. Arthur M. Greenwood, Cultural History.
E. C. Herber, History.

I. N. Hume, Cultural History.
F. W. MacKay, Numismatics.

Science and Technology

Derek J. Price.

BUREAU OF AMERICAN ETHNOLOGY

J. P. Harrington.
Sister M. Inez Hilger.

M. W. Stirling.
A. J. Waring, Jr.

ASTROPHYSICAL OBSERVATORY

C. G. Abbot.

FREER GALLERY OF ART

Oleg Grabar.
Grace Dunham Guest.

Max Loehr.
Katherine N. Rhoades.

NATIONAL AIR MUSEUM

Frederick C. Crawford.

John J. Ide.

NATIONAL ZOOLOGICAL PARK

E. P. Walker.

CANAL ZONE BIOLOGICAL AREA

C. C. Soper.

Report of the Secretary of the Smithsonian Institution

LEONARD CARMICHAEL

For the Year Ended June 30, 1961

To the Board of Regents of the Smithsonian Institution:

GENTLEMEN: I have the honor to submit a report showing the activities and condition of the Smithsonian Institution and its branches for the fiscal year ended June 30, 1961.

GENERAL STATEMENT

Just 115 years ago, Joseph Henry presented to the first Board of Regents of the Institution, at their request, a "Program of Organization of the Smithsonian Institution." While this document was being formulated, Henry was still a professor at Princeton and actively engaged in teaching and experimental work in physics. He was a man of broad influence. His eminence in science had already led his contemporaries to describe him as being next to Franklin in the list of great American physical scientists. The program that he outlined for the Smithsonian was so good that he was almost at once offered the position of Secretary of the Institution. After much hesitation he accepted the post and spent the next 32 years skillfully putting into practice and developing the plan that he had evolved.

Today, as we look at Henry's program for the Smithsonian and study the steps that he took to give it reality, we are struck by his wisdom and especially by his foresight. Before writing the basic program, Henry acquainted himself with the life and the attitudes of the distinguished English scientist, James Smithson, whose bequest established the Institution. This study led Henry to place great emphasis on the words Smithson himself had used to describe the objective of his establishment, that it should be "for the increase and diffusion of knowledge among men."

It is almost startling to note, in spite of intervening wars and many social and economic changes, that the constructive activities of the Smithsonian Institution in 1961 can still accurately be subsumed under the headings of the *increase* and *diffusion* of knowledge as directed by Smithson and as made a reality by Joseph Henry.

By means of research publications, popular publications, museum activities, lectures, international exchange of scientific documents, and a voluminous correspondence, the Institution during the current year, as in Henry's time, has effectively diffused knowledge. By investigations in a wide range of fields, the Smithsonian has also continued the research for which it has long been world-famous and that has increased the true sum of human knowledge. It can therefore be said with assurance that the current year has been outstanding in the two main activities which both Smithson and Henry saw as fundamental at the Smithsonian.

Much progress was made during the year on the new buildings that will soon help in a most basic way these great twin objectives. Construction progressed on the additional monumental building of the Institution which when completed will house and display the notable collections of the Smithsonian in the fields of history and technology. The laying of the cornerstone of this building, with appropriate ceremonies, took place on May 19. Work was also begun on the building of the long-needed East Wing of the Natural History Building. Details of these building operations are given on later pages of this report.

Good progress was also made in the continuing gradual renovation of all exhibits now displayed in existing Smithsonian buildings. It may be appropriate and useful to recapitulate here the work that has been completed in this great program since it began some eight years ago, inasmuch as such a summary has not previously been presented in any annual report of the Institution.

1. FOSSIL PLANTS AND INVERTEBRATES

The new Hall of Fossil Plants and Invertebrate Animals shows in a modern series of artistically arranged exhibits the scientific record of the early development of life on this planet. At the very beginning of the hall care is taken to show and explain what a fossil is, what animals and plants have been found as fossils, how animals become entombed in rocks, and how the geologic time scale was formed. A special case displays what may well be the oldest fossil known. Visitors see not only some of the Smithsonian's outstanding fossil preparations but also full-scale reproductions by means of colored models of typical groups of the plants and animals that lived all over the globe in the warm seas of millions of years ago. An exhibit called "Giants of the Past" shows some of the largest known invertebrate fossils. As in all modern Smithsonian exhibits, this hall displays only a small fraction of the total collections of fossil plants and invertebrates that belong to the Institution. Those selected for public display are shown in such a way as to give each visitor a vivid, interesting, and accurate introduction to the basic science of paleontology. The remaining collections in this, as in all fields, are available for study by qualified students.

2. FOSSIL FISHES AND AMPHIBIANS

The Hall of Fossil Fishes, Amphibians, and Primitive Reptiles displays selections from the Smithsonian's superb collections of these fossil creatures which represent the most primitive groups of back-boned animals. Here are many actual skeletons of some of these great ancient animals that ruled the land and the seas before modern animals evolved. This hall portrays in a particularly clear way the development of jaws and the anatomical changes related to the transition from life in water to life on the land. A habitat group illustrates for the visitor what some of these animals were actually like when they ranged the globe. A life-size diorama shows conflict between two kinds of pelycosaurs, or fin-backed reptiles, as might have happened 260 million years ago.

3. PREHISTORIC MAMMALS

In the Hall of the Age of Mammals in North America lifelike dioramas and scientifically accurate and artistically significant murals recreate a mammalian world that existed before modern man appeared. Here are shown skeletons of some of the marine and land mammals that swam, climbed, ran, or even flew millions of years ago. To give but one example, in a well-lighted case is the complete fossil skeleton of a 55-foot-long primitive whale. The remarkable series of skeletons exhibited in this hall were painstakingly collected by Smithsonian scientists in the field over many years and were then skillfully prepared for display in the museum laboratory of the Institution.

4. GEMS AND MINERALS

The Smithsonian Institution has one of the world's great collections of minerals. Competent observers declare that the Smithsonian's new Hall of Minerals is the best single exhibition of its kind in the world. The immediately adjacent Gem Room is also spoken of as the best exhibition of gems on public display in the United States. Thousands of specimens, many of them of great rarity and beauty, are featured in cases at an ideal height and so lighted as to show colors properly. The galleries are arranged so that the student of mineralogy can learn about both the crystalline structures of minerals and the chemical composition of the specimens displayed. But the hall is also significant from an esthetic and natural-history point of view for persons interested in minerals and gems as beautiful objects rather than as basic specimens for the science of mineralogy. One dramatic case shows selected minerals under ultraviolet light, which causes them to fluoresce with glows of many different colors.

Here too, by the use of a rotating disk, the radioactivity of a natural uranium ore is demonstrated.

This hall displays only 3 percent of the total Smithsonian's mineral collection, which has been gradually assembled by transfer to the Institution of minerals collected by other Government agencies, by purchases made possible by the expenditure of funds given to the Smithsonian exclusively for this purpose, and by gifts of minerals and gems by many citizens, not only of America but also of countries throughout the world. In the Gem Room in a specially constructed safe is the Hope Diamond, the largest deep blue diamond in the world. Because of its rarity and aura of romantic mystery it is of intense interest to visitors.

5. THE JADE ROOM

Immediately adjoining the Gem Hall is a room devoted to a collection of carved jade given to the Smithsonian in 1958 by the executors of the estate of the late Mrs. Maud Monel Vetlesen. This collection shows many large and beautifully carved jade objects from the 17th and 18th centuries. Many objects displayed here, such as the jade and gold scepters of old imperial China, are world famous.

Adjacent to the Jade Room is a new but still temporary display of outstanding examples of meteorites from the Institution's large collection of these natural objects that so unpredictably come to the earth from outer space.

6. LATIN AMERICAN ARCHEOLOGY

The Hall of Latin American Archeology brings together a unified range of important objects selected from the Smithsonian's extensive study collections of articles made by inhabitants of Central and South America before the coming of Columbus. The exhibits portray the wide range of early cultures in Latin America from those of simple hunting and fishing people to the high civilizations of the Incas, Mayas, and Aztecs.

The emphasis of this hall is given to cultural development and the interchange of material objects by Indians before the advent of Europeans. The great accomplishments of pre-Columbian Indians in developing a number system, a calendar, and the cultivation of plants are shown. Some of the stone sculpture is remarkably modern in its feeling and execution. Here, as in all other new Smithsonian halls, the visitor is not presented with ponderous cases of the almost endlessly repeated ceramic, stone, gold, silver, and other objects that are in the possession of the Institution. This old, so-called "visual storage," method of exhibition has for good reasons been abandoned. The objects on public display today are carefully chosen to give a coherent picture of each topic under consideration. Such general instruction cannot be conveyed to the nonexpert visitor by case after case of almost identical artifacts.

It should be added parenthetically that from the standpoint of scientific American archeology and ethnology the study collections of the Smithsonian are perhaps even more important than the collections on public display. Each year these study collections are becoming organized in a more accessible way, so that they may be used effectively by qualified research scientists.

7. NORTH AMERICAN ARCHEOLOGY

The Hall of North American Archeology displays selected objects from the collections of the Smithsonian dealing with prehistoric cultures of the Eskimo and the American Indians of the far North, the North Pacific coast, California, and the Southwest. The visitor gains a synoptic view of different styles of life of human beings in these areas of the continent in the centuries before the coming of the white man. Outstanding exhibits deal with primitive methods of quarrying, mining, making artifacts of stone, cultivating crops, and developing ornaments, household utensils, and many varieties of carved and sculptured pipes used in smoking tobacco. The objects displayed in this one new hall were selected from cataloged collections which number over 600,000 items. A second North American Indian Hall, which will show the prehistoric cultures of other North American Indians, is now being prepared for public display.

8. NATIVE PEOPLES OF THE AMERICAS

This anthropological hall shows typical examples of the life characteristic of the native peoples in both North America and South America. Large glass-sided rooms have been installed depicting outstanding patterns of behavior of particular Indian tribes from California, the Southwest, and south to the Fuegians at the lowest tip of South America. Here full-scale figures prepared under the direction of expert physical anthropologists and modeled by skillful sculptors illustrate ways of life considered by anthropologists to be of special significance in relation to each group represented. Some of these world-famous models have been shown in older exhibits at the Smithsonian for many years, but before the development of the present modern, well-lighted, well-organized presentations many of them were not exhibited to best advantage. The present-day Smithsonian staff owes a debt of gratitude to their skillful and devoted predecessors who as much as 60 years ago created these scientifically correct figures that can now for the first time be displayed adequately. In this hall, also, by means of small dioramas, other typical phases of general life of the Indians of the Caribbean, of California, and of other regions of the continent are portrayed.

9. INDIAN AND ESKIMO ARTS AND CUSTOMS

The American Indian Hall dealing with the Eskimo and with the Indians of the Eastern woodlands, the Great Plains, and the North Pacific coast differs markedly from the one just described. In this hall or series of halls are displayed notable items from the Smithsonian's vast study collections which preserve for scientists hundreds of thousands of objects or artifacts of the tribes here considered. Many of the objects shown here in the beautifully lighted and carefully labeled cases are unduplicated elsewhere in the world. Today in the art world much is said of the importance of primitive sculpture and painting, but the work of the American Indians has not always been emphasized. In this hall one sees masks and figures that well illustrate the deep artistic feelings of their creators. The Smithsonian, as the central museum of the United States, has long been the repository for collections of Indian objects belonging to the Government and dating back even into the colonial period. The Institution also preserves hundreds of thousands of objects collected by the great Western explorers of our young country. Army officers on isolated posts in the old West also were valued collectors for the Smithsonian. Objects from these and other sources have through the years been carefully cataloged, protected, and preserved at the Smithsonian. In this Hall of Indian and Eskimo Arts and Customs many of these priceless treasures are on public display for the first time. In one case are originals by George Catlin selected from the 450 paintings of this master in the collection of the Smithsonian. One of these paintings, for example, shows, almost as a modern color photograph would, Indians quarrying red pipestone to use in making ceremonial tobacco pipes. Thus in the same case the visitor can see examples of completed pipes as well as Catlin's on-the-spot painting showing exactly how Indians, who were then hardly influenced at all by Europeans, carried on this skillful work. It is interesting to note that the soapstone quarried here is scientifically called "catlinite" in honor of the artist who painted the very pictures here on display. In this hall is shown an unusual example of a Great Plains tepee. This large, portable living establishment of skins, like many other specimens at the Smithsonian, was first displayed at the Centennial Exhibition in Philadelphia in 1876, at the close of which 66 freight car loads of important specimens were brought to the Smithsonian for permanent preservation. When this hall was being set up this tepee was still wrapped in old Philadelphia newspapers of the 1870's. This fact dramatically illustrates how important the present renovation of Smithsonian exhibits is for the American people and for visitors to our shores. As a result of these new displays, many of the great treasures of the Nation for the first time can be studied and understood by the millions of Americans of the present generation who come in ever-increasing numbers to the museum.

10. THE WORLD OF MAMMALS

Scientifically, the Smithsonian has sometimes been called the Nation's biological bureau of standards. It has been given this name because in the Smithsonian's collections zoological and botanical specimens are used every day by hundreds of scientists for comparison and identification of new or unknown specimens. In connection with this work, for example, the Institution has developed one of the great collections of the furs of mammals of the world. Many of these pelts are kept in special storage rooms at low temperature for scientific study. In the new World of Mammals Hall, however, the visitor has an opportunity to see and study, in many instances in habitat placements, some of the most interesting and important mammals of the globe. These specimens are not presented monotonously as one "stuffed" animal after another in case after case. Rather, they are displayed so as to teach the basic principles of biology that are related to nutrition, locomotion, evolution, ecology, and survival. Here the student of zoology can see the many different ways in which the mammals of the world have adapted themselves to tropic heat and arctic snows. The ecological approach of many of these displays gives new significance to the exhibits that they present. Some of the groups of animals are dramatically arranged. Changing lights, for example, make it possible for the visitor to see first how lions view their prey, and then how the would-be prey, in this case zebras, view their would-be predators. Many of the great African mammals displayed were collected by President Theodore Roosevelt during his history-making African Expedition of 1909–10, sponsored by the Smithsonian Institution.

11. NORTH AMERICAN MAMMALS

In the hall just described, emphasis is given to mammals of the world exclusive of the great North American mammals. In this specifically North American Mammal Hall is a series of 12 large habitat groups showing the great and now often very rare wild animals of the Northern Hemisphere of America. Each of these large exhibits not only shows numbers of specimens of such animals as bison, elk, moose, and bear but also presents each group, often showing both adult and young animals, against a skillfully painted background of the terrain typical of the habitat of the animal. The mounted specimens in the foreground are shown in settings of carefully reproduced trees, rocks, and other natural items. The rapid restriction of the range of some of these great animals, and even their virtual extinction, make it important to show here each of these groups. Species such as bighorn sheep and wolves, for example, now occupy in the wild state only a fraction of the area that was once theirs when the continent was first known to European settlers. This presentation is important in zoological training. It gives a record of animals that played a large part in providing through their furs much of the wealth of colonial America as well as food and clothing for the pioneers of the new land.

12. BIRDS OF THE WORLD

Ornithology is one of man's oldest scientific interests. This is attested by the frequent reference to birds in the Bible and in the writings of ancient classical authors. The Smithsonian possesses one of the world's great collections of birds. The new Bird Hall of the Institution has been organized to show the principal birds of the world in natural, effective, and pleasing settings. But the hall goes far beyond a mere presentation of specimens. It depicts the biology of bird life in relation to feeding habits, aerial locomotion, nest building, and the rearing of young. On the ceiling are lifelike paintings of birds in flight so skillfully done that they seem to be seen in full round of three-dimensional form as if arrested in flight. A unique case called "Birds and Man" portrays the role of birds in mythology and art. In addition to the displays in this hall, the Smithsonian has, of course, in its study collections, bird specimens from almost every geographical region of the globe.

13. LIFE IN EARLY AMERICA

The Hall of Life in Early America is an easy transition from the characteristics of the Indian population of the country and the mammals and birds of America to the life of early European settlers before the mechanization of the industrial revolution changed the American way of life. It shows the early life of the European settlers in America by demonstrating the tools and furniture that they used. For many years generous donors have brought together at the Smithsonian large collections of objects used by Americans in what may be called the era of the handcrafts. In the present hall are displayed selected items from these collections, including implements and furniture that the colonists brought with them from England, Ireland, Germany, Spain, Scandinavia, and many other countries. Next is shown the adaptation that was made on these shores of these imported objects as a new and truly American culture gradually emerged. One may see an entire house built in New England about 1690. In this building, which was taken down board by board and brick by brick and transported to Washington and reassembled, are objects that were actually used during the early period when the house was

inhabited by the artisans who built it.   Many of them were collected
and given to the Smithsonian by the donor of the house, Mrs. Arthur
M. Greenwood.   In this hall are shown other rooms depicting styles
of life in different colonies—for example, a small but elegant paneled
room of a Virginia gentleman.   The visitor may see also a notable
mahogany Philadelphia highboy and a number of cases of fine silver
made in the South, Pennsylvania, New York, and New England.
American forged iron, glass, pottery, pewter, and textiles are all displayed.   Another feature is an entire schoolroom of an early period
showing the simple desks and equipment of elementary education in
the formative days of our country.   This hall has been visited by
millions each year since its opening.   Not only are its displays significant for Americans, who can learn from them how their predecessors
of European stock lived in pre-industrial revolution days, but also
the hall is especially interesting and important for foreign visitors,
who may absorb something of the evolution of the present style of life
of the United States during the early difficult and formative years
of the country.

14. GOWNS OF THE FIRST LADIES

The First Ladies Hall in a sense carries forward in one special area
the same philosophy shown in the large American cultural history
hall just described.   Here, in a series of special rooms, reproduced from
various periods at the White House, are dresses actually worn by the
wife or the official hostess of each President of the United States.   In
developing this series an effort was made to put in place furniture and
other objects actually used in the Executive Mansion in Philadelphia
before the White House was built and in the White House itself in
different periods.   This series is especially appropriate in this truly
national museum setting of the Smithsonian.   For example, the room
in which the dresses of Martha Washington, Dolley Madison, and
Abigail Adams are exhibited contains objects that were owned and
used by President and Mrs. Washington.   The visitor views this full
series of simulated White House rooms from a setting treated in a
dignified manner to suggest the White House itself.   A large and
beautiful early Victorian chandelier hanging in the middle of the
visitors' space does much to enhance this atmosphere.   In small wall
cases are other objects related to the presidential families of America,
including fine examples of White House china of various periods,
jewelry, and decorations used by the Presidents and their wives
throughout the history of the country.

15. TEXTILE MACHINERY AND FIBERS

The Textile Machinery and Fiber Hall shows the evolution of man's
efforts to make materials of plant and animal fibers from prehistoric
times to the present.   It supplements well the First Ladies Hall

because it demonstrates how dress fabrics themselves and many other textiles are created. It also demonstrates how the techniques of textile production have changed through the years. The visitor begins by looking at spindles recovered by archeologists from the sites of early human habitations. He then sees the development of more and more effective machinery for the manufacture of textiles. Some notable "firsts" are shown, for example, the actual model made by Whitney himself of the cotton gin and the first American spinning frame constructed by Slater in Rhode Island in the 18th century. Visitors may see a most rare and beautiful dress made years ago entirely of silk from silkworms grown in America—the silk fibers processed in America and then hand sewn in America. Modern synthetic metallic and glass fibers and a wide variety of the textiles and textile machines that have made possible the modern multiplicity of industrial and decorative fabrics are included in the displays. One of the notable exhibits of this hall is a Jacquard loom more than a century and a half old which has been put in perfect working order by Mr. Arthur Wullschleger, who gave it to the Institution. This wonderful punch-card device weaves tapestries and patterned brocades without requiring a laborious setting by human hands. The student of the history of ideas looks at this machine with surprise as he wonders why such a device which uses punch cards that are very similar in size and shape to modern punch cards, was not applied to other industrial programing tasks until many years after the Jacquard loom had proved so well its practical usefulness. In this textile hall are many typical forms of textiles arranged so that each visitor may touch and feel them. In museums visitors expect to see signs reading "Please Do Not Touch." Here the Smithsonian has reversed the injunction to "Please Touch." Experts in textiles know that only by feeling fabrics can the visitor actually gain a satisfactory knowledge of different types of materials.

16. TEXTILE PROCESSING

Immediately above the textile hall just described is another new hall devoted to the display of textiles used in human clothing, household decoration, and many industrial functions. This hall shows the history of sewing machines and other devices used in processing the textiles of civilization. Here one may also see illustrated the different types of dyeing and printing that have been used through the years for the embellishment of textiles and collections of great textile types such as lace and embroidery. No one who thinks of our modern world can fail to realize the role that the sewing machines of factory and home have played in the emancipation of women from monotonous toil. The collection of these interesting and effective machines at the

Smithsonian is one of the best in the world. The thoughtful visitor who studies them learns not only a mechanical but also a sociological lesson of importance.

17. POWER MACHINERY

In the Hall of Power Machinery the visitor sees how human beings have progressed from the use of their own puny muscles to the great power devices of our industrial age. Here original machines and patent models illustrate the contribution of engineers and inventors such as Stevens, Corliss, Otto, and Diesel. By diagrams and pictures, waterwheels and windmills are shown. Included is a working model of a classical heat engine that was used to open and close temple doors in ancient Greece. Major displays demonstrate the invention and the development of the steam engine portrayed by a series of working models of great early steam engines which may be activated by each visitor at the push of a button. Also on display are the beginnings and indeed the full development of the internal combustion engine and some of the early devices of Edison and others that show the rise of the use of electricity as a power source. A permanent display of the role of atomic energy in peacetime activity and defense is not yet open to the public, but a number of temporary exhibits on this subject have been presented from time to time by the Smithsonian.

18. FARM MACHINERY

In the Hall of Farm Machinery are shown a selection of the implements and devices which man has contrived to further his basic work of securing food from the soil. The emphasis is upon the history of American agricultural implements. Here, for example, the visitor may trace the evolution of the plow as used by North American settlers from Europe from the earliest days to the present. One interesting phase of this development shows how President Thomas Jefferson used his mathematical and scientific knowledge to make one of the first real improvements in the plow in several thousand years. Also shown are some of the "historic firsts" of the more complex agriculture machinery which has made America famous throughout the world. These exhibits show how the development and use of labor-saving machinery for planting, cultivating, and harvesting crops helped solve the problems of feeding America's rapidly growing urban population after the Civil War.

19. PRINTING ARTS

Another specialized group of industrial devices is shown in the new Printing Arts Hall. The gradual development of pictorial and text printing is illustrated in these displays. The famous printing press used by Benjamin Franklin in London in 1726 is here. The emphasis is upon the various processes by means of which printing blocks and later movable type have been used down through the centuries, together with the techniques and tools involved. Here is also demonstrated how black-and-white and color pictorial prints have been made, especially in recent years. Examples are shown of the work of some of the great printmakers of the world, including such outstanding artists as Rembrandt and Dürer. In the study collections of this division are examples of the work of many of the great printmakers of the last six centuries.

20. MILITARY HISTORY

The Military History Hall is divided into two large sections, one devoted to the United States Navy and Marine Corps, the other to the United States Army. Elaborate exhibits of the development of aviation, both civil and military, are shown in the National Air Museum to which reference is made below. The Naval-Marine Corps Hall shows the evolution, by the use of models and contemporary prints and charts, of the Navy from the first commissioned vessel of 1775 to the atomic submarine. Many portraits and memorabilia of the great Naval and Marine leaders of our Nation are exhibited. One who studies the exhibits of this hall can clearly see how the rise of the modern Navy is related to the evolution of sources of power for naval vessels as illustrated in the nearby Power Hall. Here also can be seen the vessels and equipment that led to the emergence of the sea strength of the United States from the small sailing craft of the colonies to the present Navy of this country as a preeminent world power. The change from wooden to steel warships and the development of modern naval armaments are portrayed. Also shown are a few selected examples of objects recovered from the ocean floor by the use of the new techniques of marine archeology.

The hall showing the rise of the American Army begins with examples of uniforms and equipment of colonial troops. At the entrance is placed the actual field uniform worn by General Washington when he was conducting his great campaigns of the War of Independence. The visitor can also follow the evolution of American arms and equipment down through the years. Attention is given to present-day uniforms and the arms used in each of the great wars of the Nation. Outstanding objects here include a beautiful bronze cannon brought to the colonies by General Lafayette, uniforms of both Union and Confederate officers of the Civil War, General Sheridan's horse on which he made his famous ride, a complete display of modern military missiles, including those with atomic warheads, and a very complete display of American military heraldry including the battle ribbons of all the Nation's great Army regiments.

21. NUMISMATICS

The Numismatic Hall, or Hall of Monetary History and Medallic Art, can best be described as an amazingly complete world museum of the history of money. Here are shown real examples of the first coins ever minted in ancient Greece. Following the case that shows these very early coins are others in which a visitor can see illustrated the spread of coinage throughout the ancient Mediterranean world. Also shown are means of exchange other than coins and samples of the gold and other monetary forms of non-European nations. The special feature is the great collection of colonial American and United States coins and paper money for which the Smithsonian has long been famous. The newly opened presentation of coins has a completely novel objective, for it is organized to teach the history and geography of the world in relation to money. Many of the outstanding gold pieces from the Institution's great Straub collection are on display, as are also coins of the recently presented Du Pont collection of Russian money. Many examples in the well-lighted cases are from the United States mint collection, which is now part of the over-all Smithsonian collection. Examples of almost every coin ever struck in America are thus on view or in the study collections of the Institution. The visitor to this hall who comes to it with intellectual curiosity will learn not only the fascinating story of coinage, sculpture, design, and medallic art through the centuries, but also much else that is important in the history of economics and even of civilization itself.

22. HALL OF HEALTH

Years ago, national representatives of American medical organizations urged the Smithsonian to establish a hall of health. For many years the original hall was open, but gradually it became shabby and outmoded. The modern Health Hall at the Smithsonian, on the contrary, presents the basic anatomical and physiological processes of human beings as they are known to modern science. The hall shows something of the mechanisms by means of which electronics and other technologies assist the physician in measuring and recording the human heart beat, blood pressure, respiration, visual and auditory acuity, and the like. Here the visitor can watch his own heart beat on a cathode-ray tube by holding a receiver on his chest. In this hall is located a fascinating transparent human figure which by a series of lights and a concomitant electronically reproduced lecture shows in a vivid and accurate way the principal organ systems of the human frame and how they work.

23. HISTORY OF MEDICINE, DENTISTRY, AND PHARMACY

Immediately adjacent to the Hall of Health is the Hall of Medicine, Dentistry, and Pharmacy, where the evolution of many of the devices used by physicians, surgeons, dentists, and pharmacists down through the years is shown. The development of such now common aids to the physician's practice as the stethoscope and blood-pressure instrument is traced. Some of the more elaborate devices of modern medicine and surgery such as the artificial heart and the X-ray apparatus are also exhibited. Here too is displayed a complete medieval pharmacy with an almost unique and very beautiful collection of early pharmaceutical ceramics and glassware.

THE NATIONAL AIR MUSEUM

Of all the notable renovations of exhibit presentations at the Smithsonian, none has been more outstanding than the recent transformation of the small temporary Air and Space Building. The National Air Museum, a special unit of the Institution, has in its custody probably the world's greatest collection of aircraft and instruments and objects related to aviation. Nearly all the great treasures of this museum are in storage. Some of its outstanding possessions, such as the first Wright plane and the Lindbergh plane, are on display in the Arts and Industries Building. The main museum displays of aviation, however, are now shown in a building built as a temporary test center for Liberty Motors during the First World War. This galvanized-iron building on Independence Avenue behind the original Smithsonian Building has been renovated in such a way that the new exhibits installed in it can be moved without loss to a new and permanent building when such a building is constructed. Even the present "temporary" structure in its renovated form gives a vivid demonstration of the public's interest in aviation. This small, far from commodious structure has now become one of the great attractions of Washington. During the first 12 months after this renovated building was opened, more than a million visitors sought it out and studied its exhibits portraying man's conquest of air and space. Here are shown a few examples from the Smithsonian's possibly unrivaled collection of kites. The basic principles of the aerial navigation of birds as studied by the first aviation scientists are displayed. In the center of the building are a few of the actual early aircraft of peculiar significance in the history of aviation. Models of hundreds of types of balloons and heavier-than-air craft are shown. Here also are presented many early and important types of aircraft engines. One of the notable exhibits is a collection of the great early liquid-fuel rockets made by America's, and indeed the world's, pioneer scientific student of devices for the exploration of space, the late

Dr. Robert H. Goddard. The unique specimens of Goddard's work were given to the Smithsonian by Mrs. Goddard in tribute to the early support that the Smithsonian gave to Dr. Goddard's scientific work. Other more modern space-flight specimens on display are the first recovered American Space Flight nose cone, the Able-Baker space flight apparatus, the first recovered orbiting satellite (Discoverer XIII), and many other "firsts" of modern air-space science.

Immediately outside this temporary building are displayed not models, but actual examples, of present-day rockets, including a United States Army Jupiter C, a United States Navy Vanguard, a Navy Polaris, and an Air Force Atlas.

In the paragraphs above reference has been made to the present progress of the renovation of exhibits at the Smithsonian. Mention could also be made to improvements and better lighting used in the display of the outstanding collections of oriental objects and paintings at the Smithsonian's Freer Gallery of Art. The National Collection of Fine Arts of the Smithsonian has also improved some of its temporary galleries. Notable new installations, including rooms for the decorative arts, have been opened at the National Gallery of Art, which is a bureau of the Smithsonian Institution.

The summaries that have been presented in the immediately preceding pages have been given to bring the reader of this report up to date in regard to one aspect of the work of the Smithsonian. This is a report of progress. It suggests something of the accomplishments of the past 8 years in transforming the formerly old and then sadly outmoded museum presentations at the Smithsonian Institution into modern effective and educational exhibits. During 1953, the year in which this work began, 3,429,429 visitors came to the Smithsonian buildings on the Mall. In the year covered by the present report, as noted elsewhere, 7,103,474 came to these same buildings. There can be no doubt that the renovations summarized here have met warm public acceptance.

This whole great program of renovation has been possible only because of the enthusiastic support that has been given to it by the Board of Regents of the Institution, by the Congress, and by the labors of the Smithsonian's devoted and skillful staff of curators and exhibit workers. Because of this work it is now beginning to be possible for many millions of American citizens and for foreign visitors also to see the great national treasures of the Smithsonian in an orderly and also in an educationally significant way.

Other new halls are in the process of development and will be open to the public as soon as the complex work of constructing them can be completed by the small staff of the Institution. These other new halls include a Hall of Dinosaurs, a Hall of Pleistocene Mammals, a

Comparative Anatomy Hall, a large Hall of Botany and Wood, a Hall of Ocean Life, a Hall of Reptiles and Fishes, a Hall of Man emphasizing the methods and accomplishments of physical anthropology, and a Classical Archeology Hall, a Peoples of Asia and Africa Hall, a Peoples of the Pacific Hall, a second North American Archeology Hall, a second Geology Hall, and a Hall of Insects of the World. Work on still other major displays of collections already in storage at the Smithsonian is underway so that they may be presented in the new Museum of History and Technology Building when this structure is completed.

In introducing the present report, reference was made to the emphasis given by James Smithson and Joseph Henry to the twin ideas of the diffusion and the increase of knowledge among men. Although the museum displays described in the foregoing pages constitute an important means of diffusing scientific and technological knowledge, the Institution employs many other means to promote this diffusion. One of these has traditionally been publications, and during the year represented by this report the publication program was advanced by 97 titles issued under Smithsonian imprint; and nearly 775,000 copies of Smithsonian publications were distributed, an increase of about 18 percent over the previous year. Details of these publications are given on later pages of the report. It may be pointed out that the publications of the Smithsonian are known worldwide, and the "exchange publications" that come without charge to Washington in response to Smithsonian publications from scientific research organizations all over the world play an important role in maintaining in America a complete library of scientific research. Such a collection is basic in modern American life, not only in national defense but also in the development of the cultural and industrial life of the country.

It is difficult in brief compass to describe the research activities of the Institution. The reader of this report, however, is especially urged to note the pages that present the results of research studies conducted during the current year by the Institution. The Astrophysical Observatory of the Smithsonian, for example, is concerned in the development of the science that is basic to a modern understanding of astronomy and space. Only a few years ago research in astrophysics seemed interesting but highly theoretical. Today the significance of investigations in this area for our national defense and welfare is recognized everywhere. Research investigations are also conducted in almost all the other specialized divisions of the Institution as reported on later pages of this report. Special emphasis should be given to the fact that it is the research activities of the members of the Institution's scientific staff that have established its worldwide reputation and won for it academic distinction.

THE ESTABLISHMENT

The Smithsonian Institution was created by act of Congress in 1846, in accordance with the terms of the will of James Smithson, of England, who in 1826 bequeathed his property to the United States of America "to found at Washington, under the name of the Smithsonian Institution, an establishment for the increase and diffusion of knowledge among men." In receiving the property and accepting the trust, Congress determined that the Federal Government was without authority to administer the trust directly, and, therefore, constituted an "establishment," whose statutory members are "the President, the Vice President, the Chief Justice, and the heads of the executive departments."

THE BOARD OF REGENTS

The membership of the Board of Regents remained unchanged except for the new Vice President of the United States, the Honorable Lyndon B. Johnson, who became an ex-officio member to succeed the Honorable Richard M. Nixon on January 20, 1961. The roll of Regents at the close of the fiscal year was as follows: Chief Justice of the United States Earl Warren, Chancellor; Vice President Lyndon B. Johnson; members from the Senate: Clinton P. Anderson, J. William Fulbright, Leverett Saltonstall; members from the House of Representatives: Frank T. Bow, Overton Brooks, Clarence Cannon; citizen members: John Nicholas Brown, Arthur H. Compton, Robert V. Fleming, Crawford H. Greenewalt, Caryl P. Haskins, and Jerome C. Hunsaker.

The usual informal dinner meeting, preceding the annual meeting, was held on January 12, 1961, in the main hall of the Smithsonian Building amid exhibits showing the most recent developments in the work of the Smithsonian bureaus. Col. Howard I. Chapelle spoke on "Description of the American Watercraft Collection"; Dr. Charles O. Handley, Jr., on "Mammal Survey of Panama"; Dr. T. Dale Stewart on "Reconstructing Heads of Ancient Man"; Dr. Harold P. Stern on "Hokusai in the Freer Gallery of Art"; and Dr. Fred L. Whipple on "Dust in Space."

The annual meeting was held on January 13, 1961. The Secretary presented his published annual report on the activities of the Institution. The Chairman of the Executive and Permanent Committees of the Board, Dr. Robert V. Fleming, gave the financial report for the fiscal year ended June 30, 1960.

The Regents participated in the ceremonies for the laying of the cornerstone of the Museum of History and Technology on the afternoon of May 19, 1961, and met at 5 o'clock that day in the Regents Room for the spring meeting of the Board.

FINANCES

A statement on finances, dealing particularly with Smithsonian private funds, will be found in the report of the executive committee of the Board of Regents, page 221. Funds appropriated to the Institution for its regular operations for the fiscal year ended June 30, 1961, totaled $8,114,000. Besides this direct appropriation, the Institution received funds by transfer from other Government agencies as follows: From the District of Columbia for the National Zoological Park, $1,304,000; from the National Park Service, Department of the Interior, for the River Basin Surveys, $123,895.

VISITORS

Visitors to the Smithsonian group of buildings on the Mall reached a total of 7,103,474, an all-time high and 608,844 more than the previous year. April 1961 was the month of largest attendance, with 1,082,827; August 1960 second, with 1,051,733; May 1961 third, with 990,230. Table 1 gives a summary of the attendance records for the five buildings; table 2, groups of school children. These figures, when added to the 1,032,340 recorded at the National Gallery of Art bring the year's total number of visitors at the Institution buildings on the Mall to 8,135,814.

TABLE 1.—*Visitors to certain Smithsonian buildings during the year ended June 30, 1961*

(1) Year and month	(2) Smithsonian Building	(3) Arts and Industries Building	(4) Natural History Building	(5) Air and Space Building	(6) Freer Building	(7) Total
1960						
July	151, 286	385, 718	269, 451	135, 672	16, 021	958, 148
August	178, 859	365, 810	316, 074	171, 414	19, 576	1, 051, 733
September	55, 579	153, 369	103, 240	58, 073	12, 011	382, 272
October	50, 835	130, 833	112, 431	47, 384	8, 079	349, 562
November	50, 864	110, 213	117, 335	49, 581	8, 088	336, 081
December	22, 786	58, 899	53, 439	23, 703	4, 608	163, 435
1961						
January	34, 523	67, 348	73, 588	25, 023	5, 419	205, 901
February	24, 812	70, 596	59, 541	29, 469	4, 428	188, 846
March	57, 184	157, 668	135, 663	54, 715	8, 645	413, 875
April	154, 793	483, 752	283, 071	144, 790	16, 421	1, 082, 827
May	116, 978	457, 832	286, 067	115, 758	13, 595	990, 230
June	126, 027	470, 333	238, 073	132, 276	13, 855	980, 564
Total	1, 024, 526	2, 912, 371	2, 047, 973	987, 858	130, 746	7, 103, 474

TABLE 2.—*Groups of school children visiting the Smithsonian Institution during the year ended June 30, 1961*

Year and month	Number of children	Number of groups	Year and month	Number of children	Number of groups
1960			*1961*		
July	6, 233	199	January	7, 804	223
August	3, 896	157	February	12, 510	365
September	2, 048	82	March	41, 558	1, 004
October	13, 061	362	April	85, 084	1, 817
November	21, 995	579	May	115, 996	2, 623
December	8, 238	254	June	44, 650	1, 042
			Total	363, 073	8, 707

Report on the United States National Museum

Sɪʀ: I have the honor to submit the following report on the condition and operations of the U.S. National Museum for the fiscal year ended June 30, 1961:

COLLECTIONS

During the year 971,150 specimens were added to the national collections and distributed among the eight departments as follows: Anthropology, 19,764; zoology, 369,701; botany, 103,160; geology, 229,676; science and technology, 4,231; arts and manufactures, 5,521; civil history, 237,323; and armed forces history, 1,774. The total number is less than half as many as recorded last year, when an extraordinary number of postage stamps, approaching a million and a half, was accessioned. Most of this year's accessions were acquired as gifts from individuals or as transfers from Government departments and agencies. The complete report on the Museum, published as a separate document, includes a detailed list of the year's acquisitions, of which the more important are summarized below. Catalog entries in all departments now total 54,963,805.

Anthropology.—Through an arrangement with Dr. Ralph S. Solecki, of Columbia University, whereby the Smithsonian Institution sponsored his 1957 expedition to Iraq, the division of archeology received 8,770 artifacts from Shanidar cave and neighboring sites. In addition to a few specimens from the historic and protohistoric cultural periods, the representation is mainly from the proto-Neolithic and the Mousterian, the whole indicating a time span of around 65,000 years. The division also received, by transfer from the River Basin Surveys, 5,153 artifacts collected at numerous prehistoric sites in South Dakota and Wyoming. Mrs. Virginia M. Pollak added to her earlier generous donations a wooden ibis from the Ptolemaic-Roman period of Egypt.

Of special interest among the new accessions in the division of ethnology are two rare Chinese scrolls written in the Chinese and Manchurian languages and representing awards in the years 1753 and 1868 for loyal services to the Chinese Government, donated by Dr. David C. Graham, honorary research associate in biology. A late 19th century Chinese four-panel lacquer screen was received from the estate of John T. Owens. The decoration thereon, showing four birds in a natural setting, has been executed by inlaying mother-of-pearl, rose quartz, white and stained ivory, and semiprecious stones. A group of 54 ethnological specimens of Eskimo manufacture, collected in Alaska in 1908, was presented by Dr. F. F. Fellows, West Linn, Oreg. A representative collection of 104 smoking pipes, mainly from the Near East, India, China, and Japan, was given by Dr. Leo Stoor, of Cleveland. A good collection of 84 Micronesian objects was obtained in exchange from John H. Brandt, of New York City. Among the rare specimens in this group is a type of necklace from Yap no longer obtainable from the natives.

The division of physical anthropology added to its collection of American Negro skeletal remains 14 skulls and a few miscellaneous bones recovered by the District of Columbia coroner, Dr. A. Magruder MacDonald, when an abandoned cemetery near the Calvert Street bridge in Washington was exposed in the course of building operations. The Zoller Laboratory of Dental Anthropology of the University of Chicago presented the division with 11 standard models for classifying crown characters of human deciduous teeth. The models, accompanied by an explanatory manual, were prepared by Dr. Kazuro Hanihara, of Sapporo Medical College, Japan, and are based on a series of 600 subjects representing various racial groups.

Zoology.—The division of mammals acquired a total of 4,076 specimens, comprising 42 accessions. Dr. Robert E. Kuntz forwarded nearly 1,000 specimens from Formosa and 400 from North Borneo, collected by field parties of U.S. Naval Medical Research Unit No. 2. Bernard R. Feinstein, of the Museum staff, working in cooperation with the Army Medical Research and Development Command and the Bernice P. Bishop Museum, sent 600 mammals from South Vietnam. Dr. Robert Traub forwarded 121 additional specimens collected by the U.S. Army Medical Research Unit. Capt. Vernon J. Tipton sent 273 mammals collected in Panama by the Army Preventive Medicine Division. E. V. Komarek presented 83 mammals, mostly carnivores, from the southeastern States, as well as an additional lot of 53 small mammals from the Southwest; Russell E. Mumford and Ralph D. Kirkpatrick each sent additional mammals from Indiana; and the Virginia State Department of Health, through J. T. Banks and T. M. Mullman, presented 44 mammals collected in the course of epidemiological surveys.

The same sources that were responsible for several of the mammal collections referred to above contributed some important accessions for the division of birds. From the lowlands of North Borneo, a series of 512 bird skins was received from the U.S. Naval Medical Research Unit No. 2. A total of 565 bird skins, 6 alcoholic specimens, and 20 skeletons from South Vietnam resulted from the activities sponsored by the Bernice P. Bishop Museum and the Army Medical

Research and Development Command. Received by transfer from the U.S. Fish and Wildlife Service were 1,411 bird skins and 6 alcoholic specimens from Formosa.

Noteworthy collections received in the division of reptiles and amphibians include 19 salamanders from Alabama, donated by Leslie Hubricht. A fine series of Virginia amphibians, collected by the late Walter B. Newman, was received as a gift from his mother, Mrs. Helen B. Newman. By transfer from the U.S. Army Medical Research Unit, through Lt. Col. H. J. Baker, came 29 snakes, mostly from Selangor, an area from which the Museum has had few specimens. A series of 28 Venezuelan reptiles and amphibians collected for the Museum by Dr. C. O. Handley, Jr., and D. L. Rhymer contains some frogs that are valuable for comparison with Colombian material now being studied. Another valuable addition to the amphibian group from Thailand are 39 specimens collected in South Vietnam by Bernard R. Feinstein.

The division of fishes accessioned a large collection consisting of 2,702 specimens from the Fourth Smithsonian-Bredin Caribbean Expedition. The U.S. Fish and Wildlife Service, through Harvey R. Bullis, Jr., and Daniel M. Cohen, contributed another large important collection, totaling 1,114 fishes. Dr. Eugenie Clark, of the Cape Haze Marine Laboratory of Florida, and Dr. H. Steinitz, of the Hebrew University of Jerusalem, donated 778 marine fishes collected in the Red Sea by Dr. Clark; these specimens are very valuable because the Red Sea area is the type locality of numerous kinds of fishes, some of which are endemic. Dr. Hurst Shoemaker, of the American University of Beirut, donated 361 fishes from Lebanon. Among the valuable collections received for identification were 453 Formosan fishes through Dr. Robert E. Kuntz, U.S. Naval Medical Research Unit No. 2, and 728 specimens from Africa and South America from Dr. Herbert R. Axelrod, of Tropical Fish Hobbyist Publications, Jersey City.

A very valuable accession acquired by the division of insects is the John C. Lutz collection of Hemiptera, consisting of 87,371 specimens. Particularly rich in Neotropical species, this assemblage contains 668 types of various kinds, including holotypes of 15 species. Another very important accession is the N. Baranov collection of Palaearctic tachnid flies, consisting of 4,611 specimens representing 305 genera, 68 of which are new to the collections, and 812 species, of which 499 were not previously available for study in the Museum. Other notable contributions include: 3,306 miscellaneous specimens from North and South America, donated by Dr. Charles P. Alexander; 2,915 Hawaiian insects presented by A. J. Ford, of Honolulu; 2,938 miscellaneous specimens from Pakistan, contributed by Dr. J. Maldonado Capriles; 2,127 Lepidoptera from Wisconsin given by William E.

Sieker; 7,848 miscellaneous insects from various parts of the world given by N. L. H. Krauss; and 1,128 specimens of Hymenoptera donated by Dr. Karl V. Krombein.

Contributing materially to another record-breaking year for accessions in the division of marine invertebrates were 54,480 amphipod crustaceans, including 15 type specimens, received from the Scripps Institution of Oceanography, University of California. From the Universitetets Zoologiske Museum, Copenhagen, through Dr. H. Volsøe, were received 9 deep-sea invertebrates from the world-renowned Danish Deepsea Expedition of the *Galathea*, including paratypes of unusual holothurians, starfishes, polychaete worms, and sea anemones. The Rijksmuseum van Natuurlijke Historie, Leiden, The Netherlands, through Dr. L. B. Holthuis, donated 402 crustaceans, including two scyllarid lobsters and an authoritatively identified set of European isopods. A collection of 5,528 miscellaneous Antarctic invertebrates from Operation Deep Freeze IV was received from Stanford University, through Dr. Donald E. Wohlschlag. Another large series of 5,256 miscellaneous marine invertebrates was collected for the Museum in Bermuda by Mrs. LaNelle W. Peterson.

The most important accession in the division of mollusks consisted of 12,200 specimens collected at Jaluit Atoll, in the southern Marshall Islands, by Dr. Harald A. Rehder. The Fourth Smithsonian-Bredin Caribbean Expedition added 6,000 mollusks from Yucatán. Dr. Wendell P. Woodring collected 485 specimens of marine mollusks on the Atlantic coast of Panama. From the Institute of Oceanology of the Academy of Sciences of the USSR, through Dr. E. A. Filatova, came 607 specimens of fresh-water mollusks from the USSR.

Botany.—One of the most important accessions in the department was the *Cladonia* collection of the late Alexander W. Evans, comprising 39,204 specimens, received in exchange from the Osborn Botanical Laboratory of Yale University. Unusually fine specimens of *Rhododendron* and *Primula*, numbering 2,895, collected in Asia by George Forest, were received in exchange from the Royal Botanic Garden, Edinburgh, Scotland. Others, also in exchange, were: 7,786 specimens of Asia and South America, mostly significant historical collections, from the Museum National d'Histoire Naturelle, Paris; 1,287 plants of Indonesia from the Herbarium Bogoriense; and 527 photographs of plants in the Philip Miller Herbarium from the Bailey Hortorium, Ithaca, N.Y.

The American Musuem of Natural History forwarded 15,780 specimens collected by L. J. Brass on the Sixth Archbold Expedition to New Guinea. The University of California sent 497 specimens of South American plants collected by W. Eyerdam on the Sixth Botanical Garden Expedition to the Andes, in return for identifications.

Dr. Mason E. Hale and Dr. Thomas R. Soderstrom collected 3,841 specimens in Mexico, consisting mostly of lichens, and Dr. John E. Ebinger collected 5,086 specimens in Panama, primarily on Barro Colorado Island. There were transferred from the U.S. Geological Survey, Department of the Interior, 2,650 Alaskan plants collected by Lloyd Spetzman.

The division of woods received in exchange from the Yale School of Forestry 474 wood samples collected by Dr. John J. Wurdack and L. S. Adderley in Venezuela; 966 slides of Malayan woods from the Forest Research Institute, Kepong, Selangor, Malaya, through P. K. Balan Menon; 314 wood samples with voucher herbarium specimens collected in Sarawak, from the University of Oxford, England, and 1,784 microscope slides of pollen from the Rancho Santa Ana Botanic Garden. Dr. William L. Stern presented 609 samples of wood he collected in Panama.

Geology.—Among the noteworthy gifts received in the division of mineralogy and petrology are a very fine cubic crystal of diamond, weighing 82.5 carats, from Sierra Leone, and a three-quarter carat diamond crystal in matrix from the Bulfontein Mine, South Africa, both presented by Dorus Van Itallie; a large group of wulfenite crystals from the Glove Mine, near Amado, Ariz., and a gem-quality twin crystal of chrysoberyl from Minas Gerais, Brazil, both donated by Bernard T. Rocca, Sr.

Important additions to the mineral collection received in exchange are becquerelite and fourmarierite from Republic of the Congo (Leopoldville); raspite, Australia; cronstedtite, Hungary; and benitoite, California. Newly described species received in exchange are schoderite and metaschoderite, Nevada; masuyite and lueskite, Republic of the Congo (Leopoldville); yavapaite, Arizona; and wolsendorfite, Germany.

The Roebling collection was increased by 1,625 specimens by purchase from the Roebling fund or by exchange. Among the most important of these are a collection of 40 specimens of wulfenite, each of exceptional quality, from Arizona; several adularia crystals from Switzerland; a well-formed cube of uraninite four inches on an edge, from Morogoro, Tanganyika; and a very fine large gadolinite crystal from southern Norway. Several specimens of outstanding quality were added to the Canfield collection by purchase. These include a 90-carat peridot crystal from Zebirget, Egypt; a very large sphene crystal from Baja California; bournonite, England; and apatite, Italy.

Gems obtained for the Isaac Lea collection by purchase from the Chamberlain fund include a pink scapolite from Burma weighing 12.33 carats; a blue topaz from Texas weighing 146.35 carats; a peridot from Arizona weighing 22.9 carats; and a 9.53 carat yellow tourmaline from Brazil.

During the past year the meteorite collection continued its growth. Seven meteorites new to the collection were obtained: Abee, Canada; Bruderheim, Canada; Kandahar, Afghanistan; Treysa, Germany; Utzenstorf, Switzerland; Aroos, Russia; and Moab, United States.

The division of invertebrate paleontology and paleobotany acquired some important fossil collections. The famous Greene collection, comprising 110,000 specimens and consisting mostly of Devonian corals, was given by the American Museum of Natural History. A bequest was received from the estate of Mrs. Ruby F. Renfro of approximately 50,000 specimens of Pennsylvanian, Permian, and Cretaceous fossils of north-central Texas and a small collection from Europe. Other gifts include 1,000 Devonian invertebrate fossils from the upper Dundee limestone and the Silica shale, Michigan and Ohio, donated by Dr. Erle G. Kauffman, 36 fossil crabs from the Miocene of Virginia, from George Webb; and 167 smaller Foraminifera from the Mississippian of southern Indiana, Kentucky, Tennessee, and Ohio, presented by Dr. J. E. Conkin.

Fieldwork made possible from funds of the Walcott bequest yielded 600 echinoids from the Paleocene, collected in Georgia by Dr. Porter M. Kier in collaboration with Dr. Druid Wilson of the U.S. Geological Survey; 2,500 Upper Cretaceous, Paleocene, and Eocene invertebrate fossils collected in Maryland by Dr. Erle G. Kauffman, with Dr. Norman F. Sohl and Dr. Harlan R. Bergquist of the U.S. Geological Survey; and 1,000 Pennsylvanian fossils collected in Texas by Dr. G. Arthur Cooper and Dr. Richard E. Grant.

The division of vertebrate paleontology received an outstanding accession of about 202 specimens representing fish, amphibians, and reptiles from various Permian formations in Texas and Kansas. These specimens were collected by Dr. Nicholas Hotton III and John E. Gassaway, through funds provided by the Walcott bequest. Particular mention is made of a nearly complete and articulated skeleton of the small predaceous amphibian *Acroplous vorax* taken from the Permian Speiser formation of Kansas, and a large part of a skeleton of the primitive cotylosaurian reptile *Labidosaurus* sp., from the Permian Arroyo formation of Texas. The jaws, part of the skull, and several vertebrae of a very large baleen whale were collected from the Miocene Yorktown formation near Hampton, Va., by Dr. Nicholas Hotton III, Kurt F. Hauschildt, and Dr. Frank C. Whitmore, Jr. Dr. Hotton, assisted by William E. Moran, a former employee, also secured a partial skeleton, including the greater part of a skull, of a rare embolomerous amphibian from the Mauch Chunk formation of Mississippian age.

Science and technology.—Two astrolabes of unusual interest were acquired by the division of physical sciences. Through the generosity of Lessing J. Rosenwald a very fine medieval English instrument was received, having zoomorphic star pointers as a notable feature. Although undated and unsigned, it is dated by the calendar scale about 1325. A second astrolabe received this year is an Hispano-Moorish instrument by Muhammad ibn-Sahli. This specimen exhibits a mixture of Islamic, Christian, and Jewish characteristics in its decoration.

Two major refrigerating machines for exhibit in the new hall of power machinery were received this year: the first commercially successful centrifugal refrigeration compressor from Carrier Corporation, which was generously restored by the Frick Company, and a typical steam-driven reciprocating ammonia compressor from Clifton Springs Sanitarium and Clinic.

About 3,000 large original tracings, on cloth, of heavy mining machinery for the period 1875–1902 were received from Calumet and Hecla, Inc. This valuable collection representing an important part of the creative work of Erasmus D. Leavitt (1836–1916), a widely known and highly honored mechanical engineer, was located by Robert M. Vogel, associate curator. The archival collections of the division have grown, largely through the efforts of Mr. Vogel, to a major repository of source materials in the history of mechanical and civil engineering.

Among the outstanding gifts in the section of marine transportation is a model of the brigantine sloop *Ferret*. This Admiralty model is a gift of Lansdell K. Christie. The Grace Line, Inc., presented a model of the passenger liner *Santa Paula*. In the section of land transportation a colonial chaise, including funds for its restoration, was received from Stewart Huston. A collection of fire-fighting apparatus was donated by Dr. Karl B. Bretzfelder. The Baltimore & Ohio Railroad Co. gave a collection of glass plate negatives and car drawings, through L. W. Sagle.

The division of electricity has been particularly fortunate in obtaining the Palmer collection of early electrical equipment from Princeton University. The collection is an important one and provided most of the illustrations in M. Maclaren's *Rise of the Electrical Industry during the 19th Century*. It was exceptionally rich in examples of laboratory meters, telephonic apparatus, power switchgear, and incandescent lamps. Two other large groups of specimens were also acquired: one from Brown University, consisting primarily of motors and generators, together with some interesting wireless telegraph equipment, and one from the Weston Instrument Company, composed of early commercial meters.

The acquisition of a David Rittenhouse half-size tall clock, which has an astronomical type dial, enhanced the collection of timekeeping instruments. This clock is one of Rittenhouse's earlier works, and it is probably the product of his own hands. Several other outstanding clocks were also obtained, including one by Gideon Roberts, who introduced mass-produced wooden clocks.

Among the accessions in medical sciences is a significant collection of dental instruments, received from the S. S. White Dental Manufacturing Company. The New England Hospital for Women and Children Nurses Alumnae Association donated an early uniform worn by Linda Richards and other personal memorabilia, including a Tolles microscope. Miss Richards was the first woman to receive a diploma from any American training school for nurses. A number of medals, diplomas, and other memorabilia have been received from the estate of Abraham Flexner, in accordance with his bequest.

Arts and manufactures.—A significant acquisition in the division of textiles is a collection of over 100 19th-century sewing machines presented by the Singer Manufacturing Company, through Bogart F. Thompson. Added to the fine group already accumulated, these give the Museum the world's leading historical collection of sewing machines. An outstanding collection of over 200 sewing birds, hemming clamps, and related needlework accessories was donated by Miss Mabel Whiteley. Of special interest also is the receipt of a collection of lace and embroidery from Mrs. Herbert Arthur May. The laces include examples of Chantilly, Brussels, Maltese, and Venetian needlepoint.

Several interesting items were acquired by the division of ceramics and glass. A rare Castleford urn with painted decorations was presented by Mrs. George H. Myers. Mrs. William A. Sutherland donated 28 pieces of porcelain, including an English Lowestoft teapot, a China trade porcelain fruit basket, Sevres tea set, and a Liverpool coffee pot, all of the 18th century. R. Whornton Wilson gave a unique piece of Americana, consisting of an Oriental Lowestoft cider jug and cover, with painted decorations including the inscription "Jefferson and Liberty," surmounted by an American eagle and 17 stars.

A fine group of chiaroscuro woodcuts was acquired by the division of graphic arts. The group included two examples by the important early 16th-century pioneer, Antonio da Trento, *St. Matthew* and *The Martyrdom of St. Paul and St. Peter; The Descent from the Cross*, by Ugo da Carpi, founder of the chiaroscuro process in Italy; work by the most important 17th-century practitioners include *Aeneas Carrying Anchises* by Ludolph Businck; *Death of Lucretia* by Paulus Moreelse; and *Sibyll with Books* and *Virgin with Jesus and John* by Bartolomeo Coriolano. The 18th century is represented by John Baptist Jackson's *Pieta* and the outline block for his *The Virgin in the Clouds* and *Six Saints*. A Lechrome National Photocolor One-

Shot Color Camera was presented to the section of photography by Ralph E. Wareham. This type of camera simultaneously exposes a complete set of color separation negatives which are used to produce color prints. Technicolor Corporation donated a display of motion-picture film strips explaining their Technirama process of cinematography.

The division of manufactures and heavy industries acquired several significant specimens. In the section of petroleum, Universal Oil Products Company and Esso Standard Oil Company, in association with the M. W. Kellogg Company, prepared models and flow charts illustrative of phases in the development of petroleum refining. William C. Cleveland, consultant in the section of general manufacturing, has been successful in locating more than 100 machines typical of the development of the metalworking trades. These will provide an excellent basis for a treatment of the history of fasteners of all kinds. A number of important pieces of equipment have been transferred by nuclear physics laboratories at Argonne, Chicago, and Washington, D.C.

Civil history.—President John F. Kennedy gave the Smithsonian Institution a magnificent volume, the *Atlas Nouveau*, compiled by Nicolas Sanson and published in 1692. The richly illustrated atlas, intended for the instruction of the Dauphin of France, is bound in handsome contemporary red leather and gilt binding.

Former President Dwight D. Eisenhower donated a Portuguese standing lamp in silver, a carved teakwood elephant and rider presented to him by His Majesty Bhumibol Adulyadej of Thailand, and an elaborately carved scene from the Mahabharata in ivory and sandalwood, presented to him by the President of India. Mr. Eisenhower also gave the twin microphones over which his voice was frequently carried during his 50,000-mile campaign of 1952.

Mrs. Dwight D. Eisenhower presented a pink embroidered organdy dress given her by Mrs. Carlos P. Garcia, wife of the President of the Philippines. Ralph E. Becker continued his donations of political campaign paraphernalia of the past. Significant among the gifts is a preserve crock inscribed "25,000 Majority General Jackson"—a protest against the fact that in the election of 1824 General Jackson rolled up a majority of greater than 25,000 popular votes over his nearest rival, John Quincy Adams. He lost the election, however; since no candidate had a majority of the total vote, the House of Representatives chose Mr. Adams from the three candidates having the highest number of electoral votes.

Noteworthy among accessions received in the division of philately and postal history is a specialized collection of early Peru donated by Bernard Peyton, consisting of more than 13,000 stamps and covers in 16 albums. The material portrays the postal history of Peru from the period of Royal Spanish Service to the end of the 19th century. Essays, proofs, and color trials augment the approved stamps, and each issue is thoroughly explored by means of cancellations. One album presents the Pacific Steam Navigation Company's stamps and essays including use on covers. The provisional stamps made necessary by the occupation of Chilean forces in 1879–82 are of great historical value. George L. Lee presented a collection of Egyptian stamps from the Royal Imperforata Printings prepared for Kings Fuad and Farouk. This unusual material was sold by the present Egyptian Government in 1954. Mr. Lee also gave a used copy of the 5-cent Canadian St. Lawrence Seaway stamp with inverted center. This modern printing error, of which only slightly more than 100 are known, including 11 used copies, was discovered in 1959 not long after date of issuance. Widespread interest and limited supply have caused a sharp appreciation for this variety.

A most important single addition to the numismatic collections was received from Cornelius Van Schaak Roosevelt, grandson of President Theodore Roosevelt, who donated a high-relief experimental $20 gold piece dated 1907, owned originally by President Roosevelt. This exceedingly rare and significant piece is one of the first strikings of high-relief $20 gold pieces designed by the American sculptor Augustus Saint-Gaudens at the President's request. It marks a unique venture in modern monetary history, a venture which found the President of the United States and a famous sculptor working together and devoting much of their time and energy to the task of producing a new coin design of real artistic merit. Willis du Pont donated a very significant additional group of Russian coins and medals of the latter part of the 18th century. Mrs. Louise Merrick Schermerhorn presented a group of rare gold certificates including a group of three notes dated 1864, 1866, and 1877, typifying the earliest issues of United States gold certificates. To the section of medallic art were added, as a gift from Norman Stack, two rare Washington medals made in 1790 by Manly and in 1805 by Eccleston. The Medallic Art Company of New York donated an interesting group of models and dies used for the striking of the J. F. Kennedy Inaugural Medal, as well as a process set of medals showing the various steps in the striking and finishing of the medal.

Armed Forces history.—The division of military history received a unique Revolutionary War militia color carried at the Battles of Trenton and Germantown, presented by Francis W. Headman in memory of his son, Francis W. Headman, Jr. A rare Medal of Honor, awarded for gallantry in the siege of Pekin, 1900, was presented by Lt. Col. Calvin P. Titus, the recipient. Fieldwork at Sackets Harbor, N.Y., Fort Adams, Miss., and at underwater sites in Bermuda yielded significant historical materials for the collections. President

John F. Kennedy donated an ancient Greek amphora recovered from the Mediterranean Sea.

Outstanding among the objects received during the year in the division of naval history were collections of German and Japanese ordnance and electronic equipment of World War II, Japanese uniforms, and uniform items of Fleet Admiral Nimitz and Vice Admiral Lockwood. Two items associated with Pearl Harbor were received. A unique monogrammed dish for the Confederate Navy was added to the Civil War collections.

EXPLORATION AND FIELDWORK

Dr. T. Dale Stewart, head curator of anthropology, continued his research in Iraq and during the summer participated in the 1960 Shanidar Expedition sponsored jointly by the Smithsonian Institution and Columbia University. This research extends the collaboration between Dr. Stewart and Dr. Ralph S. Solecki, formerly on the staff of the Smithsonian Institution. Dr. Stewart's participation in this fourth Shanidar expedition was based on the consideration that the skull of No. 2 had been recovered last season but that the rest of the skeleton had been left in situ. After working 6 weeks on this skull in Baghdad, Dr. Stewart went to Shanidar to join Dr. and Mrs. Solecki. They spent 2 weeks uncovering the skeleton of No. 2, which unfortunately proved to be incomplete, consisting only of a few vertebrae and two leg bones. However, at the end of this period more parts of No. 3 were found and almost immediately three new skeletons. When Dr. Stewart left Shanidar in mid-August he was able to take back to Baghdad parts of five Neanderthal skeletons. This continuing exploration, therefore, is turning out to be extremely profitable and future studies of this Neanderthal material may be expected to be of considerable significance.

In the summer of 1960 an interesting discovery was made near Littleton, Colo., of a late Pleistocene bone bed with possible human associations. Because this discovery was of interest both to vertebrate paleontologists and to archeologists, Dr. Waldo R. Wedel, curator of archeology, and Dr. C. Lewis Gazin, curator of vertebrate paleontology, collaborated in outlining a project to the National Science Foundation which has resulted in a grant to make possible a thorough exploration of the Colorado site. To begin this work, in June 1961, Dr. Wedel spent about 2 weeks at the site together with George S. Metcalf, museum aide. The first stages of this digging uncovered some human artifacts and indicated that the subsequent work might be of unusual interest.

Dr. Clifford Evans, associate curator of archeology, and his wife, Dr. Betty J. Meggers, honorary research associate, during the summer of 1960 made a comparative study of certain south American collections in various European museums. During this period they also participated in the 34th International Congress of Americanists in Vienna and the 6th International Congress of Anthropological and Ethnological Sciences in Paris. In August they engaged in fieldwork in southern France, examining the famous Paleolithic sites that are important to archeologists.

Dr. Gordon D. Gibson, associate curator of ethnology, spent most of the year in ethnological fieldwork and in collecting among the Herero of South West Africa and Bechuanaland. Dr. Gibson returned by way of Egypt and other North African countries in order to obtain material for exhibits in the planning state in a new hall of Asiatic, Pacific, and African ethnology. Since this fieldwork was still in progress at the end of the fiscal year, a more complete account of it will be left for the next annual report.

For a period of about 3½ months, Dr. Eugene I. Knez, associate curator of ethnology, visited numerous museums and conducted fieldwork in various European countries, Pakistan, India, Burma, and other countries of southeastern Asia, Hong Kong, Taiwan, Korea, and Japan to obtain, through local scientists and officials, contemporary ethnological materials for use in a renovated exhibit hall now being prepared in the Museum of Natural History. The work proved to be extremely successful, both in terms of ethnological materials acquired for the exhibit program and personal contacts made with local scientists and scholars.

In the spring of 1960, Dr. Henry W. Setzer, associate curator of mammals, participated in the Smithsonian-Collins expedition to Libya, organized and led by Robert L. Pomeroy and Alan C. Collins. The party traveled overland from Benghazi by way of Cufra Oasis to Faya in northern Tchad, investigating the little-known Tibesti Mountains on the Libyan-Tchad frontier, and returned to the Mediterranean coast by way of Sebha Oasis. In all, they traveled about 5,000 miles, and Dr. Setzer obtained a valuable collection of mammals. En route to join the expedition, he spent a brief period at the British Museum (Natural History) in London, comparing type specimens of various European and African mammals.

Toward the end of the year Dr. Charles O. Handley, Jr., associate curator of mammals, and D. I. Rhymer, office of exhibits, collected in the higher parts of the Clinch Mountains, near Saltville, Va. This exploration was a part of Dr. Handley's continuing studies of mammals of the southeastern United States. The 250 forest mammals obtained complement the large collection of meadow mammals taken in the same region in 1957 by Dr. Handley and associates.

Field studies in the survey of the variation and distribution of the birds of the Isthmus of Panamá under Dr. Alexander Wetmore, honorary research associate and retired Secretary of the Smithsonian

Institution, were continued from January through March. The work began with 10 days devoted mainly to water birds on the lower Río Chagres at Juan Mina. Following this Dr. Wetmore accompanied a party from the Gorgas Memorial Laboratory for Tropical Medicine to eastern Darién. Through cooperation of the air arm of the U.S. Army, the men with their equipment were transferred by helicopter from the town of El Real, on the lower Río Tuira, to Cerro Pirre, where camp was established on the headwaters of the Río Seteganti about 10 kilometers from the Colombian boundary. Birds collected for study skins served also as a source of blood samples to be checked for disease, and of ectoparasites, particularly mites, by other members of the party. The area is one of special interest as the mountain is isolated and has a number of species of South American affinity little known in Panamá.

Most of the remainder of the time available this year was given to studies in the upper basin of the Río Chagres. In mid-February Dr. and Mrs. Wetmore, with two assistants from the Gorgas Laboratory, crossed to the head of Madden Lake by dugout canoe and continued up the Río Boquerón to the mouth of the Quebrada Peluca near the base of Cerro Bruja. Through the kindness of W. H. Esslinger, chief hydrographer, Meteorological and Hydrographic Branch of the Canal Zone, quarters were available here, and also later at Candelaria, in small buildings housing stream gauge equipment for record of runoff waters that feed Madden Lake. At the end of 2 weeks the party moved to the Río Pequení for further studies. Both areas were still heavily forested, with few human inhabitants and fewer trails. Travel was mainly by walking and wading along the beds of streams. Although this was the dry season, rain fell daily. The specimens and notes obtained are especially valuable since this is an intermediate area between the eastern and western sections of the isthmus that has been little known from the standpoint of its biology. The men from the Gorgas Laboratory prepared a considerable series of blood smears and also made collections of biting insects of interest as possible carriers of disease. The season closed with a week at La Jagua in the savanna region east of Pacora.

The division of birds lent the services of Bernard R. Feinstein, museum aide, to the U.S. Army Medical Research and Development Command for much of the year. Mr. Feinstein has been spending the year in South Vietnam collecting with an expedition that is partially sponsored by the Bernice P. Bishop Museum, of Honolulu.

In June, William D. Field, associate curator of insects, spent 2 weeks in field research in the Great Smoky Mountains National Park and other areas of Georgia and South Carolina. Among many valuable additions he made to the national collection of butterflies during the trip, special mention should be made of the very rare species

Strymon kingi and *Megathymus harrisi*, both of which are new to the Museum's collections.

Dr. Oliver S. Flint, Jr., associate curator of insects, spent two periods collecting Trichoptera and related groups for the Museum. In May he obtained collections of such material in the area of New York State near Cornell University in connection with a trip to study museum collections. Early in June he made extensive collections in the vicinity of Highlands, N.C., and other areas of the Great Smoky Mountains and the Blue Ridge. The collections obtained at these localities contained many species and at least two genera not previously in the national collections.

In September Dr. Frederick M. Bayer, associate curator of marine invertebrates, accompanied by Anthony Di Stefano, of the office of exhibits, made a collecting trip to Florida to obtain material and notes for the coral shore exhibit of the Hall of Oceanic Life. Their work was greatly facilitated by the cooperation of the staff of the Marine Laboratory of the University of Miami. Soldier Key, lying 5 miles south of Cape Florida on the south end of Biscayne Key, provided a good representation of the flora and fauna of the coral shore area. The field party made complete photographic notes on the shoreline and shore vegetation, as well as taking a series of underwater photographs. The specimens were taken from the upper, lower, and reef flat platforms, including marine animals, algae, and other plants. Many plaster casts were made in the field and all material obtained was returned to Washington, where it will serve as a basis for the planned exhibit.

In August and September, Charles E. Cutress, Jr., associate curator of marine invertebrates, and Raymond Hays, of the office of exhibits, spent nearly 4 weeks in Oregon collecting specimens and data for a rocky shore habitat group being planned for the Hall of Oceanic Life. An excellent collecting site was found about 6 miles from the Oregon Institute of Marine Biology at Charleston, and the facilities of this Institute enabled the field party to make the best possible use of their time. In addition to obtaining many thousands of specimens of invertebrates, fishes, and plants, the party took numerous color photographs covering the animals and plants collected as well as the site. In addition, sketches and color notations were made in preparation for the proposed exhibit.

In October, Dr. Harald A. Rehder, curator of mollusks, worked in the Pacific area, particularly on Jaluit Atoll, in the southern Marshall Islands. This atoll is of much interest to biologists working in the Pacific because it was nearly completely devastated by a typhoon several years ago. Since that time two or three visits have been made to the area to observe the sequence of events following such a natural disaster. Dr. Rehder explored and studied various islands in the atoll, their shorelines and reefs, and collected mollusks and other marine life. At the 42 field stations made on the various islands composing the atoll a fairly complete collection of the reef and shallow-water mollusks was made, amounting to thousands of specimens. This collection will give the National Museum a good representation of the reef fauna of the southern Marshalls and will complement existing collections from the other parts of the Marshall Islands.

Between the middle of November and the middle of February, Dr. Joseph P. E. Morrison, associate curator of mollusks, and Thomas G. Baker, of the office of exhibits, made intensive explorations in New Caledonia to acquire specimens and data for a coral-reef group being planned in the new Hall of Oceanic Life. The cooperation of various residents of Noumea, New Caledonia, including staff members of the Oceanographic Institution and the South Pacific Commission, made it possible for them to spend much time on the reefs near Noumea and to make productive dives from small boats. The barrier reef off the coast of New Caledonia presents diverse habitats, and a very rich fauna was observed in many spots. It is anticipated that the materials and photographs returned to the Museum will permit the exhibits staff to design and build an exceptionally fine replica of a Pacific coral reef, although some further exploration may be necessary in order to obtain certain fishes and a few other typical elements of the fauna.

Dr. Richard S. Cowan, associate curator of phanerogams, in mid-June, accompanied by four staff members of the office of exhibits, examined nine sites along the eastern coast of Virginia and North Carolina for the purpose of selecting one that would serve as a basis for constructing a coastal-life group in the future hall of plant science. A large number of photographs were made, sketches and watercolor paintings of scenes and objects were executed, and the leaves of plants were cast in plaster for future use in our exhibits laboratory.

Dr. Velva E. Rudd, associate curator of phanerogams, spent about 3 weeks in Mexico, where she attended the First Botanical Congress of that country. Subsequently she traveled about 900 miles in Mexico studying the different types of vegetation, such as montane pine forest, cactus, desert, and tropical selva. Specimens were obtained for the National Herbarium, and many botanists in Mexico were encouraged to make collections and send them to Washington for study.

Early in August, Dr. G. A. Cooper, head curator of the department of geology, accompanied by Henry B. Roberts, museum aide, and Dr. Druid Wilson of the U.S. Geological Survey, made a very profitable trip to the vicinity of Hampton, Va., where they collected Miocene fossils along the James River. Two borrow pits were visited, Wilson's Pit and Rice's Pit, which have a great surface from which to collect in contrast to the usual cliff sections found in the Chesapeake Bay area. Consequently hundreds of very fine specimens were obtained. Perhaps the large areas available for searching account for the fact that a fair number of new species have been turned up from these particular pits.

In September, Dr. George S. Switzer, curator of mineralogy and petrology, accompanied by Paul E. Desautels, associate curator of that division, collected excellent mineralogical material at the Sowerbutt Quarry in the vicinity of Butler, N.J. In August Dr. Switzer visited Norway and Denmark, partly to attend meetings of the International Geological Congress and the International Mineralogical Association in Copenhagen. Before the meeting Dr. Switzer joined a field excursion to mineral occurrences in southern Norway, visiting the Kongsberg silver mines, the serpentine deposits at Modum, the Skutterud cobalt mine, the granite pegmatites of the Iveland district, the Ødegärden phosphate deposits, and the nepheline syenite pegmatites of Langesundfjord.

In February Edward P. Henderson, associate curator of mineralogy and petrology, accompanied by Dr. Chao of the U.S. Geological Survey and Dr. Cohen of the Mellon Institute of Pittsburgh, visited various localities in Georgia that had produced tektites. Five tektite localities were investigated, and it was found that the formation from which these tektites come are more complex than the local geologists had previously thought. Since the Georgia tektites have been chemically dated as being 29 million years old, and this date has been established by two separate investigators, the findings of tektites in different parts of Georgia will make it possible to date accurately some of the widely scattered beds in some sedimentary formations that contain very few fossils.

Dr. Richard S. Boardman, associate curator of invertebrate paleontology and paleobotany, during the summer months visited several European museums and universities studying collections and also explored areas for purposes of collecting. During June he collected invertebrate fossils from many of the classic Lower Paleozoic localities in Britain. These localities include many of the faunas used as standards for comparisons for stratigraphic and geologic time intervals over the world. During July and parts of August and September he collected in Norway and Sweden. The Island of Gotland produced an even ton of remarkably preserved invertebrate fossils, which will provide an important research collection as well as many specimens of exhibit potential.

In connection with the Hall of Invertebrate Paleontology then being renovated, Dr. Porter M. Kier, associate curator of invertebrate paleontology and paleobotany, accompanied by Dr. Erle G. Kauffman, assistant curator of that division, explored Scientists' Cliffs, Md., to obtain sediment from the Miocene outcrop to enable them to reconstruct an echinoid-bearing slab for the echinoderm exhibit. They also obtained many Miocene mollusks. Early in June Dr. Kier joined Dr. Raymond Douglass, of the U.S. Geological Survey, in Nevada, where they searched for Upper Cambrian carpoids. These are primitive echinoderms, and no specimens as old as the Upper Cambrian have been found outside of one locality in France. Two specimens were located in Nevada, and these are sufficiently well preserved to show characters never before reported in these animals. In the same general area a collection of trilobites was made, and many topotypic corals were obtained from the Pennsylvanian in the vicinity of Ely, Nev.

During the year Dr. Richard Cifelli, associate curator of invertebrate paleontology and paleobotany, made three expeditions in the Atlantic in collaboration with staff members of the Woods Hole Oceanographic Institution. In August he joined the oceanographic vessel *R. V. Crawford*, which then traveled in a southeasterly direction and occupied the same stations that were studied a year earlier by the scientists working from the *R. V. Chain*. Hydrographic observations were made and 200-meter oblique plankton tows were taken at each station. A separate net was used for Foraminifera and a total of 15 samples was collected. After completing work at the last station in the Sargasso Sea, the vessel returned directly to Woods Hole. In January Dr. Cifelli joined the research vessel *R. V. Chain* at Woods Hole and accompanied it along the regular Woods Hole AEC traverse to Bermuda. Despite the cold, windy weather the scientists were able to occupy all the 15 stations along this traverse, and Dr. Cifelli collected a plankton sample for Foraminifera from each. This was his third series from the traverse.

Dr. Cifelli's third trip, also on board the *R. V. Chain*, was in the equatorial Atlantic Ocean. The principal area of investigation was the Romanche Trench. This feature lies on the Equator at about longitude 18° W. and is a region of considerable geologic interest. The depth of the Trench is over 8,000 meters, but in contrast to other ocean deeps it is not situated adjacent to an island chain or continental land mass. Rather, it lies on the Mid-Atlantic Ridge itself. Dr. Cifelli joined the *Chain* in Freetown, Sierra Leone, on April 19 and accompanied it to Woods Hole. Coring, bottom sampling, and bottom dredging were emphasized during this phase of the cruise. The group obtained five cores, six bottom samples, and one dredge. All the cores contained rich layers of Foraminifera and one of them was taken from the deepest part of the trench. In addition, plankton tows were taken every night along the traverse from the Romanche Trench to Woods Hole. Dr. Cifelli obtained 52 plankton samples, which will be a valuable addition to the national collections, since they cover a very large range of latitude.

In August, Dr. Erle G. Kauffman, associate curator of invertebrate paleontology and paleobotany, joined a paleontological expedition sponsored and financed by the University of Michigan. The objective was to obtain vertebrate and invertebrate fossil remains and detailed stratigraphic data from the Upper Cretaceous and the Lower Tertiary coal-bearing formations of the Alaskan interior. Fossils other than those of plants had not previously been recorded from these beds. Beginning work in the vicinity of Healy, Alaska, the group examined in detail every major outcrop of the Tertiary coal-bearing formation and some of the Upper Cretaceous deposits, including the type sections in the Healy-McKinley area. Numerous well-preserved plant fossils were obtained but no animal remains were discovered. A representative flora was returned to the Smithsonian. Cross-bedding studies of the coal-bearing formation were made at many localities, and these studies enabled the group to define more clearly the position and size of the Tertiary coal basins and the direction of transport and source area for the Tertiary Clastic sediments. A final week was spent on the Kenai Peninsula in the vicinity of Homer, Alaska, where beds of the Kenai formation, also a Tertiary coal-bearing deposit, are well exposed in the sea cliffs. Again a search for animal life proved fruitless, although abundant plant fossils were encountered and collected. A great deal of new information concerning the stratigraphy and sedimentology of the Alaskan coal-bearing deposits was gathered, although the principal goal of the expedition, the discovery of fossil animals in these deposits, was not achieved. During a brief trip in July to Brightseat, Md., Dr. Kauffman was accompanied by museum aide Henry B. Roberts. The purpose of this expedition was to study the fauna and stratigraphy of the Upper Cretaceous Monmouth formation and the Brightseat formation and to note the nature of their contact at the type section. More than 3,000 invertebrate specimens were collected, including several species previously unknown from the Maryland Cretaceous and perhaps a few species new to science.

Dr. C. Lewis Gazin, curator of vertebrate paleontology, carried on extended research in Europe. In addition to studying historic fossil collections in many European museums and attending the International Geological Congress at Copenhagen and various paleontological symposia, Dr. Gazin also visited various collecting localities and obtained important material for the national collections. In France he visited the various collecting sites for Paleocene mammals in the Cernay area and all the known quarries where Sparnacian or Lower Eocene mammals have been found. He also worked at the Cormeilles Quarry near Paris, where a remarkable display of Early Tertiary horizons from the Ludian or Gypse de Paris through the Sannoisian to the Stampian could be seen. This is very near Sannois, the type locality for the Sannoisian Lower Oligocene. In Spain, in the vicinity of Barcelona, Dr. Gazin visited important localities where strata are exposed from the Eocene to the Pliocene. Although the local collections are essentially from the Upper Tertiary, a surprising amount of Eocene, generally regarded as barren, is exposed in the area.

A party consisting of Dr. Nicholas Hotton, 3d, associate curator of vertebrate paleontology, Kurt Hauschildt, museum aide, and Dr. Frank C. Whitmore, of the U.S. Geological Survey, made two expeditions during the year to Hampton, Va., to collect portions of a whale skeleton from the Yorktown formation. They collected the following parts of the whale: Right mandible, right maxilla, two complete ribs, about 15 vertebrae representing thoracic, lumbar, and caudal regions, and assorted small bones, mostly chevrons. This skeleton has been tentatively identified as that of a species of *Balaenoptera*. It lay about 8 feet below the top of the Yorktown (Miocene) formation as exposed at the site.

In November, Dr. Hotton collected vertebrates of Mississippian age and prospected other Mississippian localities at Greer, W. Va., and vicinity. He was accompanied by William E. Moran, formerly a member of the staff of the division of vertebrate paleontology. The Mississippian Period is of critical importance in the study of tetrapod evolution, since it marks the time of the initial radiation of the amphibians and the probable origins of the reptiles. Unfortunately, most Mississippian sediments are of marine origin, so that the rarity of terrestrial deposits of that age makes them doubly important. Three quarries were visited and much material of significance was obtained, including a partial skeleton of an embolomerous amphibian. In February Dr. Hotton left for South Africa for a collecting season in the famous Permian Karroo beds. In this work he was furnished every accommodation by his colleagues at the University of Witwatersrand in Johannesburg. Considerable success was achieved in obtaining many skulls and other skeletal portions of a variety of Permian and Triassic vertebrate forms, none of which were previously represented in the collections of the Smithsonian Institution.

Staff members of the Museum of History and Technology visited many museums in the United States and abroad during the year, mostly to observe exhibit techniques or to procure materials for exhibition in the new building. The fieldwork of these staff members generally involves trips of this sort, or visits to numerous individuals and institutions about the country in an attempt to procure exhibit materials or to learn something about developments that will be useful in the Smithsonian's expanding efforts.

For a week in September, John C. Ewers, Assistant Director of the Museum of History and Technology, was able to renew his research interests in the Blackfeet Indians in Montana. Many changes have taken place since he last visited the Blackfeet Reservation in

1953. Among these have been a rapid decline in the use of the Black-feet language by the Indians, the virtual disappearance of living links between the traditional buffalo-hunting culture and the present, the probable discontinuance of the tribal sun dance in 1959, the transference of Indian education from Indian Service schools to public schools of the State of Montana, and the abolition of Indian prohibition followed by the opening of several taverns in the town of Browning. Mr. Ewers obtained pertinent information which enabled him to bring up to date his studies of the history of the Blackfeet arts and crafts.

During the last half of August and early September Mendel L. Peterson, head curator of armed forces history, explored underwater sites in Bermuda. He took part in an investigation of four shipwreck sites, three of which dated from the 17th century and the fourth from the early 19th century. A collection of several hundred objects was recovered and forwarded to the Smithsonian. The most interesting wreck site examined is believed to be that of the *San Antonio*, a ship of the Spanish treasure fleet which was wrecked on the southwestern reefs of Bermuda in 1621. Outstanding among the hundreds of objects recovered are two wine jars of different shape and size in perfect condition. Both are of extremely rare types. Additional items recovered were money cowries, blue glass trade beads, tanbark, tanned leather, a very large number of red-ware shards, Talavera shards, and some jars of numerous shapes. Among the ordnance materials found were solid iron shot of two sizes, an extremely rare stone shot, small spheroid pebbles used in swivel guns, and three varieties of wire musket shot believed to be unique. A second ship investigated was the *Sea Venture*, which was wrecked in 1609 and resulted in the settlement of Bermuda. There is no doubt about the identity of this ship; an irrefutable chain of evidence has been discovered on the site, and the location of the wreck and circumstances of its stranding coincide perfectly with eyewitness accounts of the event. The two remaining ships are the *Virginia Merchant*, destroyed in 1660, and the *Caesar*, an English merchant ship bound for Baltimore that struck reefs southwest of Bermuda in 1818.

EXHIBITIONS

In the introductory statement of this Report the work completed in the Smithsonian's exhibits-modernization in the past 8 years has been summarized. Twenty-two National Museum halls are described in some detail in that recapitulation. It therefore seems appropriate here to record only a few additional details that pertain particularly to events of the past year.

During the year six modernized exhibition halls were opened to the public.

The third and last section of the textile hall gallery, presenting the origin and history of lacemaking and rugmaking and popular types of American needlework, was completed for public inspection on December 9, 1960. Included in this display are old American quilts, samplers dating from the 18th and 19th centuries, laces beginning with 16th-century drawnwork and also machine-made laces of the 19th century, and needlework handkerchiefs.

The completely renovated Hall of Monetary History and Medallic Art was formally opened in the Arts and Industries Building on March 18, 1961, in the presence of the Secretary of the Treasury, the Under Secretary of the Treasury, Senator Clinton P. Anderson and Representative Frank T. Bow, Regents of the Smithsonian Institution, members of the diplomatic corps, donors, collectors, and representatives of numismatic organizations from all sections of the United States. The central series of 19 specially designed cases traces the major aspects of the development of money economy from primitive barter to the establishment of our modern monetary system. The hall also features the world's largest collection of gold coins, given to the Smithsonian Institution by the late Paul A. Straub. Almost 4,000 silver coins complement this series.

The story of life through the ages from the oldest known fossils, dated 1,600 million years ago, to the Cenozoic Era mammals is depicted in three halls in the Natural History Building. The synoptic display of fossil plants features those that contributed to the formation of coal. Fossil backboneless animals such as sponges, corals, snails, clams, trilobites, and other extinct shelled animals are shown in geological time sequence. The second hall, that of fossil fishes and amphibians was informally opened in June 1960. This year a life-sized group was completed, showing an encounter between two kinds of pelycosaurs, or fin-backed reptiles, as it might have happened about 260 million years ago. The third hall, the Age of Mammals in North America, traces the succession of mammals in the five epochs of Tertiary time from Paleocene to Pliocene, a period of 70 million years. Skeletons of the better-known groups of mammals are supplemented by a display of skulls for each of these epochs. The large mural painting by Jay H. Matternes depicting some of the characteristic mammals with contemporary reptiles and plants of the Bridger middle Eocene has been completed, and a second mural, showing a Harrisonian or early Miocene life assemblage of mammals, is nearly finished. These three halls were formally opened to the public on the night of June 6, 1961.

The first of two modernized halls of North American Archeology was opened to the public on June 24, 1961. A number of the 34 exhibits in this hall portray and explain important aspects of aboriginal North American life. About half of the exhibits in the hall interpret the prehistoric cultures of the North American Arctic, the North Pacific Coast, California, and the Southwest by means of selected artifacts, graphic materials, and life-sized and miniature groups.

A temporary meteorite exhibit, placed in the areaway connecting the jade room and this archeology hall on the second floor of the Natural History Building, was also opened to the public on June 24, 1961.

The modernized Hall of Petroleum, adjoining the iron and steel exhibit in the Arts and Industries Building, provides a brief historical account of the growth of the petroleum industry since the discovery of the Drake well at Titusville, Pa., in 1859. This hall, completed in June 1961, features animated models showing the two earliest methods of drilling employed in the United States—the springpole and the Drake rig. A small display of geophysical exploration equipment, made possible by the generosity of Seimos GmbH, Humble Oil Co., Continental Oil Co., Schlumberger, and Everett Lee DeGolyer, Jr., reviews the principal methods employed to expand knowledge of America's oil resources. With the cooperation of Standard Oil Co. (Indiana), Universal Oil Products Co., Esso Standard Oil Co., M. W. Kellogg Co., C. P. Dubbs, and the Massachusetts Institute of Technology (Prof. Harold Weber), an account of the major developments in oil refining is presented. The experimental still used by Drs. Burton and Humphries at Whiting, Ind., which led to the first large-scale thermal cracking of crude, was graciously donated to the Museum by Dr. Robert Wilson. A polymerization plant model shows one of the earliest processes for increasing the high-octane content of gasoline, which was important in making fuel available for the allied air forces in 1939–40. The historic fluid-catalytic cracking process which was evolved in 1941 to provide the best qualities of fuel needed by the U.S. Air Force is also shown, as well as a platinum-catalyst reforming process demonstrated as a sample of the postwar effort to convert lower-grade to a higher-grade fuel.

Construction of Hall 8, in which will be displayed the material culture of the peoples of the Pacific Islands and South and Southeast Asia, was completed in May 1961. New construction was commenced in the adjacent Hall 7, which will contain the exhibits for the peoples of Africa and eastern Asia. Continued progress was made on the contractual construction of the large west hall fixtures for the display of oceanic life. Architect's plans for the modernization of the large east Hall 2, which will contain the dinosaurs and the Mesozoic reptiles, were completed and the construction contract let in June 1961.

At the end of the eighth year of the continuing modernization of exhibits program, 9 of the 15 galleries on the first floor and 4 second-floor halls in the Natural History Building have been renovated and opened to public view.

Curatorial planning of exhibits for the large Hall of Oceanic Life, now under construction, comprised the major exhibits project of the department of zoology during the year. All members of the curatorial staffs of the divisions of fishes, marine invertebrates, and mollusks were actively engaged in this project, and those of the divisions of mammals and reptiles and amphibians were involved to some extent. Four field trips have been made to collect materials for this hall. Dr. Joseph P. E. Morrison and James Watson obtained materials for the marshy-shore and sandy-beach groups near Ocean Spring, Miss., and Beaufort, N.C. For the Pacific coast rock-shore and tidepool habitat group, Charles E. Cutress, Jr., and Raymond E. Hays visited Cape Arago, Oreg. Coral-shore specimens were collected by Dr. Frederick M. Bayer and Anthony DiStefano at Soldier Key off Miami, Fla. Dr. Morrison and Thomas G. Baker gathered material and information for the coral-reef exhibit in New Caledonia. Five casts of fishes near record size have been donated by Al Pflueger of North Miami, Fla.

Because of the necessarily long period of time during which the large east Hall 2 and the northeast Hall 6 will be closed, a selection of dinosaurs and Pleistocene animals of popular interest has been placed on display in the rotunda of the Natural History Building.

During the year 16 new exhibits interpreting the history of medicine, dentistry, and pharmacy were installed on the east gallery of the Arts and Industries Building, bringing the total of modernized exhibits in the field of medical sciences to 28. These new displays illustrate the practice of bloodletting through the ages, the development of surgical anesthesia, spectacles, medicine chests, antique drug jars, tools of the apothecary, and dental instruments. A new exhibit on the eye was installed in the hall of health.

A special exhibition of the "geophysical globe," a new relief globe of superior accuracy, was held in the rotunda of the Arts and Industries Building during April 1961. A diorama prepared for exhibition in the hall of electricity of the Museum of History and Technology, depicting the broadcast of a program from the studio of KDKA (one of the pioneer commercial broadcasting stations in the world) during the winter of 1921–22, was placed on public display. A special exhibition, featuring the model of the 1819 steamship *Savannah*, was displayed in the watercraft hall in celebration of National Maritime Week, May 21–27, 1961. The locomotive "Pioneer," which served the Cumberland Valley Railroad in 1851, was placed on exhibition in the east hall of the Arts and Industries Building in February 1961. Two landmark machine tools of 1865–75, completely restored and made operative by William Henson, were placed on exhibition in the southwest gallery of the Arts and Industries Building. The first, a No. 1 Brown and Sharpe Universal Milling Machine, is set up to mill the flutes of twist drills, which was one of the first operations undertaken by this type of machine. The other tool, a Jones and Lamson turret lathe, is equipped with authentically reconstructed turret tools to produce brass oil cups. A temporary exhibition of fine prints, drawings, and photographs of 18th- and 19th-century civil engineering works, planned by Associate Curator Robert M. Vogel, was displayed from February 1 to April 30, 1961. A particularly attractive display of decorative watches was installed in the hall of timekeeping and the Schlage antique lock collection was shown for a period of 2 months in the rotunda of the Arts and Industries Building.

An experimental fuel cell tractor, developed by the Allis-Chalmers Manufacturing Co., was placed on special display in the hall of farm machinery in October 1960. Throughout the year a rotating exhibition of color photographs lent by the Soil Conservation Service of the U.S. Department of Agriculture was maintained at the east end of this hall.

A special exhibit featuring 250 masterpieces of ancient Greek coinage, prepared by Mrs. Clain-Stefanelli from material lent by a private collector, was displayed from December 1960 to March 11, 1961, in the rotunda of the Arts and Industries Building and from March 18 to May 26, 1961, in the monetary history hall. Several small temporary exhibits of a topical nature were arranged by the division of political history. An inaugural exhibit was displayed from December 1960 to March 1961, and during the same period state gifts presented to President Eisenhower were shown. Early voting machines and presidential commemorative material were exhibited during February 1961. During the year the White House china collection expanded so that representative pieces from almost every administration are now on exhibition. A selected group of historical items from the Postal History Museum of the Post Office Department, which was transferred to the Smithsonian Institution April 1, 1961, was placed on exhibition in the philately hall. On May 26, 1961, a rare American wooden statue of William Pitt, carved in 1801 by Joseph Wilson for the eccentric "Lord" Timothy Dexter of Newburyport, Mass., a gift of Mrs. Arthur M. Greenwood, was placed on exhibition in the cultural history hall. From January 15 to February 5, 1961, the first public showing of the recently acquired Harry T. Peter's "America on Stone" lithography collection was held in the foyer of the Natural History Building.

A complete display of United States military decorations and medals, and a Civil War 12-pounder gun on its carriage were added to the existing displays in the hall of military history. A number of warship models, relating particularly to the Civil War, were added to the exhibits in the hall of naval history, while other models were progressively retired for major restoration. This restoration normally involves complete repainting and re-rigging, and frequently requires extensive research in the interest of detailed historical accuracy.

During the month of September 1960 a special exhibition of memorabilia of Gen. John J. Pershing was placed on view in the rotunda of the Arts and Industries Building in conjunction with the national celebration of General Pershing's birth. Roman antiquities recovered from the Mediterrranean and the Sea of Galilee by the Link expedition during the previous summer were displayed from April 1 to April 26, 1961. The division of military history prepared a special exhibition of military epaulets for the annual meeting of the Company of Military Collectors and Historians which was held May 19–21, 1961, at Gettysburg, Pa.

Dr. A. C. Smith, Director of the Museum of Natural History, assumed the chairmanship of the committee coordinating and supervising the modernization of the natural history exhibits following the retirement of Dr. Herbert Friedmann as head curator of zoology. Dr. Friedmann served with distinction as a member of the exhibits planning committee since its formation in 1950, and played an active and substantial role in the organization and development of the exhibits modernization program.

The major objective of the exhibits program of the Museum of History and Technology, which is being coordinated by Assistant Director John C. Ewers, is the development of exhibits for the new building now under construction. Many of the exhibits destined for future display in this new museum building are now being installed in the Arts and Industries Building until the Museum of History and Technology Building is completed for occupancy. Exhibits for a number of halls in this new building were prepared in the exhibits laboratory and carefully stored until they can be installed. These included displays for the halls of costumes, political history, ceramics, everyday life in the American past, physics, railroads, Armed Forces history, and ordnance.

Exhibits Chief John E. Anglim provided the over-all supervision of exhibits for the United States National Museum. The exhibits work for the Museum of History and Technology was supervised by Benjamin W. Lawless, with the assistance of Robert Widder in design, Bela S. Bory in production, and Robert Klinger in the model shop. Rolland O. Hower, assisted by Thomas G. Baker and Julius Tretick, supervised the renovation of exhibition halls in the Museum of Natural History. The design of the modernized halls in existing buildings has been greatly aided by Richard S. Johnson, design branch chief, and John H. Morrissey, architectural branch chief of the architectural and structural division of the Public Buildings Service, General Services Administration, and by Luther H. Flouton, Charles J. Nora, and Julius J. Dickerson, design architects of that agency. Carroll Lusk, museum lighting specialist of Syracuse, N.Y., provided valuable consultative assistance to designers of exhibition halls for the Museum of History and Technology. George Weiner, with the assistance of Constance Minkin, Basil Andronicos, and Edna Owens, continued the editing of the curator's drafts of exhibit labels.

DOCENT SERVICE

The Junior League of Washington continued its outstanding volunteer guided tour program for schools within the Greater Washington area, with the cooperation of G. Carroll Lindsay, curator of the Smithsonian Museum Service, working with Mrs. Dean Cowie, chairman of the Smithsonian Volunteer Committee of the Junior League of Washington, and Mrs. E. Tillman Stirling, cochairman. At the conclusion of the tour season Mrs. Cowie was succeeded as chairman by her cochairman, Mrs. Stirling. Mrs. Vernon Knight will serve as cochairman of the Docent Committee for the forthcoming year.

During the 1960–61 season, tours were conducted in the Halls of Everyday Life in Early America, Native Peoples of the Americas, Gems and Minerals, Textiles, and Power. Tours in each of the halls were scheduled twice each day, 5 days a week from October through January. In February tours were offered four times daily in the Halls of Everyday Life in Early America and Native Peoples of the Americas, while they were continued in the other three halls on the same schedule of twice daily. Tours were conducted through April.

A total of 579 tours were conducted, in which 16,207 children participated. This represents a marked increase over last year's participation. It is important to express in this report the deep gratitude of all connected with the Smithsonian for the notable service to the community and the Institution given by these able and dedicated volunteer workers.

In addition to Mrs. Cowie and Mrs. Stirling, the members of the Docent Committee were: Mrs. George Armstrong, Mrs. A. Stuart Baldwin, Mrs. William Dixon, Mrs. William Ford, Mrs. Clark Gearhart, Mrs. George Gerber, Mrs. Everett Hutchinson, Mrs. Charles Kelly, Mrs. Vernon Knight, Mrs. Edward Lamont, Mrs. Ralph Lee III, Mrs. Dickson Loos, Mrs. John E. Malone, Mrs. John Manfuso, Mrs. Ernest May, Mrs. William McClure, Mrs. Robert McCormick, Mrs. Arnold McKinnon, Mrs. Peter Macdonald, Mrs. Joseph Metcalf, Mrs. William Minshall, Mrs. Minot Mulligan, Mrs. James Rasbury, Mrs. Robert Rogers, Mrs. W. James Sears, Mrs. William Sloan, Mrs. Walter Slowinski, Mrs. James Stallings, Mrs. John Voorhees, Mrs. Richard Wallis, and Mrs. Marc White.

BUILDINGS AND EQUIPMENT

On May 19, 1961, the cornerstone of the Museum of History and Technology was laid, with the Regents of the Smithsonian Institution and members of the Joint Congressional Committee participating in placing the mortar for the stone. The Honorable Earl Warren, Chief Justice of the United States Supreme Court and Chancellor of the Smithsonian Institution, together with Senator Clinton P. Anderson, Regent of the Smithsonian Institution and Chairman of the Joint Congressional Committee for the Museum of History and Technology, spoke of the history and purpose of the new building. At the close of the fiscal year the building was approximately 50 percent complete.

A contract was awarded for the construction of the east wing extension as well as alterations and air conditioning of the existing Natural History Building January 3, 1961, to the George Hyman Construction Co. Construction was started January 6, 1961, and the project on June 30, 1961 was 17.5 percent complete. This east wing extension will provide 195,000 net square feet of needed space for workrooms and laboratories for the scientific work of the Museum of Natural History.

In the Museum of Natural History, an additional 1,152 square feet of floor area has been added to the division of marine invertebrates by the installation of second-floor levels in rooms 82, 83, and 83B. Additional lighting, utilities, and air-conditioning equipment have been provided. A second-floor level has been installed in the supply division stockroom adding approximately 1,496 square feet to this area. The mineral hall has been repainted and the floor in the jade hall has been restored to its original finish. The deteriorated plaster in the north stairway has been removed and replaced, and all surfaces have been repainted. Additional space has been provided for the exhibits laboratory in the west court.

In the Arts and Industries Building, all loose, damaged plaster has been removed from the north entrance, surfaces replastered, and the entire area repainted. The hall of military history has been completely redecorated.

The buildings management department furnished the custodial and mechanical services which included the installation of needed new doors, rewiring exhibit cases, and the improvement of the security alarm system.

CHANGES IN ORGANIZATION AND STAFF

Effective June 16, 1961, the title of the division of industrial cooperation in the department of arts and manufactures within the Museum of History and Technology of the United States National Museum was changed to the division of manufactures and heavy industries.

Frank M. Setzler, head curator of the department of anthropology, retired December 31, 1960, after 30 years service. Dr. Herbert Friedmann, head curator of the department of zoology, retired May 31, 1961, after 32 years service. Dr. Friedmann is now director of the Los Angeles County Museum.

Charles G. Dorman, assistant curator of political history, transferred to the National Park Service, effective July 9, 1960. Dr. David H. Dunkle, associate curator of vertebrate paleontology, transferred to the U.S. Geological Survey on September 18, 1960. Dr. Anthony N. B. Garvan, head curator of the department of history, resigned October 16, 1960, to accept a professorship at the University of Pennsylvania. John D. Shortridge, associate curator of cultural history, resigned June 1, 1961. Eugene S. Ferguson, curator of mechanical and civil engineering, resigned June 23, 1961, to accept a professorship at Iowa State University, Ames, Iowa. Dr. William J. King, curator of electricity, resigned June 23, 1961, to accept an appointment with the American Institute of Physics, New York City.

Dr. Richard H. Howland was appointed head curator of the department of civil history, effective November 7, 1960. The head curator vacancy in the department of anthropology was filled by the promotion of Dr. T. Dale Stewart, effective March 5, 1961. Eugene N. Ostroff accepted an appointment as associate curator in charge of the section of photography, division of graphic arts, on July 25, 1960. Dr. Oliver S. Flint, Jr., was appointed associate curator of insects, effective January 1, 1961. Dr. Thomas R. Soderstrom was appointed effective October 3, 1960, assistant curator of grasses.

Respectfully submitted.

REMINGTON KELLOGG, *Director.*

Dr. LEONARD CARMICHAEL,
Secretary, Smithsonian Institution.

Report on the Bureau of American Ethnology

Sir: I have the honor to submit the following report on the field researches, office work, and other operations of the Bureau of American Ethnology during the fiscal year ended June 30, 1961, conducted in accordance with the act of Congress of April 10, 1928, as amended August 22, 1949, which directs the Bureau "to continue independently or in cooperation anthropological researches among the American Indians and the natives of lands under the jurisdiction or protection of the United States and the excavation and preservation of archeologic remains."

SYSTEMATIC RESEARCHES

Dr. Frank H. H. Roberts, Jr., Director of the Bureau, devoted a portion of the year to general supervision of the activities of the Bureau and the River Basin Surveys. In midsummer he inspected the work of excavating parties operating in the Big Bend and Oahe Reservoir areas in South Dakota and a portion of the Oahe Basin in North Dakota, as well as a field party working in the Wilson Reservoir area in Kansas. Three of the parties represented the River Basin Surveys and three were from cooperating agencies. In addition, Dr. Roberts visited one excavation that was not a part of the salvage program. The work at that location consisted of investigations in the remains of Fort Kearney, Nebr., a historic army post being studied by the Nebraska State Historical Society. During part of the trip Dr. Roberts was accompanied by Dr. John M. Corbett and Carroll A. Burroughs of the Washington office of the National Park Service, and during the entire trip by Paul L. Beaubien, regional archeologist, Region Three, National Park Service. While at Pierre, S. Dak., the group took part in an informal conference attended by leaders of all the parties and many of their student helpers working in the Plains during the summer. A wide range of archeological problems in the Missouri Basin was discussed.

In September Dr. Roberts went to Mesa Verde National Park where he served as chairman of the Advisory Group for the Wetherill Mesa Project, a cooperative undertaking between the National Park Service and the National Geographic Society. The group spent 3 days discussing and inspecting the excavations underway in two large cliff ruins and studied the operations of the field laboratory handling the materials recovered during the digging. Recommendations were made pertaining to the continuance of the investigations and improvements in the handling and cataloging of specimens.

In November Dr. Roberts went to Norman, Okla., to attend the Plains Conference for Archeology and participate in discussions relating to the history of the Indians in that general area.

Early in April at Mule Creek, Wyo., Dr. Roberts made arrangements for establishing a camp and starting a series of excavations in a Paleo-Indian site—a cooperative project between the National Geographic Society and the Smithsonian Institution. Upon the completion of these activities he proceeded to Lawton, Okla., where he was the principal speaker at the dedication of the Museum for the Great Plains on April 9. Returning to the Washington office, he began preparations for sending a field party to the site at Mule Creek and in that connection left Washington early in June for Lincoln, Nebr., where he was joined by Dr. William M. Bass, who was to be the chief field assistant, and several other members of the party. They picked up two vehicles and field equipment and proceeded to Mule Creek to set up camp, and on June 12 began excavations. Dr. Roberts remained with the party until June 19. The party, however, continued operations under Dr. Bass and was busy digging at the end of the fiscal year. As a result of the work up to that time an extensive deposit of bison bones, probably representing an extinct species, and a number of artifacts have been recovered. The site is one that dates about 9,000 years ago.

Dr. Roberts completed a manuscript, "The Agate Basin Complex," which is to be published in Mexico in a volume containing articles about the Paleo-Indian. He also did the technical editing of a series of seven reports on archeological excavations and studies in three reservoir areas, to appear in Bulletin 185 of the Bureau of American Ethnology.

At the beginning of the fiscal year, Dr. Henry B. Collins, anthropologist, was in Europe studying collections in the principal museums and attending two international anthropological congresses. He visited Lascaux and a number of other Paleolithic cave and rock shelter sites in the Dordogne region of France and examined Megalithic sites and monuments in the Morbihan and Finistere districts of Brittany. Dr. Collins attended the 34th International Congress of Americanists in Vienna, July 18–25, and the 6th International Congress of Anthropological and Ethnological Sciences in Paris, July 30–August 6. At the latter he presented a paper discussing the present status of evidence bearing on the origin of Eskimo culture.

Dr. Collins continued to participate in the activities of the Arctic Institute of North Amercia as a member of its Board of Governors, as a member of the Publications Committee that supervises preparation of the journal *Arctic* and two other publication series, and of the Research Committee that plans and supervises the Institute's extensive program of Arctic research. He also continued to serve as chairman of the Directing Committee responsible for preparation of the Arctic Institute's *Arctic Bibliography*, a comprehensive work which abstracts and indexes the contents of publications in all fields of science, and in all languages, pertaining to the Arctic and sub-Arctic regions of the world. Volume 9 of *Arctic Bibliography* (1,599 pages), containing abstracts of 7,192 scientific publications on the Arctic, was published in September 1960. Of the publications abstracted in this volume, 3,170 had appeared in English, 2,548 in Russian, 790 in Swedish, Norwegian, and Danish, 338 in German, and 346 in other languages. Volume 10, similar in size and content to volume 9, is in press, and work is proceeding on volume 11.

The project which Dr. Collins organized last year for the purpose of translating Russian publications on the archeology, ethnology, and physical anthropology of northern Eurasia made progress under the editorship of Dr. Henry N. Michael of Temple University. The first volume to be completed is S. I. Rudenko's "The Ancient Culture of the Bering Sea Area and the Eskimo Problem," the only comprehensive Russian work on the archeology of northeastern Siberia. It is now in press and will appear as the first number in a special publication series of the Arctic Institute of North America. The Advisory Committee, of which Dr. Collins is chairman, has selected material—monographs and shorter papers—for five additional volumes which are now being translated. The work is being carried out with the support of a grant from the National Science Foundation.

Dr. Collins prepared a paper on the interrelationships of early Eskimo and pre-Eskimo cultures in Alaska, Canada, and Greenland and their affinities with Temperate Zone cultures in America and Asia to be published in a volume of the *Special Publications* series of the Arctic Institute of North America, and another paper on the environmental factors involved in the origin and development of Eskimo culture in the American Arctic.

Dr. William C. Sturtevant, ethnologist, spent July and August 1960 in Europe. He attended the 34th International Congress of Americanists in Vienna and the 6th International Congress of Anthropological and Ethnological Sciences in Paris. The remainder of the period was spent in museum research. In 11 museums of England, Austria, France, the Netherlands, and Sweden Dr. Sturtevant studied several hundred early specimens collected from eastern North American Indians. He located, described, and photographed many important specimens and collections, mostly from the northeast—there are surprisingly few early southeastern specimens in Europe. To one familiar with collections in the United States the number and good condition of early northeastern Indian objects in Europe are striking.

A secondary objective of Dr. Sturtevant's study in Europe was a search for possible European prototypes of modern eastern North American Indian artifacts. Although he visited seven museums of peasant and folklore materials, this project was less successful than the first, both because of time limitations and because European collecting and research in some important categories of artifacts (e.g., basketry) are insufficiently developed.

In November 1960, Dr. Sturtevant attended an informal conference on Iroquois research in New Haven, Conn., the annual meeting of the Southern Historical Association in Tulsa, Okla. (where he delivered a paper on "History, Ethnohistory, and Folk History: Seminole Examples"), and the American Indian Ethnohistoric Conference in Bloomington, Ind. He also visited several museums and archival collections in Oklahoma City, Norman, and Tulsa. There are several important collections of southeastern Indian artifacts and documents in Oklahoma.

Dr. Sturtevant also continued his research on various tribes of eastern North America. His paper "The Significance of Ethnological Similarities between Southeastern North America and the Antilles" was issued as Yale University Publications in Anthropology No. 64 (1960), and shorter comments by him appeared in Bureau of American Ethnology Bulletin 180 and in Current Anthropology, vol. 2, No. 3 (both 1961). A somewhat revised version of his "Anthropology as a Career" (Smithsonian Publication 4343) was issued October 7, 1960.

Dr. Wallace L. Chafe, linguist, completed work on two manuscripts. One of them, "Seneca Thanksgiving Rituals," which is in press as Bureau of American Ethnology Bulletin 183, contains important Seneca religious texts, as well as transcriptions of the music that accompanies one of the rituals. The other, "Handbook of the Seneca Language," a nontechnical description of Seneca orthography and grammar with an extensive glossary of Seneca terms encountered in the anthropological literature, will be published as a Bulletin of the New York State Museum. Dr. Chafe also continued the preparation of a Seneca dictionary.

Beginning in October, Dr. Chafe mailed over 600 questionnaires in a survey of the approximate numbers and ages of speakers of the extant North American Indian languages. These were addressed to individuals who have had contact with the various Indian groups. The responses have been numerous and informative, and efforts are now being made to fill in the gaps. Fieldwork for the project is being conducted in cooperation with the American Philosophical Society.

Dr. Chafe spent considerable time throughout the year processing Arikara and Caddo linguistic material already collected and preparing to do further fieldwork on Caddo. He was also fortunate in being able to do some work with a speaker of Oklahoma Cherokee living in Washington.

RIVER BASIN SURVEYS

The River Basin Surveys, a unit of the Bureau of American Ethnology organized to cooperate with the National Park Service and the Bureau of Reclamation of the Department of the Interior and the Corps of Engineers of the Department of the Army in the Inter-Agency Archeological and Paleontological Salvage Program, continued its activities throughout the year. Attention was directed to areas that are to be flooded or otherwise destroyed by the construction of large dams in the various river systems of the United States. The year's investigations were supported by a transfer of $123,895 from the National Park Service to the Smithsonian Institution. Of that sum, $103,895 was for work in the Missouri Basin and $20,000 for studies along the Chattahoochee River in Alabama and Georgia. On July 1, 1960, the Missouri Basin Project had a carryover of $9,420, and that, with the new appropriation, provided a total of $113,315 for the Missouri Basin Project. The grand total of funds available in 1960–61 for the River Basin Surveys was $133,315.

Activities in the field were mainly concerned with excavations, although there were some limited surveys in two areas. The funds available for the last fiscal year were slightly greater than those for the preceding one, but because of increased costs there was little gain in the amount of work accomplished. On July 1, 1960, there were three excavating parties working in the Missouri Basin in South Dakota. One of them was digging sites in the Big Bend Reservoir area, and the other two were working in the Oahe Reservoir area farther north. The Missouri Basin parties completed their field activities the latter part of August and returned to the headquarters at Lincoln, Nebr.

In September a party resumed explorations and excavations along the Chattahoochee River in Alabama and subsequently extended its efforts to the Georgia side of the river in the Walter F. George Reservoir area. Work continued there until the end of December. During October a small party spent a brief period investigating a site that was being destroyed by gravel operations in the upper reaches of the Big Bend Reservoir area in South Dakota and also collected material from the immediate construction areas of the Big Bend Dam.

The 1961 field season got under way in May, when a small party went to the Merritt Reservoir area in Nebraska to make a final check on possible archeological manifestations at that location. Two previous surveys there had failed to reveal cultural materials, but it was thought that because of shifting sand dunes and construction activities something previously missed might have been uncovered. Nothing of that nature was found, and the party moved to the Big Bend area in South Dakota where it was expanded and began a series of excavations in some burial mounds. A second party went to the Big Bend area on June 13 and started excavations in a large village site on the west side of the river 4 miles above the dam site. A third party started working on the west side of the Missouri River in the Oahe Reservoir Basin on June 19. It was digging in a large village site located about 5 miles south of Mobridge, S. Dak. All three parties had the season's program well under way and were busily digging at the close of the fiscal year. During the fiscal year, 11 parties representing institutions cooperating in the Missouri Basin program worked in four reservoir areas in Kansas, Nebraska, and South Dakota. There were 24 parties from cooperating institutions working in other basins throughout the country.

As of June 30, 1961, the River Basin Surveys had carried on reconnaissance work or had excavated in 255 reservoir basins located in 29 States. In addition, two lock projects and four canal areas have been examined. During the years since the program got under way 4,952 sites have been located and recorded, and of that number 1,157 were recommended for excavation or limited testing. Because complete excavation has not been possible in any but a few exceptionally small ones, when the term "excavation" is used it implies digging only as much of a site as is thought essential to provide a reasonable sample of the materials and information to be found there. Preliminary appraisal reports have been issued for most of the reservoir areas which were surveyed. In some cases no archeological manifestations were noted and no general report was issued. During the past fiscal year no new reconnaissance work was undertaken and no such reports were distributed.

By the end of the fiscal year, 519 sites in 54 reservoir areas located in 19 different States had either been tested or dug sufficiently to provide good information about them. The sites in which digging has been done cover a wide range of cultural characteristics. Some of them pertain to early hunting and gathering peoples of about 10,000 years ago, while others represent communities lived in by early historic Indians and the remains of frontier, army, and trading posts of European origin. Between the two extremes are a series of sites attributable to sedentary horticultural groups extending from approximately the 6th to the 13th centuries A.D.

Reports on the work have been published in the Smithsonian Institution Miscellaneous Collections, in Bulletins of the Bureau of American Ethnology, and in various scientific journals and historical quarterlies. Bulletin 176, containing River Basin Surveys Papers Nos. 15–20, was distributed in December 1960. These papers consist of a series of reports on historic sites excavated in the Garrison, Oahe, and Fort Randall Reservoir areas in North and South Dakota. Bulletin 179, containing River Basin Surveys Papers Nos. 21–24, a series of reports on work in Texas, Iowa, and along the Columbia River, is in proof form and should be distributed in the early part of the next fiscal year. The papers in that Bulletin were listed in the report for 1959–60 and need no further comment here. During the year, River Basin Surveys Paper No. 25, a report on the "Archeology of the John H. Kerr Reservoir Basin, Roanoke River, Virginia-North Carolina," by Carl F. Miller, was sent to the printer and will appear as Bulletin 182. Another series of River Basin Surveys Papers, Nos. 26–32, to comprise Bulletin 185, was edited and sent to the printer in June. These reports are: "Small Sites in and about Fort Berthold Indian Reservation, Garrison Reservoir, North Dakota" and "Star Village: A Fortified Historic Arikara Site in Mercer County, North Dakota," by George Metcalf; "The Dance Hall of the Santee Bottoms on the Fort Berthold Reservation, Garrison Reservoir, North Dakota," by Donald D. Hartle; "Crow-Flies-High (32MZ1), a Historic Hidatsa Village in the Garrison Reservoir Area, North Dakota," by Carling Malouf; "The Stutsman Focus: An Aboriginal Culture Complex in the Jamestown Reservoir Area, North Dakota," by Richard P. Wheeler; "Archeological Manifestations in the Toole County Section of the Tiber Reservoir Basin, Montana," by Carl F. Miller; "Archeological Salvage Investigations in the Lovewell Reservoir Area, Kansas," by Robert W. Neuman.

The figures showing the distribution of reservoir projects throughout the country and those in which excavations have been made did not change during the current fiscal year and for that reason need not be repeated. Readers desiring that information can obtain it by referring to the Bureau's 77th Annual Report, for the fiscal year 1959–60. The excavations conducted during the present fiscal year were all in reservoir areas previously listed. Figures pertaining to the work done by State and local institutions under agreements with the National Park Service have not been included in recent reports because complete information about them is not available in the River Basin Surveys office.

The River Basin Surveys received helpful cooperation throughout the year from the National Park Service, the Bureau of Reclamation, the Corps of Engineers and other army personnel, and from various State and local institutions. The field personnel of all the cooperating agencies assisted the party leaders in numerous ways, and in all areas the relationship was excellent. Both in Washington and in the field the National Park Service continued to serve as a liaison between the various agencies. It also was responsible for the preparation of estimates and justifications for the funds needed to carry on the salvage program. The Commanding Officer at Fort Benning in Georgia provided valuable assistance in numerous ways while investigations were being made in the portion of the Walter F. George Reservoir basin which lies in the Fort Benning Reservation. In addition, the Georgia Historical Commission, the University of Georgia, and various local clubs and groups of citizens in both Alabama and Georgia assisted the leader of the River Basin Surveys party while he was working along the Chattahoochee River. In the Missouri Basin the project engineers for the Oahe Reservoir provided space for temporary living accommodations and also for the storage of equipment. In a number of cases the construction agency lent mechanical equipment which was most helpful in the stripping of the topsoil from sites and the backfilling of trenches and test pits. In the Missouri Basin the Corps of Engineers also cooperated with the staff of the Missouri Basin Project of the River Basin Surveys in the preparation of a number of small informative pamphlets telling about several of the reservoirs along the Missouri River.

General supervision of the program was from the main office in Washington, but the activities in the Missouri Basin operated from the field headquarters and laboratory at Lincoln, Nebr. At the beginning of the year the latter provided office assistance and some equipment for the Chattahoochee River Project, but subsequently most of that activity was transferred to the main office in Washington. The Lincoln laboratory processed all the materials collected by excavating parties in the Missouri Basin and also some of those from the Chattahoochee.

Washington office.—Dr. Frank H. H. Roberts, Jr., continued to direct the main headquarters of the River Basin Surveys at the Bureau of American Ethnology throughout the year. Carl F. Miller, archeologist, was based at that office and from time to time assisted the Director in some of the general administrative problems. Harold A. Huscher, archeologist, worked under the general supervision of the Washington office, but at the beginning of the fiscal year was based on the field headquarters for the Missouri Basin Project at Lincoln, Nebr. After completing his field activities along the Chattahoochee River, Alabama-Georgia, in late December, he joined the Washington office and continued to work there the remainder of the fiscal year.

Mr. Miller spent the entire time in the Washington office working on materials and data he had collected during previous seasons in the field. He spoke before various groups interested in archeological subjects and answered numerous inquiries pertaining to artifacts and cultural materials from the southeastern archeological area. He also identified artifacts from 15 collections of southeastern material. In October he attended the sessions of the Eastern States Archeological Federation in Toronto, Canada, and in May he presented a paper on

"The Archeology of the Clarksville Site, 44 Mc 14, Mecklenburg County, Virginia," before a joint session of the Archeological Societies of Virginia and North Carolina held at Clarksville. He completed a short paper, "The Physical Structure of Rock Mound at 9 ST 3, Georgia," which was published in Southern Indian Studies, vol. 11, pp. 16–19. Mr. Miller furnished data that were used in the preparation of the "Ethnological Map of Virginia," which was published by Hearn Brothers, Detroit, Mich.

At the beginning of the fiscal year Harold A. Huscher, while on annual leave, assisted Dr. Richard G. Forbis, Glenbow Foundation, Calgary, Alberta, in the excavation of the remains of a fortified earth-lodge village at Cluny in the Blackfoot Reserve on the Bow River about 65 miles east of Calgary. Returning from Canada he drove south by way of the front ranges and the high plains, visiting a number of the more important Early Man-type sites, such as those at Sage-creek and Agate Basin in Wyoming, Dent and Apex Spring in Colorado, and Homo Novusmundus in New Mexico. In mid-August he returned to duty at Lincoln, Nebr., where he made preparations for resuming the archeological investigations in the Walter F. George Dam and Lock area along the Chattahoochee River. Shortly after his arrival at Eufaula, Ala., at the end of August, he started his fieldwork. After returning to the Washington office in January he devoted his time to bringing up to date the several years' backlog of maps and field notes pertaining to the Chattahoochee investigations. In May the processed collections of the two previous years' fieldwork in Alabama-Georgia were moved from Lincoln to Washington for storage at the U.S. National Museum, and Mr. Huscher proceeded to combine that material with the collections he had made during the current season. At the close of the fiscal year he was busy selecting bone and shell specimens and items pertaining to the early colonial period for identification by various Smithsonian specialists.

Alabama-Georgia.—During the period from mid-September to the end of December Harold A. Huscher, using a power-driven screen of $\frac{3}{8}$-inch mesh and a small crew of local laborers, tested a series of 15 sites below Eufaula, Ala., in the southwestern quadrant of the Walter F. George Reservoir Basin. Most of the sites fall into two general classes. The first group consists of those with a predominance of Mississippian pottery, characterized by the early Mississippian globular pots with loop handles, comparable to the Macon Plateau types in Georgia and the Gordon types in Tennessee. Such pottery actually has a long time span, continuing down to the opening of the historic period (Pinellas, Fort Walton). The second group includes sites with an overlay of late Creek pottery such as the Chattahoochee Brushed variants and Kasihta Red-film in association with trade metal, china, and glass.

Most major sites in this reservoir, however, are proving to be in the multiple-component category with several time levels represented. The stratification is usually gradational rather than sharply demarcated, hence the digging is by arbitrary levels. At sites favorably located on the terrace points near stream junctions, underlying Early Woodland and Archaic manifestations usually will be definitely identifiable, though not sharply separable, at depths of 2.0–5.0 feet below the present surface. The following are the most important sites investigated during the fall season:

The Spann's Landing site, 1HE34, is located in Alabama 3 miles above the dam axis, in a loop of the Chattahoochee River opposite Grace's Bend, and a little more than a mile below the Mandeville Mound site (1CLA1)[1] in Clay County, Ga. This site extends for more than 800 feet along the crest of a low natural levee, with the greatest concentration of material at the north or upstream end. A series of 14 squares 10-x-10 feet were laid out there in two rows, so spaced as to give an adequately distributed sampling. Of the 14 squares, 8 pits were actually dug, to varying depths down to 5.0 feet. There is a sparse overlay of brushed pottery, indicating some use of the area during the Late Creek period, but the most intense occupation was during Mississippian times, and probably fairly early Mississippian times, as indicated by the pottery remains. One productive cache pit yielded parts of several pots of the Pinellas arcaded ware ("pumpkin pot," "melon pot"), a type described from Florida and attributed to a late peripheral Mississippian manifestation. It is, however, considered diagnostic of a possibly earlier Mississippian period as described by Caldwell for the great Rood's Landing site (9SW1), 30 miles farther north, and the Mississippian cap on the large Mandeville Mound (Stark's Clay Landing, 9CLA1), as reported by McMichael and Kellar. Along the Chattahoochee the arcaded pots with temper and handle variants may have a much longer time range, apparently continuous, than in Florida, extending back to the earlier Macon Plateau period, with the Singer-Moye site (9SW2), south of Lumpkin on the headwaters of Pataula Creek, one of the earliest major sites. At depths of 2.5–4.0 feet below the present surface at Spann's Landing, fiber-tempered pottery comparable to the Stallings Island and Orange Plain types of the latest Archaic and earliest

---

[1] Site designations used by the River Basin Surveys are trinomial in character, consisting of symbols for State, County, and site. The State is indicated by the first number, according to the numerical position of the State name in an alphabetical list of the United States; thus, for example, 32 indicates North Dakota, 39 indicates South Dakota. Counties are designated by a two-letter abbreviation; for example, ME for Mercer County, MN for Mountrail County, etc. The final number refers to the specific site within the indicated State and County.

Woodland occurred consistently, as well as early point types, the latter regularly consisting of the decomposed flint first described from the Macon area by Kelly.

1HE51, a site in Alabama at the junction of Hardridge Creek and the Chattahoochee River, 2.5 miles above the dam axis, was tested by six 10-foot squares, ranging in depth down to 5 feet. The predominant occupation there was Early Woodland, with fiber-tempered, Deptford, and Swift Creek pottery types recognized. However, no productive pit area was located. A number of large, heavy-stemmed projectile points, again in the decomposed flint characteristic of the Archaic in this area, were recovered from the deeper levels. Several less important sites near Hardridge Creek were tested by from one to six 10-foot squares, to obtain a broad spectrum sample of the range of pottery in the area. One site, 1HE56, yielded a number of sherds of all-over fingernail-incised pottery, the only site where this specialty has risen to a significant frequency.

Somewhat farther north, between White Oak and Cheneyhatchee Creeks, another series of sites was tested in order to check on exposures of Chattahoochee Brushed pottery, since a Late Creek village, Okitiyakni, had supposedly been somewhere in the general area. 1BR46, 47, and 2A were found to yield significant amounts of brushed pottery, and one area of pits was located at 46. There a large fragment of a restorable pot, which agrees closely with published descriptions of the Late Creek ware from the Southeast and from Oklahoma, was found in direct association with trade metal. Eleven squares in all were dug at these sites, but no structural remains were identified. Eight 10-x-10-foot squares were dug at five other nearby locations, but information recovered was less important. One site at the south side of Barbour Creek (1BR10) was checked by four 10-x-10-foot squares, and consistently found to yield Gulf Woodland forms, some in direct association with a level of basin-shaped hearths. One of the latter was filled with irregular fist-sized fragments of burned clay, possibly fired for use as cooking "stones" or to provide pottery temper.

In November 1960 an immediate salvage job became necessary on Hatcheechubbee Creek, in Russell County, Ala., some 17 miles north of Eufaula, where a highway relocation project was destroying an Early Woodland site, 1RU74. Known as the Kite site, it was discovered in 1959 by Sergeant David W. Chase. It lay on a point of terrace between the creek and a small unnamed spring branch from the north. There four 10-foot squares were laid out parallel to the right-of-way and taken down to depths up to 5 feet. The upper layers yielded several types of Early Woodland sherds of the Deptford and Swift Creek series, and a considerable range of thick fiber-tempered sherds (Stallings, Orange) was obtained at slightly lower levels. A series of stone artifacts was obtained in the deeper part of the tests. They consisted of the very characteristic decomposed flint of the Archaic. Several burned rock areas were noted, but no pits were found. The site, though not rich, was interesting in that there was much less intrusion from above, with the close mixing of time periods that makes some of the larger, more productive sites so confusing.

Beginning November 19, the remaining time was devoted to work on two mound sites. Trenched previously, they were 9QU1, and 9QU5, south of Georgetown, Ga., in Quitman County.

9QU1, Moore's "Mounds near Georgetown, Quitman County, Georgia" (Mounds of Lower Chattahoochee and Lower Flint Rivers, Journ. Acad. Nat. Sci. Philadelphia, 2d ser. vol. 13, pt. 3, pp. 426-456, 448), locally called the "Gary's Fishpond Mound" or the "Gary's Fishpond Site," consists of extensive village remains and a large low mound, now almost completely plowed down and carried away. The site was tested in the spring of 1960 by digging a T-trench along the east margin of the mound, and seven 10-x-10-foot trenches in the adjacent village areas. Although actually only the roots of the mound are left, it appeared desirable to attempt to determine more exactly the period of its building. Since the outwash apron of the mound was found to be intact, it seemed the site offered an opportunity for getting direct separation of mound, mound fill, and pre-mound periods, with the additional prospect of locating separate pits or features that would give individual "pure" samples.

The original grid was reset and a larger area in the western half of the mound remnants was stripped, revealing the roots of a circular mound faced with clay. It probably was originally about 200 feet in circumference at the base. A section trench cut through the western margin revealed that the clay facing had been carefully built up at a steep angle. The actual base of the mound was about 4 feet below the present surface in this area. A palisade of spaced large-diameter posts followed just outside the curve of this clay wall, but the posts did not appear to have been set into the wall. The indications were of some sort of a clay-faced "caracol" type mound. Additional bedding lines outside the circular periphery indicated a possibility that some kind of overlying rectangular mound had been built on the core of the original circular mound. An area 20-x-20 feet was excavated in mottled fill in the calculated center of the circular mound revealing numbers of post holes in interrupted alignments, running NW.–SE. and NE.–SW., though no clearly defined structure could be made out. Because of increasing inclemency of the weather the planned excavation of this center pit down into the submound could not be completed in the available time and the site was closed down.

However, additional work is certainly indicated for that location and will be scheduled for the early part of the new field season.

Several lots of midden excavated in the central 20-x-20-foot pit contain a high frequency of a carefully finished plain ware with thickened rims and no handles. This does not seem to be the local Weeden Island type, but may be evidence of contacts with or an actual occupation of the site by Early Mississippian peoples carrying a culture somewhat like that which becomes Coles Creek and Moundville farther west. If such were the case, the overlying rectangular structure would then relate to the later Fort Walton-Lamar period which seems to account for the greater part of the pottery from this site. The one recognizable structural pattern found, other than the mound, was located in the nearby village and consisted of large post holes at spaced intervals, outlining a corner and two adjacent walls of what was probably a house of the later period.

Additional work was done at 9QU5, a site referred to locally as the "Mound on the Lower Lampley Place" or the "Mound below Cool Branch." For brevity the site and mound will be referred to as the "Cool Branch Mound Site." This site had been tested previously by a 5-foot trench from the east margin to the approximate center of the mound. The mound proper was built of basket-loaded clay, apparently at one single stage of building, and there was a submound posthole pattern indicating some sort of premound building.

Thirteen additional 10-x-10-foot test pits were dug at this site, eight in an east-west line across the north margin, paralleling the edge of the terrace, and five bracketing the mound proper. Using a tractor scraper, the surface of the mound was stripped, revealing the approximate edges of a regular rectangular clay-platform mound, with the corners oriented to the cardinal points. The mound was then bulldozed away to a level approximately 0.5 foot above the contact of the clay mound with the underlying river-silt surface of the terrace, as determined in the previous trenching. The center of the mound was then cleared by hand shoveling, revealing the post holes of a rectangular submound structure of closely set posts, corners closed, approximately 27-x-36 feet over all. This building was oriented with the overlying mound, though lying partly outside the baseline on the northwest side. As nearly as could be determined from the bulldozed surface without actually tracing out the lines by shoveling, the southwest margin being the least certain, the original base dimensions of the mound were about 55-x-55 feet. At the center of the submound structure was a pile of red iron ore (hematite) probably representing a symbolic ceremonial fire. The sand beneath was stained red but did not seem actually to have been burned. Two beautiful spud celts, one of a fine-grained greenstone, were found together in the mound fill about a foot above the contact. Both had been broken by the bulldozing. The spud is commonly found in Mississippian mound sites westward to the Mississippi River.

A 5-x-10-foot test below the actual submound level revealed wall trenches of a rectangular open-cornered building, oriented NE.-SW., and in one of the series of 10-x-10-foot trenches, 75 feet southeast of the main mound, a straight section of wall trench was found. These features could not be examined further in the time available. Another test 400 feet northwest of the mound center and about 100 feet back from the terrace edge, also uncovered a house-wall trench at depths of 1.5 to 2.0 feet. Using a tractor, about a thousand square feet were stripped, tracing out the wall lines, but time did not permit complete study of the patterns. Rectangular, open-cornered houses, closely spaced but apparently not adjoining, were arranged in rows running NE.-SW. Hearths appeared to be in the forecourt to the southeast, rather than within the houses. No clearly defined occupation floor could be identified, hence the associations are not certain. Most of the pottery from that part of the site seems earlier than the houses, which presumably slightly antedate the mound, but continue into the mound period, since there is no evidence of a later house type. House evidence is so difficult to obtain along the Chattahoochee River, however, that negative evidence cannot be relied upon, and the known house areas at this site should be excavated further to get as complete house plan evidence as possible.

During the field season parties from the University of Alabama and the University of Georgia, under agreements with the National Park Service, also worked at sites in the Walter F. George Reservoir area.

Missouri River Basin—For the fifteenth consecutive year the Missouri Basin Project continued to operate from the field headquarters and laboratory in Lincoln, Nebr. Dr. Robert L. Stephenson served as chief of the project throughout the year. Activities included surveys, excavations, analysis of materials, and reporting on results. During the summer months the work was mainly concerned with excavations. Analyses and preparation of reports received the major attention throughout the other months of the year. The special chronology program begun in January 1958 continued to receive attention.

At the beginning of the fiscal year the permanent staff, in addition to the chief, consisted of 3 archeologists, 1 administrative assistant, 1 clerk-stenographer, 1 illustrator, 1 file clerk on the permanent staff, and 12 crewmen on the temporary staff. One paleontologist, on loan from the National Park Service, was added to the temporary staff for a month for the purpose of analyzing nonhuman bone material from the sites excavated over the past three seasons. In June, 2 assistant field archeologists, 1 cook, and 25 field crewmen were added to the temporary staff.

At the end of the fiscal year there were 3 archeologists in addition to the chief, 1 administrative assistant, 1 administrative clerk, 1 secretary, 1 scientific illustrator, 1 photographer, and 4 museum aides on the permanent staff, and 2 assistant field archeologists, 1 cook, and 25 field crewmen on the temporary staff.

During the year there were 10 Smithsonian Institution River Basin Surveys field parties at work in the Missouri Basin. Three of these were in the Oahe Reservoir area and two were in the Big Bend Reservoir area of South Dakota during July and August. One small field party conducted investigations during October and November in the Big Bend Reservoir area. One party investigated the Merritt Reservoir area in Nebraska during May and June. Two parties were excavating in the Big Bend Reservoir area and one in the Oahe Reservoir area during June.

Other fieldwork in the Missouri Basin during the year included 11 parties from State institutions operating under cooperative agreements with the National Park Service and in cooperation with the Smithsonian Institution in the Inter-Agency Archeological Salvage Program.

There was a slight increase in appropriated funds for fiscal year 1961, but since most of the new money was to cover wage-scale increases beginning in July, the fiscal situation brought into even sharper focus than before the critical problem of accomplishing the minimum necessary salvage at a time when two of the largest reservoirs, Big Bend and Oahe, were nearing completion and, in fact, Oahe was beginning to flood some of the important unexcavated archeological sites. However, when the parties took to the field in June it was possible to shift the methods of fieldwork from sampling of large numbers of sites back to the intensive excavation of a smaller number of key sites. The sampling techniques of the preceding two field seasons had been successful but some of the more intensive excavations were again needed.

At the beginning of the fiscal year, Dr. Warren W. Caldwell and a crew of eight were engaged in minor test excavations at two sites in the Big Bend Reservoir of South Dakota. Site 39LM222, near the mouth of Medicine Creek, in Lyman County, was a diffuse village of the La Roche complex. A small, circular house with closely spaced wall posts, four center posts, and a long entry passage, lay just above an earlier structure of indeterminate pattern. A shallow ditch surrounding the deeper house suggested that the house itself may have formed a bastion, or strong point, in the fortification system. Segments of both superimposed houses were excavated. Portions of a third house were also dug and it proved to have been a small, circular building differing little in structural details from the uppermost of the two superimposed houses. Pottery and other artifacts were

1. Use of power screen speeds testing of sites in Walter F. George Reservoir area, Alabama. River Basin Surveys.

2. Tracing bottom edge of large mound along Chattahoochee River in Georgia. River Basin Surveys.

1. Floor pit for rectangular earth lodge in Oahe Reservoir area, South Dakota. Remains of posts are visible along left wall. River Basin Surveys.

2. Excavating base of low mound in Oahe Reservoir area in North Dakota. Bison remains buried with human bodies may be seen at left. Traces of logs at right cover human skeletons. River Basin Surveys.

homogenous throughout the site, indicating a single La Roche-Iona-Russell Ware tradition and but one occupation. This would place the village in the late sedentary-farmer period of the 15th to 17th centuries. The second site of the group, 39LM224, is located but a mile downstream from 39LM222, and represented another La Roche village of diffuse pattern, but with only four houses apparent from the surface. One of them, a burned circular structure with widely spaced wall posts and long entry passage was partially excavated.

On July 19, Dr. Caldwell moved to the Oahe Reservoir area in old Armstrong County (now a part of Dewey County), above the mouth of the Cheyenne River on the west bank of the Missouri, and hired a new crew of laborers. The Oahe Reservoir, already beginning to flood, had begun to cover some of the sites in that vicinity. One of those still above water was site 39AR201, the remains of a large compact village of 18 long-rectangular houses placed in rows but without apparent fortifications. The remnants of one of the structures were excavated and other tests were made in the site. This extremely long, narrow house had been nearly twice as long as it was wide and its ruins were covered by 4.5 feet of overburden. There had been a low bench along the rear wall into which a shallow trench had been dug to receive the rear wall posts. Dentalium, native copper, and abundant human bone scraps lay on the floor and an ochre-covered human bundle burial associated with a bison skull was found in the southeast corner. Pottery was consistently Thomas Riggs Ware. This site represented a village of the Thomas Riggs Focus of middle-period sedentary farmers in the Missouri Valley and may date from the 15th century. Less than 500 yards downstream the remains of another large Thomas Riggs village, site 39AR210, were tested and found to resemble 39AR201 in all respects except that there had been a rectangular, bastioned fortification system. This site had been flooded by the Oahe Reservoir and reexposed by a drop in the water level. Recovery of archeological details was minimal, owing to their having been obscured by the flood waters, but a good artifact sample was collected. The Caldwell party completed the season's work after 9 weeks in the field.

The third River Basin Surveys party in the field at the beginning of the year, consisting of a crew of six under the direction of Robert W. Neuman, was excavating at the Boundary Mound site (32SI1) on the North Dakota-South Dakota boundary line in the Oahe Reservoir area, Sioux County, N. Dak. The site consisted of four dome-shaped burial mounds, ranging from 3 to 5 feet in height and 60 to 80 feet in diameter. Three of the mounds were excavated. Each contained a rectangular central burial pit covered with timbers and lined with matting. Bison remains (skulls, partial skeletons, and complete skeletons in articulation) were found around the timbers. The burial pits were 3 to 4½ feet deep and contained from 6 to 14 secondary human burials, the bones of several being coated with red pigment. Artifacts were generally associated with a single individual in each pit. They included side-notched projectile points, triangular knives, bipointed drills, an obsidian end scraper, sandstone atlatl weights, a catlinite object, cigar-shaped bone objects, tubular bone beads, bone awls, a bone pendant, a bear canine pendant, shell pendants, and worked human mandibles as well as those from dogs and beaver. This mound group comprised burial tumuli of the Woodland period with relationships to the east and southeast of the area. They probably date from the period of 1,500 years ago and earlier.

The Neuman party continued investigations in other burial-mound sites along the right bank of the Missouri River between Mandan, N. Dak., and Mobridge, S. Dak. Site 32M0207 is a group of three mounds in Morton County, N. Dak., some 20 miles south of Mandan. One of them was excavated but yielded only a single secondary human burial and no artifacts. The Schmidt site (32M020) is a group of eight burial mounds 12 miles south of Mandan in Morton County. One mound, 75 feet in diameter and 1.3 feet high, was excavated. It contained a single secondary human burial in a rectangular, central, timber-covered burial pit. Articulated bison bones lay near the charred timbers that had covered the pit. The only artifacts recovered were a few fragmentary stone tools from the surface near one of the unexcavated mounds. The Swift Bird site (39DW233) is a group of two burial mounds and three shallow, circular depressions. One of the mounds, 70 feet in diameter and 3 feet high, was excavated. A single primary burial lay on the mound floor. Artifacts associated with the burial include dentalium beads, a tubular bone bead, and a shell pendant in the shape of a thunderbird. It is of interest to note that no pottery was found in association with any of these burial mounds. The Neuman party completed the season's work on September 1, after 12 weeks in the field.

The fourth Missouri Basin Project field party at work at the beginning of the fiscal year was a crew of three, under the direction of G. Hubert Smith, investigating historic sites in the Oahe Reservoir area. Activities at the site of Fort Sully (39SL45) in Sully County consisted of excavations of building foundations and refuse dumps and latrine pits in several parts of the site. Pits dug near the hospital and the barroom locations were particularly informative. The excavations provided detailed outlines of some of the main structures of this military post of the 1866–94 period. They also produced one of the largest known collections, obtained under controlled conditions, of military and civil objects of this period. Especially noteworthy is a large array of glassware, including "art glass," hundreds of bottles, medical-department glassware, and household glass. Many of these objects are complete or little damaged and are marked as to origin or purpose. Objects of earthenware in great quantity, including Oriental earthenware, and numerous items of metal and leather were recovered. Strictly military objects are in the minority but unusual items of both military and civilian use will form a valuable comparative collection and future exhibit material. Even specimens of printer's type, for printing official orders, were found.

Investigations at the site of Fort Bennett (1870–91) in Stanley County, directly opposite Fort Sully, having been abandoned in June owing to flooding by the Oahe Reservoir, were resumed in August when the pool level had receded somewhat. The site was uncovered but the ground was so thoroughly waterlogged that excavation was impractical. Photographs were take for record purposes and some historic specimens were collected. The experience gained there, as at other flooded sites, clearly emphasizes the hopelessness, in a great majority of cases, of trying to do archeological work in sites that have once been flooded and reexposed when the waters receded, whether the sites in question be historic or prehistoric.

On August 10 the fifth Missouri Basin Project field party, consisting of Smith and his crew, moved into the Big Bend Reservoir area to conduct preliminary tests at site 39ST202, believed to be that of Fort George, a trading post of the 1840's. Only the scantiest contemporary record of this post has been found, although it was visited by Audubon and is reputed to have been of some importance as an opposition post in the fur trade. Tests there located former log habitations and occupational debris of the period. The site is located in Stanley County at the northeast corner of the Brule Indian Reservation. This field party also took charge of an emergency excavation of six human burials accidentally located by construction activities at the Big Bend Dam site and reported by the Corps of Engineers. The interments were in wooden coffins and contained glass beads and other late objects suggesting the early reservation period, though no record of such graves has been found. The Smith party completed 9 weeks in the field and returned to Lincoln August 19.

During the period October 26 to November 6, one Missouri Basin Project field party investigated a site being destroyed by gravel operations in the upper reaches of the Big Bend Reservoir area. Robert W. Neuman and a crew of two examined and tested the areas of the Arzberger site (39HU6), which were being cut away as a gravel quarry. A rich midden and several cache pits were exposed and excavated. Artifacts were collected and data compiled, but there appeared to be little material that had not already been discussed in a report on this site. During the same period Neuman also made a flight over the lower portion of the Oahe Reservoir and took aerial photos of several sites that had been flooded and reexposed by a drop in the pool level. On the return trip to Lincoln this party also visited sites in the immediate construction area of the Big Bend Dam (at the request of the Corps of Engineers) and while there collected specimens for dendrochronological use. It also visited an earth-lodge village site near Wessington Springs, S. Dak., and examined several amateur collections in southwest Minnesota and northwest Iowa.

The 1961 summer field season in the Missouri River Basin began in the Merritt Reservoir area on May 25. Robert W. Neuman and an assistant spent 11 days in a final intensive search of the flood-pool area of this dam on the Snake River in Cherry County, Nebr. The dam is well along in construction and, despite two previous surveys that provided very little archeological evidence, it was thought that a final investigation should be made. The shifting sand dunes in this area, combined with the construction activities, might have revealed some cultural remains of the earlier periods. Such was found not to be the case and no archeological manifestations were noted. This reservoir area can be written off as completed.

The second Missouri Basin Project field party consisted of a crew of nine under the direction of Robert W. Neuman. This party began work on June 6 in the construction area of the Big Bend Reservoir (actually the upper reaches of the Fort Randall Reservoir) at site 39BF225. At that location there is a group of three low burial mounds situated on the terrace just west of the Talking Crow site (39BF3) in Buffalo County, S. Dak. By the end of the fiscal year Neuman had trenched two of these mounds and found three components present: (a) Historic with coffin burials, (b) the mound component with secondary pit burials, and (c) a premound, nonceramic component.

The third Missouri Basin Project field party of the season was composed of a crew of 10 directed by Dr. Warren W. Caldwell. It began work on June 13 at the Pretty Head site (39LM232). This site is located on the right bank of the Missouri River, 4 miles above the Big Bend Dam site in Lyman County, S. Dak. By the end of the year excavations were well under way in several middens, and in the remains of one long-rectangular house.

The fourth Missouri Basin Project field party of the 1961 season was a crew of 10 directed by Dr. Robert L. Stephenson. This party began work on June 19 in the upper reaches of the Oahe Reservoir in Corson County, S. Dak., on the west side of the Missouri River some 5 miles south of Mobridge. There a series of small sites extending from the Blue Blanket Island site (39WW9) downstream into Dewey County to site 39DW232 was to be investigated with intensive excavations at the Potts Village site (39CO19) and the Le Compte Creek site (39DW234). The latter are the remains of circular house villages with fortifications and suggest a possible link between the later part of the long-rectangular-house period and the earlier part of the circular-house period. The two main sites each appear to have a single bastion in the fortification system. Excavations were well underway by the end of the year.

Cooperating institutions working in the Missouri Basin at the beginning of the fiscal year included five field parties from State agencies in North Dakota, South Dakota, Nebraska, Kansas, and Missouri. W. Raymond Wood of the University of Oregon had a crew at work for the State Historical Society of North Dakota at the Huff site (32M011) in the upper reaches of the Oahe Reservoir some 18 miles below Mandan, N. Dak. Wood's party excavated eight houses and 200 feet of palisade, and cross-sectioned the fortification ditch. This was the location of a fortified, bastioned village of long-rectangular houses with the houses loosely arranged in rows. One unusual house was nearly square and had four center posts comparable to the circular houses of other sites. Dr. Preston Holder of the University of Nebraska had a crew at work at the Leavenworth site (39C09), 7 miles north of Mobridge in Corson County, S. Dak., in the Oahe Reservoir. This site, visited by Lewis and Clark in 1804 and attacked by Col. Henry Leavenworth in 1823, was an Arikara village (or pair of villages) of circular houses. Holder's crew excavated four houses and tested several midden areas. Dr. Wesley R. Hurt, Jr., with a University of South Dakota crew, spent July and August excavating portions of the No Heart Creek site (39AR2) in old Armstrong County on the right bank of the Missouri River in the Oahe Reservoir. This small, compact, fortified, La Roche-type village had an unusual series of small bastions and entryways. Thomas A. Witty with a crew from the Kansas State Historical Society excavated four sites and tested several others in the Wilson Reservoir area on the Saline River in Russell and Lincoln Counties, Kans. All four excavated sites relate to the Central Plains Phase. Dr. Carl H. Chapman had a University of Missouri crew in the field surveying and testing sites in the Kasinger Bluff Reservoir on the Osage River in Henry, Benton, and St. Clair Counties, west-central Missouri.

At the end of the fiscal year six field parties representing four cooperating institutions were in the field in the Missouri Basin. Dr. Preston Holder was back at the Leavenworth site (39C09) in the Oahe Reservoir for a second season of work by the University of Nebraska. Dr. Carl H. Chapman was back at the Kasinger Bluff Reservoir in Missouri with a University of Missouri field party surveying and testing sites in that area. In addition, Chapman had a survey crew at work in the Stockton Reservoir area in Cedar and Dade Counties, Mo. Thomas A. Witty had a crew at work excavating the Woods site (14CY30) and testing several other sites in the Milford Reservoir on the Republican River in Geary County, Kans., for the Kansas

State Historical Society. Dr. Wesley R. Hurt had a crew at work by boat, testing several sites being exposed by wave action along the shores of Lewis and Clark Lake (Gavins Point) and Fort Randall Reservoirs, for the University of South Dakota. Roger T. Grange had a crew from the Nebraska State Historical Society at work in the Red Willow Reservoir area in Frontier County, southwestern Nebraska, excavating two sites near the dam construction area. All the parties mentioned above were operating under agreements with the National Park Service and were cooperating with the Smithsonian Institution in the research program.

During the time that the archeologists were not in the field they were engaged in the analysis of their materials and in the laboratory and library research. They also prepared manuscripts of technical scientific reports and wrote articles and papers of a more popular nature.

The Missouri Basin Chronology Program, begun by the staff archeologists of the Missouri Basin Project in January 1958, continued to operate and made considerable progress throughout the year. Continued cooperation and participation by more than 30 individuals representing 30 research institutions throughout the Plains area has been rewarding. This year major emphasis was placed upon the dendrochronological section of the program. Harry E. Weakly of the U.S. Department of Agriculture, Dr. Warren W. Caldwell of the Missouri Basin Project, and Ward Weakly of the University of Nebraska concentrated the tree-ring studies on a limited area along the Missouri River between Fort Thompson and the Cheyenne River in South Dakota. This takes in all the Big Bend Reservoir area and the lower portions of the Oahe Reservoir. A master chart has been constructed for this area using oak, ash, and cedar, that extends from the present back to A.D. 1302. Archeological wood, mainly cedar house posts, from a number of sites has been dated by the master chart. The dates look good, and in general correlate well with other chronological data, but until further checks have been made, release of these dates would be premature. In addition to the master chart, a "floating" sequence of nearly 300 years has been constructed, based upon timbers from houses of the Over Focus and the Thomas Riggs Focus. There also appears to be a high degree of correlation between the South Dakota master chart and the several charts that have been previously developed for areas of Nebraska.

The radioactive carbon-14 section of the program has continued to develop, and in conjunction with the University of Michigan Memorial Phoenix Laboratory, under the direction of Prof. H. R. Crane, a series of four new dates has been released. *Sample M-1079a,* charcoal from a house post of the late component at the Crow Creek site (39BF11) in the Fort Randall Reservoir, S. Dak., excavated by

Marvin F. Kivett for the Nebraska State Historical Society as a part of the Inter-Agency Archeological Salvage Program, gave a date of 560±150 years ago. *Sample M–1080a*, charcoal from Feature 4 of the Good Soldier site (39LM238) in the Big Bend Reservoir of South Dakota, gave a date of 2,380±150 years ago. This sample was excavated by Robert W. Neuman of the Missouri Basin Project staff. *Sample M–1081*, charcoal from zone D of the Logan Creek site (25BT3) in northeastern Nebraska, excavated by Marvin F. Kivett for the Nebraska State Historical Society, gave a date of 7,250±300 years ago. *Sample M–1082*, wood from a house post in a small long-rectangular house (F. 2) of the Fay Tolton site (39ST11) in the Oahe Reservoir, gave a date of 860±150 years ago. This sample was excavated by Dr. Donald D. Hartle, then of the Missouri Basin Project staff. An experiment in the decontamination of charcoal treated with paraffin failed completely. A log, one end of which had been coated with paraffin and the other end not so treated, had had the treated end deparaffined and both sections were run for carbon-14 analysis. The two dates from the same piece of charred wood were several centuries apart.

The laboratory and office staff spent its full effort during the year in processing specimen materials for study, photographing and illustrating specimens, preparing specimen records, and typing, filing, and illustrating record and manuscript materials. Accomplishments of the laboratory and office staff are listed in tables 1 and 2.

The Missouri Basin Project staff archeologists and archeologists of the National Park Service and cooperating States agencies working in the Missouri Basin met on July 30 in a roundtable field conference in Pierre, S. Dak. This 17½th Plains Conference, now a regular summer event, and a supplement to the annual Thanksgiving Plains Conference, was devoted to discussions of current fieldwork and technical problems of field identifications. During the Thanksgiving weekend, members of the staff participated in the 18th Plains Conference for Archeology, held in Norman, Okla. On April 14, members of the staff participated in the seventy-first annual meeting of the Nebraska Academy of Sciences in Lincoln.

Dr. Robert L. Stephenson, Chief, devoted a large part of his time during the year to managing the office and laboratory in Lincoln and preparing plans and budgets for the 1961 field season. He compiled a 7-volume summary of construction data and archeological work in all the 789 named reservoir sites in the Missouri Basin for use in future planning in the Lincoln office. He completed the revision of a large technical monograph, "The Accokeek Creek Site: A Middle Atlantic Seaboard Culture Sequence," previously accepted as his doctoral dissertation at the University of Michigan, and continued with preliminary analysis of materials he recovered from the excavations at the Sully site (39SL4) in the Oahe Reservoir in 1956–57–58. He also continued work on a monograph reporting the "Archeological Investigations in the Whitney Reservoir, Texas," and two smaller manuscripts, all nearing completion at the end of the year. Throughout the year he served as chairman of the Missouri Basin Chronology Program; as assistant editor of "Notes and News in the Plains Area," for *American Antiquity;* and as associate editor for the *Plains Anthropologist.* At the 18th Plains Conference, held in Norman, Okla., on Thanksgiving weekend, he served as chairman of the session on "Field Reports" and as a panel discussant for the session on "The Aksarben Aspect."

Dr. Stephenson presented a paper, "The Housing Problem," at the seventy-first annual meeting of the Nebraska Academy of Sciences in Lincoln on April 14. During the year he wrote a number of book reviews for various scientific journals. He also wrote a brief article, "Comments on 'Relationships between the Caddoan Area and the Plains' by Robert E. Bell," for publication in the *Bulletin* of the Texas Archeological Society. On May 7 he was the guest speaker at the annual meeting of the Iowa Archeological Society, talking on the subject, "Drowning Our Heritage." Throughout the year he gave seven other talks on various aspects of Missouri Basin Salvage Archeology before regular meetings of local civic organizations and school groups. In July he drove to Moscow, Idaho, to deliver a load of archeological specimens from the Missouri Basin to Dr. Alfred Bowers of the University of Idaho and to consult with Dr. Bowers on the analysis of the material. While there he met with the executive dean of the University of Idaho to confer on problems involved in anthropological programs in the University. In May he was invited to Accokeek, Md., as a consultant to the Accokeek Foundation on an archeological research program for the Accokeek area. He took annual leave to serve as part-time assistant professor of anthropology on the faculty of the University of Nebraska during both the first and second semesters of the academic year. At the end of the year he was conducting investigations in prehistoric Indian village sites in the Oahe Reservoir area.

Dr. Warren W. Caldwell, archeologist, when not in charge of field parties, devoted most of his time to analyses of specimen materials he had recovered from salvage excavations in previous years. He completed final revisions of his manuscript "Archeological Investigations at the Hickey Brothers Site, 39LM4, Lyman County, South Dakota," in collaboration with Lee G. Madison and Bernard Golden; and of the manuscript "The Garrison Dam and Reservoir," in collaboration with G. Hubert Smith. He continued the detailed analysis of materials from the Black Partizan site (39LM218) in the Big Bend Reservoir, S. Dak., and in collaboration with Harry E. Weakly con-

tinued work on the dendrochronological materials from the Big Bend
and Oahe Reservoirs of South Dakota. In May he consulted with
Dr. Douglas Osborne of the National Park Service regarding complete revision and expansion of his monograph, "The Archeology of
Wakemap; A Stratified Site near the Dalles of the Columbia," for
publication in the National Park Service series. He also completed
"Dendrochronology and the Missouri Basin Chronology Program,"
which was published in *The Tree Ring Bulletin*, vol. 23, No. 3. In
addition, he wrote several book reviews. On July 30 he served as
chairman of the 17½th Plains Conference in Pierre, S. Dak., and
over Thanksgiving weekend he gave a report on his current fieldwork
at the 18th Plains Conference in Norman, Okla. On April 14 he presented a paper at the seventy-first annual meeting of the Nebraska
Academy of Sciences held in Lincoln, entitled "Some Thoughts on
Guns and Indians." During the year he continued to serve as chairman of the dendrochronology section of the Missouri Basin Chronology Program; as assistant editor for reviews and literature for the
Plains Anthropologist, and as Plains collaborator for the Society for
American Archeology publication, *Abstracts of New World Archaeology*. On annual leave he continued to serve as part-time assistant
professor of anthropology on the faculty of the University of Nebraska. At the end of the year he was again engaged in excavating
archeological sites in the Big Bend Reservoir area.

Robert W. Neuman, archeologist, when not in the field conducting
excavations, was analyzing archeological materials he had previously
excavated in the Big Bend Reservoir area. He completed four manuscripts and had them accepted for publication: "The Olson Mound
(39BF223) in Buffalo County, South Dakota"; "Salvage Archeology at a Site near Fort Thompson, South Dakota"; "A Bibliography of Archeological References Relating to the Central and Northern Great Plains Prior to 1930"; and "Domesticated Corn from a Fort
Walton Mound in Houston County, Alabama." The first three will
be published in the *Plains Anthropologist;* the fourth in the *Florida
Anthropologist*. An article, "Indian Burial Mounds in the Upper
Missouri River Basin," was published in *Progress* of the Interior
Missouri Basin Field Committee. During the year he served as chair-
man of the carbon-14 section of the Missouri Basin Chronology Pro-
gram. On Thanksgiving weekend he presented two papers at the
18th Plains Conference in Norman, Okla., entitled "Excavations at
Four Mound Sites in the Oahe Reservoir" and "The Brother of All
Document, 1888." During late April and early May he drove to
Washington, D.C., and Knoxville, Tenn., to deliver a load of Missouri
Basin archeological specimens and to confer with archeologists at
both cities. At the end of the year he was again in the field conducting archeological excavations.

G. Hubert Smith, archeologist, after completing his fieldwork in August, was on duty the remainder of the year in the Lincoln office analyzing materials and preparing reports of work previously accomplished at historic sites in the Missouri Basin. His principal effort was directed toward preparation of a large monograph combining his own and several other investigators' work at the site of Fort Berthold and Like-a-Fishhook Village (32ML2) in the Garrison Reservoir, and by the end of the year he was well along on this manuscript. He also prepared an article, "Historical Archeology in the Missouri Basin Reservoir Areas," that was published in the *Plains Anthropologist* in November, and wrote (in collaboration with Warren W. Caldwell) a manuscript, "The Garrison Dam and Reservoir," for publication by the U.S. Army Corps of Engineers. Throughout the year he served as assistant editor for historic sites archeology for the *Plains Anthropologist* and as chairman of the historic documentation section of the Missouri Basin Chronology Program. He participated in the 18th Plains Conference, held in Norman, Okla., over Thanksgiving weekend with a report of his current field activities. On September 23–24 he participated as a discussant at the "Conference on Historic Buildings and Sites" at Iowa State University at Ames. On January 26–28, at the annual meeting of the Society of Architectural Historians, in Minneapolis, Minn., he presented an illustrated paper on "Frontier Buildings on the Upper Missouri," and on May 20 a similar paper, "Early Historic Buildings in the Missouri Basin," at the annual meeting of the Nebraska Association of Architects, held in Lincoln. On April 14 he spoke at the seventy-first annual meeting of the Nebraska Academy of Sciences in Lincoln on "Early Historic Sites and Buildings on the Upper Missouri: Some Problems of Evidence." At the close of the year he was at work in the Lincoln office on his monograph on site 32ML2.

TABLE 1.—*Specimens processed July 1, 1960—June 30, 1961*

Reservoir	Number of sites	Catalog numbers assigned	Number of specimens processed
Big Bend	6	496	2, 161
Fort Randall	1	83	1, 339
Walter F. George	57	2, 341	24, 101
Lewis and Clark	1	25	135
Oahe	15	2, 417	8, 145
Sites not in reservoirs	3	151	226
Site totals	83	5, 513	36, 107
Collections not assigned site numbers	1	3	46
Combined totals	84	5, 516	36, 153

As of June 30, 1961, the Missouri Basin Project had cataloged 1,255,716 specimens from 2,141 numbered sites and 59 collections not assigned site numbers.

Specimens restored: Two pottery vessels and one vessel section.
Specimens repaired: Fourteen nonpottery artifacts.
Specimens transferred to other agencies:
To the United States National Museum:
Archeological specimens from 425 sites in 10 reservoir areas.
Unworked shell from 16 sites in three reservoir areas.
To the University of Nebraska State Museum:
Identified, unworked animal bone from 120 sites in seven reservoir areas.

TABLE 2.—*Record material processed July 1, 1960–June 30, 1961*

MISSOURI BASIN PROJECT

Reflex copies of records	8,465
Photographic negatives made	1,507
Photographic prints made	8,916
Photographic prints mounted and filed	1,894
Transparencies mounted in glass	498
Kodachrome pictures taken in lab	160
Cartographic tracings and drawings	66
Artifacts sketched	45
Plates lettered	40
Profiles drawn	11
Plate layouts made for manuscripts	12

Cooperating institutions.—During the fiscal year a number of institutions cooperated in the Inter-Agency Salvage Program in several areas. In addition to those previously mentioned in the sections pertaining to Alabama-Georgia and the Missouri Basin, the following work was carried on under agreements with the National Park Service:

The University of Arkansas made studies in the Beaver Reservoir area on the White River and the Millwood Reservoir on Little River. The University of Kentucky conducted investigations in the Nolin Reservoir area on the Nolin River. The University of North Carolina worked at the Wilkesboro Reservoir on the Yadkin River. The University of Tennessee carried on activities in the Milton Hill Reservoir on the Clinch River. The Carnegie Museum of Pittsburgh studied archeological manifestations in the Shenango Reservoir area on the Shenango River. The New Jersey State Museum conducted investigations at Tocks Island. The University of Illinois had a project at the Shelbyville Reservoir on the Kaskaskia River, and Southern Illinois University made a series of excavations in the Carlyle Reservoir Basin on the same river. The Wisconsin State Historical Society conducted investigations in the Kickapoo Reservoir area on the Kickapoo River. The University of Texas carried on a series of surveys in the Texas Gulf Project. The Kansas State Historical

Society excavated in the Council Grove Reservoir on the Grand (Neosho) River. The University of Arizona continued its investigations in the Painted Rock area on the Gila River. The Museum of Northern Arizona continued its studies in the Glen Canyon Reservoir area on the Colorado River, as did the University of Utah in the same area and in the Flaming Gorge and Plainfield Reservoir Basins. The Museum of New Mexico worked in the Navajo Reservoir area along the San Juan River. The College of the Sequoias conducted investigations in the Terminus Reservoir area on the Kaweah River in California. Idaho State College worked in the Bruce's Eddy area on the North Fork of the Clearwater River. Washington State College continued its excavations in the Lower Monumental and Ice Harbor areas along the Columbia River and the University of Washington worked on the Priest Rapids-Wanapum Project in the Middle Columbia River district. The University of Oregon investigated sites in the John Day Reservoir Basin on the John Day River. Several institutions volunteered to carry on survey work without an agreement with the National Park Service. They include groups in Pennsylvania, New York State, Ohio, Indiana, southern California, and West Virginia. In the latter State the West Virginia Geological Survey did reconnaissance work in the Summerville Reservoir area on the Gauley River.

ARCHIVES

The Bureau archives continued under the custody of Mrs. Margaret C. Blaker, archivist. In May 1961 Mrs. Blaker visited the Haverford College Library, Haverford, Pa., where she examined pictorial and manuscript material in the Quaker Collection concerning American Indians, and in June, visited the library of Hampton Institute, Hampton, Va., and examined an extensive collection of field and studio photographs relating to Indians who were students at Hampton in the period 1880–1900. On July 10, 1960, Mrs. Caroline R. Cohen was appointed as junior anthropologist and was assigned to assist in the archives.

MANUSCRIPT COLLECTIONS

The papers of Dr. Frans M. Olbrechts, relating to his studies of the Cherokee Indians of North Carolina in 1926–31 when he was a collaborator of the Bureau, were transmitted to the Bureau archives by Dr. Olbrechts' widow, Mrs. Margriet Olbrechts of Wezembeek-Oppem, Belgium, through Dr. A. E. Meeussen, Koninklijk Museum, Tervuren, Belgium. Dr. Olbrechts died at Aix-la-Chapelle, March 24, 1958. The subject matter of the papers consists of the following categories: Vocabularies, grammar, texts, disease-name papers, Wilnoti formula papers, botany, myths, and miscellaneous ethnographic notes.

An 18-page inventory has been prepared, and the papers, which occupy 28 boxes, are available for study and microfilming.

The manuscript collection continued to be utilized by anthropologists and other students. About 300 manuscripts were consulted by searchers who visited the archives in person or purchased microfilm and other reproductions totaling 7,146 pages. An equal number of manuscripts was consulted by the archivist in obtaining information for over 90 mail inquiries. In the course of this examination, new and more detailed descriptions of manuscripts were also prepared for the permanent catalog and for future distribution in response to specific inquiries.

PHOTOGRAPHIC COLLECTIONS

The Bureau's collection of North American Indian photographs, which is one of the most extensive and most active of its kind, continued to grow through the generosity of interested individuals who either lent pictures for copying, or presented them as gifts.

Sixty original photographs of Mesquakie Indians, mainly taken by J. L. Hudson of Tama, Iowa, and apparently dating in part from the 1860's, were lent for copying by Norman Feder of New York City. Mr. Feder also lent a series of about 40 copy prints of Prairie Pottawotomie of the latter part of the 19th century.

Over 150 photographic slides of American Indian subjects were received on loan from Mrs. Doris Collester of East Riverdale, Md. Of especial interest are several dozen slides of Apache, Pima, and Maricopa Indians dated 1871 or in years of the following decade. Many of the slides bear the name of Moore, Bond & Co., Chicago or Moore, Hubbell, & Co., Chicago, as distributor, although the original source of most of the photographs is still unknown.

Forty-six photographs relating to Cree and Chipewyan Indians in Alberta, Saskatchewan, and Mackenzie, Canada, taken by Dr. Francis Harper on an expedition of the Geological Survey of Canada to the Great Slave Lake in 1914 were obtained from the Geological Survey of Canada, through the courtesy of Dr. Francis Harper and Dr. J. M. Harrison, Director of the Survey.

A scrapbook of James Earl Taylor, artist-correspondent for *Frank Leslie's Illustrated Weekly Newspaper* from 1863 to 1883, was received as a gift from the Pennsylvania Historical and Museum Commission, through John Witthoft. The scrapbook contains several hundred original photographic prints of western Indians, several photographs of Army officers, linecuts of western military posts, and other material assembled for the artist's reference, as well as reproductions of a number of Taylor's own illustrations.

Seventeen photographs of important men of the Osage, Caddo, Arapaho, Cherokee, Creek, Chickasaw, and Seminole tribes were borrowed for copying from the Quaker Collection, Haverford College Library, Haverford, Pa., through the courtesy of Dr. Thomas E. Drake. The portraits are all on similar mounts of the carte de visite style, and most are inscribed with the subjects' names and the dateline September 1865, Fort Smith, Ark. Only one of the photographs has a photographer's imprint. It is a portrait of Left Hand and Powder Face, Arapahoes, with Superintendent Enoch Hoag. On the reverse is stamped, "W. H. Lamon, Photograph Artist, Corner Massachusetts & Henry Sts., Lawrence, Kansas." Four views of Kickapoo bark- and mat-covered lodges in Chief Wapamashawa's village, Indian Territory, were also borrowed from the Quaker collection and copied.

Thirteen photographs, including 10 relating to Kiowa, Wichita, and Apache Indians, by Irwin of Chickasha, Indian Territory, 1892–ca. 1894, were lent for copying by Vernon M. Riley of Chino, Calif.

Five photographs relating to Omaha and Ponca Indians of the latter 19th century, and a group photograph of the officers of the American Association for the Advancement of Science at Ann Arbor, 1885, including the Reverend J. Owen Dorsey and Mrs. Erminnie A. Smith (both formerly associated with this Bureau) were lent for copying by Mrs. Virginia Dorsey Lightfoot of Takoma Park, Md.

Five photographs of Osage Indians, taken in 1871 by T. M. Concannon at the Osage Agency, Indian Territory, were received as a gift from Mrs. Ernest J. Martin of Drain, Oreg.

Nine photographs relating to Indians of the Southwest who were connected with projects of the U.S. Bureau of Reclamation in that area in 1941–60 were donated by the Bureau of Reclamation.

Ten copy photographs of Ute Indians of the 1870's and 1880's were received in exchange from Dr. Omer C. Stewart of Boulder, Colo.

Six recent photographs of Quapaw Indians of Oklahoma were presented by Mrs. Velma Nieberding of Miami, Okla.

A collection of between 100 and 200 mounted photographs and glass slides was received as a transfer from the library of the United States Department of the Interior. At year's end these photographs had not yet been arranged and individually listed. They relate to a variety of North American Indian tribes.

During the year prints were prepared from several hundred snapshot negatives by Matilda Coxe Stevenson that had not been previously cataloged. Most of the photographs were made at Zuñi Pueblo, ca. 1904. They include numerous views relating to dances and ceremonials and a lesser number pertaining to domestic activities. In spite of the fact that some of the photographs are not of high quality photographically, many are surprisingly clear and informative, and the collection as a whole warrants careful study.

In addition to the Zuñi views, in the Stevenson collections there are a relatively small number of photographs relating to the pueblos of Cochití, ca. 1904, San Ildefonso, ca. 1908, and Santa Clara, ca. 1911. A 16-page caption list of the entire collection has been prepared.

The photographic files continued to be used extensively by scholars and the general public. The year's total of approximately 600 purchase orders and written and personal inquiries concerning photographs is about equal to that of last year, while the total of over 2,000 prints distributed exceeds last year's figure.

ILLUSTRATIONS

Work during the past fiscal year consisted of the preparation of numerous charts, graphs, diagrams, and maps, the restoration of photographs, photo retouching, and the drawing of a variety of Indian artifacts. Also many miscellaneous drawings, diagrams, etc., were prepared for other branches of the Institution.

LIBRARY

Detailed information about the Bureau library is contained in the report of the librarian on the Smithsonian Library, but it is well to emphasize the fact that the Bureau library is still serving a useful purpose in providing reference material not only for members of the staff but for students and professionals in the Washington area and visitors from other parts of the country. However, it should be pointed out that the library is not wholly fulfilling the function that it should because of the lack of a librarian. A full-time librarian would not only greatly expedite the use of the facility by members of the staff, but would also be extremely helpful to those who find it necessary to consult publications in the Bureau library, many of which are not available in many other places. Furthermore, through an intimate knowledge of the material now available, a librarian would be able to see that new publications pertaining to the Bureau's researches are acquired promptly when they become available. For many years the Bureau library was one of the outstanding places in North America for anthropological research, and it well merits a return to its former status.

EDITORIAL WORK AND PUBLICATIONS

The Bureau's editorial work continued during the year under the immediate direction of Mrs. Eloise B. Edelen. There were issued one Annual Report and two Bulletins, as follows:

Seventy-seventh Annual Report of the Bureau of American Ethnology, 1959–60. ii+35 pp., 2 pls. 1961.

Bulletin 176. River Basin Surveys Papers, Nos. 15–20, Frank H. H. Roberts, Jr., editor. ix+337 pp., 65 pls., 25 figs. 1960.

    No. 15. Historic sites archeology on the Upper Missouri, by Merrill J. Mattes.

Bulletin 176—Continued

No. 16. Historic sites archeology in the Fort Randall Reservoir, South Dakota, by John E. Mills.

No. 17. The excavation and investigation of Fort Lookout Trading Post II (39LM57) in the Fort Randall Reservoir, South Dakota, by Carl F. Miller.

No. 18. Fort Pierre II (39ST217), a historic trading post in the Oahe Dam area, South Dakota, by G. Hubert Smith.

No. 19. Archeological investigations at the site of Fort Stevenson (32ML1), Garrison Reservoir, North Dakota, by G. Hubert Smith. With an introduction by Robert L. Stephenson and an appendix by Carlyle S. Smith.

No. 20. The archeology of a small trading post (32MN1) in the Garrison Reservoir (Kipp's Post) South Dakota, by Alan R. Woolworth and W. Raymond Wood.

Bulletin 180. Symposium on Cherokee and Iroquois culture, edited by William N. Fenton and John Gulick. VI+292 pp. 1961.

No. 1. Foreword by the editors.

No. 2. Iroquois-Cherokee linguistic relations, by Floyd G. Lounsbury.

No. 3. Comment on Floyd G. Lounsbury's "Iroquois-Cherokee Linguistic Relations," by Mary R. Haas.

No. 4. Iroquois archeology and settlement patterns, by William A. Ritchie.

No. 5. First comment on Wlliam A. Ritchie's "Iroquois Archeology and Settlement Patterns," by William H. Sears.

No. 6. Second comment on William A. Ritchie's "Iroquois Archeology and Settlement Patterns," By Douglas S. Byers.

No. 7. Cherokee archeology, by Joffre L. Coe.

No. 8. Comment on Joffre L. Coe's "Cherokee Archeology," by Charles H. Fairbanks.

No. 9. Eastern Woodlands community typology and acculturation, by John Witthoft.

No. 10. Comment on John Witthoft's "Eastern Woodlands Community Typology and Acculturation," by John M. Goggin.

No. 11. Cherokee economic cooperatives: the Gadugi, by Raymond D. Fogelson and Paul Kutsche.

No. 12. The rise of the Cherokee state as an instance in a class: The "Mesopotamian" career to statehood, by Fred O. Gearing.

No. 13. Comment on Fred O. Gearing's "The Rise of the Cherokee State as an Instance in a Class: The 'Mesopotamian' Career to Statehood," by Annemarie Shimony.

No. 14. Cultural composition of the Handsome Lake religion, by Anthony F. C. Wallace.

No. 15. Comment on Anthony F. C. Wallace's "Cultural Composition of the Handsome Lake Religion," by Wallace L. Chafe.

No. 16. The Redbird Smith movement, by Robert K. Thomas.

No. 17. Comment on Robert K. Thomas's "The Redbird Smith Movement," by Fred W. Voget.

No. 18. Effects of environment on Cherokee-Iroquois ceremonialism, music, and dance, by Gertrude P. Kurath.

No. 19. Comment on Gertrude P. Kurath's "Effects of Environment on Cherokee-Iroquois Ceremonialism, Music, and Dance," by William C. Sturtevant.

No. 20. The Iroquois fortunetellers and their conservative influence, by Annemarie Shimony.

No. 21. Change, persistence, and accommodation in Cherokee medico-magical beliefs, by Raymond D. Fogelson.

Bulletin 180—Continued

No. 22. Some observations on the persistence of aboriginal Cherokee personality traits, by Charles H. Holzinger.

No. 23. First comment on Charles H. Holzinger's "Some Observations on the Persistence of Aboriginal Cherokee Personality Traits," by David Landy.

No. 24. Second comment on Charles H. Holzinger's "Some Observations on the Persistence of Aboriginal Cherokee Personality Traits," by John Gulick.

No. 25. Iroquoian culture history: A general evaluation, by William N. Fenton.

Publications distributed totaled 29,845, as compared with 31,547 for the fiscal year 1960.

COLLECTIONS

The following collections were made by staff members of the Bureau of American Ethnology or of the River Basin Surveys and transferred to the permanent collections of the department of science and technology, the department of civil history, and the department of anthropology, U.S. National Museum:

FROM BUREAU OF AMERICAN ETHNOLOGY

Acc. No.

236067. Dictaphone. Through Dr. Frank H. H. Roberts, Jr.

234469. 31 Belgian postage stamps. Through Mrs. Margaret C. Blaker.

FROM RIVER BASIN SURVEYS

225806. 160 land and fresh-water mollusks from Arkansas and South Dakota. Through Dr. Robert L. Stephenson.

232081. Indian skeletal remains from Big Bend Reservoir, Buffalo County, S. Dak.

232741. 5,153 archeological items and skeletal material from Fall River County, S. Dak., and Crook and Fremont Counties, Wyo., 1957.

233812. Indian skeletal materials from the McNary Reservoir region.

MISCELLANEOUS

Dr. M. W. Stirling, Dr. John P. Harrington, Dr. A. J. Waring, and Sister Inez Hilger continued as research associates. Dr. Stirling, assisted by Mrs. Marion Stirling, using the Bureau's laboratory facilities, completed work on the materials from the Ecuadorian field trip undertaken while he was Director of the Bureau, and turned in a manuscript which will be published in the Bureau's series of anthropological papers.

The following bibliographies and leaflets were issued during the fiscal year:

SIL–50, 3d rev., 2/61: Selected list of portraits of prominent Indians in the collections of the Bureau of American Ethnology.

SIL–53, rev., 2/61: Photographic collections of the Bureau of American Ethnology.

SIL–76, rev., 7/60: Statement regarding the Book of Mormon.

SIL–92, rev., 1/61: Origin of the American Indian.

SIL–134, rev., 10/60: American Indian languages.
SIL–175, rev., 3/61: Selected references on present-day conditions among U.S. Indians.
SIL–264, 11/60: Selected references on the Indian and the Frontier.
SIL–276, 1/61: Linguistic considerations in the interpretation of place names.

Other bibliographies were revised during the year. They are: the "Battle of the Little Bighorn" (should be available for distribution by September 1961), and the popular "Bibliography of American Indian Medicine" (available before December 1961.)

The nearly 3,900 letters received in the Director's office plus a few hundred received by staff members are a good indication of the continued interest in the American Indian. In addition, several thousand letters requesting Bureau publications are received yearly in the Editorial and Publications Division. Many complete sets of the Bureau's bibliographies were sent out upon requests from college and university professors and libraries, and to other educational organizations. Approximately 10,200 informational items, including typescript and printed articles, bibliographies, and other leaflets, plus more than 300 photographic lists were mailed from the main Bureau office in response to requests for such materials. Many specimens were mailed in or brought to the office for identification and data on them were supplied.

Respectfully submitted.

FRANK H. H. ROBERTS, JR., *Director.*

Dr. LEONARD CARMICHAEL,
Secretary, Smithsonian Institution.

Report on the Astrophysical Observatory

Sir: I have the honor to submit the following report on the operations of the Smithsonian Astrophysical Observatory for the fiscal year ended June 30, 1961:

The Astrophysical Observatory includes two divisions: the Division of Astrophysical Research in Cambridge, for the study of solar and other types of energy impinging on the earth; and the Division of Radiation and Organisms in Washington, for the investigation of radiation as it relates directly or indirectly to biological problems. Shops are maintained in Washington for work in metals, woods, and optical electronics, and to prepare special equipment for both divisions; and a shop conducted in cooperation with the Harvard College Observatory in Cambridge provides high-precision mechanical work. The field station at Table Mountain, Calif., carries out solar observations. Twelve satellite-tracking stations are in operation, in Florida, Hawaii, and New Mexico in the United States and abroad in Argentina, Australia, Curaçao, India, Iran, Japan, Peru, South Africa, and Spain.

DIVISION OF ASTROPHYSICAL RESEARCH

The Observatory research staff made significant contributions to knowledge of solar astrophysics, meteors, meteorites, artificial satellites, geophysics, and space science. The continuing refinement of observational techniques and the development of new analytical methods provided valuable data and opened up new areas of astrophysical investigation.

The Observatory continued, with mutual benefit, its close liaison with Harvard College Observatory, the Massachusetts Institute of Technology, Boston University, and other research centers.

Solar astrophysics.—Dr. Paul W. Hodge studied the properties of the field stars and globular clusters in the Large Magellanic Cloud and found that they apparently differ from our galaxy in color, magnitudes, luminosity, and evolutionary pattern. These findings are important in establishing the true extragalactic distance scale.

Stephen E. Strom completed his study of absorption below 100 A. to determine the optical depth of the interstellar medium as a function of wavelength in the X-ray region. He found that the region above 40 A. is essentially "black" (in terms of presently conceived fluxes) and that, owing to the K-absorption limit of oxygen, there is an interesting "jump" at 23.3 A. in the curve of optical depth versus wavelength.

Dr. Charles A. Whitney continued his research in stellar atmospheres. From computations based on novel analytical methods, carried out by Angelo J. Skalafuris, he has formulated a simplified analytical description of the cooling rate behind shock waves. This work corrects the erroneous results of an earlier investigator, and also serves to check the range of validity of assumptions of "optically thin" perturbations (i.e., neglect of reabsorption of shock radiation). In his investigation of the gas dynamics of stellar atmospheres, also assisted by Mr. Skalafuris, he is concentrating initially on the structure of shock fronts in pure hydrogen, and in successive stages will work toward a unified theory incorporating the effects of radiation and the wide departures from thermodynamic equilibrium. Dr. Whitney's continuing project on the cause and nature of stellar pulsation has closely approached a definitive statement of the cause of pulsation aided by the success of Dr. John P. Cox, who served as consultant, in obtaining exact solutions for the nonadiabatic linearized wave equation. Miss Sylvia Boyd began compilation of spectrographic and photometric data on pulsating stars, which will undergo analysis in the light of the Cox-Whitney theory; Dr. R. G. Teske's investigation, under Dr. Whitney's supervision, of spectrum-line formation in pulsating stellar atmospheres indicates the need for revision of earlier interpretations.

To provide a foundation for the analysis of astrophysical data expected from future orbiting observatories, Dr. Whitney began preliminary work on methods of constructing accurate model stellar atmospheres. Using electronic computations provided by SAO, he is extending and modifying recent theoretical developments, including the work of Dr. Max Krook and his students. Owen Gingerich's completed computer program for the construction of accurate model atmospheres in radiative equilibrium has demonstrated the inadequacy of much earlier work in solar radiation and its implications for the model of the sun's atmosphere. Shiv Kumar has virtually completed the construction of several models for the atmosphere of very hot stars.

Dr. Richard McCrosky, with the use of infrared-sensitive detectors on the 61-inch telescope of the Harvard College Observatory, continues his observations of Raman-scattered Lyman α to determine the presence of hydrogen molecules in interstellar space.

Dr. Max Krook is proceeding with his theoretical research into the further development and application of methods for determining the structure of nongray atmospheres. In collaboration with Dr. Whitney, he is now calculating a number of model atmospheres. He is also applying the methods developed in continuum theories in gas dynamics to problems of the flow of rarefied gases, various problems in the dynamics of ionized gases, and the exact solution of one-dimensional problems in the kinetic theory of gases.

Fred A. Franklin made progress in his dynamical and photometric studies of the rings of Saturn and of the interaction between the rings and particles of the solar corpuscular stream. The results should apply to other astronomical problems and should yield precise values of the solar corpuscular flux.

At the Table Mountain station, Dr. Alfred G. Froiland, employing the atmospheric coefficients obtained by Smithsonian work, devised a method for determining the ozone in the vertical path.

Meteoritical studies.—The Director and Dr. Luigi G. Jacchia completed their analysis and discusssion of the orbits of 413 accurately reduced meteors. Dr. Jacchia will continue his study of the reduced material.

The Director has been investigating the distribution of semimajor axes among comet orbits and has derived the following law for the frequency distribution of lifetimes of long-period comets: Potential lifetimes of new comets are distributed according to the negative three-halves power of the lifetime in number of revolutions. His theories on the structure of the cometary nucleus will form a chapter in a forthcoming book on the solar system. From rocket, satellite, and space-probe data the Director completed a study of the influx of micrometeoritic dust on earth. The work adds significantly to knowledge of the structure and evolution of the solar system and has practical importance for the engineering and operation of space vehicles.

Robert E. Briggs is continuing his study of the distribution of interplanetary dust particles in space. This work should provide valuable data for current and future research on the nature of interplanetary space and the origin and properties of the dust particles.

Dr. John A. Wood has been conducting a study of variations in chemical composition between individual chondrules extracted from a chondrite (Bjurböle). He is analyzing these small chondrules with a direct-current arc emission spectrograph. He has also been making a theoretical analysis of the diffusion of nickel in the nickel-iron phases of iron meteorites, to determine cooling rates and thermal histories which could account for the curious nonequilibrium nickel concentration profiles noted by Uhlig and others in irons. His brief analysis and description of the new meteorite Ras Tanura (Saudi Arabia) is being prepared for publication.

Dr. E. L. Fireman, Dr. David Tilles, and James DeFelice measured the radioactive isotopes tritium and argon-37 in recovered satellite material. The tritium content of some material from the Discoverer XVII satellite was unusually high but decreased rapidly with increasing depth. Discoverer XVII was exposed to an intense solar flare (3+ magnitude). The high tritium content and its depth dependence in the satellite material lead to the conclusion that the solar flare contains 0.4 percent tritium. This is the first measurement of a radioactive isotope from the sun.

Dr. Fireman completed measurements of argon-37, argon-39, and tritium in several freshly fallen meteorites, and showed that the cosmic-ray flux is higher at a distance of one astronomical unit from the earth than at three. He has also obtained preliminary measurements on radioactive isotopes in the Bruderheim meteorite. His analysis of uranium, potassium, argon-140, and krypton-xenon in iron meteorites will help determine the age and early history of the meteorites.

Dr. Paul W. Hodge continues his study of the rate of accretion by the earth of meteoritic matter and will determine especially the physical and chemical properties of fine dust particles collected by jet aircraft at altitudes varying from 30,000 to 90,000 feet. Collections at even greater heights, up to 250,000 feet, will be attempted.

Dr. Richard E. McCrosky, with the collaboration of the Harvard College Observatory, U.S. Air Force, Lincoln Laboratories, and National Aeronautics and Space Administration, continues his attempt to reproduce the meteor phenomena by a study of artificial meteors. The results should help calibrate the mass-luminosity scale of natural meteors. From a project designed to recover a larger number of meteorites as soon as possible after their fall, Dr. McCrosky will seek data on the cosmic-ray intensity in the vicinity of the earth and throughout the orbit of the meteorite. His findings will add to our present inadequate knowledge of the numbers, masses, and orbits of meteorites.

Dr. McCrosky continued his planning of a program to locate and recover meteorites as soon as possible after their fall, by photographing meteors in flight and analyzing the photographic records to find the place of fall. The program will also augment our knowledge of the number, masses, and orbits of large meteors. Preliminary design of the stations is complete; the general location of the stations in the network in the Midwest has been determined; and a machine program for computation of impact points has been completed. The program has not yet received financial support. In view of the scientific results that can be expected from this project, it should be funded as soon as possible.

Dr. F. Behn Riggs, Jr., designed and developed an electron probe microanalyzer to make possible a point-by-point chemical analysis of polished surfaces of sectioned meteorites without destruction of samples. Analyses of micrometeorites, along with other experiments in bringing the electron beam into the air, have resulted in a useful evaluation of unsolved technical problems.

Pedro E. Zadunaisky has begun an analysis of the motion of Halley's Comet in order to check current theories about the forces perturbing the elliptic motion of a comet.

Opening a new field for study, Dr. Tilles will construct a high-sensitivity mass spectrometer and from recovered satellite samples will measure the isotopic composition of the gases in solar winds and flares. He will also study the stable isotopes of noble gases in meteorites and terrestrial rocks.

Satellite-tracking program.—The optical tracking of artificial satellites with NASA support continues to provide data for the prediction of orbits and for basic research in the space sciences. The program comprises a worldwide organization of Moonwatch teams, the operation of 12 precision photographic stations in various parts of the world, the calculation of satellite ephemerides, photographic image reduction, detailed analysis by electronic computers, and precise reduction of satellite positions.

From May 1, 1960, to May 1, 1961, Moonwatch observations of 57 satellites and their orbiting components provided data for correcting ephemerides and for acquiring and reacquiring satellites. The stations also conducted a number of searches for orbiting objects.

Dr. Gustav A. Bakos's analysis of Moonwatch observations indicates that they compare favorably with those made by radar and with field reduced observations by SPOT.

Major developments in operational techniques of the Baker-Nunn camera stations were accomplished in two fields—the automation of matched-track and off-culmination observing methods, and the design and development of auxiliary equipment that enables the entire network to be synchronized to within a few milliseconds of time. These developments will prove extremely valuable in the forthcoming research in geodesy using direct triangulation methods.

Specifications were drawn for a new electronic time standard for the stations that would be capable of maintaining uniform and precise time to an accuracy of one-half millisecond. This clock, which will greatly improve observational accuracy, is unique in its field.

Five stations in the Baker-Nunn network worked in conjunction with the Jodrell Bank Radio Telescope in making optical observations of flare stars.

Of 13,556 films received from the Baker-Nunn camera stations, the photoreduction center completed reductions of 8,961. From July 1960 through April 1961 the computations center sent 32,592 predictions to the 12 Baker-Nunn camera stations, 11,160 transits of satellites were observed, and 14,361 reduced positions were reported.

The communications center cleared more than a million words per month, 95 percent of which represent satellite data received or sent throughout the world.

The research and analysis division has made valuable contributions to our basic knowledge of the earth and the upper atmosphere, described in detail under *Space Science*. In summary, the division has achieved greater accuracy in the analysis of the earth's gravitational potential field, established the gravitational ellipticity around the earth's equator, and determined the geodetic positions of the observing stations with greater exactness. The division has measured variations of atmospheric density in relation to solar activity and interplanetary storms, and studied the effect of solar light pressure on satellites.

Dr. Károly Lassovszky is continuing his astrometric study of satellite positions determined from Baker-Nunn films. From approximately 800 measurements on 34 images of different length he analyzed the frequency distribution of settings, the relationship between this distribution and the length of the image, and the relationship between the "magnitude error" and the length of image. Position determinations have been made using reference stars at different distances. On the basis of these results, we can conclude that the accuracy is influenced neither by the distortion of the emulsion nor by the optical distortion within an area of a diameter of 5 cm. (5°8). The standard error of a position determined from numerous measurements made with Mann comparators on Baker-Nunn films is $\pm 1''1$, both in right ascension and in declination. The project should help evaluate the techniques of analysis and measurement now used for the precise reduction of satellite data. Dr. Lassovszky will also investigate the rapid and secular variations in brightness of satellites.

At the Florence meeting of COSPAR, April 10–14, 1961, the Director and Dr. George Veis presented a paper on the Observatory's "Experience in Precision Optical Tracking of Satellites for Geodesy." The Baker-Nunn cameras can photograph satellites to an accuracy of about $\pm 2''$ (seconds of arc) in topocentric position and ± 1 millisecond in time. The locations of the cameras have been connected, with standard geodetic techniques, to the major geodetic systems and to a tentative uniform one. From an analysis of the observations, geodetic information of dynamic character has been obtained; i.e., the coefficients of the second, third, fourth, and fifth order zonal harmonics of the earth's gravity field as well as the coefficients of the second order sectorial harmonic. The launching of a well-planned and controlled flashing-light geodetic satellite for international use would reduce markedly the complexity and expense of observing stations and promote international geodesy in a remarkable fashion.

Space science.—Imre G. Izsak, in the first attempt to derive two important geophysical constants from the motion of satellites, has made a good estimate of the ellipticity of the earth's equator. He has also obtained a second-order solution of Vinti's dynamical problem.

In his study of satellite orbits with very small eccentricities he has found that the orbit has two perigees and two apogees during each revolution. He is continuing his investigation of the harmonics of the earth's gravitational potential.

Dr. Don A. Lautman has undertaken a numerical integration program to provide precise ephemerides of artificial satellites. He will check general perturbation theories and attempt to obtain orbits of satellites not at present subject to general theory, as well as of those whose perturbations are too large or too complicated to be handled conveniently by general perturbation theories.

Dr. Yoshihide Kozai has shown that the effects of solar-radiation pressure must be considered in the derivation of geodetic constants from satellite data. He is continuing his studies of astronomical constants and of the geodetic uses of artifical satellites. By analysis of deviations of computed orbits from those observed by Baker-Nunn cameras, he is attempting to determine the tesseral harmonics of the earth's gravitational potential and to obtain accurate coordinates of the camera stations. He will employ recently determined values from the motion of satellites to examine the relations between astronomical constants and to eliminate inconsistencies. Dr. Kozai's determinations from satellites of the spherical harmonics to the fifth order of the earth's gravitational field are generally accepted as the most precise available.

Pedro E. Zadunaisky, from a preliminary study of atmospheric drag on nonspherical satellites, has attempted to find a "mean" attitude of satellites in relation to their velocity vectors. He will continue with more refined techniques and a different group of satellites at higher altitudes. His analysis will contribute to our knowledge of atmospheric densities and of the motion of satellites around their center of gravity. His special study of the perturbations on the orbit of Echo I caused by atmospheric drag and solar-radiation pressure gave good agreement between theory and observation.

Dr. Gustav A. Bakos is progressing with his analysis of the seasonal changes of the earth's albedo. The project has significance for our understanding of the relationship which he has demonstrated between large-scale meteorological phenomena and the observed reflectivity of the earth.

Stephen E. Strom has developed the computer program and preliminary ray-tracing method for the study of the effect of the ionosphere on radio-astronomical observations.

Dr. Mario D. Grossi, with these computations and tracings as tools, will investigate the effect of the ionosphere, the Van Allen belts, and the earth's magnetic field on radio-astronomical observations in the MF and HF bands.

Dr. Luigi G. Jacchia's studies of atmospheric drag on artificial satellites have already contributed profoundly to our knowledge of atmospheric densities above the height of 200 km. His conclusions as to variations of the atmosphere with time, solar activity, and geographic position, as well as his determinations of the atmospheric density profile, have received general international acceptance. He will continue to explore the problems of solar-terrestrial effects.

Dr. G. Colombo has made a study of the motion of Explorer IV (Satellite 1958 Epsilon) around its center of mass, as inferred from observations of several kinds, and the possible causes of the strong variations of the elements of the tangential precessional motion. Although a precise knowledge of the residual magnetization of the body of the satellite and the ferromagnetic components of the payload is needed for an exact computation, he draws attention to the unexpected pronounced effect of the interaction between the earth's magnetic field and the shell (of stainless steel) of the satellite.

Dr. Leo Goldberg, with Dr. William Liller, is directing the design and construction of two ultraviolet scanning spectrometers for flight in the S–17 Satellite within the framework of the program of Orbiting Solar Observatories of the National Aeronautics and Space Administration. The combined spectral range of the spectrometers will be 75 A. to 1500 A. and the resolving power will vary between 0.3 A. at the longer wavelengths and 1.0 A. at the shortest wavelengths. Design of the spectrometers is now in the final stages. Calibration and testing of the instrument packages will be carried out in a new laboratory recently installed in the Space Science Building.

The work of the laboratory will also be expanded in the fall to include a broad program of basic research on the vacuum ultraviolet radiation of atoms and molecules of astrophysical importance with one- and two-meter vacuum spectrographs and a shock tube and flash tube as sources. The scanning spectrometers are scheduled for rocket flights at the end of 1961 and for flight aboard the S–17 Satellite during the last quarter of 1962.

Dr. Goldberg has been engaged in a study and survey of astronomical experiments that may be performed with satellite vehicles. The conclusions of the survey have been published in two chapters of "Science in Space" in collaboration with Dr. E. R. Dyer, Jr.

The Director and Dr. Robert J. Davis, astrophysicist in charge, together with other Observatory scientists, have progressed with the planning and development of the "Celescope" project, a group of astronomical telescopes to be carried in sounding rockets and later orbited in artificial earth satellites. Specifications for the satellite payload (telescope system) have been prepared, and final negotiation for the manufacture of the instruments is being awaited. With the aid of television images in three colors and slitless spectrograms of the entire celestial sphere, these instruments will provide a means of extending astronomical observations to the far ultraviolet and X-ray regions of the spectrum.

The immediate objective of the project is to map about 100,000 stars and record their brightnesses. Further analysis in special detail of objects discovered by this survey is planned.

The first rocket flight carrying a prototype Celescope of simplified design should confirm our theoretical analyses and test some of the more critical elements of the Celescope's electronic system. Experiments have been delayed by rocket failure but should resume in February 1962.

The payload for the satellite will consist of imaging television-type detectors sensitive to certain ultraviolet spectra. These video images will be scanned and converted from analog to digital form prior to signal transmission to ground stations to preserve all the important stellar information. Models of this digital equipment have been designed and built in Celescope laboratories and will serve as guides for manufacturers building the satellite payload. The first telescope should go into orbit in 1963–64. The Celescope program is supported by NASA.

PUBLICATIONS

Publications of the Smithsonian Contributions to Astrophysics included numbers 2 through 4 of volume 4 and numbers 4 through 8 of volume 5.

The following papers by staff members of the Astrophysical Observatory appeared in various journals:

ALLER, L. H. *See* Goldberg, Muller, and Aller.

BAEZ, A. V. A proposed X-ray telescope for the 1 to 100–A region. Journ. Geophys. Res. vol. 65, pp. 3019–3020, 1960.

BROWN, J. *See* Goldberg, Mohler, and Brown.

DAVIS, R. J. U.S. plans for space telescopes for planets, stars, and nebulae. Mem. Soc. Roy. Sci. Liège, ser. 5, vol. 4, p. 25, 1961.

———. *See* also Strom, Strom, and Davis.

DEFELICE, J. *See* Fireman and DeFelice; Fireman, DeFelice, and Tilles; Tilles, DeFelice, and Fireman.

DYER, E. R., JR. *See* Goldberg and Dyer.

FIREMAN, E. L. *See* Tilles, DeFelice, and Fireman.

FIREMAN, E. L., and DEFELICE, J. Argon-37, argon-39, and tritium in meteorites and the spatial constancy of cosmic rays. Journ. Geophys. Res., vol. 65, pp. 3035–3041, 1960.

FIREMAN, E. L.; DEFELICE, J.; and TILLES, D. Tritium in recovered satellite material (abstract). Bull. Amer. Phys. Soc., vol. 6, No. 3, p. 276, 1961.

FIREMAN, E. L., and KISTNER, G. A. The nature of dust collected at high altitudes. Geochim. et Cosmochim. Acta, vol. 23, No. 5, 1961.

GINGERICH, O. A computer program for non-grey stellar atmospheres. Mem. Soc. Roy. Liège, ser. 5, vol. 4, 1960.

GOLDBERG, L. Project West Ford—properties and analyses; Introduction. Astron. Journ., vol. 66, pp. 105–106, 1961.

GOLDBERG, L. Solar experiments. Astron. Journ., vol. 65, pp. 274–277, 1960.
———. Solar experiments—US. plans. Mem. Soc. Roy. Liège, ser. 5, vol. 4, pp. 30–38, 1961.
———. The sun. Science in Space (Space Science Board Rep.), 1960.
———. The sun. Bull. Atomic Scientists, vol. 17, pp. 210–213, 1961.
GOLDBERG, L., and DYER, E. R., JR. Galactic and extragalactic astronomy. Science in Space (Space Science Board Rep.), 1960.
———. The sun. Galactic and extragalactic astronomy. *In* Science in Space, edited by L. V. Berkner and H. Odishaw, chaps. 17, 18, 1961.
GOLDBERG, L.; MOHLER, W. U.; and BROWN, J. The measurement of the local doppler shift of the Fraunhofer lines. Astrophys. Journ., vol. 132, pp. 184–194, 1960.
GOLDBERG, L.; MULLER, E. A.; and ALLER, L. H. The abundance of the elements in the solar atmosphere. Astrophys. Journ., suppl. 5, No. 45, pp. 1–138, 1960.
HAGIHARA, Y. Gaps in the distribution of asteroids. Smithsonian Contr. Astrophys., vol. 5, No. 6, 1961.
———. On the motion of satellites with critical inclination. Smithsonian Contr. Astrophys., vol. 5, No. 5, 1961.
HODGE, P. W. NGC 2209: An unusual cluster of the large Magellanic cloud. Publ. Astron. Soc. Pacific, vol. 72, pp. 308–311, 1961.
———. Studies of the large Magellanic cloud: V. The young populous clusters. Astrophys. Journ., vol. 133, pp. 413–419, 1961.
HODGE, P. W., and WRIGHT, F. W. The space density of atmospheric dust in the altitude range 50,000 to 90,000 feet. Tech. Rep., Air Force Cambridge Research Center (AFCRL 451), 1961.
HODGE, P. W.; WRIGHT, F. W.; and HOFFLEIT, D. An annotated bibliography on interplanetary dust. Smithsonian Contr. Astrophys., vol. 5, No. 8, 1961.
HOFFLEIT, D. *See* Hodge, Wright, and Hoffleit.
IZSAK, I. G. On satellite orbits with very small eccentricities. Astron. Journ., vol. 66, pp. 129–131, 1961.
———. Periodic drag perturbations of artificial satellites. Astron. Journ., vol. 65, pp. 355–357, 1960.
JACCHIA, L. G. Artificial earth satellites. Scientia, ser. 6, vol. 54, 1960.
———. A variable atmospheric-density model from satellite accelerations. Journ. Geophys. Res., vol. 65, pp. 2275–2782, 1960.
JACCHIA, L. G., and WHIPPLE, F. L. Precision orbits of 413 photographic meteors. Smithsonian Contr. Astrophys., vol. 4, No. 4, 1961.
KISTNER, G. A. *See* Fireman and Kistner.
KOZAI, Y. Effect of precession and nutation on the orbital elements of a close earth satellite. Astron. Journ., vol. 65, pp. 621–623, 1960.
———. Note on the motion of a close earth satellite with a small eccentricity. Astron. Journ., vol. 66, pp. 132–134, 1961.
———. The gravitational field of the earth derived from motions of three satellites. Astron. Journ., vol. 66, pp. 8–10, 1961.
KUMAR, S. S. On gravitational instability II. Publ. Astron. Soc., Japan, vol. 12, p. 290, 1960.
———. On gravitational instability III. Publ. Astron. Soc., Japan, vol. 13, p. 121, 1961.
McCROSKY, R. E. Observations of simulated meteors. Smithsonian Contr. Astrophys., vol. 5, No. 4, 1961.
McCROSKY, R. E., and POSEN, A. Elements of photographic meteors. Smithsonian Contr. Astrophys., vol. 4, No. 2, 1961.
MOHLER, W. U. *See* Goldberg, Mohler, and Brown.
MULLER, E. A. *See* Goldberg, Muller, and Aller.

NODVIK, J. S. *See* Rustgi, Nodvik, and Weissler.

POSEN, A. *See* McCrosky and Posen.

RIGGS, F. B., JR. Vacuum sealing of gold wire leads to a differential thermopile. Rev. Sci. Instr., vol. 32, No. 3, p. 366, March 1961.

RUSTGI, O. P.; NODVIK, J. S.; and WEISSLER, G. L. Optical constants of germanium in the region O–27 EV. Phys. Rev., vol. 122, p. 1131, 1961.

STROM, K. M. *See* Strom, S. E., and Strom, K. M.; Strom, Strom, and Davis.

STROM, S. E., and STROM, K. M. Interstellar absorption below 100 A. Publ. Astron. Soc. Pacific, vol. 73, pp. 43–45, 1961.

STROM, S. E.; STROM, K. M.; and DAVIS, R. J. A general method of analysis for n-lens, m-mirror systems (abstract). Journ. Opt. Soc. Amer., vol. 72, p. 43, 1961.

TILLES, D. *See* Fireman, DeFelice, and Tilles.

TILLES, D.; DEFELICE, J.; and FIREMAN, E. L. Argon-37 in recovered satellite material (abstract). Bull. Amer. Phys. Soc., ser. 2, vol. 2, No. 3, p. 277, 1961.

WEISSLER, G. L. *See* Rustgi, Nodvik, and Weissler.

WHIPPLE, F. L. The dust cloud about the earth. Nature, vol. 189, No. 4789, pp. 127–128, Jan. 14, 1961.

———. The earth's dust belt. Astronaut. Sci. Rev., vol. 3, No. 2, pp. 17–19, April–June 1961.

———. General conclusions. Mem. Soc. Roy. Sci. Liège, ser. 5, vol. 4, 1961.

———. Particulate contents of space. *In* Medical and Biological Aspects of the Energies of Space, P. Campbell, editor, 1061.

———. *See also* Jacchia and Whipple.

WRIGHT, F. W. *See* Hodge and Wright; Hodge, Wright, and Hoffleit.

The Special Reports of the Astrophysical Observatory distribute catalogues of satellite observations, orbital data, and preliminary results of data analysis prior to journal publication. Numbers 45 through 63, issued during the year, contain the following material:

Special Report No. 45, July 11, 1960.
List of coordinates of stations engaged in the observation of artificial earth-satellites, by D. V. Mechau.
Special Report No. 46, July 11, 1960.
The effect of a variable scale height on determinations of atmospheric density from satellite accelerations, by L. G. Jacchia.
Special Report No. 47 (C–15), Sept. 9, 1960.
Catalogue of satellite observations: Satellites 1958 Alpha, 1958 $\beta 1$, 1958 $\beta 2$, 1958 $\delta 2$, for Jan. 1–May 31, 1960, by D. V. Mechau.
Special Report No. 48 (C–16), Sept. 9, 1960.
Catalogue of satellite observations: Satellites 1959 $\alpha 1$ and 1959 $\alpha 2$ for Jan. 1–May 31, 1960, by D. V. Mechau.
Special Report No. 49 (C–17), Sept. 9, 1960.
Catalogue of satellite observations: Satellites 1959 Eta and $\iota 2$ for Jan. 1–May 31, 1960, by D. V. Mechau.
Special Report No. 50, Oct. 3, 1960.
The orbit of Satellite 1958 Alpha (Explorer I) during the first 10,500 revolutions, by P. E. Zadunaisky.
Special Report (unnumbered), Dec. 20, 1960.
Index to SAO Special Reports Nos. 1–50.
Special Report No. 51, Oct. 17, 1960.
Satellite orbital data: Satellites 1958 $\beta 1$ and 1958 $\beta 2$ by B. Miller; Satellites 1958 $\delta 2$ and 1959 $\nu 1$, by Y. Kozai, for Sept. 1959–April 1960, compiled by D. V. Mechau.

Special Report No. 52, Nov. 21, 1960.

A theory of satellite motion about an oblate planet: A second-order solution of Vinti's dynamical problem, by I. G. Izsak.

Special Report No. 53, Dec. 5, 1960.

The orbits and the accelerations of Satellites 1959 α1 and 1959 α2, by R. C. Nigam.

Special Report No. 54 (C–18), Dec. 19, 1960.

Catalogue of satellite observations: Satellites 1958 Alpha, 1958 β1, 1959 β2, 1958 δ2, 1958 Epsilon, for June 1–Aug. 31, 1960, by D. V. Mechau.

Special Report No. 55 (C–19), Dec. 19, 1960.

Catalogue of satellite observations: Satellites 1959 α1, 1959 α2, 1959 Eta, 1959 ι1, for June 1–Aug. 31, 1960, by D. V. Mechau.

Special Report No. 56, Jan. 30, 1961.

A method of analysis for lens and mirror systems, by R. J. Davis, S. E. Strom, and K. M. Strom.

A determination of the ellipticity of the earth's equator from the motion of two satellites, by I. G. Izsak.

Effects of solar radiation pressure on the motion of an artificial satellite, by Y. Kozai.

Special Report No. 57 (C–20), Mar. 3, 1961.

Catalogue of satellite observations: Satellites 1960 β1 (carrier rocket Tiros I), for Apr. 1–June 1, 1960; 1960 β2 (Tiros I), for Apr. 2–Aug. 31, 1960; 1960 γ1 (carrier rocket, Transit I B), for Apr. 13–June 3, 1960; 1960 γ2 (Transit I B) for Apr. 14–July 25, 1960, by D. V. Mechau.

Special Report No. 58 (C–21), Mar. 3, 1961.

Catalogue of satellite observations: Satellites 1960 ι1 (Echo I), and 1960 ι2 (carrier rocket, Echo I), for Aug. 12–Aug. 31, 1960, by D. V. Mechau.

Special Report No. 59, Mar. 3, 1961.

The positions of the Baker-Nunn camera stations, by G. Veis.

Special Report No. 60, Mar. 10, 1961.

The effect of radiation pressure on the secular acceleration of satellites, by S. P. Wyatt.

Special Report No. 61, Mar. 20, 1961.

Experimental and theoretical results on the orbit of Echo I, by P. E. Zadunaisky, I. J. Shapiro, and H. M. Jones.

Special Report No. 62, May 26, 1961.

The atmospheric drag of artificial satellites during the October 1960 and November 1960 events, by L. G. Jacchia.

Special Report No. 63, May 29, 1961.

Effect of the diurnal atmospheric bulge on satellite accelerations, by S. P. Wyatt.

OTHER ACTIVITIES

Members of the staff presented papers at meetings of the American Astronomical Society, the American Physical Society, the American Geophysical Union, the National Telemetering Conference, the American Meteorological Society, the American Astronautical Society, the American Philosophical Society, the Optical Society of America, the International Association of Geodesy, the Institute of Aeronautical Sciences, the National Aeronautics and Space Administration.

Dr. Fireman presented a paper at the International Atomic Energy Commission in Vienna and at a meeting of the Meteoritical Society in Los Angeles. The Director, Dr. Veis, Mr. Izsak, and Dr. Jacchia attended a COSPAR meeting in Florence, Italy. Drs. Fireman, McCrosky, and Riggs held a meeting with the director of the American Meteorite Museum in New York. The Director and Mr. Izsak met with the Space Science Board in New York City. Mr. Izsak, with Dr. Kozai and Mr. Rolff, participated in the Space Age Geodesy Symposium at Columbus, Ohio.

Dr. Davis held consultations with scientists at the University of Wisconsin on the Orbiting Astronomical Observatory. Dr. Riggs attended the Pittsburgh Diffraction Conference and participated in an A.S.T.M. panel meeting on electron probe microanalysis. The Director, Dr. Veis, and Mr. Izsak attended the 12th assembly of the International Union of Geodesy and Geophysics in Helsinki in July. Dr. Hynek visited South Dakota in connection with unmanned balloon flights. Dr. Lautman, Dr. Kozai, and Mr. Nigman attended the Yale Summer Institute in New Haven. Drs. Whipple, Davis, Jacchia, and Whitney participated in the symposium on Aeronomy sponsored by the International Association of Geomagnetism and Aeronomy at Copenhagen in July.

Dr. Whitney attended the I.A.U. symposium in Varenna, Italy, August 1960, where he presented a paper prepared jointly with Dr. P. Ledoux on present-day knowledge of the gas dynamics of variable stars. Dr. Whitney also presented, at the International Meetings of Aeronomers in Copenhagen, July 1960, a survey of methods of deriving atmospheric densities from satellite accelerations.

The Director served as president of the Tenth Astrophysical Symposium on Far Ultraviolet Spectra of Astronomical Bodies at the University of Liège, Belgium. As president of the Subcommission 22a, the Director prepared and submitted a world-wide meteoritical report to Commission 22 of the International Astronomical Union. The objective, to further international research in the field of meteorites, was forwarded by literature in the area and contributions from other members of the Committee. The Director also acted as consultant to the Scientific Advisory Board of the U.S. Air Force during the year as well as to the Committee on Science and Astronautics of the House of Representatives.

STAFF CHANGES

The following scientists joined the staff: Dr. Leo Goldberg, solar astrophysics; Drs. Giuseppe Colombo, Yusuke Hagihara, and George Veis, research and analysis, satellite-tracking program; Drs. Richard B. Southworth, David Tilles, and John A. Wood, meteoritical studies; Dr. Om P. Rustgi, Celescope.

Dr. J. Allen Hynek resigned as associate director to become director of the Dearborn Observatory, Northwestern University.

Kenneth H. Drummond resigned as assistant director (management), to accept a similar position at the University of California,

La Jolla. Carlton W. Tillinghast, Jr., became the new assistant director.

As of June 30, 1961, 309 persons were employed at the Observatory.

BUILDINGS AND EQUIPMENT

In addition to two other leased buildings, the Astrophysical Observatory occupies the recently completed Harvard University Space Science Building on the grounds of the Harvard College Observatory. Dedication took place in December 1960.

FUNDS AVAILABLE, FISCAL YEAR 1961

Satellite-tracking Program (NASA)	$3,900,000
Celescope (NASA 51–60)	695,543
Army Ballistics Missile Agency (ABMA)	19,964
Air Force Contract 1596	22,547
Air Force Contract 6627	4,998
Air Force Contract 7414	67,786
National Aeronautics and Space Administration Grant H–3647	50,000
National Science Foundation Grant 16337	20,000
National Science Foundation Grant 16067	25,000
Total	4,805,838

DIVISION OF RADIATION AND ORGANISMS

Prepared by W. H. KLEIN, Chief of the Division

The research activities of the Division were continued in the general field of photobiology, and the principal efforts were directed toward a more complete description of the regulatory responses of plants that are mediated by radiant energy. The technics of biochemistry, biophysics, cytology, and plant physiology were used in evaluating both qualitatively and quantitatively the metabolic and morphological changes occurring at the cellular and subcellular level in such photoregulatory processes.

The time course of chlorophyll synthesis at various stages of development for dark-grown Black Valentine bean plants was determined. A lag phase in the rate of chlorophyll synthesis occurs when seedlings are 6 or more days old. The rate of chlorophyll synthesis can be increased by a low-level pretreatment of red radiant energy, and this red effect can be completely eliminated by following it with far-red radiant energy. Since it appeared to be a possibility that the rate-limiting factor might be a substance which was depleted from the leaves or cotyledons at about 6 days or synthesized as a result of the red pretreatment, a number of compounds were tested by infiltrating leaves to determine their effect on the lag phase. In leaves infiltrated with delta amino levulinic acid, chlorophyll synthesis was found to occur without a lag phase during the first hour of subsequent irradiation. However, a pretreatment with red energy of delta amino levulinic acid infiltrated leaves did not increase chlorophyll synthesis, and beyond an hour of irradiation at low intensities, the rate of chlorophyll synthesis declined. At high intensities, the newly synthesized chlorophyll is destroyed.

The regulation of chlorophyll formation and the development of the photosynthetic apparatus as affected by inhibitors of protein synthesis were studied. Chlorophyll formation was inhibited at a concentration of 10 μgm./ml., and 60–80 percent inhibition occurred at 4,000 μgm./ml. Green pigments accumulating in the presence of antibiotic were chlorophylls a and b, and they were found to be present in the same ratio as in leaves treated with water instead of chloramphenicol. However, the effectiveness of chlorophyll in catalyzing photosynthesis decreased with increased concentration of chloramphenicol. Chloramphenicol does not affect the photosynthetic ability of leaves greened in its absence.

Leaves greened in the presence of chloramphenicol did not differ in their content of TPN-dependent glyceraldehyde-3-phosphate dehydrogenase from water-treated controls. Levels of carboxydismutase were somewhat lower in treated leaves. However, Hill reaction activity of a green particle fraction from leaves greened in chloramphenicol solution was only a tenth of that of the same fraction from control leaves.

The rate of chlorophyll synthesis in Black Valentine bean leaves was demonstrated to be another physiological response which is subject to the mediation of the red, far-red photomorphogenic receptor. The rate of pigment production by the chlorophyll-synthesizing mechanism in etiolated leaves can be influenced by a short preirradiation with red and far-red radiant energy. A treatment consisting of several minutes of red light, followed by an overnight period in darkness, results in appreciable stimulation in the subsequent rate of chlorophyll synthesis in continuous white light. The stimulation induced by a red pretreatment can be nullified by subsequent exposure to far-red, either immediately after the red induction or even after interposing as much as 9 hours of darkness. When red and far-red are administered alternately for several cycles, the quality of the terminal treatment controls the rate of chlorophyll synthesis. The effect of the red, far-red system on the chlorophyll-synthesizing mechanism may be due to the synthesis of pigment precursors or to changes in plastid size and/or number.

The expansion of dark-grown leaves is promoted markedly by exposure to red radiant energy. For leaf disks, the induction by red is a logarithmic function of dose over the range of 0.1 to 100 mj./cm.^{2} when given in 100 seconds. For reversal, the dose response curve is a linear function of dose, and the maximum effectiveness of the far-red occurs about 30 minutes after induction. Preliminary measurements of the spectral sensitivity of leaf disk expansion indicate that at 546 and 577 mμ, the promotive effect is as great for equal quantum flux as at 660 mμ.

For leaves stimulated by red energy, an additional growth stimulation of expansion is exerted by cobalt ions, which also promote expansion in the dark. The maximum growth promotion due to cobalt was found to be 3×10^{-4}M. and was not found to be affected by 2,4-dinitrophenol (DNP) which uncouples oxidative phosphorylation. Adenosine triphosphate (ATP) levels in the leaf tissue were not affected by cobalt alone. However, complete deletion of ATP by DNP did not occur if cobalt ion was added simultaneously. It appears that this effect is not due to the formation of a complex between DNP and cobalt ion which is inactive in the oxidative phosphorylation process. Experiments with isolated mitochondria indicate that the cobalt ion inhibits the activity of adenosine triphosphatase, thereby increasing the net gain of ATP from oxidative phosphorylation.

The yield of chromosome aberrations induced by a given dose of X-rays is increased by supplemental far-red radiation. Since far-red energy is effective as either a pretreatment or posttreatment, it is apparently the rejoining mechanism rather than breakage per se that is affected. Alternatively, the increase of X-ray-induced aberrations may result from mitotic delay induced by far-red. These possibilities are not necessarily mutually exclusive since some particular phase of the mitotic cycle, e.g., that portion of mitotic interphase during which DNA synthesis takes place, may be preferentially affected.

Studies were conducted of cell population kinetics of root systems of broad bean, *Vicia faba*, using flash labeling with tritiated thymidine assayed by autoradiographs of squashed preparations. The relative frequency of labeled nuclei in each of the various stages of mitosis was determined for dark-grown and far-red treated material. The average duration of the mitotic cycle in *Vicia faba* was found to be 19.1 hours. Cell division required 1.8 hours, and 17.3 hours were spent in mitotic interphase. During this latter portion of the cycle, DNA synthesis occupied 9.0 hours, while presynthetic and postsynthetic interphase averaged 5.1 and 3.2 hours, respectively. There was no evidence of mitotic delay in far-red treated material. Mitotic indices, which averaged 9.2 for the far-red and 8.8 for the control series, were comparable throughout.

The responses of sporangiophores of *Phycomyces blakesleeanus* to diverging unilateral blue-light stimuli given in air were determined. It was found that 3-minute stimuli given through a thin cylindrical lens (approximately the same diameter as the sporangiophore) placed

0.15 mm. away from the sporangiophore, and with its long axis parallel to the axis of the sporangiophore, produced negative curvatures. All experiments were performed in a water-saturated atmosphere in order to prevent negative avoidance responses due to the proximity of the lens. The data support Buder's conclusion that the focusing advantage is the principal effect which produces the light gradient necessary for phototropism. When compared to data obtained from sporangiophores immersed in inert liquid fluorochemicals, the attenuation across the growing zone appears to be of the order of 10 percent. Therefore, for blue stimuli, under any irradiation conditions in which the focusing advantage is less than 10 percent, negative curvatures are produced by unilateral stimuli.

Preliminary observations were made of the growth rates of sporangiophores at intensities greater than 1.5 milliwatt/cm.^{2}, for which phototropic indifference occurs with unilateral stimuli. It was found that the growth rate increased markedly for these high intensities from the normal adapted level of 3–4 mm./hr. to 5–6 mm./hr. and was maintained at this high level for several hours.

Instruments for measuring the spectral distribution of sunlight in six wavebands from 250 mμ to 5,000 mμ were completed and mounted on the roof of the North Tower of the Smithsonian Building. Automatic recorders have been installed on the tenth floor of the Tower and measurements are being made continuously from an hour before sunrise to an hour after sunset.

PUBLICATIONS

SISLER, EDWARD C., and KLEIN, WILLIAM H. Effect of red and far-red irradiation on nucleotide phosphate and adenosine triphosphate levels in dark-grown bean and Avena seedlings. Physiologia Plantarum, vol. 14, pp. 115–123, 1961.

SHROPSHIRE, W., Jr.; KLEIN, W. H.; and ELSTAD, V. B. Action spectra of photomorphogenic induction and photoinactivation of germination in Arabidopsis thaliana. Plant and Cell Physiol., vol. 2, pp. 63–69, 1961.

OTHER ACTIVITIES

During the course of the year, members of the staff attended a number of national and international scientific meetings. Dr. W. H. Klein traveled to the International Photobiology Congress in Copenhagen, Denmark, and was one of the United States representatives at the Seed Irradiation Conference in Karlsruhe, Germany. He also visited a number of laboratories in Denmark, Germany, and the Netherlands. Members of the staff who were present at the annual meeting of the American Institutes of Biological Sciences in Stillwater, Okla., were Dr. L. Loercher, L. Price, and Dr. E. C. Sisler. Papers from the Division included in the program of this meeting were: "Chlorophyll Synthesis in X-irradiated Etiolated Bean Leaf Tissue," by L. Price and W. H. Klein, and "Effect of Red and Far-red Irradiation on

Nucleotide Phosphate and Adenosine Triphosphate in Seedlings," by E. C. Sisler and W. H. Klein.

Dr. W. Shropshire participated in a Departmental Colloquium on Photobiology at Purdue University and visited laboratories at several universities in the eastern United States to confer with other investigators working in the field of phototropism.

At the 1961 meetings of the Southern Section of the American Society of Plant Physiologists at Jackson, Miss., L. Price and V. B. Elstad presented papers.

Dr. Klein opened a lecture series at Duke University, Durham, N.C., by presenting two lectures on the subject "Photoinduced Reactions in Plants and Their Action Spectra."   Dr. M. Margulies attended the annual meeting of the Federation of American Societies for Experimental Biology in Atlantic City, N.J.   Dr. R. L. Latterell presented a paper at the Radiation Research Society meetings held in Washington, D.C.

Dr. Shropshire and Dr. Klein visited marine biology and photobiology laboratories in Washington and California.

Respectfully submitted.

FRED L. WHIPPLE, *Director.*

Dr. LEONARD CARMICHAEL,
   Secretary, Smithsonian Institution.

Report on the National Collection of Fine Arts

Sir: I have the honor to submit the following report on the activities of the National Collection of Fine Arts for the fiscal year ended June 30, 1961:

SMITHSONIAN ART COMMISSION

The 38th annual meeting of the Smithsonian Art Commission was held in Washington on Tuesday, December 6, 1960. Members present were Paul Manship, chairman; Leonard Carmichael, secretary; Gilmore D. Clarke, David E. Finley, Walker Hancock, Bartlett H. Hayes, Ogden M. Pleissner, Charles H. Sawyer, and Archibald G. Wenley. James C. Bradley, Assistant Secretary of the Smithsonian Institution, Theodore W. Taylor, Assistant to the Secretary, and Thomas M. Beggs, Director, National Collection of Fine Arts, were also present.

The Commission recommended reappointment of David E. Finley, Charles H. Sawyer, Paul Manship, and Archibald G. Wenley for the usual 4-year term.

The following officers were reelected for the ensuing year: Paul Manship, chairman; Robert Woods Bliss, vice chairman; and Leonard Carmichael, secretary.

The following were reelected members of the executive committee for the ensuing year: David E. Finley, chairman; Robert Woods Bliss, Gilmore D. Clarke, Archibald G. Wenley, with Paul Manship and Leonard Carmichael, ex officio.

Mr. Beggs reported on the functions of the National Collection of Fine Arts and its relation to the other Government galleries in Washington. Mr. Beggs quoted from the publication, "Art and Government, Report to the President by the Commission of Fine Arts on Activities of the Federal Government in the Field of Art, Washington, D.C., 1953," citing especially a summary of testimony it contained, which distinguished briefly between the main purposes of the three Smithsonian bureaus of fine art. He called attention to the Act of Congress of May 17, 1938, Section 4, which defines the responsibilities of the National Collection of Fine Arts. Among these are stressed authority to accept gifts of art works of both past and present and to accept funds from private sources for their purchase and especially to encourage the development of American contemporary art. A list of references on the subject was provided.

Mr. Clarke reported that the subcommittee appointed to advise in the development of plans for housing the National Collection of Fine Arts in the Old Patent Office Building had met on December 5 and had discussed the progress made on plans for renovation of the Patent Office Building. He reviewed the architect's plans and specifications. The adaptability of the building to gallery purposes was pointed out, and the major structural change, the construction of a loading ramp and platform, was outlined. Special features discussed were off-street parking and car storage, a dining area, and the practicability of an auditorium.

Mr. Bradley stated that an appropriation had been made to the General Services Administration for the construction of a new Civil Service Building and that consequently the original Patent Office Building probably would be turned over to the Smithsonian at an earlier date than previously expected, possibly by the spring of 1963.

Dr. Carmichael requested the Commission's advice on a new operation proposed for the Smithsonian Institution. He briefly outlined the program to obtain a collection of industry-sponsored art to be used as a nucleus for traveling exhibitions, decoration of Federal offices, and possibly the decoration of Embassies and American libraries overseas, which would be supported by private funds.

The Commission recommended acceptance of the following objects for the National Collection of Fine Arts:

Marble, Napoleon Bonaparte (1808–73) by Pierre Jean David d'Angers (1788–1856). Offered by Mr. and Mrs. Fortunato Porotto, Washington, D.C.

Bronze, Abraham Lincoln (1809–65) by Augustus St. Gaudens (1847–1907). Offered by Cornelia Kremer, Washington, D.C.

Four heroic-size marble busts by William Couper (1853–1942): Jean Louis Rudolph Agassiz (1807–73), Spencer Fullerton Baird (1823–88), Benjamin Franklin (1706–90) and Joseph Henry (1797–1878). Offered by the American Museum of Natural History, New York City.

Black Belgian marble, Falcon, by Bessie Stough Callender (1889–1951). Bequest of Harold Callender, Paris, France.

Decorative wall hanging by Mary Ellen Crisp. Offered by the artist, Biddeford, Maine.

The Commission recommended the following be held for submission to the National Portrait Gallery Commission:

Oil, Judge Isaac Samuels Pennylacker (1807–47) by undetermined artist. Bequest of Dr. Bernard Samuels, Front Royal, Va.

ART WORKS LENT AND RETURNED

Institutions	Loans	Returned
American Federation of Art		1
Army Signal Corps	2	
Atomic Energy Commission		4

	Loans	Returned
Bureau of the Budget	20	2
Chrysler Art Museum	1	
Civil Service Commission		4
Corcoran Galley of Art	1	1
El Paso Museum	3	3
George Washington University	1	1
Justice, Department of	4	
Lincoln Museum	1	
Lyman Allyn Museum	8	8
Military Appeals, Court of		1
Municipal Court	4	
National Gallery of Art		1
North Carolina Museum of Art	1	1
Richard Reasoner		12
State, Department of	8	4
Toronto, Art Gallery of	5	5
Truxton-Decatur Naval Museum	1	
United States District Court	3	1
United States National Museum, Division of Military History		8
Vancouver Art Gallery	4	4
Virginia Museum of Fine Arts	1	
The White House	9	26
Whitney, Gertrude Vanderbilt, Museum of Western Art	1	1
Whitney Museum of American Art	5	5
Wichita, University of	1	
Winnipeg Art Museum	5	5
	89	98

SMITHSONIAN LENDING COLLECTION

The following four oils, transferred from the White House, were added December 6, 1960:

Undetermined title, by Gatti Annibale (1827–1909). Presented to the President by H. E. Giovanni Gronchi, President of the Republic of Italy.

Canada Ojeda, by Ameliano del Castillo. Presented to the President by the Director of Radio Station "La Voz de Guadix," Enrique Caroles Tarrago, Guadix, Granada, Spain.

Prado do Les Aninas, by Benjamin Palencia. Presented to the President by the Mayor of Madrid, Jose De Romani, Finat y Escrina, Count of Mayalde.

Francisco De Vitoria, by Varquer. Presented to the President by H. E. General Francisco Franco.

ART WORKS LENT AND RETURNED

Institutions	Loans	Returned
Federal Communications Commission		3
Florida Artists Group	35	35
Florida Gulf Coast Art Center	35	35
Labor, Department of		3
Lehigh University		1
Meltzer Gallery		24
Naples, Florida Artists Group	35	35

Institutions	*Loans*	*Returned*
Post Office Department	4	
U.S. District Court	4	
The White House		6
	113	142

THE HENRY WARD RANGER FUND

The following paintings purchased previously but not assigned have been allocated to the institutions indicated:

Title and artist	*Assignment*
214. Yesterday and Before and Before, by Loring W. Coleman (1918–).	The Canton Art Institute, Canton, Ohio.
228. Sag Harbor, by Nicolai Cikovsky (1894–).	Yankton College, Yankton, S. Dak.

According to a provision of the Henry Ward Ranger bequest, that paintings purchased by the Council of the National Academy of Design from the fund provided by the bequest and assigned to American art institutions may be claimed during the 5-year period beginning 10 years after the death of the artist represented, the following paintings were recalled for action of the Smithsonian Art Commission at its meeting December 6, 1960.

No. 105.   The Pale Light of Dawn, by Spencer Nichols, N. A. (1875–1950), was returned to the Society of Liberal Arts, Joslyn Memorial, Omaha, Nebr., where it was originally assigned in 1932.

No. 37.   The Bathers, by Spencer Nichols, N. A. (1875–1950), was returned to the Art Hall, Beloit College, Beloit, Wis., where it was originally assigned in 1924.

The following paintings, purchased by the Council of the National Academy of Design since the last report, have been assigned as follows:

Title and artist	*Assignment*
234. Wreck of the Sea Prince (watercolor), by John C. Pellew (1903–).	College of Fine and Applied Arts, University of Illinois, Urbana, Ill.
235. Espresso Magnifico, by Franklin Robbins (1917–).	City College, New York, N.Y.
236. Equestrian Acrobats, by Jon Corbino (1905–).	Howard University, Washington, D.C.
237. Bass Rocks (watercolor), by Morton Roberts (1927–).	Iowa State University, Ames, Iowa.
238. White Mountain (watercolor), by Adolf Dehn (1895–).	Assignment pending.
239. Venezia (watercolor), by Robert T. Handville (1924–).	University of Denver, Denver, Colo.
240. Nut Street Station (watercolor), by Dong Kingman (1911–).	Assignment pending.
241. My Neighbor's Place (watercolor), by Harry Anderson (1906–).	West Point Museum, West Point, N.Y.

Title and artist	*Assignment*
242. Posted (watercolor), by John De Tore (1902–).	Malden Public Library, Malden, Mass.
243. Barn in Friendship (watercolor), by Frederick P. Krause (1918–).	The Leland Stanford Junior University, Stanford University, Calif.
244. Morning in the Cove (watercolor), by Milford Zornes (1908–).	Rock Springs High School Art Project, Rock Springs, Wyo.
245. Reclining Woman (watercolor), by John Russell (1928–).	Rensselaer County Historical Society, Troy, N.Y.

SMITHSONIAN TRAVELING EXHIBITION SERVICE

In addition to the 65 exhibits held over from previous years as indicated, 56 new shows were introduced. The total of 121 of these were circulated to 314 museums in the United States.

EXHIBITS CONTINUED FROM PRIOR YEARS

1955–1956: Chinese Ivories from the Collection of Sir Victor Sassoon.

1956–1957: Contemporary German Prints; Architectural Photography II; Japan II by Werner Bischof; and The World of Edward Weston.

1957–1958: The American City in the 19th Century; Recent American Prints; Japanese Woodblock Prints; Theatrical Posters of the Gay Nineties; Birds by Emerson Tuttle; Contemporary Portuguese Architecture; Nylon Rug Designs; Burmese Embroideries; Japanese Dolls; Thai Painting; The Anatomy of Nature; Photographs of Sarawak; Glimpses of Switzerland; Art in Opera II—Carmen; The Four Seasons; Children's Paintings from Morocco; Drawings by European Children; Photographs of Angkor Wat; and Pup, Cub and Kitten.

1958–1959: German Artists of Today; Advertising in 19th Century America; The Engravings of Pieter Brueghel the Elder; Three Danish Printmakers; Charles Fenderich—Lithographer of American Statesmen; Drawings from Latin America; Contemporary Religious Prints from the Sloniker Collection; Religious Subjects in Modern Graphic Arts; Contemporary French Tapestries I; Our Town; Stone Rubbings from Angkor Wat; Shaker Craftsmanship; The Unguarded Moment, Photographs by Erich Salomon; Children's Paintings from India; A Child Looks at the Museum; and Swiss Children's Paintings.

1959–1960: The Art of Seth Eastman; Contemporary Greek Painting; Early Drawings by Toulouse-Lautrec; Watercolors and Drawings by Thomas Rowlandson; Prints and Drawings by Jacques Villon; American Prints Today; Brazilian Printmakers; Lithographs of Fantin-Latour; Arts and Cultural Centers; Bernard Ralph Maybeck; Enamels; Eskimo Art; Contemporary French Tapestries II; Contemporary American Glass; Story of American Glass; Bazaar Paintings from Calcutta; Gandhara Sculpture; Sardinian Crafts; Arctic Riviera; Photographs by Robert Capa II; Outer Mongolia; Pagan; Portraits of Greatness; Contrasts; and Paintings by Young Africans.

EXHIBITIONS INITIATED IN 1961

Paintings and Sculptures

Title	*Source*
Work by Torres Garcia	Rose Fried Gallery; private collectors.
Three Swiss Painters	The Akron Art Institute; Basel Kunthalle and Winterthur Museum.
The Technique of Fresco Painting	Michelangelo Muraro, Deputy Superintendent of Monuments in Venice; Italian Embassy.
Folk Painters of the Canadian West	National Gallery of Canada, Ottawa; Canadian Embassy.
Paintings by Ch'i Pai-Shih	Yakichiro Suma, Director of the Chuo University in Tokyo.
Birds of Greenland	Gitz-Johnsen; Embassy of Denmark, The Carlsberg Foundation, Copenhagen.
A Tribute to Grandma Moses	Galerie St. Etienne, New York; Dr. Otto Kalir.

Drawings and Prints

The America of Currier and Ives	Prints and Photographs Division, Library of Congress.
View 1960	Thomas M. Messer, Director of the Institute of Contemporary Art, Boston.
Drawings by Sculptors	Museums; private collectors; artists; Miss Jane Wade, Otto Gerson Gallery, New York City.
The Graphic Art of Edvard Munch	Lessing J. Rosenwald; National Gallery of Art.
German Color Prints	Selection from the 1959 exhibition, "Farbige Graphik"; German Embassy.
Eskimo Graphic Art	Eskimo Art, Inc., Ann Arbor, Mich.
Civil War Drawings I	American libraries; Library of Congress.
Civil War Drawings II	American libraries; Library of Congress.
American Art Nouveau Posters	Prints and Photographs Division, Library of Congress.
American Industry in the 19th Century	Prints and Photographs Division, Library of Congress.
America on Stone	Harry T. Peters Collection, Smithsonian Institution.
Printing in the Netherlands	Graphic Export Centre, Amsterdam; The Royal Netherlands Embassy.
Italian Drawings	Gabinetto Disegni Galleria degli Uffizi, Florence, Italy; Dr. Giulia Sinibaldi and Dr. Maria Fossi Todorow; Italian Embassy.

Oriental

Designed in Okinawa___________________ Ryukyuan Islands museums; Honorable Jugo Thoma, Chief Executive of the Islands; Lt. Gen. Donald P. Booth, U.S. High Commissioner.

Okinawa—Continuing Traditions_______ Ryukyuan Islands museums; Honorable Jugo Thoma, Chief Executive of the Islands; Lt. Gen. Donald P. Booth, U.S. High Commissioner.

Prints by Munakata___________________ Chisaburoh Yamada, Tokyo; Print Club of Cleveland Museum of Art.

Contemporary Japanese Drawings______ Atsuo Imaizumi, Deputy Director, National Museum of Modern Art, Tokyo; Japanese Embassy.

Japan: Design Today _________________ Japan Society, Inc., New York.

The Spirit of the Japanese Print_______ James A. Michener, Author; Charles E. Tuttle Company.

Americans—A View from the East____ Collection of Carl Boehringer.

The Way of Chinese Landscape Painting. Dr. Fritz van Briessen, German Foreign Service Officer, Tokyo; Museum of Modern Art, Tokyo.

Architecture

Swiss Industrial Architecture__________ Federation of Swiss Architects; Pro Helvetia Foundation; Swiss Embassy.

Contemporary Swedish Architecture___ National Association of Swedish Architects and Swedish Institute.

Mies van der Rohe___________________ American Institute of Architects, Washington, D.C.

Irish Architecture of the Georgian Period. Royal Institute of Architects of Ireland; Bord Failte Eireann; Irish Embassy.

One Hundred Years of Colorado Architecture. Colorado Chapter of American Institute of Architects; F. Lamar Kelsey, Chairman, Exhibits Committee.

Brasilia—A New Capital______________ Brazilian Embassy.

Design and Crafts

Scenic Designers Offstage_____________ Corning Museum of Glass; United Scenic Artists.

Design in Germany Today_____________ West German Government; Dr. Hans Eckstein, Director, Museum of Applied Arts, Munich; German Embassy.

Fibers, Tools and Weaves_____________ Paul John Smith of the American Craftsmen's Council.

Designed for Silver__________________ Museum of Contemporary Crafts; Yale University Art Gallery.

Batiks by Maud Rydin_______________ Museum of Contemporary Crafts, New York; Swedish Embassy; artist.

American Textiles___________________ Index of American Design, National Gallery of Art.

Photography

The Seasons, color photographs by Eliot Porter.	The Artist.
The World of Werner Bischof	Magnum Photos, Inc.; Embassy of Switzerland; Pro Helvetia.

Science

The Image of Physics	Miss Berenice Abbott; Physical Science Study Committee of Educational Services, Inc., Watertown, Mass.
Charles Darwin: The Evolution of an Evolutionist.	American Museum of Natural History.
The Beginnings of Flight	The William J. Hammer Collection of Aeronautical Photographs; Paul Garber, National Air Museum, Smithsonian Institution.
Two Centuries of Danish Deep Sea Research.	Hans Madsen, Zoological Museum, Copenhagen; scientific committee, Dr. Erik Bertelsen, Director, Danish Fishery Research; Dr. Anton Bruun, Dr. Ragnar Sparck and Dr. Helge Volsoe, University of Copenhagen; Danish Embassy, King Frederik and Queen Ingrid.

History

The Magnificent Enterprise. Education Opens the Door.	Campo Photocolor Exhibits; Vassar College Centennial Celebration.
The New Theatre in Germany	Pepsi-Cola Company; German Embassy.
Tropical Africa I	Twentieth Century Fund; George H. T. Kimble, Chairman, Department of Geography, University of Indiana.
Tropical Africa II	Twentieth Century Fund; George H. T. Kimble, Chairman, Department of Geography, University of Indiana.

Children's Exhibitions

Symphony in Color	John Herron Art Institute; Junior Group of the Indianapolis Symphony Orchestra.
Paintings and Pastels by Children of Tokyo.	New York Tokyo Sister City Affiliation; Tokyo Society for Art Education.
Children's Art from Italy	Junior Museum of the Metropolitan Museum of Art, New York; Professor Sergio Pagiaro.
Hawaiian Children's Art	Honolulu Academy of Arts.
Designs by Children of Ceylon	Junior Museum of the Metropolitan Museum of Art; Art Inspector of Ceylon.
Children's Paintings from Chile	Mrs. Walter Howe, wife of Ambassador of Chile; Museum of Fine Arts, Santiago.

INFORMATION SERVICE AND STAFF ACTIVITIES

In addition to the approximately 16,000 requests for information received by mail and telephone, inquiries made in person at the office numbered 1,500. In all, 167 works of art were examined by the Director.

Special catalogs were published for the following traveling exhibitions: Italian Drawings, Sardinian Crafts, Irish Architecture of the Georgian Period, and The World of Werner Bischof. A special catalog of Traveling Exhibitions for 1961–62 was also published. A 64-page illustrated brochure containing a cover design and introduction by Thomas M. Beggs was published for the Arts and Archeology of Viet-Nam exhibition.

The director visited several European countries to study art galleries, their establishment, and their relationships with government and other organizations, to confer with museum officials, collectors, and donors to the collections, and also to inspect historic buildings in process of restoration.

Six paintings in oil on canvas from the permanent collections were cleaned and revarnished, and 28 picture frames were repaired and refinished with the assistance of Buildings Management Service, which constructed and finished frames for four etchings.

Albert C. Wagner restored the French Ship model (No. 442) in the Gellatly Collection and Joseph Ternbach restored the following items from that collection: two Oriental pins, gold and glass (No. 187); Saint, alabaster (No. 377); Spanish King, wood (No. 569); St. George, wood (No. 381); St. Peter, alabaster (No. 378).

Contracts were let for the relining and restoring by Harold F. Cross of the following: Ariadne, by Wyatt Eaton; Charles G. Abbot, by Nicholas Brewer; Pegasus, by Albert P. Ryder; Robert Hare, by Alvan Clark; Richard Delafield, by Charles C. Curran; Cup of Death, by Elihu Vedder; Laura Alice, by Alice Pike Barney; The Brown Kimona, by Irving Wiles; Italian Woman and Child, by Alice Pike Barney; and two small landscapes by Alice Pike Barney.

Henri G. Courtais is under contract for renovation of the following paintings: St. Ursula, by undetermined artist; Virgin Enthroned, by Abbott H. Thayer; Thomas George Hodgkins, by Robert Gordon Hardie; Spencer Fullerton Baird, by Robert Gordon Hardie; Richard Rush, by T. W. Wood; Joseph Henry, by Henry Ulke;; Charles Doolittle Walcott, by Samantha B. Huntley; Ruins, by Francesco Guardi; Young Girl Seated, by Thomas Dewing; Music, by Thomas Dewing; The Golden Age, by John LaFarge; Amagansett to East Hampton, by George Bogert; Duchess of Ancaster, by Sir Joshua Reynolds; Mrs. Price, by William Hogarth; Smuggler's Notch, by Chauncey Ryder; The Island, by Edwin W. Redfield; and Viscountess Hatton, by Sir Peter Lely.

SPECIAL EXHIBITIONS

July 15 through August 7, 1960. Folk Art from Rumania, circulated by the Smithsonian Traveling Exhibition Service, consisted of colorful costumes, embroideries, rugs, ceramics, icons, musical instruments, photomurals of villages and buildings, together with a reconstructed room from a cottage in the district of Transylvania. A brochure was privately printed.

August 14 through September 8, 1960. Fourth Biennial Creative Crafts Exhibition, sponsored by the Ceramic Guild of Bethesda, Cherry Tree Textile Designers, Clay Pigeons Ceramic Workshop, Designers-Weavers, Potomac Craftsmen, and the Kiln Club of Washington, consisted of 220 items including 116 ceramics and glass, 77 textiles, 15 metalwork, 6 jewelry, and 6 mosaic. A catalog was privately printed.

September 17 through October 6, 1960. 67th Annual Exhibition of the Society of Washington Artists, consisted of 70 paintings and 27 sculptures. A catalog was privately printed.

October 13 through November 10, 1960. Two Centuries of Danish Deep Sea Research, circulated by the Smithsonian Traveling Exhibition Service, consisting of maps, photographs, charts, specimens, and scientific equipment. A brochure was privately printed.

October 26 through December 8, 1960. Art and Archeology of Viet Nam, sponsored by the Embassy of Viet Nam, centered about the Cham Civilization supplemented by contemporary crafts. It consisted of 148 archeological items (including the Oc-eo treasure) lent by the Vietnamese National Museums of Saigon and Hue and augmented by loans from the Peabody Museum, Harvard University, Musees Royaux du Cinquantenaire, Brussels, Belgium, and private collectors. There were also shown, in Hall 22, Natural History Building, 196 contemporary crafts items from Viet Nam.

Following its showing at the National Collection of Fine Arts, the exhibition was divided to be circulated in two sections as follows: Archeological section—Baltimore Museum of Art; Cleveland Museum of Art; University Museum of University of Pennsylvania, Philadelphia; City Art Museum of St. Louis; Portland Art Museum; and University of California, Berkeley; contemporary crafts section—Columbia University; Brandeis University; Michigan State University; and Fine Arts Gallery of San Diego. An illustrated catalog was printed.

November 27, 1960, through January 5, 1961. Twenty-third Anniversary of the Metropolitan Art Exhibition, sponsored by the American Art League, consisted of 163 items, including 129 paintings, 14 prints and drawings, and 20 sculptures. A catalog was privately printed.

December 9, 1960, through January 10, 1961. Aviation Paintings and Drawings by Charles H. Hubbell, sponsored by the National Air Museum, consisted of 150 paintings. A catalog was privately printed.

January 15 through February 5, 1961. The Victorian American, circulated by the Smithsonian Traveling Exhibition Service, consisting of a selection of 100 lithographs from the Harry T. Peters Collection.

February 11 through March 5, 1961. The World of Werner Bischof, sponsored by the Ambassador of Switzerland and circulated by the Smithsonian Traveling Exhibition Service, consisted of 80 photographs.

March 12 through April 2, 1961. The 64th Annual National Exhibition of the Washington Water Color Association, consisting of 104 paintings. A catalog was privately printed.

April 9 through April 30, 1961. New Jersey Chapter American Artists Professional League, sponsored by the New Jersey State Society of Washington, D.C., consisted of 107 paintings and 2 sculptures. A catalog was privately printed.

April 20 through April 29, 1961. Coins and Currency of Yesteryears, sponsored by the Washington Numismatic Society.

May 6 through May 28, 1961. The New Theater in Germany, sponsored by the Ambassador of the Federal Republic of Germany and circulated by the Smithsonian Traveling Exhibtion Service, consisted of photographs showing German stage design, architecture, drama schools, and organization of theaters. A brochure was privately printed.

May 7 through May 28, 1961. The Twenty-Eighth Annual Exhibition of the Miniature Painters, Sculptors, and Gravers Society of Washington, D.C., consisting of 179 items. A catalog was privately printed.

May 26 through 30, 1961. Exhibition commemorating the 100th Anniversary of the birth of Rabindranath Tagore, sponsored by the Embassy of India, consisted of 40 reproductions of paintings by Tagore.

June 3 through 25, 1961. Washington Religious Art Exhibition, sponsored by the National Conference of Christians and Jews, Washington, D.C., Region, consisted of 103 items including 74 paintings and prints, 16 sculptures, 10 ceramic and glass objects and 3 textiles. A catalog was privately printed.

June 9 through August 13, 1961. The World of Shells, a special exhibition in connection with the annual meeting of the American Malacological Union.

Respectfully submitted.

THOMAS M. BEGGS, *Director.*

Dr. LEONARD CARMICHAEL,
  Secretary, Smithsonian Institution.

Report on the Freer Gallery of Art

Sir: I have the honor to submit the forty-first annual report on the Freer Gallery of Art, for the year ended June 30, 1961.

THE COLLECTIONS

Forty-one objects were added to the collections by purchase as follows:

BRONZE

60.18. Chinese, Shang dynasty. Vessel of the type *ting*. Decorations in relief and in intaglio with cuprite and quartz filling up the fossae. One inscription inside of one or maybe two characters. Over-all height, 0.245; diameter, 0.186.

60.19 Chinese, Chou dynasty, ca. 10th-9th century B.C. Ceremonial vessel of the type *kuei*, with two handles, a cover and three short legs. The cast decorations (fluting and animal bands) are mostly in low relief except for the handles which are in the round. Patination of gray-green tin oxide is spotted here and there with touches of cuprite. Inscription of 36 characters in top and bottom. Height, 0.249; diameter, 0.263.

60.20 Chinese, Chou dynasty, Vessel of the type *yu*. Body of vessel is decorated with two bands near top and base, and cover of vessel has one band. Bail handle is more ornate, being affixed by rings and terminating in animal heads in the round. Patina is dark green, and decorations are in low relief and intaglio. Inscription in top and bottom is in 28 characters. Over-all height, 0.222; width, 0.197.

61.3. Chinese, Han dynasty, 206 B.C.-A.D. 221. Dragon. Decoration over-all in intaglio and very low relief. This animal is cast in the round; light gray-green patina. Height, 0.193; length, 0.366; width, 0.137.

METALWORK

61.12. Chinese, Ming dynasty, 16th century. Squat tripod of copper covered with cloisonné enamels in red, white, blue, green, yellow, and aubergine on light blue ground; lotus scrolls around sides and fruit underneath; elaborate gilt feet and handles of later date; carved wood cover and jade finial. Minor repairs. Over-all height, 0.181; height without cover, 0.140; diameter, 0.190.

61.22. Persian, Parthian period, 3d-1st century B.C. Heart-shaped gold ornament, possibly part of buckle, with two boars in a thicket indicated by leaves; cast mostly in high relief with black resin filling the void in back, heads in the round. Ten small loops evenly spaced along edge of back served for sewing on. Height, 0.053; width, 0.050; depth, 0.010.

PAINTING

60.24. Chinese, Ming dynasty, by Tung Ch'i-ch'ang (1555–1636). Landscape: ink on paper. One inscription and six seals on the painting. Kakemono: height, 1.282; width, 0.383.

60.15
Recent addition to the collections of the Freer Gallery of Art.

60.16
Recent addition to the collections of the Freer Gallery of Art.

60.25

Recent addition to the collections of the Freer Gallery of Art.

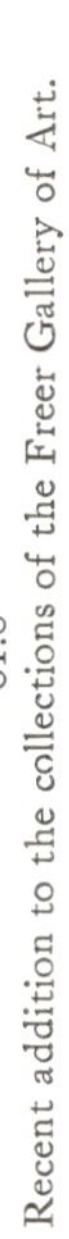

61.8

Recent addition to the collections of the Freer Gallery of Art.

60.25. Chinese, Ch'ing dynasty, by Hua Yen (1682–1755). Ten album leaves of
       birds, flowers, etc.; ink and colors on paper. Average dimensions:
       height, 0.318; width, 0.454. (Illustrated.)

60.26. Chinese, Ming dynasty, 16th century, dated 1547, by Ch'iu Ying. Narcissus
       and flowering apricots in ink and colors on paper. Kakemono: height,
       0.495; width, 0.246.

61.10. Chinese, Ming-Ch'ing dynasty, by Ch'en Hung-shou (1599–1652). Album
       of eight leaves: landscapes and figures. Signature of artist and one
       seal plus one collector's seal on each leaf. Inscriptions (quatrains) by
       the artist on opposite leaves, each with signature and two seals. Two
       inscriptions and eight seals on double leaf following paintings; ink
       and colors on paper. Average dimensions: height, 0.335; width, 0.273.

61.11. Chinese, Ch'ing dynasty, by Kung Hsien (b. ca. 1610, d. 1689). Winter
       landscape; two seals on painting and two on mount. Album leaf in
       ink on paper. Height, 0.205; width, 0.340.

60.14. Indian, third quarter of 16th century (ca. 1560–80), Mughal period, school
       of Akbar. "Sa'īd arrives with Khūsh Khurrām on the roof of the
       castle; sees two girls wrestling." Miniature from Hamza-nāma, executed
       for Emperor Akbar. One of a set: 49.18 and 60.15. Painting: height,
       0.676; width, 0.513.

60.15. Indian, third quarter of 16th century (ca. 1560–80), Mughal period, school
       of Akbar. "Umar in disguise of surgeon Mizzmuhil arrives before the
       Fort of Antalya (?)." Miniature from Hamza-nāma, executed for
       Emperor Akbar. One of a set: 49.18 and 60.14. Painting: height,
       0.673; width, 0.512. (Illustrated.)

60.27. Indian, end of 16th century, Mughal period, school of Akbar. "Prince
       Salīm with a courtier and attendants in a tent." Painted in gold and
       colors; framed by gold-flecked borders of various widths to form part
       of an album. Inscription in *devanagari* characters on back. Painting:
       height, 0.170; width, 0.114.

60.28. Indian, ca. 1595, Mughal period, school of Akbar. "Akbar, enthroned,
       gives an audience before a pavilion." Painted in gold and colors. Akbar's
       nose and forehead repainted; small piece of pigment below vizier's
       mouth chipped off. Framed by inner buff border with floral decoration
       in gold; outer border rose-colored and gold-specked. Painting: height,
       0.261; width, 0.142.

60.17. Japanese, Ashikaga period, Idealistic Chinese school, 16th century, at-
       tributed to Gakuō. Rocky landscape with wild geese; ink and colors on
       paper. Kakemono: length, 0.440; width, 0.330.

60.21. Japanese, early Momoyama period, Tosa school, late 16th century. Battle
       scene. Fan-shaped; ink, color, and gold leaf on paper. Kakemono:
       height, 0.245; width, 0.545.

60.22. Japanese, Edo period, Nanga school, by Ikeno Taiga (1723–76). "One
       hundred old men gathering for a drinking party"; ink, color, and gold
       on silk. Makimono: height, 0.538; width, 2.923.

60.23. Japanese, early Ashikaga period, by Kaō (fl. in 14th century). Kanzan;
       ink monochrome on paper. Kakemono: height, 1.025; width, 0.309.

60.31. Japanese, Edo period, Decorative school, by Sākai Hōitsu (1761–1828).
       "The thirty-six master poets"; ink, colors, and gold on silk. Kakemono:
       height, 1.361; width, 0.677.

61.1– Japanese, Edo period, Nanga school, by Baiitsu (1789). Landscape.
61.2.   A pair of six-fold screens in ink and slight colors on paper. Painting:
       height, 1.530; width, 3.556.

61.4– Japanese, Edo period, Nanga school, by Buson (1716–83). Landscape,

61.5.   figures and wind in willows. A pair of six-fold screens in ink and colors on silk. Height, 1.665; width, 3.710.

61.6. Japanese, Heian period, Buddhist school, 12th century. Nyoirin Kannon; ink, colors, silver, and gold on silk. Kakemono: height, 0.777; width, 0.405.

61.8. Japanese, Ashikaga period, Tosa school, artist unknown. *Utatane Monogatari* (The tale of Utatane); ink and color on paper. Makimono; height, 0.138; width, 10.873. (Illustrated.)

POTTERY

60.13. Chinese, Shang dynasty. Figure of a crouching stag with horns; fine-grained light buff stoneware; hollow with opening in back; linear designs all over body and head. Height, 0.172; length, 0.175; width, 0.063.

60.16. Chinese, T'ang dynasty, *San-ts'ai* ware. Figure of a seated man with black beard and Armenian features holding a wine skin; buff stoneware with transparent glaze. Height, 0.332; width, 0.173. (Illustrated.)

60.29. Chinese, T'ang dynasty, *San-ts'ai* ware. Figure of a standing female; buff stoneware with transparent glaze; finely crackled; unglazed head shows remains of painting. Height, 0.353; width, 0.156.

61.13. Chinese, Ch'ing dynasty. Ovoid vase with tall cylindrical neck; fine-grained white porcelain with transparent glossy glaze decorated in colored enamels over glaze; a landscape with palaces; poem of 14 characters; three simulated seals; four-character Ch'ien-lung mark in blue enamel on base. Height, 0.196; width, 0.098.

61.14. Chinese, Ming dynasty, early 15th century. Large dish with plain rim and unglazed base; fine white porcelain with transparent, thick glaze with some orange-peel effect; decorated in underglaze blue; a control landscape with rock, coxcomb, etc., and eight flower and fruit sprays in cavette; outside, "three friends." Height, 0.095; diameter, 0.680.

61.15. Chinese, Ch'ing dynasty, early 18th century (K'ang-hsi). Dish with rim of interlocking rings; fine white porcelain with transparent glaze, decorated in overglaze famille verte enamels and gold, dragons and floral patterns, iron-red dragon on base. Height, 0.045; width, 0.105.

61.16. Chinese, T'ang dynasty. Low round box with cover; creamy white porcelain, medium grain, with transparent, smooth, off-white glaze and no decoration. Height, 0.045; diameter, 0.105.

61.17. Chinese, Sung dynasty, *ting* ware. Dish with plain rim bound in brass; fine, off-white porcelain with transparent glaze with teardrops outside. Decorated with fish and lotus plants inside. Height, 0.060; diameter, 0.304.

61.18. Chinese, Sung dynasty, *ting* ware. Dish with plain rim bound in copper; fine off-white stoneware with transparent glaze with teardrops outside; decorated with molded bird and flower patterns inside. Height, 0.056; diameter, 0.291.

61.19. Chinese, Sung dynasty, northern celadon. Bowl with small foot and slightly flaring rim; grayish-brown stoneware with transparent, grayish-green bubbly glaze; molded decoration inside of two babies amid flowering vines. Height, 0.049; diameter, 0.121.

61.20. Chinese, Sung dynasty, northern celadon. Bowl with small foot and slightly flaring rim; grayish-brown stoneware with transparent, grayish-green bubbly glaze; decorated inside with molded fish among waves. Height, 0.037; diameter, 0.094.

60.30. Japanese, Momoyama period, *oribe* ware. Tray in the form of two fans
       with vertical sides and arching handles; coarse, buff stoneware with
       transparent glaze, decorated with brown, green, and white designs.
       Over-all height, 0.143; width, 0.234.
61.9. Japanese Momoyama period, *shino* ware. Round dish with lip folded in
       and squarish at the rim; three low loop feet and three spurmarks;
       rough stoneware with thick, bubbly crackled, mottled reddish-brown
       and gray glaze; decorated with floral designs in white slip under glaze.
       Height, 0.057; width, 0.170.
61.7. Mesopotamian, 10th century. Bowl of pale yellow-brown luster painted
       on a tin glaze; the design on the interior is a horseman turned toward
       the right holding a flag; broken and repaired, but only tiny pieces
       missing and replaced by plaster. Height, 0.058; diameter, 0.235.
61.21. Persian, mid-12th century, *lakabi* ware; large platter with carved design
       of horseman wielding a sword; set against arabesque background.
       Broken and mended with few missing pieces replaced by plaster.
       Height, 0.086; diameter, 0.408.

REPAIRS TO THE COLLECTION

Fifteen Chinese, Japanese, and Korean objects were restored, repaired, or remounted by T. Sugiura. In addition, one large rubbing
was mounted for the University of Michigan and repairs or remount-
ing completed for six Japanese screens in private collections. Repairs and regilding of 18 frames for American paintings were done
outside the Gallery.

CHANGES IN EXHIBITIONS

Changes in exhibitions amounted to 134, as follows:

American art:
  Oils ___ 18
Chinese art:
  Bronze ___ 8
  Paintings ___ 2
  Pottery ___ 6
  Stone sculpture ___ 1
Christian art:
  Crystal ___ 1
  Glass ___ 2
  Gold ___ 6
Indian art:
  Paintings ___ 2

Japanese art:
  Paintings ___ 18
  Pottery ___ 5
  Wood sculpture ___ 2
Korean art:
  Bronze ___ 3
  Jade ___ 7
  Metalwork ___ 6
  Paintings ___ 3
  Pottery ___ 19
Near Eastern art:
  Metalwork ___ 2
  Paintings ___ 12
  Pottery ___ 10
  Stone sculpture ___ 1

LIBRARY

One of the high spots of the year was the "Bronze Symposium"
held at the Freer Gallery, which brought specialists from all over
the United States, Canada, and Australia. An exhibition of books
in this special field was arranged in the library and proved a busy
place during the visitors' free time.

During the year 594 acquisitions were added to the library by title,
267 by gift and exchange from other institutions and individuals,

and 327 by purchase. Among the outstanding purchases were *Nihon shūcho shina-kodō seika* (selected relics of ancient Chinese bronzes from collections in Japan), compiled by Sueji Umehara and issued in a limited edition in six volumes, 1960–61; *Shōsōin Homotsu* (treasures of the Shōsōin), which is to be completed in 1962 in three folio volumes; *Figure prints of Old Japan, a pictorial pageant of actors and courtesans of the eighteenth century reproduced from the prints in the collection of Marjorie and Edwin Grabhorn*, with an introduction by Harold P. Stern, San Francisco, 1959. Xerographic copies of microfilms of two rare manuscripts were made.   (1) *Tōban shimpin zukan* (album of sword guard masterpieces). This illustrated manuscript written in 1783 (De Rosny's catalogue) and never published is now in the Kungliga Biblioteket, Stockholm, Nordenskjöld Collection, No. 525. In 1912 Henri L. Joly made a copy and translation and issued privately 15 copies, none of which has been located. (2) *Wu Ch'i-chen shu-hua chi* (record of calligraphy and painting seen by the author, Wu Ch'i-chen), written in mid-17th century giving the descriptions of the works, comments, and information on the collections owning them, with the dates on which he saw them. Six volumes of text with one volume of catalogue or index. A copy of the manuscript is in the *Ssu-k'u-ch'üan-shu* (the good repository of manuscripts of Chinese books) but the book was never printed(?). The copy in the Gunnar Martin Collection, Stockholm, was presumably copied from the *Ssu-k'u-ch'üan-shu* manuscript, and is the only copy outside China(?). The book is of particular importance because the author saw many of the important collections of his day and records their contents carefully. Many of the paintings he describes are still extant in the Ku-kung Collection, the Freer Gallery of Art, and other collections. Two outstanding gifts were *Chinese painting*, by James F. Cahill, Geneva, Skira, 1960 (gift of author); *Persian painting* by Basil Gray, Geneva, Skira, 1961 (gift of publisher).

The year's record of cataloging included a total of 967 entries of which 534 analytics were made, and 197 new titles of books, pamphlets and scrolls were cataloged. Only one-ninth of the cards required were available in printed cards from the Library of Congress.

The current state of the cataloging has given opportunity for special projects. Mrs. Hogenson began indexing the correspondence of Charles Lang Freer. Mrs. Usilton prepared a subject index for Technical Studies in the Field of Fine Arts, vols. 1-10; revised and enlarged the Bibliography for the *Chinese Outline;* and continued to serve as assistant editor of *IIC Abstracts: Abstracts of the Technical Literature of Archaeology and the Fine Arts.*

There were 162 requests for bibliographic information by telephone and letter. In all, 515 scholars and students who were not members of the Freer staff used the library. Thirteen of these saw and studied the Washington Manuscripts and five came to see the library installation. Students at Columbia University and Catholic University of America, who were completing their graduate work in library science, made surveys of the library as a part of their required studies.

Lou Cushing Harden, University of Rochester, served as volunteer for the intern program for the summer. This program is intended to give students a rounded experience in the general operation and purposes of a gallery, and to broaden their familiarity with the field of art in general.

PUBLICATIONS

Two publications were issued by the Gallery as follows:

Ars Orientalis, Vol. IV. 17 articles in English, French, or German, 21 book reviews, 1 bibliography, 5 notes, 2 memorials. 462 pp., 143 collotype pls., text ill. (Smithsonian Institution Publication 4431.)

Second presentation of the Charles Lang Freer Medal, a brochure issued in conjunction with the presentation to Prof. Ernst Kühnel, May 3, 1960, honoring this eminent scholar for his outstanding contributions and achievements in the field of Near Eastern art.

Publications of staff members were as follows:

CAHILL, JAMES F. Chinese art treasures. (See under Pope.)

————. Chinese painting. Geneva, Skira, 1960. 211 pp. with 100 col. ills. (Treasures of Asia.)

————. The Chinese Imperial art treasures. *Horizon, a magazine of the arts*, vol. 3 (Jan. 1961), pp. 14–25, 8 col. pls.

————. "Concerning the I-p'in style of painting," by S. Shimada. Translated by James F. Cahill. *Oriental Art*, n.s., vol. 7 (summer 1961), pp. 66–74.

————. Confucian elements in the theory of painting. In "The Confucian Persuasion," edited by Arthur F. Wright. Stanford, Stanford University Press, 1960, pp. 115–140.

————. A rejected portrait by Lo P'ing; pictorial footnote to Waley's *Yüan Mei*. *Arthur Waley anniversary volume*, London, Lung Humphries, 1959, pp. 32–39, pls.

————. The Six Laws and how to read them. *Ars Orientalis*, vol. 4 (1961), pp. 372–381.

————. Review of "Some T'ang and pre-T'ang texts on Chinese painting." Edited and translated by W. R. B. Acker. *Ars Orientalis*, vol. 4 (1961), pp. 440–444.

ETTINGHAUSEN, RICHARD. Automata: Islam. *Encyclopedia of world art*, New York, 1960, vol. 2, cols. 185–186, pl. 77. (Also published in Italian edition, Rome, 1960.)

————. The Emperor's choice. *De Artibus opuscula XL: Essays in honor of Erwin Panofsky*, edited by Millard Meiss, New York, N.Y. University Press, 1961, vol. 1, pp. 98–120, and vol. 2, figs. 1–19 on pls. 27–35.

————. The iconography of a Kāshān luster plate. (Co-author, Grace D. Guest.) *Ars Orientalis*, vol. 4 (1961), pp. 25–64, 74 figs. on 22 pls.

ETTINGHAUSEN, RICHARD. The Illuminations in the Cairo Mosche-b. Asher-Codex of the Prophets . . ., by R. H. Pinder Wilson with contributions by R. Ettinghausen. *Der Herbäische Bibeltext Seit Franz Delitzsch*, by Paul Kahle. Stuttgart, W. Kohlhammer Verlag, 1961, pp. 95–98.

————. Paintings of the sultans and emperors of India in American collections. Bombay, Lalit Kalā Akademi, 1961, 19 pp. 14 col. pls.

————. Taklīf (inlay). *Urdu encyclopedia of Islam*, Lahore, 1960, vol. 1, pp. 597–607, 4 pls.

————. Review of "The Chester Beatty Library: A catalogue of the Persian manuscripts and miniatures, vol. 1, MSS. 101–105," by A. J. Arberry, M. Minovi, and E. Blochet. *Ars Orientalis*, vol. 4 (1961), pp. 393–396.

————. Review of "The Chester Beatty Library: A catalogue of the Turkish manuscripts and miniatures," by V. Minorsky. *Ars Orientalis*, vol. 4 (1961), pp. 385–392.

————. Review of "Indian painting: Fifteen color plates," by W. G. Archer. *Ars Orientalis*, vol. 4 (1961), pp. 397–399, pls. 1–2.

————. Review of "The Nala-Damayantī drawings," by Alvan Clark Eastman. *Ars Orientalis*, vol. 4 (1961), pp. 396–397.

————. Review of "Persian miniatures; the story of Rustum." Introduction and notes by William Lillys. *Artibus Asiae*, vol. 22 (1959), p. 268.

————. Review of "Turkisches Puppentheater. Versuch einer Geschichte des Puppentheaters im Morgenland," by Otto Spies. *The Muslim World*, vol. 50, No. 3 (July 1960).

GETTENS, RUTHERFORD J. European conservation laboratories. *Museum News*, vol. 39 (Dec. 1960–Jan. 1961), pp. 23–27, ills.

————. Teaching and research in art conservation. *Science*, vol. 133 (Apr. 21, 1961), pp. 1212–1216, 3 ills.

KATSUKI, TAKASHI. Review of "The beauty of ceramics," by Seizo Hayashiya. Tokyo, Kawade Shobo, 1960. *Far Eastern Ceramics Bulletin*, vol. 12, No. 43 (June–Dec. 1960), p. 47.

————. Review of "Chinese ceramics, one hundred selected masterpieces from collections in Japan, England, France and America," ed. by Fujio Koyama. Tokyo, Nihon Keizai, 1960. *Far Eastern Ceramic Bulletin*, vol. 12, No. 43, (June–Dec. 1960), p. 48–49.

————. Translation of "Chōsen tōji gaisetsu," or general observations on Korean ceramics, by Fujio Koyama. *Far Eastern Ceramic Bulletin*, vol. 12, No. 43 (June–Dec. 1960), pp. 19–38, 6 pls.

POPE, JOHN ALEXANDER. Chinese art treasures, exhibited in the United States by the Government of the Republic of China, Washington, 1961, 286 pp., pls. (part col. and mount.) Text by John A. Pope, Aschwin Lippe, and James F. Cahill.

————. Chinese art treasures cross the Pacific. *The Connoisseur*, New York, vol. 147 (June 1961), pp. 231–240, col. front., 20 figs.

————. Review of "Dated Buddha images of Northern Siam," by A. B. Griswold. *Ars Orientalis*, vol. 4 (1961), pp. 446–452.

STERN, HAROLD P. America; a view from the East. *Antiques*, vol. 79 (Feb. 19, 1961), pp. 166–169, ills.

————. A ninth-century eleven-headed Kannon. *Worcester Art Museum Annual*, vol. 8 (1960), pp. 1–7, front., 4 pls.

————. Obituary, James Marshall Plumer. *Oriental Art*, n.s., vol. 7 (spring 1961), p. 47.

———. Review of "Hokusai," by J. Hillier. London, Phaidon Press, 1955. *Journal of Asian Studies*, vol. 19 (Nov. 1959), pp. 87–88.

———. Review of "Graphic art of Japan, the Classical school," by Owen E. Holloway. Hollywood-by-the-Sea, Florida, Translantic Arts, 1957. *The Art Bulletin*, vol. 42 (Dec. 1960), pp. 311–312.

PHOTOGRAPHIC LABORATORY

The photographic laboratory made 10,378 items during the year, as follows: 7,363 prints, 864 negatives, 2,013 color slides, 100 black-and-white slides, 38 color-film sheets. In all, 3,133 slides were lent during the year.

BUILDING AND GROUNDS

The exterior walls appear to be sound and in good condition, but plans are under way for roof repair during the next year.

Painting of structural steel in the attic was begun but not completed. The cleaning of the interior limestone was finished, which improved the general appearance greatly. All concrete floors were painted and given a protective coat of wax.

In storage 14 all stone storage was confined to two walls by refitting with new steel and wood shelving. The remaining area will be fitted in the near future for the expansion of storage of various art objects plus an examining table. Storage 16A is now under construction to provide more space for storage and a research work area.

The doors leading from the main office to the anteroom were re-designed and fitted with glass. The dais in Gallery V was completely refinished. In the auditorium new drapes and stage curtain were installed. A new projector was installed, and with this second projector and the enlarged screen it is now possible to show two slides side by side for comparison purposes for the lecture series.

Old boxwood plants from the courtyard were transplanted to the north entrance of the building and smaller replacements were made in the court. Lantana was planted around the fountain for the summer season and appears to be doing well.

ATTENDANCE

The Gallery was open to the public from 9 to 4:30 every day except Christmas Day. The total number of visitors to come in the main entrance was 130,949. The highest monthly attendance was in August, 19,576.

There were 2,140 visitors who came to the Gallery office for various purposes—for general information, to submit objects for examination, to consult staff members, to take photographs or sketch in the galleries, to use the library, to examine objects in storage, etc.

AUDITORIUM

The series of illustrated lectures was continued as follows:

1960

October 11.	Dr. Nelson I. Wu, Yale University, "In Search of a New Style in Chinese Painting." Attendance, 155.
November 15.	Dr. John D. Cooney, Brooklyn Museum, "Disasters in Collecting." Attendance, 142.

1961

January 10.	Dr. Richard Edwards, University of Michigan, "Painting of the Southern Sung." Attendance, 142.
February 14.	Professor Benjamin Rowland, Harvard University, "The Translation of Indian Art to Central Asia." Attendance, 203.
March 14.	Henry Trubner, Royal Ontario Museum, "Han Pictorial Design." Attendance, 113.
April 11.	Professor George H. Forsyth, Jr., University of Michigan, "The Fortified Monastery of St. Catherine at Mt. Sinai." Attendance, 202.

From June 12 to 14 a seminar on "Technical Studies of Ancient Metal Artifacts" was held, the chief purpose of which was to gather together specialists in ancient metals and other interested persons from fields of Chinese art and conservation. Problems in analysis, composition, fabrication, and alteration of ancient metal artifacts were discussed with particular reference to Chinese ceremonial bronzes in the Freer collections. Question periods and informal discussions followed each of the 15 papers read by specialists from the United States, Canada, and one from Australia. Attendance, 57, 44, and 52.

Outside organizations used the auditorium as follows:

The Bellhaven Woman's Club held a short business meeting in the morning.	October 18. Attendance, 40.
The United States Department of Agriculture held meetings as follows:	
Foreign Agriculture	November 14. Attendance, 198. May 22. Attendance, 499.
Federal Extension Service	November 16. Attendance, 290. March 20. Attendance, 131.
Food and Drug Administration	November 23. Attendance, 95. December 21. Attendance, 68. February 15. Attendance, 76. March 15. Attendance, 63. April 19. Attendance, 101. May 17. Attendance, 89. June 21. Attendance, 72.
Marketing Division, Economic Research Conference	November 28–30. Attendance, 150, 195, and 109. December 2. Attendance, 85.
Farmers' Co-op Service	December 13 and 15. Attendance, 115 and 119.
4–H Clubs	March 23. Attendance, 176.

The Washington Film Society showed the following films:

"The Story of Gosta Berling" (1923) Sweden.	April 6 and 7. Attendance, 254.
"Los Olivadados" (1951) Mexico.	April 13 and 14. Attendance, 168.
"Munna" (1957) India, and "Song of Ceylon" Great Britain (1934).	April 20 and 21. Attendance, 313.
"Where Chimneys are Seen" (1953) Japan, and "Fable for Friendship."	April 27 and 28. Attendance, 211.
"Farrebizue" (1947) France, and "Trut" (1944) Sweden.	May 4 and 5. Attendance, 194.
Three short films from the British Free Cinema.	May 11 and 12. Attendance, 209.
"The White Reindeer" (1956) Finland, and "Glimmering" (1948) France.	May 25 and 26. Attendance, 168.
"Goja" (1951) Tunisia, and "Time Out of War" (1955) France.	June 1 and 2. Attendance, 154.
"Bab El-hadid" (1959) Egypt, and "N.Y., N.Y." (1950) United States.	June 8 and 9. Attendance, 275.
Alfred Friendly, of the Washington Post, lectured on "Bushmen (African) Paintings."	May 10. Attendance, 170.
Washington Society of the Archaeological Institute of America showed three films: "Roman Mosaics," "Colors in the Dark," and "Book Festivities."	May 18. Attendance, 229.

On May 2, seven members of the Washington Society of the Archaeological Institute of America held a Board Meeting in the Staff Room, Dr. Ettinghausen, president, presiding.

STAFF ACTIVITIES

The work of the staff members has been devoted to the study of new accessions, objects contemplated for purchase, and objects submitted for examination, as well as to individual research projects in the fields represented by the collections of Chinese, Japanese, Persian, Arabic, and Indian materials. Reports, oral and written, and exclusive of those made by the technical laboratory (listed below), were made on 7,221 objects as follows: For private individuals, 5,438; for dealers, 874; for other museums, 909. In all 1,373 photographs were examined, and 780 Oriental language inscriptions were translated for outside individuals and institutions. By request, 23 groups totaling 550 persons met in the exhibition galleries for docent service by the staff members. Two groups totaling 24 persons were given docent service by staff members in the storage rooms.

Among the visitors were 64 distinguished foreign scholars or persons holding official positions in their own countries who came here under the auspices of the Department of State to study museum administration and practices in this country.

During the year the technical laboratory carried on the following activities:

Objects examined by various methods including microscopic, microchemical, X-ray diffraction, ultraviolet light, spectrochemical analysis, and specific gravity determination:

Freer objects examined____ 19
Outside objects examined____ 93

The following projects were undertaken by the laboratory during the year:

1. For a period of three weeks, February 24 to March 15, Miss Elisabeth West worked as a guest in the Conservation Center of the Institute of Fine Arts, New York University, where she continued the spectrochemical analyses of inscribed ceremonial bronzes from the Freer collections.

2. In April 1961, R. J. Gettens, at the Conservation Center of the Institute of Fine Arts, New York University, gave a seminar entitled "Use of the Microscope in Examination of Works of Art." Attendance, 8.

3. R. J. Gettens continued as editor and Miss West as assistant editor of *IIC Abstracts* published by the International Institute for Conservation of Historic and Artistic Works, London, England.

4. Continued systematic collection of data on the technology of ancient copper and bronze in the Far East.

By invitation the following lectures were given outside the Gallery by staff members (illustrated unless otherwise noted):

1960

August 11.
Dr. Ettinghausen, at the Twenty-fifth International Congress of Orientalists, Moscow, U.S.S.R., "Pre-Mughal-Indo-Muslim Manuscripts."

September 15.
Dr. Ettinghausen, at the American School of Oriental Research, Jerusalem, Israel, "The Interrelationship of India and the Near East in the Middle Ages."

October 20.
Dr. Cahill, at Yale University, New Haven, Conn., "The Coming Discovery of Chinese Paintings."

November 1.
Dr. Ettinghausen, at Ankara University, Turkey, "Variety of Arts in Museums of Iran, Pakistan, and Turkey."

November 13.
Dr. Cahill, at Miami University, Oxford, Ohio, "The Coming Discovery of Chinese Paintings."

November 14.
Dr. Cahill, at Miami University, Oxford, Ohio, "Great Chinese Paintings in Far Eastern Collections."

November 17.
Dr. Cahill, at Mary Washington College, Fredericksburg, Va., "In Search of Chinese Paintings."

November 28.
Dr. Cahill, at the Japan-America Society, Washington, D.C., "The Southern School in Japanese Painting."

1961

January 12.
Dr. Stern, at Regents' Dinner, Smithsonian Institution, Washington, D.C., "Hokusai."

January 19.	Dr. Ettinghausen, at Hermitage Foundation, Norfolk, Va., "Islamic Art in the Mediterranean World."
February 3.	Dr. Ettinghausen began teaching a semester's course on "Islamic Painting" at New York University.
February 6.	Dr. Cahill began an academic course of lectures on Chinese paintings at the American University, Washington, D.C.
February 14–15.	Dr. Ettinghausen, at University of Southern Illinois, Carbondale, Ill., "Mughal Painting: A Critical Comparison."
February 23.	Dr. Stern, at the University of Michigan, Ann Arbor, Mich., "Japanese Paintings of the Tokugawa Period."
February 24.	Dr. Cahill, at the Institute of Contemporary Arts, Washington, D.C., "Chinese Art and the Contemporary West."
March 10.	Dr. Ettinghausen, at the Foreign Service Institute, Washington, D.C., "Islamic Art."
March 16.	Dr. Cahill, at Walters Art Gallery, Baltimore, Md., "Great Chinese Paintings in Far Eastern Collections."
March 24.	Dr. Ettinghausen, at Macalester College, St. Paul, Minn., "Islamic Art."
March 30.	Dr. Cahill, at the Chinese Art Society, Asia House, New York City, "Chinese Art and the Contemporary West."
April 3.	Dr. Pope, at the Far Eastern Luncheon Association, Carlton Hotel, Washington, D.C., "The Chinese Exhibition." (Not illustrated.)
April 12.	Dr. Stern, at the Birmingham Museum of Art, Birmingham, Ala., "Japanese Painting of the Tokugawa Period."
April 15.	R. J. Gettens, at the Conservation Center, Institute of Fine Arts, New York University, "A Proposed Handbook for Analysis of Materials of Art and Archaeology."
May 23.	R. J. Gettens, at the American Association of Museums meeting, Detroit, Mich., "Maya Blue: An Unsolved Problem in Ancient Pigment."
May 23.	Elisabeth West, at the American Association of Museums meeting, Detroit, Mich., "Efflorescent Salts on Museum Objects."
June 6–11.	Dr. Cahill, at the National Gallery of Art, Washington, D.C., gave seven lectures on "The Chinese Exhibition."

Members of the staff traveled outside Washington on official business as follows:

1960

July 1.	Dr. Stern, in New York City, examined objects at dealers and in museums and private collections.
July 18–December 16.	Dr. Ettinghausen attended the 25th International Congress of Orientalists in Moscow on behalf of the Smithsonian Institution and the American Council of Learned Societies, as well as the Cultural Seminar on Art and Archaeology of the CENTO Powers, in Ankara, on behalf of the Department of State. He also studied Islamic objects, paintings, and manuscripts in the museums and libraries of Dublin, London, Oxford, Paris, Hamburg, Bukhara, Kabul, Teheran, Damascus, Jerusalem, Qusair, 'Amra, Cairo, Istanbul, Ankara, Konya, Bursa, Vienna, Milan, Florence, Bologna, Rome, Palermo, and Madrid.

September 7–14.	Dr. Stern, in New York City, examined objects at dealers and in museums and attended exhibitions at the Museum of Modern Art and the Metropolitan Museum.
September 8–23.	Elisabeth H. West spent two weeks in England visiting laboratories and conferring with members of various staffs in London: Research Laboratory; British Museum; National Gallery of Art; Victoria and Albert Museum; Institute of Archaeology; Courtauld Institute of Art; University of London; and the Percival David Foundation of Chinese Art. Oxford: Research Laboratory for Archaeology and the History of Art.
October 22.	Dr. Cahill, in New York City, examined Chinese paintings belonging to dealers and museums, and attended an exhibition of Chinese paintings at Asia House.
November 5.	Dr. Cahill, in New York City, examined Chinese paintings belonging to a private collector.
December 14–18.	Dr. Stern and T. Sugiura, in New York City, attended an official meeting of the Rockefeller Foundation; attended the opening of the Modern Japanese Craft Show at the Museum of Decorative Arts; an exhibition of Japanese screens at the Willard Gallery; the Rappert exhibition at Asia House; and examined objects.

1961

January 6.	Dr. Ettinghausen, in New York City, examined objects.
January 9–10.	Dr. Pope, in Boston, attended the final meeting of the Far Eastern Ceramic Group.
January 19.	Dr. Ettinghausen, in New York City, examined objects at dealers.
January 23.	Mr. Gettens, in New York City, attended meetings of the Conservation Committee at the Institute of Fine Arts, New York University.
January 26.	Dr. Cahill, in New York City, broadcast over THE VOICE OF UNESCO, Riverside Radio program WRVR, on "Books and the Artist."
February 17.	Dr. Ettinghausen, in New York City, examined objects.
February 17–March 20.	Dr. Pope, in Geneva, Switzerland, for consultations regarding printing of the catalogue for the Chinese Exhibition.
February 21–April 10.	Dr. Stern, in Chicago, Seattle, San Francisco, Santa Barbara, Los Angeles, Kansas City, and Cleveland, examined objects in museums, private collections and at dealers.
March 29–April 1.	Dr. Cahill, in New York City, examined objects.
April 22.	Dr. Cahill, in Chicago, examined objects.
April 28–May 2.	Dr. Pope, in Chicago, examined objects.
May 4, 5.	Mrs. Lnor O. West, in the Boston area, attended the meetings of the Museum Store Managers Association held in the Museum of Fine Arts, Worcester Art Museum, and Old Sturbridge Village.
May 12–16.	Dr. Pope, in Philadelphia, appeared on the University Museum's WCAU–TV program, WHAT IN THE WORLD, later going on to New York City to examine objects.

May 18–24.   Dr. Stern, in Philadelphia, examined objects at the Phila-
                  delphia Museum of Art, and later, in New York City.

As in former years, members of the staff undertook a wide variety
of peripheral duties outside the Gallery, served on committees, held
honorary posts, and received recognitions.
    Respectfully submitted.

                                        A. G. WENLEY, *Director.*

Dr. LEONARD CARMICHAEL,
    Secretary, Smithsonian Institution.

Report on the National Air Museum

Sɪʀ: I have the honor to submit the following report on the activities of the National Air Museum for the fiscal year ended June 30, 1961:

Administrative studies and planning continued for the new National Air Museum Building, pending the appropriation of planning funds.

Many interesting and historically significant accessions were received during the year. Among the more notable ones were a full-size mock-up of an inertial guidance platform used for navigation in space-flight vehicles, from the Autonetics Division of North American Aviation, Inc.; an early Curtiss-built OX–5 aircraft engine, from the Massachusetts Institute of Technology; the RVX 1–5, first recovered nose cone after a flight of intercontinental range, from the U.S. Air Force; three additional volumes of Dr. Robert Goddard's notes on his experiments, from Mrs. Goddard; the XF8U–1 "Crusader" airplane (the "One X"), from Chance Vought Aircraft Company and the U.S. Navy; the Hiller "Flying Platform," from the U.S. Army and Navy; memorabilia of Norman Prince of the Lafayette Escadrille, from Frederick H. Prince, Jr.; Discoverer XIII, first recovered orbiting satellite, from the U.S. Air Force; the "Que Sera Sera," first airplane to land at the South Pole, from the U.S. Navy; 150 volumes of Pilots and Engine Manuals, from the Shell Companies Foundation; the first camera to take stabilized motion pictures of the earth from space, from the General Electric Company; the radio transmitter used by Adm. Richard E. Byrd in his historic first flight over the South Pole; and a painting of astronaut Alan B. Shepard, from Congressman James Fulton.

The name of the old Aircraft Building was changed to the Air and Space Building to reflect the many famous firsts of space flight now exhibited. During the fiscal year, 987,858 visitors to this renovated display were counted. It is expected that the Mercury capsule "Freedom 7" will be placed in this building shortly.

Information service continued to increase during the year. The museum now averages about 400 letters per month, furnishing historical, technical, and biographical information on air and space flight to authors, researchers, schools, government agencies, and the public.

ADVISORY BOARD

No formal meetings of the Advisory Board were held. Individual members were consulted from time to time.

SPECIAL EVENTS

The following special presentation ceremonies were held during the year. The RVX 1–5 nose cone, presented by Gen. Bernard A. Schriever, USAF; a Beechcraft Executive airplane, presented by George L. Lee, Sr., chairman of the board of the Red Devil Tool Co.; the Able-Baker space flight equipment, presented by Lt. Gen. J. H. Hinrichs, U.S. Army; the XF8U–1 "Crusader," presented by Charles J. McCarthy of Chance-Vought Company and Adm. James S. Russell of the Navy; the Discoverer XIII satellite, presented by Gen. Thomas D. White, Chief of Staff, USAF; and the first space camera, presented by Hilliard W. Page, general manager of the missile and space vehicle department of the General Electric Company.

The Director attended the Air Force Association Annual Meeting in San Francisco at which he was honored with the Alpha Eta Rho Aviation Fraternity Award for contributions to Aviation Education. He also attended the annual meeting of the National Aeronautic Association, the Lester D. Gardner Lecture by Gen. James H. Doolittle at MIT, the dedication of the Paul Moore Research and Development Center at Republic Aviation Corporation, and visited numerous Army, Navy, Air Force, and NASA bases. He spoke frequently on these visits, emphasizing the importance of the proper preservation and recording of the history of space flight now being made.

Paul E. Garber, head curator and historian, and curators Louis S. Casey and Kenneth E. Newland represented the air museum at a number of aviation meetings during the year. Mr. Garber delivered 27 lectures.

IMPROVEMENTS IN EXHIBITS

There have been continuous experimentation and improvements in the Museum's exhibits, reflected particularly in the renovated Air and Space Building which has proved to be a valuable testing ground for new methods of display, in anticipation of the new building.

REPAIR, PRESERVATION, AND RESTORATION

Continued improvement in the facilities at the Silver Hill, Md., restoration and preservation division has been accomplished. This is now a busy little aircraft "factory," made out of storage space, preserving and restoring aircraft and engines for display in the new building. Examples of the work done are found in the Air and Space Building.

ASSISTANCE TO GOVERNMENT DEPARTMENTS

Service and information was provided during the year to various Government departments including the Federal Aviation Agency, National Aeronautics and Space Administration, Justice Department, U.S. Navy, U.S. Air Force, Post Office Department, and Bureau of Standards.

PUBLIC INFORMATION SERVICE

This service grows in volume, and requires the majority of the time of the curatorial staff. The historical research involved is valuable not only to the the authors, researchers, historians, students and teachers served, but also to the Museum staff as potential material for eventual Museum publications.

REFERENCE MATERIAL AND ACKNOWLEDGMENTS

Much useful material was added to the reference files, library, and photographic files of the Museum during the year. This is very valuable to the staff for providing information, authenticating data, and for historical research.

The cooperation of the following persons and organizations in providing this material is sincerely appreciated and acknowledged:

AIR FORCE LOGISTIC COMMAND, Wright-Patterson Air Force Base, Ohio: Two copies of the Index of Serial Numbers assigned to aircraft through fiscal year 1958.

AITKEN, WILLIAM D., Jacksonville Beach, Fla.: One photostat of page 2 of the Boston Herald, Dec. 5, 1909, magazine section and three photographs.

AMOS, VINCENT S., St. Petersburg Beach, Fla.: 20 volumes aviation periodicals.

ANDO, HIDEYO, Tokyo, Japan: Nine 4-x-5'' photographs of Japanese aircraft.

ARMY BALLISTIC MISSILE AGENCY, REDSTONE ARSENAL, Huntsville, Ala.: 16-mm. sound motion picture of "Recovery of Able-Baker Nose Cone," edited copy of ABMA-film No. 89, copy 3 unclassified.

ARNOLD, MRS. H. H., Sonoma, Calif.: A group of 36 photographs.

BACKARD, P. H., Lockheed Aircraft Service Inc., Ontario, Calif.: Book, "The Flying Flea," by Henri Mignet.

BELL AEROSYSTEMS Co., Buffalo, N.Y.: Motion picture, "Report on Jet Propulsion."

BOEING AIRPLANE Co., Seattle, Wash.: Photographs, several lithographed 3-view drawings of aircraft (Boeing).

BROCKHAMPTON PRESS, Leicester, England: Book, "Hovercraft," by Angela Croome,

BROWN, W. NORMAN, Toronto, Canada: Five 4½-x-6'' photographs.

BUCKLEY, MRS. W. W., Washington, D.C.: One 16-x-20'' photograph of a Farman airplane taking off from street between White House and State, War, and Navy Building.

CANNON, JAMES, OFFICE OF PUBLIC INFORMATION, U.S. ATOMIC ENERGY COMMISSION, Washington, D.C.: Two photographs of atomic bombs (WWII).

COLEMAN, "COLE," New Orleans, La.: One 12-x-15½'' photograph of Lindbergh.

COX, JERE, BRANIFF AIRWAYS, Dallas, Texas: 19 8-x-10'' photographs (14 of Braniff type of aircraft and 5 of presentation ceremonies and T. E. Braniff); organization chart; chart showing Braniff routes; also four fact sheets.

DOUGLAS AIRCRAFT Co., INC., Santa Monica, Calif.: Two sets of drawings of Douglas "World Cruisers."

DOWNER AIRCRAFT INDUSTRIES, INC., Alexandria, Minn.: Photographs, miscellaneous data on Bellanca 260.

EARLY BIRD ORGANIZATION, E. A. Goff, Jr.: Early Bird files.

FAIRCHILD ENGINEERING AND AIRCRAFT CORP., Hagerstown, Md.: Specifications of the Fairchild F27 and F27A.

FRAZAR, MRS. PEARL, San Diego, Calif.: Program of the International Air Meet at Grant Park, Chicago, Aug. 12–20, 1911.

GEUTING, JOSEPH T., Washington, D.C.: Copy of "The 1961 Aerospace Year Book."

GIBSON, CHRISTIAN D., RAYMOND CORP., Greene, N.Y.: 16 issues of Industrial Aviation magazine, May 1944–August 1945.

GLENBOW FOUNDATION, Calgary, Alberta, Canada: Eight 8-x-10'' photographs, 14 5-x-7'' photographs, all of JL–6 type of aircraft.

GODDARD, MRS. ROBERT H., Worcester, Mass.: 1929 transcription of the material in Vols. 1 and 2 of set of 20 volumes. Report on the development of liquid-propelled rocket. Consists of 8 sections (337 pages) of transcript, and 8 reports of August 1929, containing 398 2¾-x-4¾'' photographs.

GREESON, OTIS H., Washington, D.C.: 13 photographs of miscellaneous aircraft and shows.

HAGERT, HENRY, Moorestown, N.J.: 28 copies of "Aero and Hydro" magazine from December 1912 to July 1913.

HAWKS, CHARLES R., FEDERAL AVIATION AGENCY, Los Angeles, Calif.: 39 boxes of engineering data on obsolete aircraft.

HOFFMAN, MAJ. WM. WECKHAN, New York, N.Y.: One photo album; three artillery School Manuals, WWI; one pictorial, "Belgium at War"; one translation of the campaign of the Belgium Army.

INTERNATIONAL CIVIL AVIATION AGENCY, Montreal, Canada: 16-mm. films, "Approach to Land GCA" and "Approach to Land ILS."

JOHNSON, F. ROY, Murfreesboro, N.C.: Copies of two old prints of Henry Gatling's pre-Civil War gliders.

KNABENSHUE, MRS. H. ROY, Arcadia, Calif.: Books, photographs, photo albums, magazines, newspaper clippings, airship log books, maps, drawings.

KORN, EDWARD A., East Orange, N.J.: Three photographs.

LIBRARY OF CONGRESS, Nathan R. Einhorn, Washington, D.C.: Miscellaneous.

LOCKHEED AIRCRAFT INTERNATIONAL, INC., Los Angeles, Calif.: Brochure containing news releases, photographs, and general information on Lockheed LASA–60 aircraft.

MARTIN CO., Baltimore, Md.: Drawings and photographs of Martin aircraft. Picture history of the Martin Co. with 3-view drawings.

MASSIN, ALEX, Toronto, Ontario, Canada: 16 commemorative air mail envelopes.

MAYERMAN, SAMUEL, Philadelphia, Pa.: Four bound volumes of "American Aviation."

McGUINN, CAPT. MICHAEL E. III, New York, N.Y.: Drawing of 1906 and 1909 Ellehamer plane, magazines and clippings on Ellehamer.

MEAD, MRS. CLARENCE, Seattle, Wash.: Five photographs of Post-Rogers crash scene.

MEYER, CORD, New York, N.Y.: Identification card of Lt. A. B. Thaw, II.

MOLSON, KEN M., Islinzton, Ontario, Canada: Book by Alan Sullivan, Lt. RAF, "Aviation in Canada, 1917–1918."

MYERS, FRANK A., Cleveland, Ohio: 20 pages of photostats of 1910–11 Harvard Boston Aero Meets as reported in *The Boston Evening Transcript*, September 1910, August and September 1911.

NAVY, DEPARTMENT OF THE, BUREAU OF AERONAUTICS, Washington, D.C.: 53 photograph albums.

NOORDUYN, ROBERT H., Irving, Texas: One photograph of Fokker T–2, one booklet of Fokker aircraft.

NORTHWEST AIRLINES, INC., Ronald McVickar, Washington, D.C.: History, photographs of their airlines and two annual reports, 1958 and 1959.

PAGE, GEORGE A., and PURDUM, VERNON, AERONCA MANUFACTURING CORP., Middletown, Ohio: 36 drawings of Aeronca aircraft, E113A installation drawing, low wing data report, production quantity listing (1930–44) miscellaneous performance data sheets (2).

PAGE, GEORGE, JR., Reynoldsburg, Ohio: National Geographic Magazine, 1918–46, including photographs, negatives, blueprints (Curtiss). News clipping of Ballooning.

PARKER, FRED: One photograph scrapbook, two photographs, one book.

POLITELLA, DARIO: Book, "Operation Grasshopper."

RESEARCH STUDIES INSTITUTE, Maxwell AFB, Ala.: Documents on the B–29 "Enola Gay" and organization.

REYNOLDS, B. C., Santa Barbara, Calif.: Roland Rohlf's chronology. Four transcripts of personal interviews.

RUSSELL, FRANK F., New York N.Y.: Three photograph albums and assorted photographs.

SEBOLD, R. C., GENERAL DYNAMICS CORP., San Diego, Calif.: Two sets of 3-view drawings, 1:16 scale of Convair F2Y–1 and Convair XFY–1 airplanes.

SHIPMAN, ERNEST, INTERNATIONAL BUSINESS MACHINES CORP., New York, N.Y.: Photographs, photo album, correspondence, pamphlets, Hammer collection.

SIKORSKY AIRCRAFT, Stratford, Conn.: Photographs and reference material on the Sikorsky S–61 and HSS–2 helicopters.

STRICKLAND, MRS. P. O'MALLEY, FEDERAL AVIATION AGENCY, Washington, D.C.: Copy of "Leslie Takes the Skyroad."

VERNON, VICTOR, St. Petersburg, Fla.: Two scrapbooks.

VICTORY, DR. JOHN F., Washington, D.C.: Bound book "L'Aeronautica Italiana Nell 'Immagine, 1487–1875."

WEBSTER, CLIFFORD L., West Palm Beach, Fla.: 135 photographs and 5 flight log books.

WEEKS, MRS. HAROLD E., Brooklyn, N.Y.: Book of bound copies of *The Weekly Bulletin* of the School of Instruction, Army Balloon School, Arcadia, Calif., dated 1918 through 1919.

WENTZEL, VOLKMAR, NATIONAL GEOGRAPHIC SOCIETY, Washington, D.C.: Photograph of early airship.

WILLIAMS, COL. DAVID M., Alexandria, Va.: Photo copy of diary.

ACCESSIONS

Additions to the National Aeronautical and Space collections received and recorded during the fiscal year 1961 totaled 266 specimens in 110 separate accessions, as listed below. Those from Government departments are entered as transfers; others were received as gifts or loans.

AERONCA MANUFACTURING CORP., Middletown, Ohio: An Aeronca E–113 engine cut-away. (N.A.M. 1176.)

AIR FORCE, DEPARTMENT OF THE, Wright Patterson Air Force Base, Ohio: Four aircraft engines of World War I period. (N.A.M. 1213.) Ballistic Missile Division, Calif.: Capsule that contained the measuring and recording instruments during the Discoverer XIII experiment. (N.A.M. 1183.) Through Marquardt Aircraft Company, Ogden, Utah: A Marquardt YRJ–43–MA–3 ram-jet engine, serial No. 00001, embodying the latest developments in the ram-jet propulsion system. (N.A.M. 1184A.) Air Force Museum, Fairborn, Ohio: A Russian Yakovlev 18 (YAK–18), post-World War II advanced trainer and nuisance raider. (N.A.M. 1153.) Air Research and Development Command, Dayton, Ohio: RVX 1–5, the first nose cone recovered after a flight of intercontinental range.   (N.A.M. 1159.)

AMERICAN MACHINE & FOUNDRY CO., Springdale, Conn.: Model of a ground-effect machine developed by Walter Crowley.   (N.A.M. 1233.)

ARMY, DEPARTMENT OF THE, ARMY BALLISTIC MISSILE AGENCY, Huntsville, Ala.: Exact duplicate mockup of monkey Baker space capsule covered with lucite walls (N.A.M. 1173); Able-Baker Project recovered nose cone (N.A.M. 1164); two Explorer I satellites (first U.S. satellite in orbit) and two final-stage power packs (N.A.M. 1163).   ARMY ORDNANCE MISSILE COMMAND, Redstone Arsenal, Ala.: 12 varied-scale models of Army missiles and launch vehicles. (N.A.M. 1175.)   ARMY EXHIBITS, Cameron Station, Va.: 1:24 scale model of Jupiter C with Explorer I satellite mounted on it.   (N.A.M. 1151.)

ARNOLD, Mrs. H. H., Sonoma, Calif.: Memorabilia of Gen. H. H. Arnold, including his personal flags of rank, dress uniform worn at his wedding, and eight academic hoods for the various honorary degrees he received (N.A.M. 1246); duty uniform of Gen. Arnold.   (N.A.M. 1149).

AUSMUS, REINHARDT, Sandusky, Ohio: Two early aircraft propellers.   (N.A.M. 1236.)

AUTONETICS DIVISION, NORTH AMERICAN AVIATION, INC., Downey, Calif.: Full-size mockup of inertial guidance platform used for navigation in nuclear submarines and space vehicles.   (N.A.M. 1146.)

AVIATION GAS TURBINE DIVISION, WESTINGHOUSE ELECTRIC, Kansas City, Mo.: Westinghouse J–32 gas turbine engine produced in 1943–44 and the smallest of this type of engine produced, developing 300 lbs. thrust at 35,000 rpm. (N.A.M. 1180.)

AZBE, VICTOR J., St. Louis, Mo.: Original letter written by Otto Lillienthal to his brother Gustav, Oct. 25, 1886.   (N.A.M. 1152.)

BATES, MORTIMER F., Burbank, Calif.: 1912 aviator's helmet purchased from Roold in Paris in 1912.   (N.A.M. 1182.)

BEECH AIRCRAFT CORP., Wichita, Kans.: Model of the Beech AT–7, a World War II twin-engine advance pilot training aircraft.   (N.A.M. 1230.)

CAIN, CHARLES W., Milwaukee, Wis.: An ashtray of aluminum from the tank of the Bellanca airplane "Columbia" which twice flew across the Atlantic Ocean in 1927 and 1930.   (N.A.M. 1154.)

CARMELO, ALFREDO, Bethesda, Md.: Painting of Bevo Howard's Jungmeister aerobatic plane.   (N.A.M. 1240.)

CHANCE VOUGHT AIRCRAFT, INC., Dallas Tex.: Model of the Regulus I surface-to-surface missile (N.A.M. 1168); the Chance Vought XF8U–1 "Crusader," popularly known as the "One X" (N.A.M. 1174).

CONVAIR, DIVISION OF GENERAL DYNAMICS, San Diego, Calif.: Two scale models of the Convair Atlas launch vehicle (N.A.M. 1224); 8–x–10′ photo montage mural of the launching of an Atlas (N.A.M.) 1215).

CURTISS-WRIGHT CORP., Woodridge, N.J.: 1:16 scale model of Curtiss A–1 aircraft, the first U.S. Navy aircraft.   (N.A.M. 1221.)

DOOLITTLE, GEN. JAMES H., Los Angeles, Calif.: Six items of personal memorabilia: special awards, plaques, etc.   (N.A.M. 1145.)

DUPONT, F. V., Cambridge, Va.: Model of the Wright "B" airplane.   (N.A.M. 1244.)

FEDERAL AVIATION AGENCY, Oklahoma City, Okla.: Radio equipment.   (N.A.M. 1172.)

FULTON, CONGRESSMAN JAMES, Pittsburgh, Pa.: Loan of a painting of Alan Shepard, America's first man-in-space, painted by James Scalese of Pittsburgh. (N.A.M. 1241.)

GENERAL ELECTRIC, Philadelphia, Pa.: First camera to take pictures of earth from outer space. (N.A.M. 1218.)

GODDARD, MRS. ESTHER C., Worcester, Mass.: Vols. 21, 22, and 23 of Dr. Goddard's notes on his experiments. (N.A.M. 1165).

GOLDEN, BERNIE, Asbury Park, N.J.: A propeller manufactured by the Simmons Co. of Washington, D.C., of a very early vintage. Fitted with sprocket attachment for chain drive. (N.A.M. 1148.)

GRUMMAN AIRCRAFT CORP., Bethpage, N.Y.: Model of the Grumman F1OF Jaguar fighter aircraft. (N.A.M. 1238.)

HALL, ERNEST, Warren, Ohio: Fragments of aircraft and engines built by the Wrights, Curtiss, and Bleriot. (N.A.M. 1237.)

HARTMAN, ARTHUR J., Burlington, Iowa : Oil painting of early hot-air balloon ascension at a county fair and a full-size cut-off release with model parachute. (N.A.M. 1251.)

HEINTZ, RALPH M., Los Gatos, Calif.: Antenna weight used on the "Floyd Bennett" during its flight over the South Pole in 1929 (N.A.M. 1232) ; aircraft transmitter used by Richard E. Byrd in his historic first flight over the South Pole (N.A.M. 1223).

HYLAN, RAY, Henrietta, N.Y.: Boeing F4B–4 single-engine biplane Navy fighter of the early 1930 period. (N.A.M. 1243.)

ITALIAN GOVERNMENT, Air Attache, Washington, D.C.: Model of a Macchi 202 fighter, the most advanced fighter design produced by Italy in World War II. (N.A.M. 1147.)

JOUETT, COL. JOHN, Washington, D.C.: Trophy urn presented to a group of Americans for their service to the Republic of China during World War II. (N.A.M. 1239.)

KLEAN, LESTER E., Bensenville, Ill. : Model of the Curtiss JN4–D–2. (N.A.M. 1166.)

LOCKHEED AIRCRAFT CORP., Burbank, Calif. : 1 : 16 scale model of the Navy submarine-launched missile, the "Polaris." (N.A.M. 1249.)

MARTIN COMPANY, Baltimore, Md.: Model of early monoplane patrol bomber (N.A.M. 1225) ; model of the SM68 Titan missile produced by the Martin Company for the U.S. Air Force (N.A.M. 1222).

MASSACHUSETTS INSTITUTE OF TECHNOLOGY, Cambridge, Mass.: Curtiss-built OX–5 engine with manufacturer's number 6329. (N.A.M. 1157.)

MASSIN, ALEX, Toronto, Ontario, Canada : Set of 12 U.S. Air Force insignia, (N.A.M. 1214.)

McDONNELL AIRCRAFT CORP., St. Louis, Mo. : 1 : 3 scale model of the Mercury capsule with escape tower (N.A.M. 1231) ; model of the McDonnell F4H–1 Phantom II (N.A.M. 1235) ; 12 1 : 16 scale models of aircraft produced by the donor (N.A.M. 1242).

MEAD, CLARENCE H., Seattle, Wash. : Pontoon flat cap from Post-Rogers plane wreck. (N.A.M. 1167.)

MESSERSCHMITT, A. G., Augsburg (through German Air Attache), Washington, D.C.: Model, 1 : 16 size, of the famed Messerschmitt BF 109 single-seat, single-engine fighter of World War II. (N.A.M. 1162.)

MIKESH, CAPT. ROBERT C., Washington, D.C. : Models of two Japanese fighters. (N.A.M. 1226.)

MILLER, L. B., Tarpon Springs, Fla. : Leather flight coat-jacket that belonged to Amelia Earhart. (N.A.M. 1227.)

MODERN ART FOUNDRY, New York, N.Y.: Purchase of bronze casting of plaster bust of Dr. S. P. Langley. (N.A.M. 1229.)

NATIONAL AERONAUTICS AND SPACE AGENCY, Washington, D.C. : 14 framed photographs of former members of the National Advisory Committee for Aeronautics (N.A.M. 1161) ; 8-x-10'' piece of skin used in construction of 100'-diameter "Echo" passive communication satellite (N.A.M. 1160).

NAVY, DEPARTMENT OF THE, Washington, D.C.: Production version of Pratt & Whitney J–57 jet engine (N.A.M. 1156). NAVAL AIR STATION, Patuxent, Md.: Hiller Rotorcycle, one-place, portable helicopter (N.A.M. 1245). EXHIBITS SECTION, Washington, D.C.: Models of technically and historically significant Navy aircraft (N.A.M. 1234). OFFICE OF NAVAL RESEARCH, Washington D.C.: Hiller ducted platform (N.A.M. 1177). BUREAU OF WEAPONS, Washington, D.C. Culver TD2C–1 target drone aircraft (N,A.M. 1196) ; Grumman TBF–1 Avenger, U.S. Navy torpedo bomber (N.A.M. 1197) ; Curtiss SB2C–5 "Hell-diver" aircraft (N.A.M. 1198) ; Grumman F8F–1D "Bearcat" aircraft, last of the reciprocating-engine carrier-based fighters developed for World War II (N.A.M. 1199) ; first airplane to have landed at the South Pole, "Que Sera Sera," an R4D (N.A.M. 1200) ; Vought V–173 "Flying Pancake" full-size flying model, built to examine the practicability of a low aspect ratio wing configuration (N.A.M. 1201) ; specimen of Japanese attack aircraft developed in anticipation of a "last ditch" defense of the Japanese homeland (N.A.M. 1202) ; Grumman F4F (FM–1) manufactured by Eastern Aircraft (N.A.M. 1203) ; North American SNJ–4 (AF AT–6), advanced trainer used by both the U.S. Navy and the U.S. Army Air Force during World War II (N.A.M. 1204) ; Vought F4U–1B "Corsair," single-engine, single-place, inverted-gull-wing fighter of World War II (N,A.M. 1205) ; Ryan FR–1 "Fireball," single-place twin-engine low-wing aircraft (N.A.M. 1206) ; specimen of the Kaman K–225 helicopter, the first such vehicle powered by a gas turbine engine (N.A.M. 1207) ; Piasecki PV–3 tandem-rotor helicopter, designed as a medium-range rescue and cargo vehicle (N.A.M. 1208) ; Arado Ar–196A, twin float reconnaissance monoplane used on the German battleship "Prince Eugene" (N.A.M. 1209) ; Dornier Do–335 "Pfiel (Arrow)" twin-tandem-engined heavy fighter, developed by the German Air Force about 1942 (N.A.M. 1210) ; an example of the Vought OS2U–3 scout observation type aircraft (N.A.M. 1186) ; Grumman F6F–3 single-engine, single-place, low-wing monoplane fighter of World War II vintage (N.A.M. 1187) ; Douglas D–558–2 "Skyrocket," rocket-powered research aircraft, first to exceed twice the speed of sound (N.A.M. 1188) ; Douglas SBD–6, of a type used extensively in the Pacific theater of operations during World War II (N.A.M. 1189) ; Interstate TDR–1 twin-engine, low-wing monoplane, designed as a remote-control torpedo launching vehicle (N.A.M. 1190) ; Naval Aircraft Factory N3N–3, single-engine two-place biplane trainer of World War II vintage (N.A.M. 1191) ; Sikorsky JRS–1 amphibian aircraft (N.A.M. 1192) ; Boeing (Stearman) N2S–5 Kaydet, two-place, biplane, primary training aircraft (N.A.M. 1193) ; Grumman JRF–2 "Petulant Porpoise" modified to take different experimental hull configurations (N.A.M. 1193) ; Hiller HOE–1 ram-jet-powered helicopter (N.A.M. 1195) ; Navy-Curtiss TS–1 (TR–1), single-place biplane fighter-trainer of 1922 vintage (N.A.M. 1219) ; components of Navy-Curtiss NC–4, the first airplane to cross the Atlantic Ocean (N.A.M. 1220) ; group of 34 exhibition models of varying scale of Navy aircraft types (N.A.M. 1253).

PACKARD, PATRICK H., Ontario, Calif.: Airplane designed by M. Henri Mignet, the first of this design built in the United States at the direction of Powell Crosley. (N.A.M. 1158.)

PALEN, COLE, Rhinebeck, N.Y.: Seven early aircraft instruments, mostly of World War I vintage. (N.A.M. 1179.)

PIPER AIRCRAFT CORP., Lock Haven, Pa.: Models 1:16 size of the Piper Apache PA–23, Aztec PA–23–50, and the Comanche PA–24 aircraft.   (N.A.M. 1217.)

PRINCE, FREDERICH H., JR., Long Island, N.Y.: Memorabilia of Norman Prince.   (N.A.M. 1181.)

RED DEVIL TOOLS, Union N.J.: Beechcraft Model D–18–S, an example of an executive transport.   (N.A.M. 1171.)

RICKENBACKER, CAPT. E. V., New York, N.Y.: A German World War I flyer's crash helmet and a log book showing flight operations of the 94th Squadron (Rickenbacker's).   (N.A.M. 1247.)

ROCKWELL, COL. PAUL, Asheville, N.C.: Bronze reproduction of gold medal struck to commemorate the launching of the French aircraft carrier "LaFayette."   (N.A.M. 1248.)

RYAN AERONAUTICAL CORP., San Diego, Calif.: Two 1:20 scale models of Ryan-developed aircraft, the FR–1 "Fireball" and the X–13 "Vertijet."   (N.A.M. 1155.)

SHAFFER, CLEVE F., San Francisco, Calif.: Experimental liquid-fuel rocket motor and spring scale for measuring thrust, used by donor during period 1927 to 1932.   (N.A.M. 1252.)

SHELL COMPANIES FOUNDATION, INC., Washington, D.C.: Handbooks, erection and maintenance manuals for aircraft and engines.   (N.A.M. 1212.)

SHOEMAKER, JOS., ESTATE OF, Bridgeton, N.J.: Two aircraft of 1909–11 vintage.   (N.A.M. 1211.)

SMITHSONIAN INSTITUTION, SECRETARY'S OFFICE, Washington, D.C.: Two guilded metal copies of the Langley Medal which was awarded to Dr. Robert Hutchings Goddard posthumously, June 28, 1960.   (N.A.M. 1178.) ; DEPARTMENT OF ARTS AND MANUFACTURES: Three examples of airplane tail-wheel tires produced by the B. F. Goodrich Company.   (N.A.M. 1185.)

TODD, H. S., Miami Springs, Fla.: A unique 5-cylinder, radial model aircraft engine, complete with accessories and a 3-blade adjustable-pitch propeller.   (N.A.M. 1150.)

TRACY, DANIEL, Lakewood, Ohio: Model 1:16 size of the Curtiss R–6 racer, winner of the 1922 Pulitzer Prize Race.   (N.A.M. 1216.)

UNITED CONTROL CORP., Seattle, Wash.: Aircraft warning tone generator for Cessna 210.   (N.A.M. 1170.)

WALKER, L. L., JR., Houston, Tex.: A group of 10 historically and technically significant engines (N.A.M. 1250) ; wooden timing disk for a Hispano-Suiza engine.   (N.A.M. 1184.)

WATERMAN, WALDO, San Diego, Calif.: The Waterman Aerobile, a unique example of the airplane-automobile combination.   (N.A.M. 1228.)

WRIGHT, ORVILLE, ESTATE OF, Dayton, Ohio: The original Wright Brothers' aeroplane, invented and built by Wilbur and Orville Wright, and flown by them at Kitty Hawk, N.C., December 17, 1903.   (N.A.M. 1169.)

Respectfully submitted.

PHILIP S. HOPKINS, *Director.*

DR. LEONARD CARMICHAEL,
   Secretary, Smithsonian Institution.

Report on the National Zoological Park

SIR: I have the honor to submit the following report on the activities of the National Zoological Park for the fiscal year ended June 30, 1961:

GIFTS

From the standpoint of both popular interest and rarity, the outstanding gift of the year was the white tigress, Mohini of Rewa, which arrived on December 4, 1960. This beautiful animal, cream colored with brown to black stripes and ice-blue eyes, was the gift of the Metropolitan Broadcasting Corporation of New York and Ralph Scott of Washington, D.C. The Director of the National Zoological Park, accompanied by Bert Barker, senior keeper of small mammals, flew to India to select the tiger from a litter of four white cubs raised by the Maharajah of Rewa and escort it to Washington. Thomas J. Abercrombie, staff member of the National Geographic Magazine, joined the Zoo men in Rewa to make photographs. The Maharajah had captured a male white tiger cub in 1951, and when it was adult mated it to a normal-colored Bengal tiger. The young were all the usual orange color. Then he mated the white male to one of the female offspring, and the resulting four cubs were all white. A subsequent litter, from the same parents, had one orange and two white cubs. Mohini was formally presented to President Eisenhower on the White House lawn by John Kluge, president of the Board of the Metropolitan Broadcasting Corporation, as a gift to the children of America. Mohini, when she arrived, was a little over 2 years old and weighed about 200 pounds. Her name is Hindi for Enchantress, and she continues to enchant the throngs who daily come to see her. She is the only white tiger in any zoo in the world at this time.

Through the efforts of Mrs. Ira J. Heller, the "Share Your Birthday Foundation"—an organization to promote international good will among children—brought an Indian elephant as a gift from the children of India and the Maharajah of Mysore to the children of America. Ambika is a female approximately 9 years old and weighs 2,820 pounds. She arrived in the United States on April 14, 1961, after a 47-day voyage on the S.S. *Steel Architect* of the Isthmian Line. Between various appearances before school children in other cities she is on deposit in the National Zoological Park, which will eventually be her permanent home.

The Montana State Fish and Game Department, of Helena, Mont., sent to the Zoo five bighorn sheep and one Rocky Mountain goat, thus helping to build up the collection of North American game animals.

The Department of External Affairs, Canadian Government, Ottawa, gave a pair of Canadian beavers. On May 31 they were formally presented by the Speaker of the Canadian Senate, Mark Drouin, and the Speaker of the Canadian House, Roland Michener, and accepted on behalf of the Smithsonian Institution by Assistant Secretary Remington Kellogg. Representative Cornelius E. Gallagher of New Jersey, representing the Interparliamentary Union, also spoke at the presentation. The beavers were placed in the newly renovated pool in the section of the Park long known as Beaver Valley.

Sir Edward Hallstrom of the Taronga Zoological Park Trust of Sydney, Australia, sent eight lesser flying phalangers, a welcome addition to the collection.

Through John Hoke of the American Consulate in Paramaribo, the Government of Surinam sent a three-toed sloth. While the two-toed sloth is commonly seen in zoos and has frequently bred in the National Zoological Park, the three-toed is a rarity as it does not adapt well in captivity. This animal lived from July 2, 1960, to January 29, 1961, and produced a young one after it arrived. The baby, unfortunately, died after 14 days. When Mr. Hoke returned from his Surinam mission, he brought two more three-toed sloths and gave them to the Zoo on June 19, 1961.

The Hogle Zoo in Salt Lake City, Utah, sent the Park two kit foxes, a species that had not been represented in the collection for several years.

J. Lear Grimmer, Associate Director, made another field trip to British Guiana to study the life history of the hoatzin and returned with three red agoutis and a large collection of birds and reptiles, including the brown-throated conure, the black-headed conure, yellow-headed marsh bird, black-throated cardinal, crested oropendula, three species of ground doves, Cook's boa, and the rainbow boa.

Space does not permit a complete list of all gifts received during the year, but in addition to those already mentioned, the following are of interest:

Alston, F. J., Charlotte, N.C., sea lion.
Armstrong, Wallace J., Washington, D.C., African lungfish, 2 angelfish, peacock cichlid.
Balakirshnan, M. P., Kerala, India, Malabar squirrel.
Brady, James, Arlington, Va., night monkey.
Bump, Dr. Gardiner, New Dehli, India, jungle cat (*Felis chaus*), coppersmith (barbet).
Cate, Mrs. Robert, Washington, D.C., 2 toucans.
Department of Preventive Medicine, Entomology Branch, Fort Sam Houston, Tex., cacomistle.

1. Three ring-tailed lemurs from Madagascar are the first to be exhibited at the National Zoological Park in many years.

2. A young serval cat, born May 2, 1961, in the National Zoological Park.

1. A clouded leopard.   National Zoological Park.

2. The white tiger from Rewa.   National Zoological Park.

1. A mother two-toed sloth and her two-month-old baby.   National Zoological Park.

2. Male kookaburra (on the right) and three of his offspring.   The second clutch of eggs can be seen in the nest at the base of tree.   National Zoological Park.

Fish and Wildlife Service, Annapolis, Md., Virginia deer; Boothbay Harbor, Maine, 5 great black-backed gulls, 3 harbor seals; Eastern Shore, Md. (through Vern Stott), 2 pied-billed grebes, 6 whistling swans, 3 golden-eyed ducks, bufflehead; Turkey Bay, Md., whistling swan.

George's Pet Store, Bladensburg, Md., spider monkey.

Harbaugh, George, Mount Rainier, Md., spiny-tailed iguana.

Joy, Chief Petty Officer J. E., San Angelo, Tex., 22 western diamond-backed rattlesnakes.

Kuntz, Dr. Robert, Taipei, Taiwan, 11 green snakes, water snake, 6 green vipers (*Trimeresurus stejnegeri*), 3 green vipers (*T. gramineus*), striped rat snake.

Moynihan, Dr. Martin H., Barro Colorado Island, C.Z., 4 spider monkeys.

Muckels, R. N., Irongate, Va., spider monkey.

Nye, Alva G., McLean, Va., golden eagle.

Pinkston, Miss Nell S., Arlington, Va., tovi parakeet.

Pomeroy, Mr. and Mrs. Eugene, American Embassy, Benghazi, Libya, 2 spiny-tailed lizards.

Roeder, H. Edward, Churchtown, Md., red-crowned mangabey.

Sather, Ken, Round Lake, Minn., 3 red-breasted geese.

Stambaugh, Dean, Washington, D.C., 2 troupials, 1 yellowhammer.

Statland, Samuel, Washington, D.C., 5 African clawed frogs.

Swain, Mark, Las Vegas, Nev., puma.

Wetmore, Dr. Alexander, Washington, D.C., crowned hawk eagle.

Xanten, William Jr., Washington, D.C., collection of North American snakes.

PURCHASES

Among important purchases of the year were an African rhinoceros, three Cape buffaloes, three brindled gnus, a clouded leopard, and three ring-tailed lemurs. The Director, while in New Delhi making arrangements for the shipment of the white tiger, purchased a sizable collection of native birds, including bulbuls, tits, thrushes, parrots, and parakeets.

Other purchases of interest were:

Rocky Mountain goat	2 South American lapwings
3 Patagonian cavies	2 pileated tinamous
Emu	Quetzal
5 lesser African flamingoes	2 purple gallinules
4 Dalmatian pelicans	7 Nanday parrots
2 black-necked swans	2 Illiger's macaws
4 coscoroba swans	Concave-casqued hornbill
Harpy eagle	

EXCHANGES

By the judicious use of exchanges with other zoos and with individuals the following animals were obtained:

Barcelona Zoo, Barcelona, Spain, 2 Goliath frogs.

Breazeale, Edgar, Edmonton, N.C., 6 chukar quail, 8 bobwhite quail.

Calgary Zoo, Calgary, Alberta, 2 Arctic foxes.

Cincinnati Zoo, Cincinnati, Ohio, jaguar.

Crandon Park Zoo, Miami, Fla., 3 green frogs, 4 Cuban tree frogs, 2 oak toads, 5 spadefoot toads.

Department of Commerce, Bureau of Fisheries, 2 hellbenders.

Emperor Valley Zoo, Port-of-Spain, Trinidad, 2 spider monkeys, blue tanager, 2 palm tanagers, maroon or silver-beaked tanager, violet tanager, 3 jacarini finches, 2 saffron finches, 4 purple sugarbirds, 4 yellow-winged sugarbirds, 4 bananaquits, 3 black-headed sugarbirds, 6 scarlet ibis.

Hanson, Charles, Oak Harbor, Ohio, 3 banded geckos, 2 *Uta* sp., California king snake, 2 glossy snakes, bull snake, mud snake, 2 fox snakes, garter snake (black phase), 2 island water snakes.

New York Zoological Park, New York, N.Y., 4 falcated teals, 2 triangular spotted pigeons.

Okit, W., Winston-Salem, N.C., black swan, 2 mutant pheasants.

Philadelphia Zoological Garden, Philadelphia, Pa., 4 prairie dogs.

Phillips, Mrs. Jerry, Waldorf, Md., 4 wood ducks.

Portland Zoo, Portland, Oreg., 2 alligator lizards, Columbian ground squirrel, 3 North American porcupines, 2 ring-tailed cats, 10 least chipmunks, 11 golden-mantled squirrels, 2 murres, 3 herring gulls, 6 Washington ground squirrels, chickaree, 4 chukar quail, 2 Onogadoria chickens, 2 Pacific rattlesnakes, rubber boa.

San Diego Zoo, San Diego, Calif., 2 Indian monitors, 8 valley quail, 4 Gambel's quail, 4 burrowing owls, toco toucan.

Southwest Wild Animal Farm, Blackstone, Mass., 4 peach-faced lovebirds.

Thomas, Charles, Washington, D.C., silver pheasant.

Tote-em-In Zoo, Wilmington, N.C., 2 Asiatic chipmunks, 2 European hedgehogs, 3 Indian monitors, 3 black racers.

Whiteman, Robert L., Fairfax, Va., 2 hog-nosed snakes, 3 water snakes, 2 ribbon snakes, 3 worm snakes.

The following animals were sent to other zoos and to private collectors in exchange:

Alipore Zoo, Calcutta, India, 4 scarlet ibises, 2 roseate spoonbills, 12 wood ducks, 2 Gambel's quail, 2 California Valley quail, 2 bobwhite quail, 2 coscorobas, sulphur-and-white-breasted toucan, white-lined toucanet, 3 cackling geese, 4 red-breasted marsh birds, cardinal, Gila monster, Mexican bearded lizard, 2 armadillos.

Barcelona Zoo, Barcelona, Spain, 10 prairie dogs.

Breazeale, E., Edmonton, N.C., 4 Canadian geese.

British Guiana Zoo, Georgetown, British Guiana, 4 domestic rabbits, 4 peafowl.

Calgary Zoo, Calgary, Alberta, Cape hunting dog, 2 brown pelicans, 2 barred owls, 3 night herons.

Ceylon Zoological Gardens, Colombo, Ceylon, 6 prairie dogs.

Cincinnati Zoo, Cincinnati, Ohio, 2 lion cubs.

Copenhagen Zoo, Copenhagen, Denmark, 6 cardinals, white-throated sparrow, 2 zebra finches, white-headed nun, blue jay, robin, 2 Java finches, 2 baldpates, 30 common Anolis.

de Lauerolle, Vasantha, Berkeley, Calif., Indian python.

Detroit Zoo, Royal Oak, Mich., 2 Pacific rattlesnakes, 2 pygmy rattlesnakes, 2 western rattlesnakes, 2 Amazon spotted turtles, 1 copperhead, 4 Taiwan cobras, 2 flat-headed turtles, South American red-lined turtle, large side-necked turtle, Murray turtle, Indian monitor, 3 Cook's boas.

Franklin Park Zoo, Boston, Mass., 3 red deer, 2 white fallow deer, 2 Virginia deer.

Hanson, Charles, Oak Harbor, Ohio, 2 Cook's boas.

Houston Zoo, Houston, Tex., South American rat snake, 2 common iguanas, 2 Indian monitors, 6 pilot black snakes, black tegu, 2 African bull frogs, fox snake, 2 Amazon spotted turtles, gibba turtle, Pacific rattlesnake, 2 manushi, glossy snake, 4 palm vipers, 2 flat-headed turtles, Formosan striped rat snake, Formosan rat snake, 2 South American red-lined turtles, milk snake, 2 Indian wolf snakes, 2 large snake-necked turtles, 2 Murray turtles, boa constrictor, Indian python, 2 Taiwan cobras, snorkel viper, 6 tree boas, Cuban boa, Indian cobra.

Portland Zoo, Portland, Oreg., Nile hippopotamus, 2 eastern box turtles, 2 yellow-bellied turtles, 2 eastern painted turtles, Florida water turtles, red-lined turtle, 2 western diamond-backed rattlesnakes, 2 African porcupines.

Sacramento Zoo, Sacramento, Calif., 2 Cape hunting dogs.

Salisbury Snake Farm, Southern Rhodesia, anaconda.

San Antonio Zoo, San Antonio, Tex., black leopard, water civet, 2 golden-bellied badgers, lesser panda, giant Indian squirrel, 2 kelp gulls, 2 American ospreys, 2 cotton teal, 10 Quaker parakeets, 3 ring-necked teal, llama, 2 Formosan masked civets, 3 Newman's genets, Patagonian cavy, sika deer, laughing thrush, 2 Formosan red-billed pies, 2 plain-breasted ground doves.

Seattle Zoo, Seattle, Wash., 3 mute swans.

Southwick Wild Animal Farm, Blackstone, Mass., 1 wild turkey.

Thomas, Charles, Washington, D.C., 2 cockatiels.

Toledo Zoo, Toledo, Ohio, 2 Cape hunting dogs.

Tote-em-In Zoo, Wilmington, N.C., 8 fallow deer, 5 Virginia deer, elk, yak, Columbian ground squirrel, 4 eastern flying squirrels.

BIRTHS AND HATCHINGS

The number of young animals born in the Zoo was gratifying and included several "firsts," either for this Zoo or for the United States. The pair of Margay cats that had a young one last year produced another kitten, which was cared for by the mother. A baby serval was taken away from its mother and raised by hand. The Canadian beavers, which were gifts from the Canadian Government, had a young one just after arriving in the park and before the formal presentation by Canadian officials, and so it was on view during the ceremony. The Dorcas gazelles were equally obliging and had their fawn at the time when President Bourguiba of Tunisia, who gave the original pair to Mrs. John Eisenhower, was in Washington.

A pair of kookaburras, a gift in 1954 from Sir Edward Hallstrom of the Taronga Zoological Park Trust in Sydney, Australia, began laying eggs in February 1961. The nest was built in an opening at the base of a hollow tree, and the birds excavated the site until the nest was 2 or 3 inches below ground level. Three eggs were laid, and the male and female birds took turns incubating them, neither bird leaving the nest until the other had replaced it during the 25 days of incubation. On four occasions the female was observed calling the male by rapping on the tree with her bill, and the male responded immediately and entered the nest. The kookaburras had always been fed on dead mice, and before the eggs hatched the keepers began accustoming the adults to eating mice that had been cut up in small pieces. These chopped mice, supplemented with cockroaches that had been injected with multivitamins, were fed directly to the young birds by the parents after the old birds had crushed them thoroughly either in their bills or by rapping them against the tree. Thirty days after hatching, the first bird left the nest, but they continued to be fed by the parents until they were 2 months old. Before the first brood was self-reliant, the female began laying eggs again, and two more young were hatched on June 5.

Following the procedure of previous years, all births and hatchings are listed below, whether or not the young were successfully raised. In many instances the record of animals having bred in captivity is of importance.

MAMMALS

Common name	Scientific name	Number
Rat kangaroo	*Potorous* sp.	2
Night monkey	*Aotus trivirgatus*	2
Squirrel monkey	*Saimiri sciureus*	2
Hybrid macaque	*Macaca philippiensis* x *M. irus*	1
Rhesus monkey	*Macaca mulatta*	1
Barbary ape	*Macaca sylvanus*	3
Moustached monkey	*Cercopithecus cephus*	1
DeBrazza's guenon	*Cercopithecus neglectus*	2
White-handed gibbon	*Hylobates lar*	1
Chimpanzee	*Pan satyrus*	1
Two-toed sloth	*Choloepus didactylus*	1
Three-toed sloth	*Bradypus tridactylus*	1
Beaver	*Castor canadensis*	1
Prairie dog	*Cynomys ludovicianus*	3
African crested rat	*Lophiomys* sp.	1
White-footed mouse	*Peromyscus* sp.	1
Deer mouse	*Peromyscus maniculatus*	5
African porcupine	*Hystrix galeata*	3
Patagonian cavy	*Dolichotis patagona*	4
Dingo	*Canis antarcticus*	1
Common jackal	*Canis aureus*	6
Timber wolf	*Canis lupus nubilus*	3
Cape hunting dog	*Lycaon pictus*	5
European brown bear	*Ursus arctos*	5
Grizzly bear	*Ursus horribilis*	2
Hybrid bear F2	*Thalarctos maritimus* x *Ursus middendorffi*	4
Coatimundi	*Nasua narica*	3
Newman's genet	*Genetta genetta neumanii*	4
Water civet	*Atilax paludinosus*	3
Serval	*Felis serval*	2
Margay cat	*Felis wiedii*	1
Lion	*Panthera leo*	2
Peccary	*Pecari tajacu*	1

Common name	Scientific name	Number
Nile hippopotamus	*Hippopotamus amphibius*	1
Llama	*Lama glama*	4
Bactrian camel	*Camelus bactrianus*	1
White fallow deer	*Dama dama*	4
Axis deer	*Axis axis*	2
Red deer	*Cervus elaphus*	2
Sika deer	*Cervus nippon*	4
Virginia deer	*Odocoileus virginianus*	7
Reindeer	*Rangifer tarandus*	3
Dorcas gazelle	*Gazella dorcas*	1
Barbary sheep	*Ammotragus lervia*	1
Rocky Mountain sheep	*Ovis canadensis*	1

BIRDS

Common name	Scientific name	Number
Mute swan	*Cygnus olor*	6
Whooper swan	*Olor cygnus*	3
Wood duck	*Aix sponsa*	2
American pintail	*Anas acuta*	9
Mandarin duck	*Dendronessa galericulata*	22
Golden pheasant	*Chrysolophus pictus*	4
Jungle fowl	*Gallus gallus*	7
Wild turkey	*Meleagris gallopava*	2
Quaker parakeet	*Myopsittacus monachus*	8
Burrowing owl	*Spectyto cunicularis hypugaea*	1
Kookaburra	*Dacelo gigas*	5

REPTILES

Common name	Scientific name	Number
Snapping turtle	*Chelydra serpentina*	11
Box turtle	*Terrapene carolina*	24
Painted turtle	*Chrysemys picta*	8
Yellow-bellied turtle	*Pseudemys scripta* sp	47
Red-lined turtle	*Pseudemys scripta callirostris*	55
Red-bellied turtle	*Pseudemys rubriventris*	12
Red-lined turtle	*Pseudemys elegans*	16
Eastern water snake	*Natrix sipedon*	14
Florida green water snake	*Natrix cyclopion floridana*	29
Island water snake	*Natrix insularum*	45
Garter snake	*Thamnophis sirtalis*	11
Ribbon snake	*Thamnophis sauritus*	4
Black racer	*Coluber constrictor*	4
Pilot black snake	*Elaphe obsoleta*	13
Taiwan cobra	*Naja naja atra*	7
Northern copperhead	*Ancistrodon contortrix*	12

FISHES

Common name	Scientific name	Number
African mouthbreeder	*Pelmatochromis guentheri*	15

The importance of a zoological collection rests, to a large extent, upon the diversity and scope of its representation throughout the whole of the animal kingdom. The National Zoological Park has enjoyed some measure of success in efforts to add representative species belonging to little-known or absent families.

The total number of accessions for the year was 1,371. This includes gifts, purchases, exchanges, deposits, births, and hatchings. Several minor species, which are best displayed in large numbers, do not have an individual count, merely being listed as "many."

STATUS OF THE COLLECTION

Class	Order	Family	Species or subspecies	Individuals
Mammals	15	51	244	627+
Birds	22	77	419	1,196+
Reptiles	4	23	161	414+
Amphibians	2	11	25	108+
Fish	4	8	21	86+
Arthropods	3	3	3	Many
Mollusks	1	1	1	Many
Total	51	174	874	2,431+

ANIMALS IN THE COLLECTION ON JUNE 30, 1961

MAMMALS

MONOTREMATA

Family and common name	*Scientific name*	*Number*
Tachyglossidae:		
Echidna, or spiny anteater	*Tachyglossus aculeatus*	1

MARSUPIALIA

Didelphidae:		
Opossum	*Didelphis marsupialis*	5
Dasyuridae:		
Tasmanian devil	*Sarcophilus harrisii*	1
Phalangeridae:		
Sugar glider	*Petaurus breviceps*	4
Squirrel glider	*Petaurus norfolcensis*	7
Phascolomidae:		
Hairy-nosed wombat	*Lasiorhinus latifrons*	2
Mainland wombat	*Wombatus hirsutus*	1
Macropodidae:		
Red kangaroo	*Macropus rufus*	1
Tree kangaroo	*Dendrolagus matschici*	3
Rat kangaroo	*Potorous* sp.	7

INSECTIVORA

Erinaceidae:		
European hedgehog	*Erinaceus europaeus*	2

CHIROPTERA

Family and common name	Scientific name	Number
Vespertilioninae:		
Little brown bat	*Myotis lucifugus*	1

PRIMATES

Family and common name	Scientific name	Number
Lemuridae:		
Ring-tailed lemur	*Lemur catta*	3
Lorisidae:		
Great galago	*Galago crassicaudatus*	2
Senegal galago	*Galago senegalensis*	2
Dwarf galago	*Galago senegalensis zanzibarisus*	2
Slow loris	*Nycticebus coucang*	1
Common potto	*Perodicticus potto*	2
Cebidae:		
Night monkey	*Aotus trivirgatus*	3
Brown capuchin monkey White-throated capuchin Capuchin	*Cebus capucinus*	10
Squirrel monkey	*Saimiri sciureus*	7
Black spider monkey	*Ateles fusciceps*	5
Spider monkey	*Ateles geoffroyi*	5
Woolly monkey	*Lagothrix* sp.	1
Callithricidae:		
Cottontop marmoset	*Saguinus oedipus*	1
Black-and-red tamarin	*Saguinus nigricollis*	1
Cercopithecidae:		
Toque, or bonnet monkey	*Macaca sinica*	3
Javan macaque	*Macaca irus mordax*	2
Crab-eating macaque	*Macaca irus*	1
Philippine macaque	*Macaca philippinensis*	2
Macaque hybrid	*Macaca philippinensis* X *Macaca irus*	2
Rhesus monkey	*Macaca mulatta*	4
Formosan monkey	*Macaca cyclopis*	2
Red-faced macaque	*Macaca speciosa*	1
Barbary ape	*Macaca sylvanus*	13
Moor macaque	*Macaca maurus*	1
Gray-cheeked mangabey	*Cercocebus albigena*	1
Agile mangabey	*Cercocebus galeritus agilis*	1
Golden-bellied mangabey	*Cercocebus galeritus chrysogaster*	1
Red-crowned mangabey	*Cercocebus torquatus*	2
Sooty mangabey	*Cercocebus fuliginosus*	5
Crested mangabey	*Cercocebus aterrimus opdenboschii*	2
Blacked-crested mangabey	*Cercocebus aterrimus*	3
Chacma baboon	*Papio comatus*	1
Mandrill	*Mandrillus sphinx*	1
Gelada baboon	*Theropithecus gelada*	1
Vervet guenon	*Cercopithecus aethiops pygerythrus*	1
Green guenon	*Cercopithecus aethiops sabaeus*	2

Family and common name	Scientific name	Number
Cercopithecidae—Continued		
Guenon, hybrid	*Cercopithecus aethiops* X *C. A. pygerythrus*	2
Moustached monkey	*Cercopithecus cephus*	3
Diana monkey	*Cercopithecus diana*	1
Roloway monkey	*Cercopithecus diana roloway*	1
Preuss's guenon	*Cercopithecus l'hoesti preussi*	1
DeBrazza's guenon	*Cercopithecus neglectus*	3
White-nosed guenon	*Cercopithecus nictitans*	1
Lesser white-nosed guenon	*Cercopithecus nictitans petaurista*	1
Allen's monkey	*Allenopithecus nigroviridis*	2
Spectacled, or Phayre's langur	*Presbytis phayrei*	1
Entellus, or Hanuman monkey	*Presbytis entellus*	2
Langur	*Presbytis* sp.	1
Pongidae:		
White-handed gibbon	*Hylobates lar*	5
Wau-wau gibbon	*Hylobates moloch*	1
Gibbon, hybrid	*Hylobates agilis* X *H. lar pileatus*	1
Gibbon, hybrid	*Hylobates lar* X *H.* sp	2
Sumatran orangutan	*Pongo pygmaeus*	2
Bornean orangutan	*Pongo pygmaeus abelii*	1
Chimpanzee	*Pan satyrus*	4
Gorilla	*Gorilla gorilla*	2

EDENTATA

Family and common name	Scientific name	Number
Myrmecophagidae:		
Giant anteater	*Myrmecophaga tridactyla*	1
Bradypodidae:		
Three-toed sloth	*Bradypus tridactylus*	1
Two-toed sloth	*Choloepus didactylus*	6
Dasypodidae:		
Nine-banded armadillo	*Dasypus novemcinctus*	1

LAGOMORPHA

Family and common name	Scientific name	Number
Leporidae:		
Domestic rabbit	*Oryctolagus cuniculus*	7

RODENTIA

Family and common name	Scientific name	Number
Aplodontidae:		
Mountain beaver	*Aplodontia rufa*	1
Sciuridae:		
Gray squirrel (black)	*Sciurus carolinensis*, melanistic phase	2
Gray squirrel (albino)	*Sciurus carolinensis*	3
Fox squirrel	*Sciurus niger*	1
Chickaree	*Tamiasciurus douglasii*	1
Giant Indian squirrel	*Ratufa indica*	2
Asiatic squirrel	*Callosciurus nigrovittatus*	1
Formosan tree squirrel	*Callosciurus erythraeus*	3
Asiatic forest squirrel	*Callosciurus caniceps*	3
Striped ground squirrel	*Lariscus insignis*	1
Long-nosed squirrel	*Dremomys rufigenis*	1
Woodchuck, or groundhog	*Marmota monax*	2

Family and common name	Scientific name	Number
Sciuridae—Continued		
Prairie dog	Cynomys ludovicianus	6
Round-tailed ground squirrel	Citellus tereticaudus	1
California ground squirrel	Citellus beecheyi	1
Washington ground squirrel	Citellus washingtoni	5
Golden-mantled ground squirrel	Citellus lateralis	4
Eastern chipmunk	Tamias striatus	2
Eastern chipmunk (albino)	Tamias striatus	1
Yellow-pine chipmunk	Eutamias amoenus	7
Indian palm squirrel	Funambulus palmarum	1
Formosan flying squirrel	Petaurista grandis	1
Eastern flying squirrel	Glaucomys volans	6
Castoridae:		
Beaver	Castor canadensis	8
Cricetidae:		
Golden hamster	Mesocricetus auratus	1
White-footed mouse	Peromyscus sp.	11
Pine vole	Pitymys pinetorum	2
Gerbil	Gerbillus pyramidum	2
Fat-tailed gerbil	Pachyuromys duprasi	Many
Hairy-tailed jird	Sekeetamys calurus	1
Jird	Meriones sp.	8
Muridae:		
Egyptian spiny mouse	Acomys cahirinus	10
Egyptian spiny mouse	Acomys dimidiatus	Many
Multimammate mouse	Mastomys sp.	2
Crested rat	Lophiomys sp.	4
Slender-tailed cloud rat	Phloeomys cumingii	1
Gliridae:		
African dormouse	Graphiurus murinus	1
Hystricidae:		
Malay porcupine	Acanthion brachyura	1
African porcupine	Hystrix galeata	7
Caviidae:		
Patagonian cavy	Dolichotis patagona	6
Dasyproctidae:		
Red agouti	Dasyprocta sp.	3
Chinchillidae:		
Peruvian viscaccia	Lagidium viscaccia	1

CARNIVORA

Family and common name	Scientific name	Number
Canidae:		
Dingo	Canis antarcticus	3
Coyote	Canis latrans	1
Common jackal	Canis aureus	3
Timber wolf	Canis lupus nubilus	2
Texas red wolf	Canis niger rufus	2
Arctic fox	Alopex lagopus	2
Red fox	Vulpes fulva	1
Kit fox	Vulpes macrotis	2
Fennec	Fennecus zerda	2
Big-eared fox	Otocyon megalotis	1
Raccoon dog	Nyctereutes procyonoides	3

Family and common name	Scientific name	Number
Canidae—Continued		
Cape hunting dog	*Lycaon pictus*	2
Ursidae:		
Spectacled bear	*Tremarctos ornatus*	1
Himalayan bear	*Selenarctos thibetanus thibetanus*	2
Japanese black bear	*Selenarctos thibetanus japonicus*	1
Korean bear	*Selenarctos thibetanus ussuricus*	2
Black bear	*Euarctos americanus*	2
European brown bear	*Ursus arctos*	3
Iranian brown bear	*Ursus arctos occidentalis*	2
Alaskan Peninsula bear	*Ursus gyas*	2
Grizzly bear	*Ursus horribilis*	2
Sitka brown bear	*Ursus sitkensis*	1
Polar bear	*Thalarctos maritimus*	2
Hybrid bear	*Thalarctos maritimus* X *Ursus middendorffi*	4
Malay sun bear	*Helarctos malayanus*	2
Sloth bear	*Melursus ursinus*	2
Procyonidae:		
Raccoon	*Procyon lotor*	10
Raccoon (black phase)	*Procyon lotor*	1
Raccoon (albino)	*Procyon lotor*	1
Coatimundi	*Nasua narica*	4
Cacomistle, or ring-tailed cat	*Bassariscus astutus*	5
Kinkajou	*Potos flavus*	4
Olingo	*Bassaricyon gabbi*	2
Lesser panda	*Ailurus fulgens*	3
Mustelidae:		
Ferret	*Mustela eversmanni*	1
Marten	*Martes americana*	1
Fisher	*Martes pennanti*	1
Tayra	*Eira barbara*	1
Grison	*Galictis vittata*	1
Zorilla, or striped weasel	*Ictonyx capensis*	2
Wolverine	*Gulo luscus*	1
American badger	*Taxidea taxus*	1
Golden-bellied ferret-badger	*Helictis moschata subaurantiaca*	3
Common skunk	*Mephitis mephitis*	3
California spotted skunk	*Spilogale putorius phenax*	1
South American flat-tailed otter	*Pteronura brasiliensis*	1
Viverridae:		
Genet	*Genetta genetta neumanii*	8
Genet (black phase)	*Genetta genetta neumanii*	1
Formosan spotted civet	*Viverricula indica*	2
Ground civet	*Viverra tangalunga*	1
Linsang	*Prionodon linsang*	1
African palm civet	*Nandinia binotata*	2
Formosan masked civet	*Paguma larvata taivana*	1
Binturong	*Arctictis binturong*	1

Family and common name	*Scientific name*	*Number*
Viverridae—Continued		
African gray mongoose	*Herpestes ichneumon*	1
Black-footed mongoose	*Bdeogale* sp.	2
African water civet	*Atilax paludinosus*	5
Striped African mongoose	*Crossarchus fasciatus*	2
White-tailed civet	*Ichneumia albicauda*	1
Cryptoproctidae:		
Fossa	*Cryptoprocta ferox*	1
Hyaenidae:		
Striped hyena	*Hyaena hyaena*	2
Felidae:		
Jungle cat	*Felis chaus*	2
Pallas's cat	*Felis manul*	2
Serval cat	*Felis serval*	4
Ocelot	*Felis pardalis*	2
Margay cat	*Felis wiedii tigrina*	4
Puma	*Felis concolor*	3
Lynx	*Lynx canadensis*	1
Bobcat	*Lynx rufus*	2
Leopard	*Panthera pardus*	5
Black leopard	*Panthera pardus*	2
Lion	*Panthera leo*	3
Bengal tiger	*Panthera tigris*	3
Bengal tiger (white phase)	*Panthera tigris*	1
Jaguar	*Panthera onca*	2
Clouded leopard	*Neofelis nebulosa*	1
Snow leopard	*Panthera uncia*	3
Cheetah	*Acinonyx jubata*	2

PINNIPEDIA

Otariidae:		
California sea-lion	*Zalophus californianus*	6
Patagonian sea-lion	*Otaria flavescens*	1
Phocidae:		
Harbor seal	*Phoca vitulina*	3

TUBULIDENTATA

Orycteropodidae:		
Aardvark, or antbear	*Orycteropus afer*	1

PROBOSCIDEA

Elephantidae:		
African elephant	*Loxodonta africana*	1
Forest elephant	*Loxodonta cyclotis*	1
Indian elephant	*Elephas maximus*	2

HYRACOIDEA

Procaviidae:		
Hyrax	*Procavia syriaca*	1

PERISSODACTYLA

Equidae:		
Mongolian wild horse	*Equus przewalskii*	1
Burro, or donkey	*Equus asinus*	1
Grant's zebra	*Equus burchelli boehmi*	3

Family and common name	Scientific name	Number
Equidae—Continued		
Grevy's zebra	Equus grevyi	2
Tapiridae:		
Brazilian tapir	Tapirus terrestris	1
Rhinocerotidae:		
Great one-horned Indian rhinoceros	Rhinoceros unicornis	1
White, or square-lipped rhinoceros	Ceratotherium simum	2
African black rhinoceros	Diceros bicornis	1

ARTIODACTYLA

Family and common name	Scientific name	Number
Tayassuidae:		
Collared peccary	Pecari tajacu	3
Hippopotamidae:		
Hippopotamus	Hippopotamus amphibius	2
Pygmy hippopotamus	Choeropsis liberiensis	4
Camelidae:		
Llama	Lama glama	6
Guanaco	Lama glama guanicoe	3
Alpaca	Lama pacos	4
Bactrian camel	Camelus bactrianus	2
Cervidae:		
White fallow deer	Dama dama	6
Axis deer	Axis axis	5
Red deer	Cervus elaphus	8
American elk	Cervus canadensis	2
Sika deer	Cervus nippon	10
Père David's deer	Elaphurus davidianus	1
Virginia deer	Odocoileus virginianus	9
Reindeer	Rangifer tarandus	13
Forest caribou	Rangifer caribou	1
Giraffidae:		
Nubian giraffe	Giraffa camelopardalis	1
Antilocapridae:		
Pronghorn	Antilocapra americana	1
Bovidae:		
Sitatunga	Tragelaphus spekii	1
Brindled gnu	Connochaetes taurinus	3
Anoa	Anoa depressicornis	2
Zebu	Bos indicus	1
Yak	Poephagus grunniens	3
Gaur	Bibos gaurus	3
African buffalo	Syncerus caffer	4
American bison	Bison bison	2
Wisent, or European bison	Bison bonasus	2
Dorcas gazelle	Gazella dorcas	3
Rocky mountain goat	Oreamnos americanus	8
Tahr	Hermitragus jemlahicus	1
Ibex	Capra ibex	1
Blue sheep	Pseudois nayaur	1
Aoudad	Ammotragus lervia	4
Big-horn sheep	Ovis canadensis	5
Dall sheep	Ovis dalli dalli	2

BIRDS

SPHENISCIFORMES

Family and common name	*Scientific name*	*Number*
Spheniscidae:		
King penguin	*Aptenodytes patagonica*	4
Adélie penguin	*Pygoscelis adeliae*	2

STRUTHIONIFORMES

Struthionidae:		
Ostrich	*Struthio camelus*	1

RHEIFORMES

Rheidae:		
Rhea	*Rhea americana*	1

CASUARIIFORMES

Casuariidae:		
Cassowary	*Casuarius* sp.	2
Dromiceidae:		
Emu	*Dromiceius novaehollandiae*	5

TINAMIFORMES

Tinamidae:		
Pileated tinamou	*Crypturus soui panamensis*	1

PROCELLARIIFORMES

Diomedeidae:		
Black-footed albatross	*Diomedea nigripes*	2

PELECANIFORMES

Pelecanidae:		
Rose-colored pelican	*Pelecanus onocrotalus*	2
White pelican	*Pelecanus erythrorhynchos*	3
Brown pelican	*Pelecanus occidentalis*	1
Dalmatian pelican	*Pelecanus crispus*	4
Phalacrocoracidae:		
Double-crested cormorant	*Phalacrocorax auritus auritus*	4
Farallon cormorant	*Phalacrocorax auritus albociliatus*	1
European cormorant	*Phalacrocorax carbo*	6
Anhingidae:		
Anhinga, or snakebird	*Anhinga anhinga*	1
Indian darter	*Anhinga melanogaster*	2

CICONIIFORMES

Ardeidae:		
Reddish egret	*Dichromanassa rufescens*	3
Reddish egret (white phase)	*Dichromanassa rufescens*	1
Cattle egret	*Bubulcus ibis*	3
American egret	*Casmerodius albus*	1

Family and common name	*Scientific name*	*Number*
Ardeidae—Continued		
Snowy egret	*Leucophoyx thula*	2
Great white heron	*Ardea occidentalis*	2
Eastern green heron	*Butoribes virescens*	3
Louisiana heron	*Hydranassa tricolor*	3
Black-crowned night heron	*Nycticorax nycticorax*	12
Little blue heron	*Florida caerulea*	1
Least bittern	*Ixobrychus exilis*	1
Tiger bittern	*Tigrisoma lineatum*	2
Cochleariidae:		
Boat-billed heron	*Cochlearius cochlearius*	1
Balaenicipitidae:		
Shoebill	*Balaeniceps rex*	1
Ciconiidae:		
American wood ibis	*Mycteria americana*	3
European white stork	*Ciconia ciconia*	4
Indian adjutant stork	*Leptoptilos dubius*	1
White-bellied stork	*Abdimia sphenorhyncha*	2
Threskiornithidae:		
White ibis	*Eudocimus albus*	2
Scarlet ibis	*Eudocimus ruber*	4
Black-faced ibis	*Theristicus melanopis*	1
Blackheaded ibis	*Threskiornis melanocephala*	1
White-faced glossy ibis	*Plegadis mexicana*	2
Eastern glossy ibis	*Plegadis falcinellus*	5
Roseate spoonbill	*Ajaia ajaja*	6
Phoenicopteridae:		
Chilean flamingo	*Phoenicopterus chilensis*	2
Cuban flamingo	*Phoenicopterus ruber*	1
Old World flamingo	*Phoenicopterus antiquorum*	1
Lesser flamingo	*Phoeniconais minor*	2

ANSERIFORMES

Anhimidae:		
Crested screamer	*Chauna torquata*	4
Anatidae:		
Coscoroba swan	*Coscoroba coscoroba*	4
Mute swan	*Cygnus olor*	6
Black-necked swan	*Cygnus melancoriphus*	2
Whooper swan	*Olor cygnus*	4
Whistling swan	*Olor columbianus*	11
Trumpeter swan	*Olor buccinator*	2
Black swan	*Chenopis atrata*	2
Egyptian goose	*Alopochen aegyptiacus*	1
White-fronted goose	*Anser albifrons*	3
Indian bar-headed goose	*Eulabeia indica*	5
Emperor goose	*Philacte canagica*	2
Blue goose	*Chen caerulescens*	6
Lesser snow goose	*Chen hyperborea hyperborea*	2
Greater snow goose	*Chen hyperborea atlantica*	5
Ross's goose	*Chen rossii*	4
Red-breasted goose	*Branta ruficollis*	4

Family and common name	Scientific name	Number
Anatidae—Continued		
Canada goose		
Lesser Canada goose		
Cackling goose	*Branta canadensis*	30
White-cheeked goose		
Canada goose X blue goose, hybrid	*Branta canadensis X Chen caerulescens*	2
Wood duck	*Aix sponsa*	Many
Wood duck X red-headed duck, hybrid	*Aix sponsa X Aythya americana*	1
Pintail duck	*Anas acuta*	10
Chestnut-breasted teal	*Anas castanea*	1
Gadwall	*Anas strepera*	5
European wigeon	*Anas penelope*	5
Mallard duck	*Anas platyrhynchos*	25
Mallard duck, albino	*Anas platyrhynchos*	1
Mallard duck X American pintail duck, hybrid.	*Anas platyrhynchos X Anas acuta*	1
Indian spotted-billed duck	*Anas poecilorhyncha*	1
Black duck	*Anas rubripes*	9
Greater scaup duck	*Aythya marila*	7
Lesser scaup duck	*Aythya affinis*	5
Red-headed duck	*Aythya americana*	9
Ring-necked duck	*Aythya collaris*	3
Canvasback duck	*Aythya valisineria*	7
Bufflehead duck	*Bucephala albeola*	1
American goldeneye	*Bucephala clangula americana*	1
Black-bellied tree duck	*Dendrocygna autumnalis*	2
Fulvous tree duck	*Dendrocygna bicolor*	1
Mandarin duck	*Dendronessa galericulata*	18
Baldpate	*Mareca americana*	10
Rosy-billed pochard	*Metopiana peposaca*	1
Red-crested pochard	*Netta rufina*	1
Cotton teal	*Nettapus coromandelianus*	4
Comb duck	*Sarkidiornis melanota*	1
South African sheldrake	*Casarca cana*	1
Ruddy shelduck	*Casarca ferruginea*	2
European shelduck	*Tadorna tadorna*	1

FALCONIFORMES

Family and common name	Scientific name	Number
Cathartidae:		
Andean condor	*Vultur gryphus*	1
King vulture	*Sarcoramphus papa*	1
Black vulture	*Coragyps atratus*	6
Hooded vulture	*Necrosyrtes monachus*	1
Ruppell's vulture	*Gyps rueppellii*	3
Turkey vulture	*Cathartes aura*	9
Sagittariidae:		
Secretarybird	*Sagittarius serpentarius*	2
Accipitridae:		
African yellow-billed kite	*Milvus migrans*	2
Brahminy kite	*Haliastur indus*	1
Black-faced hawk	*Leucopternis melanops*	1
Red-winged hawk	*Heterospizias meridionalis*	1

Family and common name	Scientific name	Number
Accipitridae—Continued		
Red-tailed hawk	*Buteo jamaicensis*	3
Red-shouldered hawk	*Buteo lineatus*	1
Swainson's hawk	*Buteo swainsoni*	1
Mauduyt's hawk-eagle	*Spizaetus ornatus*	1
Great black hawk	*Ictinaetus malayensis*	1
Golden eagle	*Aquila chrysaetos*	3
Imperial eagle	*Aquila heliaca*	2
White-breasted sea eagle	*Haliaetus leucogaster*	1
Pallas's eagle	*Haliaetus leucoryphus*	1
Bald eagle	*Haliaetus leucocephalus*	5
Buzzard eagle	*Buteo poecilochrous*	1
Harpy eagle	*Harpia harpyja*	2
Guianan crested eagle	*Morphnus guianensis*	1
Monkey-eating eagle	*Pithecophaga jefferyi*	1
Bateleur eagle	*Terathopius ecaudatus*	2
Bearded vulture	*Gypaetus barbatus*	1
Falconidae:		
Sparrow hawk	*Falco sparverius*	5
Duck hawk	*Falco peregrinus anatum*	1
Red-footed falcon, or crane hawk	*Falco vespertinus*	1
Forest falcon	*Micrastur semitorquatus*	2
Chimango	*Milvago chimango*	2
Chimachima hawk	*Milvago chimachima*	1
Audubon's caracara	*Polyborus cheriway*	3
White-throated caracara	*Phalcoboenus albogularis*	3

GALLIFORMES

Family and common name	Scientific name	Number
Megapodiidae:		
Brush turkey	*Alectura lathami*	1
Cracidae:		
Blue-cered curassow	*Crax alberti*	1
Wattled curassow	*Crax globulosa*	2
Panama curassow	*Crax panamensis*	1
Nocturnal curassow	*Nothocrax urumutum*	1
White-headed piping guan	*Pipile cumanensis*	1
Phasianidae:		
Erckel's francolin	*Francolinus erckeli*	1
Hildebrandt's francolin	*Francolinus hildebrandti*	2
Bob-white	*Colinus virginianus*	1
Chukar quail	*Alectoris graeca*	4
Gambel's quail	*Lophortyx gambeli*	2
Valley quail	*Lophortyx vallicola*	6
Argus pheasant	*Argusianus argus*	1
Golden pheasant	*Chrysolophus pictus*	7
Onogadori chicken	*Gallus gallus*	2
Red junglefowl	*Gallus gallus*	6
Nepal pheasant	*Gennaeus leucomelanus*	2
Black-backed kaleege pheasant	*Gennaeus melanonotus*	2
Silver pheasant	*Gennaeus nycthemerus*	1
Peafowl	*Pavo cristatus*	5
Ring-necked pheasant	*Phasianus colchicus*	4
Ring-necked pheasant, albino	*Phasianus colchicus*	2

Family and common name	*Scientific name*	*Number*

Phasianidae—Continued

Ring-necked pheasant X green pheasant, hybrid	*Phasianus colchicus* X *P. versicolor* ___	1
Bhutan, or gray peacock pheasant____	*Polyplectron bicalcaratum*_______	2
Reeves's pheasant_________________	*Syrmaticus reevesi___________*	2

Numididae:

| Vulturine guineafowl_______________ | *Acryllium vulturinum___________* | 3 |

Meleagrididae:

| Ocellated turkey___________________ | *Agriocharis ocellata___________* | 2 |
| Wild turkey_______________________ | *Meleagris gallopavo___________* | 5 |

GRUIFORMES

Gruidae:

Siberian crane____________________	*Grus leucogeranus___________*	1
Demoiselle crane__________________	*Anthropoides virgo___________*	1
Sarus crane______________________	*Antigone antigone___________*	2
African crowned crane_____________	*Balearica pavonina___________*	6

Psophiidae:

| Trumpeter________________________ | *Psophia crepitans___________* | 2 |

Rallidae:

Cayenne wood rail________________	*Aramides cajanea___________*	2
Virginia rail______________________	*Rallus limicola___________*	1
King rail_________________________	*Rallus elegans___________*	1
Purple gallinule___________________	*Ionornis martinica___________*	2
South Pacific swamp-hen___________	*Porphyrio poliocephalus_________*	1
American coot____________________	*Fulica americana___________*	1

Eurypygidae:

| Sun bittern_______________________ | *Eurypyga helias___________* | 1 |

Cariamidae:

| Cariama, or seriama_______________ | *Cariama cristata___________* | 1 |

Otididae:

| Senegal bustard___________________ | *Eupodotis senegalensis_________* | 2 |

CHARADRIIFORMES

Jacanidae:

| Common jacana___________________ | *Jacana spinosa___________* | 2 |

Haematopodidae:

| Oystercatcher_____________________ | *Haematopus ostralegus_________* | 2 |

Charadriidae:

Golden plover____________________	*Charadrius apricarius_________*	2
Australian banded plover__________	*Zonifer tricolor___________*	3
European lapwing_________________	*Vanellus vanellus___________*	4
South American lapwing___________	*Belonopterus cayennensis_______*	4
Crocodile bird____________________	*Pluvialis aegyptius___________*	7

Scolopacidae:

| Pectoral sandpiper_______________ | *Erolia melanotos___________* | 1 |

Recurvirostridae:

| Black-necked stilt_________________ | *Himantopus mexicanus_________* | 1 |

Burhinidae:

| South American thick-knee_________ | *Burhinus bistriatus___________* | 1 |

Stercorariidae:

| MacCormick's skua_______________ | *Catharacta maccormicki_________* | 2 |

Family and common name	Scientific name	Number
Laridae:		
Ring-billed gull	Larus delawarensis	3
Kelp gull	Larus dominicanus	3
Laughing gull	Larus atricilla	1
Herring gull	Larus argentatus	3
Western, or California gull	Larus argentatus californicus	2
Great black-backed gull	Larus marinus	2
Silver gull	Larus novaehollandiae	8
Franklin's gull	Larus pipixcan	2
Noddy tern	Anous stolidus	2
Common tern	Sterna hirunde hirunde	4

COLUMBIFORMES

Family and common name	Scientific name	Number
Columbidae:		
Band-tailed pigeon	Columba fasciata	2
High-flying Budapest pigeon	Columba livia	9
Black-billed pigeon	Columbia nigrirostris	1
Triangular spotted pigeon	Columba guinea	2
Crowned pigeon	Goura victoria	1
Blue ground dove	Claravis pretiosa	5
Ruddy ground dove	Chaemepelia rufipennis	7
Indian emerald-winged tree dove	Chalcophaps indica	10
Bleeding-heart dove	Gallicolumba luzonica	2
Diamond dove	Geopelia cuneata	1
Plain-breasted ground dove	Columbigallina minuta	12
Ground dove	Columbigallina passerina	5
Ring-necked dove	Streptopelia decaocto	7
Blue-headed ring dove	Streptopelia tranquebarica	2
White-winged dove	Zenaida asiatica	1
Mourning dove	Zenaidura macroura	3

PSITTACIFORMES

Family and common name	Scientific name	Number
Psittacidae:		
Kea parrot	Nestor notabilis	2
Red lory	Domicella garrula	2
Banksian cockatoo	Calyptorhynchus magnificus	1
White cockatoo	Kakatoe alba	2
Solomon Islands cockatoo	Kakatoe ducrops	1
Sulphur-crested cockatoo	Kakatoe galerita	4
Bare-eyed cockatoo	Kakatoe sanguinea	5
Great red-crested cockatoo	Kakatoe moluccensis	1
Leadbeater's cockatoo	Kakatoe leadbeateri	7
Cockatiel	Nymphicus hollandicus	7
Yellow-and-blue macaw	Ara ararauna	3
Red-and-blue macaw	Ara chloroptera	3
Red-blue-and-yellow macaw	Ara macao	2
Illiger's macaw	Ara maracana	2
Brown-throated conure	Conurus aeruginosus	2
Petz's parakeet	Aratinga canicularis	1
Rusty-cheeked parrot	Aratinga pertinax	2
Tovi parakeet	Brotogeris jugularis	1
Yellow-naped parrot	Amazona auropalliata	5

Family and common name	*Scientific name*	*Number*
Psittacidae—Continued		
Finsch's parrot	*Amazona finschi*	1
Blue-fronted parrot	*Amazona aestiva*	1
Red-fronted parrot	*Amazona bodini*	1
Double yellow-headed parrot	*Amazona oratrix*	3
Black-headed, or Nanday parrot	*Nandayus nanday*	9
Lineolated parakeet	*Bolborhynchus lineolatus*	7
White-winged parakeet	*Brotogeris versicolurus*	1
Malabar, or blue-winged parrot	*Psittacula columboides*	4
Blossom-headed parakeet	*Psittacula cyanocephala*	10
Greater ring-necked parakeet	*Psittacula eupatria*	3
Rose-breasted parakeet	*Psittacula alexandri*	1
Moustached parakeet	*Psittacula fasciata*	1
Lesser ring-necked parakeet	*Psittacula krameri*	6
Barraband's parakeet	*Polytelis swainsoni*	1
Quaker parakeet	*Myopsittacus monachus*	17
Budgerigar, or grass parakeet	*Melopsittacus undulatus*	4
Rosy-faced lovebird	*Agapornis roseicollis*	2
Masked lovebird	*Agapornis personata*	1
Black-headed caique, or seven-color parrot	*Pionites melanocephala*	2
Yellow-thighed caique	*Pionites leucogaster xanthomeria*	1

CUCULIFORMES

Musophagidae:		
Purple-headed turaco	*Gallirex porphyreolophus*	1
South African turaco	*Tauraco corythaix*	2
White-bellied go-away bird	*Corythaixoides leucogaster*	1
Plantain-eater	*Crinifer africanus*	1
Cuculidae:		
Koel	*Eudynamys scolopacea*	1
Roadrunner	*Geococcyx californianus*	2
Coucal, or crow-pheasant	*Centropus sinensis*	3

STRIGIFORMES

Tytonidae:		
Barn owl	*Tyto alba*	1
Strigidae:		
Great horned owl	*Bubo virginianus*	6
Screech owl	*Otus asio*	3
Spectacled owl	*Pulsatrix perspicillata*	1
Malay fishing owl	*Ketupa ketupu*	2
Snowy owl	*Nyctea nyctea*	4
Barred owl	*Strix varia*	16
Burrowing owl	*Speotyto cunicularia hypugaea*	3
Nepal brown wood owl	*Strix newarensis*	1
Short-eared owl	*Asio flammeus*	1
Saw-whet owl	*Aegolius acadicus*	2

COLIIFORMES

Coliidae:		
Mousebird	*Colius striatus*	1

TROGONIFORMES

Family and common name	Scientific name	Number
Trogonidae:		
Cuban trogan	*Priotelus temnurus*	2

CORACIIFORMES

Alcedinidae:		
Kookaburra	*Dacelo gigas*	8
Coraciidae:		
Lilac-breasted roller	*Coracias caudata*	2
Indian roller	*Coracias benghalensis*	2
Bucerotidae:		
Pied hornbill	*Anthrococeros malabaricus*	1
Concave-casqued hornbill	*Buceros bicornis*	1
Abyssinian ground hornbill	*Bucorvus abyssinicus*	1
Gray hornbill	*Tockus birostris*	2
Great black casqued hornbill	*Ceratogymna atrata*	1
Malayan hornbill	*Aceros undulatus*	1
Crowned hornbill	*Tockus alboterminatus*	1
Yellow-billed hornbill	*Tockus flavirostris*	1

PICIFORMES

Capitonidae:		
Asiatic great barbet	*Megalaima virens*	1
Crimson-breasted or coppersmith barbet	*Megalaima haemacephala*	1
Toucan barbet	*Semnornis ramphastinus*	1
Ramphastidae:		
White-lined toucanet	*Aulacorhynchus albivittatus*	2
Sulphur-breasted toucan	*Ramphastos carinatus*	1
White-and-sulphur-breasted toucan	*Rhamphastos vitellinus*	1
Ariel toucan	*Ramphastos ariel*	1
Cuvier's toucan	*Ramphastos cuvieri*	1
Picidae:		
Golden-backed woodpecker	*Brachypternus benghalensis*	2
Scaly-bellied woodpecker	*Picus squamatus*	1

PASSERIFORMES

Tyrannidae:		
Eastern kingbird	*Tyrannus tyrannus*	1
Pittidae:		
Indian pitta	*Pitta brachyura*	1
Alaudidae:		
Horned lark	*Eremophila alpestris*	2
Corvidae:		
Magpie	*Pica pica*	5
Yellow-billed magpie	*Pica nuttalli*	1
Asiatic tree pie	*Crypsirina formosae*	2
Magpie jay	*Calocitta formosa*	1
Blue jay	*Cyanocitta cristata*	3
Steller's jay	*Cyanocitta stelleri*	4
European jay	*Garrulus glandarius*	2
African white-necked crow	*Corvus albus*	2
American crow	*Corvus brachyrhynchos*	3
Raven	*Corvus corax*	2

Family and common name	Scientific name	Number
Corvidae—Continued		
Indian crow	*Corvus splendens*	1
Formosan red-billed pie	*Cissa caerulea*	6
Occipital blue pie	*Cissa occipitalis*	1
Hunting crow	*Cissa chinensis*	3
Inca jay	*Xanthoura yncas*	1
Cracticidae:		
White-backed piping crow	*Gymnorhina hypoleuca*	1
Paridae:		
Red-headed tit	*Aegithaliscus concinnus*	1
Great tit	*Parus major*	1
Gray tit	*Parus major*	3
Tufted titmouse	*Parus bicolor*	3
Chickadee	*Parus atricapillus*	1
Yellow-cheeked tit	*Parus xanthogenys*	1
Sittidae:		
Chestnut-bellied nuthatch	*Sitta castanea*	1
Timaliidae:		
White-crested laughing thrush	*Garrulax bicolor*	4
Tit-babbler	*Yuhina flavicollis*	1
Black-headed sibia	*Heterophasia capistrata*	2
Silver-eared mesia	*Mesia argentauris*	6
Pekin robin	*Liothrix luteus*	4
White-capped redstart	*Chaimarrhornis leucocephalus*	2
Pycnonotidae:		
Red-eared bulbul	*Pycnonotus jocosus*	1
Black-headed bulbul	*Pycnonotus atriceps*	3
Red-vented bulbul	*Pycnonotus cafer*	5
White-cheeked bulbul	*Pycnonotus leucogenys*	6
White-eared bulbul	*Pycnonotus leucotis*	1
Troglodytidae:		
Carolina wren	*Thryothorus ludovicianus*	1
Mimidae:		
Mockingbird	*Mimus polyglottos*	1
Catbird	*Dumetella carolinensis*	3
Turdidae:		
Robin, albino	*Turdus migratorius*	1
European song thrush	*Turdus ericetorum*	2
Blackbird	*Turdus merula*	2
Cliff chat	*Thamnolaea cinnamoneiventris*	1
Motacillidae:		
White wagtail	*Motacilla alba*	2
Sturnidae:		
Rose-colored pastor	*Pastor roseus*	1
Purple starling	*Lamprocolius purpureus*	3
Burchell's long-tailed starling	*Lamprotornis caudatus*	1
Amethyst starling	*Cinnyricinchus leucogaster*	1
Tricolored starling	*Spreo superbus*	1
Starling	*Sturnus vulgaris*	2
Jungle mynah	*Acridotheres tristis*	1
Lesser hill mynah	*Gracula religiosa indica*	1
Greater Indian hill mynah	*Gracula religiosa intermedia*	2

Family and common name	Scientific name	Number
Nectariniidae:		
Scarlet-chested sunbird	*Chalcomitra rubescens*	1
Eastern double-collared sunbird	*Cinnyris mediocris*	2
Variable sunbird	*Cinnyris venustus*	2
Scarlet-tufted malachite sunbird	*Nectarinia johnstoni*	2
Beautiful sunbird	*Nectarinia pulchella*	1
Tecasse sunbird	*Nectarinia tacazze*	1
Zosteropidae:		
White-eye	*Zosterops palpebrosa*	8
Coerebidae:		
Black-headed sugarbird	*Chlorophanes spiza*	2
Purple sugarbird	*Cyanerpes coerulea*	4
Blue or yellow-winged sugarbird	*Cyanerpes cyaneus*	4
Bananaquit	*Coereba flaveola*	1
Parulidae:		
Ovenbird	*Seiurus aurocapillus*	1
Ploceidae:		
Red-naped widowbird	*Coliuspasser laticauda*	10
Giant whydah	*Diatropura procne*	1
Baya weaver	*Ploceus baya*	3
Vitelline masked weaver	*Ploceus vitellinus*	3
Mahali weaver	*Ploceipasser mahali*	1
Red bishop weaver	*Euplectes orix*	1
Yellow-crowned bishop weaver	*Euplectes afra*	2
White-headed nun	*Lonchura maja*	4
Bengalese finch	*Lonchura* sp.	6
Cut-throat weaver finch	*Amadina fasciata*	1
Lavender finch	*Estrilda coerulescens*	2
Strawberry finch	*Estrilda amandava*	5
Red-eared waxbill	*Estrilda astrild*	1
Common waxbill	*Estrilda troglodytes*	1
Zebra finch	*Poephila castanotis*	13
Gouldian finch	*Poephila gouldiae*	1
Java finch	*Padda oryzivora*	8
Icteridae:		
Yellow-headed marshbird	*Xanthocephalus xanthocephalus*	1
Rice grackle	*Psomocolax oryzivora*	1
Purple grackle	*Quiscalus quiscula*	12
Swainson's grackle	*Holoquiscalus lugubris*	1
Boat-tailed grackle	*Megaquiscalus major*	2
Glossy cowbird	*Molothrus bonariensis*	3
Brown-headed cowbird	*Molothrus ater*	2
Bay cowbird	*Molothrus badius*	2
Colombian red-eyed cowbird	*Tangavius armenti*	1
Red-winged blackbird	*Agelaius phoeniceus*	4
Red-breasted marshbird	*Leistes militaris*	10
Troupial	*Icterus icterus*	2
Crested oropendola	*Xanthornus decumanus*	1
Thraupidae:		
Blue tanager	*Thraupis cana*	1
White-edged tanager	*Thraupis leucoptera*	2
Violet tanager	*Euphonia violacea*	2

Family and common name	Scientific name	Number
Thraupidae—Continued		
Black-and-white tanager	*Cissopis leveriana*	1
Yellow-rumped tanager	*Ramphocelus icteronotus*	1
Passerini's tanager	*Ramphocelus passerinii*	1
Red tanager	*Piranga rubra*	1
Fringillidae:		
Rice grosbeak	*Oryzoborus crassirostris*	1
Evening grosbeak	*Hesperiphona vespertina*	6
Brazilian cardinal	*Paroaria cucullata*	1
Black-throated cardinal	*Paroaria gularis*	7
Black-eared cardinal	*Paroaria gularis nigro*	2
Cardinal	*Richmondena cardinalis*	3
European linnet	*Carduelis cannabina*	6
European goldfinch	*Carduelis carduelis*	3
European goldfinch X canary, hybrid	*Carduelis carduelis X Serinus canarius*	1
Canary	*Serinus canarius*	2
Green finch	*Chloris chloris*	2
Lesser yellow finch	*Sicalis luteola*	2
Saffron finch	*Sicalis flaveola*	6
White-lined finch	*Spermophila lineola*	5
European bullfinch	*Pyrrhula pyrrhula*	2
Melodious grassquit	*Tiaris canora*	1
Chaffinch	*Fringilla coelebs*	1
Slate-colored junco	*Junco hyemalis*	1
Buff-throated saltator	*Saltator maximus*	1
Tawny-bellied seedeater	*Sporophila minuta*	7
Song sparrow	*Melospiza melodia*	1
Dickcissel	*Spiza americana*	5
White-throated sparrow	*Zonotrichia albicollis*	1
White-crowned sparrow	*Zonotrichia leucophrys*	2
Yellowhammer	*Emberiza citrinella*	1
European bunting	*Emberiza calandra*	2
Jacarini finch	*Volatinia jacarini*	3
Tropical seed finch	*Oryzoborus torridus*	3

REPTILES

LORICATA

Family and common name	Scientific name	Number
Alligatoridae:		
Caiman	*Caiman sclerops*	2
Black caiman	*Melanosuchus niger*	8
American alligator	*Alligator mississipiensis*	9
Chinese alligator	*Alligator sinensis*	2
Crocodilidae:		
Broad-nosed crocodile	*Osteolaemus tetraspis*	2
African crocodile	*Crocodylus niloticus*	2
Narrow-nosed crocodile	*Crocodylus cataphractus*	1
Salt-water crocodile	*Crocodylus porosus*	1
American crocodile	*Crocodylus acutus*	2
Gavialidae:		
Indian gavial	*Gavialis gangeticus*	1

CHELONIA

Family and common name	Scientific name	Number
Chelydridae:		
Snapping turtle	*Chelydra serpentina*	Many
Alligator snapping turtle	*Macrochelys temminckii*	1
Kinosternidae:		
Musk turtle	*Sternotherus odoratus*	3
Mud turtle	*Kinosternon subrubrum*	7
South American mud turtle	*Kinosternum cruentatum*	2
Emydidae:		
Box turtle	*Terrapene carolina*	Many
Three-toed box turtle	*Terrapene c. triunguis*	2
Ornate box turtle	*Terrapene ornata*	1
Florida box turtle	*Terrapene bauri*	1
Kura kura box turtle	*Cuora amboinensis*	2
Diamondback turtle	*Malaclemys terrapin*	3
Map turtle	*Graptemys geographica*	2
False map turtle	*Graptemys pseudogeographica*	2
Barbour's map turtle	*Graptemys barbouri*	4
Painted turtle	*Chrysemys picta*	Many
Western painted turtle	*Chrysemys picta belli*	15
Cumberland turtle	*Pseudemys scripta troostii*	23
South American red-lined turtle	*Pseudemys scripta callirostris*	2
Yellow-bellied turtle	*Pseudemys scripta scripta*	15
Red-bellied turtle	*Pseudemys rubriventris*	10
Red-eared turtle	*Pseudemys scripta elegans*	12
Southern water turtle	*Pseudemys floridana*	17
Florida red-bellied turtle	*Pseudemys nelsoni*	2
Central American turtle	*Pseudemys ornata*	2
Cuban water turtle	*Pseudemys decussata*	1
Chicken turtle	*Deirochelys reticularia*	1
Spotted turtle	*Clemmys guttata*	4
Wood turtle	*Clemmys insculpta*	6
Iberian pond turtle	*Clemmys leprosa*	2
European pond turtle	*Emys orbicularis*	3
Blanding's turtle	*Emys blandingii*	2
Reeve's turtle	*Chinemys reevesii*	4
Testudinidae:		
Giant Aldabra tortoise	*Testudo elephantina*	2
Galápagos tortoise	*Testudo vicina*	2
Duncan Island tortoise	*Testudo ephippium*	2
South American tortoise	*Testudo tabulata*	1
Star tortoise	*Testudo elegans*	2
European tortoise	*Testudo graeca*	1
Pelomedusidae:		
African water turtle	*Pelomedusa subrufa*	2
African black mud turtle	*Pelusios nigricans*	1
Amazon spotted turtle	*Podocnemis unifilis*	2
Chelydidae:		
South American side-necked turtle	*Batrachemys nasuta*	2
Australian side-necked turtle	*Chelodina longicollis*	3
Small side-necked turtle	*Hydromedusa tectifera*	2
Large side-necked turtle	*Phrynops hilarii*	8
Krefft's turtle	*Emydura krefftii*	8

Family and common name	Scientific name	Number
Chelydidae—Continued		
Murray turtle	Emydura macquarrii	3
South American gibba turtle	Mesoclemmys gibba	2
Flat-headed turtle	Platemys platycephala	3
Trionychidae:		
Southern soft-shelled turtle	Trionyx ferox	5
African soft-shelled turtle	Trionyx triunguis	2

SAURIA

Family and common name	Scientific name	Number
Gekkonidae:		
Giant gecko	Gekko stentor	1
Nelson's gecko	Aristelliger nelsoni	1
Banded gecko	Coleonyx variegatus	1
Iguanidae:		
Common iguana	Iguana iguana	3
Carolina anole	Anolis carolinensis	Many
Nelson's anole	Anolis nelsoni	1
Giant anole	Anolis equestris	1
Texas horned lizard	Phrynosoma cornutum	1
Crested lizard	Leiocephalus varius	3
Blue scaly lizard	Sceloporus cyanogenys	1
Fence lizard	Sceloporus undulatus	2
Spiny-tailed iguana	Ctenosaura acanthura	1
Scincidae:		
Mourning skink	Egernia luctuosa	2
White's skink	Egernia whitei	4
Greater five-lined skink	Eumeces fasciatus	1
Broad-headed skink	Eumeces laticeps	1
Great plains skink	Eumeces obsoletus	1
Sand skink	Scincus officinalis	4
Stump-tailed skink	Tiliqua rugosa	1
Malayan skink	Mabuya multifasciata	2
Gerrhosauridae:		
Plated lizard	Gerrhosaurus major	1
Teiidae:		
Black tegu	Tupinambis nigropunctatus	1
Varanidae:		
Dumeril's monitor	Varanus dumerili	1
Indian monitor	Varanus flavescens	1
Malayan monitor	Varanus salvator	1
Indian monitor	Varanus bengalensis	1
Pakistan monitor	Varanus griseus	2
Australian lace monitor	Varanus varius	3
Helodermatidae:		
Mexican beaded lizard	Heloderma horridum	1
Beaded lizard (black phase)	Heloderma horridum	1
Gila monster	Heloderma suspectum	1
Anguidae:		
Glass lizard	Ophisaurus ventralis	3

SERPENTES

Family and common name	Scientific name	Number
Boidae:		
Anaconda	Eunectes murinus	1
Tree boa	Boa enydris enydris	1
Cook's tree boa	Boa enydris cooki	6

Family and common name	*Scientific name*	*Number*
Boidae—Continued		
Boa constrictor	*Constrictor constrictor*	1
Emperor boa	*Constrictor imperator*	1
Cuban ground boa	*Tropidophis melanura*	1
Rainbow boa	*Epicrates cenchria*	4
Cuban tree boa	*Epicrates angulifer*	3
Ball python	*Python regius*	1
Indian rock python	*Python moluras*	2
Regal python	*Python reticulatus*	1
Colubridae:		
Water snake	*Natrix sipedon*	2
European grass snake	*Natrix natrix*	1
Diamond-backed water snake	*Natrix rhombifera*	1
Red-bellied water snake	*Natrix erythrogaster*	1
Island water snake	*Natrix insularum*	1
Mangrove snake	*Natrix compressicauda*	1
Florida green water snake	*Natrix cyclopion floridana*	1
Queen snake	*Natrix septemvitta*	2
Garter snake	*Thamnophis sirtalis sirtalis*	3
Ribbon snake	*Thamnophis sauritus*	6
Ring-necked snake	*Diadophis punctatus edwardsii*	1
Black racer	*Coluber constrictor constrictor*	5
Red racer	*Masticophis flagellum*	1
Asiatic rat snake	*Elaphe taeniura*	1
Lesser Indian rat snake	*Elaphe carinata*	1
Pilot black snake	*Elaphe obsoleta obsoleta*	3
Pilot black snake (albino)	*Elaphe obsoleta obsoleta*	1
Fox snake	*Elaphe vulpina*	2
Corn snake	*Elaphe obsoleta guttata*	2
Lindheimer's rat snake	*Elaphe obsoleta lindheimeri*	1
Chicken snake	*Elaphe quadrivittata*	1
Aesculapian snake	*Elaphe longissima*	1
King snake	*Lampropeltis getulus getulus*	1
Speckled king snake	*Lampropeltis getulus holbrooki*	3
California king snake	*Lampropeltis getulus californiae*	2
Sonoran king snake	*Lampropeltis getulus splendida*	1
Scarlet king snake	*Lampropeltis triangulum doliata*	1
Milk snake	*Lampropeltis triangulum*	1
Tropical king snake	*Lampropeltis polyzonus*	1
Mole snake	*Lampropeltis rhombomculata*	1
Cat-eye snake	*Leptodeira annulata*	1
Eastern worm snake	*Carphophis amoenus*	1
DeKay's snake	*Storeria dekayi*	1
Green whip snake	*Dryophis prasinus*	1
File snake	*Simocephalus capensis*	1
Wolf snake	*Lycodon flavomaculatus*	2
Green-headed tree snake	*Leptophis mexicanus*	1
Elapidae:		
Indian cobra	*Naja naja*	2
Taiwan cobra	*Naja naja atra*	7
Egyptian cobra	*Naja haje*	1
Krait	*Bungarus multicinctus*	1

Family and common name	*Scientific name*	*Number*
Acrochordidae:		
Elephant trunk snake	*Acrochordus javanicus*	1
Crotalidae:		
Southern copperhead	*Ancistrodon contortrix contortrix*	1
Northern copperhead	*Ancistrodon controtrix mokeson*	2
Western broad-banded copperhead	*Ancistrodon contortrix laticinctus*	1
Water moccasin, or cottonmouth	*Ancistrodon piscivorus*	3
Mamushi	*Ancistrodon halys blomhoffi*	1
Asian snorkel viper	*Ancistrodon acutus*	2
Green palm viper	*Trimeresurus gramineus*	2
Stejneger's palm viper	*Trimeresurus stejnegeri*	1
Wagler's pit viper	*Trimeresurus wagleri*	1
Mamushi, or Asiatic viper	*Trimeresurus elegans*	1
Habu, or Asiatic viper	*Trimeresurus flavoviridis*	1
Southern Pacific rattlesnake	*Crotalus viridis helleri*	1
Prairie rattlesnake	*Crotalus viridis viridis*	1
Western diamondback rattlesnake	*Crotalus atrox*	24
Timber rattlesnake	*Crotalus horridus*	2

AMPHIBIANS

CAUDATA

Amphiumidae:		
Congo eel	*Amphiuma means*	1
Cryptobranchidae:		
Hellbender	*Cryptobranchus alleganiensis*	2
Ambystomidae:		
Spotted salamander	*Ambystoma maculatum*	2
Jefferson's salamander	*Ambystoma jeffersonianum*	1
Salamandridae:		
Red-bellied newt	*Cynops pyrrhogaster*	10
Red-spotted newt	*Diemictylus viridescens*	19

SALIENTIA

Bufonidae:		
American toad	*Bufo americanus*	1
Giant toad	*Bufo marinus*	5
Cuban toad	*Bufo peltocephalus*	6
Oak toad	*Bufo quercicus*	2
Pelobatidae:		
Spadefoot toad	*Scaphiopus holbrooki*	14
Pipidae:		
Surinam toad	*Pipa pipa*	14
African clawed frog	*Xenopus laevis*	5
Leptodactylidae:		
Colombian horned frog	*Ceratophrys calcarata*	2
Argentine horned frog	*Ceratophrys ornata*	1
Hylidae:		
Barking tree frog	*Hyla versicolor*	2
Green tree frog	*Hyla cinerea*	4
Cuban tree frog	*Hyla septentrionalis*	4
Squirrel tree frog	*Hyla squirella*	1
Gray tree frog	*Hyla versicolor*	2

Family and common name	Scientific name	Number
Microhylidae:		
Great Plains narrow-mouthed toad__	*Microhyla olivacea*__________	1
Ranidae:		
African bull frog_________________	*Rana adspersa*_______________	4
American bull frog________________	*Rana catesbeiana*____________	1
Green frog________________________	*Rana clamitans melanota*________	5
Leopard frog______________________	*Rana pipiens*________________	Many

ARTHROPODS

DECAPODA

Cenobitidae:		
Land hermit crab_________________	*Coenobita clypeatus*____________	Many

ARANEIDA

Theridiidae:		
Black-widow spider________________	*Latrodectus mactans*___________	1

ORTHOPTERA

Blattidae:		
Tropical giant cockroach___________	*Blaberus giganteus*___________	Many

MOLLUSKS

PULMONATA

Planorbidae:		
Pond snail________________________	*Helisoma trivolvis*___________	Many

FISHES

NEOCERATODONTOIDEI

Protopteridae:		
African lungfish__________________	*Protopterus annectens*_________	2

OSTARIOPHYSOIDEI

Characidae:		
Piranha _________________________	*Serrasalmus niger*___________	1
Metynnis ________________________	*Metynnis rooseveltii*__________	1
Black tetra_______________________	*Gynmocorymbus ternetzi*_______	3
Cyprinidae:		
Zebra fish________________________	*Brachydanio rerio*___________	3
Clown barb_______________________	*Barbus everetti*_____________	1
Tiger barb________________________	*Puntius partipentazona*________	2
White Cloud Mountain fish_________	*Tanichthys albonubes*_________	15
Electrophoridae:		
Electric eel_______________________	*Electrophorus electricus*________	1

CYRINODONTOIDEI

Poeciliidae:		
Flag-tailed guppy_________________	*Lebistes reticulatus*__________	10
Guppy __________________________	*Lebistes reticulatus*__________	15
Black mollie______________________	*Mollienesia latipinna*_________	2
Platy, or moonfish________________	*Xiphophorus maculatus*_________	1

PERCOMORPHOIDEI

Family and common name	Scientific name	Number
Anabantidae:		
Climbing perch	*Anabas testudineus*	3
Cichlidae:		
Peacock cichlid	*Astronotus ocellatus*	1
Egyptian mouthbreeder	*Haplochromis multicolor*	3
Angelfish	*Pelmatochromis guentheri*	2
African mouthbreeder	*Pterophyllum eimekei*	2
Jack Dempsey fish	*Cichlasoma biocellatum*	15
Jewelfish	*Hemichromis bimaculatus*	1
Lorcariidae:		
South American catfish	*Plecostomus plecostomus*	2

FINANCES

Funds for the operation of the National Zoological Park are appropriated annually under the District of Columbia Appropriation Act. The operation and maintenance appropriation for the fiscal year 1961 totaled $1,304,000, which was $138,800 more than for the fiscal year 1960. The increase consisted of $22,000 to cover salary increases for General Schedule employees in accordance with Public Law 86–568; $16,000 to cover salary increases for police employees in accordance with Public Law 86–379; $25,800 to cover salary increases for Wage Board employees; $12,900 for within-grade salary advancements for both General Schedule and Wage Board employees; $8,500 for Federal Employees Health Benefits; $46,100 to establish 11 new positions; $7,500 for the purchase of new equipment.

Of the total appropriation, 83.5 percent ($1,089,002) was used for salaries and related personnel costs and 16.5 percent ($214,998) for the maintenance and operation of the Zoo. Included in the latter figure were $74,000 for animal food; $18,000 for fuel for heating; $34,257 for materials for building construction and repairs; $9,725 for the purchase of animals; $9,600 for electricity; $5,400 for telephone, postal, and telegraph services; and $5,000 for veterinarian equipment and supplies. The balance of $35,675 in operational funds was expended for other items, including freight, sundry supplies, uniforms, gasoline, road repairs, equipment replacement, and new equipment.

In addition to the regular appropriation, $240,000 for safety improvements was appropriated for capital outlay. This was to carry out the second phase of the safety program.

PERSONNEL

On October 10, 1960, Dr. William M. Mann, Director of the National Zoological Park from 1925 until 1956, died at the age of 74. During his regime he had built up the collection of animals from about 1,600 to more than 3,000 specimens; he had supervised the building of modern quarters for birds, reptiles, large mammals, and small mammals, as well as of machine shops, the Zoo restaurant, and police headquarters. He led numerous expeditions to South America, Indonesia, and Africa to collect animals for the Zoo. It was during his tenure of office that the National Zoological Park grew from a second-rate Zoo to one of world-wide importance.

Russell Morrison, supervisory keeper, came to the Zoo March 1, 1931, and was assigned to the reptile house. He died of a heart attack while on duty August 14, 1960.

Malcolm Davis, who first came to the Zoo on November 16, 1927, retired on July 1, 1960, to accept a research position in private industry. He had for many years been in charge of the bird house and was associate head keeper at the time of his retirement. He had been on many expeditions to collect animals, including three voyages to Antarctica to bring back penguins.

Other retirements were those of Bertelle Ford, keeper, employed at the Zoo from December 5, 1942, to October 31, 1960; Leonard Ford, supervisory animal keeper, December 29, 1950, to June 15, 1961; William G. Modena, December 16, 1936, to July 31, 1960, assistant superintendent of maintenance and construction; Charles Dean, operating engineer, August 16, 1927, to December 31, 1960; and Ada McNeil, custodial laborer, from November 10, 1952, to July 31, 1960.

Reily Straw, a welder, was promoted to take Mr. Modena's place as assistant superintendent of maintenance and construction. Donald Swartzback of the grounds department was made supervisor of the new tree section.

A night-keeper program was initiated this year to insure care of the animals 24 hours a day. This is essential particularly in the case of baby animals that are being hand fed or sick animals that need medication during the night.

In fiscal year 1961 there were 197 authorized positions at the Zoo, divided as follows: Administrative office, 16; animal department, 76, an increase of 6 over the previous year (2 night keepers, 2 commissary stewards, 2 laborers); mechanical department, 61; police department, 33, an increase of 3; and grounds department, 11, an increase of 2.

Mrs. Fruza C. Kussrow was appointed budget analyst on July 18, 1960, and Frank Maloney came in as engineer on April 16, 1961.

FRIENDS OF THE NATIONAL ZOO

"Friends of the National Zoo," a group of civic-minded District residents, were active again this year. On December 16, 1960, John Perry, president of the organization, presented to the Smithsonian Institution a "master plan" which had been made by Meade Palmer and Morris Trotter, landscape architects. This substitutes a pedestrian "greenway" for the dangerous automobile road that now goes through the center of the Zoo and suggests locations for new buildings such as a new monkey house, monkey island, lion house, hoofed-stock complex, administration building, and auditorium. Dr. Carmichael presented the master plan to the Board of Regents at their annual meeting in January 1961.

The "Friends" were responsible for a brass plaque which was placed at the base of the flag that flies at the Connecticut Avenue entrance to the Zoo. This flagpole was dedicated in September 1959, "as an expression of warm affection for Dr. William M. Mann, former Director of the Zoo," and on the day of Dr. Mann's funeral the flag was flown at half-staff.

June 5, 1961, was designated as Zoo Night for the "Friends." About 200 of them gathered at the Police Station at 8 p.m. and were taken on a conducted tour.

INFORMATION AND EDUCATION

The Zoo continues to handle a large correspondence with persons all over the world and from every part of this country, who write to the Zoo, as a national institution, for information regarding animals. Telephone calls come in constantly asking for identification of animals, proper diets, or treatment of disease. Visitors to the office as well as to the animal exhibits are constantly seeking information.

On his trip to India for the white tiger, the Director had an opportunity to visit zoos in Hawaii, Japan, the Philippines, Malaya, and Thailand, as well as India, and to photograph various types of new construction and design. He has lectured on these Oriental zoos to civic and scientific groups. His article on "Enchantress, the White Tiger" was published in the National Geographic Magazine for May 1961.

J. Lear Grimmer, Associate Director, continued his fieldwork in British Guiana and spent 7 weeks there studying the life history of the hoatzin. For 2 weeks he was joined by William Widman, senior keeper. Mr. Grimmer left again for British Guiana in June 1961, accompanied by Keeper Charles Hall.

The Director and Travis E. Fauntleroy, Jr., assistant to the Director, attended the annual convention of the American Association of Zoological Parks and Aquariums at Long Beach, Calif., in September 1960. Mr. Fauntleroy stopped at Brookfield (Chicago), San Francisco, San Diego, and San Antonio to study management methods in these well-known zoos. The Director visited Vancouver, B.C., Seattle, Wash., Portland, Oreg., San Francisco, and San Diego, studying recent construction at these zoos. In February, the Director and Dr. James F. Wright attended the Midwinter Conference of Midwest Zoo Directors in St. Louis, where the Director presented a paper on Oriental Zoos and Dr. Wright spoke on the immobilization of animals.

In Washington, the Director spoke on three radio programs and appeared on television, showing a number of Zoo animals.

Senior Keeper William F. Widman and Supervisory Keeper Holmes M. Vorous have written an article on the hatching of kookaburras in the Zoo, which will be published in England by Avicultural Magazine in the autumn of 1961.

Senior Keeper Mario DePrato and Holmes M. Vorous accompanied a shipment of live reptiles to the Detroit Zoo in August 1960, arriving there in time for the opening of the new reptile house. While in the Midwest they visited zoos in Toledo, Cleveland, and Pittsburgh, studying methods of exhibiting and handling animals.

Ordinarily the Zoo does not conduct guided tours of the Park, but exceptions were made for a group of children from the Columbia Lighthouse for the Blind and for four other groups of handicapped children.

On July 14, 1960, 1,523 foreign exchange students visited the Zoo; the schoolboy patrol, consisting of 9,740 students from all parts of the country, came to the Park on May 13, 1961; and a group of African students toured the Park on June 21, 1961.

While the Zoo does not conduct a regular research program as such, effort is made to study the animals and improve their health, housing, and diet in every way possible.

REPORT OF THE VETERINARIAN

The veterinarian, Dr. James F. Wright, reports that the major veterinary problems at the National Zoological Park for this year, as in past years, stem from the lack of facilities and help to investigate disease in the collection, absence of suitable hospitalization and quarantine, and the need for a full-time arrangement for orphan-animal care.

The central nervous system disease of monkeys mentioned in last year's report is still under investigation by the Armed Forces Institute of Pathology. Necropsies have been performed on seven monkeys which during life had shown the typical signs of acute amaurotic epilepsy as described by Langdon and Cadwallader in 1915 and again by Van Bogaert and Scherer in 1935. These cases include two immature Barbary apes (died January 5, 1960, and April 8, 1961), an immature pig-tailed macaque (July 20, 1959), an immature hybrid (Philippine x Javan) macaque (January 6, 1960), an immature drill (April 9, 1960), an immature mandrill (June 24, 1960), and an immature hybrid gibbon (*Hylobates lar* x *H*. sp.) which was raised in a keeper's home from the day of birth and was thus rather free of the Park environment. Three monkeys in the collection, a gray-cheeked mangabey, a black-crested mangabey, and a mandrill, all female adults, have the typical seizures of this malady periodically but act normal in every way except during the attacks. The black-crested mangabey is, as nearly as can be determined, blind without obvious gross defect in either eye. For almost a year, these three animals have received daily doses of diphenylhydantoin sodium, which apparently has suppressed the occurrence and severity of the seizures to a minor degree. Ingestion of toxic quantities of lead has always been considered a strong possibility in causing this condition, but it has been determined that no lead-base paints have been used in the animal areas, and an analysis of the water supply at the monkey house disclosed less than acceptable minimums of this element.

A maned wolf (*Chrysocyon jubatus*), received from a dealer in South America, died after a short illness in February 1961. The only antemortem signs were inappetence and inanition leading to a comatose state on the day before death. Antibiotics, canine antidistemper serum, and intravenous therapy were without observable effect. A necropsy performed immediately after death by the Pathology Institute disclosed the following conditions: heartworm (*Dirofilaria* sp.), lungworm (*Filaroides osleri*), and hookworm infestations; presence of the giant kidney worm (*Dioctophyma renale*); parasitic nodules of *Spirocerca lupi* in the aorta and other great vessels; large ulcerated areas in the stomach; and negri bodies of rabies in microscopic preparations of brain tissue. Just prior to death blood samples were taken from this animal for blood-picture study and serology. The interesting finding of these studies was the presence of serum antibodies to the disease caused by *Leptospira canicola*. The serum titre was a very high 1:6400.

A female maned wolf, which was obtained from the same source in January 1960, died in August 1960, with the same antemortem signs. The necropsy report describes only an infestation with the lungworm *Filaroides osleri*. The central nervous system of this individual was not examined because the carcass was requested for the U.S. National Museum.

Juvenile osteoporosis occurred in a pair of bobcats and a mountain lion, all being raised with the parents and all showing similar signs of onset-lameness in one hind limb progressing to severe lameness and ultimately posterior paralysis. Radiographs taken of one of the bobcats showed a fracture of the femur, a folding fracture of the pelvis, and collapse of the lumbar vertebrae with resultant compression of the spinal cord. Necropsy reports by Dr. Wayne Riser established the condition as juvenile osteoporosis. For future cases he recommended the addition of potassium iodide to the ration as well as increased calcium and vitamin D (one-half teaspoonful daily of a solution of 50 mg. KI to 100 cc. of water).

In the report for 1960 it was stated that attempts were being made to develop a diagnostic test for tuberculosis in wild hoofed animals through serum antibodies. Blood samples were obtained from two elands and a giraffe suspected of being infected with this disease. These samples were checked serologically by investigators of the Department of Agriculture, whose preliminary report indicated that no specific antibodies for the tuberculosis antigen were present in the serums of these animals. Since the samples were examined, all three animals have died with the necropsy diagnosis of pulmonary tuberculosis. These pathological findings have been supported by reports from Dr. Alfred G. Karlson of the Mayo Foundation, who isolated and identified the bovine variety of the tuberculosis organism from tissues of these animals.

A lammergeyer, or bearded vulture (*Gypaetus barbatus*), which was acquired from a dealer in West Germany in June 1960, developed wartlike lesions on both feet after one month in the collection. In two more days similar lesions were noticed on the lower lid of the right eye. The left eyelid became involved in another three weeks. The growths were fleshy in nature with no vesicle formation noted, although there did appear to be some secondary infection and discharge from the sites. Except for an erratic appetite, which may have been caused by shipment, it was not apparent that this condition had any general debilitating effect on the bird. The largest growth was easily removed from the eyelid for pathological examination; the smaller "nodules" all dropped off after three or four weeks. As this bird was returning to normal, similar lesions were noticed on a king penguin. Again the condition occasioned the bird no distress and disappeared in about one month. While the penguin was recovering, a black-footed albatross developed some nodules in and around the beak which disappeared in about six weeks. Finally an Adélie penguin was found with numerous growths around the beak and eyelids. Whereas the aforementioned birds recovered, this penguin died before the lesions had disappeared. The pathologists found pathognomonic evidence of fowl-pox infection in this penguin and in the tissue submitted from the lammergeyer vulture. It is probable that the virus was introduced from the vulture brought from overseas by air shipment. The black-footed albatross and the king penguin are also presumed to have been infected with this virus. There has been no subsequent appearance of this condition to date.

Two three-toed sloths (*Bradypus tridactylus*) were acquired during the past year from South America: a male, which lived only four days after arriving in poor condition, and a female, which lived from September until February 1961 and produced a baby, which lived for 14 days. Both the adult sloths had severe anemias and bone marrow hypoplasia, according to the pathologists' report.

A female spotted hyaena died May 12, 1961. No report has come in as yet from the AFIP except that the animal had mammary tumors. Both this hyaena and the male, which died in 1960, were received at the Park July 1, 1947.

The use of the intramuscular, long-acting barbiturate "Capchur-barb" was continued, both in the projectile syringe and by hand syringe. Among the animals requiring sedation or anesthesia with this drug were two American alligators, an eland antelope, a pronghorn antelope, zebu cow, American elk, raccoon, bighorn sheep, puma, capuchin monkey, Java macaque, lesser panda, and Grevy's zebra. Another anesthetic preparation that was found most useful was the rectal thiopental sodium (Pentothal-Abbott). This drug is packaged in disposable plastic syringes for immediate use with a graduated plunger and two separate applicators per syringe. This type of sedation or anesthesia was used for short procedures and for restraint on primates and carnivores.

Dr. Wright made two trips to a game farm in Florida and one to the quarantine station in New Jersey at the request of the Department of Agriculture for the purpose of immobilizing captive wild animals with the projectile syringe method. The drug used in these immobilizations was succinylcholine chloride, with one exception described below. The list of animals successfully immobilized with succinylcholine includes 23 Grant's zebra, 11 Grevy's zebra, 8 Damara zebra, 17 eland, 4 greater kudu, 4 beisa oryx, 2 blackbuck, 2 aoudad, 1 hartebeest, 1 brindled gnu, 3 nilghai, 1 American bison, 3 red deer, 1 giraffe, 1 spotted hyaena, and 1 white-handed gibbon. In addition to these, 5 white-tailed gnus were immobilized with the drug gallamine triethiodide (Flaxedil-Lederle). On the basis of reports received from investigators in Africa it seemed that this latter drug was more satisfactory for immobilizing wildebeest. However, both gallamine and succinylcholine have been used successfully in this type of animal. Complete reports on these immobilizations are in preparation.

Dr. Wright's paper "The Immobilization of Captive Wild Animals with Succinylcholine II," prepared in collaboration with Dr. Warren R. Pistey of the New England Institute for Medical Research, was published by the Canadian Journal of Comparative Medicine, vol. 25, No. 3, March 1961.

A demonstration of the use of the projectile syringe was given at the University of Maryland for a combined meeting of the Maryland State Veterinary Medical Association, the District of Columbia Veterinary Medical Association, American Animal Hospital Association, and the District of Columbia Academy of Veterinary Medicine.

Dr. F. R. Lucas, Livestock Sanitary Laboratory, Centreville, Md., provided clinical laboratory services including microscopic tissue reports.

Identification of parasites from specimens in the collection were made by M. B. Chitwood and W. W. Becklund of the Parasite Classification and Distribution Investigations, Beltsville Parasitological Laboratory, U.S. Department of Agriculture.

Necropsies of major and important specimens were performed by the pathologists of the Armed Forces Institute of Pathology, Walter Reed Army Medical Center. Necropsy materials not needed by the Institute were offered to Dr. Thomas Peery of the George Washington School of Medicine for comparative pathology study.

Isolations and identifications of suspected tubercular tissues were made by Dr. Karlson of the Mayo Foundation.

Following are the statistics for the mortality rates during the past fiscal year and a table of comparison with the past 6 fiscal years:

Mortality, fiscal year 1961			*Total mortality, past 6 fiscal years*	
	Death	Attrition*		
Mammals	102	32	1956	618
Birds	163	17	1957	549
Reptiles	132	71	1958	550
			1959	472
	—	—	1960	532
	397	120	1961	517

*Attrition is the term used for those losses due mainly to the trauma of shipment and handling after accession at the Zoo, or before an animal can adapt to cage habitation within the collection.

The old pair of Nile hippopotamuses, Pinky and Bongo, were "retired" from the Zoo in the summer of 1959 and placed on deposit at a private zoo in Virginia to make room for a younger pair. The male, Bongo, who had come to the Zoo on April 7, 1914, died on December 4, 1959, after 45 years 7 months 27 days in captivity. The female, who was 11 years old when she was obtained on April 25, 1939, died on December 31, 1960.

Other animals that had been in the collection for a relatively long time and died this year were: A kiang (*Equus onager*) received October 14, 1934, died August 16, 1960, after 25 years 10 months 2 days; South American lungfish (*Lepidosiren paradoxa*), received May 6, 1932, died January 18, 1961, after 28 years 8 months and 12 days. An Indian fresh-water turtle (*Batagur baska*) was a very old specimen when it arrived on September 17, 1947. It died May 19, 1961, after 13 years 8 months 2 days. It was the only one in captivity in the United States and probably the oldest specimen of its kind in any zoo.

A horned toad, *Ceratophrys ornata*, collected by Frances Shippen on the National Zoological Park Expedition to Argentina (received in the Zoo June 27, 1939) is still living. A salt-water crocodile (*Crocodylus porosus*), purchased July 12, 1932, when about 8 years old, is still living and is believed to be the largest in captivity.

COOPERATION

At all times special efforts are made to maintain friendly contacts with other Federal and State agencies, private concerns and individuals, and scientific workers for mutual assistance. As a result, the Zoo receives much help and advice and many valuable animals, and in turn it furnishes information and, whenever possible, animals it does not need.

In cooperation with the State Department and the White House, the National Zoological Park arranged for the fulfillment of President Eisenhower's promise to General DeGaulle to send him three pronghorn antelopes for the Paris Zoo. The antelopes selected had been in the collection here and were thus accustomed to captivity. They had originally come from the State Fish and Game Department of Montana, which will send replacements to the National Zoological Park. The pronghorns, the only ones in any European zoo, were flown from Andrews Air Force Base on August 2, 1960, on an Air Force C–130 cargo plane. Lt. Col. Perry Penn, 62d Squadron commander, and Capt. Donald Gould, aircraft commander, were in charge, and the Director of the Zoo accompanied the shipment. All arrangements were made at the request of President Eisenhower. In addition, the plane carried two Virginia deer fawns and an assortment of small mammals, birds, and reptiles. The plane stopped at Prestwick, Scotland, and unloaded there two bear cubs, birds, and alligators for the zoos in Edinburgh and Bristol, before continuing on to Orly Field in France.

Through the cooperation of the U.S. Fish and Wildlife Service Senior Keeper William Widman made a number of collecting trips on Chesapeake Bay to secure waterfowl for the Zoo.

Special acknowledgment is due George Kirk and John Pulaski, in the office of the U.S. Dispatch Agent in New York City, and Stephen E. Lato, Dispatch Agent in San Francisco, who are frequently called upon to clear shipments of animals coming from abroad, often at great personal inconvenience. The animals have been forwarded to Washington without the loss of a single individual.

When it is necessary to quarantine animals coming into this country, they are taken to the U.S. Department of Agriculture's station in Clifton, N.J. During the past year Dr. B. C. Swindell and Andy Goodel, two of the officials stationed there, have been most cooperative in keeping the National Zoological Park informed as to the well-being of animals and birds being held there for quarantine.

Animals that die in the Zoo are offered to the United States National Museum. If the Museum does not need them, they are sent on request to reasearch workers in other institutions.

The Zoo cooperated with the National Capital Parks and lent small animals to Park naturalists and to the Nature Center in Rock Creek Park for demonstration.

Gifts of plants were received from Mount Vernon, the Botanical Gardens, National Bureau of Standards, District of Columbia Waterworks, St. Elizabeth's Hospital, the Naval Observatory, and the Soldiers' Home. A very welcome gift was a 15-by-40-foot greenhouse, from the Bureau of Standards, to supply tropical plants for forage and for planting in indoor cages.

VISITORS

In cooperation with Albert Mindlin and Samuel Rosenthal, analytical statisticians of the Management Office of the District of Columbia, a new method of estimating the visitor attendance is being developed for greater statistical reliability.

Number of bus groups visiting the Zoo in fiscal year 1961

Locality	Number of groups	Number in groups	Locality	Number of groups	Number in groups
Alabama	30	1, 213	Mississippi	14	541
Arizona	1	28	Montana	1	25
Arkansas	2	70	New Hampshire	1	40
California	1	40	New Jersey	12	963
Connecticut	7	259	New Mexico	1	26
Delaware	13	498	New York	269	10, 753
District of Columbia	177	7, 021	North Carolina	218	8, 652
Florida	33	1, 166	Ohio	32	1, 241
Georgia	124	4, 995	Pennsylvania	294	11, 775
Illinois	6	241	Rhode Island	16	604
Indiana	5	200	South Carolina	52	2, 076
Iowa	5	188	Tennessee	52	2, 022
Kansas	2	60	Texas	2	92
Kentucky	16	618	Vermont	1	35
Louisiana	2	90	Virginia	735	29, 449
Maine	2	441	West Virginia	66	2, 352
Maryland	954	38, 159	Wisconsin	5	182
Massachusetts	11	64			
Michigan	9	303	Total	3, 171	118, 043
Minnesota	6	213			

Groups from foreign countries

	Number of groups	Number in groups		Number of groups	Number in groups
Asia	3	150	Haiti	1	58
Ecuador	1	30	Japan	2	70
Exchange students	40	1,523			
Finland	2	80	Total	51	1,966

About 2 p.m. each day the cars then parked in the Zoo are counted and listed according to the State, Territory, or country from which they come. This is, of course, not a census of the cars coming to the Zoo but is valuable in showing the percentage of attendance by States of people in private automobiles. Many District of Columbia, Maryland, and Virginia cars come to the Zoo to bring guests from other States. The tabulation for the fiscal year 1961 is as follows:

	Percentage		*Percentage*
Maryland	32.3	California	0.7
Virginia	23.2	Connecticut	.7
District of Columbia	21.1	South Carolina	.6
Pennsylvania	3.9	Michigan	.6
New York	2.3	Illinois	.5
North Carolina	1.9	Georgia	.4
Ohio	1.4	Delaware	.4
New Jersey	1.3	Indiana	.4
West Virginia	1.2	Tennessee	.4
Florida	1.1	Texas	.4
Massachusetts	.9		

The remaining 4.3 percent came from other States, Azores, Bahamas, British Columbia, Canada, Canal Zone, Cuba, England, Finland, France, Germany, Guatemala, Japan, Mexico, Newfoundland, Norway, Okinawa, Philippines, Switzerland, and the Virgin Islands.

On the days of even small attendance there are cars parked in the Zoo from at least 15 States, Territories, the District of Columbia, and foreign countries. On average days there are cars from about 22 States, Territories, the District of Columbia, and foreign countries; and during the periods of greatest attendance the cars represent no less than 34 different States, Territories, and countries. Parking spaces in the Zoo now accommodate 1,079 cars when the bus parking place is utilized and 969 cars when it is not used.

POLICE DEPARTMENT

The practice of using men for police duty on a temporary basis during the busy season continues to prove a highly satisfactory arrangement, releasing the regular officers for special details and assignments, as well as patrol duty.

Refresher courses in first-aid training were given by Sgt. A. L. Canter, Pvt. C. S. Grubbs, and Keeper Lester Ratliff.

Sgt. A. L. Canter, Pvts. G. H. Adams, M. J. Devlin, Jr., and A. S. Kadlubowski attended an extensive course on the handling of juveniles administered by the Youth Aid Division of the District of Columbia Metropolitan Police Department.

The police force conducted 1,647 investigations of traffic violations, 137 investigations of a general nature, picked up 42 truant children and took appropriate action and returned 269 lost children to their parents or groups. The First Aid Station handled 1,575 cases, mostly for minor injuries. Visitors who stopped in the police headquarters for information numbered 8,202. Eyeglasses and sunglasses found in the Park and unclaimed were turned over to the Society for the Prevention of Blindness, and unclaimed articles of clothing, etc., were given to the Goodwill Industries.

The Mounted Color Guard, now numbering six officers, continued to participate in local parades.

SAFETY SUBCOMMITTEE

Lt. John R. Wolfe is chairman of the National Zoological Park Safety Subcommittee, which consists of Dr. James F. Wright, administration office; Lt. C. E. Brink, police department; Bert J. Barker, animal department; Reily Straw, maintenance and construction; Michael Dubik of the grounds department; and Mrs. W. M. Holden of the Smithsonian Institution as subcommittee secretary. Monthly meetings of the Safety Subcommittee were held to discuss safety measures and make recommendations to the Director.

In addition to the safety manual issued to the animal department in January 1960, a new safety manual for the maintenance and construction department was issued in October 1960, and one for the grounds department in January 1961. A safety manual for the police department is now being printed.

A survey of all Park buildings was conducted on September 27, 1960, by Harold McCoy of the Federal Civil Defense Organization, accompanied by Captain James and Lt. Brink of the Zoo police. This was in regard to "Fall Out Space," and the total number of square feet of floor space and the number of persons who could be sheltered in case of bombing were established.

Reily Straw represented the Subcommittee at the National Safety Conference's annual convention in Chicago in October 1960.

Sgt. A. L. Canter and Pvt. G. H. Adams attended the General Services Administration "Driver Training School" and are now qualified to test Park employees and other Smithsonian employees for issuance of Government drivers' permits.

Sergeant Canter and Private Adams attended the Federal Safety Council's meeting on the use of safety belts in Government vehicles and gave a report to the subcommittee.

Five fire extinguishers were added to fill the requirements of the District of Columbia Fire Marshall. Directional signs to the extinguishers have been painted and installed. First-aid boxes have been placed in all Park buildings. Exit signs have been installed in all buildings frequented by the public. A shifting conveyor was made in the mechanical shop for use in moving large animals. Red flags and danger signs have been purchased for use on moving vehicles and when work is being done on trees. Public pay telephones have been relocated to aid the public and relieve inside communications, and 14 new telephones and extensions were added to the Park telephone system to improve communications and supply contact in isolated areas.

The police pistol range has been improved, the work being done by the police in their off-duty time with assistance from the grounds and maintenance department.

An oxygen inhalator was added to the police first-aid room for use in case of heart patients, electrical shock, etc. Dr. Wright instructed the police in its use and operation.

BUILDINGS AND GROUNDS

Much of the work accomplished during the past fiscal year was done to insure the safety of visitors, employees, and animals. The District of Columbia Department of Buildings and Grounds, from funds appropriated in FY 60, installed 5,000 feet of standardized visitors' safety fencing in front of many outdoor exhibits. They also repaired the roofs of the small-mammal building, elephant house, and bird house, and the walls and ceiling of the reptile house. The ceiling of the reptile house was sprayed with an accoustical compound, which reduces noise in the building by at least 50 percent. Because of the bad echo, this house had been extremely noisy when filled with people.

The new gorilla cage, which was made by remodeling the former gibbon cage, is now adequate for the apes which came here as babies but are now nearly full-grown animals. This cage has electrically controlled doors for the shifting cage, heavy ¾-inch steel bars, ¼-inch plate glass on the inside quarters, and protective wiring on the outside. The outside enclosure has a roof of corrugated fiberglass panels so that the gorillas can enjoy being outdoors, protected from rain and excessive heat.

Fronts of the other great-ape cages, used by chimpanzees and orangutans, were moved back to allow for more keeper space between the bars and the glass. Formerly there was a possibility that a chimpanzee might reach out through the bars and seize a keeper passing by. While this work was being done, the interior of the cages was brightly painted.

Remodeling of the alligator and crocodile exhibit in the reptile house was done primarily for safety reasons, but resulted in an improvement in the general appearance. The old coping was removed, and ¼-inch glass fronts installed up to a height of 8 feet. A 42-inch guard rail prevents the visitors from tapping on the glass. Inward-curving spikes keep the alligators back from the glass. A child with a 28-inch eye level is able to see all but 10 inches of the water.

In the small-mammal house, the old guard rail was topped with an angled railing that keeps visitors back and makes it impossible for them to reach over and put fingers in the cages.

An attractive new exhibit during the summer of 1961 was the installation of a group of 10 capuchin monkeys on a small island in the waterfowl pond near the crossroads. Trees were cut back so that there is no possibility of the monkeys' jumping from branch to branch to freedom, and the surrounding water is sufficient barrier to keep them from climbing the low fence that surrounds the area. With a small tree-house shelter against inclement weather, the monkeys have done well, and the ducks and geese have accepted the new arrivals with equanimity.

"Beaver Valley," the wooded ravine below the bear dens, which fell into disuse during World War II, was finally restored, and new pools and fencing put in. In addition to the large beaver pond, on which a pair of mute swans raised their young, there are pools for harbor seals, otters, and other aquatic mammals.

Three dens in the main bear line were repaired with reinforced concrete floor slabs, copings, gutters, partition walls, and ironwork. Five cages in the short bear line above the reptile house were also repaired. This meant breaking up old deteriorated concrete walkways, floor slabs, and pools, and replacing them with new concrete.

Major alterations were made to the interior of the old cookhouse, which will now be used as an operating room for animals. An extension to the parking area fronting the pachyderm house was completed, and repairs were made to holes in the main roadways. A new floor was installed in the director's office, as the old one had been badly damaged by termites, and the office was painted.

There was constant repair to old water and sewer systems, to electric lines, heating lines, steam bypasses and return lines, and boilers in the central heating plant. Some new heating lines, conduits, sewer lines, and storm-water lines were installed. All cleaning of ground areas and burning and hauling of trash to the District dump was done by the mechanical department.

The grounds department found that with new equipment, in particular a Skyworker for trimming high branches, and enlarged personnel, including two dendricians or tree culturists, the 5-year backlog of work was reduced in a satisfactory manner. Two more flower beds were planted and others slightly enlarged. Barberry bushes were planted in strategic spots to deter visitors from walking in unsafe areas. Trees were planted for both shade and forage.

Four more employees in the grounds department attended and completed classes in first aid; instructions were given to some of the keepers and police in the use of the Skyworker in case of emergencies; and all men in the grounds crew were given a one-hour horticultural classroom lesson monthly.

The Washington Star, on June 18, 1961, carried an article in the gravure section entitled "Washington's Toughest Gardening Job," describing the work done by Michael Dubik, supervisory head gardener, and his staff of 10 men.

PLANS FOR THE FUTURE

Owing to the intense interest in plans for the development and growth of the National Zoological Park, the architectural and engineering firm of Daniel, Mann, Mendenhall & Johnson began architectural studies and engineering estimates for a redevelopment of the Zoo. These plans will be completed by September 1961.

Respectfully submitted.

THEODORE H. REED, *Director.*

Dr. LEONARD CARMICHAEL,
Secretary, Smithsonian Institution.

Report on the Canal Zone Biological Area

SIR: It gives me pleasure to present herewith the annual report on the Canal Zone Biological Area for the fiscal year ended June 30, 1961.

SCIENTISTS, STUDENTS, AND OBSERVERS

Following is the list of 43 scientists, students, and observers who visited Barro Colorado Island last year and stayed for several days in order to conduct scientific research or observe the wildlife of the area. Fourteen other scientific visitors each spent a day and a night on the island. In addition, scientists of other research and technical organizations in the Canal Zone and the Republic of Panama made use of station facilities.

Name	*Principal interest*
Barghoorn, Dr. and Mrs. Elso S., Harvard University.	Limnology.
Baskin, Jonathan N., Harvard University.	Study of army ants, dorylines and pomerines.
Bennett, Dr. and Mrs. Charles, Jr., University of California.	Microclimatology.
Blest, Dr. Andrew D., University College, London.	Behavior of Lepidoptera.
Brennan, Dr. and Mrs. James, Middle America Research.	Wildlife observation.
Bumzahem, Mr. and Mrs. Carlos B., University of Illinois.	Herpetology.
Colby, Susan, Smithsonian Institution.	Inspection of facilities.
Craven, Mrs. Harriet P., Fallen Leaf, Calif.	Wildlife observation.
Ebinger, Dr. and Mrs. John, Yale University.	Botany.
Eisenmann, Eugene, New York City.	Ornithology.
Fast, Arthur H., Arlington, Va.	Wildlife observation.
Greenfield, Ray, Honolulu, Hawaii.	Wildlife observation.
Hodgson, Mr. and Mrs. Edward S., Commonwealth Scientific and Industrial Research Organization, Australia.	Ecology.
Klopfer, Dr. Peter H., Duke University.	Tropical ecology.

Name	*Principal interest*
Larsen, Mr. and Mrs. Henry, Geneve, Switzerland.	Wildlife observation.
Lundy, William, Panama Canal Co.	Wildlife observation.
MacArthur, Dr. Robert, Duke University.	Tropical ecology.
Martin, Otis O., Smithsonian Institution.	Fiscal survey.
O'Neill, John P., Norman, Okla.	Ornithology.
Pennoyer, Capt. Ralph G., Virginia Society of Ornithology.	Wildlife observation.
Pohl, Harold, Orange Coast College.	Wildlife observation.
Rubinoff, Mr. and Mrs. Ira, Harvard University.	Ichthyology.
Selsor, C. Jackson, San Diego, Calif.	Wildlife observation.
Smith, Lloyd M., Orange Coast College.	Wildlife observation.
Stirling, Mrs. Matthew W., Washington, D.C.	Wildlife observation.
Stott, Kenhelm, San Diego, Calif.	Wildlife observation.
Straatman, R., CSIRO, Canberra, Australia.	Entomology.
Stuart, Dr. Alastair M., University of Chicago.	Termite behavior.
Sweeney, Mrs. Edward C., Washington, D.C.	Wildlife observation.
Taylor, Mr. and Mrs. R. W., Harvard University.	Ant behavior.
Willis, Edwin, University of California.	Ecology and behavior of birds following army ants.
Williams, Pfc. Carl, Headquarters U.S. Army, Caribbean.	Wildlife observation.
Zimmerman, Mr. and Mrs. John L., University of Illinois.	Physiology of tropical birds.

VISITORS

Approximately 212 visitors were permitted to visit the island for a day.

RAINFALL

During the dry season (January through April) of the calendar year 1960, rains of 0.01 inch or more fell during 52 days (163 hours) and amounted to 26.64 inches, as compared to 1.91 inches during 1959. During the wet season of 1960 (May through December), rains of 0.01 inch or more fell on 172 days (757 hours) and amounted to 113.43 inches, as compared to 92.97 inches during 1959. Total rain for the year was 140.07 inches. During 36 years of record, the wettest year was 1935 with 143.42 inches, and the driest year was 1930 with only 76.57 inches. February was the driest month of 1960 (0.95 inch) and December the wettest (22.35 inches). The maximum records for short periods were: 5 minutes, 1.30 inches; 10 minutes, 1.65 inches; 1 hour, 4.11 inches; 2 hours, 6.33 inches; 24 hours, 10.87 inches.

TABLE 1.—*Annual rainfall, Barro Colorado Island, Canal Zone*

Year	Total inches	Station average	Year	Total inches	Station average
1925	104. 37	--------	1943	120. 29	109. 20
1926	118. 22	113. 56	1944	111. 96	109. 30
1927	116. 36	114. 68	1945	120. 42	109. 84
1928	101. 52	111. 35	1946	87. 38	108. 81
1929	87. 84	106. 56	1947	77. 92	107. 49
1930	76. 57	101. 51	1948	83. 16	106. 43
1931	123. 30	104. 69	1949	114. 86	106. 76
1932	113. 52	105. 76	1950	114. 51	107. 07
1933	101. 73	105. 32	1951	112. 72	107. 28
1934	122. 42	107. 04	1952	97. 68	106. 94
1935	143. 42	110. 35	1953	104. 97	106. 87
1936	93. 88	108. 98	1954	105. 68	106. 82
1937	124. 13	110. 12	1955	114. 42	107. 09
1938	117. 09	110. 62	1956	114. 05	107. 30
1939	115. 47	110. 94	1957	97. 97	106. 98
1940	86. 51	109. 43	1958	100. 20	106. 70
1941	91. 82	108. 41	1959	94. 88	106. 48
1942	111. 10	108. 55	1960	140. 07	107. 41

TABLE 2.—*Comparison of 1959 and 1960 rainfall, Barro Colorado Island (inches)*

Month	Total 1959	Total 1960	Station average	Years of record	1960 excess or deficiency	Accumulated excess or deficiency
January	0. 32	2. 96	2. 17	35	+. 79	--------
February	0. 15	. 95	1. 36	35	−. 41	+. 38
March	0. 11	4. 47	1. 27	35	+3. 20	+3. 58
April	1. 33	18. 26	3. 39	36	+14. 87	+18. 45
May	8. 89	15. 55	10. 98	36	+4. 57	+23. 02
June	8. 29	11. 53	10. 84	36	+. 69	+23. 71
July	8. 86	11. 46	11. 63	36	−. 17	+23. 54
August	8. 62	7. 02	12. 21	36	−5. 19	+18. 35
September	14. 69	9. 49	10. 18	36	−. 69	+17. 66
October	9. 03	19. 50	14. 06	36	+5. 44	+23. 10
November	10. 18	16. 53	18. 16	36	−1. 63	+21. 47
December	24. 41	22. 35	11. 16	36	+11. 19	+32. 66
Year	94. 88	140. 07	107. 41	--------	--------	+32. 66
Dry season	1. 91	26. 64	8. 19	--------	--------	+18. 45
Wet season	92. 97	113. 43	99. 22	--------	--------	+14. 21

BUILDINGS, EQUIPMENT, AND IMPROVEMENTS

The existing facilities on Barro Colorado Island were improved in a number of ways during the last year. The top floor of the Old Laboratory was renovated to provide additional living accommodations for visiting scientists. The reconstruction of Barbour House at its new site, necessitated by the 1959 landslide, was completed. Extensive repairs were made to the dock, and a new landing stage, to facilitate loading and unloading of gas and diesel oil drums, was constructed. Routine maintenance activities included painting some buildings, and minor repairs to several houses and aviaries. One generator was overhauled, and a new electric ⅓-hp. water pump was installed. New rain-recording equipment is in process of being installed by the Hydrographic Office of the Panama Canal Company. Expansion of the library continued.

OTHER ACTIVITIES

Scientific research conducted on Barro Colorado Island during the past year encompassed every field of tropical natural history except anthropology.

The Resident Naturalist continued his research on the behavior of several groups of tropical birds and monkeys. Field observations of the behavior of tropical American carnivores were completed.

Dr. John Ebinger, of Yale University, conducted botanical studies in addition to adding considerably to the collection of botanical specimens and reorganizing the station herbarium.

John Zimmerman continued the research on the physiology of tropical birds begun in 1959 by Dr. Charles Kendeigh of the University of Illinois. Other research projects continued dealt with temperature and humidity gradients conducted by Dr. Charles F. Bennett, Jr., and the analysis of the behavior of Lepidoptera by Dr. Andrew Blest. A summary of Dr. Blest's earlier work on Barro Colorado Island appeared in the Annual Report of the Smithsonian Institution for 1959.

Termites and ants, both of which have been favored subjects for study from the inception of the station, continued to provide material for several scientists. Those birds that follow army ants were the subject of a year-long investigation by Edwin Willis of the University of California.

FINANCES

Trust funds for the maintenance of the island and its living facilities are obtained by collections from visitors and scientists, table subscriptions, and donations.

The following institutions continued their support to the laboratory through the payment of table subscriptions: Eastman Kodak Co.,

New York Zoological Society, and Smithsonian Institution. Donations are also gratefully acknowledged from Eugene Eisenmann and C. M. Goethe.

PLANS AND REQUIREMENTS

The only major building project in view is the reconstruction of the boathouse for which work plans have been made. Plans have also been made to overhaul the *Snook*, the large motor launch.

The improvement of the library will continue.

Within the next few years several major items of equipment will need to be replaced.

ACKNOWLEDGMENTS

The Canal Zone Biological Area can operate only with the excellent cooperation of the Canal Zone Government and the Panama Canal Company. Thanks are due especially to the former Lt. Gov. John D. McElheny, and the Executive Secretary Paul Runnestrand and his staff; the Customs and Immigration officials; and the Police Division. Also deeply appreciated are the technical advice and assistance provided by P. Alton White, Chief of the Dredging Division, and members of his staff; and C. C. Soper of the Eastman Kodak Co.

Respectfully submitted.

MARTIN H. MOYNIHAN,
Resident Naturalist.

Dr. LEONARD CARMICHAEL,
Secretary, Smithsonian Institution.

Report on the International Exchange Service

Sir: I have the honor to submit the following report of the activities of the International Exchange Service for the fiscal year ended June 30, 1961:

The International Exchange Service was initiated by the Smithsonian Institution in the early years of its existence for the interchange of scientific publications between learned societies and individuals in the United States and those of foreign countries. It serves as a means of developing and executing, in part, the broad and comprehensive objective of the Institution, "the diffusion of knowledge."

The Smithsonian Institution is the official United States agency for the exchange with other nations of governmental, scientific, and literary publications. The International Exchange Service is the bureau designated to carry out the functions assigned to the Smithsonian Institution in various conventions, treaties, and international agreements relating to the international exchange of publications.

Publications were received from approximately 250 domestic sources including United States Government bureaus and departments, congressional committees and members of Congress, universities, agricultural experiment stations, learned societies, organizations, and individuals for transmission to foreign addressees in more than 100 foreign countries. Among the publications received for transmission abroad are the following: Language, Journal of the Linguistic Society of America; Journal of the National Education Association; Journal of the American Dental Society; Journal of Science, Iowa State College; Virginia Journal of Science, University of Virginia; Novitates, American Museum of Natural History; Expedition, University Museum, University of Pennsylvania; Brevoria, Museum of Comparative Zoology, Harvard College; Anthropological Record, University of California; Yale University Bulletin; Yearbook of the Carnegie Institution of Washington; Zoologica, New York Zoological Society; Transactions of the American Geophysical Union; Transactions of the American Association of Physicians; Transactions of the American Society of Mechanical Engineers; American Midland Naturalist; Museum of Art Register, University of Kansas; Paleontological Contributions, University of Kansas; Oregon Law Review, University of

Oregon; Studies in English, University of Texas; Proceedings of the American Philosophical Society; Contributions, Scripps Institution of Oceanography; and Annals of the Missouri Botanical Garden.

The number of packages of publications received for transmission during the year was 1,272,604, an increase of 130,606 over the previous fiscal year. The weight of the packages received was 923,179 pounds, an increase of 45,543 over the previous fiscal year.

The packages of publications are forwarded by ocean freight to the port of entry selected by the foreign exchange bureau to whom the shipment is consigned. They are then distributed by the foreign exchange bureau to the intended addressees.

In the countries where there is no exchange bureau, the publications are mailed directly to the addressees. However, if the weight of the packages (intended for one addressee) would make it more economical to forward by ocean freight, the packages are so transmitted to the port selected by the addressee, who must make all arrangements for accepting the shipment at that port of entry.

The total weight of the packages forwarded during the year amounted to 895,010 pounds, of which 571,181 pounds were forwarded by ocean and domestic freight, and 323,829 pounds were forwarded by mail or other means. This was 24,226 pounds more than was forwarded during the previous fiscal year. The number of cases shipped to the foreign exchange bureaus was 3,375, or 74 less than during the previous fiscal year. Of these cases 1,028 were for the full depository recipients of official United States publications which were compiled and forwarded in accordance with bilateral treaties made between the United States and other countries for the exchange of official publications.

Shipments are made to Formosa. No shipments are being made to the mainland of China, North Korea, and Communist-controlled area of Viet-Nam.

FOREIGN DEPOSITORIES OF GOVERNMENTAL DOCUMENTS

The recipients of the official United States publications are determined as a result of bilateral treaties entered into between the United States and the various foreign countries for the mutual exchange of their official publications. The treaty stipulates whether the recipient will receive all the official publications of the United States Government or only a selected list. The recipient receiving all the official publications is classified as a full depository. The recipient receiving a selected list is classified as a partial depository. The International Exchange Service receives copies of all the official United States publications. These are sorted and transmitted to the depositories designated by the Library of Congress. During the past fiscal year there were 598,238 pieces weighing 184,264 pounds assembled for transmission to the full depository recipients, and 71,940 pieces weighing 31,108 pounds assembled and transmitted to the partial depository recipients.   The names and addresses of the full and partial depositories are given in the following list:

DEPOSITORIES OF FULL SETS

ARGENTINA: División Biblioteca, Ministerio de Relaciones Exteriores y Culto, Buenos Aires.
AUSTRALIA: Commonwealth National Library, Canberra.
   NEW SOUTH WALES: Public Library of New South Wales, Sydney.
   QUEENSLAND: Parliamentary Library, Brisbane.
   SOUTH AUSTRALIA: Public Library of South Australia, Adelaide.
   TASMANIA: Parliamentary Library, Hobart.
   VICTORIA: Public Library of Victoria, Melbourne.
   WESTERN AUSTRALIA: State Library, Perth.
AUSTRIA: Administrative Library, Federal Chancellery, Vienna.
BRAZIL: Biblioteca Nacional, Rio de Janeiro.
BULGARIA: Bulgarian Bibliographical Institute, Sofia.[1]
BURMA: Government Book Depot, Rangoon.
CANADA: Library of Parliament, Ottawa.
   MANITOBA: Provincial Library, Winnipeg.
   ONTARIO: Legislative Library, Toronto.
   QUEBEC: Library of the Legislature of the Province of Quebec.
CEYLON: Department of Information, Government of Ceylon, Colombo.
CHILE: Biblioteca Nacional, Santiago.
CHINA: National Central Library, Taipei, Taiwan.
   National Chengchi University, Taipei, Taiwan.
COLOMBIA: Biblioteca Nacional, Bogotá.
COSTA RICA: Biblioteca Nacional, San José.
CUBA: Dirección de Asuntos Culturales, Ministerio de Relaciones Exteriores, Habana.[2]
CZECHOSLOVAKIA: University Library, Prague.
DENMARK: Institut Danois des Échanges Internationaux, Copenhagen.
EGYPT: Bureau des Publications, Ministère des Finances, Cairo.
FINLAND: Parliamentary Library, Helsinki.
FRANCE: Bibliothèque Nationale, Paris.
GERMANY: Deutsche Staatsbibliothek, Berlin.
   Free University of Berlin, Berlin-Dahlem.
   Parliamentary Library, Bonn.
GREAT BRITAIN:
   ENGLAND: British Museum, London.
   LONDON: London School of Economics and Political Science.   (Depository of the London County Council.)
HUNGARY: Library of Parliament, Budapest.[1]
INDIA: National Library, Calcutta.
   Central Secretariat Library, New Delhi.
   Parliament Library, New Delhi.
INDONESIA: Ministry for Foreign Affairs, Djakarta.
IRELAND: National Library of Ireland, Dublin.
ISRAEL: State Archives and Library, Hakirya, Jerusalem.

---

[1] Shipment suspended.
[2] Change in address.

ITALY: Ministero della Pubblica Istruzione, Rome.
JAPAN: National Diet Library, Tokyo.[3]
MEXICO: Secretaría de Relaciones Exteriores, Departamento de Información para el Extranjero México, D.F.
NETHERLANDS: Royal Library, The Hague.
NEW ZEALAND: General Assembly Library, Wellington.
NORWAY: Utenriksdepartmentets Bibliothek, Oslo.
PERU: Sección de Propaganda y Publicaciones, Ministerio de Relaciones Exteriores, Lima.
PHILIPPINES: Bureau of Public Libraries, Department of Education, Manila.
POLAND: Bibliothèque Nationale, Warsaw.[1]
PORTUGAL: Biblioteca Nacional, Lisbon.
SPAIN: Biblioteca Nacional, Madrid.
SWEDEN: Kungliga Biblioteket, Stockholm.
SWITZERLAND: Bibliothèque Centrale Fédérale, Berne.
TURKEY: National Library, Ankara.
UNION OF SOUTH AFRICA: State Library, Pretoria, Transvaal.
UNION OF SOVIET SOCIALIST REPUBLICS: All-Union Lenin Library, Moscow.
UNITED NATIONS: Library of the United Nations, Geneva, Switzerland.
URUGUAY: Oficina de Canje Internacional de Publicaciones, Montevideo.
VENEZUELA: Biblioteca Nacional, Caracas.
YUGOSLAVIA: Bibliografski Institut FNRJ, Belgrade.[3]

DEPOSITORIES OF PARTIAL SETS

AFGHANISTAN: Library of the Afghan Academy, Kabul.
BELGIUM: Bibliothèque Royale, Bruxelles.
BOLIVIA: Biblioteca del Ministerio de Relaciones Exteriores y Culto, La Paz.
BRAZIL: MINAS GERAIS: Departmento Estadul de Estatistica, Belo Horizonte.
BRITISH GUIANA: Government Secretary's Office, Georgetown, Demerara.
CANADA:
    ALBERTA: Provincial Library, Edmonton.
    BRITISH COLUMBIA: Provincial Library, Victoria.
    NEW BRUNSWICK: Legislative Library, Fredericton.
    NEWFOUNDLAND: Department of Provincial Affairs, St. John's.
    NOVA SCOTIA: Provincial Secretary of Nova Scotia, Halifax.
    SASKATCHEWAN: Legislative Library, Regina.
DOMINICAN REPUBLIC: Biblioteca de la Universidad de Santo Domingo, Ciudad Trujillo.
ECUADOR: Biblioteca Nacional, Quito.
EL SALVADOR:
    Biblioteca Nacional, San Salvador.
    Ministerio de Relaciones Exteriores, San Salvador.
GREECE: National Library, Athens.
GUATEMALA: Biblioteca Nacional, Guatemala.
HAITI: Bibliothèque Nationale, Port-au-Prince.
HONDURAS:
    Biblioteca Nacional, Tegucigalpa.
    Ministerio de Relaciones Exteriores, Tegucigalpa.
ICELAND: National Library, Reykjavik.
INDIA:
    BOMBAY: Secretary to the Government, Bombay.
    BIHAR: Revenue Department, Patna.

---

[3] Receives two sets.

KERALA: Kerala Legislature Secretariat, Trivandrum.
UTTAR PRADESH:
   University of Allahabad, Allahabad.
   Secretariat Library, Lucknow.
   WEST BENGAL: Library, West Bengal Legislative Secretariat, Assembly
     House, Calcutta.
IRAN: Imperial Ministry of Education, Tehran.
IRAQ: Public Library, Baghdad.
JAMAICA:
   Colonial Secretary, Kingston.
   University College of the West Indies, St. Andrew.
LEBANON: American University of Beirut, Beirut.
LIBERIA: Department of State, Monrovia.
MALAYA: Federal Secretariat, Federation of Malaya, Kuala Lumpur.
MALTA: Minister for the Treasury, Valletta.
NICARAGUA: Ministerio de Relaciones Exteriores, Managua.
PAKISTAN: Central Secretariat Library, Karachi.
PANAMA: Ministerio de Relaciones Exteriores, Panamá.
PARAGUAY: Ministerio de Relaciones Exteriores, Sección Biblioteca, Asunción.
PHILIPPINES: House of Representatives, Manila.
SCOTLAND: National Library of Scotland, Edinburgh.
SIAM: National Library, Bangkok.
SINGAPORE: Chief Secretary, Government Offices, Singapore.
SUDAN: Gordon Memorial College, Khartoum.

INTERPARLIAMENTARY EXCHANGE OF THE OFFICIAL JOURNAL

There are now being sent abroad 87 copies of the Federal Register and 100 copies of the Congressional Record. This is an increase over the preceding year of three copies of the Congressional Record with no change in the recipients of the Federal Register. The countries to which these journals are being forwarded are given in the following list.

DEPOSITORIES OF CONGRESSIONAL RECORD AND FEDERAL REGISTER

ARGENTINA:
   Biblioteca de la H. Legislatura de Mendoza, Mendoza.[4]
   Biblioteca del Poder Judicial, Mendoza.[5]
   Boletin Oficial de la República Argentina, Buenos Aires.
   Cámara de Diputados Oficina de Información Parlamentaria, Buenos Aires.
AUSTRALIA:
   Commonwealth National Library, Canberra.
   NEW SOUTH WALES: Library of Parliament of New South Wales, Sydney.
   QUEENSLAND: Chief Secretary's Office, Brisbane.
   VICTORIA: Public Library of Victoria, Melbourne.[5]
   WESTERN AUSTRALIA: Library of Parliament of Western Australia, Perth.
BELGIUM: Bibliothèque du Parlement, Palais de la Nation, Brussels.[4 5]
BRAZIL: Biblioteca da Câmara dos Deputados, Brasilia, D.F.[4 6]
BRAZIL: Secretaria da Presidencia, Rio de Janeiro.[4]
BRITISH HONDURAS: Colonial Secretary, Belize.
CAMBODIA: Ministry of Information, Phnom Penh.

---

[4] Congressional Record only.
[5] Federal Register only.
[6] Added during the year.

CANADA:

    Clerk of the Senate, Houses of Parliament, Ottawa.

    Library of Parliament, Ottawa.

CEYLON: Ceylon Ministry of Defense and External Affairs, Colombo.[4]

CHILE: Biblioteca del Congreso Nacional, Santiago.[4]

CHINA:

    Legislative Yuan, Taipei, Taiwan.[4]

    Taiwan Provincial Government, Taipei, Taiwan.

CUBA:

    Biblioteca del Capitolio, Habana.

    Biblioteca Pública Panamericana, Habana.[5]

CZECHOSLOVAKIA: Ceskoslovenska Akademie Ved. Prague.[4]

EGYPT: Ministry of Foreign Affairs, Egyptian Government, Cairo.[4]

FINLAND: Library of the Parliament, Helsinki.[4,6]

FRANCE:

    Bibliothèque Assemblée Nationale, Paris.

    Bibliothèque Conseil de la République, Paris.

    Library, Organization for European Economic Cooperation, Paris.[4]

    Research Department, Council of Europe, Strasbourg.[4]

    Service de la Documentation Étrangère, Assemblée Nationale, Paris.[4]

GERMANY:

    Amerika Institut der Universität München, München.[4]

    Archiv, Deutscher Bundestag, Bonn.

    Bibliothek des Instituts für Weltwirtschaft an der Universität Kiel, Kiel-Wik.

    Bibliothek Hessischer Landtag, Wiesbaden.[4]

    Deutsches Institut für Rechtswissenschaft, Potsdam-Babelsberg II.[5]

    Deutscher Bundesrat, Bonn.[4]

    Deutscher Bundestag, Bonn.[4]

    Hamburgisches Welt-Wirtschafts-Archiv, Hamburg.

    Westdeutsche Bibliothek, Marburg, Hessen.[4,6,7]

GHANA: Chief Secretary's Office, Accra.[4]

GREAT BRITAIN:

    Department of Printed Books, British Museum, London.

    House of Commons Library, London.[4]

    N.P.P. Warehouse, H.M. Stationery Office, London.[5,8]

    Printed Library of the Foreign Office, London.

    Royal Institute of International Affairs, London.[4]

GREECE: Bibliothèque, Chambre des Députés Hellênique, Athens.

GUATEMALA: Biblioteca de la Asamblea Legislativa, Guatemala.

HAITI: Bibliothèque Nationale, Port-au-Prince.

HONDURAS: Biblioteca del Congreso Nacional, Tegucigalpa.

HUNGARY: Országos Széchenyi Konyvtár, Budapest.

INDIA:

    Civil Secretariat Library, Lucknow, United Provinces.[5]

    Indian Council of World Affairs, New Delhi.[4]

    Jammu and Kashmir Constituent Assembly, Srinagar.[4]

    Legislative Assembly, Government of Assam, Shillong.[4]

    Legislative Assembly Library, Lucknow, United Provinces.

    Kerala Legislature Secretariat, Trivandrum.[4]

    Madras State Legislature, Madras.[4]

    Parliament Library, New Delhi.

---

[7] Three copies.
[8] Two copies.

Gokhale Institute of Politics and Economics, Poona.[4]
IRELAND: Dail Eireann, Dublin.
ISRAEL: Library of the Knesset, Jerusalem.
ITALY:
    Biblioteca Camera dei Deputati, Rome.
    Biblioteca del Senato della Republica, Rome.
    International Institute for the Unification of Private Law, Rome.[5]
    Periodicals Unit, Food and Agriculture Organization of the United Nations, Rome.[5]
JAPAN:
    Library of the National Diet, Tokyo.
    Ministry of Finance, Tokyo.
JORDAN: Parliament of the Hashemite Kingdom of Jordan, Amman.[4]
KOREA: Library, National Assembly, Seoul.
LUXEMBOURG: Assemblée Commune de la C.E.C.A., Luxembourg.
MEXICO:
    Dirección, General Informacion, Secretaría de Governación, Mexico, D.F.
    Biblioteca Benjamin Franklin, México, D.F.
    Aguascalientes: Gobernador del Estado de Aguascalientes, Aguascalientes.
    BAJA CALIFORNIA: Gobernador del Distrito Norte, Mexicali.
    CAMPECHE: Gobernador del Estado de Campeche, Campeche.
    CHIAPAS: Gobernador del Estado de Chiapas, Tuxtla Guitiérrez.
    CHIHUAHUA: Gobernador del Estado de Chihuahua, Chihuahua.
    COAHUILA: Periódico Oficial del Estado de Coahuila, Palacio de Gobierno, Saltillo.
    COLIMA: Gobernador del Estado de Colima, Colima.
    GUANAJUATO: Secretaría General de Gobierno del Estado, Guanajuato.[5]
    JALISCO: Biblioteca del Estado, Guadalajara.
    MÈXICO: Gaceta del Gobierno, Toluca.
    MICHOACÁN: Secretaría General de Gobierno del Estado de Michoacán, Morelia.
    MORELOS: Palacio de Gobierno, Cuernavaca.
    NAYARIT: Gobernador de Nayarit, Tepic.
    NUEVO LÈON: Biblioteca del Estado, Monterrey.
    OAXACA: Periódico Oficial, Palacio de Gobierno, Oaxaca.[5]
    PUEBLA: Secretaría General de Gobierno, Puebla.
    QUERÉTARO: Secretaría General de Gobierno, Sección de Archivo, Querétaro.
    SINALOA: Gobernador del Estado de Sinaloa, Culiacán.
    SONORA: Gobernador del Estado de Sonora, Hermosillo.
    TAMAULIPAS: Secretaría General de Gobierno, Victoria.
    VERACRUZ: Gobernador del Estado de Veracruz, Departamento de Gobernación y Justicia, Jalapa.
    YUCATÁN: Gobernador del Estado de Yucatán, Mérida.
NETHERLANDS: Koninklijke Bibliotheek, The Hague.[5]
NEW ZEALAND: General Assembly Library, Wellington.
NORWAY: Library of the Norwegian Parliament, Oslo.
PANAMA: Biblioteca Nacional, Panama City.[4]
PHILIPPINES: House of Representatives, Manila.
POLAND: Kancelaria Rady Panstwa, Biblioteka Sejmowa, Warsaw.
PORTUGUESE TIMOR: Repartição Central de Administração Civil, Dili.[5]
RHODESIA AND NYASALAND: Federal Assembly, Salisbury.[5]
RUMANIA: Biblioteca Centrala de Stat RPR, Bucharest.
SPAIN: Boletin Oficial del Estado, Presidencia del Gobierno, Madrid.[5]

SWITZERLAND: Bibliothèque, Bureau International du Travail, Geneva.[5]
   International Labor Office, Geneva.[5,8]
   Library, United Nations, Geneva.
TOGO: Ministere d' Etat, de l'Interieur, de l'Information et de la Presse, Lome.
UNION OF SOUTH AFRICA:
   CAPE OF GOOD HOPE: Library of Parliament, Cape Town.
   TRANSVAAL: State Library, Pretoria.
UNION OF SOVIET SOCIALIST REPUBLICS: Fundamental'niia Biblioteka Obshchest-
   vennykh Nauk, Moscow.
URUGUAY: Diario Oficial, Calle Florida 1178, Montevideo.
YUGOSLAVIA: Bibliografski Institut FNRJ, Belgrade.[8]

FOREIGN EXCHANGE SERVICES

Exchange publications for addressees in the countries listed below
are forwarded by freight to the exchange services of those countries.
Exchange publications for addressees in other countries are forwarded
directly by mail.

LIST OF EXCHANGE SERVICES

AUSTRIA: Austrian National Library, Vienna.
BELGIUM: Service des Échanges Internationaux, Bibliothèque Royale de Bel-
   gique, Bruxelles.
CHINA: National Central Library, Taipei, Taiwan.
CZECHOSLOVAKIA: Bureau of International Exchanges, University Library,
   Prague.
DENMARK: Institut Danois des Échanges Internationaux, Bibliothèque Royale,
   Copenhagen.
EGYPT: Government Press, Publications Office, Bulaq, Cairo.
FINLAND: Delegation of the Scientific Societies, Helsinki.
FRANCE: Service des Échanges Internationaux, Bibliothèque Nationale, Paris.
GERMANY (Eastern): Deutsche Staatsbibliothek, Berlin.
GERMANY (Western): Deutsche Forschungsgemeinschaft, Bad Godesberg.
HUNGARY: Service Hongrois des Echanges Internationaux, Országos Széchenyi
   Konyvtár, Budapest.
INDIA: Government Printing and Stationery, Bombay.
INDONESIA: Minister of Education, Djakarta.
ISRAEL: Jewish National and University Library, Jerusalem.
ITALY: Ufficio degli Scambi Internazionali, Ministero della Pubblica Istruzione,
   Rome.
JAPAN: Division for Interlibrary Services, National Diet Library, Tokyo.
KOREA: Korean Library Association, Seoul.
NETHERLANDS: International Exchange Bureau of the Netherlands, Royal Li-
   brary, The Hague.
NEW SOUTH WALES: Public Library of New South Wales, Sydney.
NEW ZEALAND: General Assembly Library, Wellington.
NORWAY: Service Norvégien des Échanges Internationaux, Bibilothèque de
   l'Université Royale, Oslo.
PHILIPPINES: Bureau of Public Libraries, Department of Education, Manila.
POLAND: Service Polonais des Échanges Internationaux, Bibliothèque Nationale,
   Warsaw.
PORTUGAL: Seccão de Trocas Internacionais, Biblioteca Nacional, Lisbon.
QUEENSLAND: Bureau of International Exchange of Publications, Chief Secre-
   tary's Office, Brisbane.
RUMANIA: International Exchange Service, Biblioteca Centrala de Stat, Bu-
   charest.

SOUTH AUSTRALIA: South Australian Government Exchanges Bureau, Government Printing and Stationery Office, Adelaide.

SPAIN: Junta de Intercambio y Adquisición de Libros y Revistas para Bibliotecas Públicas, Ministerio de Educación Nacional, Madrid.

SWEDEN: Kungliga Biblioteket, Stockholm.

SWITZERLAND: Service Suisse des Échanges Internationaux, Bibliothèque Centrale Fédérale, Berne.

TASMANIA: Secretary of the Premier, Hobart.

TURKEY: National Library, Ankara.

UNION OF SOUTH AFRICA: Government Printing and Stationery Office, Cape Town.

UNION OF SOVIET SOCIALISTS REPUBLICS: Bureau of Book Exchange, State Lenin Library, Moscow.

VICTORIA: Public Library of Victoria, Melbourne.

WESTERN AUSTRALIA: State Library, Perth.

YUGOSLAVIA: Bibliografski Institut FNRJ, Belgrade.

The number of packages and the weight of the packages received from sources in the United States for transmission abroad, and the packages received from foreign sources intended for domestic addressees are classified in the following table:

| Classification | Received by the Smithsonian Institution for transmission | | | |
| | For transmission abroad | | For distribution in the United States | |
	Number of packages	Weight in pounds	Number of packages	Weight in pounds
United States parliamentary documents received for transmission abroad	746, 298	354, 886		
Publications received from foreign sources for United States parliamentary addressees			10, 819	14, 613
United States departmental documents received for transmission abroad	249, 019	235, 823		
Publications received from foreign sources for United States departmental addressees			4, 721	11, 651
Miscellaneous scientific and literary publications received for transmission abroad	205, 972	220, 240		
Miscellaneous scientific and literary publications received from abroad for distribution in the United States			55, 775	85, 966
Totals	1, 201, 289	810, 949	71, 315	112, 230
Grand total	1,272,604 packages		923,179 pounds	

Respectfully submitted.

J. A. COLLINS, *Chief.*

Dr. LEONARD CARMICHAEL,
Secretary, Smithsonian Institution.

Report on the National Gallery of Art

SIR: I have the honor to submit, on behalf of the Board of Trustees, the twenty-fourth annual report of the National Gallery of Art, for the fiscal year ended June 30, 1961. This report is made pursuant to the provisions of section 5(d) of Public Resolution No. 14, Seventy-fifth Congress, first session, approved March 24, 1937 (50 Stat. 51).

ORGANIZATION

The statutory members of the Board of Trustees of the National Gallery of Art are the Chief Justice of the United States, the Secretary of State, the Secretary of the Treasury, and the Secretary of the Smithsonian Institution, ex officio. The four general trustees continuing in office during the fiscal year ended June 30, 1961, were Ferdinand Lammot Belin, Chester Dale, Paul Mellon, and Rush H. Kress. Duncan Phillips, a general trustee, resigned from the Board of Trustees on December 1, 1960, and on May 3, 1961, John Hay Whitney was elected a general trustee of the National Gallery of Art to serve in that capacity for the remainder of the term expiring July 1, 1963. On May 4, 1961, Chester Dale was reelected by the Board of Trustees to serve as President of the Gallery and Paul Mellon was elected Vice President.

The executive officers of the Gallery as of June 30, 1961, are as follows:

Huntington Cairns, Secretary-Treasurer.
John Walker, Director.

Ernest R. Feidler, Administrator.
Huntington Cairns, General Counsel.
Perry B. Cott, Chief Curator.

The three standing committees of the Board, as constituted at the annual meeting on May 4, 1961, were as follows:

EXECUTIVE COMMITTEE

Chief Justice of the United States, Earl Warren, Chairman.
Chester Dale, Vice Chairman.

Secretary of the Smithsonian Institution, Leonard Carmichael.
Paul Mellon.
John Hay Whitney.

FINANCE COMMITTEE

Secretary of the Treasury, C. Douglas Dillon, Chairman.
Chester Dale, Vice Chairman.
Paul Mellon.

Secretary of the Smithsonian Institution, Leonard Carmichael.
John Hay Whitney.

PERSONNEL

At the close of the year full-time Government employees on the staff of the National Gallery numbered 312, as compared with 314 employees at the close of the previous fiscal year. The United States Civil Service regulations govern the appointment of employees paid from appropriated public funds.

Continued emphasis was given to the training of employees under the Government Employees Training Act. Under the provisions of this act, the Gallery secured training and development of several of its employees in their profession to help maintain the standing and prestige of the Gallery. Among those for whom training was provided during the year were the assistant chief curator, the curator of painting, the curator of education, and the associate curator of education.

APPROPRIATIONS

For the fiscal year ended June 30, 1961, the Congress of the United States in the regular annual appropriation for the National Gallery of Art provided $1,848,000 to be used for salaries and expenses in the operation and unkeep of the Gallery, the protection and care of works of art acquired by the Board of Trustees, and all administrative expenses incident thereto, as authorized by Joint Resolution of Congress approved March 24, 1937 (20 U.S.C. 71–75; 50 Stat. 51). Congress also included in a supplemental appropriation act $72,000 to cover pay increases not provided for in the regular appropriation. The total appropriation for the fiscal year was $1,920,000.

The following expenditures and encumbrances were incurred:

Personal services	$1,569,500.00
Other than personal services	350,395.29
Unobligated balance	104.71
Total	1,920,000.00

ATTENDANCE

There were 1,032,340 visitors to the Gallery during the fiscal year 1961, an increase of 67,150 over the total attendance of 965,190 visitors during the fiscal year 1960. The average number of visitors daily was 2,843.

ACCESSIONS

There were 1,387 accessions by the National Gallery of Art as gifts, loans, or deposits during the fiscal year.

GIFTS

During the year the following gifts or bequests were accepted by the Board of Trustees:

PAINTINGS

Donor	Artist	Title
Coe Foundation, New York, N.Y.	Beechey	General Sir Thomas Picton.
Do	Cotes	Miss Elizabeth Crewe.
Do	Gainsborough	William Yelverton Davenport.
Do	Miereveld	Portrait of a Lady with a Ruff.
Chester Dale, New York, N.Y.	Stuart	Lady Liston.
The Fuller Foundation, Inc., Boston, Mass.	Reynolds	Squire Musters.
Do	Gainsborough	Master John Heathcote.
Do	Turner	The Dogana and Santa Maria della Salute, Venice.
Colonel and Mrs. Edgar W. Garbisch, New York, N.Y.	Greenwood	Mrs. Welshman.
The Adele R. Levy Fund, Inc., New York, N.Y.	Renoir	Madame Henriot.
National Gallery of Art Purchase Fund—	Copley	The Copley Family.
Andrew W. Mellon Gift.	de Heem	Vase of Flowers.
Mrs. Lillian S. Timken, New York, N.Y.	Fry	Landscape.
Do	----do	Potters in Landscape.
Do	----do	Obv.: Seascape. Rev.: Landscape with Palm Tree.
Do	----do	Sheep by Stream and Field.

SCULPTURE

Donor	Artist	Title
Stanley Mortimer, Litchfield, Conn.	Italian School, XVI Century.	Farnese Hercules.

DECORATIVE ARTS

Donor	Artist	Title
Coe Foundation, New York, N.Y.	Flemish Gothic Tapestry.	The Return from the Hunt.

GRAPHIC ARTS

During the year Mrs. E. C. Chadbourne gave a colored mezzotint portrait of George III with autograph of George I. An etching entitled "Pastorale" by Hans Thoma was given by Rabbi Hugo B. Schiff, and a water color entitled "The Clipper Ship *Minnie G. Loud*" by Roux was given by Robert Peet Skinner.

OTHER GIFTS

During the fiscal year 1961 gifts of money were made by The A. W. Mellon Educational and Charitable Trust, Old Dominion Foundation,

Avalon Foundation, Calouste Gulbenkian Foundation, The Fein Foundation, James N. Rosenberg, Irving R. Saal, Mrs. John T. Terry, and various donors in memory of Mrs. Dorothy V. Keppel. An additional cash bequest was received from the estate of William Nelson Cromwell.

EXCHANGE OF WORKS OF ART

In exchange for nine works of art in the Samuel H. Kress Collection, the Kress Foundation gave the National Gallery of Art the following pieces of sculpture:

Artist	*Title*
Tino di Camaino	Madonna and Child with Queen Sancia, Saints and Angels.
Giovanni di Balduccio	Charity.
Bonino da Campione	Justice.
Do	Prudence.
Orcagna	Angel with Tambourine.
Do	Angel with Hurdy-Gurdy.
Quercia, Jacopo della	Madonna of Humility.
Master of the Mascoli Altar	Angel of the Annunciation.
Do	Virgin of the Annunciation.
Do	St. Peter.
Do	St. Paul.
Benedetto da Maiano	Madonna and Child.
Fiamberti	Madonna and Child.
Robbia, Andrea della	The Adoration of the Child.
Robbia, Luca della	Nativity.
Solari, Cristoforo	Madonna and Child.
Michelangelo (attr. to)	Apollo and Marsyas.
Sansovino	Madonna and Child.
Coysevox	Louis of France, The Grand Dauphin.
French School, Early 18th Century	Louis, Duc de Bourgogne.
Desjardins	Louis XIV.
Riemenschneider	St. Burchard of Würzburg.

In exchange for a print by Odilon Redon entitled "Profile de Lumière" in the Lessing J. Rosenwald Collection, Mr. Rosenwald gave the National Gallery of Art a superior impression of the same print.

WORKS OF ART ON LOAN

The following works of art were received on loan by the Gallery:

From	*Artist*	*Title*
Robert Woods Bliss, Washington, D.C.		28 objects of Pre-Columbian Art.
Mrs. Mellon Bruce, New York, N.Y.	Goya	Condesa de Chinchón.
Chester Dale, New York, N.Y.	Bellows	Blue Morning.
Do	Monet	The Seine at Giverny.
Jerome Hill, New York, N.Y.	Delacroix	The Arab Tax.
Do	do	Fanatics of Tangiers.

To	*Artist*	*Title*
Samuel H. Kress Foundation, New York, N.Y.	Master of Badia a Isola.	Madonna Enthroned with Angels.
Do	Signorelli	Madonna and Child with Saints.
Do	Tintoretto	Summer.
Mrs. Eugene Meyer, Washington, D.C.	Dufresne	Still Life.
Do	Renoir	Nude.
Do	do	Man Lying on a Sofa.

WORKS OF ART ON LOAN RETURNED

The following works of art on loan were returned during the fiscal year:

To	*Artist*	*Title*
Robert Woods Bliss, Washington, D.C.		6 objects of Pre-Columbian Art.
Mrs. Mellon Bruce, New York, N.Y.	Pissarro	Spring at Louveciennes.
Stephan Walter Cassirer, Copenhagen, Denmark.	Cézanne	Pears.
The Calouste Gulbenkian Foundation, Lisbon, Portugal.	Egyptian, Saite Period.	Statuette of the Courtier Bes.
Do	Egyptian, Saite Period.	Head of a Priest.
Samuel H. Kress Foundation, New York, N.Y.		30 paintings and 8 sculptures.
Mrs. Eugene Meyer, Washington, D.C.	Dufresne	Still Life.
Do	Renoir	Nude.
Do	Renoir	Man Lying on a Sofa.
Richard W. Norton, Shreveport, La.	Bingham	The Result of the Election.

WORKS OF ART LENT

During the fiscal year the Gallery lent the following works of art for exhibition purposes:

To	*Artist*	*Title*
American Federation of Arts, New York, N.Y.	Daumier (bronze)	Le Dédaigneux (Prunelle).
Do	Daumier (bronze)	Le Rieur Edente.
Do	Daumier (bronze)	Le Stupide (Chevandier de Valdrome).
Birmingham Museum of Art, Birmingham, Ala.	Sully	Andrew Jackson.
University of California, UCLA Art Galleries, Los Angeles, Calif.	Boucher	Tête-à-Tête (drawing).
Do	Moreau le Jeune	La Petite Loge (drawing).
Corcoran Gallery of Art, Washington, D.C.	Ryder	Mending the Harness.
Do	Ryder	Siegfried and the Rhine Maidens.

To	*Artist*	*Title*
El Paso Museum of Art, El Paso, Tex.	Stuart	Betsey Hartigan.
Do	West	Self-Portrait.
Do	Trumbull	William Rogers.
Do	Eichholtz	The Ragan Sisters.
Do	Copley	Henry Laurens.
Do	Peale	Benjamin Harrison.
Department of Justice, Washington, D.C.	Dupré	The Old Oak.
Do	Diaz de la Peña	Forest Scene.
Do	Tanner	Engagement between the Monitor and Merrimac, Hampton Roads.
Do	Unknown	Lexington Battle Monument.
Do	do	Leaving the Manor House.
Do	do	Village by the River.
Do	do	Regatta Near Sandy Hook.
Smithsonian Institution, Washington, D.C.	Roux	The Clipper Ship "Minnie G. Loud."
Department of State, American Embassy, London.	Beechey	General Sir Thomas Picton.
Do	Cotes	Miss Elizabeth Crewe.
Do	Gainsborough	William Yelverton Davenport.
Do	Miereveld	Portrait of a Lady with a Ruff.
Do	Flemish Gothic Tapestry.	The Return from the Hunt.
Department of State, Washington, D.C.	Brussels, 17th-Century Tapestry.	America.
Do	Harpignies	Landscape.
Do	Feke	Portrait of a Lady.
Do	Benbridge	Portrait of a Man.
Do	Peale	George Washington.
Do	Lambdin	Abraham Lincoln.
Do	Romney	Sir Archibald Campbell.
Virginia Museum of Art, Richmond, Va.	Stuart	Mrs. Richard Yates.
The White House, Washington, D.C.	Hassam	Allies Day, May 1917.
Do	Audubon	Farmyard Fowls.
Do	Bard	Steamer St. Lawrence.
Do	Unknown	Flowers and Fruit.
Do	Winterhalter	Queen Victoria.
Do	MacKay	Catherine Brower.
Do	Volk	Abraham Lincoln.
Do	Schrag	Solitude (engraving).
Do	Marini	Cavalier Rouge (colored lithograph).
Woodlawn Plantation, Mt. Vernon, Va.	Polk	General Washington at Princeton.

EXHIBITIONS

The following exhibitions were held at the National Gallery of Art during the fiscal year 1961:

Prints by Toulouse-Lautrec. From the Rosenwald Collection. Continued from previous fiscal year through August 15, 1960.

French 18th-Century Prints and Drawings. From the Widener Collection. Continued from previous fiscal year through September 14, 1960.

Prints by Hogarth. From the Rosenwald Collection. August 16, 1960, through December 1, 1960.

Exhibitions of recent accessions. Paintings from the Timken Collection, August 30, 1960, through September 30, 1960; "Madame Henriot" by Renoir, February 26, 1961, through March 15, 1961; "Squire Musters" by Reynolds, "Master John Heathcote" by Gainsborough, and "The Dogana and Santa Maria della Salute, Venice" by Turner, May 6, 1961, through June 4, 1961.

Italian Drawings from Five Centuries. Lent by Italian Museums. October 9, 1960, through November 6, 1960.

Italian Prints. From the Rosenwald Collection. October 9, 1960, through November 6. 1960.

Manuscript Illuminations, XIth–XVth Century. From the Rosenwald Collection. October 9, 1960, through February 2, 1961.

The Splendid Century: French Art of the Seventeenth Century. Sponsored by the Government of France and arranged by the Direction Générale des Affaires Culturelles and the Association Française d'Action Artistique. November 10, 1960, through December 15, 1960.

Christmas Prints. From various donors. December 2, 1960, through March 5, 1961.

The Civil War, A Centennial Exhibition of Eyewitness Drawings. From 18 collections and private lenders. January 8 through February 12, 1961.

Rembrandt Etchings. From various donors. February 3 through March 21, 1961.

The Marie and Averell Harriman Collection. From the collection of the Honorable and Mrs. W. Averell Harriman. April 16 through May 14, 1961.

Chinese Art Treasures. Sponsored by the Government of the Republic of China. May 28, 1961, to continue into the next fiscal year.

Early American Lighting Devices. From the Index of American Design. March 5, 1961, to continue into the next fiscal year.

TRAVELING EXHIBITIONS

Rosenwald Collection.—Special exhibitions of prints, drawings, and sculpture from the Rosenwald Collection were circulated during the fiscal year to 30 museums, universities, schools, and art centers in the United States.

Index of American Design.—During the fiscal year 1961, 22 traveling exhibitions (753 plates and 60 lithographs) were circulated in this country to 15 States and the District of Columbia.

CURATORIAL ACTIVITIES

Under the direction of Dr. Perry B. Cott, chief curator, the curatorial department accessioned 43 gifts to the Gallery during the fiscal year 1961. Advice was given regarding 670 works of art brought

1. Reynolds: Squire Musters. National Gallery of Art. Given in memory of Governor Alvan T. Fuller by the Fuller Foundation.

2. Gainsborough: Master John Heathcote. National Gallery of Art. Given in memory of Governor Alvan T. Fuller by the Fuller Foundation.

Turner: The Dogana and Santa Maria della Salute, Venice. National Gallery of Art. Given in memory of Governor Alvan T. Fuller by the Fuller Foundation.

Copley: The Copley Family.　National Gallery of Art Purchase Fund, Andrew W. Mellon Gift.

Renoir: Madame Henriot. National Gallery of Art. Gift of the Adele R. Levy Fund, Inc.

1. Renoir: Girl with a Basket of Fish. National Gallery of Art.   Gift of William Robertson Coe.

2. Renoir: Girl with a Basket of Oranges. National Gallery of Art.   Gift of William Robertson Coe.

to the Gallery for expert opinion and 25 visits to collections were made by members of the staff in connection with offers of gifts. About 3,700 inquiries, many of them requiring research, were answered verbally and by letter.

Dr. Cott addressed the North Carolina State Art Society on the occasion of the opening of the Samuel H. Kress Collection in the North Carolina Museum of Art at Raleigh.

Miss Elizabeth Mongan, curator of graphic arts, lectured on Graphic Arts at Notre Dame University; the Renaissance Society, Cambridge, Mass.; and the Art Institute of Chicago.

Dr. H. Lester Cooke, curator of painting, lectured at the Smithsonian Institution and at Georgetown University.

Dr. Katherine Shepard, assistant curator of graphic arts, served again as secretary of the Washington Society of the Archaeological Institute of America. She gave a graduate course in Ancient Sculpture the first semester and a graduate course in Ancient Painting the second semester, at Catholic University.

John Pancoast, registrar, gave a graduate seminar in Italian Renaissance Sculpture at Catholic University.

The Richter Archives received and cataloged over 180 photographs on exchange from museums here and abroad, 2,178 photographs were purchased, and about 5,000 reproductions have been added to the Richter Archives.

RESTORATION

Francis Sullivan, resident restorer of the Gallery, made regular and systematic inspection of all works of art in the Gallery and periodically removed dust and bloom as required. He relined 12 paintings and gave special treatment to 36. Sixteen paintings were X-rayed as an aid in research. Mr. Sullivan supervised the construction of a vacuum hot-table and used it as an adjunct in the relining of paintings. Experiments were continued with the application of 27H and other synthetic varnishes developed by the National Gallery of Art Fellowship at the Mellon Institute of Industrial Research, Pittsburgh, Pa. Proofs of all color reproductions of Gallery paintings were checked and approved, and technical advice on the conservation of paintings was furnished to the public upon request.

PUBLICATIONS

William P. Campbell, assistant chief curator, wrote the introduction and catalog notes for the catalog of the exhibition *The Civil War, A Centennial Exhibition of Eyewitness Drawings*.

Miss Elizabeth Mongan, curator of graphic arts, wrote introductions for two exhibition catalogs.

Dr. H. Lester Cooke, curator of painting, wrote an article entitled "Great Masters of Impressionist Art: the Dale Collection," *National Geographic Magazine*, May 1961. He was also coauthor of "Roman Drawings at Windsor Castle," Phaidon Press, 1960, and wrote articles for *America Illustrated*.

Dr. Katharine Shepard, assistant curator of graphic arts, reviewed a book for the *American Journal of Archaeology*, April 1961.

Miss Anna M. Voris, museum curator, wrote an article on "Art Galleries" for the *American Oxford Encyclopedia*.

During the fiscal year 1961 the Publications Fund published the remaining two in a series of ten booklets, *Schools of Painting in the National Gallery of Art*, and began the sale of boxed sets in slipcases. Two new catalogs were published, *The Civil War* and *Exhibition of the Marie and Averell Harriman Collection*, as well as a new edition of *Twentieth Century Painting from the Chester Dale Collection*. New material placed on sale by the Publications Fund included "Horace Walpole" by Wilmarth Sheldon Lewis, the 1960 A. W. Mellon Lecturer in the Fine Arts; "The Revolution," a recording by Richard Bales of the Gallery staff; "Ratapoil," a sculpture reproduction of a work by Daumier in the Rosenwald Collection; "Roman Drawings at Windsor Castle" by Hereward Lester Cooke of the Gallery staff and Sir Anthony Blunt; and two new collotype reproductions of portraits by Roberti in the Kress Collection.

Five new color and eight new monotone postcards and an 11 x 14" reproduction of the Chalice of the Abbot Suger of Saint-Denis were published. The Christmas card selection included seven new color and four new black-and-white subjects.

In connection with the exhibition of Chinese Art Treasures, a special sales area was set up in the central lobby at which fifty 2 x 2" slides published by the Fund were sold, as well as postcards, small and large prints, scrolls, books, and the exhibition catalog.

EDUCATIONAL PROGRAM

The program of the Educational Office was carried out under the direction of Dr. Raymond S. Stites, curator in charge of educational work, and his staff. The staff lectured and conducted tours on the works of art in the Gallery's collection.

Attendance for the General Tours, Tours of the Week, and Picture of the Week talks, totaled 38,839, and that of the auditorium lectures on Sunday afternoons totaled 12,433 persons.

Special lectures, tours, and conferences were arranged for 376 groups and individuals, and the total number of persons served in this manner was 14,088. These included groups of visitors from Government agencies, club and study groups, foreign students, religious organizations, convention groups, and women's organizations. These special services were also given to school groups from all over the country.

The program of training volunteer docents continued and instruction was given to approximately 100 volunteers. By special arrangement with the school systems of the District of Columbia and the surrounding counties of Maryland and Virginia these volunteers conducted tours for 1,724 classes with a total of 51,920 children, an increase of 5,336 children over last year's total.

The staff of the Educational Office delivered 10 lectures in the auditorium on Sunday afternoons, and 30 lectures were given by guest lecturers. André Grabar delivered the Tenth Annual Series of the A. W. Mellon Lectures in the Fine Arts, beginning April 16, 1961, and continuing for six consecutive Sundays. His subject was "Christian Iconography and the Christian Religion in Antiquity."

The slide library of the Educational Office has a total of 41,989 slides in its permanent and lending collections. During the year 1,368 slides were added to the collections; 285 persons borrowed a total of 11,613 slides from the collections.

Members of the staff participated in activities outside the Gallery. Dr. Stites gave a total of 54 lectures in various cities throughout the country and in Washington, D.C., and wrote four magazine articles. Dr. Margaret Bouton, associate curator, gave a night course in the history of art at the American University, and Marcel Franciscono, docent, gave a night course in the history of art at George Washington University. The staff members prepared material for use by the volunteer docents and kept up the program of editing this material regularly. This material is also lent to slide borrowers and is sold with slide sets and photographs through the Publications Fund.

A printed calendar of events was prepared and distributed monthly to a mailing list of 7,553 names. Twenty-one new 13-minute radio talks were prepared and recorded by members of the staff for use during intermission of the broadcasts of the Gallery's Sunday evening concerts.

EXTENSION SERVICE

The Extension Service was separated from the Educational Office and placed under the supervision of Dr. Grose Evans, curator of the Index of American Design. This service circulates to the public the traveling exhibits, Gallery films, and slide lecture sets. There are 17 traveling exhibits in circulation, lent free of charge except for transportation charges. The exhibits were circulated 95 times and seen by approximately 46,000 viewers. There are three Gallery films in circulation; these have been lent 45 times during the year and seen by 12,200 persons. A total of 622 slide sets with texts on a variety of objects in the collection were lent 1,563 times and seen by 93,780 viewers.

This year the Extension Service reached approximately 151,980 viewers. Last year's estimated total was 67,480.

LIBRARY

During the year the library, under the supervision of Miss Ruth E. Carlson, acquisitioned 827 books and 655 pamphlets; 266 books, 40 pamphlets, 45 subscriptions to periodicals, and 2,178 photographs were purchased from private funds; Government funds were used to purchase 16 books and 24 subscriptions to periodicals, and for the binding of 114 volumes of periodicals. Gifts to the library included 460 books, and 407 pamphlets. The library acquired through exchange 85 books, 208 pamphlets, 1,572 periodicals, and 180 photographs.

The library cataloged and classified 1,343 publications, recorded 2,497 periodicals, filed 5,570 catalog cards, routed charges for 7,169 periodicals, and filed 3,012 book charges. This year the library sold 213 duplicate books, and 578 periodicals were sent to the U.S. Book Exchange. The library borrowed 1,409 books on interlibrary loan, 1,287 of these from the Library of Congress.

The library is the depository for black-and-white photographs of works of art in the Gallery's collections. These are maintained for use in research by the staff, for exchange with other institutions, and for sale to the public. Approximately 8,191 photographs were stocked in the library during the year and 1,452 orders for 6,407 photographs were filled. There were 307 permits for reproduction of 767 subjects processed in the Library.

INDEX OF AMERICAN DESIGN

The work of the Index of American Design during the year was carried on under the direction of Dr. Grose Evans, curator. In all, 55 sets of color slides (2,750 slides) were circulated throughout the United States. The photographic files were increased by 51 negatives and 231 prints, and these photographs were used for exhibits as well as for study and to fill requests for publication. Twenty-seven permits to reproduce 121 subjects were issued. Approximately 429 visitors used Index material for purposes of research, publication, and design.

The curator continued to participate in the orientation program of the U.S.I.A. personnel, and also delivered lectures to club and school groups. Expert opinions were rendered to 10 persons. He also attended sessions of the Williamsburg Forum and the Alexandria Forum, and traveled to New England and three other cities to study American architecture and furnishings. In addition, Dr. Evans has been conducting a course for George Washington University, "The Story of Painting," on television, WTOP, since June 12, 1961, covering painting from the Cave Age to the present. The lectures are divided into 45 sessions of one-half an hour, presented Monday, Wednesday, and Friday at 6:30 a.m.

MAINTENANCE OF THE BUILDING AND GROUNDS

The Gallery building, the mechanical equipment, and the grounds have been maintained at the established standards throughout the year.

The renewal program of all solid portions of the roof was completed.

The Phantasia marble borders in the East and West Garden Courts, which had raised and broken, were removed and replaced with a domestic marble, "Compania Rose." This does not require reinforcement by steel rods which were the primary cause of the failure of the Phantasia marble.

One of the elevators in the north lobby was converted from manual to automatic.

The Gallery greenhouse was operated to full capacity in providing flowering plants for the decoration of the Gallery throughout the year.

Fourteen hundred Gallery-grown landscape-size azaleas were replanted in redesigned beds on the grounds as substitutes for overgrown and nematode-infested small-leaf hollies and euonymous. The azaleas are effective as foliage plants throughout the year and give the landscaping additional color in spring and early summer.

Spreading Japanese yews were substituted for the nematode-damaged, small-leaf hollies on the south side of the building.

The experimental planting of various zoysia grasses continued in the Madison Drive and Seventh Street parkings and other exposed lawn areas.

LECTOUR

The Gallery's electronic guide system, Lectour, continued to be an effective tool for art education purposes. During the fiscal year 1961 Lectour was available in 20 different exhibition areas and was used by 74,487 visitors. It has been installed in 10 additional gallery rooms and broadcasts will be available to the public during the ensuing fiscal year.

Lectour broadcasts were prepared for special exhibitions of Civil War paintings, Italian drawings, and Chinese art treasures.

OTHER ACTIVITIES

Thirty-seven Sunday evening concerts were given in the East Garden Court. The National Gallery orchestra conducted by Richard Bales played 10 of these concerts. Two of the 10 concerts were made possible by the Music Performance Trust Fund of the American Federation of Musicians. In addition, a string orchestra conducted by Richard Bales furnished music during the opening of the new Print Room and the Widener Rooms on October 8, 1960, and at the opening of the Civil War Exhibition on January 7, 1961. The concert on Sunday evening, October 23, 1960, was dedicated to United Nations Day and four Sunday evening concerts during May 1961 were devoted to the National Gallery of Art's 18th American Music Festival. All concerts were broadcast in their entirety in stereophonic sound by station WGMS, AM and FM. Intermission talks during these broadcasts were given by members of the Gallery's Educational Office.

During the year 8,059 copies of 16 press releases were approved and issued in connection with the various exhibitions and Gallery activities. A total of 138 permits to copy and 81 photographic permits were issued.

In response to requests 2,275 copies of the pamphlet "A Cordial Invitation from the Director," and 1,650 copies of the Gallery's Information Booklet were sent to members of the House and Senate for distribution to their constituents; and 26,225 copies of the pamphlet "A Cordial Invitation from the Director," and 2,655 copies of the Information Booklet were sent to various organizations holding conventions in Washington.

A total of 95 publications on the Gallery's collections and exhibitions were sent to various museums in accordance with the Exchange Program.

Henry B. Beville, the Gallery's photographer, and his staff processed 22,124 prints, 17,142 color slides, 570 black-and-white slides, 3,510 negatives, 558 color transparencies, 146 sets of color separation negatives, 5 infrared photographs, and 3 ultraviolet photographs during the fiscal year.

AUDIT OF PRIVATE FUNDS OF THE GALLERY

An audit of the private funds of the Gallery will be made for the fiscal year ended June 30, 1961, by Price Waterhouse & Co., public accountants, and the certificate of that company on its examination of the accounting records maintained for such funds will be forwarded to the Gallery.

Respectfully submitted,

HUNTINGTON CAIRNS, *Secretary.*

Dr. LEONARD CARMICHAEL,
Secretary, Smithsonian Institution.

Report on the Library

SIR: I have the honor to submit the following report on the activities of the Smithsonian library for the fiscal year ended June 30, 1961:

As in the past the emphasis of the library has been on the providing of the literature and library services necessary for the promotion of the Smithsonian's various programs.

The number of items received by the library during the year was 67,275, including books, journals, pamphlets, microfilms, maps, photostats, and atlases. Of this total, 2,178 books were purchased, and subscriptions were placed for 675 scientific and technical journals. The balance of the materials came by exchange and gifts. The library's active exchange program, on a worldwide basis, continued to supply the journals, proceedings, and memoirs of scientific and learned societies which form the backbone of many of the library's collections. New exchanges established totaled 289, and 1,867 pieces were specifically requested to supply items missing from sets. A concentrated effort was made to bring the files of Russian journals up to date. Duplicate or ephemeral materials forwarded to other libraries amounted to 45,765 items including 41,159 sent to the Library of Congress.

Gifts from interested donors, many of them rare or out-of-print items, contributed to the library's resources. Some of the outstanding ones include:

A collection of 91 books and papers on pipes and smoking, from Dr. Leo Stoor, Cleveland, Ohio.

The Tatler, 1709–1711; the Lucubrations, vols. 1–4, by Isaac Bickerstaffe, Esq., London, 1749, from Mrs. Edward N. Townsend, Long Island, N.Y.

Atlas nouveau, by Sanson-Nicolas, Paris, 1692, from President John F. Kennedy.

Trees, Shrubs and Woody Vines of the Southwest, by Robert A. Vines. From the author, Texas University, Austin, Texas.

150 catalogs of medical instruments and apparatus, donated by the S. S. White Dental Co., Philadelphia, Pa.

American Heritage Picture History of the Civil War, 2 vols., donated by J. W. Eardesley, Washington, D.C.

Commemorative Biographical Record of New Haven County, Connecticut, J. H. Beers & Co., 1902. Donated by Claude Pearce, Arlington, Va.

Great Moments in News Photography, by John Faber. From Mr. Faber, Mountain Lakes, N.J.

Photochronograph and its Application, 1894, donated by Fr. Hayden of Georgetown College Observatory, Washington, D.C.

The Birds of California, by W. L. Dawson, 4 vols., donated by C. U. S. Roosevelt, Washington, D.C.

500 pieces of philatelic materials donated by Mrs. F. J. Shippen, Detroit, Mich.

14 volumes on American history, from Mrs. Arnold Miles, Washington, D.C.

The catalog section cataloged 7,983 volumes, recataloged 750 volumes, transferred 859 items, and checked in 31,443 periodicals. New procedures were adopted for the recording of serials in the serial record (formerly the periodical record). Because of more efficient methods of handling and processing, the recording of serials is on a current basis. The complete revamping of the serial record will result in still less time being required for checking of bibliographic data and for the recording of serials. This long-range project, which has had an excellent beginning, is one of the major steps in putting the library on an effective operating basis.

In cooperation with the Library of Congress the staff checked the library's serial holdings, which will be recorded in the third edition of the Union List of Serials. This bibliographic tool of national importance is used constantly by our staff.

The skilled hand binders repaired and restored 3,431 volumes of materials that required expert care and treatment, while 6,200 volumes of books and journals were prepared for binding or rebinding by a commercial binder. The continued program of weeding and discarding unused or duplicate materials from the collections resulted in 10,658 items being withdrawn.

The reference section answered a total of 32,094 reference and bibliographical requests, handled 2,840 pieces of correspondence that asked for specific types of information, and circulated 28,822 items. No record is kept of the circulation of books and journals assigned to the divisional libraries where they circulate freely within the division. Through interlibrary loans, 5,235 items were borrowed from other libraries, chiefly the Library of Congress; in addition, 935 pieces were lent. The facilities of the reading rooms in the main and branch libraries were used by 14,520 visitors, including many scholars and scientists. Floor plans were drawn by members of the staff for the library's expanded space which will ease the severely crowded stack and work areas.

The book collection that serves the staff of the Museum of History and Technology continued on a very active basis. Progress was seen in the growth and development of the collections and in the service provided. The staff answered 11,765 reference questions, replied to 894 letters, lent 12,599 publications, and assisted 3,982 persons coming to the library seeking specific types of information. One of the most significant achievements was the organization of 2,297 trade catalogs according to a special cataloging and classification scheme. With the addition of two temporary library assistants, good progress was made toward shaping the collection into a live, workable library. The shifting of the old card catalog into a new one and the cataloging of the collection of books on the history of medicine were completed. The preparation and distribution of a bimonthly accession list has fulfilled a long-felt need to inform members of the Museum staff of new library acquisitions.

The library for the Smithsonian Astrophysical Observatory began operation on a full-time basis this past year. New equipment has been installed and an active acquisitions program is under way to supply library materials. Many problems are to be resolved before this library can become fully effective.

The library staff continued to translate into English miscellaneous items in foreign languages which were referred to the library for translation. The Institution's participation in the National Science Foundation Russian translation program has resulted in the publishing of one volume: "Musk Deer and Deer," by K. K. Flerov.

Members of the staff continued active membership and participation in the Special Libraries Association and the American Library Association, with representation at the annual conventions of both organizations. The librarian continued as the Smithsonian representative on the U.S. Book Exchange. During the year, members of the staff visited the Smithsonian Astrophysical Observatory library, Cambridge, Mass., the Harvard University libraries, and the Canal Zone Biological Area library at Barro Colorado Island.

Librarians from other research organizations and museums both in the United States and in other countries visited the library, the publications distribution section, and the International Exchange Service for the exchange of professional knowledge and publications.

In spite of difficulties, the library has had a fruitful year. The addition of temporary staff eased the flow of work in some areas.

SUMMARIZED STATISTICS

ACCESSIONS

	Volumes	Total recorded volumes, 1961
Smithsonian main library (including the Natural History Museum)	2, 671	340, 349
Museum of History and Technology	8, 241	
Astrophysical Observatory (including Smithsonian Astrophysical Observatory, Cambridge, Mass.)	212	13, 612
Radiation and Organisms (formerly counted with the Astrophysical Observatory)	82	1, 869
Bureau of American Ethnology	629	38, 891
National Air Museum	107	816
National Collection of Fine Arts	68	14, 305
National Zoological Park	3	4, 296
Total	12, 013	414, 138

Unbound volumes of periodicals and reprints and separates from serial publications, of which there are many thousands, have not been included in these totals.

EXCHANGES

New exchanges arranged____ 289
Specially requested publications received______________________________ 1, 867

CATALOGING

Volumes cataloged____ 12, 763
Catalog cards filed____ 59, 795

PERIODICALS

Periodical parts entered____ 31, 443

CIRCULATION

Loans of books and periodicals______________________________________ 28, 822

Circulation in the divisional libraries is not counted except in the Division of Insects.

BINDING AND REPAIR

Volumes sent to the bindery____ 6, 200
Volumes repaired in the library______________________________________ 3, 431

Respectfully submitted.

RUTH E. BLANCHARD, *Librarian.*

Dr. LEONARD CARMICHAEL,
   Secretary, Smithsonian Institution.

Report on Publications

Sir: I have the honor to submit the following report on the publications of the Smithsonian Institution and its branches for the year ended June 30, 1961:

The publications of the Smithsonian Institution are issued partly from federally appropriated funds (Smithsonian Reports and publications of the National Museum, the Bureau of American Ethnology, and the Astrophysical Observatory) and partly from private endowment funds (Smithsonian Miscellaneous Collections, publications of the Freer Gallery of Art, and some special publications). The Institution also edits and publishes under the auspices of the Freer Gallery of Art the series Ars Orientalis, which appears under the joint imprint of the University of Michigan and the Smithsonian Institution. In addition, the Smithsonian publishes a guidebook, a picture pamphlet, postcards and a postcard folder, a color-picture album, color slides, a filmstrip on Smithsonian exhibits, a coloring book for children, and popular publications on scientific and historical subjects related to its important exhibits and collections for sale to visitors. Through its publication program the Smithsonian endeavors to carry out its founder's expressed desire for the diffusion of knowledge.

During the year the Institution published 10 Smithsonian Miscellaneous Collections papers; 1 Annual Report of the Board of Regents and separates of 24 articles in the General Appendix; 1 Annual Report of the Secretary; 4 special publications; and reprints of 3 special publications and 2 popular publications.

The U.S. National Museum issued 1 Annual Report, 4 bulletins, 1 paper in the series Contributions from the U.S. National Herbarium, 7 papers in the series Contributions from the Museum of History and Technology, and 21 Proceedings papers.

The Bureau of American Ethnology issued 1 Annual Report and 2 Bulletins.

The Astrophysical Observatory issued 8 papers in the series Smithsonian Contributions to Astrophysics.

The National Collection of Fine Arts published 1 catalog, and the Smithsonian Traveling Exhibition Service, under the National Collection of Fine Arts, published 4 catalogs and 3 folders.

The Freer Gallery of Art issued one brochure and volume 4 of Ars Orientalis.

DISTRIBUTION

In all, 774,444 copies of publications and miscellaneous items were distributed. *Publications:* 141 Contributions to Knowledge, 28,606 Smithsonian Miscellaneous Collections, 7,838 Annual Report volumes and 22,795 pamphlet copies of Report separates, 44,307 special publications, 87 reports of the Harriman Alaska Expedition; 66,722 publications of the National Museum; 29,845 publications of the Bureau of American Ethnology; 18,424 publications of the National Collection of Fine Arts; 150 publications of the Freer Gallery of Art;[1] 15,145 publications of the Astrophysical Observatory; 384 War Background Studies; 1,582 reports of the American Historical Association; and 6,231 publications not issued by the Smithsonian Institution. Miscellaneous: 7 sets of North American Wild Flowers and 45 North American Wild Flower prints, 2 Pitcher Plant volumes, 56,666 Guide Books, 18,663 picture pamphlets, 336,199 postcards and postcard folders, 19,963 color slides, 97,740 information leaflets, 10 New Museum of History and Technology pamphlets, 443 statuettes, 2,379 Viewmaster reels, and 1 filmstrip.

SMITHSONIAN MISCELLANEOUS COLLECTIONS

In this series, under the immediate editorship of Miss Ruth B. MacManus, there were issued 10 papers as follows:

Volume 139

No. 10. Water transparency observations along the east coast of North America, by Jerome Williams, E. R. Fenimore Johnson, and Albert C. Dyer. 181 pp., 2 pls., 13 maps. (Publ. 4391.) Oct. 26, 1960. ($2.50.)

Volume 140

No. 2. Pleistocene birds in Bermuda, by Alexander Wetmore. 11 pp., 3 pls. (Publ. 4423.) July 7, 1960. (40 cents.)

No. 3. Doctor Langley's paradox: Two letters suggesting the development of rockets, by Russell J. Parkinson. 4 pp., 3 pls. (Publ. 4424.) Aug. 31, 1960. (50 cents.)

No. 4. The cephalic nervous system of the centipede *Arenophilus bipuncticeps* (Wood) (Chilopoda. Geophilomorpha, Geophilidae), by Michael A. Lorenzo. 43 pp., 5 pls., 5 figs. (Publ. 4425.) Nov. 8, 1960. (75 cents.)

No. 5. A revision of the Ordovician bryozoan genera *Batostoma, Anaphragma,* and *Amplexopora,* by Richard S. Boardman. 28 pp., 7 pls. (Publ. 4426.) Dec. 15, 1960. (75 cents.)

Volume 141

The biotic associations of cockroaches, by Louis M. Roth and Edwin R. Willis. 470 pp., 37 pls., 7 figs. (Publ. 4422) Dec. 2, 1960. ($7.50.)

---

[1] In addition to those distributed by the Gallery itself.

Volume 142

No. 1. Facts and theories concerning the insect head, by R. E. Snodgrass. 66
pp., 21 figs. (Publ. 4427.) Nov. 4, 1960. (75 cents.)

No. 3. Some osteological features of modern lower teleostean fishes, by William
A. Gosline. 42 pp., 8 figs., 4 diagrams. (Publ. 4458.) June 12, 1961.
(50 cents.)

Volume 143

No. 1. Some locomotor mechanisms of birds, by Frank A. Hartman. 91 pp.,
7 figs. (Publ. 4460.) June 15, 1961. ($2.00.)

No. 2. Sixteen-day weather forecasts from satellite observations, by C. G. Abbot.
6 pp. (Publ. 4462.) May 26, 1961. (25 cents.)

SMITHSONIAN ANNUAL REPORTS

REPORT FOR 1959

The complete volume of the Annual Report of the Board of
Regents for 1959 was received from the printer on December 22, 1960:

Annual Report of the Board of Regents of the Smithsonian Institution showing
the operations, expenditures, and condition of the Institution for the year ended
June 30, 1959. x+ 693 pp., 86 pls., 125 figs., 1 map. (Publ. 4392.)

The general appendix contained the following papers (Publ.
4393-4416):

The transuranium elements, by Glenn T. Seaborg.

The IGY in retrospect, by Elliott B. Roberts.

Astronomy from artificial satellites, by Leo Goldberg.

Solar radio astronomy, by Alan Maxwell.

The new uses of the abstract, by George A. W. Boehm.

Mirages, by James H. Gordon.

Lessons from the history of flight, by Grover Loening.

The use of oceanography, by G. E. R. Deacon.

Ambergris—Neptune's treasure, by C. P. Idyll.

The rhythmic nature of animals and plants, by Frank A. Brown, Jr.

The survival of animals in hot deserts, by E. B. Edney.

Amphibians, pioneers of terrestrial breeding habits, by Coleman J. Goin.

A study of saturniid moths in the Canal Zone Biological Area, by A. D. Blest.

Evolution of knowledge concerning the roundworm *Ascaris lumbricoides*, by
Benjamin Schwartz.

The protection of fauna in the U.S.S.R., by G. P. Dementiev.

Reconstructing the ancestor of corn, by Paul C. Mangelsdorf.

The need to classify, by Roger L. Batten.

Current advances and concepts in virology, by staff members of Lilly Research
Laboratories.

In search of a home: From the Mutiny to Pitcairn Island (1789–1790), by
H. E. Maude.

The Chinook sign of freedom: A study of the skull of the famous chief Com-
comly, by T. D. Stewart.

The Muldbjerg dwelling place: An early Neolithic archeological site in the
Aamosen Bog, West Zealand, Denmark, by J. Troels-Smith.

Three adult Neanderthal skeletons from Shanidar Cave, northern Iraq, by Ralph
S. Solecki.

Sumerian technology, by Ida Bobula.

Brandywine: An early flour-milling center, by Peter C. Welsh.

The Report of the Secretary, which will form part of the Annual Report of the Board of Regents, was issued January 15, 1961:

Report of the Secretary and financial report of the Executive Committee of the Board of Regents for the year ended June 30, 1960. x+225 pp., 10 pls., 1 map. (Publ. 4429.)

SPECIAL PUBLICATIONS

Lichen handbook, by Mason E. Hale. 178 pp., 20 pls., 58 figs. (Publ. 4434.) [June] 1961. ($4.00.)

The Victorian American. Lithographs from the Harry T. Peters *America on Stone* collection, by Anthony N. B. Garvan and Peter C. Welsh. 30 pp., 21 pls. (Publ. 4466.) [May] 1961. ($1.00.)

Uniform regulations for the Army of the United States (1861), by Edgar M. Howell. 61 pp., incl. 36 pls. (Publ. 4467.) [June] 1961. ($1.00.)

REPRINTS

The Smithsonian Institution. (Revised.) 49 pp., illustr. (Publ. 4145.) [April] 1961. (50 cents.)

Masters of the air. (Revised.) 31 pp., illustr. (Publ. 4183.) [June] 1961. (50 cents.)

The world of the dinosaurs, by David H. Dunkle. 22 pp., illustr. (Publ. 4296.) [November] 1960, and [April] 1961. (50 cents.)

Anthropology as a career, by William C. Sturtevant. (Revised.) 20 pp. (Publ. 4343.) [October] 1960, and [January] 1961. (20 cents.)

Brief guide to the Smithsonian Institution. (Revised.) 82 pp., illustr. [March] 1961. (25 cents.)

Trees and shrubs of Mexico (including reprints of Parts 1–3 and 5 of volume 25, Contributions from the United States National Herbarium). In 2 parts. 1: pp. xviii+1–170, xxxvii+171–515, xxviii+517–848. 2: pp. 1313–1721. (Publ. 4461.) Apr. 28, 1961. ($20.00.)

PUBLICATIONS OF THE UNITED STATES NATIONAL MUSEUM

The editorial work of the National Museum continued during the year under the immediate direction of John S. Lea, assistant chief of the division. The following publications were issued:

REPORT

The United States National Museum annual report for the year ended June 30, 1960. Pp. vi+175, illus., January 13, 1961.

BULLETINS

219. The national watercraft collection, by Howard I. Chapelle. Pp. xi+327, 204 figs. Nov. 23, 1960.

220. Type specimens of reptiles and amphibians in the U.S. National Museum, by Doris M. Cochran. Pp. xv+291. Apr. 4, 1961.

221. Type specimens of birds in the United States National Museum, by Herbert G. Deignan. Pp. x+718. Mar. 17, 1961.

223. The parasitic weaverbirds, by Herbert Friedmann. Pp. viii+196, 3 figs., 16 pls. (4 color), Dec. 30, 1960.

225. Contributions from the Museum of History and Technology, Papers 12–16, by members of the staff and others:

Paper 12. Hermann Stieffel, soldier-artist of the West, by Edgar M. Howell. Pp. 1–16, 11 figs.   July 8, 1960.

Paper 13. North Devon pottery and its export to America in the 17th century, by C. Malcolm Watkins. Pp. 17–60, 36 figs. (1 color). Dec. 30, 1960.

Paper 14. Tea drinking in 18th-century America: Its etiquette and equipage, by Rodris Roth. Pp. 61–91, 22 figs., 1 color pl. Jan. 30, 1961.

Paper 15. Italian harpsichord-building in the 16th and 17th centuries, by John D. Shortridge. Pp. 93–107, 12 figs. Dec. 15, 1960.

Paper 16. Drug supplies in the American Revolution, by George B. Griffenhagen. Pp. 109–133, 4 figs. Mar. 9, 1961.

228. Contributions from the Museum of History and Technology, Papers 19 and 20, by members of the staff and others.

Paper 19. Elevator systems of the Eiffel Tower, 1889, by Robert M. Vogel. Pp. 1–40, 41 figs. Feb. 21, 1961.

Paper 20. John Ericsson and the age of caloric, by Eugene S. Ferguson. Pp. 41–60, 11 figs. Jan. 25, 1961.

CONTRIBUTIONS FROM THE NATIONAL HERBARIUM

Volume 35

Part 2. A taxonomic revision of the Humiriaceae, by José Cuatrecasas. Pp. iii+25–214, 38 figs., 24 pls. Apr. 14, 1961.

PROCEEDINGS

Volume 110

Title page, table of contents, and index. Pp. i–iii, 599–619, August 19, 1960.

Volume 111

No. 3429. A revision of the genus *Ogcodes* Latreille with particular reference to species of the Western Hemisphere, by Evert I. Schlinger. Pp. 227–336, 9 figs., 13 pls. Sept. 9, 1960.

No. 3430. Cydnidae of the Western Hemisphere, by Richard C. Froeschner. Pp. 337–680, 13 pls. Oct. 25, 1960.

Title page, table of contents, and index. Pp. i–iv, 681–692. Mar. 15, 1961.

Volume 112

No. 3431. Lace-bug genera of the world (Hemiptera: Tingidae), by Carl J. Drake and Florence A. Ruhoff. Pp. 1–105, 5 figs., 9 pls. July 7, 1960.

No. 3436. Revision of the milliped genus *Cherokia* (Polydesmida: Xystodesmidae), by Richard L. Hoffman. Pp. 227–264, 7 figs., 1 pl. Oct. 12, 1960.

No. 3437. Reexamination of species of Protura described by H. E. Ewing, by F. Bonet and S. L. Tuxen. Pp. 265–305, 103 figs. Oct. 13, 1960.

No. 3438. Studies in neotropical Mallophaga, XVII: A new family (Trochiliphagidae) and a new genus of the lice of hummingbirds, by M. A. Carriker, Jr. Pp. 307–342, 12 figs. Oct. 13, 1960.

No. 3439. The pelagic amphipod genus *Parathemisto* (Hyperiidea: Hyperiidae) in the North Pacific and adjacent Arctic Ocean, by Thomas E. Bowman. Pp. 343–392, 19 figs. Oct. 13, 1960.

No. 3440. Assassin bugs of the genus *Ghilianella* in the Americas (Hemiptera, Reduviidae, Emesinae), by J. Maldonado-Capriles. Pp. 393–450, 146 figs. Sept. 9, 1960.

No. 3441. Welcome Mound and the effigy pipes of the Adena people, by Frank M. Setzler. Pp. 451–458, 1 fig., 4 pls. Sept. 9, 1960.

No. 3442. Descriptions of new bats from Panama, by Charles O. Handley, Jr. Pp. 459–479. Oct. 6, 1960.

No. 3443. Cultural sequences in Hokkaido, Japan, by Lt. Col. Howard A. MacCord. Pp. 481–503, 5 figs., 14 pls. Dec. 5, 1960.

No. 3444. Noctuid moths of the Scopulepes group of *Hemeroplanis* Hübner, by E. L. Todd. Pp. 505–515, 6 figs., 1 pl. Sept. 13, 1960.

No. 3445. *Lithoglyptes spinatus*, a burrowing barnacle from Jamaica, by Jack T. Tomlinson and William A. Newman. Pp. 517–526, 10 figs. Dec. 20, 1960.

No. 3446. Notes on Mysidacean crustaceans of the genus *Lophogaster* in the U.S. National Museum, by O. S. Tattersall. Pp. 527–547, 7 figs. Dec. 20, 1960.

No. 3447. The fairy shrimp *Brachinecta campestris* from Northwestern United States (Crustacea: Phyllopoda), by James E. Lynch. Pp. 549–561, 5 figs. Dec. 5, 1960.

No. 3448. Stargazer fishes from the western North Atlantic (family Uranoscopidae), by Frederick H. Berry and William W. Anderson. Pp. 563–586, 1 fig., 4 pls. Apr. 12, 1961.

Volume 113

No. 3450. *Paraconger*, a new genus with three new species of eels (family Congridae), by Robert H. Kanazawa. Pp. 1–14, 3 figs., 2 pls. Jan. 26, 1961.

No. 3451. Revision of the milliped genus *Deltotaria* (Polydesmida: Xystodesmidae), by Richard L. Hoffman. Pp. 15–35, 4 figs. Mar. 17, 1961.

No. 3452. Four new species of *Pseudocyclops* (Copepoda: Calanoida), from Puerto Rico, by Thomas E. Bowman and Juan G. González. Pp. 37–59, 11 figs. Mar. 20, 1961.

PUBLICATIONS OF THE BUREAU OF AMERICAN ETHNOLOGY

The editorial work of the Bureau continued under the immediate direction of Mrs. Eloise B. Edelen. The following publications were issued during the year:

ANNUAL REPORT

Seventy-seventh Annual Report of the Bureau of American Ethnology, 1959–60. ii+35 pp., 2 pls. 1961.

BULLLETINS

Bulletin 176. River Basin Surveys Papers, Nos. 15–20, Frank H. H. Roberts, Jr., editor. ix+337 pp., 65 pls., 25 figs. 1960.

No. 15. Historic sites archeology on the Upper Missouri, by Merrill J. Mattes.

No. 16. Historic sites archeology in the Fort Randall Reservoir, South Dakota, by John E. Mills.

No. 17. The excavation and investigation of Fort Lookout Trading Post II (39LM57) in the Fort Randall Reservoir, South Dakota, by Carl F. Miller.

No. 18. Fort Pierre II (39ST217), a historic trading post in the Oahe Dam area, South Dakota, by G. Hubert Smith.

No. 19. Archeological investigations at the site of Fort Stevenson (32ML1), Garrison Reservoir, North Dakota, by G. Hubert Smith. With an introduction by Robert L. Stephenson and an appendix by Carlyle S. Smith.

No. 20. The archeology of a small trading post (Kipp's Post, 32MN1) in the Garrison Reservoir, North Dakota, by Alan R. Woolworth and W. Raymond Wood.

Bulletin 180. Symposium on Cherokee and Iroquois culture, edited by William N. Fenton and John Gulick. vi+292 pp. 1961.

No. 1. Foreword by the editors.

No. 2. Iroquois-Cherokee linguistic relations, by Floyd G. Lounsbury.

No. 3. Comment on Floyd G. Lounsbury's "Iroquois-Cherokee Linguistic Relations," by Mary R. Haas.

No. 4. Iroquois archeology and settlement patterns, by William A. Ritchie.

No. 5. First comment on William A. Ritchie's "Iroquois Archeology and Settlement Patterns," by William H. Sears.

No. 6. Second comment on William A. Ritchie's "Iroquois Archeology and Settlement Patterns," by Douglas S. Byers.

No. 7. Cherokee archeology, by Joffre L. Coe.

No. 8. Comment on Joffre L. Coe's "Cherokee Archeology," by Charles H. Fairbanks.

No. 9. Eastern Woodlands community typology and acculturation, by John Witthoft.

No. 10. Comment on John Witthoft's "Eastern Woodlands Community Typology and Acculturation," by John M. Goggin.

No. 11. Cherokee economic cooperatives: the Gadugi, by Raymond D. Fogelson and Paul Kutsche.

No. 12. The rise of the Cherokee state as an instance in a class: The "Mesopotamian" career to statehood, by Fred O. Gearing.

No. 13. Comment on Fred O. Gearing's "The Rise of the Cherokee State as an Instance in a Class: The 'Mesopotamian' Career to Statehood," by Annemarie Shimony.

No. 14. Cultural composition of the Handsome Lake Religion, by Anthony F. C. Wallace.

No. 15. Comment on Anthony F. C. Wallace's "Cultural Composition of the Handsome Lake Religion," by Wallace L. Chafe.

No. 16. The Redbird Smith Movement, by Robert K. Thomas.

No. 17. Comment on Robert K. Thomas's "The Redbird Smith Movement," by Fred W. Voget.

No. 18. Effects of environment on Cherokee-Iroquois ceremonialism, music, and dance, by Gertrude P. Kurath.

No. 19. Comment on Gertrude P. Kurath's "Effects of Environment on Cherokee-Iroquois Ceremonialism, Music, and Dance," by William C. Sturtevant.

No. 20. The Iroquois fortunetellers and their conservative influence, by Annemarie Shimony.

No. 21. Change, persistence, and accommodation in Cherokee medico-magical beliefs, by Raymond D. Fogelson.

No. 22. Some observations on the persistence of aboriginal Cherokee personality traits, by Charles H. Holzinger.

No. 23. First comment on Charles H. Holzinger's "Some Observations on the Persistence of Aboriginal Cherokee Personality Traits," by David Landy.

No. 24. Second comment on Charles H. Holzinger's "Some Observations on the Persistence of Aboriginal Cherokee Personality Traits, by John Gulick.

No. 25. Iroquoian culture history: A general evaluation, by William N. Fenton.

PUBLICATIONS OF THE ASTROPHYSICAL OBSERVATORY

The editorial work of the Smithsonian Astrophysical Observatory continued under the immediate direction of Ernest E. Biebighauser. The year's publications in the series Smithsonian Contributions to Astrophysics are as follows:

Volume 4

No. 2. Orbital elements of photographic meteors, by Richard E. McCrosky and Annette Posen. Pp. 15–84, 19 figs. 1961.

No. 3. Orbital elements of meteors, by Gerald S. Hawkins and Richard B. Southworth. Pp. 85–95. 1961.

No. 4. Precision orbits of 413 photographic meteors, by Luigi G. Jacchia and Fred L. Whipple. Pp. 97–129, 6 figs. 1961.

Volume 5

No. 4. Observations of simulated meteors, by Richard E. McCrosky. Pp. 29–37, 3 figs. 1961.

No. 5. On the motion of satellites with critical inclination: Libration of an earth satellite with critical inclination, by Yusuke Hagihara, pp. 39–51, 3 figs.; Motion of a particle with critical inclination in the gravitational field of a spheroid, by Yoshihide Kozai, pp. 53–58, 1 fig. 1961.

No. 6. Gaps in the distribution of asteroids, by Yusuke Hagihara. Pp. 59–67, 2 figs. 1961.

No. 7. Major flares and geomagnetic activity, by Barbara Bell. Pp. 69–83, 13 figs. 1961.

No. 8. An annotated bibliography of interplanetary dust, by Paul W. Hodge, Frances W. Wright, and Dorrit Hoffleit. Pp. 85–111. 1961.

PUBLICATIONS OF THE NATIONAL COLLECTION OF FINE ARTS

Art and archeology of Viet Nam, Asian crossroad of cultures. 63 pp., illustr. 1960. (Publ. 4430.) ($1.00.)

Italian drawings. 78 pp., 42 ills. 1960.

Irish architecture of the Georgian period. 17 pp., illustr. 1960.

The world of Werner Bischof. 12 pp., 48 ills. 1961.

Smithsonian Institution Traveling Exhibitions. 1961–1962 catalog. 40 pp.

Three folders: Sardinian crafts, New exhibitions, and Architectural exhibitions.

PUBLICATIONS OF THE FREER GALLERY OF ART

Ars Orientalis, vol. IV. (17 articles by various authors, 5 notes, 21 book reviews, 2 obituaries, 1 bibliography.) 462 pp., 143 pls., 61 text figs. [June] 1961.

Second presentation of the Charles Lang Freer Medal. (A brochure issued in connection with the presentation of the medal to Prof. Ernst Kühnel, May 3, 1961.)

REPORTS OF THE AMERICAN HISTORICAL ASSOCIATION

The annual reports of the American Historical Association are transmitted by the Association to the Secretary of the Smithsonian Institution and are by him communicated to Congress, as provided in the act of incorporation of the Association. The following report was issued during the year:

Annual Report of the American Historical Association for 1959. Vol. 1. Proceedings. 1960.

REPORT OF THE NATIONAL SOCIETY, DAUGHTERS OF THE AMERICAN REVOLUTION

In accordance with law, the manuscript of the sixty-third annual report of the National Society, Daughters of the American Revolution, was transmitted to Congress on March 13, 1961.

OTHER ACTIVITIES

The chief of the division continued to represent the Smithsonian Institution on the board of trustees of the Greater Washington Educational Television Association, Inc., of which the Institution is a member. He also represented the Institution at the annual meeting of the Association of American University Presses held early in May at Oklahoma City and Norman, Okla.

PAUL H. OEHSER,
Chief, Editorial and Publications Division.

Dr. LEONARD CARMICHAEL,
Secretary, Smithsonian Institution.

Other Activities

LECTURES

In 1931 the Institution received a bequest from James Arthur, of New York City, a part of the income from which was to be used to endow an annual lecture on some aspect of the sun. The 27th Arthur lecture was delivered in the auditorium of the Natural History Building on the evening of February 2, 1961, by Dr. Herbert Friedman, Superintendent of the Atmosphere and Astrophysics Division of the U.S. Naval Research Laboratory. This lecture will be published in full in the general appendix of the Annual Report of the Board of Regents of the Smithsonian Institution for 1961.

Dr. Erik Sjoqvist, of the Department of Art and Archaeology of Princeton University, delivered a lecture on "Morgantina, an Unknown Greek City in Sicily" in the auditorium of the Natural History Building on the evening of January 24, 1961. This was sponsored jointly by the Smithsonian and the Archaeological Institute of America.

Alfred Friendly, managing editor of the *Washington Post*, lectured on "Bushman Paintings" in the Freer Gallery of Art auditorium on the evening of May 10, 1961.

Several lectures were sponsored by the Freer Gallery of Art and the National Gallery of Art. These are listed in the reports of these bureaus.

Many other lectures on technical subjects were given at the Institution during the year.

SCIENCE INFORMATION EXCHANGE

The Science Information Exchange, an agency operated within the Smithsonian Institution, is a clearinghouse for current scientific research in process. The basic purpose of the Exchange is to foster and facilitate effective planning and management of scientific research activities supported by United States agencies and institutions by promoting the exchange among participating agencies of administrative data about all types of current research. Thus the Exchange provides a means of communication concerning on-going research which precedes publication of research findings, and which prevents unknowing duplication.

Abstracts of research-in-process have been for some years registered by investigators engaged in biological, medical, and psychological research and in limited aspects of research in the social sciences. Through an extensive system of subject indexing, these abstracts are provided upon request and without charge to research institutions. For granting agencies and properly constituted committees it prepares extensive surveys of research in broad areas.

In September 1960 the Governing Board of the Bio-Sciences Information Exchange (the name of the agency as originally organized in 1950) was reconstituted as the Governing Board, Science Information Exchange, to reflect the inclusion of the physical sciences in the scope of the operation. Dr. Orr E. Reynolds, of the Department of Defense, was elected chairman. An ad hoc committee for the physical sciences was established under the chairmanship of Dr. Urner Liddel, and recruitment for professional staff in the physical sciences began.

The volume of registration and of use of the Exchange in the field of the life sciences has continued to grow, and it is believed that similar volume and use for the physical sciences will develop. It is expected that the actual scope of coverage and service, by subject matter and by types of research projects, will evolve and expand gradually.

A systems survey by Booz, Allen, and Hamilton was begun in November 1960 and completed in May 1961. Consultant services by the Computer Usage Corporation have assisted in the orderly conversion to magnetic tape and in formulating plans for expanded activities.

An associate director for the life sciences, Dr. David Hersey, was selected but will not enter on duty until the next fiscal year.

SMITHSONIAN MUSEUM SERVICE

The Smithsonian Museum Service, through appropriate educational media, interprets to museum visitors and to the general public the objects, specimens, and exhibits in the several Smithsonian museums and develops interpretative and educational material relating to the work of the Institution in the fields of science, natural history, art, and history. The Museum Service also cooperates with the volunteer docents of the Junior League of Washington, D.C. A more complete report of this activity, directed by G. Carroll Lindsay, curator, is carried in the Report of the United States National Museum.

The Museum Service provided assistance to professional and subprofessional groups and individuals visiting the museums of the Institution or planning to do so. Assistance in the form of lectures, answers to inquiries, and special tours of certain museum areas was rendered to college and university groups visiting the Institution and to other groups and individuals from the United States and abroad, visiting or planning to visit the Smithsonian in a professional capacity. Arrangements were made through the Museum Service for Smithsonian participation in the Workshop on Community Resources sponsored by the University of Maryland. Through the facilities of this workshop, a five-day program outlining the history of the Institution and the work of the various Smithsonian museum and research bureaus was presented to 40 graduate students from the University of Maryland. This workshop has, since its inception in 1958, provided an opportunity for more than 150 local school teachers and university faculty members to become acquainted with cultural resources of the Institution of value in school curricula.

The Museum Service cooperated with the Greater Washington Educational Television Association in the preparation of a half-hour educational television presentation based on the early musical instrument collection of the Smithsonian.

Through the Museum Service distribution of certain duplicate specimens and objects from the United States National Museum was made to the Overbrook School for the Blind for use in that school's training of blind children. Special "touch" exhibits and demonstrations were arranged for visiting groups of children from the Columbia Lighthouse for the Blind.

The program for visitor orientation to Smithsonian museums and exhibits was continued through the installation of another electronically controlled slide lecture device in the Lobby of the Museum of Natural History. Floor diagrams showing exhibit locations and listings of exhibits and location of each were installed in the Museum of Natural History.

Arrangements for various Smithsonian public functions and events including lectures, films, and the opening of new halls and exhibits were made by the Museum Service. More complete information about these activities will be found under appropriate headings elsewhere in the Annual Report of the Secretary of the Smithsonian Institution. Mailing lists for announcements of these events were maintained and kept current. The Smithsonian *Calendar of Events*, a listing of special events of the Institution was prepared and distributed monthly.

Report of the Executive Committee of the Board of Regents of the Smithsonian Institution

For the Year Ended June 30, 1961

To the Board of Regents of the Smithsonian Institution:

Your executive committee respectfully submits the following report in relation to the funds of the Smithsonian Institution, together with a statement of the appropriations by Congress for the Government bureaus in the administrative charge of the Institution.

SMITHSONIAN INSTITUTION

PARENT FUND

The original bequest of James Smithson was £104,960 8s 6d—$508,318.46. Refunds of money expended in prosecution of the claim, freight, insurance, and other incidental expenses, together with payment into the fund of the sum of £5,015, which had been withheld during the lifetime of Madame de la Batut, brought the fund to the amount of $550,000.

The gift of James Smithson was "lent to the United States Treasury, at 6 per centum per annum interest" (20 USC. 54) and by the Act of March 12, 1894 (20 USC. 55) the Secretary of the Treasury was "authorized to receive into the Treasury, on the same terms as the original bequest of James Smithson, such sums as the Regents may, from time to time see fit to deposit, not exceeding, with the original bequest the sum of $1,000,000."

The maximum of $1,000,000 which the Smithsonian Institution was authorized to deposit in the Treasury of the United States was reached on January 11, 1917 by the deposit of $2,000.

Under the above authority the amounts shown below are deposited in the United States Treasury and draw 6 percent interest:

	Unrestricted funds	Income 1961
James Smithson	$727, 640	$43, 658. 40
Avery	14, 000	840. 00
Habel	500	30. 00
Hamilton	2, 500	150. 00
Hodgkins (General)	116, 000	6, 960. 00
Poore	26, 670	1, 600. 20
Rhees	590	35. 40
Sanford	1, 100	66. 00
Total	889, 000	53, 340. 00

	Restricted funds	Income 1961
Hodgkins (Specific)	$100, 000	$6, 000. 00
Reid	11, 000	660. 00
Total	111, 000	6, 660. 00
Grand total	1, 000, 000	60, 000. 00

In addition to the $1,000,000 deposited in the Treasury of the United States there has been accumulated from income and bequests the sum of $3,871,350.59 which has been invested. Of this sum, $3,734,473.88 is carried on the books of the Institution as the Consolidated Fund, a policy approved by the Regents at their meeting on December 14, 1916. The balance is made up of several small funds.

CONSOLIDATED FUND

(Income for the unrestricted use of the Institution)

Fund	Investment 1961	Income 1961
Abbott, W. L., Special	$21, 344. 95	$1, 100. 60
*Avery, Robert S., and Lydia	56, 590. 75	2, 917. 95
Gifts, royalties, gain on sale of securities	395, 583. 11	20, 397. 09
Hachenberg, George P. and Caroline	5, 761. 97	297. 09
*Hamilton, James	578. 35	29. 84
Hart, Gustavus E.	697. 84	36. 00
Henry, Caroline	1, 732. 75	89. 37
Henry, Joseph and Harriet A.	70, 231. 84	3, 621. 31
*Hodgkins, Thomas G. (General)	43, 399. 98	2, 237. 79
Morrow, Dwight W.	110, 789. 10	5, 712. 49
Olmsted, Helen A.	1, 148. 62	59. 21
*Poore, Lucy T. and George W.	233, 177. 42	12, 023. 11
Porter, Henry Kirke	410, 317. 07	21, 156. 85
*Rhees, William Jones	677. 83	34. 94
*Sanford, George H.	1, 275. 36	65. 74
*Smithson, James	1, 749. 06	90. 16
Taggart, Gansen	512. 44	22. 14
Witherspoon, Thomas A.	184, 890. 65	9, 533. 36
Total	1, 540, 459. 09	79, 425. 04

*In addition to funds deposited in the United States Treasury.

CONSOLIDATED FUND

(Income restricted to specific use)

Fund	Investment 1961	Income 1961
Abbott, William L., for investigations in biology	$149, 362. 74	$7, 675. 50
Armstrong, Edwin James, for use of Department of Invertebrate Paleontology when principal amounts to $5,000.00	1, 710. 21	70. 78

CONSOLIDATED FUND—Continued

Fund	Investment 1961	Income 1961
Arthur, James, for investigations and study of the sun and annual lecture on same	$57,298.65	$2,954.43
Bacon, Virginia Purdy, for traveling scholarship to investigate fauna of countries other than the United States	71,779.58	3,701.12
Baird, Lucy H., for creating a memorial to Secretary Baird	34,495.02	1,778.64
Barney, Alice Pike, for collection of paintings and pastels and for encouragement of American artistic endeavor	41,092.28	2,118.80
Barstow, Frederick D., for purchase of animals for Zoological Park	1,432.35	73.86
Canfield collection, for increase and care of the Canfield collection of minerals	54,796.73	2,825.45
Casey, Thomas L., for maintenance of the Casey collection and promotion of researches relating to Coleoptera	17,958.19	925.96
Chamberlain, Francis Lea, for increase and promotion of Isaac Lea Collection of gems and mollusks	40,345.65	2,080.30
Dykes, Charles, for support in financial research	61,682.94	3,180.48
Eickemeyer, Florence Brevoort, for preservation and exhibition of the photographic collection of Rudolph Eickemeyer, Jr	15,572.70	802.97
Hanson, Martin Gustav and Caroline Runice, for some scientific work of the Institution, preferably in chemistry or medicine	12,736.57	656.74
Higbee, Harry, income for general use of the Smithsonian Institution after June 11, 1967	26.69	.48
Hillyer, Virgil, for increase and care of Virgil Hillyer collection of lighting objects	9,415.97	485.49
Hitchcock, Albert S., for care of the Hitchcock Agrostological Library	2,260.72	116.55
Hrdlička, Aleš and Marie, to further researches in physical anthropology and publication in connection therewith	68,539.55	3,360.75
Hughes, Bruce, to found Hughes alcove	27,423.90	1,414.05
Loeb, Morris, for furtherance of knowledge in the exact sciences	124,864.24	6,438.27
Long, Annette and Edith C., for upkeep and preservation of Long collection of embroideries, laces, and textiles	777.91	40.09
Maxwell, Mary E., for care and exhibition of Maxwell collection	28,101.35	1,448.94
Myer, Catherine Walden, for purchase of first-class works of art for use and benefit of the National Collection of Fine Arts	28,939.20	1,492.16
Nelson, Edward W., for support of biological studies	31,861.40	1,642.86

CONSOLIDATED FUND—Continued

Fund	Investment 1961	Income 1961
Noyes, Frank B., for use in connection with the collection of dolls placed in the U.S. National Museum through the interest of Mr. and Mrs. Noyes	$1, 376. 47	$70. 99
Pell, Cornelia Livingston, for maintenance of Alfred Duane Pell collection	10, 619. 83	547. 57
Petrocelli, Joseph, for the care of the Petrocelli collection of photographic prints and for the enlargement and development of the section of photography of the U.S. National Museum	10, 621. 07	574. 62
Rathbun, Richard, for use of division of U.S. National Museum containing Crustacea	15, 238. 20	785. 72
*Reid, Addison T., for founding chair in biology, in memory of Asher Tunis	25, 483. 68	1, 314. 01
Roebling Collection, for care, improvement, and increase of Roebling collection of minerals	172, 910. 49	8, 915. 65
Roebling Solar Research	33, 028. 76	1, 703. 02
Rollins, Miriam and William, for investigations in physics and chemistry	198, 652. 57	9, 985. 51
Smithsonian employees' retirement	33, 655. 55	1, 766. 50
Springer, Frank, for care and increase of the Springer collection and library	25, 692. 44	1, 324. 74
Strong, Julia D., for benefit of the National Collection of Fine Arts	14, 324. 85	738. 62
Walcott, Charles D. and Mary Vaux, for development of geological and paleontological studies and publishing results of same	685, 644. 88	35, 318. 99
Walcott, Mary Vaux, for publications in botany	82, 932. 44	4, 276. 19
Younger, Helen Walcott, held in trust	104, 571. 77	5, 122. 45
Zerbee, Francis Brinckle, for endowment of aquaria	1, 359. 02	70. 09
Total	2, 298, 586. 56	117, 772. 34

*In addition to funds deposited in the United States Treasury.

FREER GALLERY OF ART FUND

Early in 1906, by deed of gift, Charles L. Freer, of Detroit, gave to the Institution his collection of Chinese and other Oriental objects of art, as well as paintings, etchings, and other works of art by Whistler, Thayer, Dewing, and other artists. Later he also gave funds for construction of a building to house the collection, and finally in his will, probated November 6, 1919, he provided stocks and securities to the estimated value of $1,958,591.42, as an endowment fund for the operation of the Gallery. The fund now amounts to $9,721,210.13.

SUMMARY OF ENDOWMENTS

Invested endowment for general purposes	$2,429,459.09
Invested endowment for specific purposes other than Freer endowment	2,441,891.50
Total invested endowment other than Freer	4,871,350.59
Freer invested endowment for specific purposes	9,721,210.13
Total invested endowment for all purposes	$14,592,560.72

CLASSIFICATION OF INVESTMENTS

Deposited in the U.S. Treasury at 6 percent per annum, as authorized in the U.S. Revised Statutes, sec. 5591		$1,000,000.00
Investments other than Freer endowment (cost or market value at date acquired):		
Bonds	$1,530,633.40	
Stocks	2,295,685.77	
Real estate and mortgages	28,756.00	
Uninvested capital	16,275.42	
		3,871,350.59
Total investments other than Freer endowment		$4,871,350.59
Investments of Freer endowment (cost or market value at date acquired):		
Bonds	$4,993,135.06	
Stocks	4,724,660.49	
Uninvested capital	3,414.58	
		9,721,210.13
Total investments		$14,592,560.72

EXHIBIT A

BALANCE SHEET OF PRIVATE FUNDS

June 30, 1961

ASSETS

Current funds:
General:
Cash:

United States Treasury current account		$510, 434. 04
In banks and on hand		355, 166. 47
		865, 600. 51
Less uninvested endowment		19, 690. 00
		845, 910. 51
Travel and other advances		12, 724. 00
Total general funds		858, 634. 51

Restricted:

Cash—United States Treasury current account	$1, 738, 733. 99	
Investments—United States Treasury Notes	1, 635, 712. 56	
Total restricted funds		3, 374, 446. 55
Total current funds		4, 233, 081. 06

Endowment funds and funds functioning as endowment:
Investments:
Freer Gallery of Art:

Cash	$3, 414. 58	
Stocks and bonds	9, 717, 795. 55	
	9, 721, 210. 13	

Consolidated:

Cash	$15, 709. 70	
Stocks and bonds	3, 718, 764. 18	
	3, 734, 473. 88	
Loan to United States Treasury	1, 000, 000. 00	
Other stocks and bonds	107, 554. 99	
Cash	565. 72	
Real estate at book value	28, 756. 00	4, 871, 350. 59

Total endowment funds and funds functioning as endowment	14, 592, 560. 72
Total	18, 825, 641. 78

FUND BALANCES

Current funds:		
General:		
Unexpended funds—unrestricted		$858,634.51
Total general funds		858,634.51
Restricted (Exhibit C):		
Unexpended income from endowment	$1,084,076.28	
Funds for special purposes (gifts, grants, etc.)	2,290,370.27	
Total restricted funds		3,474,446.55
Total current funds		4,233,081.06
Endowment funds and funds functioning as endowment (Exhibit D):		
Freer Gallery of Art		$9,721,210.13
Other:		
Restricted	$2,441,891.50	
General	2,429,459.09	4,871,350.59
Total endowment funds and funds functioning as endowment		14,592,560.72
Total		18,825,641.78

EXHIBIT B

PRIVATE FUNDS

STATEMENT OF CURRENT GENERAL FUND RECEIPTS AND DISBURSEMENTS AND CHANGES IN CURRENT GENERAL FUND BALANCES

Year ended June 30, 1961

	Operations	Publications	Gifts and grants
Current receipts:			
Endowment income:			
Freer Gallery of Art	$561, 579. 06		
Other restricted funds	51, 689. 33		
Unrestricted	132, 765. 04		
Investment income	50, 269. 06		
Gifts and grants	192, 098. 38		$5, 247, 913. 18
Publications and photographs		$90, 006. 23	
Miscellaneous	7, 935. 90	38. 85	
Appropriated from endowment fund	556. 82		
Total current receipts	996, 893. 59	90, 045. 08	5, 247, 913. 18
Current expenditures:			
Salaries:			
Administrative	123, 831. 39		
Research	22, 045. 95		2, 198, 724. 26
Other	174, 221. 63		
Total salaries	320, 098. 97		2, 198, 724. 26
Purchase for collection	293, 305. 14		

Researches and exploration and related administrative expenses:					
Travel		15,964.11			
Equipment and supply		4,041.69			
Other		7,483.22		3,049,188.92	
Publication and photographs		30,931.12	56,842.33		
Buildings, equipment and grounds:					
Buildings and installations		11,539.36			
Court and grounds maintenance		1,756.54			
Technical laboratory		1,731.99			
Contractual services—custodian and legal fees		24,246.17			
Supplies and expenses:					
Meetings, special exhibits		16,484.72			
Lectures		3,408.07			
Photographs and reproductions		10,946.39			
Library		4,003.65			
Stationery and office supplies		58.08			
Postage, telephone and telegraph		235.41	1.70		
Employees' withholding payments	$601,886.59				
Less employee withholding	554,126.98	47,759.61			
Total current expenditures		793,994.24	56,844.03	5,247,913.18	
Excess of current receipts over current expenditures		202,899.35	33,201.05		$236,100.40
Transfer to endowment principal—Ganson Taggart Fund					(500.00)
Total					235,600.40
Balance at beginning of year					623,034.11
Balance at end of year					858,634.51

EXHIBIT C

PRIVATE FUNDS

STATEMENT OF CHANGES IN CURRENT RESTRICTED FUND BALANCE

Year ended June 30, 1961

	Funds for special purposes		
	Unexpended income	Gifts, grants, etc.	Total
Balance at beginning of year_____	$1, 127, 115. 28	$1, 331, 791. 41	$2, 458, 906. 69
Add:			
Income from restricted endowment:			
Freer Gallery of Art_______	436, 006. 08	---------------	436, 006. 08
Other restricted funds_____	258, 908. 76	---------------	258, 908. 76
	694, 914. 84	---------------	694, 914. 84
Less custodial costs________	37, 170. 41	---------------	37, 170. 41
Net income from restricted endowment_____	657, 744. 43	---------------	657, 744. 43
Sale of publications________	17, 599. 03	1, 674. 38	19, 273. 41
Gifts and grants___________	---------------	6, 127, 382. 33	6, 127, 382. 33
Other______________________	3, 035. 70	169, 394. 08	172, 429. 78
	1, 805, 494. 44	7, 630, 242. 20	9, 435, 736. 64
Deduct:			
Transfer to current income:			
Freer Gallery of Art_______	525, 806. 14	---------------	525, 806. 14
Other restricted funds_____	50, 291. 84	5, 247, 913. 18	5, 298, 205. 02
Unrestricted______________	132, 765. 04	42, 068. 49	174, 833. 53
	708, 863. 02	5, 289, 981. 67	5, 998, 844. 69
Income added to principal, net____________________	9, 116. 16	---------------	9, 116. 16
Returns to National Science Foundation_______________	---------------	51, 729. 57	51, 729. 57
Transfer to (from) gifts and grants__________________	1, 839. 31	(1, 839. 31)	---------------
Transfer to endowment funds_	1, 599. 67	---------------	1, 599. 67
	721, 418. 16	5, 339, 871. 93	6, 061, 290. 09
Balance at end of year_________	1, 084, 076. 28	2, 290, 370. 27	3, 374, 446. 55

EXHIBIT D

PRIVATE FUNDS

STATEMENT OF CHANGES IN PRINCIPAL OF ENDOWMENT FUNDS AND FUNDS FUNCTIONING AS ENDOWMENT

Year ended June 30, 1961

Balance at beginning of year		$13,771,652.40
Add:		
Gifts and bequests (including transfer of Ganson Taggart Fund)	$30,849.67	
Income added to principal as prescribed by donor	9,116.16	
Net gain on investments	781,499.31	821,465.14
Total		14,593,117.54
Deduct amounts appropriated to current funds for retirement payments		556.82
		14,592,560.72
Balance at year end consisting of:		
Unrestricted	$2,429,459.09	
Restricted for:		
Freer Gallery of Art	9,721,210.13	
Other collections and research	2,441,891.50	
		14,592,560.72

The practice of maintaining savings accounts in several of the Washington banks and trust companies has been continued during the past year, and interest on these deposits amounted to $12,593.72.

Deposits are made in banks for convenience in collection of checks, and later such funds are withdrawn and deposited in the United States Treasury. Disbursement of funds is made by check signed by the Secretary of the Institution and drawn on the United States Treasury.

The Institution gratefully acknowledges gifts and grants from the following:

Academic Press Co., contribution to the Rathbun Memorial Fund.

Edward D. Adler, contribution to the Smithsonian Institution.

American Cocoa Research, grant to help defray costs of art work in connection with the publication of a Taxonomic Monograph of the Genus *Theobroma* by Dr. Jose Cuatrecasas.

American Petroleum Institute, grant-in-aid toward the establishment of a permanent exhibit and animated petroleum map in the United States National Museum.

American Petroleum Institute, grant to cover expenses of Dr. G. Arthur Cooper in connection with his participation in the Geology Domain Committee Symposium to be held in Houston, Texas.

Atomic Energy Commission, additional grant for support of research and study of the biochemical effects of ionizing and nonionizing radiation on plant metabolism during development.

Atomic Energy Commission, additional grant for support of research entitled "Systematic Zoological Research on the Marine Fauna of the Tropical Pacific Area."

Bernice P. Bishop Museum, grant to assist in defraying expenses of Dr. Bernard R. Feinstein in connection with field work in Viet Nam and neighboring countries.

Bredin Foundation, grant for the support of research entitled "Ocean Food Chain Cycle."

Mrs. John S. Burdette, contribution for the restoration of a platform rocker given by her to the Smithsonian Institution.

Alan C. Collins, grant for a research expedition to Tibesti Mountains of Libya.

Curtiss-Wright Corporation, gift for the construction of a replica of the first naval aircraft, the Curtiss A–1.

Department of the Air Force, additional grant for research entitled "Study of Atmospheric Entry and Impact of High Velocity Meteorites."

Department of the Air Force, additional grant for upper atmosphere stellar image study.

Department of the Air Force, additional grant for support of research entitled "The Accretion of Interplanetary Matter by the Earth."

Department of the Air Force, additional grant for research directed toward the study of stellar scintillation.

Department of the Air Force, grant for the support of research entitled "The Reduction of Satellite Observations to Determine Atmospheric Density."

Department of the Army, Ordnance Corps, additional grants for research entitled "Procurement of Satellite Tracking and Orbit."

Department of the Army, Quartermaster Corps, grant for support of a report on "The Biotic Associations of the Blattaria" by Roth and Willis.

Eastern Federation of Mineralogical and Lapidary Societies, grant to defray expenses of Paul E. Desautels while attending the 1960 convention in Asheville, North Carolina.

Felix and Helen Juda Foundation, gift to the Freer Gallery of Art Publication Fund.

Mr. Reuben H. Fleet, gift for the purchase of a scale model of Consolidated NY–1 Aircraft for the National Air Museum.

Alex. Gordon 3d, contribution to the Smithsonian Institution.

Mr. E. P. Henderson, gift for the Meteorite Fund.

Mr. Stewart Huston, gift for the restoration of an 18th Century Chaise.

Institute of Andean Research, grant for Archeological Research in Ecuador on Project J of the Institute of Andean Research Program, "Interrelationships of New World Cultures."

International Association for Plant Taxonomy, gift to cover expenses of Dr. A. C. Smith in connection with travel to Brussels while attending the meeting of the Editorial Committee of the International Code of Botanical Nomenclature.

Jersey Production Research Corporation, additional grant for support of a research project on Echinoid Spines.

Jewitt Foundation, grant for the support of research entitled "Ecology and Morphology of the Hoatzin."

Edwin A. Link, additional gift for the support of the Marine Archeological Project.

Link Foundation, additional gift for the support of special publications dealing with aviation and the Smithsonian Institution Collections.

McDermott Foundation, gift to purchase a telescope which will be loaned indefinitely to the Dallas Moonwatch Team.

Metropolitan Broadcasting Corporation, grant to cover expenses relating to the shipment of the White Tigress from India to the National Zoological Park.

Mitch Miller Foundation, grant for the support of research entitled "Ecology and Morphology of the Hoatzin."

Mrs. George Maurice Morris, gift to establish the Miriam H. Morris Fund.

National Academy of Sciences, travel grants for J. F. Gates Clarke, William Stern, S. H. Reisenberg, and H. G. Diegnan to attend the Tenth Pacific Science congress.

National Aeronautics and Space Administration, additional grants for the support of the Satellite Tracking Program.

National Aeronautics and Space Administration, additional grants for the support of astronomical research studies.

National Aeronautics and Space Administration, additional grant for the acquisition of the "Beyer Tektite Collection."

National Geographic Society, grant for Paleo-Indian investigations at Agate Basin, Eastern Wyoming.

National Institute of Health, grant toward the purchase of the Melander Collection of Diptera.

National Science Foundation:

Grant for research entitled "Obsidian Dating."

Additional grant for research entitled 'Oldest Fossil Bryozoa of the United States."

Additional grant for research entitled "Comparative Analysis of Behavior in Tropical Birds."

Additional grant for research entitled "Morphology and Paleoecology of Permian Brachiopods."

Additional grant for research entitled "Endocrine Basis of Parasitic Breeding in Birds."

Additional grant for research entitled "Metabolic Aspects of the Digestion of Wax."

Additional grant for research entitled "Taxonomic Study of the Phanerogams of Colombia."

Grant for research entitled "Permo-Triassic Reptiles of South Africa."

Grant for partial support for the "Preparation and Publication of *Supplement to Annotated Bibliography of Termites*, 1955–1960."

Grant for research entitled "A Revision of the Beetles of the Genus Neobrotica Jacoby."

Additional grant for research entitled "Systematics of Chilopoda and Diplopoda."

Additional grant for research entitled "Revisionary Study of the Blattoidea."

Additional grant for research entitled "Systematic Studies of South American Microlepidoptera."

Additional grant for research entitled "Early Tertiary Mammals of North America."

Grant for research entitled "Construction of Highly Sensitive Mass Spectrometer for analyzing Rare Gases in Meteorites."

Grant for research entitled "Culture History of South Arabia."

National Science Foundation—Continued

Grant for research entitled "Foreign Cambrian Trilobites with American Affinities."

Grant for research entitled "Systematic Significance of Echinoid Spines."

Grant for research entitled "Botanical Exploration of Southern Brazil."

Grant for research entitled "Research on Stellar Atmosphere."

Grant for research entitled "Extensive Studies, over a long period of time, in the worldwide Order Hemiptera."

Additional grant for research entitled "Taxonomy of the Bamboo."

Grant for research entitled "Settlement pattern in the Missouri Valley."

Grant for research entitled "Caddo Language Study."

Grant for research entitled "A Late Pleistocene Fauna and Possible Human Associations near Littleton, Colorado."

New York Academy of Sciences, gift to defray expenses of Dr. M. T. Newman while attending the conference on "Genetic Perspectives in Disease Resistance and Susceptibility."

Office of Naval Research, additional grant to provide expert consultants to advise the Navy Advisory Committee.

Office of Naval Research, additional grant to perform psychological research studies.

Office of Naval Research, additional grant for support of research entitled "Information on Shark Distribution and the Distribution of Shark Attack all over the World."

Office of Naval Research, additional grant for study concerning the development of a proposal for an institute or laboratory of human performance standards.

Office of Naval Research, additional grant for research in connection with studies on the marine fauna of the South Pacific Ocean.

Office of Naval Research, additional grant to perform aeronautical research studies.

Mrs. John B. Oliver, gift to the Historic Dresses Fund.

Pan American Union, grant for travel expenses of Dr. Clifford Evans and Dr. Betty Meggers to Barranquilla, Colombia, to attend the conference on Methodology.

Mr. B. T. Rocca, gift to the Smithsonian Institution.

Rancho Santa Ana Botanic Garden, grant for joint botanical collecting expedition to the Hawaiian Islands.

St. Petersburg Shell Club, grant to defray expenses of Dr. Harald Rehder to St. Petersburg to attend the annual Shell Show.

Dr. Jeanne S. Schwengel, gift to defray travel expenses of Dr. Harald A. Rehder from Washington to Honolulu in connection with his trip to Jaluit Atoll in the Marshall Islands.

Shell Companies Foundation, gift to purchase 180 volumes of "Collection of Pilots and Engine Handbooks."

Texas Gulf Sulphur Co., grant for the construction of two Frasch Models.

U.S. Department of Agriculture, grant for the support of research in the Order Diptera.

Wenner-Gren Foundation, grant to defray travel expenses of Dr. T. Dale Stewart while attending the Wenner-Gren Foundation Symposium Number 16.

Woods Hole Oceanographic Institution, grant to cover travel expenses of Dr. Richard Cifelli to participate in Woods Hole Oceanographic Institution research cruises in the North Atlantic.

Yale University, gift to defray travel expenses of Dr. William L. Stern in connection with a trip to New Haven, Connecticut.

For support of the Science Information Exchange:
  Atomic Energy Commission
  Department of Defense
  Department of the Navy
  Federal Aviation Agency
  National Aeronautics and Space Administration
  National Institute of Health
  National Science Foundation
  Veterans' Administration

Included in the above list of gifts and contributions are reimbursable contracts.

The foregoing report relates only to the private funds of the Institution.

The following appropriations were made by Congress for the Government bureaus under the administrative charge of the Smithsonian Institution for the fiscal year 1961:

Salaries and Expenses____ $8, 114, 000. 00
National Zoological Park____ 1, 304, 000. 00

The appropriation made to the National Gallery of Art (which is a bureau of the Smithsonian Institution) was $1,920,000.00.

In addition, funds were transferred from other Government agencies for expenditure under the direction of the Smithsonian Institution as follows:

Working Funds, transferred from the National Park Service,
  Interior Department, for archeological investigations in river
  basins throughout the United States____________________________ $123, 895. 00

The Institution also administers a trust fund for partial support of the Canal Zone Biological Area, located on Barro Colorado Island in the Canal Zone.

AUDIT

The report of the audit of the Smithsonian Private Funds follows:

THE BOARD OF REGENTS,
Smithsonian Institution,
Washington 25, D.C.

We have examined the balance sheet of private funds of Smithsonian Institution as of June 30, 1961 and the related statement of current general private funds receipts and disbursements and the several statements of changes in funds for the year then ended. Our examination was made in accordance with generally accepted auditing standards, and accordingly included such tests of the accounting records and such other auditing procedures as we considered necessary in the circumstances.

Land, building, furniture, equipment, works of art, living and other specimens and certain sundry property are not included in the accounts of the Institution; likewise, the accompanying statements do not include the National Gallery of Art and other departments, bureaus and operations administered by the Institution under Federal appropriations. The accounts of the Institution are maintained on the basis of cash receipts and disbursements, with the result that the accompanying statements do not reflect income earned but not collected or expenses incurred but not paid.

In our opinion, subject to the matters referred to in the preceding paragraph, the accompanying statement of private funds presents fairly the assets and funds principal of Smithsonian Institution at June 30, 1961; further, the accompanying statement of current general private funds receipts and disbursements and several statements of changes in funds, which have been prepared on a basis consistent with that of the preceding year, present fairly the cash transactions of the private funds for the year then ended.

PEAT, MARWICK, MITCHELL & CO.

WASHINGTON, D.C.
September 11, 1961

Respectfully submitted.

(s) CLARENCE CANNON,
(s) CARYL P. HASKINS,
(s) ROBERT V. FLEMING,
Executive Committee.

GENERAL APPENDIX

to the

SMITHSONIAN REPORT FOR 1961

ADVERTISEMENT

The object of the GENERAL APPENDIX to the Annual Report of the Smithsonian Institution is to furnish brief accounts of scientific discovery in particular directions; reports of investigations made by staff members and collaborators of the Institution; and memoirs of a general character or on special topics that are of interest or value to the numerous correspondents of the Institution.

It has been a prominent object of the Board of Regents of the Smithsonian Institution from a very early date to enrich the annual report required of them by law with memoirs illustrating the more remarkable and important developments in physical and biological discovery, as well as showing the general character of the operations of the Institution; and, during the greater part of its history, this purpose has been carried out largely by the publication of such papers as would possess an interest to all attracted by scientific progress.

In 1880, induced in part by the discontinuance of an annual summary of progress which for 30 years previously had been issued by well-known private publishing firms, the Secretary had a series of abstracts prepared by competent collaborators, showing concisely the prominent features of recent scientific progress in astronomy, geology, meteorology, physics, chemistry, mineralogy, botany, zoology, and anthropology. This latter plan was continued, though not altogether satisfactorily, down to and including the year 1888.

In the report of 1889, a return was made to the earlier method of presenting a miscellaneous selection of papers (some of them original) embracing a considerable range of scientific investigation and discussion. This method has been continued in the present report for 1961.

Reprints of the various papers in the General Appendix may be obtained, as long as the supply lasts, on request addressed to the Editorial and Publications Division, Smithsonian Institution, Washington 25, D.C.

Some Astronomical Aspects of Life in the Universe[1]

By Su-Shu Huang

Institute for Advanced Study, Princeton, N.J.[2]

[With 3 plates]

THREE different ways by which matter interacts are gravitational, nuclear, and chemical. As our knowledge now stands, it appears that the behavior of all matter in the universe—from shining stars to exuberant life on the earth—may eventually be explained in terms of these interactions. Indeed, the emergence of life in general, and on earth in particular, is a net result of all three.

All forms of life must rely for maintenance on a stellar source of energy. Therefore, the nature and evolution of a star control the emergence and development of life. There is no doubt now that stars condense from gas and dust in the interstellar clouds, a newly formed star's temperature being very low because the interstellar gas is quite cool. As the star contracts, its temperature increases, and it moves from the lower right-hand corner of the Hertzsprung-Russell diagram toward the left side. Figure 1 shows the early evolutionary tracks of stars of different masses, which can be roughly represented by straight lines.[3]

Gravitational contraction stops when the internal temperature becomes high enough for thermonuclear reactions to begin to convert hydrogen into helium. These reactions supply energy equal to that radiated by the star, which therefore maintains an equilibrium condition with constant luminosity for a long time. Such a state of affairs corresponds to a star on the main sequence.

The time of contraction to the main sequence depends on the mass, as shown in table 1. The time scales given here are longer than usu-

[1] Reprinted by permission from Sky and Telescope, vol. 21, No. 6, June 1961.

[2] On leave from Goddard Space Flight Center, National Aeronautics and Space Administration.

[3] For a detailed description of a star of solar mass contracting to the main sequence, see "Early Solar Evolution," Robert R. Brownlee and Arthur N. Cox, Sky and Telescope, May 1961, p. 252.—Ed.

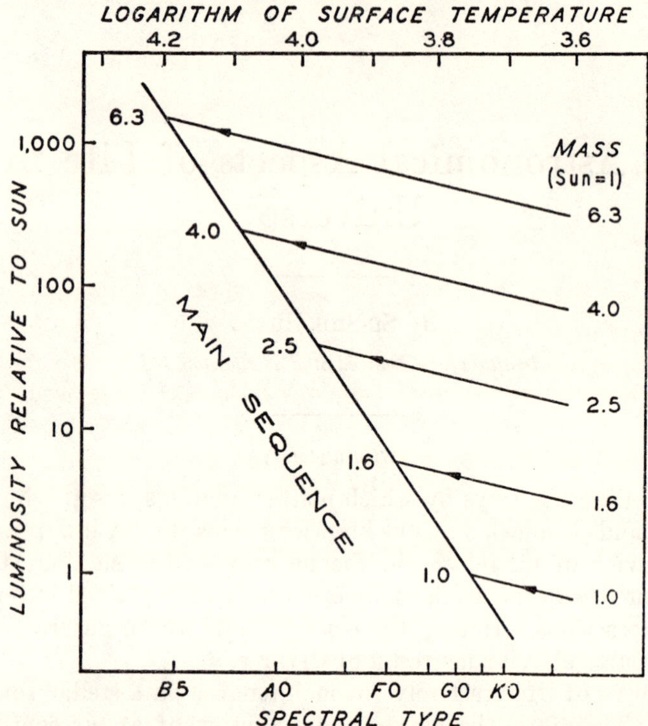

FIGURE 1.—A contracting newborn star evolves leftward in this diagram to the main sequence, where a long stay should favor development of life on any planets the star may have.

ally cited because we have taken into account the change in luminosity of the star during its contraction.

A star of a certain mass will arrive at the main sequence with a definite spectral type and luminosity, and its character changes only slightly during the long period in which the hydrogen in its core is being consumed. Once the central hydrogen is exhausted, the star evolves quite rapidly toward the right, to become a giant or supergiant—very different in size and surface brightness from before.

It is obvious from the table that time scales on the main sequence are much longer than those of contraction. This explains why about 90 percent of observed stars are to be found on the main sequence. The stay of a more massive star on the main sequence is shorter than that of a less massive star, as it dissipates its energy much faster. Thus, an O star remains in this state for only a few million years, compared to an M star's 100 billion.

From this brief look at stellar life histories, it is clear that gravitation holds a star together while nuclear interactions release the energy it radiates. The third kind of reaction, chemical, does not play a significant role in shaping a star, yet chemical action is responsible for the emergence and evolution of living organisms. And although we can predict that in about 10 billion years or less our sun will become a white dwarf, there is no way of telling how man will evolve in even 10 million years.

What is the reason for this? Gravitational interaction is very simple and is described by Newton's law of gravitation. The number of possible nuclear interactions is very large indeed, since there are hundreds of different atomic nuclei; nevertheless, we could still list all conceivable reactions. Hence we can compute them and even predict the evolution of stars by the law of gravitation and our knowledge of nuclear physics.

But how big is the total number of chemical reactions—both inorganic and organic—that one may conceive? Unable to estimate such a number, I am probably safe in saying that it is larger than any astronomical figure we can find in our textbooks. It is this wealth of chemical activity that makes a prediction of the emergence and evolution of living organisms difficult, if not permanently elusive.

If we cannot compute the time scale of biological evolution, we must find it out empirically. Here on earth it took about 3 billion years for humans to evolve from atoms. I have suggested earlier that since biological evolution occurs through the random processes of mutation and selection, its average time scale is probably of the same order of magnitude—a few billion years. On this basis, for successful biological evolution on a planet, the luminosity of its parent star must

TABLE 1

Mass (sun=1)	Time scales in billions of years		Characteristics on main sequence		
	Gravitational contraction	Main-sequence stage	Spectral type	Radius (sun=1)	Luminosity (sun=1)
17.0	0. 00012	0. 008	B0	9. 0	29, 000
6.3	. 0011	. 08	B5	4. 2	980
3.2	. 0041	. 4	A0	2. 8	100
1.9	. 022	2	A5	1. 51	12. 0
1.5	. 042	4	F0	1. 25	4. 8
1.3	. 056	6	F5	1. 24	2. 7
1.02	. 094	11	G0	1. 02	1. 2
1.00	. 11	13	G2 (sun)	1. 00	1. 0
0.91	. 14	17	G5	. 92	. 72
0.74	. 23	28	K0	. 74	. 35
0.54	. 60	70	K5	. 54	. 10

be constant for at least this long. Thus we see from the table that only those main-sequence stars at and below spectral type F can support life. Others evolve too fast and do not maintain constant luminosities long enough.

A second limitation on the development of life on a planet is its star's ability to warm up a large space around it. Stars are fireplaces in the cold and dark of space, each having a region of propitious temperature in which life may develop and survive. It is evident, for example, that the habitable zones of cool stars of spectral type M are much smaller than that of the sun. Therefore, the chance of finding a planet revolving permanently inside the habitable zone of an M star is less than for somewhat hotter stars. However, M-type dwarfs are far more numerous than any other single spectral type, and the total number of them supporting life may be appreciable.

Combining the previous two arguments, we conclude that intelligent life has the highest chance of being found in the vicinities of stars of medium temperature, like the sun. A further limitation applies to binary and multiple systems, which constitute about one-third of all stars. A planet associated with a binary may or may not have a stable orbit, and in the latter case could wander out of the habitable zone and destroy life that might have developed earlier.

As for a life-supporting planet itself, one of its most important qualifications is maintenance of an atmosphere suitable for the chemical processes of living beings. An atmosphere makes possible the existence of water or other substances in liquid form on the planet's surface; it is simply inconceivable that living organisms can be maintained without the aid of some substances in liquid form.

The earth holds its air because its gravitational attraction prevents gas molecules, which are in a state of thermal motion, from escaping. The moon and Mercury are devoid of atmospheres partly because of their smaller surface gravities; hence, a larger planet is required.

But it is not advantageous to the emergence of life, especially of a high form, if the planet is too big. Since the most abundant element in the universe is hydrogen, a newly formed planet must have a high percentage of it, particularly in its outer envelope, because of hydrogen's light weight. In other words, we expect a new planet's atmosphere to be chemically in a reducing state. As A. I. Oparin has pointed out, life may first appear under reducing conditions, but it seems unlikely that life of a high form would emerge under such a dominantly hydrogen atmosphere.

My tentative conclusion is based upon the energy metabolism of living beings. In an oxidizing atmosphere, like the earth's, the combustion of glucose,

$$C_6H_{12}O_6 + 6O_2 \longrightarrow 6CO_2 + 6H_2O,$$

which supplies most of the body's needs for energy, yields about 700 kilogram-calories of free energy per mole. On the other hand, in a reducing atmosphere the free energy has to be derived from fermentation of glucose to ethyl alcohol and carbon dioxide, according to

$$C_6H_{12}O_6 \longrightarrow 2C_2H_5OH + 2CO_2,$$

which amounts to only about 60 kilogram-calories per mole.

Consequently, under reducing conditions a living being has to consume more than 10 times as much food as in an oxidizing environment in order to derive the same amount of free energy. Therefore, it is doubtful that a mind such as man's would appear through evolution in a reducing atmosphere, because living beings would be too preoccupied with seeking food.

If hydrogen must first escape from the air before a high form of life emerges, the planet must not be too large. Plausible values for the radius would be between 1,000 and 20,000 kilometers, which includes the moon and Mercury. The former could hold air if its density were high, and the latter would have a suitable atmosphere if its distance from the sun were greater.

The problem of life on other worlds is ultimately related to the formation of the complex molecules that are essential to life processes. Life on the earth, as we all know, depends upon carbon-containing molecules and on water. The fundamental question of bioastronomy is whether living beings elsewhere must also depend on the carbon bond, with water as a solvent. Although a definite answer cannot be provided, I have several arguments in favor of an affirmative one.

From what other element can complex molecules be built? A glance at the periodic table shows silicon, located directly below carbon, to be a likely candidate. Indeed, silicon is largely responsible for the great variety of molecules found in the earth's crust. However, silicon appears to have a higher affinity for fluorine and other halogens than for hydrogen. While its cosmic abundance is as much as one-fifth that of carbon, the percentage of halogens in the cosmos is negligible compared with hydrogen. As a result, complex compounds of silicon have much less chance to form than do those involving carbon.

There are several empirical results favoring carbon as an essential life constituent. M. Calvin and his associates made the first successful experiment in prebiological chemistry when they obtained formaldehyde and formic acid in a cyclotron from a mixture of carbon dioxide and water. In 1953, S. L. Miller found that the amino acids—the building blocks of proteins—are formed, together with other organic compounds, when an electric discharge is passed through a mixture of methane, ammonia, and water vapor, in concentrations approximately

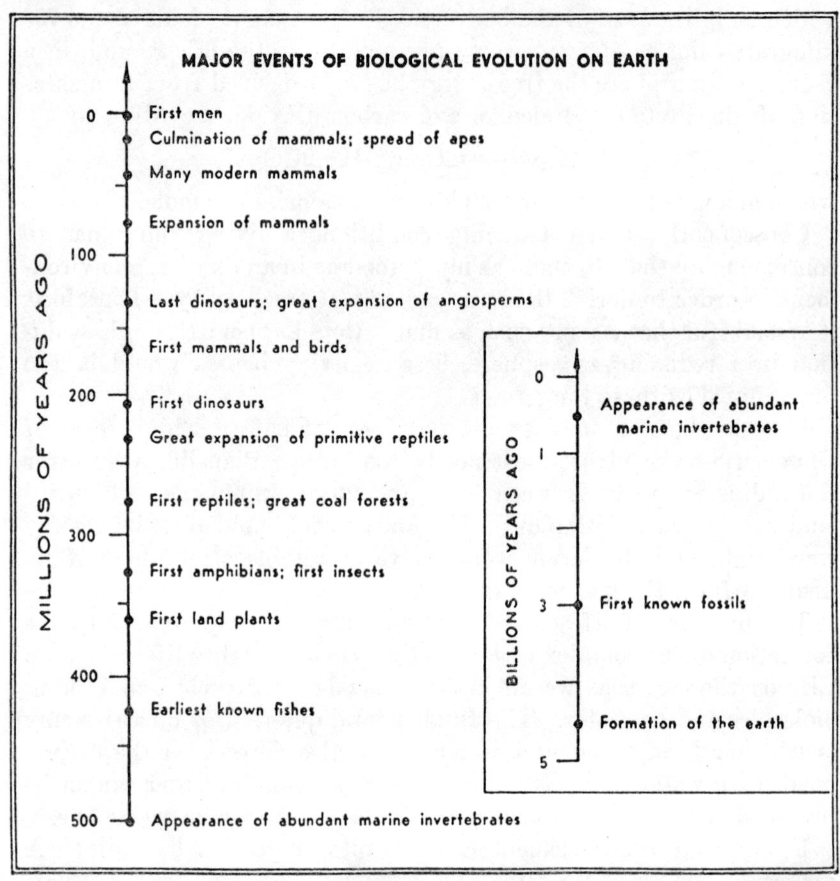

Figure 2.—Right: The author's chart of the major events in the evolution of life on our planet. The compressed scale (inset) shows some very early events in the earth's history.

equal to those given by H. C. Urey for the primitive atmosphere of the earth.

Calvin also discovered organic compounds in meteorites. Very recently B. Nagy, D. J. Hennessy, and W. G. Meinschein detected paraffinic hydrocarbons, closely akin to those found on earth in living matter, in a fragment of a stony meteorite that fell in France nearly a century ago. They believe this to be the first empirical evidence for the existence of life beyond our own planet. Such an interpretation has not been unanimously accepted by authorities on this subject. However, if the meteorite's hydrocarbons are not due to contamination, they indicate definitely that the formation of organic compounds is not limited to the surface of the earth, although the mechanism of formation may be debated for a long time to come.

All these results suggest that complex compounds of carbon can be formed easily from inorganic substances when conditions are suitable. We may not be seriously wrong if we assume that life everywhere in the universe depends on carbon compounds.

The question of life elsewhere in the solar system is no longer as speculative as it was even a decade ago, and in 10 years we may have definite proof concerning the present existence of living beings on other planets. But if no life is found, it does not prove that none ever appeared—such proof requires actual excavation of a planet's surface, which may take a few decades to achieve.

Mars is most frequently mentioned as a possible former or present abode of life. Despite its small gravitational attraction (with only 10 percent of the earth's mass), its surface gravity is 37 percent of ours and it retains an atmosphere. There is no hydrogen or helium; none is expected. Spectroscopic observations show carbon dioxide is present, but the search for oxygen has been negative. Mars' atmosphere contains less than 1/1,000 as much oxygen as the earth's, yet there is doubtless much nitrogen.

Although spectroscopic observations have failed to detect water vapor on Mars, its presence may be indicated by the seasonal variations of the polar caps. However, the physical nature of the polar caps is still debatable. Some observers consider them to be made of ice, but others, like C. C. Kiess and his collaborators (Sky and Telescope, June 1960, p. 469), explain the caps as solid nitrogen tetroxide.

The temperature of Mars' equatorial region can reach a maximum of about 30° C., but in general is lower than on earth. Since not much water exists in the Martian atmosphere to keep heat from radiating away into space at night, the temperature probably reaches as low as −100° C. Whether life can be maintained under these conditions has interested astronomers for a long time.

Dark green areas in the equatorial regions suggest that plant life of some form is present on Mars. The color and shade of these markings change with the seasons in a way that indicates the growth and decay of vegetation (darker in spring and lighter in autumn). Because of the very severe climate, no higher terrestrial plants could survive. However, special kinds, such as lichens, might live. A lichen is a symbiotic plant composed of two different organisms: fungus and alga. These can flourish together under conditions that would be fatal if either had to meet them alone.

The fungus, which does not perform photosynthesis, derives food from the alga, which does. But the fungus helps maintain the water supply necessary for growth of the alga. Consequently, this symbiotic plant occurs all over the earth, enduring many kinds of extreme climate, from burning deserts to freezing mountaintops. However, it is not necessarily lichens themselves that we observe in the dark-green areas of Mars.

Rather, we wish to emphasize here that the severe climate on Mars does not exclude the possibility of the maintenance of life there. Indeed, observations by W. M. Sinton strongly imply that an infrared absorption band characteristic of many organic compounds is present in the Martian spectrum, which strengthens the belief in some form of vegetation on that planet.

Because Mars lacks oxygen, most astronomers agree that we should not expect to find a high form of life there, and I personally believe this conclusion is probably right. But there is the unlikely possibility that intelligent beings might have existed, or still survive, on Mars. This view does not need the support of the canals, whose interpretation has aroused much controversy. But since Mars' gravity is smaller than the earth's, it was easier for hydrogen to dissipate, and biological evolution could have started earlier on the red planet than here. It is not inconceivable that intelligent beings emerged on Mars millions of years ago. One might object that the rate of evolution would be slower because chemical reactions would occur less rapidly at the low Martian temperature. On the other hand, the development of the human brain may have been completed during the glacial ages here on earth.

The other neighbor of the earth is Venus. Carbon dioxide is abundant in its atmosphere, and water vapor has recently been established by John Strong, but oxygen has never been detected. There are extensive clouds that prevent us from seeing the planet's actual surface, and we can only measure the composition of the upper atmosphere. The clouds themselves probably consist of water droplets or ice particles.

Microwave observations of Venus by C. H. Mayer and his coworkers yield a temperature of more than 300° C. As Carl Sagan has pointed out, the high temperature of the planet is consistent with an abundance of carbon dioxide and water vapor below the clouds. Both these substances produce a very efficient greenhouse effect, letting visible sunlight pass through but preventing infrared radiation from going out. Hence Venus' surface temperature probably reaches such a high value that life is impossible there.

The existence of life on other bodies in our solar system cannot be categorically denied. However, because of their chemically reducing atmospheres and low temperatures (or very high, for Mercury's sunlit side), life must be very primitive, if present at all.

Elsewhere in the universe, the fundamental problem is the existence of planets. Are stars always accompanied by some smaller bodies? We don't have a definite answer, because of observational difficulties. No earthbound telescope could detect a planet of Jupiter's size even if

The delicate dusky markings of the cloud-covered planet Venus are well shown in these photographs taken by H. Camichel with a 15-inch telescope at Pic du Midi Observatory in France. The narrow crescent (left) was recorded on October 3, 1943; the other view on the 6th of the following month. Venus's high surface temperature makes it ill suited as an abode of life.

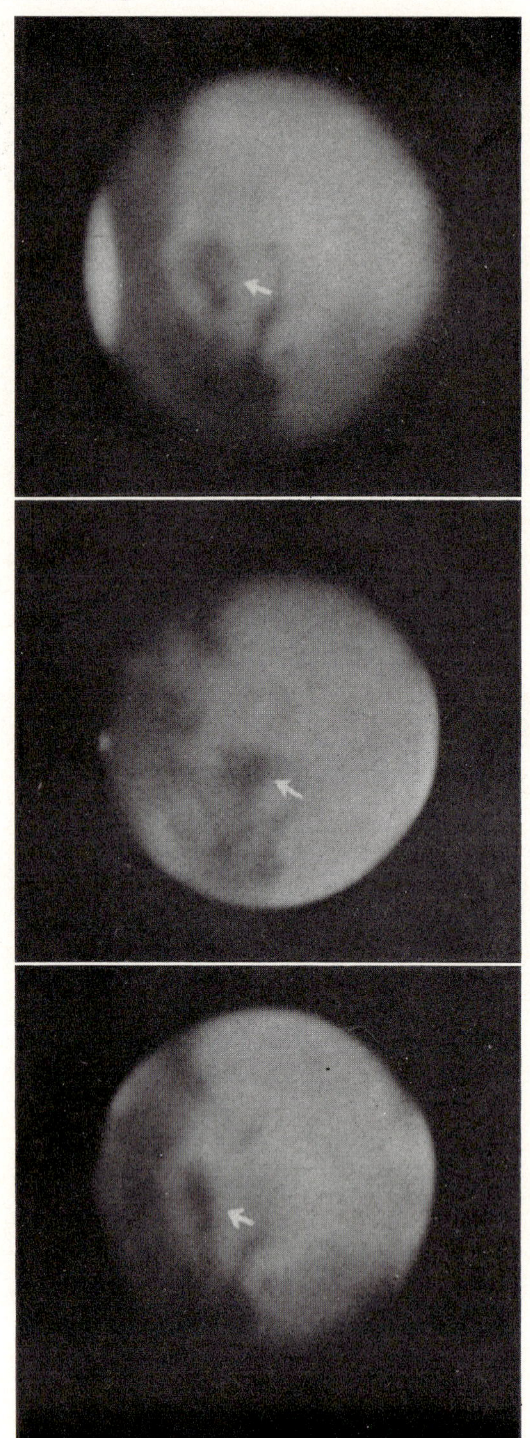

Changes in the size and form of Solis Lacus and in the strength of the canals and oases thereabout. Photograph by E. C. Slipher, Lowell Observatory.

This Sproul Observatory model made by Sarah Lee Lippincott shows the arrangement in space of all the stars known to lie within 16 light-years of the sun, which is at the center. The plexiglas sphere is 36 inches in diameter, and the distance scale is one inch per light-year. Wooden beads are used to represent the stars, with Sirius (right below center) the largest. To the right above center is Procyon, shown, like Sirius, with its white-dwarf companion. The large star at the left is Altair. Among these stellar neighbors there are 53 visible stars, including Tau Ceti and Epsilon Eridani which satisfy the author's criteria for possibly having planets where intelligent life may exist. These two stars were selected for special scrutiny in the Project Ozma attempt to detect extraterrestrial radio transmissions. Photograph from Sproul Observatory of Swarthmore College.

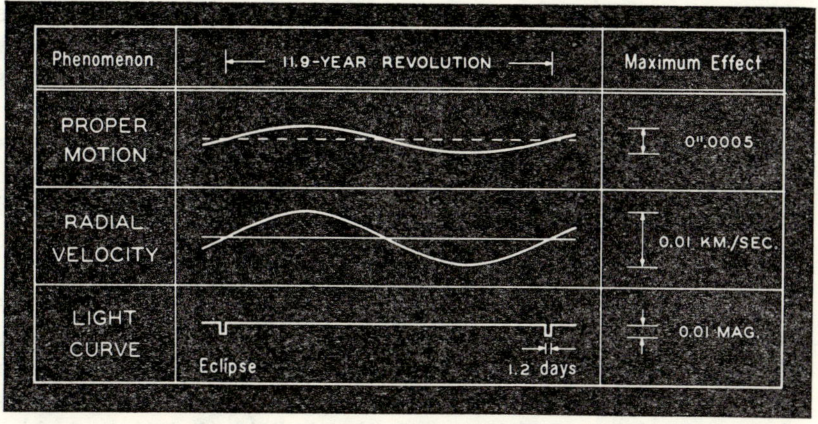

FIGURE 3.—Three kinds of observational tests are presented for the detection of a planet similar to Jupiter revolving around a solar-type star 32 light-years distant from us. Even at best, the maximum effects (right) are very minute.

it were associated with the nearest star, for the planet would be lost in the glare of the star's light. However, as Nancy G. Roman has suggested, a telescope installed in an artificial satellite would suffer much less from scattering of starlight in the earth's atmosphere and might be used for such a search.

What theoretical reasoning can be applied to this problem? Some 30 years ago astronomers felt that our solar system was formed when the sun encountered another star. Since the average distance between two neighboring stars is very large, a close encounter of this kind is a very rare event, producing only one planetary system among many millions of stars. But it has since been shown that the collision theory of planet formation is untenable.

Astronomers are now convinced that planets form from dust and gas that is either the remnant in the process of star formation or that has been acquired from the interstellar medium. If the cloud is massive enough, another star could be formed instead of planets. Thus, binary and planetary systems have apparently the same origin, and they have other properties in common.

According to G. P. Kuiper, the average separation of all components in binary systems that have been studied is about 20 astronomical units, roughly the mean distance of the major planets from the sun. Also, there is wide range in the ratio of masses of binary star components, with a few as small as 10 times the ratio of Jupiter's mass to the sun's. Unseen companions with masses about 0.01 that of the sun have been found by K. A. Strand (61 Cygni) and Sarah Lee Lippincott (Lalande 21185). Since binary stars are very numerous, planetary systems should also occur frequently.

We can also make, heuristically, a prediction regarding the stars that have a good chance of possessing planets. Years ago Otto Struve pointed out that the rapid rotation of early-type main-sequence stars did not occur in classes later than $F5$. In other words, the average angular momentum per unit mass of main-sequence stars suffers a conspicuous discontinuity at this spectral subdivision. A reasonable possibility to explain this is that planetary systems are formed around stars of later spectral types, the unobservable planets absorbing the excess angular momentum in each case.

The available evidence, therefore, suggests that most single stars on the main sequence between $F5$ and perhaps $K5$ have a good chance of supporting life of an advanced form on their planets. Only a few percent of all stars fall in this range. Within 16.3 light-years (5 parsecs) of the sun, there are 58 other individual stars, 5 of which are unseen companions. Of 26 single stars in this group, only 2 besides the sun fall within our limitations for supporting life: Epsilon Eridani, a $K2$ dwarf, and Tau Ceti, a $G4$ dwarf.

Of course, the actual chance of intelligent life appearing is less than a few percent. Even if the size of a planet revolving within a habitable zone is right, its surface topography might not be. If the entire surface were water covered, for instance, a civilization like ours could not develop. Taking everything into consideration, I venture to state that no more than 1 to 2 percent of stars may have at one time or another supported intelligent life. On this basis, there are within 1,000 light-years a few thousand stars around which life of this nature could appear.

For us on earth, a most interesting question is whether or not intelligent life exists elsewhere right now. What is the chance of finding extraterrestrial contemporaries? No one dares guess how long our civilization will endure. Granted that man does not destroy himself, he still has to face natural calamities, such as a recurrence of the ice ages. Will man's tendency to overspecialization bring about his downfall? I incline to believe that the lifetime of a technological civilization occupies only a very small fraction of the entire period of biological evolution. If so, two such civilizations in different worlds would scarcely be simultaneous.

An interstellar journey will not be within our means for a long time to come. At the speed of artificial satellites that we have launched so far, it would take hundreds of thousands of years to cover the 10 light-years of distance to Epsilon Eridani or Tau Ceti. This leaves us with only radio communication as a possible means of contacting other intelligent beings. This problem has been treated in detail in an article on Project Ozma, by Frank D. Drake of the National Radio Astronomy Observatory, in Sky and Telescope for January 1960

(p. 140). So far, Project Ozma observations have given negative results.

It is generally agreed among radio scientists that the best frequency to employ is that of the 21-cm. neutral hydrogen line. It has been suggested that the value of pi, or the fine structure constant, or any other dimensionless constant, be transmitted in order to distinguish our signal from natural sources of radio noise. I personally think a great effort of this kind inadvisable, however fundamental the constant might be.

Instead, I suggest using simple numbers: 1, 2, 3, each represented by the corresponding number of dots. They are as good a sign of intelligence as any physical or biological constant. Then we could proceed to introduce the concept of equality and other algebraic symbols (as P. Morrison has also proposed). This can be done by coding such symbols and repeating a large number of examples, just as arithmetic is taught to children. At this stage the binary, decimal, or some other number system may be introduced, and finally the x, y concept of locating a point on a plane. Once this is established, a means for interchanging information follows easily.

While the chances of success in receiving intelligible signals from outer space are extremely small, even during a long search with larger and larger radio telescopes, it is worth trying because of its fundamental importance in understanding the nature of living beings and its impact on our philosophical beliefs.

X-rays From the Sun[1]

By HERBERT FRIEDMAN

U.S. Naval Research Laboratory

ONLY A few decades ago solar X-ray emission was unknown. The sun was viewed as a glowing sphere of hot gas radiating at a temperature of 6,000° K. and incapable of producing any significant flux of X-rays. Today, with information gained from experiments carried in rockets and satellites, we know that solar X-rays shape some of the major features of the ionosphere. Sporadic, explosive outbursts of X-rays are synchronized with solar flares and linked directly with radio fadeouts. More modest eruptions are associated with active prominences and coronal condensations. The stormy character of solar X-ray emission far exceeds that of any portion of the ultraviolet or visible spectrum, and is matched only by the violent outbursts observed at radio frequencies.

At the time of a solar eclipse, a corona of faintly luminescent gas is visible above the disk. This thin white halo, with a slightly greenish cast, reaches millions of miles into space. The source of solar X-ray emission lies within the corona very near its base where the temperature is of the order of a million degrees Kelvin. How the corona reaches this remarkably high temperature when the visible surface of the sun is only 6,000° K. is explainable in terms of the dissipation of shock-wave energy. Immediately below the surface of the sun, energy is transported outward by the violent convection of hydrogen gas. Starting as sound waves generated by turbulence within the hydrogen convection zone, they propagate outward, increasing in amplitude as the density decreases until shock waves develop. Energy is thus transferred from the interior to the corona. Because the corona is so thin, it radiates poorly and only a small fraction of the sun's energy need be dissipated in the corona to achieve very high temperatures.

In the 25th annual James Arthur lecture on the sun,[2] Dr. Leo Goldberg described the earth's atmosphere as a barrier to astronomical

---

[1] The 27th annual James Arthur lecture on the sun, given under the auspices of the Smithsonian Institution on Feb. 2, 1961.

[2] See Annual Report of the Smithsonian Institution for 1959, p. 285.

research in the ultraviolet and X-ray regions of the spectrum. Very soft X-rays (10 to 100 A.) cannot penetrate to less than 100 km. above the ground. Harder X-rays (1 to 10 A.) reach progressively deeper levels down to the bottommost fringe of the ionosphere. At still shorter wavelengths, X-rays are sufficiently penetrating to be observed with balloon-borne apparatus.

The history of solar X-ray measurements begins with the use of German V-2 rockets brought to White Sands immediately after World War II. One of the primary objectives of the rocket astronomy program initiated at that time was the study of the solar spectrum beyond the atmospheric barrier in the near ultraviolet, beginning at about 3,000 A. It soon became evident that the spectral energy distribution declined so rapidly toward shorter wavelengths that photographic spectroscopy would experience great difficulty. X-ray measurements were therefore attempted with sensitive detectors such as Geiger counters and ionization chambers coupled with filters that provided spectral resolution in comparatively narrow wavelength intervals, for example, 2 to 8 A., 8 to 18 A., and 44 to 60 A.

Although spectroscopy of the ultraviolet range has made tremendous strides in the past dozen years, our knowledge of the X-ray region is as yet confined to only the broad features. High-resolution spectra still remain to be achieved, but the goal no longer appears very far off and may be well within the reach of the first orbiting solar observatories soon to be launched.

X-ray photometry from rockets has been carried on by the author and his colleagues at the Naval Research Laboratory for more than a full sunspot cycle, beginning in 1949. In a typical experiment, the detector is mounted against an aperture in the skin of the rocket looking outward. Its view of space during the course of the flight depends entirely on the spin and yaw motion of the rocket. As the rocket traverses the upper atmosphere, signals are telemetered continuously via a radio transmitter in the rocket to a receiver on the ground. When the spinning rocket reaches altitudes to which solar X-rays can penetrate, modulated signals appear in the record with a roll frequency maximizing whenever the detector looks closest to the direction to the sun. Essential to such an experiment is a visible photocell measurement, which permits the calculation of the aspect of the rocket at all times during the flight and therefrom the appropriate correction for the dependence of X-ray signals on the angle of incidence of the radiation.

Near sunspot minimum, in 1953 and 1954, the rocket measurements indicated a marked reduction in X-ray emission below 20 A. In some experiments no emission at all was detected below 10 A. With the approach to solar maximum, the over-all X-ray flux increased, but especially at the shorter wavelengths. In the 2 to 8 A. band, the minimum-to-maximum variation was a factor of several hundred; from 8 to 20 A., at least a factor of 45; in the 44 to 60 A. band, the variation was approximately sevenfold. Assuming that the X-ray spectrum had a gray body distribution, it was not possible to fit the measurements in these three wavelength intervals by a single temperature. The longer wavelength emission could be adequately described by a temperature between 0.5 and 1×10^6 degrees K., but the shorter wavelength range, below 20 A., required a temperature closer to 2×10^6 degrees K. At the higher temperature, the gray body emission needed to supply the observed counting rate at 8 to 20 A. contained only 1 percent of the flux deduced for the 20 to 100 A. range from the longer wavelength measurements. It was concluded, therefore, that the shortest wavelength X-ray emission was associated with local, hotter regions occupying no more than 1 percent of the volume of the corona, in which the temperature was of the order of 2 million degrees K. These hotter regions were presumably distributed within a corona whose general temperature did not exceed 1 million degrees K. Figure 1 is a plot of the solar spectral energy distribution illustrating the results of these measurements. The curve marked "A–16" is for 1953 and "A–43" for 1956. They represent the minimum and maximum fluxes observed during the past sunspot cycle. The shaded region added to the A–16 curve is the increment of flux measured below 20 A. and attributed to localized hot spots at 2 million degrees K.

Practically all our knowledge of the ionosphere before direct rocket measurements were available was based on radio soundings. A pulse of radio waves entering a cloud of electrons is reflected when the density of the electrons reaches a critical value proportional to the square of the frequency. The time required for the pulse to travel to the ionosphere and back to ground is a measure of the height of the reflecting region. At certain critical frequencies there appear abrupt discontinuities in reflection heights as though the electron density were distributed in several well-defined layers. These layers are named "E," "F_1," and "F_2." In the lowest region of the ionosphere, named "D," the electron density is too small to reflect megacycle-per-second frequencies. The lower ionosphere normally acts as an absorbing region for these short waves and a good reflector for very long waves, such as the static generated by thunderstorms.

The variation of intensity with altitude showed that solar X-rays were absorbed in the E-region of the ionosphere between 100 and 140 km. Furthermore, the X-ray energy absorbed there appeared adequate to account for a major portion of the ionization. A direct check on the relationship between X-rays absorbed in the E-region and the resulting electron density there can be obtained by comparing

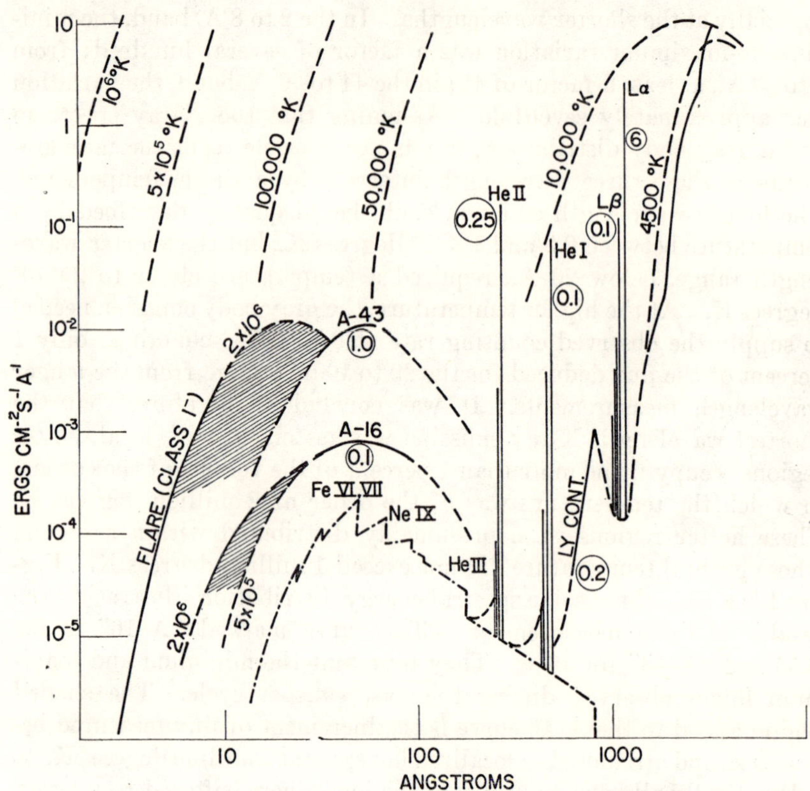

FIGURE 1.—Solar spectral energy distribution below 2,000 A. Solid lines represent rocket measurements. Dashed curves labeled with temperatures represent black-body distributions. Dot-dash curve is Elwert's (1960) theoretical continuum.

X-ray fluxes with the observed variation in critical frequency of the E-region. According to the theory of the formation of an ionospheric layer, the critical frequency is proportional to the fourth root of the intensity of ionizing radiation. The observed sevenfold variation in total flux from minimum to maximum would therefore produce a factor of $7^{1/4}$, or 1.6 in the critical frequency for E-region if X-rays were the sole source. Using values of the critical frequency corresponding to the times of rocket flights, the variations were from about 2.7 mc./sec. to 4.1 mc./sec., a factor of 1.5, in good agreement with the variation expected from the X-ray observations. Actually, there is an important contribution to the ionization of E-region by solar ultraviolet radiation, and it is theoretically difficult to evaluate the relative importance of X-ray and ultraviolet contributions. However, an analysis based on the best information available at the present time indicates that the X-ray influence is predominant.

Observations over more than two sunspot cycles have clearly established correlations between the fluxes of ionizing radiation and active centers on the sun. If the ionizing radiation were uniformly distributed over the face of the sun, an eclipse would lead to a smooth decline in the ionospheric electron density to a minimum value at totality, followed by a smooth recovery to normal in very much the same fashion, followed by the visible light curve. Instead, an irregular course of ionospheric electron-density changes has been noted in almost all observations conducted during eclipses. Monthly averages of critical frequencies show detailed agreement with the pattern followed by monthly values of sunspot numbers, indicating that at least part of the ionizing flux emanates from the vicinity of sunspots. Prior to 1958, however, no direct identification of localized sources of X-ray emission in the corona had been made.

The eclipse of October 12, 1958, offered an opportunity to launch rockets bearing ultraviolet and X-ray detectors to observe the distribution of emission sources over the disk and to determine whether any residual emission of X-rays or ultraviolet radiation was detectable at totality. During the totality phase of an eclipse, the E-region of the ionosphere does not disappear completely as would be expected if the source of the ionizing radiation were totally obscured and recombination were very fast. The residual ionization could be attributed to a sluggishness of the recombination process or to a portion of the ionizing radiation originating at sufficient height in the corona to bypass the edge of the moon.

The rocket experiment was carried out from shipboard near the Danger Islands of the South Pacific. Solid-propellant rockets were mounted on the helicopter deck of the U.S.S. *Point Defiance* and were launched at the appropriate times and in such a direction as to carry them through the eclipse shadow at E-region altitudes. Each rocket was equipped with X-ray detectors sensitive to two wavelength bands, 8 to 18 A. and 44 to 60 A., and a Lyman-α ionization chamber. Signals from these detectors and from aspect indicators were telemetered to the ground station aboard ship throughout the flight. Two rockets were launched during totality and indicated about 0.05 percent residual Lyman-α flux and from 10 to 13 percent residual X-ray flux.

A second objective of the experiment was to identify localized sources of emission over the disk. Figure 2 shows the optical distribution of active regions on the day of the rocket eclipse experiment. The area of the disk near the east limb contained a number of active regions identified by plages, whereas an equivalent area bordering the west limb was almost free of activity. Rockets were fired so as to observe exposed crescents on the east and west limbs before second contact and after third contact, as marked by the curves NN8.59F and NN8.62F in the figure. The east limb crescent, containing the plage areas, was observed to be six times as bright in X-ray emission as the west limb crescent, which was almost clear of plage activity (making allowance for the relative disk areas exposed).

In principle, X-ray image-forming devices of high light-gathering power can be achieved in the form of a grazing incidence reflection telescope or a zone plate, but no such devices have yet been perfected for use in rockets. Calculations, based on the intensity measured with X-ray photometers and the evidence of concentrated sources derived from the rocket eclipse experiment, indicated that a simple pinhole camera could produce an X-ray image with a resolution of about a tenth of a solar diameter during the flight time of an Aerobee-Hi rocket if the camera were mounted on a pointing control to aim it continuously at the sun. The first photograph of the sun in its X-ray emission was obtained in this manner on April 19, 1960. The camera was 6 inches long, with a pinhole of 0.005 inch in diameter. To exclude visible and ultraviolet light, the pinhole was covered by a plastic film of Parlodion, which was overcoated with an evaporated film of aluminum. This combination transmitted much of the X-ray spectrum below 50 A.

The X-ray photograph is reproduced in the upper left-hand portion of figure 3. The biaxial pointing control which carried the camera did not compensate for rotation about the sun-camera axis, with the result that the precession of the rocket caused the image to rotate and discrete features to be drawn into extended arcs. Furthermore, the sense of rotation varied during the course of the flight so that the image was first turned about 20° clockwise and then returned counterclockwise to complete the full arc of 160° extent. In spite of the smearing thereby produced, a clear correlation could be observed between the X-ray emission regions and the visible plage regions on the sun.

By direct measurement of the image, the mean diameter of the X-ray outline of the sun was found to be 5 percent greater than the diameter of the optical disk. The maximum diameter was 6 percent greater. Thus, within the limited definition of the camera, the X-ray emission was observed to extend to about 0.06 solar radii (43,000 km.) above the visible limb. All the measured X-ray regions in the photograph were about the size of the resolution circle when allowance was made for the smearing effect of the camera rotation. It appears that the regions of strong X-ray emission are smaller than the corresponding visible plage regions. From the fact that the sizes of the X-ray regions on the limb were nearly the same as those near the center of the disk, it would seem that the X-ray sources have a radial extension comparable to the surface projection.

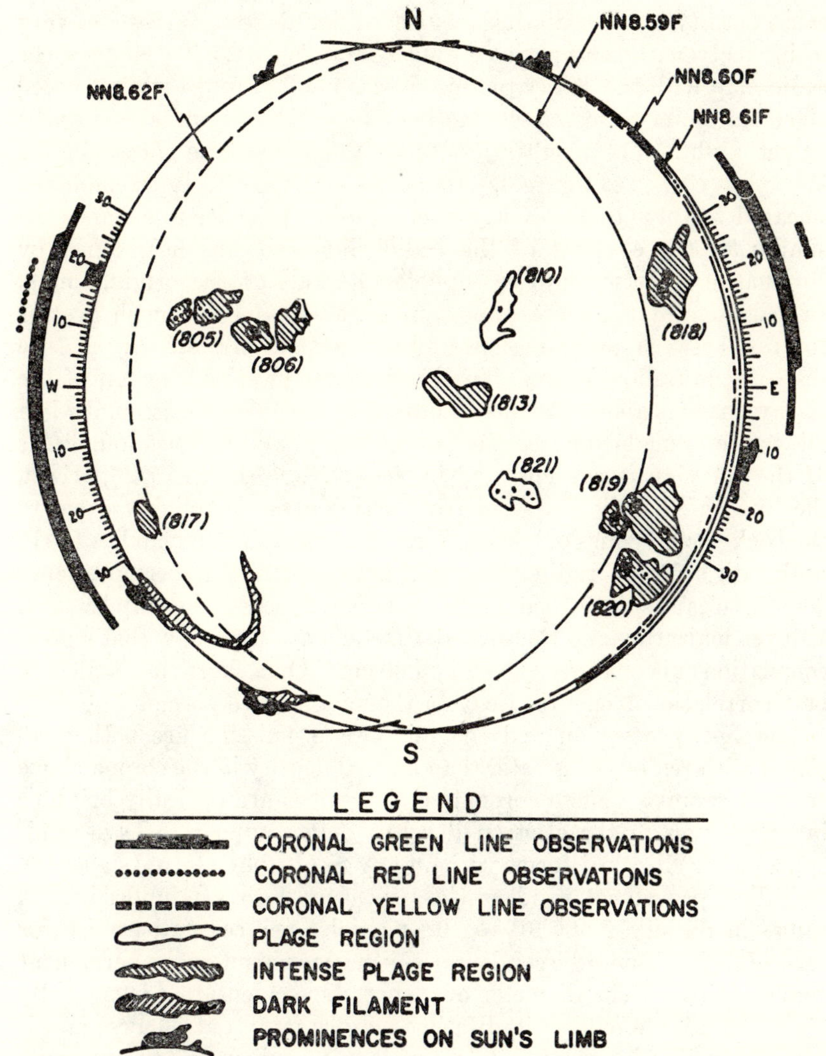

FIGURE 2.—Solar-activity map on day of rocket eclipse experiment, October 12, 1958.

A strong correlation is known to exist between visible plage regions and the regions of origin of the slowly varying component of radio microwave emission. Solar radio emissions in the decimeter wavelength range also correlate closely with variations in E-region electron density. The lower right-hand portion of figure 3 contains a radioheliograph of the sun at a wavelength of 9.1 cm., obtained at Stanford University with a microsteradian, pencil-beam interferometer, having a resolution of 3.5 minutes of arc. It is interesting to compare the radioheliograph with the X-ray disk photograph because both types of radiation require million-degree sources and vary in intensity with the square of the electron density. To compare the radio map with the X-ray picture, it was photographed while rotated about its center to match the motion of the X-ray camera during the rocket flight. The resulting smeared radio image is shown in the lower left corner of figure 3. Its major features closely resemble the smeared features of the X-ray photograph. In order to enhance the similarity, the contrast of the radioheliograph was heightened by eliminating the two lowest isophote intervals of the original map. In fact, one of the more important differences is the much greater contrast between active regions and background in the X-ray picture than in the radio picture. The bright, nearly central, region of the X-ray image is about 80 times as intense as the quiet background when allowance is made for the effect of smearing, and at least four-fifths of the emission is concentrated in the active areas. In comparison, the integrated radio emission from active areas is roughly equal to the background emission. The X-ray photograph also matches fairly well with a 21-cm. radioheliograph, but the detailed correspondence is not as clear as the 9.1-cm. map. Studies of the relationship between E-layer ionization and the solar decimeter wave flux show that a good correlation exists between 3 cm. and 30 cm. On a short time scale, the best correlation seems to occur in the range 10 to 15 cm.

The X-ray emission and the microwave emission are both associated with regions of greater than normal density in the corona above sunspot groups. These coronal condensations are optically brighter in proportion to the electron density. They appear to have semi-spherical or elliptical forms without any resolvable internal structure. So-called permanent condensations measure 1 to 2 minutes in arc, range in density from 10^9 to 10^{10} particles per cc., and persist for several days. Sporadic condensations may form out of the permanent condensations. The diameter of a sporadic condensation is typically about 0.5 minute of arc; its lifetime may be minutes to hours; and it is accompanied by the formation of loop prominences and the emission of bursts of centimeter wave emission and solar flares.

Originally, the condensations were thought to be at very elevated temperatures, as high as 6 or 7×10^6 degrees K., but they are now believed to be at near normal coronal temperatures in the range 1.6×10^6 to 0.06×10^6 degrees K. The association of X-ray emission with the coronal condensations implies an upper limit of the order of 2×10^6 degrees K. for the temperature of a condensation. It has been argued that thermal conductivity in a condensation is so high that it cannot maintain a high temperature relative to its surroundings. If a condensation were at a temperature of 6×10^6 degrees, as originally proposed, it would lose all its energy to the neighboring corona

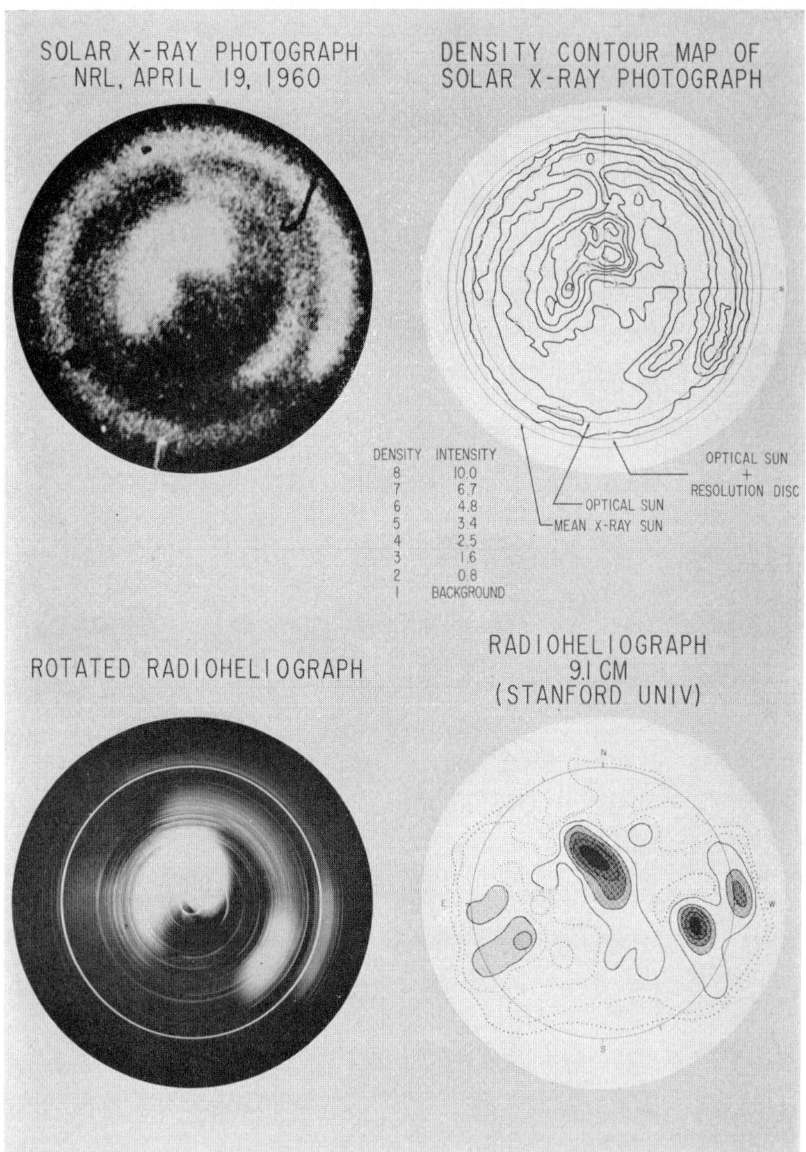

FIGURE 3.—Comparison of X-ray solar-disk photograph with radioheliograph. Lower left image was produced by photographing radioheliograph while it was being rotated in manner analogous to rotation of rocket camera during its exposure.

in less than 20 minutes. On the other hand, if a permanent condensation were actually slightly cooler than the normal corona, the excess energy radiated because of its higher density could readily be replaced by heat conduction from the surrounding corona. To help us understand such details of the structure of the corona, we may look forward to the achievement of X-ray photographs of much higher resolution. Satellites will offer the possibility of mapping such fine detail because of the longer observing times available.

Superposed on the slowly varying X-ray emission associated with plages are short-lived, transient outbursts synchronized with flare activity. Flares have only very rarely been observed in white light. When viewed in the red light of hydrogen H-α, a flare appears to develop with great speed. In a matter of minutes an area of the order of one-thousandth of the solar disk may increase tenfold in brightness. Intense radio noise is generated and shortwave radio communications are instantaneously blacked out until the flare disappears. Flares cover a tremendous spectrum in size from those just barely detectable, so-called microflares, to the most catastrophic explosions. These latter are accompanied by streams of particles of cosmic-ray energies which arrive within a matter of minutes at the earth and streams of slower moving plasma that may require a day or two to reach the earth where they are manifested by magnetic storms and auroral displays.

The earliest attempts to detect flare X-rays were made in the summer of 1956 with the Rockoon, a combination of a small, solid-propellant rocket, carried aloft on a Skyhook balloon. The procedure was to launch a Rockoon in the morning from a ship at sea and permit it to float at 80,000 feet. When a flare was detected optically or indirectly indicated by a shortwave fadeout, the rocket was fired by radio command. It was unfortunately necessary to fire the rocket at the end of the day even if a flare did not occur. Although this approach to the problem was not efficient, it succeeded in measuring the emission of one small flare during the course of the expedition and clearly revealed the importance of the accompanying X-ray flux. The result of that particular measurement is included in figure 1 and identified as the portion of the X-ray spectrum associated with a Class 1 flare.

In 1957 two-stage, rail-launched, solid-propellant rockets capable of transporting substantial payloads to ionospheric altitudes became available. Experiments were conducted with the Nike-Deacon and the Nike-Asp during the IGY. The latter rocket had the capability of carrying a 50-pound payload to about 150 miles. Instrumented rockets could be kept in constant readiness, requiring only the push of a button to launch them when a flare was observed. With this approach, a number of measurements of X-ray and ultraviolet emission were obtained during solar flares. At the peak of a moderately large flare, the entire X-ray spectrum was observed to brighten to many times its normal intensity. At the shortest wavelengths, the increases were orders of magnitude greater, although the energy content was only a small portion of the total X-ray output. X-ray quanta with energies up to 125,000 electron volts appeared, whereas the normal short-wavelength limit was of the order of a few thousand electron volts. From the spectral distribution of the observed X-ray emission, it is possible to speculate about the mechanism involved in its production. If it is assumed that the enhanced X-ray emission resulted from a heating of the coronal gas, a temperature as high as 10^8 degrees K. would be required. Alternatively, the spectrum could have been produced by streams of suprathermal electrons injected into cooler gas at a temperature not exceeding 10^7 degrees K. To choose between such widely divergent models will require much more detailed spectral information than has been obtained thus far. The energy radiated as X-rays represents a major portion of the total energy output of a solar flare and is entirely adequate to explain the accompanying ionospheric disturbances, such as the shortwave fadeout and sudden phase anomaly.

During the year 1960, a major step forward in the study of X-ray emission from solar flares was accomplished by the launching of the first satellite observatory by the U.S. Naval Research Laboratory. The satellite, called Solar Radiation I (1960 Eta 2), carried two ionization chambers to measure solar Lyman-α (1216 A.) and X-rays (2–8 A.). These detectors were mounted on the equator of the spherical satellite, to which was imparted a high spin rate upon separation from the launching vehicle. Each detector viewed the sun once per revolution, giving a spin-modulated signal which was transmitted continuously.

Figure 4 illustrates a sample record obtained during the passage of the satellite over Blossom Point, Md., on August 6, 1960, almost simultaneously with the start of a Class 1 flare, which lasted 18 minutes. Lyman-α signals are indicated by upward deflections from the midscale zero level. X-ray signals deflect downward. On the pass illustrated by the first strip of telemetered signals, the sun was quiet. A steady Lyman-α signal is indicated, but only the barest trace of X-ray intensity. As the satellite returned one orbit later, telemetry reception began almost in coincidence with the eruption of the flare at 1506 UT. At 1509 UT, the X-ray emission began to increase. Ionospheric observations and cosmic-noise measurements showed simultaneous starts of various ionospheric disturbances. Between 1510 and 1511 UT, while a microwave outburst occurred, the X-ray flux increased rapidly to full scale and remained at that level until flare maximum in H-α was reached at 1514 UT. Shortly afterward, the

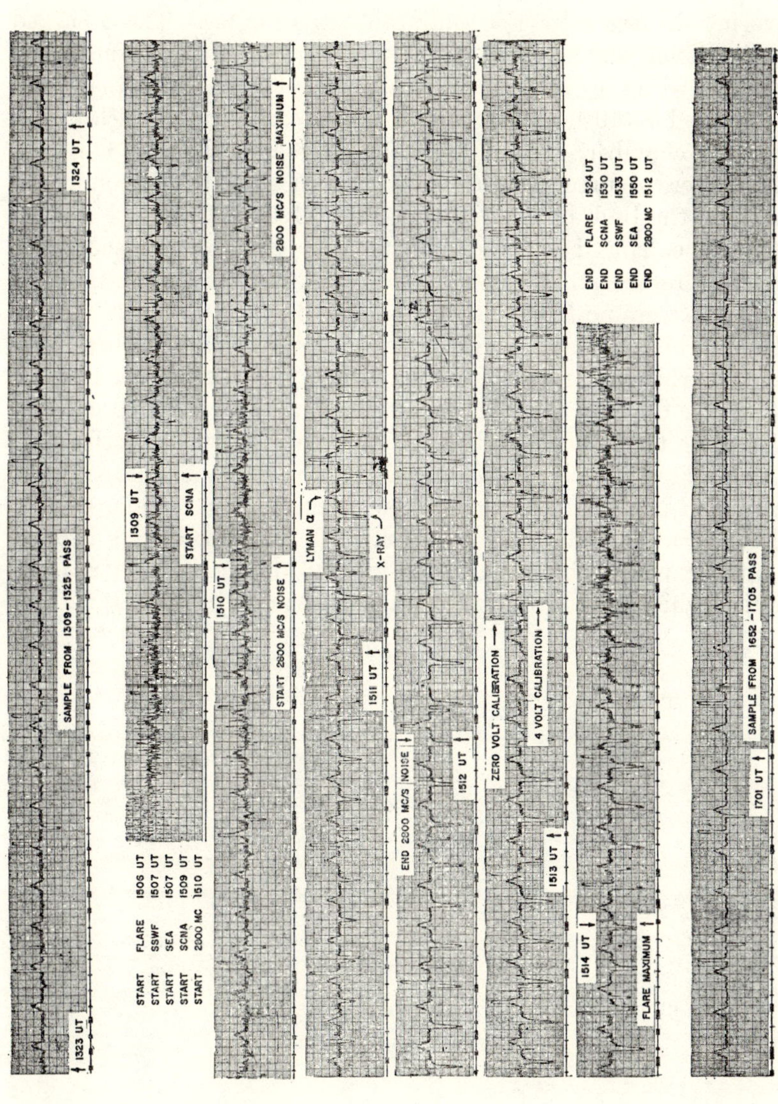

FIGURE 4.—X-ray and Lyman-α signals telemetered from Solar Radiation I on August 6, 1960, during Class 1 flare.

satellite passed out of range of the ground station. On the next pass, the sun was again quiet. At 1701 UT, the record showed only the faintest trace of X-ray emission. Throughout the entire sequence of events the Lyman-α flux remained unchanged.

Many observations are available from the records of Solar Radiation I covering the beginning and ending phases of flares. The enhanced X-ray emission started with the visible flare in every instance and terminated with the decay of the flare. In every case where the X-ray flux exceeded 5×10^{-3} erg cm.$^{-2}$ s^{-1} in the 2 to 8 A. bandwidth of the X-ray ion chamber, a shortwave fadeout was observed. On July 24, 1960, there occurred a sudden disappearance of a large prominence seen above the limb between 0900 UT and 1200 UT. As this event progressed, enhanced X-ray emission was observed on six successive telemetered records, the mean flux reaching 5×10^{-3} erg cm.$^{-2}$ s^{-1} at 1020 UT. There were no flares visible on the disk at that time.

More sophisticated solar X-ray observatories will undoubtedly be placed in orbit in the near future. It will be extremely interesting to study the detailed correlations between the radio-noise spectra accompanying these flares and X-ray spectra. As was described by Dr. Alan Maxwell in the 26th James Arthur lecture,[3] the radio emission takes a variety of forms associated with thermal excitation, plasma oscillations, and synchrotron emission. Thus far, the closest association appears to exist between X-ray emission and the centimeter-wave radiation which results from thermal excitation.

---

[3] See Annual Report of the Smithsonian Institution for 1959, p. 299.

The Challenge of Space Exploration [1]

By ROBERT C. SEAMANS, JR.

Associate Administrator
National Aeronautics and Space Administration

IT IS here proposed to discuss the program of the National Aeronautics and Space Administration (NASA) for space exploration—a program designed around the concept that men must participate directly in this exploration. Let me say at the outset that there is no dichotomy between manned and unmanned spaceflight in NASA's thinking. and planning. Each of these approaches contributes important information, techniques, and developments to the other. We are convinced that concurrent advancement of both unmanned and manned spaceflight will pay off in a total science and technology of far-reaching, even revolutionary, importance to mankind.

WHY WE MUST ACCELERATE OUR SPACE PROGRAM

I will first review the major reasons behind the President's decision to accelerate our space program, including the landing of a team of United States astronauts on the moon in this decade. The United States must make this effort for urgent scientific, technological, political, and economic reasons. In his May 25, 1961, state of the Union message, President Kennedy said:

Now is the time to act, to take longer strides—time for a great new American enterprise—time for this nation to take a clearly leading role in space achievement . . . I believe that the nation should commit itself to achieving the goal, before the decade is out, of landing a man on the moon and returning him safely to earth.

Four major reasons underlie the national decision to marshal the resources required for leadership in space: 1, the quest for scientific knowledge; 2, direct and immediate application of satellites into operational systems; 3, the risk of delay in our space competition with Communism; and 4, the technological advances and stimulus to our economy that will emerge from the space effort.

<hr>

[1] Address before the 1961 Air Force/Aerospace Corporation Symposium on Ballistic Missile and Aerospace Technology, Los Angeles, Calif., Aug. 29, 1961. The original presentation has here been somewhat updated.

SCIENTIFIC KNOWLEDGE

Space research is a vigorously expanding field, whose growth is comparable to the development of nuclear physics after World War II. It is a field which cuts across the established areas of astronomy and physics and the earth sciences, and draws together scientists of varied backgrounds. The close interaction and exchange of ideas among scientists from many different fields have proved to be highly stimulating.

One of the goals of the NASA scientific program involves lunar exploration, manned and unmanned. From the scientific standpoint, exploration of the moon is of great importance. The moon may hold the answers to some of the key questions in science. How was the solar system created? How did it develop and change? Where did life originate? The moon is devoid of atmosphere in the terrestrial sense. Having neither winds nor rains, its surface is almost changeless. Thus the moon offers scientists a chance to study the very early matter of the solar system in practically the form in which it existed billions of years ago.

The great volume of United States research in the space sciences demonstrates the intense interest of American scientists. Data flowing into astronomy and the earth sciences from United States space experiments are providing significantly new ideas and concepts to these traditional disciplines.

DIRECT APPLICATIONS

Space itself, when instrumented by man, will provide system capabilities not previously possible. Early returns from NASA experiments are already leading to early implementation of communications and meteorological satellite systems.

In 1960 NASA's Echo I passive communications satellite appealed to the world's imagination. The huge aluminized plastic sphere has been seen by people in many countries. Echo proved that it is possible to communicate between distant areas on the earth by reflecting radio signals from a satellite.

Private companies have shown interest both in the Echo concept and in "repeater" satellites that can receive messages at one point over the earth's surface and retransmit them to ground receiving stations thousands of miles distant. Satellite communications will make worldwide telephone and television services realities and will accommodate growth of global communications. This enhanced communication could well be a bond drawing people of the world closer together.

NASA's Tiros series of satellites has demonstrated the possibilities of vastly more accurate and longer-range weather forecasting. Tiros

I transmitted nearly 23,000 television pictures of the earth's cloud patterns. Tiros II, launched in November 1960, has transmitted more than 40,000 pictures and has reported important information about the atmosphere and the radiation of solar heat back from the earth.

The Weather Bureau made use in 1961 of Tiros III pictures of storm Eliza in the Pacific and hurricane Anna in the Atlantic. NASA also used Tiros III for weather support of Astronaut Grissom's July 21, 1961, Mercury suborbital flight. Twice a day as the satellite passed over the Caribbean, one of its two TV cameras was triggered to report weather conditions in the area of the flight. Also, when Major Grissom was briefed just prior to his flight, he was shown TV pictures obtained from Tiros for visual comparison during the actual flight.

According to the House Committee on Science and Astronautics, "An improvement of only 10 percent in accuracy [of weather forecasting] could result in savings totaling hundreds of millions of dollars annually to farmers, builders, airlines, shipping, the tourist trade, and many other enterprises."

RISK OF DELAY

It is not my place to discuss military missions, but there is an important interchange of components and vehicles between the NASA and the Department of Defense programs. United States mastery of space is essential insurance against finding ourselves with a technology inferior to that the Communists will develop as they press forward on the space frontier. If we allow them to surpass us, their space technology in its military aspects could jeopardize our security.

In addition to potential direct military conflicts, the free societies are in deadly competition with the Communists for the support of the uncommitted peoples of the world. Space activity has great emotional appeal, and we cannot afford the risk of being passed or appearing to be passed. Today, prestige is one of the most important elements of international relations. Essential is the belief of other nations that we have capability and determination to carry out whatever we declare seriously that we intend to do.

In the minds of millions, dramatic space achievements have become today's symbol of tomorrow's scientific and technical supremacy. There is, without a doubt, a tendency to equate space and the future. Therefore, space is one of the fronts upon which President Kennedy and his administration have chosen to act broadly, vigorously, and with continuous purpose. No other single field offers us the opportunity to gain more of what we need abroad and at the same time to achieve such a wealth of both practical and scientific results at home.

STIMULUS TO ECONOMY

Our Nation needs the stimulus, the knowledge, and the products that will evolve as we carry out our program of space exploration. The influence of the technical progress that will come into being through the integrating force and drive of a major space effort will be felt throughout the economy. Many of the instruments, equipment, power sources, and techniques that we devise to make space expeditions possible will be adaptable to other uses. The result will be substantial scientific advances and a variety of new consumer goods and industrial processes that will return tremendous benefits to us in practically every profession and activity.

Two decades ago the theme of the Temporary National Economic Committee hearings was that America's frontiers had closed and that this was what had caused the stagnation of the thirties. All frontiers then seemed to have been passed, all new territories explored, with very little left for inquiring intelligence beyond applying and developing what has already been discovered. Psychologists and philosophers have recognized the need of man's mind for new frontiers to cross. In this connection, manned and unmanned exploration of space is already stimulating basic and applied research throughout our educational, governmental, and industrial systems. The concept of an eternally shut-in human race has been proved superficial. The prospect of exploring space is providing the catalyst and tonic for new adventures of the mind and spirit.

UNMANNED SPACE FLIGHT

Since January 31, 1958, this country has successfully launched 46 earth satellites, 2 solar satellites, and 2 deep space probes. A recent one is Explorer XII which is making simultaneous measurements of many aspects of the space environment between altitudes of about 200 and 50,000 miles from the earth. The early years of space exploration have provided scientific knowledge important to direct application of satellites in operational systems for communication and weather forecasting, and have contributed to the technology needed for more advanced manned and unmanned spacecraft to come.

Some of the scientific findings are:

Discovery of two intense radiation zones trapped around the earth—the Van Allen belts.

Determination that the earth is slightly pear shaped with the stem at the North Pole.

New data regarding the makeup of the fields of magnetism in space. For example, Explorer X, a 78-pound NASA satellite, transmitted highly meaningful data on solar-terrestrial relationships—such as magnetic fields and solar winds.

Discovery that sunlight exerts appreciable physical pressure on objects in space. This pressure is shifting the orbit of the Vanguard I satellite about a mile per year and has affected the orbit of the 100-foot-diameter Echo I satellite at a rate 300 times greater.

Among our most successful experiments to date has been the Pioneer series of space probes. Pioneer V, for example—launched into solar orbit on March 11, 1960—was tracked into space to a distance of 22.5 million miles, still the greatest distance any manmade object has been tracked. Pioneer V sent back scientific data on conditions in space until communication contact was lost on June 26, 1960. This space probe gave us new and valuable information about cosmic rays, the earth's magnetic field, and solar "storms" and evidence of the existence of a large "ring current" circulating around the earth at altitudes of about 30,000 to 60,000 miles.

Advanced launch vehicles are becoming available for both scientific missions and operational systems. They will have greatly improved load-carrying capability for unmanned space experiments. For example, detailed plans have been made and work has begun on an Orbiting Geophysical Observatory, based on the use of the Agena. This observatory will be one of our first standardized satellites, with a stock-model structure, basic power supply, attitude control, telemetry, and a command system. Its modular compartments are capable of carrying 50 different geophysical experiments on a single mission. The observatory itself will be about 6 feet long by 3 feet square. The two solar "paddles" which collect energy from the sun will be about 6 feet square. The satellite will weigh 1,000 pounds and will include 150 pounds of scientific equipment.

NASA's plans for extending unmanned space exploration to the moon and beyond are maturing. Ranger spacecraft—successors to the one flown in a test on August 23, 1961—will land instruments on the moon. These instruments will determine the nature and extent of tremors and measure the force of gravity on the lunar surface.

Following Ranger will come Surveyor, a spacecraft that will be able to make a so-called "soft landing" on the moon. More delicate scientific instruments than those in Ranger can thus be employed. Surveyor will have aboard scientific instruments, including drills and tapes, to analyze the lunar surface and to determine its makeup. At the same time, high-resolution television cameras will transmit to earth pictures of the lunar terrain.

Also underway is a spacecraft that will fly close to Venus and Mars, and later perhaps other, more distant planets. This spacecraft, called Mariner, will carry instruments to measure planetary atmosphere, surface temperatures, rotation rates, magnetic fields, and surrounding radiation regions.

The NASA experimental program for developing operational systems includes, as already stated, communication and meteorological satellite projects. Our communications satellite program encompasses a coordination of passive experiments as well as investigations with active repeaters at medium altitudes—2,000 to 4,000 miles—and at synchronous altitude. NASA has arranged for two experimental projects at medium altitudes, one under Government contract and one financed by private industry. Both experiment satellites will include, in addition to the communication payload, instruments for measuring the effects of radiation on performance and life expectancy of the payload. Ground stations in this country, Europe, and South America will be employed for both projects.

A synchronous orbit system may provide world coverage, with fewer satellites, thus avoiding large costs and complexities of tracking and switching. We face technical difficulties, however, in placing and maintaining satellites in such orbits for long periods. NASA is initiating a series of experiments that will employ 40- or 50-pound payloads in synchronous orbits. The ground facilities which the Army has been developing for its Project Advent have been made available to NASA for the synchronous satellite experiment.

The Tiros series of meteorological experiments will be followed by a series using an earth-stabilized spacecraft—called Nimbus—in polar orbit. The Weather Bureau of the Department of Commerce, the responsible organization for United States weather-forecasting activities, is following through on an operational meteorological satellite system based on Nimbus. As agent for the Weather Bureau, NASA will specify the launch vehicles and spacecraft, conduct the launch operations, and control the satellites in space.

MANNED SPACEFLIGHT IS ESSENTIAL

Frequently I have been asked why we are preparing to send men on hazardous spaceflights when instrumented satellites and probes have proved so versatile and have returned such quantities of information on the near-space environment of the earth and on conditions in the vast reaches of deep space.

First, integration of a human pilot into an onboard spacecraft system greatly improves reliability. The man can make not only in-flight tests but also in-flight repairs. We have striking examples of this in missions of NASA's X-15 rocket airplane which has been flying to the fringes of space and has achieved a speed of over 4,000 miles per hour. In at least 8 out of 38 X-15 flights to date, flights would have failed without a pilot in the cockpit to correct malfunctions of equipment, instruments, or powerplant. In at least as many other cases, if X-15 missions had been unmanned, we would have obtained no information because either instruments or telemetry failed. The X–15 pilot, however, was able to land with valuable flight information recorded by his own senses.

Second, while instruments can perform many tasks of sensing and measuring better than men, the statistical information gathered and transmitted to earth by these devices constitutes only a part of the basic research necessary for understanding the larger realities of space. The most advanced apparatus can perform only as it is programed to do. Instruments have no flexibility to meet unforeseen situations. Scientific data acquired in space mechanically must be balanced by on-the-spot human senses, human reasoning, and by the power of judgment compounded of these human elements.

A man's capacity for storing information is enormous. He requires a minimum of programing. He can change his mind without elaborate and time-consuming reprograming. His mind is an excellent filter, discarding redundant data with great speed. Man also far outstrips any computer in the ability to make decisions. In this connection, I should like to quote what Dr. Carl Sagan, of the Department of Astronomy, University of California, recently wrote to Senator Paul Douglas of Illinois, to emphasize scientific reasons for manned spaceflight.

> The scientific value [of spaceflight] comes when the men perform scientific tasks. There are large numbers of mineralogical, microbiological, and astronomical questions which trained scientific personnel on the moon will be able to answer far more reliably than any presently conceived automatic instruments. . . .
>
> I feel strongly that, while an enormous amount of very significant scientific information can be obtained by unmanned vehicles, there are certain problems of the greatest significance which may well elude any unmanned system. If indigenous life exists on the planet Mars—and the bulk of contemporary evidence suggests that this is indeed the case—any but the most preliminary investigations will require a human experimenter.
>
> It is very difficult to imagine a sophisticated experimental program on the biochemistry, morphology, physiology, genetics, ecology, or behavior of even simple extraterrestrial organisms carried out by a preprogramed instrumented package. If the extraterrestrial organisms are very different from familiar lifeforms—and with 5 billion years of independent evolution, this may well be true—it is possible that an instrumented landing vehicle will not even be able to identify them as alive. A human scientist who can draw conclusions . . . on the spot is an enormous asset in all aspects of lunar and planetary exploration. . . .

Third, we must recognize that manned flight in space has a much greater impact on the world's populace than unmanned flight.

The United States has congratulated the Soviet Union on the orbital flights of Cosmonauts Gagarin and Titov. These achievements did not surprise us. We had been expecting them. Because the Russians have a significant lead on large boosters, we should be prepared for other Soviet "firsts" in space in the immediate future. This serves to underline the urgency of President Kennedy's decision to accelerate our own manned space program.

Finally, it must be realized that in the long run man cannot, by his very nature, be kept out of space. The same drive that led Columbus to explore the outer reaches of the known world will induce modern man to explore the deeps of the solar system.

MANNED SPACE FLIGHT

The historic flights of American Astronauts Alan Shepard and Virgil Grissom on May 5 and July 21, 1961, respectively, were so completely reported that I shall not repeat the details. As you know, these flights were important steps in Project Mercury, which is the first phase in the United States program for manned spaceflight.

The spaceflights of Astronauts Shepard and Grissom were made to test the man and the Mercury spacecraft, and to determine the quality of the vehicle and its systems and man's ability to handle them in space. In other words, the flights were made to learn how the astronaut, his capsule, and his equipment can best function together, as preliminary steps to putting an astronaut in orbit around the earth.

The value of these preliminary flights is attested by the success of Astronaut John Glenn's orbital flight on February 20, 1962, in which the initial objective of Project Mercury was achieved. Further three-orbit 4½-hour flights are planned in Project Mercury. Then late this year or early in 1963 we will begin flights with a Mercury spacecraft modified so that it has the capability of remaining in orbit up to 24 hours.

To follow Mercury, we are developing the two-man spacecraft Gemini, in which we will conduct orbital flights up to a week in duration, and test out techniques of maneuvering and joining spacecraft in orbit about the earth.

The third phase of our manned spaceflight program is called Project Apollo. The Apollo spacecraft will be large enough for living and working quarters to accommodate three men who will be able to operate in a "shirt-sleeves environment." The Apollo spacecraft will be injected into earth orbit by the Saturn launch vehicle which has an eight-cluster first stage with a thrust of 1,500,000 pounds, compared to the Russian booster with about 750,000 pounds of thrust, the Atlas with 360,000 pounds, and the Redstone with 78,000. The Redstone was used for the Shepard and Grissom flights, and the Atlas will be the booster for Mercury orbital flights.

The Apollo-Saturn combination will provide a manned earth satellite, in which the three-man team can perform a great variety of scientific experiments while training for sustained spaceflight. Next will come voyages deeper into space including a three-man voyage around the moon and return to earth, and finally an actual moon landing and return, planned late in this decade.

The Saturn launch vehicle which is now under development will not provide the capability for circumlunar flight and lunar landing. In the near future, we will commence the development of larger launch vehicles. Implementation of this program will result in the investment of large sums for research, development, and capital equipment. We must select the vehicle configurations wisely in order to fulfill our immediate objectives and to maximize our capabilities for other possible missions involving large payloads.

The design of the Apollo spacecraft itself must be kept as flexible as possible to meet the requirements of an orbiting laboratory, as well as circumlunar and lunar-landing flights. To achieve this flexibility, the so-called "modular concept" will be employed. In other words, various building blocks or units of the vehicle systems will be used for different phases of missions. The first component, which we call the "command center module," will house the crew during launching and entry. It will also serve as a flight control center for the remainder of missions.

The second module is a propulsion unit. In earth-orbital flights, this unit will return the craft to earth under either normal or emergency conditions. It will also be used for maneuvering in orbit and for orbital rendezvous with other satellites. For circumlunar flights, the propulsion module will return the spacecraft to earth safely from any point along the lunar trajectory and will provide midcourse and terminal guidance corrections. In addition, the propulsion module will inject the Apollo spacecraft into an orbit around the moon and eject it from that orbit toward earth. For the lunar landing mission, the propulsion unit will serve as the takeoff stage.

The third module is a propulsion stage that will decelerate the spacecraft as it approaches the moon, and will gently lower it to the moon's surface.

For the earth-orbital laboratory an additional module may be added to the spacecraft to provide capacity for scientific instrumentation and for life support during a reasonably long-lived orbit.

It is important to note that the command center module for lunar flights will have to be designed to permit entry into the atmosphere at 25,000 miles per hour, or at nearly one and one-half times the speed of a satellite returning from orbit. Developing protection against entry heating will be one of our most difficult problems. The spacecraft must have a moderate amount of maneuverability within the atmosphere to control the flight path and to allow landing at a preselected site. All designs being considered must be capable of surviving either ground or water landings.

Among requirements for the Apollo system are the following:

1. A life support system to provide a suitable environment for periods of several weeks.

2. Radiation shielding to give sufficient protection during passage to and from the moon as well as on the lunar surface.

3. A navigation system which will give position fixes, and which will compute the amount and direction of thrust for course correction when required.

4. An attitude stabilization system to be used throughout the flight. This system will permit orientation of the spacecraft for thrust control as well as for lunar landing and reentry through the atmosphere.

5. Communications for all phases of the flight.

Feasibility studies for Project Apollo were underway for many months. Initial studies were carried out in NASA's research and development centers and by industry. On July 18–20, 1961, more than 1,200 representatives of firms in the aerospace industry attended a NASA-Industry Technical Conference in Washington, where they were briefed on Apollo requirements. In mid-August, proposals were solicited from a number of industry teams for design and fabrication of the Apollo spacecraft system.

THE CHALLENGE TO THE AEROSPACE INDUSTRIES

Of the $1,671,750,000 NASA budget for fiscal year 1962, $206,750,000 was for salaries and personnel expenses of the NASA organization. Contract effort provided for the construction of new facilities and the support of the research and development activities. The fiscal year 1962 budget included $245 million for construction of new and supporting facilities and $1,220 million for research and development. This research and development encompassed propulsion systems, propellants, power supplies, structures and materials, guidance and control, instrumentation and telemetry, and aerodynamics, as well as launch vehicles and the satellite program.

The 1962 program was approximately twice the 1961 program. Funding requirements will increase still further in 1963 if we are to meet the goals recommended by President Kennedy. NASA, other Government agencies, universities, and industry all have important responsibilities in the conduct of this rapidly expanding effort. We feel that the NASA staff should be kept at a level necessary to plan the space exploration program and to organize, contract for, and oversee it, while conducting enough in-house work to maintain the caliber of our scientific and technical personnel. However, contract participation by universities and industry currently amounts to more than 85 percent of NASA budget dollars. This percentage will increase.

The special responsibilities of the aerospace industries in this prodigious undertaking involve the following important areas that deserve special attention:

Working with universities, to educate greatly increased numbers of scientists, engineers, and technicians for roles in space exploration but broadly trained for other major technological developments of future importance to this country.

Utilizing technical personnel effectively, thereby minimizing the time spent by these specially trained people on routine effort.

Organizing teams of technical and administrative personnel in imaginative ways, both within the corporate structure and between corporations working toward common objectives.

Providing technical and administrative competence in new geographic areas when special site locations are required for fabrication, testing, and tracking.

Improving the reliability of newly developed equipment by greatly increased emphasis on sound engineering, individual workmanship, and extensive testing.

Initiating research programs aimed at enhancing our space effort and modernizing facilities for fabrication and testing of components.

Utilizing the technology developed for the space program in other fields to build our economy.

CONCLUSION

I would like to conclude with thoughts that concern all who are working in the national space effort.

The first is from Dr. Guyford Stever of the Massachusetts Institute of Technology. He has said:

We aerospace engineers have a tremendous responsibility to everyone. We are the ones entrusted with the future of mankind in this field. We have a need for broader, more balanced people in the aerospace professions, those with a social awareness and an understanding of nontechnical, as well as technical subjects. The aerospace engineer must get the most out of the field and fit it into the needs of society.

He believes that aerospace scientists and engineers will bring an incredible revolution in medicine, communications, and materials—to mention only three.

A month ago the National Science Foundation issued a study called "Investing in Scientific Progress," from which I should like to quote a few lines:

From the time of Franklin and Jefferson the people of the United States have had faith in both the intellectual and the material benefits that science can bring. We have continually expanded our scientific knowledge of the physical universe, of living things, and of social organization. Our past investment in science has brought us double reward: a highly developed technology which has helped to keep us free, and a continuing enlargement of our understanding which has helped to enrich our freedom.

Today, far more than in the past, scientific progress determines the character of tomorrow's civilization.

Space exploration in general, and manned spaceflight in particular, offers us the chance for unparalleled progress. I am firmly convinced that, as a nation, we shall respond boldly and with determination to the call President Kennedy issued in his inaugural address when he urged the world—

To invoke the wonders of science instead of its terrors . . . to explore the stars, to conquer the deserts, eradicate disease, tap the ocean depths and encourage the arts and commerce.

The Smithsonian's Satellite-tracking Program: Its History and Organization[1]

By E. NELSON HAYES

Technical Writer, Smithsonian Astrophysical Observatory

[With 4 plates]

FOR CENTURIES poets have imagined voyages to the moon and planets,[2] and since the late 19th century scientists have been slowly evolving the means by which those dreams might become realities.[3]

Robert Goddard of Clark University, Worcester, Mass., outlined in 1919 a method for reaching extreme altitudes and later, supported in part by grants from the Smithsonian Institution, conducted a series of limited experiments to demonstrate the practicability of his ideas. Thereafter both in the United States and in Europe increasing attention was paid to the development of rockets for military use and for the probing of the upper atmosphere and the exploration of outer space.

The fundamental idea was that rockets of limited thrust could penetrate the upper atmosphere and bring back valuable scientific data. Later, manned rockets of greater power would reach outer space and eventually journey throughout the solar system.

BEGINNING

DEVELOPMENT OF CONCEPT

The concept of an artificial satellite orbiting the earth was a fairly late development, because such a vehicle would be of little scientific value unless it could signal information back to the earth

---

[1] The present article takes the development of the satellite-tracking program up to October 1957. It is expected that a later Smithsonian Report will contain a further article embodying results after that date.

[2] See Marjorie Nicholson, "Voyages to the Moon," Macmillan, 1948.

[3] In the 1890's the father of Russian rocketry, Konstantin Tsiolkovsky, in his famous novel "Beyond the Planet Earth" (translated by Kenneth Syers: Pergamon, 1960), defined for the first time in scientific terms the feasibility of interplanetary travel. A decade later he published "The Probing of Space by Means of Jet Devices."

or could be tracked by optical or other means. The idea had to await the invention of suitable telemetry and tracking techniques.

In the decade following World War II a number of suggestions for artificial earth satellites were made. At the Rand Corporation, a nonprofit research group sponsored by Douglas Aircraft Co., one project in 1946 investigated a number of the problems that would be encountered in the development of a scientific space program. As one aspect of his work on that project, Dr. Fred L. Whipple of the Harvard College Observatory wrote the now famous paper "Possible Hazards to a Satellite Vehicle from Meteorites," 1946, in which he proposed a "meteor bumper" of thin metal surrounding the skin of the space vessel.

Meanwhile, at White Sands, N. Mex., the U.S. Army was modifying and using the V–2 rocket, developed by Germany in World War II, to explore the upper atmosphere. Later flights of White Sands rockets were photographed with a camera-telescope developed by the Harvard Meteor Project, and from Dr. Whipple's study of those films evolved the technique of photographing earth satellites in orbit.

By 1951 the number of scientists involved in various space researches was such that they felt the need of an opportunity to exchange ideas. In the fall of that year a symposium on the physics and medicine of the upper atmosphere was held in San Antonio, Tex., under the sponsorship of the Air University School of Aviation Medicine of Randolph Field. Dr. James Van Allen, chairman of the Upper Atmosphere Rocket Research Panel, speculated on the nature and intensity of the cosmic radiation. Dr. Joseph Kaplan, chairman of an Air Force panel on geophysical research, discussed the physics of the upper atmosphere. Dr. Wernher von Braun, technical director of the guided missile development group at the Redstone Arsenal in Huntsville, Ala., considered means of returning a winged rocket vehicle from a satellite orbit to the earth. Dr. Whipple spoke on meteoritic phenomena and meteorites. Their papers and more than 30 others were published in 1952 under the title "Physics and Medicine of the Upper Atmosphere: A Study of the Aeropause."

At the second International Congress of Astronautics, held in London, England, during September 1951, three British scientists, K. W. Gatland, A. M. Kunesch, and A. E. Dixon, presented a paper on "Minimum Satellite Vehicles." At the next meeting of the Congress in Zurich, Switzerland, the following year, there were more extensive discussions and proposals, including "MOUSE," or a Minimum Orbital Unmanned Satellite of the Earth, a 100-pound object to orbit over both geographic poles.

One expression of this early work appeared as a series of articles in Collier's magazine in 1952 and as "Across the Space Frontier" published by Viking Press the same year. Gathered and edited by Cornelius Ryan of the Collier's staff and written for a popular audience, the papers included "The Heavens Open," by Whipple; "Prelude to Space Travel," by von Braun; "This Side of Infinity," by Kaplan; and "A Station in Space," by Willy Ley. The last described in some considerable detail a manned, wheel-shaped satellite 250 feet in diameter, circling the earth every 2 hours at a mean altitude of 1,075 miles. The station would serve as "a superb observation post" from which technicians could inspect every ocean, continent, country, and city on earth, and study the universe without the optical and radio interference of the atmosphere. Interestingly enough, no mention was made of the possibility of tracking the station from ground observatories. Indeed, the idea was quite the opposite: observers in the space station would "track" the earth and would determine, for example, the shape of the earth by precise photographs of the edge of moonlight as it passed across the face of our planet.

Dr. Whipple did, however, include in his chapter the following:

Predicting the position and motion of the space station itself will be one of the most difficult problems ever encountered in celestial mechanics, or the science of predicting the positions of astronomical objects. The earth's doorknob shape, with a bulge of several miles at the equator, combines with the changing direction of the moon's attraction to alter slightly but continuously the nearly circular orbit of the space station. Until recently, the calculation of such an orbit would have taken a good computer a considerable number of hours. But the orbit of the space station will change by an infinitesimal amount in the short period of each 2-hour swing. Therefore, unless the computer can calculate this new orbit in less than the 2 hours necessary for the space station to make one journey around the earth, it is obvious that his calculations can never keep abreast of the space station, let alone predict its position in the future.

The answer to the computing problem lies, of course, in the huge "electronic brain" calculation machines which we have today. Their use on the ground will be absolutely essential in plotting the motion of the space station. Following this man-made island in the sky continuously and precisely, these electronic machines will be able to make exact calculations with much greater rapidity than the speed of the space station in its 2-hour journeys around the earth.

While this space-station project, although feasible, could not have been completed in less than 15 years, its specifications were based on research that was to help make possible the launching of our first satellite, Explorer I, in 1958.

PROJECT ORBITER

In June 1957 what was to become known as Project Orbiter was defined by a group of scientists assembled in Washington. Attending this meeting were Comdr. George W. Hoover, Office of Naval Research; Wernher von Braun; Frederick C. Durant, president of the International Astronautical Federation; Fred Singer of the University of Maryland; Fred L. Whipple of Harvard; David Young of the

Aerojet-General Corporation; and several others. Von Braun was already supervising the making of Redstone missiles; he suggested that several of these be allocated to the project and that a cluster of small solid rockets be attached to the end of each in order to stabilize its flight. The launch would be made eastward at the Equator. The hope was that a 6-pound ball would be placed in orbit.

Included in this proposal was an optical tracking system of which Dr. Whipple was to have charge. He planned to borrow theodolites from various units of the Armed Services and set up three observing stations around the Equator. The Air Force was to transport material to the proposed sites.

THE INTERNATIONAL GEOPHYSICAL YEAR—IGY

Meanwhile, the United States had become an active participant in the IGY.[4] In 1952 the International Council of Scientific Unions proposed to the nations of the world that an International Geophysical Year be organized to conduct an extensive scientific study of the earth. A year later a Special Committee (to become known as the CSAGI) of the International Council scheduled the 18 months from July 1, 1957, to December 31, 1958, as the IGY. Of the nations invited to participate, 67 responded favorably.

One of the 14 fields of investigation of the IGY was rockets and satellites, the coordinator (or reporter) for which was Dr. Lloyd V. Berkner of Associated Universities, a complex of research facilities, including Brookhaven National Laboratories. The program outlined for this field in 1954 specified exploration of the high atmosphere by small earth satellites as one project.

Each participating country organized a national committee for the IGY. Chairman of the U.S. committee was Dr. Joseph Kaplan of the University of California at Los Angeles. In October 1954 the committee first gave serious consideration to launching an instrumented satellite as one phase of its program. On January 22 of the following year the Technical Panel on Rocketry of the U.S. National Committee resolved that a study group, called the LPR (Long Playing Rocket) committee, be set up under the chairmanship of Dr. Fred Whipple. Its purpose was to report on geophysical possibilities, technical feasibility, budget, controls, motor, manpower, timing, cost estimates, desired orbit, and possibly other subjects related to the launching of an artificial earth satellite.

---

[4] For accounts of the IGY, including something about the first two International Polar Years from which the IGY evolved, the reader is referred to: Sydney Chapman, "IGY: Year of Discovery," University of Michigan Press, 1959; J. Tuzo Wilson, "IGY: The Year of the New Moons," Knopf, 1961; and Walter Sullivan, "Assault on the Unknown," McGraw-Hill, 1961.

At a special meeting of the LPR committee in Washington three possible approaches to placing a small payload in orbit around the earth were outlined. The committee defined some of the technical and scientific aspects of orbiting a 10-pound object; they suggested that it should be approximately 20 inches in diameter and be painted white or have an otherwise highly reflecting surface. Such an object could be observed visually from the ground at twilight, when it would be the equivalent of a star of the sixth magnitude. Dr. Whipple stated firmly that it could be found optically with binoculars or with Askania-type cameras, and he discussed the techniques for acquiring the object once it was in orbit. The committee concluded that a satellite for payloads of up to 10 pounds could be realized within 2 or 3 years, provided sufficient funds and manpower were available. On March 10, 1955, the U.S. National Committee adopted a resolution favoring the launching of instrumented satellites.

Several months later Kaplan wrote to Dr. Alan T. Waterman, Director of the National Science Foundation, summarizing the views and proposals of the U.S. National Committee concerning the LPR project. The executive committee had already acted favorably upon a budget of approximately 10 million dollars for the launching of IGY satellites. The budget included provisions for 10 "birds" and 5 observation stations, including the necessary scientific instrumentation, related equipment, and a minimum civilian scientific staff. The report described the provisions for the five ground stations, one each in equatorial Pacific, South America, the Atlantic Ocean, Africa, and the Philippines, and defined some of the simplest and most direct experiments that could be performed through the instrumented satellite: precise geodetic measurements; the determination of upper-air densities; measurement of solar radiation; measurement of particle radiation; determination of current flows in the ionosphere associated with magnetic storms and radio blackouts; and the determination of hydrogen in interplanetary space.

The major question next to be resolved was whether Project Orbiter or some alternative was to be the official IGY satellite program of the United States. Project Orbiter had been proposed to Donald A. Quarles, the Assistant Secretary of Defense; however, the Naval Research Laboratory, under the Office of Naval Research, had been developing its own program. Both proposals were presented for decision to a special committee appointed by President Eisenhower.

On July 29, 1955, President Eisenhower announced to the world that the U.S. would launch a small instrumented earth-circling satellite as part of its IGY effort, and several weeks later the Secretary of Defense, Charles E. Wilson, added that the Department of Defense would participate in this phase of the IGY program. In his press release Wilson repeated that it would perhaps be possible under ideal conditions of weather and illumination to see the satellite with the naked eye. However, he continued, the principal means of observation and tracking would be by scientific instruments, including telescopes, theodolites, and electronic devices. Predictions of the position and path of the satellite were to be determined by electronic computers, and these data would be disseminated to all participating scientists.

On October 6, 1955, the Department of Defense announced that work had begun on Project Vanguard, the name assigned to the rocket-satellite package of the Naval Research Laboratory. The Russians had also announced that they would launch satellites during the IGY, and a number of nations, including the United Kingdom, France, Japan, Australia, and Canada, planned to include rocket launchings in their IGY programs.

THE SMITHSONIAN ASTROPHYSICAL OBSERVATORY

The Smithsonian had had wide experience in research and fieldwork. The Institution is and always has been much more than a collection of museums. The first Secretary of the Institution, Joseph Henry, was, in the words of the astronomer Simon Newcomb, "the first American after Franklin to reach high eminence as an original investigator in physical science." [5] He set the pattern and tradition of scientific investigation that has continued fruitfully for more than a century. From its very beginning the Smithsonian has maintained a staff of research scientists who have devoted themselves to a great variety of projects.

One of the earliest plans presented to the Institution was that for making weather observations on a systematic, scientific basis. The program got underway in 1847, and 2 years later the then recently perfected telegraph system was used to transmit meteorological data. Most of the observers were unpaid amateurs, a precedent for the establishment of the Moonwatch program.

Also, the Smithsonian had a paternal interest in the development of rocketry in this country, for it had sponsored the work of Robert Goddard, had helped provide financial support for his early experiments, and in 1919 had published his now famous pamphlet, "A Method for Reaching Extreme Altitudes." Alone of all Government agencies, it had glimpsed the significance and feasibility of Goddard's proposal that rockets could be used to explore the upper atmosphere. The U.S. satellite program of the IGY was a logical and inevitable result of the experiments of Robert Goddard.

In 1954, virtually on the eve of the IGY program, the retirement of L. B. Aldrich, Director of the Smithsonian Astrophysical Observa-

---

[5] Quoted by Paul H. Oehser in "Sons of Science," p. 28, Henry Schuman, 1949.

tory, required the choice of a successor. Two main divisions of research constituted the activities of the Observatory at that time: one on radiation and organisms, devoted to studies of the effect of non-ionizing and ionizing radiant energy on plants and animals; the other on astrophysical investigations proper, primarily of solar radiation, for which two field stations (at Montezuma, Chile, and Table Mountain, Calif.) were maintained to accumulate data.

Both divisions owed their origin to the prophetic imagination of Samuel P. Langley, third Secretary of the Smithsonian Institution and founder of its Astrophysical Observatory. As early as 1888 he had expressed in the Annual Report his cherished hope "of erecting and equipping an observatory for astrophysical research," where he might pursue his work on solar radiation in accordance with his concept of what he called "the new astronomy," concerned not with the formerly prime objective of finding positions of the heavenly bodies, but of learning "what they are in themselves and in relation to ourselves." In 1891 he received from the National Government his first appropriation of funds for this research.

Early in his career Langley had been associated with the Harvard Astronomy Department and had come to the Smithsonian from the observatory at Allegheny University. He was therefore strongly convinced that there should be close connections between a research establishment of the sort he envisaged and the scientists in universities both here and abroad. In addition, as President Gilman of Johns Hopkins observed at the Langley Memorial exercises held in Washington on December 3, 1906, he had proved during his Secretaryship that one "of the most remarkable characteristics of the Smithsonian has been its power of adaptation to changing circumstances . . . shown [among other ways] by expansion of other work. It has always been ready to enlarge its domain and sustain the burden of fresh responsibilities."

With such traditions in mind, Dr. Leonard Carmichael, Secretary of the Smithsonian since 1953 and formerly president of Tufts College, sought as a new Director a scientist capable of broadening significantly the research program of the Observatory to include the major fields of current astrophysics. He chose Dr. Whipple both for his eminence as an astronomer and for his experience as leader of the radar "window project" during the war and as a participant in the Harvard Meteor Project.

Both Drs. Whipple and Carmichael intended the former's appointment to open the way to close and beneficial cooperation between the Astrophysical Observatory and the Harvard College Observatory in Cambridge, Mass. Both institutions were to be distinct in all administrative and financial matters, but it was recognized that the Astrophysical Observatory of the Smithsonian would gain much by being put in the academic atmosphere of Cambridge.

Although Dr. Whipple's appointment did not become effective until July 1, 1955, he began working part time for the Smithsonian in April, and a provisional budget was drafted for the program to track the satellite of Project Orbiter.

The Astrophysical Observatory was officially transferred to the grounds of the Harvard College Observatory on July 1. The professional staff consisted of Dr. Whipple and Dr. John S. Rinehart, half of whose time was to be devoted to scientific research and half to assisting Dr. Whipple in the administration of the Observatory.

Dr. Whipple now enlarged the scope of the program of the Observatory to "embrace not only research in solar activity and its effects upon the earth, but also meteoritic studies and studies of the high atmosphere." He conceived the optical tracking of satellites as "a new and startling tool of remarkable power in the study of solar-system and geophysical phenomena."

That summer Dr. Whipple went to Europe, still believing in the strong possibility that some modification of von Braun's Orbiter project would be adopted. When he returned and learned otherwise, he immediately began to adapt his proposals for tracking Orbiter to requirements of the Vanguard satellite, which at that time was planned to weigh approximately 20 pounds and be 30 inches in diameter. Making some a priori assumptions about the satellite itself and the orbit it would follow, he calculated that the object would be as bright as visual magnitude 5 to 7, that is, near the limit of naked-eye visibility, but certainly easily observable under good atmospheric conditions by means of binoculars or wide-field optical equipment.

For this new tracking program he proposed that only the most rapid, large-aperture Schmidt optical system would be suitable for observing the satellite and that the telescope might be mechanized so that the motion of the instrument would follow the apparent motion of the satellite itself. He also outlined the value of teams of amateur visual observers (later to be named "Moonwatch") for acquiring the satellite in its first few orbits. In addition, he made provisions for a computations center to receive observational data and to prepare predictions of satellite passages, and a communications network to and from the various observing stations and teams and the suggested headquarters in Cambridge. With imaginative foresight he envisaged what was to become the optical tracking program of the Smithsonian Astrophysical Observatory.

His proposal for the Smithsonian to provide optical tracking of the IGY satellites also involved at least two unrealistic factors that were to have a crucial bearing on the events of the next few years. First, the program was geared for 18 months, that is, for the period of the IGY; no one made specific plans for the program to continue after December 31, 1958. This meant that equipment contracted for by the Observatory did not need to be designed and built to function efficiently beyond that date. It is a tribute to the skillful planning of the scientists and technicians and to the manufacturing abilities of the firms involved that most of the instruments and buildings are still in good working condition as this is written. Second, the program was geared to track only one or two satellites on the assumption that of the six "earnest tries" made by Vanguard not more than two would succeed. Few seem to have taken seriously the possibility that Russia would also launch several satellites during the IGY and that the Smithsonian Astrophysical Observatory might have the responsibility for tracking them optically.

THE IGY AND THE SMITHSONIAN

Late in 1955 the National Academy of Sciences and the National Science Foundation, acting for the U.S. National Committee of the IGY, assigned to the Smithsonian Astrophysical Observatory, through the Institution in Washington, the responsibility for the optical tracking of U.S. artificial earth satellites launched during the period from July 1, 1957, to December 31, 1958.

It had been evident from the first that the tracking of satellites was a job for astronomers. It must never be lost sight of that a satellite, once launched, is neither a missile nor a rocket, but an object basically similar to the kind that astronomers have for centuries been observing and studying. The satellite is, as far as the optical tracker is concerned, a point of light on the celestial sphere. It requires the kind of accurate positioning and clocking for which, through their parallax, double-star, and other programs, astronomers had worked out the optical techniques. No other group was capable of this type of work.

Although Dr. Whipple was convinced that optical tracking of satellites was possible, he had only the precedent of the Harvard Meteor Project to guide him, as well as, of course, his profound knowledge of astronomy. Virtually all phases of the satellite-tracking program were fundamentally new. No one could say with certainty that some redesign of the super-Schmidt camera would be able to photograph an orbiting satellite. No one could say with surety that an organization of amateur astronomers would show the diligence and dedication required to make "Moonwatch" a success. No one could define precisely the qualifications of the observers needed at the Baker-Nunn camera stations; and no one knew the exact means by which mathematicians and astronomers would determine the orbit of a satellite and prepare predictions.

This meant that the optical satellite-tracking program was to be not only a field operation but also a program of scientific research. In turn, this meant that the project needed a certain margin for error, an opportunity to fail and to profit by the failure.

The scientist is accustomed to such failure. He will undertake a research project, may carry it part or all the way through, and then realize that he has been on the wrong track. If possible, he then starts all over again. His essential task is to find the truth, and the route to that truth may be roundabout.

These problems were not unique to the satellite-tracking program. Other scientific groups entering this field of space research with great enthusiasm in 1955 tended not only to underestimate the cost, time, and personnel required, but also to slight the fundamental nature of research in their proposals to and demands of the Government. With all the hustle and bustle of the U.S. National Committee and its subcommittees, many phases of the IGY program seem to have been on an ad hoc basis, perhaps necessarily so. The result was much improvisation, much shifting and changing, and much need of explanation that sometimes appeared to be mere rationalization.

On the other hand, many factors worked in favor of the space program, and especially that of the Smithsonian. The IGY was, in the words of Dr. Berkner, "perhaps the most ambitious and at the same time the most successful cooperative enterprise ever undertaken by man."[6] As such, not only did it command the dedicated effort of thousands of scientists throughout the world, it also aroused a remarkable enthusiasm among the peoples of many countries. Millions saw in it an example of international goodwill and cooperation such as they had only too rarely known. The IGY, particularly its space projects, fired the imagination of people who, when called upon to do so, gave to it their fullest cooperation. As we shall see, hardheaded businessmen were willing to sacrifice time and money to help the Smithsonian establish its satellite-tracking program. The success of that program, despite its many headaches and heartaches, resulted in no small measure from the zealous interest and willing support of the public, as well as from the determined efforts of research scientists, field personnel, and management to work together harmoniously and productively.

PLANNING

IGY GRANT

The first IGY grant to the Smithsonian became effective January 1, 1956, and continued to the end of June of the same year. Its purpose

---

[6] From his Foreword to "IGY: The Year of the New Moons," by J. Tuzo Wilson, p. vii, Knopf, 1961.

was to initiate the optical satellite-tracking program by determining the design of the optics and the camera, estimating the cost of long lead-time equipment, negotiating the establishment of camera stations here and in foreign countries, outlining the Moonwatch organization, and defining the many other aspects of what was to become a very complex project.

THE HARVARD METEOR PROGRAM

The tracking plans that Dr. Whipple developed had in considerable measure evolved from his experiences with the Harvard Meteor Project. That project had been set up before World War II and then in 1947 vitalized by him with the assistance of Harlan Smith and Richard E. McCrosky. In 1948 the field program was transferred to New Mexico preparatory to the delivery of the super-Schmidt cameras, which had been specially designed for the project.

The first intention had been to set up a fairly complex field operation, with even the possibility of moving the cameras from southern New Mexico in winter to northern New Mexico in summer in order to take advantage of the best weather conditions. However, with a very limited budget, supported primarily by Government funds, the fieldwork was gradually simplified. Two stations, 50 miles apart, were established: one at Sacramento Peak and the other at Organ Pass. The stations were simultaneously to photograph a meteor, a technique that would enable the astronomers to determine its height, velocity, deceleration, and direction.

Since no suitable camera-telescope was available, Dr. Whipple and his staff sketched the idea of a new type to do the job. Dr. Whipple insisted that the optics of the camera should use glass transparent to the ultraviolet; he felt certain that that glass could be molded into the hemisphere required by the optical design they had in mind. He asked Dr. James G. Baker, who at that time was a consultant to the Perkin-Elmer Corporation of Norwalk, Conn., to work out the design of the camera, and Perkin-Elmer was to manufacture it. Meanwhile, the National Bureau of Standards in Washington agreed to mold the hemispheres. The super-Schmidt [7] that this team created proved a notable success and became the prototype of the Baker-Nunn satellite-tracking camera.

---

[7] The super-Schmidt is an f/.65 instrument with an aperture of 12.25 inches and a focal length of 8 inches; the angular diameter of the field of view is 52°. The mirror is 23.5 inches in diameter. The corrector plate has an aspheric surface. The equatorial mounting of the camera permits it to track the stars. A rotating shutter chops the meteor trail on the photographic plate into discrete segments.

The film on which the meteor is photographed is molded into a hemisphere to match the design of the optical system. This was the first time that photographic film was manufactured in this form, another achievement of the Harvard Meteor Project.

SPOT [8]

In November of 1955 Dr. Whipple mentioned to Dr. J. Allen Hynek, professor of physics and astronomy at Ohio State University and director of McMillin Observatory there, the strong possibility that the Smithsonian would receive the satellite-tracking grant from the IGY, and suggested that perhaps Dr. Hynek would be interested in becoming the Observatory's associate director in charge of the program. Quick to appreciate the challenge of setting up such a program, and excited by the prospect of tracking satellites, Dr. Hynek took leave of absence at Ohio State and came to Cambridge early in January 1956.

By late winter Whipple and Hynek had clearly outlined the means by which the goal of the optical tracking program could be achieved. The goal was to determine with sufficient accuracy the position and time of a satellite on the celestial sphere during the evening and morning twilight periods. The means were:

1. A relatively simple super-Schmidt camera that would use a continuous roll of film and two types of shutters: one a gross shutter operating once during each film transport cycle, and the other a rotating barrel-type shutter with a period of 5 percent of the total film transport cycle; the latter, which would interrupt the exposure for periods of about one-hundredth of a second, would be synchronized with a stroboscopic presentation of the crystal clock face that would be photographed directly on the film strip.

2. A crystal clock accurate to within 1 millisecond.

3. A network of 10 to 12 camera stations throughout the world.

4. Scores of teams of amateur astronomers to make preliminary observations of the satellite.

5. An orbit calculation and prediction section and a communications center at the Smithsonian Astrophysical Observatory in Cambridge.

The task now was to make these means realities.

THE OPTICAL TRACKING PROGRAM

It was inevitable that Dr. Baker should be asked to design the optical system of the camera. He had created the super-Schmidt camera and was considered to be the world's foremost authority on optical systems for astronomical cameras. In the summer of 1955 Dr. Whipple had gone over the various possibilities with him, and together they settled tentatively on a classical Schmidt system of approximately 16-inch clear aperture at f/1 and a field of view of

---

[8] The program is often referred to as SPOT (Smithsonian Precision Optical Tracking). Mrs. Kathryn C. Norris provided a prize for the winner of a contest to pick a suitable name, and this one by Mrs. Eileen C. Cavanaugh, was chosen from among the many entries.

perhaps 20°. Dr. Baker had then suggested that the film in the camera could be mounted to wind across a curved focal surface (the back-up plate); he had earlier used this method for a 6-inch f/1 Schmidt camera, one of his wartime projects.

In February of the following year, having formally accepted from the Observatory the assignment to design the optical system, Dr. Baker ran a family of rays through a classical Schmidt system on an IBM computer as a preliminary step toward determining possible improvements. The over-all problem was a formidable one. An f/1 Schmidt system had never been built for an aperture greater than 8 inches, and the classical Schmidt system has only one corrector plate. This new camera might require complex plates with strong aspheric optical powers and would have a much larger aperture.

To complicate matters, in the spring the Navy announced that the diameter of the Vanguard satellite had been lowered from 30 to 20 inches. This was a most critical decision. It meant that even closer attention would have to be given to the optical performance of the camera and that the factor of safety, already so narrow in the original choice, had now vanished. In addition, it became apparent that the camera had to track the satellite, rather than remain stationary and permit the satellite to record itself on the exposed film.

At this point Whipple, Hynek, and Baker decided upon a larger instrument. To restore the desired factor of safety for recording the faint image of the satellite, they found it necessary to increase the aperture to 20 inches, to hold the speed to f/1, and to seek an image diameter no larger than 20 microns. (A human hair has a diameter of about 75 microns.) At the same time they increased the desired field of view to 30° to guarantee that, despite the uncertainties of initial positions, the faint satellite image could be detected against the background of stars. They recognized that the cost of the camera would be substantially greater than had been considered before and that the classical Schmidt system was inadequate to do the job. No one, however, was fully aware then that the trail toward the goal of a satisfactory camera would be long and difficult.

The next step was to design the mechanical elements of the camera. In February Whipple and Hynek discussed the problem with Joseph Nunn of South Pasadena, Calif., who was known and highly recommended to them. The essential question was precisely whether, and if so how, the camera was to move. There were three possibilities: the first, which already seemed doubtful, was to have the camera remain stationary and let the satellite make a track on the film; the second was simply to have the camera track the satellite, w th the stars appearing on the film as chopped trailed images, and the satellite as a "point"; the third was a rather complicated oscillating movement, whereby the camera would alternate between remaining stationary and tracking the satellite. After many discussions, they chose the third method because it offered both greater flexibility of tracking technique and an extra margin of safety, ensuring that the camera could record a faint satellite as well as the star background.

Mr. Nunn made a set of preliminary drawings and sent them on to Cambridge. To indicate the real size of the device, an isometric presentation showed a 6-foot man standing next to the camera, which was approximately 12 feet high and about 12 feet long at its greatest horizontal dimension. The shoulders of the operator shown at one end of the camera came about level with the normal pivot point of the camera itself. It would be, then, a fairly large instrument.

The third requirement of the system was some means of timing the satellite observations. In the spring of the previous year Robert Davis, a graduate student at Harvard, had worked with Dr. Whipple in planning a timing system for Project Orbiter and in outlining techniques for tracking satellites. They had determined that they would need a position accuracy of about 1 or 2 seconds of arc with a reasonable but versatile camera, and this would in turn demand an accuracy of approximately 1 millisecond in the timing of the observations. After some investigation Mr. Davis ordered a model 110 frequency time standard from Norrman Laboratories in Williams Bay, Wis.

In February 1956 the Norrman time standard arrived in Cambridge. Packed in a cardboard box for shipping, it had been handled so roughly in transit that four of the control knobs had been broken and some other damage done. Nevertheless, when plugged in, it worked, giving Mr. Davis a certain confidence in its ruggedness and reliability. In the weeks that followed he tested the clock to prove that, in Cambridge at least, it would keep time to within a millisecond, although its performance in the field was an uncertainty.

The next question was, where should the Baker-Nunn camera stations be located? The Vanguard satellites were planned for low inclinations in respect to the Equator, and the stations had therefore to be in a broad band defined roughly by the 30th parallels north and south. To this requirement was added the concept of a north-south line of stations in the Western Hemisphere. Furthermore, the locations had to be where there was a minimum of cloud cover and where the landscape would permit observations of satellites reasonably near the horizon. Finally, the overseas sites had to be in countries with which it would be possible to make agreements for the establishment and maintenance of the stations.

Since astronomers form a closely knit international fraternity, Hynek's plan was simply to correspond with astronomers he knew throughout the world, enlist their cooperation, and thus arrange for sites. The U.S. National Committee, however, thought that all international arrangements should be made through the State Department. While undoubtedly Hynek's procedure would have resulted in much faster selection of the sites, the IGY approach ensured a maximum of cooperation from the local governments.

Another, though slight, delay came from the attempt to locate together the Baker-Nunn and the Minitrack stations for electronic tracking, on the assumption that this arrangement would save a good deal of time, effort, and money. It soon became apparent, however, that for technical reasons Minitrack needed large, flat areas on which antennas could be set up; they did not require clear skies, but did want their stations to be free of radio interference.

The actual choice of sites did not begin until after the IGY Barcelona meeting of September 1956. Meanwhile, however, the physical needs of the stations were clearly defined, and some preliminary negotiations were undertaken through the U.S. National Committee and the State Department.

At the same time much thought was given to the materiel that each station would need. By the middle of 1956 tentative lists had been drawn up, including photographic and darkroom equipment, power supplies, and such miscellaneous items as binoculars, flashlights, shovels, fire extinguishers, picks, and even rifles. What became increasingly apparent was that each station would need to be a relatively self-sustaining scientific laboratory located in an as yet unspecified region with unknown problems of communication and transportation.

THE VISUAL TRACKING PROGRAM

Before precise predictions could be sent to the Baker-Nunn stations so that they could make optical observations, preliminary orbital data had to be obtained. The Smithsonian needed, therefore, to have widely scattered around the globe many teams of visual observers who could, using very approximate predictions, find the object and determine its position to an accuracy within 1 degree of arc, and the time to an accuracy within 1 second. From these data, predictions precise enough for the Baker-Nunn stations could be derived.

Dr. Whipple knew that amateur astronomers could be depended upon to take an interest in this kind of observing and do it satisfactorily. Since 1911 the American Association of Variable Star Observers had been contributing data requiring the skills that would be needed to make preliminary observations of satellites. Members of the Astronomical League and the Western Amateur Astronomers were among other amateurs who had been doing comparable observing tasks for many years. Dr. Whipple suggested that individuals drawn from these and similar organizations might be willing to participate in the satellite program. When the problem was presented to Miss Grace C. Scholz (now Mrs. Armand Spitz) of the League, she helped organize a committee to recruit observers and work out techniques and instrumentation.

In February 1956 the Smithsonian appointed Dr. Armand N. Spitz, director of the Spitz Laboratories in Yorklyn, Del., and inventor of the Spitz Planetarium, to coordinate these activities. By that time the basic work of the teams had been fairly well specified: using only standard binoculars or simple monoculars and stopwatches, they were to locate and clock man's first efforts to conquer space. In the months to follow more sophisticated instrumentation was gradually developed.

The Astronomical League circulated among the amateur astronomers a plea for volunteers to participate in the visual observing program. Because this was perhaps the first opportunity for amateur scientists to take part in the IGY and contribute to it data of significant value, the response was immediate.

Although the program was to be operated on a volunteer basis, each individual member had to be selected for his skill and his willingness to accept responsibility and to undertake what would prove to be a fairly arduous and time-consuming job. His only reward was the knowledge that his work would be of unquestioned scientific value and that without his effort and that of hundreds like him the satellites might become lost for scientific observation.

Dr. Spitz lectured to interested groups throughout the country, not only to recruit individuals for the visual observing program, but also to tell the general public something about the U.S. satellite program and to enlist the support of industry. People craved information about space exploration, which was now moving out of the realm of science fiction into the arena of everyday reality. To his efforts were added those of Whipple and Hynek, who used every opportunity during their many journeys across the United States to inform the public of plans for and progress toward the launching and tracking of IGY satellites. In a sense, these three and other members of the Smithsonian staff served as liaison officers between the scientific community and the general public, preparing them to accept, understand, and appreciate the events that were to begin so suddenly and dramatically on October 4, 1957, with the successful orbiting of the Russian satellite Sputnik I.

COMPUTING AND COMMUNICATIONS

There remained two other important phases of the program to be considered: computations and communications. Computations for operational purposes involved devising means of deriving from observations a mathematical description of the orbit of the satellite so that predictions of its future passages over specified places could be made. Communications would send the predictions to the Moonwatch teams and the Baker-Nunn camera stations and receive from them their observations. A communications network could not, of course, be set up until the sites of the Baker-Nunn camera stations and of the Moonwatch teams had been determined.

During the period of the first IGY grant, Prof. Leland Cunningham of the University of California at Berkeley was employed as a consultant. He spent a good part of the summer of 1956 in Cambridge developing a theory to deal with perturbations of the satellite's orbit caused by the earth's gravity. This he was able to do with considerable success, and later one of the primary responsibilities of the computations section of the Observatory would be to program his theory for orbital calculations on the IBM–704 electronic computer. Also, Robert Davis made several preliminary studies of the perturbations that would occur in the orbit of a satellite.

DEVELOPMENT OF OBJECTIVES FOR USE OF DATA

Much thought was being given to the scientific uses that could be made of the Moonwatch and Baker-Nunn observations. There gradually evolved an understanding of how these data could later provide the basis for a more detailed and more precise knowledge of:

1. The effects on the earth and the ionosphere of solar ultraviolet light, cosmic and solar X-rays, and other radiations.

2. The physics of the upper atmosphere as it related to more accurate long- and short-range weather forecasting.

3. The points in the upper atmosphere at which energy is either absorbed or radiated, and the problem of energy balance and dynamics of the upper atmosphere.

4. The disturbances in the atmosphere that result from solar flares and solar radiation.

5. The relation between conditions in the upper atmosphere and the weather at lower levels.

6. The variations of density and temperature at different levels of the upper atmosphere.

7. The nature and cause of the aurora.

8. The forces that produce the changes and fluctuations in the earth's magnetic field.

9. The variations in composition and thickness of the earth's crust.

10. The size and exact shape of the earth.

11. The sizes and relative positions of the land masses of the earth.

These objectives were to become the responsibility of the research and analysis section of the Observatory, a unit established late in 1957.

PEOPLE [9]

Finally, something should be said about the people who came to work on the program during these months and the months to follow. Dr. Hynek had done first things first. Instead of setting up a large and complex organization, he started out by seeing to the design of absolutely essential equipment. He had found people to initiate this work before he employed anyone else except his secretary.

In the months that followed Dr. Hynek hired people with a sense of adventure, individuals who could think and act for themselves as pioneers on a new scientific frontier. Through hunt and luck, he gathered about him a group of men with talent. These included not only scientists, engineers, and technicians, but also some who, though perhaps short on professional background, showed an infectious enthusiasm and willingness and ability to get things done.

BUILDING

FUNDING

At the end of June 1956 the original IGY grant ended. Effective July 1 the Smithsonian received a group of new grants, totaling approximately 3 million dollars, to carry the tracking program through to the end of the IGY on December 31, 1958. The budget would later pose some problems. Difficulty stemmed from the fact that money could not readily be transferred from one phase of the program to another according to need, nor was there any contingency fund.

---

[9] Drs. Theodore E. Sterne, Charles A. Whitney, and Luigi G. Jacchia joined the program as physicists of the satellite-tracking program in July 1956. Dr. Don A. Lautman joined the staff in August of the same year as computing analyst, and a month later was appointed a mathematician. Dr. Max Krook was appointed astrophysicist in August 1956. Jack Slowey came to Cambridge in September of 1956 as a physicist and was appointed astronomer to the program in 1959. Dr. Karl G. Henize was appointed astronomer in charge of Baker-Nunn camera stations in September of 1956 and the following year became senior astronomer. James Knight joined the program as an engineer in September of the same year. Aubrey J. Stinnett joined the staff as a technologist in September 1956. Dr. George A. Van Biesbroeck was appointed astronomer in September of the same year and became a consultant in February 1957. Leon Campbell, Jr., joined the Observatory as a consultant in October of 1956, and the next January became supervisor of station operations for Moonwatch. Robert E. Briggs was appointed mathematician in October of 1956. Dr. Gerhard F. Schilling came to the Observatory as a consultant in December 1956, a month later was appointed atmospheric physicist, and in 1958 became a specialist as assistant to the Director. Samuel B. Whidden became a station observer in February of 1957; in May of 1959 he was appointed station coordinator for Moonwatch. Stefan Sydor joined the program in May 1957 as a consultant and a few weeks later was appointed optical advisor. Kenneth H. Drummond became a consultant in May of 1957, administrative officer in September of that year, and executive officer in December. E. Stuart Fergusson came to Cambridge in the summer of 1957 as a consultant; in September he became executive officer of the satellite-tracking program. Charles M. Peterson joined the staff as communications specialist in August 1957; the next summer he was appointed chief of communications. Dr. John White joined the Observatory as a senior observer in September 1957, but served as a public information specialist after October 4 of that year.

THE BAKER OPTICS

During the spring months of 1956 Dr. Baker made further calculations on modified Schmidt systems. Such a system might, for example, consist of a cemented doublet correcting plate and an aspheric mirror. It became quite clear, however, that the difficulties of the problem had increased faster than simple modifications of the classical Schmidt could accommodate. Dr. Baker brought this situation to Dr. Whipple's attention and requested financial support to conduct a searching examination of more involved optical systems.

Authorization to proceed was obtained in June. Dr. Baker then began detailed calculations of systems of increasing complexity to find the simplest that would meet the new requirements. Before arriving at the final solution, he analyzed exhaustively three other simpler systems and various intermediate systems, and rejected them all.[10]

Nevertheless, with the completion of calculation for the third system, Dr. Baker knew that he had "cracked" the problem. It was now largely a question of finding more suitable glass types. The design of the corrector cell itself represented a compromise; if the air spaces between the lenses of the cell are too large, the aspheric powers, even though weak, lead to unacceptable astigmatism in the outer field. If the air spaces are too small, the aspheric powers become too great for practical manufacture. Therefore, in applying the concept of the three-lens corrector cell, he had to interpolate more or less along a curve to reach a point that represented as small an air space as would be practicable for a system that could actually be manufactured. A larger air space than was decided upon would have simplified the manufacturing problem, but the astigmatism in the outer field would have made for unhappy results well outside the 20-micron

---

[10] The first of these, already mentioned, was an achromatized classical Schmidt system modified to include an aspheric primary mirror. The second system made use of two air-spaced corrector elements and an aspheric mirror. The performance of this second system was appreciably superior to that of the standard classical Schmidt but otherwise was discouraging because of residual higher-order coma, or "halo" around the image. He was forced to go to a more complicated system. Drawing on more than 20 years' experience, and choosing ordinary types of optical glass selected after much computing, he designed his third optical system, which met the monochromatic requirements; its performance was, in fact, more or less identical to that of the present satellite camera in the optimum region of the spectrum. The chromatic aberrations, or color blur, of this combination of ordinary glass types turned out, however, to be well beyond the assigned tolerances. At the extremes of the spectral range, the image formed by this system would have been 5 times larger in diameter and 25 times larger in area than the specified 20-micron spot size. The monochromatic characteristics of the system did prove the value of the three-plate corrector cell. It would not, however, have been at all safe to adopt the design, inasmuch as the effect of the color blur would have been rendered all the more disastrous because the aperture of the camera would be necessarily much obscured by the presence of film and shutter in the light beam. These shadowing effects would have been present in the enlarged star images and would have made precision measurement most difficult.

tolerance. Clearly, this same curve was also a curve of dollars, and it was necessary to be most careful to strike an acceptable balance between cost and performance.

The choice of suitable glasses for the corrector cell necessitated finding a combination of types that would remove or satisfactorily reduce the so-called secondary spectrum that had been the remaining dominant aberration of system No. 3. The catalog of Schott, the well-known German manufacturer of optical glass, listed only a few types providing negative dispersive characteristics of the proper trend throughout the spectrum. Of these only KzFS–2 seemed to be at all acceptable. Although listed as greenish in coloration, it was considerably whiter than the KzF series and, if kept thin, would provide adequate transmission in the ultraviolet. Unfortunately, this glass was also described as sensitive to acid staining and "soluble" in distilled water, though to a less degree than KzFS–3. Nevertheless, there was no way to solve the optical problem except to adopt KzFS–2 for the outermost pair of elements in the correcting trio of elements. The sensitivity of KzFS–2 to moisture and to atmospheric acid staining has continued to plague operators of the Baker-Nunn cameras, yet by no means to the degree earlier anticipated. Although the fact is perhaps not obvious, the transmitted light actually used in taking satellite pictures is far less affected by the staining of the KzFS–2 surfaces than the reflected light, not otherwise used, would indicate.

The central element of the corrector cell had to be matched to KzFS–2. Dr. Baker finally chose SK–14, a glass of fairly high index compared to KzFS–2 but known to have very good transmission.

An important but unlooked-for bonus in the choice of these two glasses was that they have very little thermal expansion, at least compared with that of many other optical glasses. In this respect they were unusually well matched, a fact that simplified the design of the means by which the elements of the corrector cell would be held in accurate alignment.

This three-element corrector cell as finally designed would provide, then, an image with a minimum of color aberration and a minimum of coma. It was now matched to a mirror 30 inches in diameter, the best glass for which was Pyrex, made by the Corning Glass Works in Corning, N.Y.

Dr. Baker completed the optical design of the camera by the end of July 1956. Already it was a much more complicated system than either he or the staff of the Observatory had ever anticipated. As the months went by, it proved to be considerably more expensive to manufacture and involved a larger, heavier camera than any of them had originally thought.

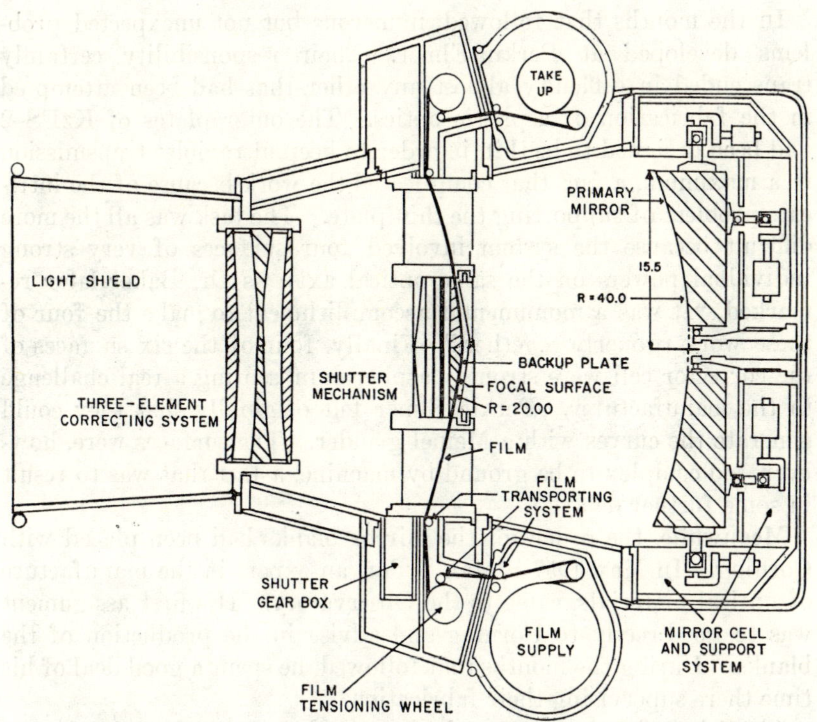

FIGURE 1.—Simplified cross-section view of the Baker-Nunn camera.

Looking back on those months of arduous work and of crucial decisions and on the periods of discouragement that preceded discovery, Dr. Baker even now sees no practical alternative to the system that was designed.[11]

Although probably only Dr. Baker could have designed the optical system of the camera, it seemed that a number of firms might be able to manufacture the lenses and mirrors once Schott and Corning had delivered the glass. However, the Perkin-Elmer Corporation, a large company with varied experience in the manufacture of optics, was the only firm that bid for the contract and had the personnel and machines to back up their bid. On November 16, 1956, a contract for the manufacture of the optics was signed by them and the Observatory.

---

[11] At best, he would now add a zero power plane-parallel hard-crown optical plate in front of the corrector cell simply in order to protect the KzFS–2 lens; while in a sense this would have been a fourth corrector, it actually would have presented no difficulties of design or manufacture and could even now be added at any time. Otherwise, called upon to do the same job today, he would still do it in precisely the same way. He would make a plea, however, to those using the cameras to think of them as highly specialized tools that need much care, periodic maintenance, and occasional renovation.

In the months that followed, numerous but not unexpected problems developed at Perkin-Elmer. Their responsibility certainly transcended in difficulty almost any other that had been attempted in the fabrication of aspheric optics. The outer plates of KzFS–2 had been designed to be thin in order to keep ultraviolet transmission to a maximum, a fact that complicated the work because of the intricate problem of supporting the thin plate. The task was all the more difficult because the system involved four surfaces of very strong individual powers on the same optical axis; as Dr. Baker later remarked, "It was a monumental accomplishment to make the four of these work properly together." Finally, four of the six surfaces of the corrector cell were strongly aspheric, presenting a real challenge to the manufacturer. Perkin-Elmer felt originally that they could generate the curves with a Meinel grinder. The surfaces were, however, too complex to be ground by machine, a fact that was to result in some further delays.

Meanwhile, the order for the mirror blanks had been placed with Corning. In May 1957 Stefan Sydor, an expert in the manufacture of optical materials, came to the Observatory. His first assignment was to go directly to Corning and advise in the production of the blanks. During the months that followed, he spent a good deal of his time there supervising their fabrication.

The Schott firm in Germany had received contracts for manufacturing the glasses for the corrector cell and for the aspheric-surface back-up plates against which the photographic film would be tensioned to lie in the focal surface. They did a magnificent job on both assignments.

By June 1957 a sufficient number of the three types of glass blanks had been received from Schott and from Corning to assure uninterrupted production during the remainder of the year. Military Air Transport Service (MATS) had already flown 40 of the 48 large glass disks for the corrector-plate assembly from Germany to Connecticut, and transported another 5 during the summer. This was one of the many ways in which the Air Force cooperated with the Observatory and facilitated the work of the program.

Perkin-Elmer erected a new optical shop for fine grinding and polishing of the optical parts of the camera, and by the summer of 1957 were grinding and polishing the test optics. Rough grinding of the spheric surface of the corrector optics was done on a machine especially built by Frank Cooke of North Brookfield, Mass. The rough grinding of the primary mirrors was done at the main plant.

During these months Sydor spent much of his time at the Perkin-Elmer plant, working 10, 12, even 14 hours a day to complete, if possible, the first set of optics by late summer.

THE NUNN CAMERA

Joseph Nunn continued to work on the design of the camera. By September 1956 he had prepared a series of pictorial drawings that indicated the general construction, and by late fall he had prepared the first blueprints indicating the details, including the optical features.

Here it will be best to describe the camera as it is now used at the photographic tracking stations.

The camera must follow the path of the satellite as it moves across the sky. A special mount is required for this purpose.

Like a star, a satellite rises into the sky from the horizon, culminates, and then sets. Here the similarity in their paths ends. Satellite culmination is not limited to the observer's meridian. Furthermore, its path on the celestial sphere is not necessarily restricted to a semicircle, nor is it symmetrical about culmination. Consequently, the angular velocity of the satellite as observed from a point on the surface of the earth may change greatly between horizon and culmination.

For these reasons the traditional telescope mount that is designed to track stars would be most inadequate to track satellites. On the other hand, a mount that would follow exactly every possible path of the satellite would be so complex as to be wholly unsuitable in the field. The mount designed is a simple yet effective compromise between these two extremes.

Set in a gimbal ring, the camera can be turned on its triaxial mounting at predetermined speeds to match the predicted motion of a satellite. This speed can be continuously varied from zero to 7,000 seconds of arc per second of time. This latter speed is equivalent to traversing the sky from horizon to horizon in 93 seconds.

The gimbal ring and the drive mechanism are fitted into the yoke of an orthodox altitude-azimuth mount. By making the necessary settings for azimuth, altitude, and track angle, the operator can direct the camera to any point in the sky above 15° elevation in such a way that the camera will be driven through that point in the same direction as that taken by the satellite during its passage. The actual point for tracking is usually about culmination, the highest elevation of the satellite as seen by the observer.

The camera photographs on a 55-mm. film. The field of view of the camera is 30° along the track of the satellite, and 5° perpendicular to that track. The camera photographs at rates ranging from one frame every 2 seconds to one frame every 32 seconds.

The path swept out by the camera is a great circular arc 130° long. In regions away from culmination, there is necessarily a divergence between the path of the camera and the path of the satellite; however, the image of the satellite does remain long enough within the field of the camera to enable the operator to obtain a sequence of photographs that define its path.

The camera mount also incorporates an oscillating mechanism that permits the operator to photograph alternately at different angular velocities. When the optimum combination of satellite image and reference star field is required, the camera can be set to photograph alternately at the angular velocity of the satellite and at the component of sidereal motion along the path of the satellite. At the first of these velocities the satellite image is stationary and well defined on the frame, while the star images are trailed into lines about 1 mm. in length. At the second velocity the star images are short and well exposed, while the satellite image is trailed.

Negotiations were now under way for awarding the contract for the construction of the camera. While a number of firms were considered, including Perkin-Elmer, who wanted to build the camera as well as to fabricate the optics, the contract was given to the Boller & Chivens Co. of South Pasadena, Calif. A small machine manufactory employing at that time probably 25 persons, the Boller & Chivens organization had in the past worked very successfully with Joseph Nunn in the production of instruments designed by him. The contract arrangements with Boller & Chivens [12] were completed on October 4, 1956, exactly one year before Sputnik I was sent into orbit.

Manufacturing the optics on the East Coast and the mechanical elements on the West Coast not only presented some difficult logistics but also complicated the fabrication of the camera itself. There was no opportunity of fitting the optics until after the corrector cell and the mirror had been made and delivered to South Pasadena, at which time, of course, the mechanical elements of the camera would be virtually completed. This made it necessary for the work to be done with extreme care so that there would be no last-minute delay because parts did not fit.

The optical components of the camera were extremely large and complex; in fact, the corrector cell optics were and still are the largest aspheric refractor lenses ever built. While the problem of mounting a 30-inch mirror had many times been solved for individual telescopes, it had not been solved for the mass production of 12 cameras. The

---

[12] This decision to award the contract to them was based in part on the possibility of Nunn and Boller & Chivens working closely together in the production of the camera, and in part, of course, on the proved ability of the firm to turn out work of high quality and on schedule. Whipple and Hynek, who had wide contacts throughout the rather specialized field of optical instrumentation, were convinced through their dealings with Joseph Nunn that Boller & Chivens would be the best firm to manufacture the camera.

various components had to be mounted in such a manner that they would maintain the proper position relative to each other and relative to the rest of the camera. At a number of conferences, Mr. Nunn, representatives of Perkin-Elmer, and the Observatory staff developed the details of the design of a series of holding rings for the corrector-cell optics and the method for mounting the mirror.

Early in 1957 a scale model of the camera was built and painted in the brilliant colors that Nunn and Stinnett had decided upon. It was a beautiful piece of equipment; Whipple and Hynek showed it proudly to groups they addressed, and certainly it did much to dramatize to the public the U.S. satellite-tracking program.

The manufacture of the camera was one of the finest achievements of American industry. Of entirely new design and of complex structure, 12 of them had to be built without the construction of a prototype, and without the testing of the individual components of the system. The cameras were built almost concurrently, and the first one completed had to work. And once the large components were put into production, there was no opportunity to change any of the details.

By June of 1957 Boller & Chivens were devoting more than 50 percent of their manufacturing facilities to the production of the camera parts. Subcontractors in the Los Angeles area were simultaneously fabricating the frame and tube sections and machining the castings for the corrector cells. Meanwhile, contracts had been placed for the manufacture of the necessary electronic equipment for the operation of the camera and the Norrman clock, including the frequency control unit for the camera drive and the automatic transfer switches for emergency power.

The Observatory had by then also determined the type of film that was needed for the camera. After a series of experiments at the Agassiz Station of Harvard Observatory, the staff chose the famous ID–2 emulsion, which is still used today for about half of the satellite-tracking work. It provided the spectral distribution that the Observatory needed, that is, reflected sunlight, and was a faster film than any of the other emulsions then available. Some 40,000 feet of this film was ordered from Eastman-Kodak and put in storage for tests of the camera in South Pasadena and at the New Mexico field station in the fall.

THE NORRMAN CLOCK

By the summer of 1956 the details of the clock to time the photographs taken by the Baker-Nunn camera had been fairly well defined. To replace the mechanical presentation of time in the Norrman clock model 110, Robert Davis had developed an electronic sweep, in which an electron beam pulses on and off in synchronism with the time. This beam is presented on an oscilloscope somewhat similar to the picture tube in a television set. The clock with the oscilloscope and the electronic sweep was installed in the dome of the 15-inch telescope at the Harvard Observatory, and the following weeks were spent developing a usable system of time presentation on the oscilloscope.

The next step was to find a radio receiver that would give reliable, consistent reception of the WWV time signals from Beltsville, Md. Davis chose a fixed-frequency receiver so that station personnel could not use the set for listening to anything except WWV!

It was then necessary to arrange for some emergency power supply, since the stations would be located in areas where the local power would not be especially reliable. Following specifications drawn up by Davis, an electrical firm in Cambridge built an emergency system similar to that used for railroad signals. It worked exactly as required but used a rather expensive type of battery. Since the cost was prohibitive, the 12 camera stations were actually supplied with emergency power systems using ordinary automotive batteries, which were to prove inadequate.

By the end of June 1956 the timing system pieced together from various components was functioning satisfactorily at the Harvard Observatory. The staff then began to think seriously of how the time presentation could be photographed inside the Baker-Nunn camera. Dr. Hynek obtained from Edward Halbach of the Milwaukee Astronomical Society a photographic slave clock that was compatible with the modified Norrman Time Standard and that illuminated whirling dials by means of an electronic photographic strobe lamp. After preliminary testing, Hynek and Davis determined that this slave clock was essentially what they would need, once an oscilloscope presentation was added to it. Now they had a complete prototype slave clock that, properly reduced in size and made to fit mechanically inside the Baker-Nunn camera, would give the time presentation required.

In July Mr. Norrman came to Cambridge and was shown the assembly. This led to his building the model 111, which was basically a model 110 with the oscilloscope, the auxiliary circuits for an electronic presentation of microtime, and other accretions. Meanwhile, Davis completed the assembly of a prototype time station and successfully tested it in August.

Davis then went to California to discuss with Joseph Nunn and with Boller & Chivens the integration of the clock and the camera. A firm decision was made that all the synchronous motors in the camera would be driven from the accurate 60-cycle current of the

Norrman clock.[13] In addition, they decided that Boller & Chivens would build the mechanical parts of the slave clock, but that the contract for the electronic components would be placed elsewhere.

By spring of the following year the first model 111 clock arrived in Cambridge. It turned out to be somewhat less reliable than had been hoped, although it did maintain the same accuracy as model 110. Furthermore, since the clock was subject to rather complex breakdowns difficult to repair, it required constant and careful maintenance that would prove to be yet another responsibility on the overburdened shoulders of the early observers. The addition of the oscilloscope and other components to model 110 had taxed to the limit the capacity and the performance of the original Norrman clock.

Meanwhile, Shapiro & Edwards of Pasadena, Calif., were awarded the contract for engineering and building the time-presentation system within the camera itself; and yagi antennas for the reception of WWV signals at 10, 15, and 20 megacycles were ordered, as well as the cable for connecting the crystal clock and camera.

Early in the summer of 1957 the model 111 was found to be capable of time interpolation during a 6-hour interval to an accuracy of 1 ten-thousandth of a second; during this test the device was continuously compared with the WWV signals from the time service station of the National Bureau of Standards.

The model 111 was put into production at the Norrman Laboratories, and in September a clock was shipped to South Pasadena, Calif., for testing with the camera itself.

FIELD ORGANIZATION

THE BAKER-NUNN CAMERA STATIONS

At the IGY conference in Barcelona, Spain, in September 1956 members of the Observatory staff held lengthy discussions with representatives from other countries for the establishment and operation of the Baker-Nunn camera stations. Sites were being considered in South Africa, Spain, Iran, India, Australia, Japan, Hawaii, the Netherlands West Indies, Argentina, and Peru, in addition to two in the United States. There were also discussions of the possibility of establishing stations in Egypt, Anglo-Egyptian Sudan, and Ethiopia.

Agreements for the maintenance of the stations were to be for a 2-year period, with the further stipulation that the contracts could be extended indefinitely upon approval of the parties concerned. The

---

[13] Tests proved that the model 111 would not only operate the slave clock but would also provide precise voltage for the frequency controlled generator that would supply the motors of the camera.

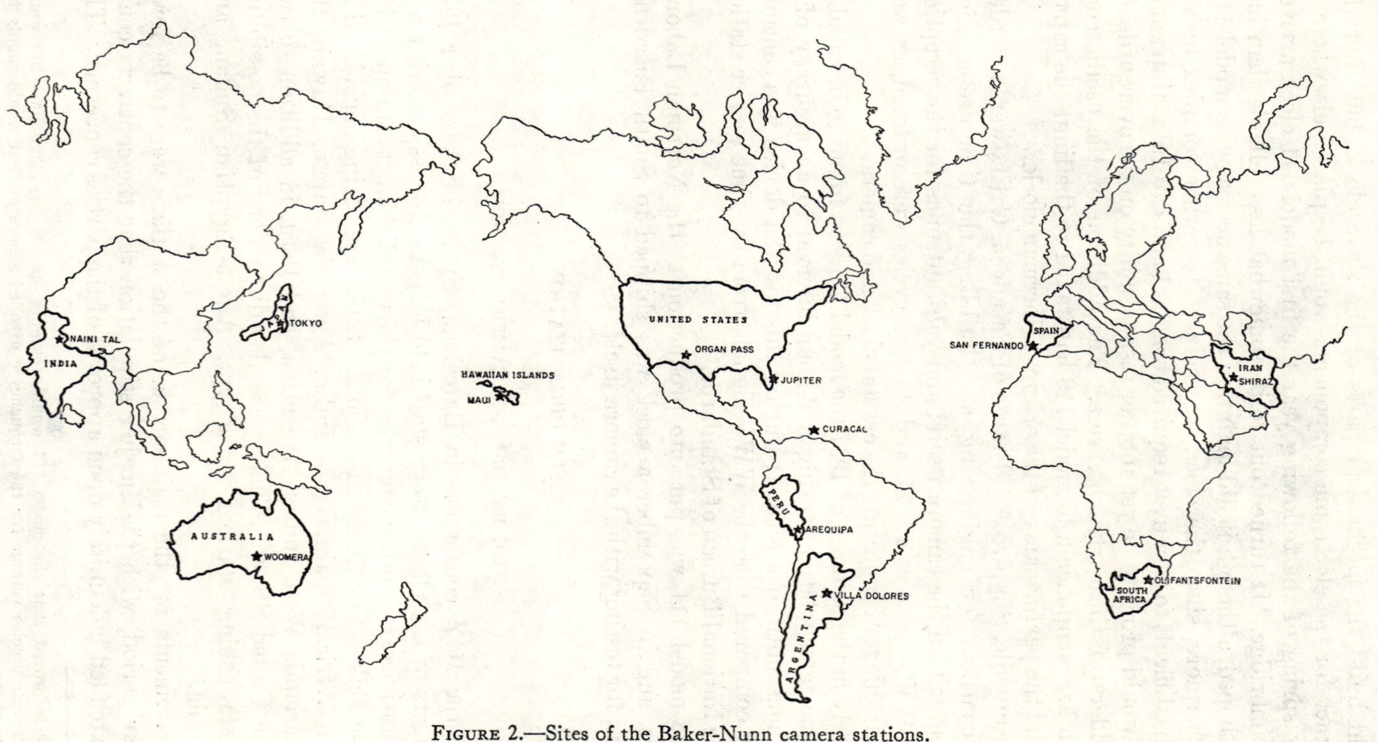

FIGURE 2.—Sites of the Baker-Nunn camera stations.

Smithsonian was to provide the scientific equipment for all the stations, as well as other materials and services as needed.

Diplomatic and exchange problems would involve not only the arrangement of contracts, but also visas, import regulations, customs duties, personal income taxes, exchange of currency, and special import restrictions. In large measure, these questions were to be resolved through the U.S. Department of State.

Early in 1957 members of the Observatory toured a number of countries to inspect suggested sites. Dr. Whipple visited proposed sites in Florida and Spain. Dr. Hynek went to Argentina, Peru, and the Netherlands West Indies, and made preliminary arrangements for the establishment of stations there. Dr. Henize undertook similar missions in Spain and the Union of South Africa (now the Republic of South Africa). Meanwhile, Japan and Australia, as part of their participation in the IGY program, agreed to equip the stations in their countries, except for camera, clock, and accessories, and to provide the observers. In most of the countries cooperation was immediately forthcoming, and arrangements proceeded smoothly.

The 12 Baker-Nunn camera stations are the following:

Organ Pass, N. Mex.—On the slope of St. Augustin Mountain overlooking the White Sands Proving Ground and the White Sands National Monument, this site is used cooperatively by the Smithsonian satellite-tracking program and the Harvard Meteor Program. The Smithsonian expanded the Harvard building to house both projects. In September 1957 material and equipment for this first Baker-Nunn camera station were received.

Olifantsfontein, South Africa.—In August of 1956 Dr. Menzel of the Harvard College Observatory and Dr. Whipple approached C. G. Hide of the Council for Scientific and Industrial Research of South Africa to arrange for the establishment of a station in that country. The site selected was Olifantsfontein, which means literally the elephant's fountain or the elephant's drinking pool, a small town halfway between Pretoria and Johannesburg, on an almost flat, bleak veldt plateau broken by occasional scrub and timber.

The South African National Committee for the IGY provided the buildings, which were completed by November 1957. Except for the camera house, these are prefabricated rondavels, circular in structure, with conical roofs of 14-foot diameter; they provide an unusual combination of native architecture and 20th-century scientific technology. Around the station are the antennas of a large broadcasting station, part of the communications system of the South African Government.

Woomera, Australia.—The Weapons Research Establishment,[14] a branch of the Department of Supply, Commonwealth of Australia, operates the station independently but in close cooperation with the Smithsonian. The site was completed by the Establishment on October 1, 1957. At this huge Woomera complex of scientific projects, the Establishment also maintains with the U.S. Naval Research Laboratory a Minitrack station, the only one that is operated jointly with a Baker-Nunn observatory.

The nearby village has about 3,000 people. The altitude varies from about 350 to 450 feet above sea level, with gentle undulations. The surface is mostly rock and clay. Ten inches of rain marks a good year.

The Baker-Nunn camera house differs considerably from the Smithsonian plans in that it was built to withstand very dusty storm conditions and to provide satisfactory housing for precision equipment in a climate where the temperature rises in the summer to 120° F. in the shade. The joint operation here of the Minitrack and the Baker-Nunn in the one set of buildings including communications, computations room, and stores, has proved the value of running one large station instead of two small ones.

San Fernando, Spain.[15]—The station is near the sea and close to the Spanish Naval Observatory, in the town of San Fernando, population 40,000, about 50 miles northwest of Gibraltar.

Arrangements were initiated in mid-1956 with M. C. Herero of the Battelle Institute in Madrid, and early in 1957 with Admiral de la Puente, director of the Spanish Naval Observatory.[16] Construction of the buildings was completed in February 1958.

The station is unique in that it is an urban establishment, but the layout and buildings could be called typical of most of the other Baker-Nunn stations built by the Smithsonian. These buildings were among those that in late 1961 were showing signs of real deterioration; they had, of course, been intended to last only the 18 months of the IGY.

Mitaka, Japan.—The station in Japan was established through the cooperation of Dr. Takesi Nagata, Secretary of the Japanese National Committee for the IGY, and Dr. Masasi Miyadi, coordinator for

---

[14] The Weapons Research Establishment itself tests and develops new weapons for the British and the Australian Governments. It has the world's largest overland rocket range, running 1,200 miles across the country, and maintains large laboratories and workshops at Salisbury near Adelaide, the capital of South Australia. Some 300 miles from Adelaide, Woomera is the field-testing station and the range head.

[15] Before this site was chosen, Almeria was rejected because of heavy cloud cover, and Izana in the Canary Islands because of gravity anomalies.

[16] The Spanish Naval Observatory has played a distinguished role in European astronomy; it was one of 14 observatories that undertook the Carte du Ciel at the turn of this century. The tradition of cooperative work is thus well established.

the IGY in that country and director of the Tokyo Astronomical Observatory. The Tokyo Observatory, which operates the station, is in Mitaka, a town of 1,000 people, about 40 miles outside Tokyo. Construction of the buildings on the Observatory grounds was completed in January of 1958.

The region around Mitaka is on the fringe of the monsoon area; in the summer, observing is limited by clouds and rain.

Naini Tal, India.—The station in India was established through the cooperation of the Uttar Pradesh Observatory at Naini Tal, and the program was coordinated by Dr. M. K. Vainu Bappu, its chief astronomer.

Some 150 miles north of New Delhi, the station is about 8 miles from Naini Tal, a town of 12,000 people. Naini Tal was the first of the hill stations of India, where the European administrators in the days of the British rule used to go to escape from the extreme conditions in summer on the plains of India. The Baker-Nunn camera was the first instrument installed at Manora Peak, the newly selected site for the Observatory.

Here also the monsoon season interferes considerably with the observing program. There is some difficulty in transportation—with no airport nearby, materials must come by rail or road from New Delhi.

Arequipa, Peru.—Arrangements for the station in Peru were made through the chairman of its National IGY Committee, Dr. J.A. Broggi, and through Fernando L. de Romana of Arequipa. Construction of the station was begun in December of 1957.

Arequipa, with a population of 95,000, the second largest city in Peru, had at one time been the location of a Harvard observing station that for 5 years had been directed by Leon Campbell, Sr. The site for the Baker-Nunn station, about 3 miles outside the city, was provided under contract agreement by the National University of San Agustín, which operates a seismic station nearby.

Arequipa and the village where the station is actually located are in an elevated valley some 8,000 feet above sea level in very mountainous country with peaks up to 20,000 feet high. It rarely rains there, although the skies are often cloudy.

Shiraz, Iran.—Arrangements for the Shiraz station were coordinated by Dr. H. K. Afshar, a member of the faculty of science of the University of Teheran. The universities of Teheran and Shiraz assumed the construction cost of the building and arranged for the lease of land.

Shiraz, in southwest Iran, has a population of 130,000. The city itself is in a fairly flat, green valley. Quite arid mountains surround it, and the station is in the foothills of these mountains on the property of the Nemazee hospital about 4 miles outside the city.

Shiraz is right on the edge of the monsoon belt, which has an adverse effect on observing conditions, as do also haze and dust. Transportation into the city is by air, even heavy equipment now being sent in by plane because there is no convenient seaport entry.

Curaçao, Netherlands West Indies.—Arrangements for this station were made through Dr. P. C. Henriquez, secretary of the Development Authority of the Netherlands Antilles Government. The Department of Public Works of the island administration provided drawings, contract arrangements, and supervision of the construction of the buildings, and some materials.

Curaçao is about 40 miles from the Venezuela coast. Together with the adjacent island of Aruba, it is the world's largest oil-refining complex. Willemstad, the capital of the island, is one of the world's major ports in terms of tonnage handled each year.

The temperature on Curaçao is about 80° F., day and night, winter and summer. Rain is infrequent, and the whole island is extremely dry. The station is about 4 miles from Willemstad, toward the center of the island, on the Santa Barbara estate owned by the Newport Mining Co.

Jupiter, Fla.—Originally, Cocoa Beach was considered as the station site, but the Observatory finally decided on Jupiter because it was away from sea spray and had what little elevation could be found in Florida. The station, some 15 miles north of Palm Beach, is located in Jonathan-Dickinson State Park, site of Fort Murphy, a U.S. military training post during World War II. By February of 1958 the camera house had been completed, and the U.S. Air Force made available to the station personnel a large administration building.

Villa Dolores, Argentina.—An agreement was drawn up between the Smithsonian and the Observatorio Nacional Argentino for the establishment of the station near Villa Dolores in the general region of Córdoba. Land was provided through the Astronomical Observatory of the University of Córdoba.

Villa Dolores is in central Argentina, over the high sierras from Córdoba 100 miles away. It is a large rural town with a population of about 30,000. The station is about 5 miles from Villa Dolores in flat, open farming country. The climate is good, but there is considerable rain.

Mount Haleakala, Hawaii.—The station is located within 50 feet of the top of Haleakala Mountain, the largest dormant volcanic crater in the world.[17] The University of Hawaii supervised the construction, and the Geophysical Institute of the University through the work of

---

[17] Originally, the Smithsonian had considered establishing the station at the Mauna Loa Observatory; however, the possibility of volcanic eruption and the logistics problems presented by 50 miles of bad roads resulted in the rejection of that site.

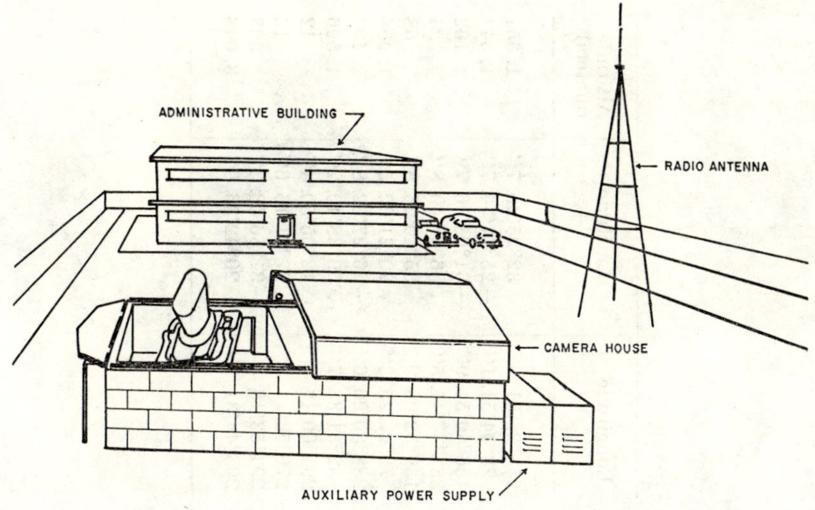

FIGURE 3.—Typical layout of a Baker-Nunn camera station.

Dr. Walter Steiger contributed much to the success of the satellite-tracking program there.

From the farming centers and cane towns of Maui, 22 miles of extremely winding road lead up the mountain to the station. Most of the observers live in a small village about 12 miles by road from the top.

On Maui there is almost every kind of climate. One side of the mountain is completely arid, the other side is a tropical rain forest. The station is about 10,000 feet in altitude, above almost all clouds; if there are clouds, they are seen as fog. Cinder dust in a strong wind is a problem, although not a serious one.

Even before these sites were actually chosen, realistic plans had to be made for constructing, equipping, and supporting the stations. Usually, the establishing of an astronomical observatory requires three to five years. Now, 12 had to be built in less than a year and a half. Furthermore, the staff of the Smithsonian had to decide what would be needed to make the stations reasonably self-contained and self-sufficient before they knew where the stations would be located.

The layout of each station and the design of the buildings were the responsibility of Elwyn Balch, who served as a construction consultant to the Observatory and who worked closely with local authorities in planning and constructing the facilities at each site.

The general layout consisted of a building to house the Baker-Nunn camera, an administration building, a powerhouse, a tool and fuel shed, and possibly a separate unit for developing film. The design for the camera house included provisions for a sliding roof that would

TABLE 1.—*Baker-Nunn camera stations*

Station No.	Location	Longitude	Latitude	Altitude (meters)
9001	Organ Pass, N. Mex	253°26′51. 8″	32°25′26. 7″	1, 651
9002	Olifantsfontein, South Africa	28°14′51. 1″	−25°77′34. 7″	1, 544
9003	Woomera, Australia	136°46′54. 9″	−31°06′06. 7″	162
9004	San Fernando, Spain	353°47′41. 5″	36°27′49. 8″	24
9005	Tokyo, Japan	139°32′06. 9″	35°40′23. 6″	58
9006	Naini Tal, India	79°27′25. 3″	29°21′32. 5″	1, 954
9007	Arequipa, Peru	288°30′20. 6″	−16°27′52. 8″	2, 452
9008	Shiraz, Iran	52°31′33. 7″	29°38′40. 2″	1, 596
9009	Curaçao, Netherlands West Indies	291°09′46. 0″	12°05′50. 4″	12
9010	Jupiter, Fla	279°53′11. 8″	27°01′16. 6″	12
9011	Villa Dolores, Argentina	294°53′18. 3″	−31°56′08. 3″	598
9012	Maui, Hawaii	203°44′31. 7″	20°42′36. 0″	3, 048

permit the camera to operate down to within 15° of the horizon; the roof would protect the camera during hours when it was not in use and during inclement weather, an especially important provision because of the KzFS–2 glass used in the corrector cell. Arrangements were made to obtain small prefabricated buildings from the Air Force to house the power facilities, fuel, and maintenance tools.

James Knight and Aubrey Stinnett were assigned the actual selection of the innumerable items required for the successful operation of the stations. These included not only the beam antennas and numerous items of electronic equipment, but also dozens of household necessities, tools, and other essential supplies.

By late spring of 1957 approximately 95 percent of all the material required for the independent operation of the 12 satellite-tracking stations had been received, cataloged, crated, and stored, and was ready for shipment. By June all material and equipment except the camera and the clock had been received at the Australia and Spain stations, and from then on each station was in its turn set up for operations preliminary to the arrival of the camera and clock.

Probably as much as 10 tons of equipment was sent to each station, all without the loss of any important item, and even without any serious mishaps. There was a fire aboard a ship carrying equipment to Japan, but it did very little damage. A truck was "lost" in Iran for several months.

The selection of the observers for the Baker-Nunn camera stations presented as many and as difficult problems as the selection of the sites and the acquisition of material. Drs. Whipple, Hynek, Henize, and several other members of the Smithsonian staff, as well as Drs. Frances Wright and Richard McCrosky of the Harvard Meteor Program, all took part in the selection of the first observers. In fact, at times there were more interviewers than interviewees.

The first task was to define precisely the kind of personality needed for the operation of a station, and the skills required to make a success of the optical observing program. There were as many different opinions as there were interviewers. It turned out that neither education nor past experience was the best criterion. The Harvard people already knew that movie writers, artists, plumbers—in fact, almost any type of person—might serve brilliantly as an observer if he had the proper attitude and a certain basic intelligence and mechanical aptitude. What was needed was a person who had eagerness, enthusiasm, a spirit of adventure, and especially a sense of responsibility—one who could impart to the interviewers the feeling that what he most wanted to do was to photograph satellites.

The first observers were essentially romantics, men who had a common interest in this new age of satellites and an intense curiosity about science and the world. They were also men of considerable versatility and strong character, as indeed they had to be, for they were about to undertake a kind of do-it-yourself project, often a one-man project until assistant observers could be obtained. They were men who could not only operate the Baker-Nunn camera but also drive nails, who could not only work cooperatively and efficiently with scientists but also deal with strangers in strange lands.

With these characteristics went another that was to create some difficulties. They were not organization men. Chosen for their ability to make decisions, they frequently proceeded to make them in contradiction to and sometimes in defiance of orders from Cambridge. Chosen for their sense of responsibility, they often felt themselves to be more responsible to the station than to the over-all operation of the Satellite-tracking Program. Chosen for their ability to improvise, they sometimes improvised in ways that lessened the scientific value of their observations. In other words, they were pioneers, with all the strengths and weaknesses of the pioneer type.

The first observer to be hired was Samuel Whidden who had had several years as an observer on the Harvard Meteor Program. While he was to assist in the details of station establishment, the preparation for station operations, and the selection and training of other observers, it is perhaps characteristic of the program that his versatility was put to work on the choice of film for the Baker-Nunn camera.

By the summer of 1957 classes for the observers had been started. Courses in basic electronics and in the maintenance of the Norrman time standard were given by Andrew B. Ledwith. Classes in spherical astronomy, photography, and the reduction of observations were presented by other members of the staff. Plans then called for the first group of observers to go to Organ Pass, N. Mex., for final training as soon as the first Baker-Nunn camera had been received there.

THE MOONWATCH PROGRAM

During the summer and early fall of 1956, the appeal of the Observatory for Moonwatch teams was heard and heeded throughout the world. That summer the Observatory issued the first Bulletin for Visual Observers of Satellites, in which the code word Moonwatch was adopted officially. Incidentally, another code name had been a strong contender—SEESAW, for "I see it, I saw it"; fortunately, it lost.

In that first Bulletin appeared a brief outline of the objectives, organization, qualifications for observers, and operational procedures of Moonwatch. Each team was to set up a "fence" of observers. When an observer watching one "picket" of the fence saw the satellite, he was to signal to the timekeeper and then obtain a precise fix of the object

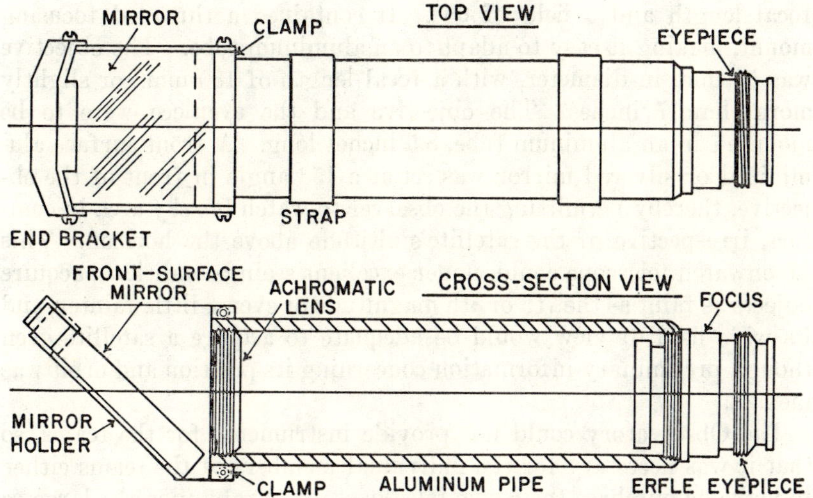

FIGURE 4.—Schematics of 50-mm. Moonwatch monoscope.

against a background of stars and on the meridian pole in the line of sight of the telescope. The group leader would then send the information to the communications center in Cambridge.

The program had three major technical problems. The first was that of precise timing of the observations. This could be done by use of either a stopwatch or a chronograph checked against accurate short-wave radio time signals broadcast by WWV or by some other national time service. The second was the accurate recording of the satellite position against the background of stars. For this purpose copies of the Skalnate Pleso Atlas of the Heavens were distributed to the teams. The third technical problem, of course, was the choice of a suitable telescope; the instrument had to be able to pick out objects of the 7th or 8th magnitude; and it had to be of simple, rugged design so that it could be easily used and would prove durable throughout the life of the program.

To determine the specifications of the telescope and the organizational details of the typical team, G. R. Wright, chairman of the National Advisory Committee, established a pilot Moonwatch station at his home in Silver Spring, Md. There a group of amateur astronomers tested some 30 different optical instruments that had been proposed for visual tracking. Three of these instruments[18] met admirably the needs of the program, and from them the Observatory drew up the specifications for what was to become known as the Moonwatch monoscope; the eyepiece was a wide-angle Erfle of 1.25-inches

---

[18] Built by Roy Walls of Washington, D.C., by Arthur S. Leonard of Davis, Calif., and by Roy M. Griffing of Los Altos, Calif.

focal length and a field of 68°. It contained a threaded focusing mount, making it easy to adapt to an aluminum tube. The objective was 51 mm. in diameter, with a focal length of 180 mm., or slightly more than 7 inches. The objective and the eyepiece were to be mounted in an aluminum tube, 8.5 inches long. A front surface aluminized or silvered mirror was set at a 45° angle in front of the objective, thereby permitting the observer to watch his sky area in comfort, irrespective of the satellite's altitude above the horizon. This Moonwatch telescope could, under excellent seeing conditions, acquire objects as faint as the 7th or 8th magnitude or even a little fainter, and its wide field of view would be adequate to acquire a satellite even though preliminary information concerning its position and orbit was inexact.

The Observatory could not provide instruments for the teams, so that it was necessary for the individual members of the teams either to make or purchase their own telescopes, or to rely upon the largesse of local firms, organizations, and others who were interested in supporting the project. The optics for the Moonwatch telescope could be purchased for about $20, and the assembly could be done in a home workshop; an estimated 40 percent of the observers built their own. Most of the others purchased the so-called EDSCOPE (a monoscope), manufactured in New Jersey, for about $50. Thus, at a relatively low cost, each Moonwatch team was able to equip itself with the needed optical instruments, and at its own expense.

At the same pilot Moonwatch station, tests were made of a number of means of keeping time. The result was the acceptance of an inexpensive chronograph that could be adjusted to a rate of 2 seconds of gain or loss per day and could be checked periodically against short-wave radio time signals.

Early in 1957 a Moonwatch steering committee was appointed to provide scientific and technical advice and to coordinate Moonwatch observations with other phases of the optical tracking program. The chairman of the committee was Dr. George Van Biesbroeck of the Yerkes Observatory, who was a consultant to the Smithsonian.

Leon Campbell, Jr., had already been appointed supervisor of Moonwatch. He had joined the staff of the Observatory in the fall of the previous year and had devoted most of his time to public information, but some also to the formal organization of the visual observing program. While Dr. Armand Spitz had instituted the initial steps of Moonwatch, his duties at the Spitz Laboratories did not allow him sufficient time to attend to the organization of the teams.

Most of the stations planned to use the typical Moonwatch monoscope. Since that telescope would not, however, be able to acquire objects much fainter than the 8th magnitude, an instrument of deeper penetration might be needed to locate fainter satellites or bright satellites at distant apogee. Thus, a network of Moonwatch stations strategically located and equipped with special telescopes was organized. These stations were to be located in Cape Town, Johannesburg, and Pretoria, South Africa; at the Kirkland Air Force Base in Albuquerque, N. Mex.; near the Holloman Air Force Base in Alamogordo, N. Mex.; at the Naval Ordnance Test Station in China Lake, Calif.; and at the Vincent Air Force Base in Yuma, Ariz. These stations were equipped with 8-power M–17 elbow telescopes of 50-mm. objective of 120-mm. diameter and a field of 2.4°; these were supplied by the Naval Research Laboratories, which also furnished limited technical guidance in their use.

By spring more than 70 Moonwatch stations had been organized in the United States and its territories, with a total of approximately 1,500 observers. The function of the visual program was now thought of in somewhat larger terms. Already the Observatory recognized the vital ways in which Moonwatch was informing the American public. The teams were to continue in increasing measure to educate their communities and to enlist laymen in activities that would promote a general interest in science.

At about this time Moonwatch solicited the aid of the Air Force, which named Col. Owen F. Clarke to act as liaison officer between the Pentagon and the Observatory. One of his first suggestions was that if Moonwatch was going to put on an alert, an idea which had been in the minds of the staff for some time, it should try to simulate the passage of a satellite: a small light trailed across the sky by a plane at 7,000 feet altitude and 120 miles per hour would give the approximate motion, magnitude, and direction of a satellite.

On May 17, 1957, Moonwatch held its first test alert, limited to stations in the continental United States. Six aircraft flights to simulate the satellites had been scheduled in widely separated parts of the country. The individual stations were not told that the "satellites" would be towed by planes so that the alert did in effect test the acquisition capabilities of six of the teams as well as show up those stations that might imagine rather than actually see a satellite. Some 75 of the 77 registered teams participated to the extent of reporting directly by telephone to headquarters in Cambridge. The alert thus also served to test communications procedures as well as to sustain the interest of the people who had cooperated so splendidly in organizing these teams.

The alert demonstrated much enthusiasm, cooperation, skill, and hard work among the teams, as well as the effectiveness of telephone communication. While the general readiness of the Moonwatch teams was highly gratifying, in some instances stations did not report clearly the position and time of the sighted object, were not familiar with the use of WWV time signals, and showed a certain amount of observing strain—that is, after 10 or 15 minutes the eyes of the observers proved to be considerably fatigued and to lose efficiency.

Meanwhile, teams were being formed abroad. At the September IGY conference in Barcelona, each participating country was asked to appoint a coordinator for satellite observations. Later the International Astronautical Federation meeting in Rome, Italy, volunteered its cooperation and facilities in establishing Moonwatch stations in many countries throughout the world.

More than a dozen teams were organized in South America. When Dr. Hynek visited countries there in his search for sites for the Baker-Nunn stations, he also publicized the purpose of, and the need for, Moonwatch teams. In Chile he met Father German Saa, Dr. Heilmaier, and Dr. Ruttlant, all of whom were interested in organizing Moonwatch teams. In Argentina he traveled with Teofilo Tabanera, president of the Argentine Astronautical Federation, who now offered his services in organizing teams. Sr. Tabanera also translated the Bulletin for Visual Observers into Spanish and circulated it throughout the Spanish-speaking countries of Latin America.

Of the foreign teams, however, none was more numerous and none more enthusiastic than those in Japan. By the summer of 1957 some 25 Moonwatch teams had been organized there, and Dr. Masasi Miyadi, director of the Tokyo Astronomical Observatory, had been appointed tracking coordinator of the Japanese IGY committee. He in turn enlisted the cooperation of the Astronomical Society of Japan, the Oriental Astronomical Association, the Japan Astronomical Study Association, and the Ikomason Astronomical Society. While the teams were led by experienced amateur and semiprofessional astronomers, most of the members were college and high-school students.

There were at least two reasons for the popularity and success of Moonwatch in Japan. The Japanese are especially interested in things scientific, particularly and traditionally those involving the use of lenses. Also, three of the large newspaper chains in Japan gave the Moonwatch program a vast amount of publicity, helped to find sites, and even equipped some of the teams. Eventually more than 80 teams were organized there.

On July 19, 1957, during the evening twilight, a second national alert involving approximately 80 Moonwatch teams in the United States was held. Simulated satellites were towed by airplanes of the Civil Air Patrol. As before, the stations phoned their reports to Cambridge. The alert showed a marked improvement in the operational techniques of the teams.

By early October 1957 Moonwatch teams had been organized in the following countries: Argentina (10 teams); Australia (5); Belgian

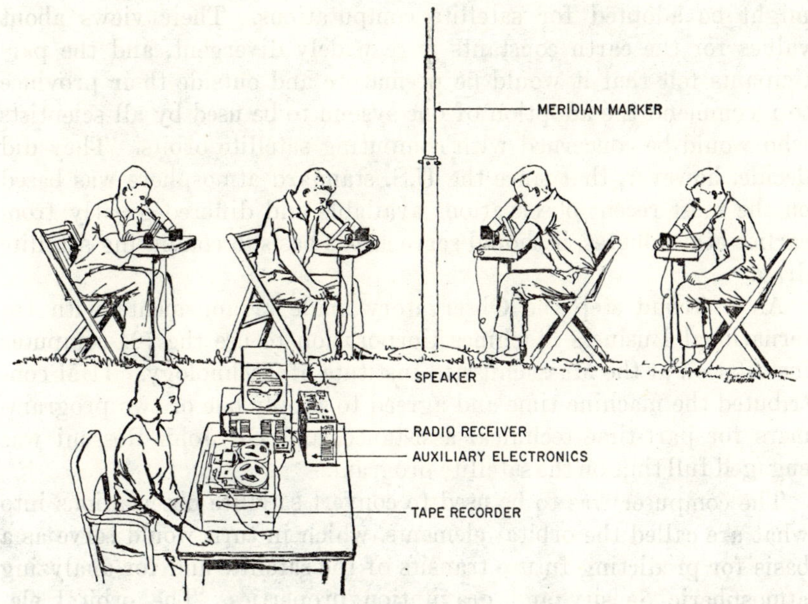

FIGURE 5.—Typical layout of a Moonwatch team in action, 1957.

Congo (1); Chile (6); Formosa (2); Denmark (1); Egypt (1); Guatemala (3); India (1); Iran (1); Italy (2); Japan (30); Liberia (1); Mexico (1); Netherlands West Indies (1); Peru (2); Philippines (2); the Union of South Africa (4); Germany (10).

HEADQUARTERS ORGANIZATION

COMPUTATIONS

The functions of the computing section of the Observatory were defined by early 1957 as: (1) to predict future motions of a satellite after initial observations had been made by the Moonwatch teams; (2) to supply the Baker-Nunn stations with all data necessary for them to photograph transits of the satellites; (3) to measure exactly the position of the satellite on the photographs taken by the Baker-Nunn stations; and finally (4) to analyze all orbital data received from the Moonwatch teams, the Baker-Nunn stations, and other sources, as a basis for evaluating geophysical constants and geodetic positions.

As a first step the Observatory held a conference on units and constants for satellite-orbit computations late in January. Attending this conference, and already members of the Smithsonian staff, were Drs. Hynek, Jacchia, Lautman, Schilling, and Sterne, and Mr. Slowey, as well as a number of other scientists. They discussed earth constants and atmospheric constants and considered what values might be adopted for satellite computations. Their views about values for the earth constants were widely divergent, and the participants felt that it would be premature and outside their province to recommend the adoption of one system to be used by all scientists who would be concerned with computing satellite orbits. They did decide, however, that since the U.S. standard atmosphere was based on the most recent observations available and differed greatly from earlier atmospheres, it should serve as the basis in computing satellite drag.

As a second step the Observatory made arrangements with International Business Machines Corporation to use the 704-computer installation at the Massachusetts Institute of Technology. IBM contributed the machine time and agreed to supply one or two programmers for part-time technical assistance, and Dr. John Rossoni was engaged full time on the satellite program.

The computer was to be used to convert satellite observations into what are called the orbital elements, which in turn would serve as a basis for predicting future transits of the satellite and for analyzing atmospheric density and gravitation properties. The orbital elements refer to the size and shape of the elliptical orbit of a satellite in motion around the earth, the orientation of that orbit in space, and the position of the satellite in its orbit at any particular time.

In accordance with the laws of Kepler, an astronomical body orbiting a larger one moves in an ellipse; the apogee is the point in that ellipse farthest from the center of the larger body, the perigee, the point nearest. The first orbital element is the semimajor axis (a) of the ellipse, that is, half the length of the long axis. The second element is the eccentricity (e), which is the degree of "flattening" of the ellipse; it can vary from 0 for a circle to 1 for a parabola.

The orientation of the plane of the orbit is given by the next two elements, the right ascension of the ascending node (Ω) and the inclination (i). The former is the angle between the vernal equinox and the point at which the orbit crosses the Equator in a northerly direction; and the inclination is the angle that the plane of the orbit makes with the plane of the Equator.

The orientation of the orbit in its plane is specified by the fifth element (ω), called the argument of perigee, which is the angle from the ascending node to the perigee point.

The sixth orbital element is the time of perigee passage (T), that is, the moment at which the satellite is at perigee.

If a satellite were orbiting a perfectly spherical body without atmosphere, and if there were no forces such as radiation from the sun or lunar gravity, the orbit would be stationary and conform to Kepler's laws. From three accurate observations of the satellite, it

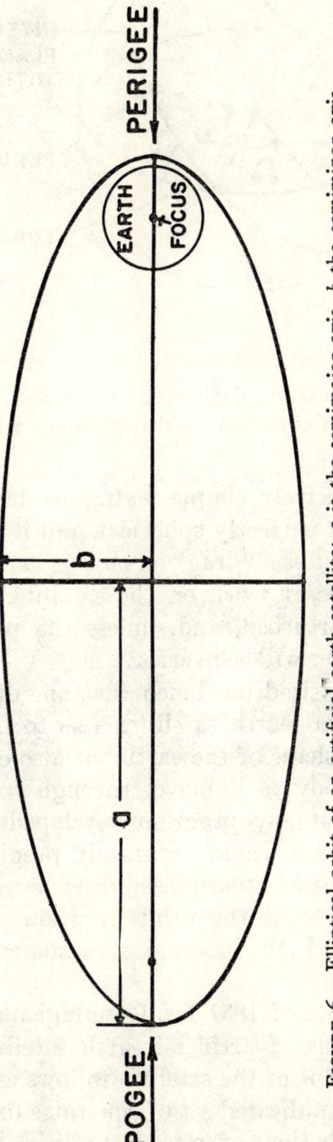

FIGURE 6.—Elliptical orbit of an artificial earth satellite; a is the semimajor axis, b the semiminor axis.

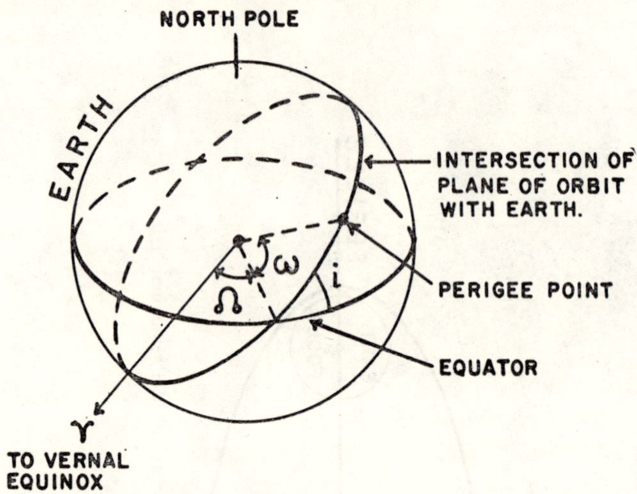

FIGURE 7.—Diagram of angular orbital elements. Ω is the right ascension of the ascending node; ω is the argument of perigee; i is the inclination; γ is the vernal equinox.

would then be a relatively simple matter to define the orbit. The earth, however, is not perfectly spherical, and it is surrounded by an atmosphere that produces a "drag" on objects moving through it; and there are other forces at work on the satellite. Consequently, the satellite's orbit is perturbed, and, unless the perturbations can be anticipated, predictions will be in error.

It cannot be emphasized too much that one of the major reasons for launching artificial earth satellites was to improve our knowledge not only of the shape of the earth but also of these other forces that act upon the body as it moves through space. No one could reasonably expect that any program developed before the launching of the first satellite would accurately predict the orbit. Furthermore, all estimates of atmospheric density were on the low side, with the consequence that the orbit programs worked out before October 4, 1957, used an inaccurate estimate of this important parameter.

During the first part of 1957 Dr. Cunningham continued to work on analytical problems of artificial earth satellites. Since, during one revolution, the orbit of the satellite follows essentially an ellipse, he derived a fairly complicated set of equations to compute the deviations from, or perturbations of, a perfect ellipse. From the practical standpoint of making predictions, the major term in these equations accounts for the rotation of the orbital plane of the ellipse in space.

Cunningham's analytical theory could in principle have been used to calculate predictions of satellite positions or satellite transits.

There was, however, one problem. No one knew what values to insert into the equations for the flatness of the earth; consequently, one could not predict the rate of rotation of the orbital plane.

Using the numerical integration procedures developed by Cunningham, Dr. Lautman worked out a second computer program. This required taking a set of initial conditions, carrying the numerical integration forward step by step to the times at which observations were available, computing the observations that would be seen if the orbit were correct, comparing those with the actual observations, and computing the differences, that is, the residuals. This is done for one estimated orbit and a dozen observations, from which are derived a dozen sets of errors or discrepancies. Then, one by one the elements of the assumed orbit are corrected, and the corrections are applied to the original orbit, new predictions are computed, the predictions are then compared with new observations, and a second set of residuals is determined. A statistical study of this ensemble of residuals leads to an estimate of the "best orbit."

The program developed by Lautman could not be used for making practical day-by-day predictions. First, it required a very good initial guess at the orbit. If the guess were poor, the next guess might be even worse, and impossible predictions would result. Second, the calculations for each improvement of the orbit were very time-consuming on the IBM–704 electronic computer. As much as an hour might be required for each stage of the improvement.

Late in the summer of 1957 the Observatory staff decided that they would probably require a third computer program which would permit the computation of an orbit from three observations. This would be especially needed since the differential correction programs demanded an initial orbit that was fairly accurate. Jack Slowey modified a method developed primarily by Robert Briggs to include the secular variations in the orbital elements due to the earth's bulge. Working closely with John Rossoni of IBM, Slowey and Lautman were debugging the program early in October.

COMMUNICATIONS

In the summer of 1957 Norris D. Pease, a communications consultant, laid out the plans for the communications center at 79 Garden Street, Cambridge. His objective was to provide means of communication between Cambridge and the satellite-tracking stations and the Moonwatch teams and to coordinate these so that there would be rapid transmittal of information. Through this network the communications center could send preliminary orbital data to the Moonwatch teams, the teams could make observations and send determinations of time and position to Cambridge; Cambridge then could prepare predictions of satellite passages over the Baker-Nunn stations and send these data to the stations; and these, in turn, after photographing the satellite, could return the results of their observations to Cambridge.

Specific links of the network were established through the facilities of military agencies and several private communications companies. For each Baker-Nunn camera station, the link had to be worked out on an individual basis. The plans as laid out by Mr. Pease called for completion of the communications center by November 1, at which time the following facilities were to be available:

First, a teletype machine Model 28, linked with the commercial network of the American Telephone & Telegraph Co.; this was to be used primarily for two-way conference calls.

Second, a teletype machine Model 19, also linked with the commercial network of the American Telephone & Telegraph Co., to be used principally for the transmission of messages to domestic sources and for the establishment of outgoing and incoming contact with overseas networks through the American Cable and Radio, Western Union, and RCA.

Third, a Navy teletype machine Model 19, to provide noncommercial contact with all government and military installations on the Military Communications Network, and to serve for the delivery of messages via military installations to various observatories and to Moonwatch leaders throughout the world.

Finally, a Western Union machine to provide commercial linkage with Cambridge and with Boston Western Union offices for transmission of domestic messages.

In August, Charles Peterson, who had formerly served as a communications expert with the U.S. Navy, was appointed supervisor of the communications of the Observatory.

ACCELERATING

The schedule called for the completion of the first camera in South Pasadena by September 30 and full operation of the station at Organ Pass by November 15, 1957. In Cambridge the Moonwatch program was progressing beyond all expectations, and computations and communications were well advanced.

Voices were heard, however, particularly in Washington circles, that the tracking program was behind schedule. There was even the striking suggestion that Project Vanguard was being slowed down because there were no facilities for tracking the satellite once it was in orbit. Meanwhile, an IGY meeting was scheduled for late September and early October in Washington. Dr. Whipple felt it was imperative that the Observatory have a working camera and that star photographs taken with it be available for showing at that meeting, in order to scotch these unfounded rumors. He asked that contracts for the optics and the camera be expedited.

From late August on, one member of the administrative staff and one or two members of the technical staff of the Observatory were assigned to temporary duty at Boller & Chivens and another such group at the Perkin-Elmer Corp. Both plants then scheduled night and weekend shifts. Boller & Chivens subcontracted some of their work to a number of small concerns in the Los Angeles area and acted as an assembler and manager in the final manufacturing process.

By the middle of September Perkin-Elmer completed the first set of optics and the first aspheric-surfaced back-up plate, and these were rushed to South Pasadena.

Meanwhile, Boller & Chivens had continued production of the camera, and a building had been constructed for its testing. Large enough to house six Baker-Nunn cameras at one time, it had a sliding roof over half of it so that the cameras could photograph the sky through an angle of nearly 90°.

The street lights around the Boller & Chivens plant might have interfered with the testing program at night, and although the city fathers could not turn them off, they did paint them out. They also had the branches trimmed off several trees in order to provide a reasonably clear horizon.

During the last week of September the first camera was completely assembled; film was run through it, and adjustments were made so that the camera could handle it properly. A photographic room was set up, and delivery was accepted of several thousand feet of the ID-2 film.

On October 2 the camera was moved out of the factory assembly area into the test building that had just been completed, although the sliding roof had not yet been put in place. That evening and the following morning, members of the Observatory then began to test the camera by photographing the stars. After careful focusing, the final alignment of the optics was only a few thousandths of an inch off from what had been calculated. The staff then decided that certain minor mechanical alterations and adjustments would have to be made, and that these would require that the camera be torn down, some machining done, and the camera put back together again.

The next day was October 4, 1957!

ACKNOWLEDGMENTS

Dr. Fred L. Whipple and Mrs. Lyle G. Boyd provided the opportunity and offered the encouragement for the writing of this little history.

A paper of this sort must be written from primary documents and also from personal reminiscences. For many of the first, I am indebted to E. Stuart Fergusson, who worked his way through many a thick file to find, copy, and annotate important papers. Also, I interviewed on tape 17 men and women who participated in these events. To those now anonymous sources I am most grateful.

The drawings were made by Ed De Matteo.

The Main Lines of Mathematics[1]

By J. L. B. COOPER

University College of South Wales and Monmouthshire

EVERYONE knows some mathematics, yet few persons have an idea of what the subject is about, even in the imprecise way in which they know that physics is about matter or zoology about animals. Most people either confuse mathematics with applied mathematics—and let me explain, to avoid this confusion, that I am using the word mathematics in its strict, and indeed its only logical, interpretation to mean pure mathematics—or think that it is not about anything at all, but it is a farrago of rules of calculation, such as one encounters in elementary arithmetic, a rather distasteful preliminary to really interesting pursuits such as keeping accounts or learning engineering. This attitude develops into and is encouraged by some prevalent theories of mathematics: the word "farrago," indeed, is one that I have borrowed from Wittgenstein. Without doubt these theories have the effect of laying an exclusive emphasis on the most uninteresting parts of mathematics, manipulative techniques and the learning of notation; and one can hardly doubt that they contribute to the mechanistic and rule-of-thumb methods of teaching the subject which are in evidence in so many schools and are complained of in several recent reports on secondary school mathematics.

These theories have behind them the authority of the most fashionable modern school of British philosophy, that of linguistic analysis, and of its predecessor, logical positivism; and with their backing have penetrated all sorts of diverse fields, up to esthetics, literary criticism, and the brains trust. So widely held are they that it would be just to describe them as a folklore about our subject.

The best-known phrase from this folklore or mythology of mathematics is the sentence "Mathematics is a language." This is not, to be exact, a tenet of any philosophical school. It is far too imprecise for that. Even with all the possible twists one can give to the meanings of the words "mathematics," "language," and "is," it is hard to find,

---

[1] Reprinted, with extensive revisions, by permission from The Advancement of Science (London), vol. 17, No. 70, March 1961.

a sense which does not make it either absurd or trivial. Literally, it is certainly absurd. It is characteristic of a language that it has no concepts of its own, that anything said in one language can be translated into another. A statement in English, when expressed in French, is no longer an English statement; but a mathematical statement cannot be made into a nonmathematical statement by any translation, while perfectly good mathematical statements—for instance: "the sum of the angles in a triangle is two right angles," "given any prime number, there is a prime number larger than it"—can be expressed, as here, in perfectly good English, and remain the same when expressed in Russian, Greek, or Japanese as far as mathematical content is concerned. As far as I know, the origin of the phrase is an aphorism of Willard Gibbs, "Mathematics is the language of the Sciences"; but this is a statement about the sciences, not about mathematics, just as the sentence "English is the language of Shakespeare's plays" is not a description of the English language. What it means is that mathematics has a highly developed notation of its own, which is used in the other sciences; and this is clearly true, unless it is misinterpreted into an identification of mathematics with its notation.

The underlying meaning of the phrase "mathematics is a language" is that mathematics has no content of its own. This is expressed with greater precision in positivist and related philosophies by saying that mathematical theories are purely a matter of definition, or consist of a set of tautologies; or, and this comes to much the same thing, that in a mathematical system the truth or falsity of the statements made depends only on the form of the statements, just as the grammatical correctness of an English sentence is determined by the form of the sentence in relation to the rules of syntax; it is this last formulation which links this view with the linguistic theory of mathematics.

To understand the degree of truth, and the errors, in these theories we must consider the structure of a mathematical theory if it is presented in an ideally exact form. Suppose that we have such a theory—say the theory of the integers, or Euclidean geometry, to give examples—set out with the greatest possible precision and rigor. We should find, to begin with, that the theory had a set of words or concepts in terms of which all the other expressions of the theory are defined: for since any concept can be defined only in terms of other concepts, and the process must start somewhere, there must be some terms which are not defined; these we call the undefined terms of the theory. Next we find a set of initial assumptions, or axioms of the theory, which take the form of a set of statements about the undefined terms. The theory itself then follows in the form of a chain of logical arguments proceeding by deduction step by step from the axioms, every step being a statement implied by the axioms and the statements previously proved.

This procedure is not quite exclusive to mathematics. It can be followed equally well in other disciplines, and is sometimes found in works on mathematical physics, in particular in dynamics, though a strict axiomatic procedure in which no assumptions are introduced apart from the axioms which are stated initially is rare outside mathematics. There are, however, two crucial differences between an axiomatic system in mathematics and one, however strictly carried through, in physics. The first is that in mathematical physics some at least of the undefined terms are intended to be names of specific things or relations in the physical world and the second is that the validity of the system depends on the correspondence between the deductions made within the systems—the theorems of the system— and the observed behavior of these physical things. The correspondence may be pretty remote and abstract, in the most developed theories, but it must in some sense be there. In a mathematical theory, on the other hand, the undefined terms need not be the names of specific things, and no observational evidence can, therefore, affect the validity of the theory.

The classical example of a mathematical system is Euclidean geometry. In its traditional form the words used in the system—point, line, distance, and so on—were held to refer to things which exist in the real world or at any rate are approximately copied by real things; and the axioms of the geometry are supposed to be true statements about these real things. They were also supposed to be self-evidently true, with the exception of the axiom of parallels; it was hoped for centuries that it could be shown that to deny the axiom of parallels would lead one to a contradiction with the other axioms, but eventually geometries were constructed in which the axiom of parallels was denied—for example, Lobachevskian geometry, in which the existence of an infinite number of lines through a given point parallel to any given line is asserted. What is more, these systems were proved to be free from contradiction.

Here is one way in which we can prove the consistency, that is, the freedom from contradiction, of Lobachevskian geometry. Draw a circle Γ in the ordinary Euclidean plane. Now we make a miniature dictionary, interpreting words which occur in Lobachevskian geometry by assigning to them meanings in terms of figures inside Γ; for clearness, the words occurring in Lobachevskian geometry will be enclosed in inverted commas to distinguish them from the same words in their normal Euclidean sense.   (See fig. 1.)

"Point" and "line" are to mean, respectively, point inside and part of a line inside Γ. We say that two "lines" are "parallel" if they

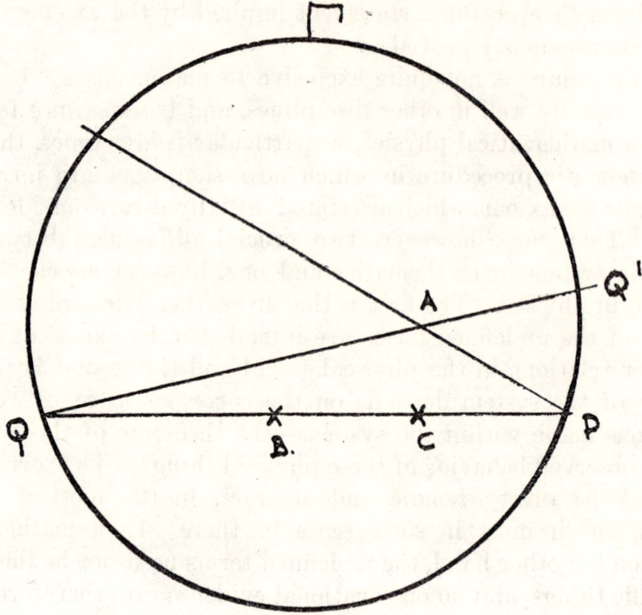

FIGURE 1.

do not meet at any "point" (therefore, if they do not meet inside Γ).
It is clear that if l is any "line" and A is any "point" not on that line,
then there are an infinite number of "lines" through A which are
"parallel" to l; in figure 1 all the "lines" in the sector between AP
and AQ' are "parallel" to l.

So far, we have managed to contradict one of the axioms of Euclidean geometry; but this is not of interest unless we can show that the
other concepts and axioms of Euclidean geometry can be defined and
retain their truth. The difficulties are the definitions of "distance"
and "angle"; these definitions are more technical, and that of "angle"
depends on a knowledge of complex logarithms; but the reader who
does not know about these may be consoled by the remark that it is
not essential that he understand the details of these definitions.

The "distance" between two points B and C is defined as follows:
If BC meets at P and Q, the "distance" from B to C is

$$\text{"}BC\text{"} = \log \frac{PB \cdot QC}{PC \cdot QB}$$

where PB and so on are the ordinary Euclidean (signed) distances.
As C tends to P or Q, its "distance" from B becomes infinite, so that
the "length" of a line is infinite as in ordinary geometry. It is easy
to check that if B, C, D are collinear, then $\text{"}BC\text{"} + \text{"}CD\text{"} = \text{"}BD\text{"}$," so
that these "distances" add in the usual manner. It is possible, though

more difficult, to prove that other Euclidean properties of distance such as that two sides of a triangle are greater than the third side hold.

To understand the definition of "angle," one must know that from any "point" A two imaginary tangents can be drawn to the circle Γ. The slopes of these tangents are complex numbers, say t_1 and t_2; if AX, AY are any two lines through A, with slopes m_1, m_2, then [2]

$$\text{"angle } \angle XAY \text{"} = \frac{1}{2i} \log \frac{(m_1 - t_1)\,(m_2 - t_2)}{(m_1 - t_2)\,(m_2 - t_1)}$$

where

$$i = \sqrt{-1}.$$

Now a geometry as rich in content as that of Euclid can be constructed. Indeed all the theorems of Euclidean geometry which do not need the axiom of parallels are true in it—the celebrated "Pons Asinorum" about isosceles triangles, theorems on congruence of triangles, for instance; but the sum of the angles of a triangle is less than two right angles, Pythagoras's theorem, is false, and there are no similar triangles which are not congruent.

Another model for non-Euclidean geometry—Riemannian geometry this time—can be obtained by considering a sphere S, and letting "point" mean a pair of points on S lying at opposite ends of a diameter, and "line" a great circle (i.e., a circle in which S is cut by a plane through its center). Here again, the theorems of Euclid which do not depend on the axiom of parallels are valid; the reason for choosing pairs of points to mean "point" is that we wish to ensure that any two "points" lie on one and only one "line"; but now there are no "parallel lines" (think of the lines of longitude on the earth, which are great circles and, though apparently parallel at the Equator, meet at the Poles) and the sum of the angles in a triangle is greater than two right angles.

Thus we have found sets of objects constructed in terms of concepts of Euclidean geometry which obey non-Euclidean geometry. A set of objects which obeys the axioms of a mathematical system is called a *model* for that system. We have here models for both Lobachevskian geometry, in which through every point in a plane with a line there is an infinite number of parallels to that line, and for Riemannian geometry, in which there are no parallels to that line.

---

[2] This definition of "angle" may be made clearer by the observation that in ordinary Euclidean geometry, the angle between two lines with slopes m_1 and m_2 is equal to

$$\frac{1}{2i} \log \frac{(m_1 - i)\,(m_2 + i)}{(m_1 + i)\,(m_2 - i)}$$

so that in Euclidean geometry the two tangents to Γ are replaced by the two lines through A of slopes i and $-i$; these are the lines joining A to the circular points at infinity.

The important conclusion we can draw from the existence of a model is that the system does not contain contradictions; that is, it is consistent. It is vital that a mathematical system be consistent; for if one can prove two contradictory statements in any logical system, one can prove any statement whatever, and in an inconsistent system any statement whatever is a theorem, so that the system is possibly useless.

From the point of view which obtained from the time of the Greeks to the 19th century, the validity of Euclidean or non-Euclidean geometry was thought to depend on their truth for points and lines in physical space. From the point of view of modern mathematics, this is a question of physics, not of mathematics; it is a difficult one for physics to settle, because even if non-Euclidean geometry is physically valid its results for small enough figures differ little from those of Euclidean geometry, just as it is impossible by studying a small part of the earth to decide whether the earth is flat or round. Actually the general theory of relativity teaches that non-Euclidean geometry holds in the real world; but this question in no way affects the mathematical status of non-Euclidean geometry, though it certainly gives an added interest to its study. Even without this the study of non-Euclidean geometry would not be an idle game; for instance, Lobachevskian geometry has important applications in the theory of functions of a complex variable. Validity of a mathematical system in the modern sense is a question of its consistency; if a geometrical system is consistent, it is a worthwhile object of mathematical study, and, experience has shown, it generally has application in subjects where the "points" of the geometry may be entities far removed in their nature from our intuitive idea of the points of space.

Our proof that non-Euclidean geometry is consistent uses models based on Euclidean geometry and therefore assumes implicitly that Euclidean geometry is consistent. We can go on to construct a model for Euclidean geometry in which the word "point" is interpreted to mean an ordered pair (or, in the case of three-dimensional geometry, an ordered trio) of real numbers; this gives a proof of the consistency of Euclidean geometry, but it assumes the consistency of the theory of the real numbers. For the real numbers, again, models exist: the most familiar is that in which a real number is taken to be an infinite decimal, that is, a sequence of integers. Thus one can construct models for the real numbers in terms of the integers and the theory of sets.

Frege and Russell and the school of mathematical logicians which followed them aimed to go still further, and to eliminate the integers as independent concepts by defining them in terms of sets. Thus one can define "one" to be the set of all sets having only a single number, "two" to be the set of all pairs, and so on; the apparent circularity is easily avoided. This important construction provides us with a way of giving a model for any part of mathematics in terms of concepts derived solely from set theory.

This process was called by Frege and Russell the reduction of mathematics to logic: but this is rather misleading, for what they meant by logic was set theory, which is vastly different from traditional logic. What the construction gives us is a proof of the consistency of mathematics depending only on the assumption that set theory is consistent: and if set theory were identical with logic in the traditional meaning of the word, its consistency would not be open to reasonable doubt. Unfortunately, hardly had the new theory of sets been established before serious antinomies were discovered arising from the arguments used in it; and even apart from these antinomies some mathematicians considered certain arguments of set theory to be suspect. These difficulties have not yet been overcome. Certainly, axiom systems for set theory have been constructed which avoid all the known antinomies and do not appear to contain any new ones; but we have no proof that these axiom systems are self-consistent, and there is strong reason to believe that we can never have such a proof.

Let us now assess the degree of truth in the theories that mathematics consists of tautologies or that it is solely a matter of definition. These theories are frequently coupled, though they are in fact distinct. They will be found, for example, in Ayer's *Language, Truth and Logic*, where they are supported by the picturesque, if scarcely verifiable, statement that "A being whose intellect was infinitely powerful would take no interest in logic or mathematics. For he would be able to see at a glance everything that his definitions implied, and, accordingly, could never learn anything from logical inference which he was not fully conscious of already." This couples the definition theory of mathematics with the theory that, within a given set of definitions—and axioms are regarded here as definitions—the truth or falsehood of any statement can be decided by a purely mechanical process—say, that a computer could be built which, on having fed to it the axioms of mathematics, could settle the truth of any theorem, given enough time; for a computer with indefinite time is the nearest we can get in this world to Ayer's being with infinite intelligence; and, if his philosophy needs divine help to save it, we are not better off in the next world, if theology is correct in holding that divine omniscience extends to the physical world as well as to mathematics.

The tautology theory of mathematics is essentially a result of generalization from two special cases. It is based, first, on the obvious fact that it is true of elementary arithmetic; the truth of an arithmetical calculation, however complicated, can be checked by a purely mechanical decision process. Second, it is based on the fact that the same is true for elementary logic, the propositional calculus. Any of the theorems of this calculus, which is to be found, for example, at the beginning of *Principia Mathematica*, can be checked by a purely mechanical process. It was this which led Wittgenstein to put forward the tautology theory of mathematics; for he accepted Russell's claim to have reduced mathematics to logic, and equated logic with the elementary propositional calculus. However, it has been proved that no mechanical decision process is possible even for the whole of mathematical logic, let alone for all of mathematics. The tautology theory should, therefore, be regarded as one which applies to some relatively trivial parts of mathematics, but not to the more interesting parts and certainly not to the whole subject.

The definition theory has more truth to it; indeed, it has a validity for any section of mathematics. It is quite correct to say that the undefined terms in any mathematical system have the properties assumed in the axioms as a matter of definition, and that any theorems of the system are true as a result of these definitions. A statement about points, lines, and so on which is valid if these things occur in a model for Euclidean geometry may be false for a model of a non-Euclidean geometry.

However, it would be just as true to say that the formulae of chemistry are a matter of definition; for if we assigned the names of the elements in a different way we would get quite different chemical formulae. Nevertheless, a statement that chemistry is a matter of definition would ignore the fact that however the names are jumbled, for a chemical system to be valid there must be some way of assigning elements to the names which makes the formulae correct; to make the analogy clear, there must be some assignment of elements to names of elements which makes the actual behavior of matter a model for the chemical system. In the same way, the assertion that mathematics is purely a matter of definition ignores the problem of the validity of mathematical systems. For particular systems, this validity can be established within mathematics, by constructing models for a given system in terms of another axiom system—say geometry in terms of the real numbers; but eventually we must come to a primary system of axioms, and if we are to have any sort of guarantee of validity for this it must be found outside mathematics.

What sort of guarantee can we have? This is a very difficult question, and it would be wrong to suggest that mathematics must be tied down to, or that it does imply, any one answer. Certainly there can be no absolute guarantee of the consistency of mathematics: any science is liable to error, and the progress of mathematics in the future may reveal unsuspected inconsistencies, as it has done in the past. However, this does not allow us to dismiss the whole problem of consistency;

to do so would be to treat mathematics as a sort of game, like a chemical system with any random combination of elements allowed: and it would make the possibility of applying mathematics an insoluble problem. We cannot take the subject seriously without a conviction that any contradictions there may be are peripheral and remediable. Such a conviction cannot, again, be based solely on an appeal to empirical experience, since, for example, mathematics deals with sets of indefinitely large magnitude and with infinite sets, and these cannot, as such, be part of empirical experience. It is because of this that empiricist philosophers try to explain mathematics away, in the ways I have described. I do not wish to involve myself in metaphysical knots; but it seems reasonable to say that the source of our convictions about mathematics must arise from a correspondence between the terms of mathematical theories and some of the things which our minds either bring to or find in our experience of the external world, or create by generalization, abstraction, and extrapolation beyond experience. I shall leave this thorny subject and go on to discuss what it is that mathematics deals with.

The subject of any mathematical theory is a *mathematical structure;* and by a mathematical structure I mean a set of objects for which some defined relations exist between its elements, or between sets of its elements or even between sets of sets of elements.

Most of the mathematical structures we encounter are complex, in the sense that they are combinations of structures with fewer relations. Complex structures can be seen as being built up out of elementary structures: I am using the word elementary in the sense of logically simple, not the pedagogic sense. There are two main types of elementary structure in mathematics, which between them appear to cover all the cases which arise in modern mathematics:

(1) *Algebraic structures*, in which the defined relations are between finite numbers of elements.

(2) *Topological structures*, in which the relations are between pairs of sets, or between individual elements and sets, or between individual elements and sets of sets.

I can best show what this means by first taking a familiar complex structure, the real numbers, and explaining the elementary structures which it involves. The real numbers have three elementary algebraic structures:

(1) The structure of addition: three numbers a, b, c may be related by the rule $a+b=c$.

(2) The structure of multiplication: three numbers may be related by $ab=c$.

(3) The structure of order: two numbers a, b may be related by $a>b$.

The structures are linked by a variety of laws: thus

A. $\quad a+b=b+a \qquad a+(b+c)=(a+b)+c$

$\qquad ab=ba \qquad\qquad a(bc)=(ab)c$

$\quad a(b+c)=ab+ac$

There is an element 0, such that $a+0=a$ for all a. For any a there is an element $-a$, such that $a+(-a)=0$.

B. There is an element 1 such that $a.1=a$ for all a.

C. For each $a=0$ there is an element b such that $ab=1$.

In addition, the real numbers have a topological structure, which is what is involved whenever we talk about such matters as limits, convergence and so on. The typical relationship which describes the topology of the real numbers is that of neighborhood:

A neighborhood of a real number a is any set which includes an interval with a as midpoint.

If we consider geometry, again, we are once more dealing with a complex structure. The structures involved in geometry are mostly algebraic: they involve finite sets of objects, in relations such as incidence—a point being on a plane, a plane passing through a line. It is only when we come to consider differential properties—tangency, curvature of curves and surfaces—that topological structures are brought in.

The characteristic differences between classical mathematics—say that of a century ago—and that of modern mathematics is that classical mathematics dealt preeminently with complex structures, modern mathematics with less complex ones.

The reason for this is very practical. If we discuss a complex structure that structure may be so tightly specified by the numerous relations which define it that, roughly speaking, only one example of the structure exists: or, to be more exact, if we have two sets of objects which both have that structure, then they are exact pictures of one another, as one Euclidean plane is an exact picture of the other: the objects in the two sets can be made to correspond univocally so that all the relations are transferred by the correspondence. For instance, anything which obeys the sets of laws A, B, C, and in addition has the order structure of the real numbers is an exact picture, in this sense, of the real numbers. On the other hand, a less complex structure may have as examples vastly different things. Thus, any set of objects which obeys the laws A and B is called a commutative ring with unit. Any deductions we make which are based exclusively on A and B will hold for any such ring. Now, the polynomials form such a ring: so do the functions of a real variable; and consequently if we restrict ourselves to the axioms for a ring, our conclusions will be valid for a wide variety of mathematical objects, whereas conclusions based on the entire set of axioms for the real numbers cannot be guaranteed to hold for any structures other than the real numbers.

An effect of this tendency to deal with structures which, because they are simpler in the logical sense, are therefore less narrowly defined, is that some important mathematical terms have come to have their meanings extended from the original sphere of reference to cover things having some structure in common with the original notion. A good example is the word "space." The use of this word has been extended to any set of elements which shares the algebraic properties of displacements in Euclidean space—namely, the possibility of being added together and of being multiplied by a number; this gives us the notion of a vector space. On the other hand, the word is used for any set of objects with a topological structure. These two ideas combine very fruitfully in the theory of topological vector spaces, and, more specifically, the theory of linear function spaces. By these are meant sets of functions: the "points" of the space are functions, $f(x)$, $g(x)$, of some variable x; functions can be added or multiplied by numbers to give other functions. Moreover, we can define the distance between functions, in various ways: for instance we might take the "distance" from $f(x)$ to $g(x)$ to be the maximum value of $|f(x)-g(x)|$ if we are dealing with continuous functions. Alternatively, we can define it, for the same, or a wider space of functions, by

$$\text{"distance from } f(x) \text{ to } g(x)\text{"} = \{\textstyle\int |f(x)-g(x)|^2 dx\}^{\frac{1}{2}}$$

A space of functions with this last definition of distance has properties very similar to those of Euclidean space; it differs in having an infinite number of dimensions, but properties like the theorems on parallels, on the sum of the angles of a triangle, Pythagoras's theorem, are as in ordinary Euclidean space; we can for instance say that two functions are "perpendicular" to one another if $\int f(x)\, g(x)\, dx = 0$.

We can transfer notions derived from Euclidean spaces to these spaces; and this has proved helpful in a number of problems both of pure mathematics and of mathematical physics. For example, when we are considering a vibrating system, such as a stretched string or a bell, the possible forms of displacement of the system are "points" in a function space, in which the "distance" above is connected with the energy of the displacement. The mechanical properties of the system enable us to define a sort of "ellipsoid" in this space; and the principal axes of the "ellipsoid" are connected with the pure, simple harmonic vibrations of the mechanical system.

The method of transferring ideas from the examples of mathematical structures which we encounter in ordinary mathematical experience to more general examples of these structures is both fruitful and dangerous—dangerous because we may be misled by arguments based solely on analogy. It is therefore necessary to make sure that our arguments are based solely on our axioms, and that we do not introduce tacitly assumptions brought over from Euclidean space. Rigor of argument is therefore highly important in this sort of mathematics; its role is to ensure that anything which we assert to follow from the axioms of a structure holds for all structures obeying those axioms and not merely for those familiar to our intuition.

I would like to illustrate the variety of things which can share a mathematical structure by discussing the example of a Boolean ring. Now a ring means any set of objects which obeys the axioms A, B. A Boolean ring is one which in addition satisfies the axioms:

$$a+a=0, \qquad a^2=a, \text{ for all elements } a$$

The simplest structure which obeys the laws of a Boolean ring consists of just two objects, 0 and 1, with the usual law of multiplication and the usual law of addition save that $1+1=0$. An example of such a ring is got by taking 0 to mean the set of all even numbers, 1 to mean the set of all odd numbers: then $1+1=0$ means that the sum of any two odd numbers is even. More complicated examples are:

(1) *Propositional logic.*—The symbols of the algebra stand for propositions, that is statements which are either true or false. If a is a proposition, $a=0$ means that a is false, $a=1$ that a is true. If a and b are two propositions, ab is the proposition which says that both a and b are true, $a+b$ says that one but not both of $a+b$ are true. Then $1+a$ says that a is false: for 1 is true, and not both of 1 and a are true. $a+a$ is always false: for either, neither, or both of a and a are true; aa is the same as a. We have then, $a+a=0$, $a^2=a$; and the other axioms of ring theory can be verified relatively easily.

(2) *Subsets of a set.*—The symbols of the algebra stand for subsets of a set, which is denoted by 1; 0 stands for the empty set. If a and b are two sets, ab is the set of objects common to a and b, $a+b$ the set of objects lying in just one of a,b. Again it is easy to verify the axioms.

(3) *Electrical switching circuits.*—The symbols of the algebra stand for electrical circuits which involve switches. $a=0$ means that the circuit a is always broken, $a=1$ that it is always connected. If two circuits are so arranged that they are always made or broken together, they are denoted by the same symbol; if the one is always made when the other is broken, one is denoted by a symbol a, say the other by $1+a$. If a and b are two circuits in series, the circuit they form together is denoted by ab; if they are in parallel, the joint circuit is $a+b+ab$. The laws of Boolean algebra are obeyed; and the symbols for a circuit give a means of working out how the circuit behaves.

To sum up: The role of mathematics is to discover and investigate structures which arise in our theoretical treatment of physical experience and in mathematics itself. Mathematical training should be directed to building up an ability to form an intuitive grasp of such structures—intuitions of geometric space, of number, of algebraic relations, and so on; the mechanical side of mathematics, the purely linguistic side, that is the ability to read notation, are important, but should not be stressed at the expense of understanding.

Reprints of the various articles in this Report may be obtained, as long as the supply lasts, on request addressed to the Editorial and Publications Division, Smithsonian Institution, Washington 25, D.C.

Early Experiments in Instrument Flying [1]

By James H. Doolittle, Lt. Gen., USAF (Ret.)

Chairman, Space Technology Laboratories, Inc.

[With 2 plates]

The development of flight has been a gradual evolutionary process. There are, however, certain landmarks along the route, and we may consider that there are roughly defined areas of progress between these landmarks.

In the very early days of flying, a slight breeze could cancel or delay a flight. I recall seeing my first air show in the winter of 1909–10 at Dominquez Field near Los Angeles. In those early days it was customary for a pilot to wet his finger in his mouth and hold it up. If there was enough air movement to cause uneven evaporation, thus making one side cooler than the other, then there was too much wind to fly. Soon, however, a modest wind was not a deterrent to flight, and a good breeze was considered desirable because it shortened takeoff and landing distance.

Next came the period when a pilot was happy only as long as he could see the horizon. He might fly in or through clouds, but he wanted clear air and a visible horizon when he came back through them.

This paper will deal with the next era, at the end of which a visible horizon was not required and during which it became possible to fly, and even land, without seeing outside an instrumented cockpit. Today aircraft fly safely and reliably in all but the most inclement weather, and I look forward to the not very distant future when the airplane— or its successor—will fly absolutely regardless of weather and will then become not only the fastest, but the most reliable form of transportation.

---

[1] The third Lester Gardner lecture given at the Massachusetts Institute of Technology, Apr. 28, 1961; somewhat modified for publication. A repeat of the lecture was given at the Smithsonian Institution on Sept. 28, 1961, by permission of the Massachusetts Institute of Technology.

BEGINNINGS OF INSTRUMENT FLYING

Whenever pilots got together for meditation and discussion in the immediate post-World War I era, the subject of "flying instinct" or flying "by the seat of the pants" was likely to come up. Views were divided. Some pilots believed that they could fly indefinitely without reference to the visible horizon—because they had done so. Others agreed that they had but claimed it was the inherent stability of their aircraft which made it possible and not pilot skill.

In the early twenties the navigational instruments most commonly used were the magnetic compass, the altimeter, and the airspeed indicator. It was customary on cross-country flights to follow railroads, or less frequently, highways, and the maps generally used were the standard Rand McNally maps of the individual States. These State maps were each about the same size and so, unfortunately, were usually not to the same scale.

The personal experiences in the pages that follow are related to illustrate conditions which affected all fliers of the era. On September 4–5, 1922, I flew a DH–4 airplane, in which additional gasoline and oil tanks had been installed, from Pablo Beach, Fla., to Rockwell Field at San Diego, Calif., with one intermediate stop for fuel at Kelly Field, San Antonio, Tex. The elapsed time was 22 hours 35 minutes. It was the first time the North American Continent had been crossed in less than 24 hours.

It was also the first airplane in which I had used a bank-and-turn indicator. To obtain the instrument it was necessary to go to the Army Air Service Engineering Base at old McCook Field in Dayton, Ohio, and "promote" an experimental model through the help of cooperative technical friends. This instrument, invented in 1917 by Elmer Sperry, Sr., built by Elmer Sperry, Jr., and first flight-tested by Lawrence Sperry with Elmer, Jr., as passenger, was not yet in common usage or generally available.

I took off just after dark, having chosen a moonlight night to facilitate night flying, but about 4 hours out I ran into solid overcast and then severe thunderstorms. For a while the lightning flashes were almost constant and, in the otherwise black night, so intense as to light up the ground clearly for a considerable area. Some flashes were so close that their familiar ozone odor could be detected, but although it seemed that one could reach out and touch them, none struck the plane.

The air was extremely turbulent and the airplane was violently thrown about its axes as well as up and down and, despite its excellent stability characteristics, was held on a relatively even keel only with great concentration and effort. After the lightning died away, the turbulence appeared to intensify, and there was about an hour in the jetblack darkness when no ground reference point could be seen and it would have been quite impossible to maintain proper attitude and course without the blessed bank and turn indicator. Although I had been flying for almost 5 years "by the seat of my pants" and considered that I had achieved some skill at it, this particular flight made me a firm believer in proper instrumentation for bad weather flying.

In 1925 I wrote a thesis at the Massachusetts Institute of Technology for a doctor of science degree in aeronautics. At first I had hoped to study, through carefully controlled flight tests, the possibility—or impossibility—of a specially trained pilot orienting himself without flight instruments and determining certain phenomena, such as wind direction, without reference to a visible horizon or point on the ground. But this subject was not sufficiently abstract for the doctorate and was changed to an analysis of "The Effect of the Wind-Velocity Gradient," employing flight tests, wind tunnel data, and mathematical analyses. The thesis begins:

There has long been an uncertainty in the minds of aviators regarding the effect of the wind on the flying qualities of an airplane. Some pilots claim that it is much easier to turn into the wind than with it, and that at any altitude they can tell the wind direction by the feel of the ship in a turn, and this even though in a dense cloud which would preclude the possibility of obtaining their relative motion from any stationary object.

Other pilots maintain that, regardless of the wind velocity or the proximity of the ground, there is no difference in the feel of the plane when turning into the wind and when turning with it. They claim that any apparent difference is due wholly to the psychological effect on the pilot, resulting from the difference in groundspeed in the two cases, and if there is any difference in the ship's performance, from a time-altitude standpoint, it is because the pilot handled the controls differently. In other words, if the pilot were blindfolded he could not tell the wind direction when turning, and a turn made into the wind would be identical with a turn made with the wind. This is, of course, considering the turn in relation to the medium in which it is being executed and not in relation to the curves traced out on the ground.

There is a similar difference of opinion regarding the effect of a strong wind on the rate of climb. Experienced pilots are about evenly divided, half feeling that a plane climbs better into the wind, and the other half feeling that the wind makes absolutely no difference.

Seven of the leading pilots of the day were questioned regarding the effect of wind on flying performance. The answers given were far from consistent, as might be expected from such a group of individualists. There was, therefore, still considerable confusion—and controversy—among the experts.

The conclusions from the thesis, somewhat oversimplified, were that in airplane flight—

1. There is no measurable effect in level flight, at altitude, due to wind direction as long as the wind is steady.

2. There is no effect on climb due to wind except very near the ground, and there the wind-velocity gradient increases the rate of climb slightly when flying into the wind and decreases it slightly when flying with the wind.

3. A steady wind has no effect on turning except very near the ground, when the wind-velocity gradient causes a slight tendency to settle when turning away from a headwind and a slight tendency to climb when turning into it. This is most noticeable in strong winds and when flying at a large angle of attack or at minimum power.

Summing up: A steady wind exercises no measurable effect on airplane performance at altitude—except, of course, on groundspeed and direction of flight. Very near the ground, however, the effect of wind-velocity gradient can be serious, particularly in the case of a heavily loaded airplane. The danger is increased by a strong tendency on the part of the pilot to pull the nose up or in beyond the most efficient angle of attack. This increases any tendency to settle and may even cause the airplane to stall and spin in.

In the early and middle 1920's the Jones-Bárány revolving chair test was given to all military pilots as a part of their periodic physical examination for flying. Normally this test was given with the pilot's eyes open, and the flight surgeon looked for variations in times and amount of the rhythmic side-to-side movement of the eyes called nystagmus.

In early 1926, Capt.—later Col.—David A. Myers, an outstanding Air Corps flight surgeon, decided to augment the routine test by giving an additional test consisting of several rotations of the chair with the pilot's eyes closed. After the rate of rotation became steady, a normal pilot, with eyes closed, could not tell which way he was turning. If the rate of rotation was slowed down and stabilized at a somewhat lower speed, the pilot thought the rotation had been stopped, and when the rotation actually was stopped he thought he was turning in the opposite direction.

The explanation is that man normally maintains his equilibrium by sight, touch, hearing, muscle, and vestibular sense. Touch and hearing are not important in flight orientation. By using the three remaining senses he can usually ascertain and maintain his position, accurately sense the rate and direction of his motion, and generally orient himself with relation to the earth. Sight is by far the most reliable of these three senses, and when sight is lost, we must get our sense of balance and motion from the muscles and from the fluid movement sensors in the vestibular canals. If an individual is merely displaced, the fluid motions return to zero very rapidly, but if one is rotated, it may take from 5 to 25 seconds for the fluid motions to stop. During this period an individual can experience a false sense of motion called vertigo. This, of course, explains why early-day pilots flying in dense fog or clouds frequently become confused and occasionally spun in and crashed.

Capt.—later Col.—William C. Ocker, an early and extremely competent Army Air Corps pilot and flight researcher, had long been interested in instrument flying and in 1918 had tested the then new bank-and-turn indicator. In mid-1926 he took Captain Myers' new "blindfold test." His first reaction was that Captain Myers had played a trick on him or, if not, that his senses had failed him. After further consideration he decided that here was proof positive that no normal pilot could consistently fly "blind" without instruments.

Ocker, who had had considerable experience flying with the bank-and-turn indicator—he frequently carried one, a quickly attachable unit complete with venturi, in his flight baggage—believed this instrument could correct the pilot's faulty senses. He designed a lightproof "black box" which contained a bank-and-turn indicator and a magnetic compass. This box was mounted on the front of the Jones-Bárány chair. The pilot sealed his face against the opening in the box and observed the bank-and-turn indicator and compass. With this piece of equipment he could correctly identify the direction and rate of his rotation. After the rotation stopped and the compass settled down, he could then determine heading.

Myers and Ocker continued their experiments, and the arrangement of black box and revolving chair were patented and subsequently used in the training of pilots. Later some pilots were to learn to fly by instruments alone before they learned to fly under normal visual conditions.

In the late 1920's and early 1930's, Captain Ocker and 1st Lt.—later Col.—Carl J. Crane collaborated in the study of instrument flying techniques and developed, among other things, a unitary arrangement of instruments which would give the pilot a maximum of useful information with a minimum of effort and fatigue. They referred to this as a "Flight Integrator."

In 1932 Major Ocker and Lieutenant Crane wrote, and the Naylor Printing Co. published, a book entitled: "Blind Flight in Theory and Practice." This book gave an excellent analysis of the problems inherent in instrument flying and their solution. It was for many years the standard reference book on instrument flying.

DANIEL GUGGENHEIM FUND FOR THE PROMOTION OF AERONAUTICS

Daniel Guggenheim was one of the great industrialists, philanthropists, and citizens of the 20th century. He was interested in everything that could lead to a fuller life and a better world. One of his many great contributions was the Daniel Guggenheim Fund for the Promotion of Aeronautics. It was established for the purpose of promoting the advance of the art, science, and business of aviation. It proved to be a very effective medium in the accomplishment of that purpose.

The fund was established in January 1926 with a grant of $2,500,-000; although $500,000 had been given the previous year to New York University for the purpose of starting aeronautical education. The fund, in cooperation with the Government, was to be administered by a board of trustees composed of men of "eminence and competence." Harry Guggenheim, gifted son of Daniel and a World War I naval aviator, was chosen president of the fund. In the initial stages of its organization, Rear Adm. H. I. Cone, an outstanding naval officer, was vice president; he was succeeded by Capt.—later Vice Adm.— Emory S. Land of the Construction Corps of the U.S. Navy, who served until the fund's work was completed. The strength of character, sound judgment, organizational ability, understanding, and capacity for cooperation of Harry Guggenheim and Capt. "Jerry" Land were, in large part, the cement which held the fund together, enabled it to function efficiently, and made possible its considerable contributions.

The general purposes of the fund were defined as follows:

1. To promote aeronautical education both in institutions of learning and among the general public.

2. To assist in the extension of fundamental aeronautical science.

3. To assist in the development of commercial aircraft and aircraft equipment.

4. To further the application of aircraft to business, industry, and other economic and social activities of the Nation.

The basic concept of the fund was "to maintain a simple, inexpensive directing organization depending on established outside agencies, whenever possible, to carry out the aims of the fund." It was to be a primer—a sparkplug—to stimulate interest and promote action.

From the first it was understood that flight safety and reliability were important considerations and that one phase of the fund's work might certainly be to study means of assuring safe and reliable flight despite weather conditions. With this in mind, a special committee of experts was organized to define the problem and a directive was prepared which authorized study regarding—

1. The dissipation of fog.

2. The development of means whereby flying fields may be located from the air regardless of fog.

3. The development of instruments to show accurately the height of airplanes above the ground, to replace barometric instruments now in general use showing height above sea level.

Consolidated NY–2 airplane with the author standing beside the rear cockpit which was hooded for the "first complete instrument flight." Lt. Ben Kelsey rode in the front open cockpit but did not touch the controls. September 24, 1929.

The author in the cockpit of the Consolidated NY–2 airplane which he used in making the first complete flight, from takeoff to landing, entirely by the use of instruments, September 24, 1939. Inset shows the two instruments, then in experimental stage, used on the flight. These instruments are now standard equipment on all airplanes, for "blind flying."

4. Improvement and perfection of instruments allowing airplanes to fly properly in fog.

5. Penetration of fog by light rays.

To assist in carrying out pertinent parts of this directive the directors of the fund decided in 1928 to establish a Full Flight Laboratory at Mitchel Field, Long Island, N.Y., with all necessary facilities and equipment. In August 1928 I was borrowed from the Army Air Corps to head this laboratory. Prof. William G. Brown of the Aeronautics Department of the Massachusetts Institute of Technology joined us as technical assistant in February 1929. Professor Brown worked with the fund's Full Flight Laboratory from then until it was dissolved at the end of 1929. His technical knowledge and unbounded enthusiasm provided a constant help and inspiration.

This was a most interesting period in my life. The good book says, "No man can serve two masters for . . . he will hold to one and despise the other." I had three: An Army boss, Lt. Col.—later Maj. Gen.—Conger Pratt, commanding officer of Mitchel Field where I was stationed; Capt.—later Vice Adm.—Land, of the Navy; and Mr. Guggenheim, a civilian. They were all such fine, understanding, and cooperative people that my existence, instead of being complex, was uncomplicated and extremely pleasant.

DEVELOPMENT OF BLIND-FLYING INSTRUMENTATION

Our first activity in the Full Flight Laboratory was to study and endeavor to analyze the work previously done on blind landing in fog.

In England tethered balloons had been lined up with the landing field and used with some success in still air and when the fog was not thick. This concept was abandoned at once as not satisfactory, for experience had indicated that the fog layer might be very thick and that still air could not be depended upon at all times when visibility was restricted—for example, in a blizzard.

In both England and France the lead-in-cable idea was tried out. In this system an electrified cable circled the field and led in to a landing. It required very sensitive sensing equipment in the airplane, and it was necessary to make a precision turn into the field at low altitude. This turn presented considerable difficulty. Lt. LeRoy Wolf of the Army Air Corps also experimented with the electrified cable concept at Wright Field. The U.S. Navy had some success with an electromagnetic cable guide at Lakehurst Naval Air Station.

The low-frequency radio range had been developed by the Bureau of Standards and the Army, and was in limited use for aerial navigation. An adaptation of this radio range in the form of a radio homing beacon seemed to offer the greatest promise for our use. It could also be readily tied in with the radio receiver and other conventional airborne equipment.

Actual blind landings had been attempted with dragging weights and with long tail skids. These either gave an indication upon touching the ground or were rigged to actuate the aircraft control. Additional background information was available, but the material outlined above was fairly representative.

The first important expenditure made by the Full Flight Laboratory was for two modern airplanes. One, a Consolidated NY–2 military training plane mounting a J–5 engine, was to be used in the instrument-landing experiments and to test instruments, equipment, or devices that might be helpful in overcoming fog flying problems. It had the large wings used by the Navy for pontoon seaplane training, but mounted, in place of the pontoons, a specially reinforced landing gear with long oleo action. As a training plane it had a very high factor of safety, was extremely rugged, and was inherently stable about all three axes. Special flying and landing wires permitted the rigging in of additional dihedral. The acceptance test flight on this airplane was made on November 3, 1928, at the factory near Buffalo, and the airplane was flown to Mitchel Field the next day. It was flown considerably in November and December and then delivered to the Radio Frequency Laboratories in Boonton, N.J., to have voice radio installed. It was at Boonton for 4 weeks this first time and frequently thereafter.

The second airplane was a Navy-type Vought Corsair 02U–1 mounting a Pratt & Whitney Wasp engine. It was to be used for cross-country practice flying and was an excellent airplane for the purpose. It was a fast, good-flying airplane, but not as rugged and stable as the NY–2. The 02U–1 was delivered to the fund on November 21, 1928, and the first cross-country flight—to Boston, with Harry Guggenheim as passenger—was made on the same day.

The Army Air Corps made a hangar available at Mitchel Field for the use of the Full Flight Laboratory. It was initially provided for the safe airplane competition, another important contribution to the fund. The Army also provided the full-time services of an excellent mechanic to maintain the laboratory's aircraft. This was Cpl.—later Sgt.—Jack Dalton. The continued excellent mechanical condition of the two aircraft thereafter was largely the result of his competence and devotion.

Lt.—later Brig. Gen.—B. S. Kelsey was made available by the Army Air Corps as flight assistant and safety pilot. When flights were made under the hood it was necessary, in the interest of safety, to have another pilot in the airplane to look out for other aircraft and also to make sure that the pilot under the hood did not get into difficulty because of possible instrument or equipment failure. Lieutenant Kelsey, from the start, was a full-fledged member of the team and did much of the experimental work. His piloting help, criticism of tests carried out, sound technical counsel, and ever-pleasant personality contributed greatly to the results achieved.

As the preliminary practice flights progressed, it soon became apparent that even with the very stable and sturdy NY–2, the available instruments were not adequate. For determining heading when maneuvering and when landing, the compass, owing to the northerly turning error, was entirely unsatisfactory, and the bank-and-turn indicator, though excellent for its purpose, was more a qualitative than a quantitative measuring instrument. Also, at the moment of touchdown in a blind landing, it was very desirable that the wings be level with the ground. This was not easy to assure, particularly when the wind was gusty. An accurate, reliable, and easy-to-read instrument showing exact direction of heading and precise attitude of the aircraft was required, particularly for the initial and final stages of blind landings. Two German artificial-horizon instruments, the Anschutz and the Gyrorector, were studied but were not deemed entirely satisfactory.

I sketched a rough picture of the dial for an instrument which I thought would do the job and showed it to Elmer Sperry, Sr., a great engineer and inventor who had established and headed the Sperry Gyroscope Co. and who was very much interested in aviation. It was, in substance, the face of a directional gyro superimposed on an artificial horizon. He advised that a single gyroscopic instrument could be designed to meet the requirements, but recommended, for simplicity of construction, two separate instruments. I agreed, and he then assigned his very ingenious son, Elmer, Jr., to work with us and to be responsible for the design and fabrication of the two instruments. We could not have had a better colleague. Elmer, also, soon became a member of the team and spent as much time at the hangar and at the evening "discussion" sessions in our quarters on Mitchel Field as the rest of us. These evening sessions were frequent and long. The wives joined their husbands and helped in the work. Out of this, as you know, came the Sperry Artificial Horizon and the Sperry Directional Gyroscope which still, with their descendants, are on the instrument panel of every airliner and military airplane today.

As time passed, literally hundreds of blind and simulated blind landings were made. To make a landing, the airplane was put in a glide at 60 m.p.h., with some power on, and flown directly into the ground. Although this was about 15 m.p.h. above stalling speed, the landing gear absorbed the shock of landing and if the angle of glide was just right the airplane did not even bounce. Actually, after a while, it was possible to make consistently perfect landings by this method. To assure just the right amount of power in the glide, a mark was made at the proper place on the throttle quadrant.

Excellent cooperation was obtained from every organization and individual with whom we worked. Among them were the Pioneer Instrument Co., the Radio Corp. of America, and the Bell Telephone Laboratories, which installed the modern radio transmitter and provided miniature earphones with molded plugs. Along with the other BTL personnel, Capt. Luff Meridith and Capt. Ray Books, recently retired from the Army Air Corps, were very helpful. At the Aircraft Radio Corp. of Radio Frequency Laboratories, which installed the excellent radio receiver, Dr. L. M. Hull, the president; Drs. A. W. Parkes, F. H. Drake, and all members of the staff were most cooperative. Assistance was also rendered by the Kollsman Instrument Co., the Sperry Gyroscope Co., and many other industrial concerns, scientists, engineers, and inventors. Very valuable support was received from the Bureau of Standards, whose experts designed and installed most of the ground and airborne radio navigation equipment. Dr. Harry Diamond, of the Bureau, and his associates spent much time with us and could not have been more cooperative.

While aural signals were satisfactory for rough aerial navigation, it soon became apparent that a visual indicator would be much better for the precise directional control required in blind landings. To meet this requirement, the Bureau of Standards, working with the Airways and Radio Division of the Department of Commerce, designed a 2-kw. semiportable two-leg range, which was used as a homing beacon, and a fan-type marker beacon. The homing range was installed on the west side of Mitchel Field. The marker beacon sat on the leg of the homing range and was located on the east side of the field.

The indicator for the homing range, carried in the airplane, was a pair of juxtaposed vibrating reeds. If the plane was to the right of the course, the right reed vibrated through the greater amplitude; if to the left of the course, the left reed vibrated more vigorously. If the plane was on course, both reeds vibrated through the same arc. As the station was approached, if the amplitude of vibration became too great, it could be reduced through use of a rheostat.

As the fan-type marker beacon was approached, a single reed started to vibrate. It reached maximum amplitude, then quickly dropped to zero when the airplane was directly overhead, rapidly built up to maximum again, and then tapered down. The homing-range indicator also had a distinct null when the airplane was directly over the range station.

As the tests progressed, the instrumentation and equipment were constantly improved until toward the end of 1929, during the final stages of the flight tests, the following instruments and equipment were carried:

1. Normal engine instruments.
2. Magnetic compass.
3. Earth inductor compass.
4. Bank-and-turn indicator.
5. Directional gyro.
6. Artificial horizon.
7. Airspeed indicator.
8. Altimeter.
9. Rate-of-climb indicator.
10. Outside air thermometer.
11. Vibrating reed homing range indicator.
12. Vibrating reed marker beacon indicator.

Considerable thought was given to the location or arrangement of each instrument in order to facilitate reading and reduce pilot fatigue. Fatigue led to errors, and piloting errors could not be tolerated in instrument landings. The airplane, in addition to its flight instruments, carried a RFL radio receiver, a BTL radio transmitter, two 6-inch Pyle National landing lights, and a parachute flare. Small instruments were preferred over the more conventional larger ones because, even though they were somewhat harder to read individually, the small instruments permitted more compact and logical arrangement and were easier to read and interpret en masse. It was soon determined that small instruments could be made easier to read by use of broader hands with white or radium paint applied to the outer half of their length. It was found that the instruments could be read more quickly, and over a long period with less fatigue, if the arrangement of the instruments and the position and direction of motion of the indicating hands was "natural." Also any abnormality or improper indication should be detectable automatically by a quick glance at the instrument panel. This did not "solve" instrument flight but did simplify it.

A larger than customary Leece-Neville generator was installed on the engine to assure an adequate and continuous electrical supply. The mast-type receiving antenna, which was employed to minimize directional effect, required considerable development before a tendency to vibrate under certain flight conditions could be corrected. A trailing wire antenna was used for transmission in normal flight. This was reeled in and a fixed wire antenna used for transmitting when landing.

The specialized ground equipment consisted of a radio receiver and transmitter which provided voice communication with the aircraft and a Kollsman sensitive altimeter with which the altimeter in the airplane was synchronized by radio. In addition, there was the visual homing range and the visual fan-type marker beacon previously mentioned, and, of course, there was available the standard Mitchel

Field Army-type aural beacon to lead an aircraft to the general vicinity of the airfield.

Two problems that were very much on the minds of the fund directors were collision of aircraft in the air and the formation of ice on the wings, structure, and propeller, and in the carburetor of aircraft when atmospheric conditions were conducive to icing. Dr. W. C. Greer and Dr. Merrit Scott at Cornell University carried out work, under fund sponsorship, on the underlying causes of ice formation on aircraft. The fund also sponsored the work done by John P. Kilgore of New Haven, Conn., on an electrically heated wing blanket for deicing. The Full Flight Laboratory did no development work on deicing equipment, but many test flights were made under icing conditions to determine effects and limitations.

BAD-WEATHER FLIGHTS DEMONSTRATED NEED FOR BLIND-LANDING EQUIPMENT AND RADIO COMMUNICATION

The NY–2 was frequently out of commission during the installation of new instruments or equipment. These were convenient periods for cross-country flying practice under unfavorable weather conditions in the 02U–1. This airplane had all necessary flight instruments but no blind-landing equipment.

An extreme example of a cross-country bad-weather flight took place on March 15, 1929. I took off from Buffalo in the 02U–1 headed for Mitchel Field. It was night, and the weather was fair and improving at Buffalo, but marginal to the south and east. This was to be a difficult flight but possible, and just the sort of thing required to establish flight "limitations." In a pinch I could return to Buffalo at any time up to the point where nearly half of the gasoline supply was used up.

I well realized that the pilot who flew within his limitations would probably live to a ripe old age, whereas the pilot who flew beyond them would not. I also knew that different pilots had different limitations. This was pointed up in the mid-1920's when I was a test pilot at old McCook Field. At that time there were few facilities and little ground equipment to do environmental testing on new airborne devices. It was therefore necessary to test them out in flight, and the test pilots spent many hours flying around the airfield to see how a new device held up under the accelerations, vibrations, and changes in temperature and pressure experienced in flight. Lt. Alex Pearson always spent these hours practicing precision flying; for instance, holding constant speed and altitude. As a result he became extremely proficient and could fly a better speed course or do a smoother saw-tooth climb than any of the rest of us.

I spent the hours flying low in the vicinity of McCook Field and on the main air routes in and out, memorizing the terrain. I knew every high building, tree, silo, windmill, radio tower, and high-tension line in the area. I could therefore fly in—or under—adverse weather safely when other equally experienced pilots did not fly. This was not because I was a better or more daring pilot than my colleagues; constant practice had simply extended my limitations. The trick was to learn your limitations, gradually expand them, but never go beyond them. I thought I was being smart, but the commanding officer, learning that I frequently flew in that area when other pilots did not, thought differently. Unaware of my training plan, he removed me from the job of chief pilot in the flying section, advising me that I did not have judgment enough to be a pilot, and assigned me to the airplane section as an aeronautical engineer.

All these things went through my mind as the weather deteriorated. I planned to fly contact all the way and therefore, in order to avoid the mountains, took the route Buffalo, Rochester, Syracuse, Utica, Schenectady, Albany, and then down the Hudson River. There was no particular problem getting to Albany, but from there on the ceiling and visibility became marginal. Soon I had passed the "point of no return" and no longer had gasoline enough to go back to Buffalo.

At one place I found it expedient to slow down and hover with the left wing of the airplane over a brightly lighted southbound passenger train traveling along the east side of the Hudson River. Presently it went through a cut, making its pursuit too hazardous, so I left the train and followed the riverbank. I considered crossing the river and landing on the parade ground at West Point, but abandoned this idea as the weather remained flyable—barely. Upon reaching the lights and heat of New York City, and finding the ceiling and visibility slightly improved, I flew south to the Battery hoping to be able to get to Mitchel Field from there, but the East River and the area to the south were "socked in" and I could not go on. I next tried to get to Governor's Island and land on the drill ground, but it was fog shrouded, as was also the Yonkers Golf Course which I next hoped to use for an emergency landing after having turned north back up the Hudson. I then returned to the Battery with the intention of crash landing in Battery Park, but a chap ran out into the middle of the park and waved me off. He apparently thought I mistook it for a flying field.

It is interesting to note that the George Washington Bridge across the Hudson at 179th Street was under construction at this time. There were as yet no suspension cables or other horizontal structure, and only the great vertical piers on each side of the river had been completed. I had passed the east pier three times without seeing it.

About this time it appeared that a crash landing in the river might be necessary, so I removed my parachute in order to be able to swim ashore. The water, on closer inspection, looked uninviting, and I decided on a final try—this time for Newark Airport—and headed across the Hudson. As soon as the river was crossed and the lights south of Jersey City appeared, it became obvious that this last chance was impractical. Thereupon I climbed up through the fog, which was only about a thousand feet thick with crystal-clear skies above, intending to fly west until past the thickly populated part of the metropolitan area and then jump. The gasoline gage had been fluttering on zero for some time. I noted about this time that my parachute harness was off and promptly put it on.

About over Kenilworth, beyond Elizabeth, I saw a revolving beacon through a hole in the fog and a flat-looking area adjacent to it with no lights. Hoping it might be an emergency field or at least an open area, although realizing that it might be a woods or a lake, I turned the landing lights on and dove through the hole and scouted the area. The bottom of the fog was still very low, and I tore the left lower wing badly on a treetop. The airplane still flew, although almost completely out of gasoline, so I returned to the most likely spot and crashlanded, taking the impact by wrapping the left wing around a tree trunk near the ground. The 02U–1 was completely washed out—quite beyond repair—but I was not even scratched or bruised.

The moral of the story is that had I been flying the NY–2 mounting blind-landing equipment and with the Full Flight Laboratory radio station alerted at Mitchel, this would have been a routine cross-country flight with "no sweat."

The flight pointed up the importance of constant radio communication between the aircraft and the ground, and the need for frequent and accurate weather reports obtainable by radio during flight in order to assure safe continuation or to indicate suitable alternate destinations. It also indicated the desirability of a special light to mark emergency fields for night landings. Later green lights were used.

In general, the weather a pilot could fly in safely was determined by airplane characteristics, ground facilities and procedures, ground and airborne equipment and instrumentation, the pilot's general skill and his specialized knowledge of the local aids to air navigation, the terrain, and the weather conditions to be expected in the area.

DEVELOPMENT OF ALTITUDE-MEASURING INSTRUMENTS

An important requirement in instrument landing was to have a precise measure of altitude when approaching the ground for a landing. The conventional barometric altimeters of the day measured, at best, to the nearest 50 or 100 feet. It would be of great value to have an altimeter that, near the ground, would measure to 10 or even 5 feet. The Kollsman Instrument Co. developed such an instrument, and I was very pleased, on August 30, 1929, in the second 02U—a more modern version—to take Paul Kollsman and his new instrument up on its first test flight. Mr. Kollsman held the sensitive altimeter in his lap during the flight and it performed perfectly. Here was another important addition to flight instrumentation. We promptly obtained one and installed it in the NY–2.

This instrument had two hands and a multiplication factor of 20 between them. Actually the fast-moving hand made one complete revolution for each 1,000 feet change in altitude, which meant a movement of about $5/32$ inch for a change of 20 feet in altitude. This was more than one order of magnitude more accurate than earlier altimeters. Although the Kollsman altimeter provided a very considerable advance in instrumentation, it still measured the barometric altitude or height above sea level. An instrument which would measure the height above the ground regardless of changes in barometric pressure would be of great value.

With this idea in mind, several companies were encouraged to work on a sonic altimeter. One built by Sperry was tested out in the NY–2. A note on a frequency of about 950 cycles was directed at the ground from a megaphone on the bottom of the airplane and picked up by a detector on the airplane after having been reflected back from the ground. The elapsed time interval was measured, as in a marine "fathometer," and the altitude above the ground thus determined. The concept was theoretically sound, but in its initial form the equipment caused considerable drag and was unduly large, heavy, difficult to install, and complicated. It also appeared that a radio altimeter measuring the phase difference of radio waves reflected back from the ground offered more promise. Several radio altimeters were under development—with fund encouragement—and the sonic altimeter experiments were therefore abandoned.

FOG-DISPERSAL EXPERIMENTS

Although major emphasis was given in the Full Flight Laboratory to flight tests designed to permit flying safely and reliably despite fog, the fund and the laboratory were also interested in experiments on the penetration of fog by light rays and on the dispersal of fog.

Studies on fog penetration were made by Dr. Anderson of the University of Washington and Dr. Barnes of Bryn Mawr College under fund sponsorship, and by Dr. Julius A. Stratton of the Massachusetts Institute of Technology for Col. E. H. L. Green. The visual, infrared, and ultraviolet portions of the spectrum were carefully explored.

It was concluded that though there was some difference in penetration due to wavelength, there was little likelihood of finding any visual light that would penetrate thick, dense fog. Dr. Stratton's further investigations gave some promise that at very short wavelengths—below 1 centimeter—there was a possibility that fog might be penetrated by dispersal. In addition to the scientific studies carried out, various inventors presented ideas for fog penetration, all of which received careful consideration.

Four basic methods of fog dispersal were originally considered:

1. *Dispersal by mechanical means.*—Here the concept was to have a large propeller or series of propellers "churn up" the fog.

2. *Dispersal by chemical means.*—Experiments carried out by Henry G. Houghton, Jr., of MIT, using hygroscopic materials, showed some promise both in the laboratory and in full-scale tests that were conducted on the estate of Colonel Green in South Dartmouth, Mass.

3. *Dispersal by electrical means.*—From the early 1920's Dr. Warren of Hartford, in collaboration with the Army Air Service, had been experimenting with cloud and fog dispersal by means of electrified sand particles dropped from an aircraft. He was occasionally successful in dispersing small clouds. Mr. Flowers experimented with fog dispersal through the use of electrified water particles and achieved some interesting results.

4. *Dispersal by heat.*—Experimentation on, and the actual accomplishment of, fog dispersal by heat has been carried on until fairly recent times.

FIDO (Fog, Intense Dispersal Of) was effectively used in World War II on 3 of the long emergency fields and 10 main landing fields in England. It consisted of powerful heat sources at intervals along the runways which heated the air to a temperature above the dewpoint, thereby dispersing the nearby fog. Approximately 2,500 bombers and fighters—mostly RAF but including some USAF—returning from missions and finding their home base (and much of England) covered in pea-soup fog were directed to the cleared "tunnels in the fog" over these FIDO fields and landed safely.

Perhaps I should mention here that the Eighth Air Force Bomber units in England were being trained and equipped to operate "blind"—without FIDO—and at the end of the war two groups could take off and land regardless of fog. Shortly the entire force would have been so trained.

In the late 1940's successful FIDO experiments were carried out at the Naval Air Base at Arcata on the coast of northern California. Arcata was chosen because it was in one of the foggiest areas on the entire Pacific coast. Southwest Airways successfully used the Navy fog-dispersal system from November 1947 until November 1949.

In 1953, a FIDO installation was made at the Los Angeles International Airport at a cost of $1,325,000 for installation, modification, and test. While the installation appeared to handle moderate fogs fairly well, it did not satisfactorily disperse dense fogs where the visibility was one-eighth mile or less. The dispersal difficulties seemed to arise from the great amount of heat required, the airport configuration, and the movement and intrusion of the fog. Further operational problems resulted from infrequent use of equipment and the high cost of installation, maintenance, and operation. It was also anticipated that there would be difficulty experienced in moving passengers to and from the airport and in moving aircraft to and from the cleared runway when the fog was really dense. The following year the FIDO program was abandoned at Los Angeles.

It appears that FIDO is a successful way of coping with intense fog only when the air is comparatively still. When there is any considerable movement of the air and fog—particularly if the movement has a component across the runway—the cleared airmass moves on and new fog comes in faster than it can be dispersed. Difficulties have also been experienced in an absolutely dead calm owing to conduction, particularly at runway intersections and elsewhere where there were no burners.

The Full Flight Laboratory's first experience with FIDO occurred in 1929. Mr. Reader, of Cleveland, operated a gravel pit and utilized a large blowtorch type of heater to dry the gravel and sand. He observed that if there was an intense fog when he turned the heater on, the fog in the immediate area dispersed. Learning of the Guggenheim fog-flying experiments, he wrote giving information of his experience and advising that he was interested in helping to solve the fog problem. He was invited to bring one of his heaters to Mitchel Field, where it was installed just east of the last hangar.

For several months thereafter we waited in vain for a dense fog. Finally, on September 24, 1929, it came. Someone, I think it was Jack Dalton, awakened just before daylight and noted that there was a zero-zero fog covering the area. Our gang was quickly called together. We immediately notified Mr. Reader, who arrived shortly thereafter. Mr. Guggenheim was also notified, but he had to come from Port Washington and didn't arrive until later. The equipment was fired up, but the fog did not disperse except in the immediate vicinity of the blowtorch. The experiment was a disappointing failure. At the time we considered the concept impractical, and the equipment was removed.

In retrospect, it appears that the trouble was probably fog movement or possibly the absence of a mineral mass to store and reflect the heat. Also, for satisfactory fog dispersal over a considerable area, about two orders of magnitude more heat energy would seem to be required.

FIRST FLIGHT FROM TAKEOFF TO LANDING BY INSTRUMENTS ALONE

Though we were all disappointed, we were there, and the fog was there, so I decided to make a real fog flight. The NY–2 was pushed out of the hangar and warmed up. The ground radios were manned, and the radio beacons were turned on. I taxied out to the middle of the field and took off. Coming through the fog at about 500 feet and making a wide swing, I came around into landing position. By the time I landed 10 minutes after takeoff, the fog had started to lift.

About this time Mr. Guggenheim, along with several other people, arrived, and we decided to do an "official," under-the-hood flight. I had just made a real flight in the fog and wanted to go alone, but Mr. Guggenheim insisted that Ben Kelsey be taken along as safety pilot. The fog had lifted considerably by this time, and he was afraid there might be other aircraft in the vicinity.

We both got into the airplane, and the hood over my cockpit was closed. The engine was again warmed up and I taxied the airplane out and turned into the takeoff direction on the radio beam. We took off and flew west in a gradual climb. At about 1,000 feet the airplane was leveled off and a 180° turn was made to the left. This course was flown several miles and another 180° turn to the left was made. The airplane was lined up on the left of the radio range located on the west side of Mitchel Field, and a gradual descent started. I leveled off at 200 feet above the ground and flew at this altitude until the fan beacon on the east side of the airfield was passed. From this point the airplane was flown into the ground, using the instrument landing procedure previously developed. Actually, despite previous practice, the final approach and landing were sloppy. This entire flight was made under the hood in a completely covered cockpit which had been carefully sealed to keep out all light. The flight, from takeoff to landing, lasted 15 minutes. It was the first time an airplane had been taken off, flown over a set course, and landed by instruments alone. This was just 10 months and 3 weeks after the first test flight of the NY–2.

INDICATIONS FROM EARLY TESTING OF INSTRUMENTS

The tests carried out thus far indicated, among other things, that before all-weather flying would be practical, there was a need for—

1. Better coordination between the long-range aural beam and the short-range visual landing beam.

2. Accurate measurement of distance along the landing beam.

3. A slant glide beam at right angle to the vertical landing beam which might be curved to become tangent to the earth rather than intersect it in a straight line.

4. The possibility of automatic volume control on the receiving radio.

5. A good gyro pilot to assist the pilot in flying the aircraft. This could be, and later was, tied in with the instrument landing systems.

6. Much more work on ignition shielding, not only to reduce noise but to permit flight in heavy rain.

At the end of 1929 the fund, feeling that it had made the necessary initial contribution and believing that further development could better be carried out by other organizations, was disbanded. The Full Flight Laboratory went out of existence with the fund, and the NY–2 was turned over to the U.S. Army Air Corps and moved to Wright Field, where instrument-landing experimentation and development were continued under the direction of 1st Lt.—Later Maj. Gen.—Albert Hegenberger.

The Bureau of Standards and the Bureau of Air Commerce of the Department of Commerce also continued their work, and on March 20, 1933, James L. Kinney, with William La Violette as mechanic and Harry Diamond as passenger, flew a Bellanca airplane by instruments from College Park, Md., to Newark Airport, a distance of about 200 miles. He landed blind, using the recently developed bent landing beam. The weather was actually below minimum.

The Collier Trophy is awarded each year to an individual or group "for the greatest achievement in aviation in America, with respect to improving the performance, efficiency, or safety of aircraft, the value of which has been thoroughly demonstrated by actual use during the preceding year." In 1934 the Collier Trophy was awarded to Capt. Albert Hegenberger, U.S. Army Air Corps, for the development and demonstration of a successful blind-landing system. On May 9, 1932, Captain Hegenberger made the first solo blind flight, depending solely upon instruments from takeoff to landing. Over a period of years he and his colleagues had greatly improved the equipment previously used and developed additional equipment. He devised a blind-landing procedure which became standard military practice. This system was put into actual use in 1934.

Flying by instruments had outgrown the early experimental phase. It was a practical reality, and aviation had entered a new era.

Three Famous Early Aero Engines[6]

By ROBERT B. MEYER, JR.

National Air Museum, Smithsonian Institution

[With 9 plates]

In 1853 Sir George Cayley of England created the first man-carrying glider. This was an important milestone in the history of heavier-than-air craft, but without power such aircraft could be used only for sport. It was not until the advent of the successful application of power to heavier-than-air craft by the Wright brothers 50 years later that flying could become practical.

During the 50-year period following 1903, improved engines made possible increasingly successful flights. Throughout the first decade the typical airplane was the powered glider. Having a large wing area and a small amount of power for their weight, these airplanes were very sensitive to wind variations, and therefore difficult to fly except in calm air. For the same reasons such airplanes were slower than the sports cars of their day. True powered airplanes were not built until World War I. Some of these had sufficient power to "hang on their propellers" briefly during certain combat maneuvers. Between World Wars I and II the helicopter advanced toward a practical stage. For the first time controlled vertical lift was obtained by heavier-than-air craft. This too would not have been possible without improved engines having a high horsepower/weight ratio. Shortly after World War II jet engines began to develop more thrust than the weight of the airframe in which they were installed. Such aircraft so powered are able to climb vertically. Thus in a span of 50 years heavier-than-air craft advanced from gliders deriving all their lift from wings to airplanes capable of deriving all their lift from engines.

It is the engine which is the key to successful, practical flight; hence the significance of this brief study of three famous aeronautical engines which first powered aircraft in 1903. Each of these engines is on display in the National Air Museum of the Smithsonian Institution. Although they are similar in that each is of the internal-combustion, four-stroke-cycle, gasoline-burning type, and each is equipped with automatic inlet valves, they differ from one another in most other respects.

Each engine will be considered separately from the standpoints of history, specifications, capabilities, and survival value. Two of them were used in heavier-than-air craft, and one powered a lighter-than-air craft. All three were ancestors of distinct types of heavier-than-air craft powerplants.

THE CLEMENT ENGINE

The first of these engines to power an aircraft was the Brazilian Santos Dumont's French built and designed Clement motor (made by Adolphe Clement, who later founded the famous Clement-Bayard firm) which propelled his airship No. 9 during the summer of 1903. To quote from his book, "My Air-ships":

I determined to build a small airship runabout for my pleasure and convenience only. . . . So I built my number 9, the smallest of possible dirigibles, yet very practical indeed. As originally constructed, its balloon capacity was but 7,770 cubic feet, permitting me to take up less than 66 pounds of ballast; and thus I navigated it for weeks, without inconvenience. Even when I enlarged its balloon to 9,218 cubic feet, the balloon of my number 6, in which I won the Deutsch Prize, would have made almost three of it, while that of my Omnibus is fully eight times its size. As I have already stated, its 3 horsepower Clement motor weighs but 26½ pounds. With such a motor one cannot expect great speed; nevertheless, this handy little runabout takes me over the Bois [Paris] at between 12 and 15 miles per hour, and this notwithstanding its egg-shaped form, which would seemingly be little calculated for cutting the air.

Further information is given in an article which appeared in the Scientific American for July 11, 1903:

The new Clement gasoline motor used on the number 9 has proved especially satisfactory. The little motor with its cylinders joined in the form of a V to a round aluminum crank box, seems like a toy and weighs but 26½ pounds, although it will develop 3 horse power. The weight per horse power (8.8 pounds), the smallest that has yet been reached, is the result of long experience in racing cars, where the weight must be cut down to a minimum. Current for the spark is supplied by a battery and induction coil of the motor-bicycle pattern. The motor is connected through a light friction clutch to the long shaft which passes back of the propeller. A bicycle wheel with a heavy rim (without the tire) forms the flywheel and lies next to the motor. . . . An airbag of 60 cubic yards lies along the inside of the balloon at the bottom, forming a pocket which can be filled out with air by a fan [blower] mounted on the motor shaft. The balloon is [therefore] always kept in shape as the gas escapes.

SPECIFICATIONS

Cylinders	2 arranged in the form of a V.
Cooling	Air.
Carburetion	Automobile-type carburetor.
Ignition	Battery, induction coil, spark plug (high-tension).
Horsepower	3.
Bore and stroke	2¼ x 2¾ in.
Displacement	21.8 cu. in.
Dimensions	17 in. high x 9½ in. wide x 9 in. long.
Weight	26½ lb.
Weight/hp. ratio	8.8 lb. per hp.
Country of manufacture	France.

Clement engine. Left side view as presently shown in the Air and Space Building, Smithsonian Institution. Visible are the left cylinder and its valve mechanism, spark-timing system, flywheel, clutch, and blower.

Clement engine. Right side view as presently exhibited. Visible are the right cylinder and its valve mechanism, spark-timing system, carburetor, clutch, and flywheel.

Clement engine. Rear view, as presently exhibited. Shown are the cylinders, valve mechanisms, flywheel, clutch, and blower.

Manly-Balzer engine. Left side view showing cylinders, exhaust ports, push rods, cooling water manifold, fuel/air intake manifold, and flywheels.

Manly-Balzer engine. Right side view showing cylinders, flywheels, and ignition-timing mechanism.

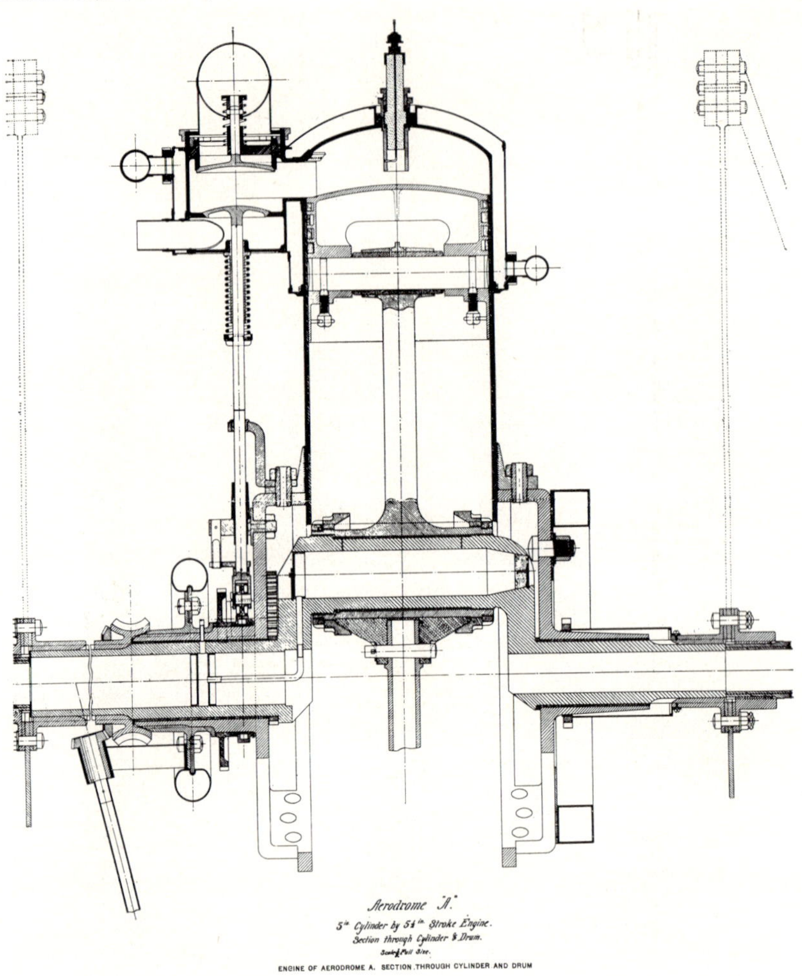

Manly-Balzer engine. Cross section of a cylinder showing spark plug, automatic intake and push-rod operated exhaust valves and their mechanisms, fuel/air intake and water manifolds, water jackets, piston, connecting rods, and crankshaft.

Wright brothers' engine. Underside view showing flywheel, oil pump, exhaust valve camshaft, rocker arms and valve springs, and igintion system camshaft.

Wright brothers' engine. Left front view showing automatic intake valves, rocker-arm actuated exhaust valves, fuel induction system, timing chain, and spark advance lever.

Wright brothers' engine. Right rear view of engine as mounted in the airplane, showing the flywheel, magneto, propeller drive chains, automatic intake valve springs, and open-ended can surface type of carburetor.

The Clement engine had two tasks to perform: the propulsion of a lighter-than-air craft, and the operation of a blower [fan] to aid in maintaining the rigidity and therefore the structural integrity of the dirigible's envelope [balloon].

As Santos Dumont stated above, this motor would propel his diminutive airship up to 15 m.p.h. Forcing it much beyond this speed would not have been practical because of the envelope's great resistance to the passage of the air. If a considerably more powerful engine had been installed, it would have weighed so much that little or no ballast could have been carried. This would have prevented safe aerial navigation.

The blower, as mentioned above, merely forced air under low pressure into a flexible compartment on the underside of the gas bag. This compensated for any reduction in stiffness of the airship's envelope due to a loss of lifting gas caused by leakage or purposeful releasing of the gas. Probably only a fraction of 1 horsepower was needed for this purpose.

This particular engine was apparently designed for the Clement Autocyclette motorcycle which was sold in 1903. However, its light weight and reasonably good weight/power ratio made it an ideal engine for the diminutive airship.

From 1903 until the advent of World War II, this motorcycle type of engine (two air-cooled cylinders in **V**-configuration) was being manufactured for single-place heavier-than-air craft. Below are listed some examples.

British J.A.P. of 1909.
French Farcot of 1913.
British Blackburne of 1923.
American Indian of 1925.
British Anzani of 1936.

Engines with their cylinders arranged horizontally on either side of the crankshaft (horizontally opposed) eventually replaced powerplants having the **V**-arrangement of the Clement. The advantages of the former type are more smoothness (the reciprocating parts counterbalanced each other) and better visibility (the cylinders did not protrude above the crankcase). This type gave way in turn to the four-cylinder engine in the same configuration. This four-cylinder version offered more smoothness owing to more frequent and smaller power impulses, as well as greater safety, for the loss of one cylinder would not cause a forced landing. After World War II most single-seat airplanes were powered by the four-cylinder horizontally opposed air-cooled engine. The Clement motorcycle type of engine therefore appears to have influenced aircraft engine design for single-seat airplanes directly for 35 years, and indirectly for more than 50 years.

THE MANLY-BALZER ENGINE

The second of these engines to power an aircraft was redesigned and rebuilt by the American Charles M. Manly. It was first used in an aircraft during the autumn of 1903.

From 1887 to 1896 Samuel Pierpont Langley, Secretary of the Smithsonian Institution, had conducted a series of experiments with heavier-than-air craft models. By 1896 his steam-driven ones had made repeated flights of from one-half to three-quarters of a mile. President McKinley learned of these successes and during 1898 authorized the expenditure of $50,000 for the construction and testing of a man-carrying heavier-than-air flying machine. Before agreeing to attempt the work for the War Department, Langley had made a search for a reliable builder who would undertake to construct a gasoline engine of not less than 12 horsepower, to weigh not exceeding 100 pounds. What then seemed to be a sound contract had been entered into for one engine which would meet these requirements. The first builder was soon found to be unreliable, and after a more extended search, a contract was entered into on December 12, 1898, with Stephen M. Balzer, an engine builder in New York City. He was to furnish an engine meeting the above-mentioned requirements by February 28, 1899. Since it had been estimated that 24 horsepower was needed, provision was made in the contract that a duplicate engine should be constructed immediately after the completion of the first one.

The ancestor of this engine was a four-stroke-cycle, air-cooled three-cylinder rotary which Balzer had built for his 1894 automobile. The automobile with its engine is on display in the Smithsonian Institution, having been given by the builder on May 16, 1899. An extra engine was delivered to Charles M. Manly of the Smithsonian Institution on September 5, 1899.

When the end of February 1899 arrived, it was found that although the engine builder had succeeded in constructing an engine which weighed 100 pounds, and which theoretically should have given something over 12 horsepower, it was impossible to make it work properly. The mechanical construction of the more important parts had been well executed, and this main portion of the contractural work was completed within the time called for by the contract. The trouble was that the engine, which was of the rotary-cylinder type, would not furnish anything like the power which had been expected of it, and which the size and number of its cylinders indicated that it should furnish.

At this point Charles Manly took command of the situation. He had been appointed Langley's assistant in these experiments two years previously at the age of 22, having graduated with distinction from the Cornell University School of Engineering.

On May 6, 1900, he visited Balzer in New York City to find out exactly what had been accomplished, and to see what might be done to improve the engine's efficiency.   He tested the engine and found it producing only 4 hp., and this low output could be maintained for only a few minutes.   After working on the problem for several weeks, Manly succeeded in obtaining a continuous rating of 8 hp. at 350 r.p.m. This being only two-thirds of the necessary power, the project was abandoned.

Manly spent the next three months searching for a suitable engine among the American and European manufacturers without success. As a last resort, he decided to redesign the Balzer engine.

By September 18, 1900, he had modified it with Balzer's help so that it developed 18½ hp. at 715 r.p.m.   It differed from its original configuration by having stationary instead of rotating cylinders, and the cylinders water cooled with damp cloths instead of being air cooled.   Later the ignition system was changed from the low-tension make-and-break type (which was difficult to keep in time and in good operating condition) to the modern high-tension type using spark plugs.   Considerable weight was saved by having a single coil and distributor for all five cylinders instead of a separate one for each.   Manly designed and made his own spark plugs which had a reliability far exceeding those available.   He accomplished this by extending the metal portion of the plug and the terminals into the cylinder and beyond the insulator, thereby preventing soot deposits from forming and causing short circuits.   With these improvements the engine developed 21.5 hp. at 825 r.p.m. while weighing but 120 pounds.

By this time it was realized that more than 24 hp. would be needed, for the aerodrome, as Langley called his flying machine, would weigh more than the original calculations indicated.   (Smithsonian Institution Information Leaflet No. 29 describes the aerodrome project.) Since it had been demonstrated that a single engine would develop sufficient horsepower, the heavier and more complicated dual-engine concept was abandoned.   The engine was therefore redesigned by Manly, with larger cylinders, to give 40 hp. with all the cylinders operating, or 28 hp. with one cylinder "dead."   He used some of Balzer's men and equipment.

Four particularly important features were incorporated in the engine:

1. Instead of the usual single-walled cylinder, the following double-walled construction was employed, making the cylinders stronger and lighter: an outer seamless shell, with an integrally formed head, made of $\frac{1}{16}$-in. steel, providing the strength.   To act as the wearing surface for the piston, a cast-iron liner, also $\frac{1}{16}$ in. thick, was shrunk

into the steel shell. Near the bottom edge of the steel shell was screwed and brazed a flange which was then bolted to the crankcase. Entering the side of the cylinder near the top was the combustion chamber, which, together with the inlet port, was machined out of a solid steel forging and brazed to the cylinder. Balzer had pioneered this type of construction.

2. Instead of using damp cloths wrapped around the cylinders for cooling purposes, which were effective for only 3 or 4 minutes, Manly developed a light-weight water jacket of sheet steel 0.02 in. thick which was brazed to each cylinder.

3. Being a heavier-than-air craft of light construction, it was realized that attitudes, accelerations, and vibrations would be encountered which were quite foreign to automotive practice. For this reason the float type of carburetor, which was usually employed on automobiles, was abandoned as being too erratic in operation at its stage of development in 1903. Instead, a Balzer type of carburetor was employed which consisted of a tank filled with porous wooden balls. Gasoline was admitted at the bottom in a steady flow and the balls became saturated, thus giving off vapors which were drawn into the intake manifold.

4. Instead of having each connecting rod attached directly to the main crankshaft bearing, Manly used a single master rod. It was attached directly to the main crankshaft bearing. To this were fastened the four link rods connected to the other pistons. In this manner the bearing area was greatly increased, which was necessary since the new engine was to develop more than twice as much power as its predecessor.

The engine was completed in December 1901 and was tested in January 1902. Under a Prony brake load of 52.4 hp. at 950 r.p.m., it ran continuously for 10 hours during three separate tests. The net dry weight of the engine proper was 124.2 lb. With 20 lb. of cooling water, flywheels, batteries, and accessories, the total weight of the powerplant was 207.5 lb., or 3.96 lb. per hp.

SPECIFICATIONS

Cylinders	5 in radial configuration.
Cooling	Water.
Carburetion	Surface type, no float.
Ignition	Battery, induction coil, spark plug (high-tension).
Horsepower	52.4 at 950 r.p.m.
Bore and stroke	5 x 5.5 in.
Displacement	540.2 cu. in.
Dimensions	37-in. diameter and 19-in. width.
Weight	207.5 lb. including cooling water.
Weight/hp. ratio	3.96 lb. per hp.
Country of manufacture	U.S.A.

There were two tasks which the Manly engine was to perform: it had to provide sufficient power to lift and to propel the aerodrome. It was calculated that 28 hp. would be enough if the weight/horsepower ratio were sufficiently low. How well the engine succeeded is revealed by the above specifications which show a continuous hp. of 52.4 and a weight/horsepower ratio of 3.96. This was the least heavy aviation engine for its power in the world until the advent of the 18-hp. three-cylinder air-cooled engine created by J. C. H. Ellehammer of Denmark in 1906. It weighed 3 lb. per hp.

For the next 40 years this same water-cooled radial type of engine was being manufactured for various types of aircraft. Below are listed some examples.

American Albatross of 1910.
French Salmson of 1919.
French Anzani of 1920.
German Rumpler design of 1923.
German BMW 803 of 1944.

The five-cylinder radial configuration was chosen by Balzer and Manly for the following principal reasons:

1. The greater smoothness of operation of an odd as compared with an even number of cylinders.

2. The greater uniformity of torque with increasing number of cylinders. Five seemed at that time to be the greatest practical odd number.

3. The reduction of weight and complication of the radial form.

This class of engine, air cooled instead of water cooled, emerged as the principal type of aircraft powerplant for the following 40 years. It is only now being replaced by jet engines. The Manly engine was therefore a 100-percent airplane engine although having automobile antecedents and was so well designed and built that it was a model for the majority of airplane engines produced throughout the world until the end of World War II.

THE WRIGHT BROTHERS' ENGINE OF 1903

The third of these engines to power an aircraft was that of the Wright brothers during the winter of 1903. Orville and Wilbur Wright designed the engine themselves and built it with the help of their machinist, Charles E. Taylor. It was apparently based on the single-cylinder natural-gas engine they had designed and built previously to power their 1901 wind tunnel.

They began to build it in December 1902, and the first tests were run on February 12, 1903. On the 13th dripping gasoline caused the bearings to freeze, and this broke the engine body and frame. It was necessary to order a new aluminum casting which was received on April 20, 1903. The rebuilt motor was shop tested in May. In a description of the motor by Wilbur Wright dated February 28, 1903, he had this to say:

We recently built a four-cylinder gasoline engine with 4″ piston and 4″ stroke, to see how powerful it would be, and what it would weigh. At 670 revolutions per min. it developed 8½ horsepower, brake test. By speeding it up to 1,000 rev. we will easily get 11 horsepower and possibly a little more at still higher speed, though the increase is not in exact proportion to the increase in number of revolutions. The weight including the 30-pound flywheel is 140 lbs.

A description of the rebuilt motor by Orville Wright dated June 28, 1903, follows: "Since putting in heavier springs to actuate the valves on our engine we have increased its power to nearly 16 horsepower, and at the same time reduced the amount of gasoline consumed per hour to about one half of what it was before."

By November 5, 1903, the engine had been tested in the Wrights' first powered airplane, the "Kitty Hawk Flyer." Considerable trouble was experienced with the propeller shafts. Finally, new ones had to be made, and so the engine did not become successfully airborne until December 17, 1903.

A detailed description of the motor follows. It consists of quotations from "The Papers of Wilbur and Orville Wright," edited by Marvin W. McFarland.

This historic motor is described by Orville Wright in an undated typewritten memorandum among the Wright papers in the Library of Congress: The motor used in the first flights at Kitty Hawk, N.C., on December 17, 1903, had (four) horizontal cylinders of 4-inch bore and 4-inch stroke. The ignition was by low-tension magneto with make-and-break spark. The boxes inclosing the intake and exhaust valves had neither water jackets nor radiating fins, so that after a few minutes' run the valves and valve boxes became red hot. There was no float-feed carburetor. The gasoline was fed to the motor by gravity in a constant stream and was vaporized by running over a large heated surface of the water jacket of the cylinders. Due to the preheating of the air by the water jacket and the red-hot valves and boxes, the air was greatly expanded before entering the cylinders. As a result, in a few minutes' time, the power dropped to less than 75 percent of what it was on cranking the motor.

The motor was worn in by driving a flat-bladed fan, of approximately five-foot diameter, mounted on the crankshaft. From measurements made in many tests with a stop watch and revolutions counter the speed at which the motor could turn this fan was known. The highest speed ever measured was 300 turns (1,200 r.p.m.) in the first fifteen seconds after starting the cold motor. The revolutions dropped rapidly and were down to 1,090 r.p.m. after several minutes' run.

The crankcase and water jacket were cast in a single block of aluminum alloy. The crankshaft was made from a block of machine steel 1⅝ inches thick and had five babbitted main bearings. A 15-inch, 26-pound flywheel was attached to the rear end of the shaft. A chain drive on the front end drove the camshaft, which operated the breaker arms and exhaust valves. A boxwood idler, 1¼ inches in diameter, without flanges, created tension on the chain.

The valve heads were made of cast iron. The stems were of steel. The intake valves operated automatically. Neither the cylinders nor the pistons were ground. The connecting rods were seamless steel tubes screwed into brass big ends.

The motor was started with the aid of a dry-battery coil box. After starting, ignition was provided by a low-tension magneto, friction-driven by the flywheel. This magneto—permanent horseshoe magnets with exciting coils—weighed 18 pounds. Insulated ignition electrodes in the cylinder heads were connected by a strap of copper. The speed of the motor was regulated on the ground by retarding the spark. A small lever on the leg of the motor controlled the timing of the spark by altering the position of the camshaft. There was no way to regulate the speed of the motor in flight.

Lubrication was supplied to the cylinders by a small oil pump driven by a worm gear on the camshaft. No pump was used in the cooling system. The vertical sheet-steel radiator was attached to the central forward upright. Gas feed was controlled by a metering valve, not adjustable during flight. A shutoff valve, made from an ordinary gaslight pet cock, was placed conveniently near the operator. The fuel tank had a capacity of 0.4 gallon. The fuel line was copper.

The weight of the 1903 engine is given as 161 pounds dry in Orville Wright's letter to Charles L. Lawrance, November 15, 1928, or 179 pounds with magneto. Complete with magneto, radiator, tank, water, fuel, tubing, and accessories, the powerplant weighed a little over 200 pounds.

Orville Wright gave some additional facts in his letter to Fred H. Colvin, March 13, 1945:

It was entirely disassembled after the flights at Kitty Hawk in December 1903, due to an accident to the crankcase, and was never reassembled until 1916, when it was put together and exhibited with the 1903 plane at the dedication of the new M.I.T. buildings.

On January 9, 1906, Orville Wright wrote Carl Dienstbach in reply to a request for an exhibit at the first Aero Club show in New York:

We could not furnish the motor used on our original flyer. The water jacket and the main frame have been very much changed; the metal of the old frame has been used in making new castings. We could send you the crankshaft and flywheel of the original engine, but we do not think it would be worth while.

The crankshaft and flywheel were sent, however, and on February 7, 1906, Orville Wright again wrote Dienstbach:

We are pleased to present the photographs to the Club and would be glad to leave with the Club some relic from our first flyer. We have no objection to the Club's retaining the crank and flywheel for the present, though we wish the privilege of claiming it if we should decide to set the original machine together again, only a few parts of which are lacking. All of the parts of the engine are still in existence excepting the body.

The crankshaft and flywheel of the 1903 motor were not returned by the Aero Club after the exhibit, and when a search was made for them some years later they could not be found. Therefore when the 1903 aeroplane and motor were assembled for shipment to England in 1928, it was necessary to substitute for the missing parts the crankshaft and flywheel of the 1904 motor. A handwritten memorandum among the Wright papers in the Library of Congress (dated 1945 and initialed O. W.) attests to this substitution: "Crankshaft and flywheel of 1904 motor, with modification to fit 1903 chain-guide bearing, now in 1903 motor."

Additional information about this engine was furnished by Charles E. Taylor in an article that appeared in the May 1928 issue of the journal Slipstream. A partial quotation follows:

Orv and Will then asked me to help them build the motor for their first power-driven machine. They had a little workshop where they built and repaired bicycles at 1927 West Third Street. As I recall we first hit upon the idea of an air-cooled motor but we decided after some figuring that it would weigh more per horsepower than a water-cooled type so we settled upon the latter. I do not know but that if we could have secured the light alloys available today we would have gone ahead with the air-cooled job.

The first thing we did as an experiment was to construct a sort of skeleton model in order that we might watch the functioning of the various vital parts before venturing with anything more substantial. Orv and Will were pretty thorough that way—they wouldn't take anything for granted but worked everything out to a practical solution without too much haste. I think that had a lot to do with their later success.

When we had the skeleton motor set up we hooked it to our shop power, smeared the cylinders with a paint brush dipped in oil and watched the various parts in action. It looked good so we went ahead immediately with the construction of a four cylinder engine. I cut the crank shaft from a solid block of steel weighing over a hundred pounds. When finished it weighed about 19 pounds. We didn't have spark plugs but used the old "make and break" system of ignition. The gas was led in and made to spread over the chamber above the heated water jackets and this immediately vaporized it. Of course, we had real gasoline in that day—fully 76 proof and you could count on it going into action at the least excuse.

The cylinders of that first motor were made of gray iron as were the pistons. As I recall those cylinders were from $\frac{1}{8}$ inch to $\frac{3}{16}$ inch in thickness. So far as I know that was the first four cylinder engine ever built. The automobile manufacturers were out of the picture then and the Oldsmobile firm was the only one I was familiar with at that time. We tried to get a motor built there but they couldn't make one near the low weight we wanted. The old one-lunger auto engines of that day really weighed more than our entire flying machine with the first motor installed.

When the engine was ready for block test we rigged up a connection with natural gas, put on a resistance fan and made several block runs in this manner. Later we used gasoline fuel and found the motor would run satisfactorily. That first motor developed around 18 h.p. and weighed around 190 pounds. We were all highly pleased at being able to hold down the weight to this figure but a short time afterward we built another motor that produced around 45 h.p. and which weighted about the same as the first one.

When we installed the first motor in the original machine it lay on its side to the right of the pilot and in such a position that the pilot's weight partially off-set that of the motor. The radiator was made from speaking tubes flattened to reduce the capacity.

Yes, I must admit there wasn't much to that first motor—no carburetor, no spark plugs, not much of anything but cylinders, pistons and connecting rods, but it worked.

SPECIFICATIONS

Cylinders___________________ 4 horizontal in-line.
Cooling_____________________ Water.
Carburetion_________________ Surface type—no float.
Ignition____________________ Low-tension magneto with make-and-break spark.
Horsepower_________________ 12.05 at 1,090 r.p.m.
Bore and stroke_____________ 4 x 4 in.
Displacement_______________ 201.1 cu. in.
Dimensions_________________ 13⅝ in. high x 23½₃₂ in. wide x 30¹¹⁄₁₆ in. long.
Weight_____________________ Slightly over 200 pounds including cooling water.
Weight/hp. ratio___________ Approximately 16.6 lb. per hp.
Country of manufacture______ U.S.A.

In June of 1903 Orville Wright wrote to a friend:

About Christmastime we began the construction of the motor, which is of four cylinders, four-inch bore and four-inch stroke. We had estimated that we would require a little over eight horsepower to carry our weight of 625 lbs. of machine and man. At this weight we would be limited to two hundred lbs. for our motor. Our motor on completion turned out to be a very pleasant surprise. Instead of eight horsepower, for which we hoped but hardly expected, it has given us 13 (non-continuous) horsepower on the brake, with a (dry) weight of only 150 lbs. in the motor.

In 1904 we built two more motors of the design of 1903, excepting that an extra half inch of water was provided for over the cylinders. One of these motors was of four-inch bore. . . . The four-inch bore motor was experimented with in the shop in 1904, 1905, and 1906, and finally was developed to the point where it would hold 24 to 25 horsepower continuously at 1,300 revolutions per minute. This was just twice the power secured from the original motor of the same size. . . .

Although the 1903 Wright brothers' motor was heavier for the horsepower it delivered than those of Santos Dumont or Professor Langley (respectively two and four times as heavy), it nevertheless fulfilled its function. On April 12, 1911, Orville Wright wrote: "We look upon reliability in running as of much more importance than lightness of weight in aeroplane motors. We attempt to design our flyers of such efficiency that extremely light motors are not needed."

Since the Wright brothers did not have the wealth of Santos Dumont or the Government grant of Langley, it was necessary for them to build their own engine. It therefore had to be of practical and simple design. A logical procedure was to adapt the automobile engine to the requirements of the airplane, which is what they did.

Following is a list of pre-World War I engines of the automobile type which were similar to the Wright brothers' 1903 engine in that they had four in-line cylinders, were water cooled, and were equipped with large flywheels.

French Clement-Bayard of 1908
French Renault of 1908
French Vivinus of 1908
French Chenu of 1909
German Daimler of 1909
English Green of 1910
Italian Fiat of 1910
American Hansen and Snow of 1910
American Sturtevant of 1911
German Adler of about 1911
German A.E.G. of about 1912

Between World Wars I and II the following American automobile water-cooled engines were converted to power the listed airplanes.

Model T Ford-engined Sessions-Smith Pietenpol "Sky Scout" of 1932
Plymouth-engined Fahlin "Plymo-Coupe" of 1935
Ford Model A-engined "Wiley Post" of 1935
Studebaker-engined Waterman "Arrowbile" of 1936
Ford V–8-engined Arrow "Sport V–8" of 1936

After World War II the following German air-cooled automobile engines were used in the listed airplanes.

Volkswagen-engined French Jodel "D–9" of 1948 onward
Volkswagen-engined French Druine "D.31 Turbulent" of 1956 onward
Volkswagen-engined Belgian Avions Fairey "T–66 Tipsy Nipper" of 1956 onward. In addition, Pollman "Hepu" Porsche engines were available for those wishing increased power.

In this country by 1960 some airplanes were already powered by the American Chevrolet Corvair air-cooled automobile engine, although up to that time no manufacturer had produced an airplane design to be powered with it.

In conclusion, let it be noted that the Santos Dumont Clement motorcycle-type engine started a trend that continued (for single-seat light aircraft) until World War II. The Wright brothers' automobile-type engine started a trend that continued through 1960 (and probably will continue for a good many years) for one- and two-seat light airplanes. The Manly-Balzer type of engine was the only one of the three that was truly an airplane engine. What started out as a static, water-cooled radial evolved to the rotary air-cooled engines of World War I, and thence to the static, air-cooled radials of World War II. These engines, because of their greater simplicity and lightness, had gained ascendancy over the automobile-type water-cooled ones with in-line cylinders by the beginning of World War II. Since that time the jet engine has come to the fore with regard to high-performance airplanes, but the radial engine through 1960 was still the choice of many operators because of its low original cost and low fuel consumption.

GRAPHICS FOR THE CLEMENT ENGINE

The following 8- × 10-in. black-and-white photographs are available from the National Air Museum of the Smithsonian Institution.

Negative No.	*Description*
*46,816–B	Rear view of Clement engine as exhibited in the Air and Space Building of the National Air Museum, showing cylinders, valve mechanisms, flywheel, clutch, and blower.
*46,816–A	Left side view of Clement engine as exhibited in the Air and Space Building of the National Air Museum, showing left cylinder and its valve mechanism, spark timing system, flywheel, clutch, and blower.
*46,816	Right side view of Clement engine as exhibited in the Air and Space Building of the National Air Museum, showing right cylinder and its valve mechanism, spark timing system, carburetor, clutch, and flywheel.
30,556	Front left view showing valve mechanism and spark advance.

GRAPHICS FOR THE MANLY-BALZER ENGINE

The following are photographs available from the Smithsonian Institution:

*30,592–A	Manly-Balzer engine. Left side view as exhibited in the Air and Space Building of the National Air Museum showing cylinders, exhaust ports, push rods, cooling water manifold, fuel/air intake manifold, and flywheels.
*30,592	Manly-Balzer engine. Right side view as exhibited in the Air and Space Building of the National Air Museum showing cylinders, flywheels, and ignition timing mechanism.
18,081	Carburetor.

The following are photographs of drawings:

19,874–A	Same view as Negative No. 30,592–A, but in addition shows starting crank.
19,874–D	Plan view showing cylinders, flywheels, starting crank, spark plugs, fuel/air and water manifolds, and ignition timing mechanism.
19,874–B	Plan and front views of ignition timing mechanism.
*19,874–C	Manly-Balzer engine. Cross section of a cylinder showing spark plug, automatic intake, and push-rod-operated exhaust valves and their mechanisms, fuel/air intake and water manifolds, water jackets, piston, connecting rods, and crankshaft.

GRAPHICS FOR THE WRIGHT BROTHERS' ENGINE

The following are photographs available from the Smithsonian Institution:

*41,898–A	Left front view. It shows the combustion chambers, automatic intake valve mechanism, exhaust valve rocker arms, external electrical connections for make-and-break ignition system, spark retard lever, water outlets, fuel line and open-ended tin can within which fuel and air were mixed, oil line, chain connecting crankshaft and camshaft with its sprockets and boxwood idler, and a part of the flywheel.

Negative No.	*Description*

38,626–F________ Left rear view. It shows the combustion chambers, the exhaust valve rocker arms and springs, the exhaust valve camshaft, external electrical connections for the make-and-break ignition system, the camshaft and part of the mechanism for operating the breakers within the combustion chambers, oil feed line and manifold, part of the timing chain, and flywheel with its oiler and sprockets for driving the propellers.

*38,388__________ Rear right view of the motor as mounted in the airplane. It shows the magneto driven by friction from the flywheel's rim, the flywheel with its oiler, and the chains connecting it with the propellers, water outlet lines, automatic intake valve springs, and open-ended can surface type of carburetor.

*41,898–C_______ Plan view of the bottom. It shows the flywheel with its sprockets and oiler, the external parts of the oil pump, the oil in line to the pump, and the oil out line to the manifold which distributes it to the crackshaft bearings, the inlet for cooling water, the exhaust valve camshaft, rocker arms, and valve springs, the ignition make-and-break system camshaft and part of the operating equipment, and part of the timing chain together with its idler.

The following are photographs of drawings. Permission to use must be obtained from the Science Museum, London, England.

38,319–D________. 6-view drawing of the entire motor.

38,320–C________ Mainly a cross-section drawing showing the combustion chamber, cylinder, crankcase, piston, connecting rod, and crankshaft.

38,320–A________ Mainly drawings of crankcase cover, valves, and valve guides.

38,320–E________ Mainly drawings of magneto, gasoline tank, and radiator.

The National Air Museum, Smithsonian Institution, has blueprints for sale as follows: No. C–3 showing plan view, No. C–1 showing left side elevation, and No. C–9 showing magneto.

N.B.—Views of all engines refer to their positions in aircraft.

*Items marked with an asterisk are illustrations that appear in this paper.

SELECTED BIBLIOGRAPHY

1. SANTOS-DUMONT, A. My air-ships. Century Co., New York, 1904.
2. Scientific American for July 11, 1903.
3. Aerosphere for 1939. Edited by Glenn D. Angle. Aircraft Publications, New York.
4. Langley memoir on mechanical flight. Pt. 2, by Charles M. Manly. Smithsonian Institution, 1911.
5. VEAL, C. B. Manly, the engineer. S.A.E. Journ., vol. 44, No. 4, April 1939.
6. Original source material by Langley, Manly, and Balzer.
7. U.S. Patent No. 573174 dated Dec. 15, 1896, by Stephen M. Balzer.
8. The Aeroplane (British), Apr. 11, 1958.
9. The papers of Wilbur and Orville Wright, including the Chanute-Wright letters and other papers of Octave Chanute. Edited by Marvin W. McFarland. McGraw-Hill Book Co., New York, Toronto, and London, 1953.

10. MACMILLAN, NORMAN. Great aircraft. St. Martin's Press, New York, 1960.
11. GIBBS-SMITH, CHARLES H. The aeroplane—an historical survey of its origins and development. Her Majesty's Stationery Office in cooperation with the Science Museum, London, 1960.
12. MARSHALL, FRED, editor of Slipstream. Building the original Wright motor. Slipstream, May 1928.

Organic Chemistry: A View and a Prospect[1]

By SIR ALEXANDER TODD

Professor of Organic Chemistry
University of Cambridge, England

ORGANIC chemistry is as old as chemistry itself, but it was first recognized as a separate division at the end of the 18th century. Its growth to become not only the largest part of chemistry, but one of the largest of all the sciences in its factual content and in the number of its adherents, has occurred essentially during the past hundred years—since indeed it acquired its necessary theoretical basis through the work of Frankland, Couper, Kekulé, van't Hoff, and Le Bel, to mention only the major names associated with the basic structural theory of carbon compounds. Today its rate of growth is as fast as ever and the output of original work is prodigious. Some idea of that output is given by the calculation made a few years ago that, assuming an organic chemist were to read for 8 hours each day, it would take him about 18 months to read all the literature in his own subject produced during one year and published in the standard European and American journals.

Parallel with the phenomenal growth of the science, there has been an equally phenomenal growth of organic chemical industry until today it is a vital factor in the economy of Britain as well as of all other industrial countries. During the 6 years ending in 1960, when chemical industry as a whole showed an annual growth rate of 6.5 percent (as against an over-all rate of 3.1 percent for industry as a whole), the annual rate of growth for certain of the main organic sectors was even higher (plastics 15 percent, general organic chemicals 13 percent, pharmaceuticals 8.4 percent). These figures reflect the constantly growing impact of organic chemistry on nearly every aspect of our material civilization, for many products of the industry based on it such as plastics, synthetic fibers, dyes, detergents, adhesives, coatings, etc., are absorbed by and form a vital part of a variety of industries not themselves ordinarily regarded as chemical. In these circum-

[1] Reprinted by permission from The Times Science Review, London, No. 42, Winter 1961.
(C) The Times Publishing Co., Ltd., 1961. All rights reserved.

stances it is interesting, at the end of about a century's growth—for the science of organic chemistry and the organic chemical industry have grown side by side in close association with one another—to look at the present position of the science and to see whether future trends are discernible. This involves not only consideration of the most recent advances, but also a brief glance at the course of development in past years; for development patterns tend to repeat themselves in science as elsewhere.

NATURAL PRODUCTS

Organic chemistry is usually defined as the chemistry of the carbon compounds, but its original definition given by Berzelius just over 150 years ago was "the chemistry of substances found in living matter." Although Berzelius's definition is inadequate insofar as a very large number of carbon compounds are known which do not occur in living matter, the older definition is worth remembering because it was interest in the chemistry of living matter that initiated the science. It is, moreover, fair to say that the study of substances found in living matter has provided most of the stimuli to the advance of organic chemistry throughout its history, and there is little reason to doubt that this will continue to be the case. But the direct study of substances present in living matter—broadly described as natural products—which is now one of the dominant features of organic chemistry has only become so during the 20th century. This is not, however, surprising. Many of the products of living matter are of extreme complexity, and they were for the most part far beyond the reach of the early organic chemists. Even when the basic theory essential for modern developments was laid down about a hundred years ago the practical techniques available were too feeble to do more than permit the study of some relatively simple examples, and the second half of the 19th century was the period in which structural and synthetic organic chemistry grew to the point at which a return to the study of complex natural substances became practicable. It was during this initial intensive phase of development that organic chemical industry also grew to be of major importance. Modern organic chemical industry had its origin in the dyestuffs industry which began just a hundred years ago in this country with W. H. Perkin's accidental discovery of mauveine in the course of an abortive attempt to synthesize quinine in the laboratory, and was spurred on by work such as that of Graebe and Liebermann on the dyestuff of madder root which led to the synthesis of alizarin. It was thus born of academic research and as it grew and prospered, so did the science of organic chemistry. From those early days up to the present time the industry and the science have been closely associated; this has been greatly to the advantage of both and may help to explain their extraordinarily rapid growth. No industry stands closer to its parent science than does the organic chemical industry and in no industry is the gap between scientific discovery and industrial development smaller.

SYNTHESIS AND THEORY

Synthetic organic chemistry, which was well established by the beginning of this century, was and remains the backbone of the organic chemical industry and it still continues as one of the main streams of research in the science. Natural-product chemistry has been, however, dominant in the academic field for close on 50 years; essentially concerned with structural elucidation, it has also had a considerable influence on synthetic chemistry, since total synthesis of a natural product is commonly regarded as the final proof of structure. Many natural products are of such complexity that novel synthetic procedures have had to be devised for them, enriching the general arsenal of synthetic methods at the chemist's command. Natural-product chemistry has, of course, also influenced the course of industry by giving it new leads to the production of materials with desirable properties in one direction or another; this has been particularly marked in the pharmaceutical industry in the fields of hormones, hormone substitutes, and synthetic drugs. But it is also noticeable in other branches—the connection between natural coloring matters and the dyestuffs industry has already been mentioned, and the plastic and polymer field owes much to work such as that of the German chemist Harries on natural rubber; many other examples could be given.

There is, however, a third important line of advance in organic chemistry which has come into special prominence during the past 20 years or so. This concerns theoretical aspects of the subject. It is true to say that organic chemistry at the beginning of this century was in danger of stagnation since its theoretical basis, although essentially sound, was relatively undeveloped, and the science, with its enormous factual content, was distinctly topheavy. Fortunately, ideas stemming from the new atomic physics were soon brought to its aid through the young science of physical chemistry, and these have led over the years to a much deeper and more precise understanding of organic structures and of the mechanism of organic chemical reactions. These theoretical advances have greatly influenced recent developments in all branches of the subject, although they have presented a number of knotty problems to the universities since they have entailed a lot of re-thinking of teaching methods; it is doubtful whether a wholly satisfactory solution to these problems has yet been found.

These three, admittedly somewhat arbitrary, divisions of organic chemistry represent the main lines of advance which, by their progress and interplay, have brought organic chemistry to its present level in the academic and industrial fields.

NEW TECHNIQUES

One final point regarding their development should, however, be made. All three divisions have owed much to the successive introduction of new techniques and indeed without the development of micro-analytical methods, chromatography—paper, ion-exchange, and more recently vapor-phase [2]—and the introduction of physical methods of analysis and identification using spectroscopy in its various forms as well as X-ray crystallography, none of them could have reached its present position. What has been achieved and how far can one estimate from the answer to that question the outlook for the future?

Carbon compounds both natural and synthetic fall into two great groups. The first comprises those substances whose molecules can be regarded as units in themselves; these are of relatively low molecular weight varying from methane (CH_4) with a molecular weight of 16 to vitamin B_{12} ($C_{63}H_{88}N_{14}O_{14}PCo$) with one of 1354. The second group is that of the so-called macromolecules which includes inter alia the polysaccharides, proteins, nucleic acids, and rubber among natural products, and the synthetic polymers and plastics among synthetic materials. These substances have very large molecules, and their molecular weight may run into millions, as in the case of nucleic acids. It is characteristic of them that they are made up of a very large number of small unit molecules all joined together in a more or less regular manner by processes of polymerization or polycondensation. Since substances of the second group cannot normally be purified by the traditional methods of crystallization or distillation it is not surprising that most of the progress in organic chemistry has hitherto been in the field of the relatively small "unit" molecules.

There indeed it has been spectacular. The structures of a very large number of complex natural products have been worked out— vitamins, hormones, antibiotics, alkaloids, steroids, coenzymes, etc.— and most of them have been synthesized; many, indeed, are today manufactured by synthesis on a commercial scale. The power of modern organic synthesis has been amply demonstrated in recent

---

[2] See, for example, "A New Kind of Chromatogram," by A. T. James, in No. 16 of The Times Science Review, London, Summer, 1955.

years by such achievements as the total synthesis of steroids, such as cholesterol and cortisone, of chlorophyll, of cozymase, and of alkaloids such as strychnine. Synthetic methods have indeed reached such a level of perfection that very few structures would seem beyond their grasp. Structural determination, which in natural-product chemistry usually precedes synthesis, has in the past 10 years or so made enormous strides by the introduction of new physical methods based on ultraviolet, infrared, and nuclear magnetic resonance spectroscopy, and on X-ray crystallography. The power of the last-named analytical tool is amply demonstrated in the brilliant work of Prof. D. Crowfoot Hodgkin on the structure of vitamin B_{12}. Such techniques have already rendered obsolescent many of the older degradative methods of the organic chemist—in which the structure of a complex molecule was arrived at by a study of the breakdown products formed from it in different conditions—and further advances in the same direction may be expected from the newer applications of mass spectroscopy which enables a mixture of molecules to be separated on the basis of their respective masses. The flowering of structural and synthetic chemistry is reflected in the triumphs of the allied industry—the stream of synthetic drugs which have given for the first time cures rather than palliatives for many diseases, pesticides and herbicides, new dyes of vastly improved performance, as well as detergents and a host of other materials now regarded as normal features in our daily life. Moreover, the spectacular development of catalytic methods of synthesis and degradation in the field of petroleum chemistry has led not only to the appearance of a wealth of new intermediates for the chemical industry, but also to a gradual ousting of coal in favor of petroleum as its raw material.

MACROMOLECULES

Progress in the study of macromolecular substances was, until comparatively recently, very slow, largely because of the absence of experimental techniques for dealing with them. But with the appearance of the newer physical techniques of separation, study of the natural macromolecules both by degradation and synthesis has begun to grow very rapidly. Among the more spectacular developments have been the structural elucidation of a number of protein or polypeptide hormones including insulin and the total synthesis of a number of the smaller members of the group such as vasopressin. Substantial progress is now being made in determining the structure of the larger natural proteins, a striking example being provided by the very recent work on myoglobin structure [3] using X-ray methods

[3] See, for example, "Molecules of Life" in No. 28 of The Times Science Review, London, Summer, 1958, and the model of the structure of myoglobin reproduced in No. 37, Autumn, 1960, p. 1.

as a primary tool. The outlook in protein chemistry, which 15 years ago was still rather bleak, is now full of promise and offers new vistas in biology and medicine. Equally spectacular have been developments in the nucleic-acid field. Since the establishment of the general structure of the nucleic acids by chemical means 10 years ago and the consequent establishment of the physical nature of the deoxyribonucleic acids which form the genic material in living cells, there has been an astonishing flowering of chemical and biological work in this field. Occupying as they do a central position in the cellular economy by controlling the transmission of hereditary characteristics and by guiding the synthesis of cellular proteins, the nucleic acids form a group of compounds whose importance in life processes can hardly be overestimated. They are also key constituents of viruses, and the relevance of their study to research on cancer is being increasingly recognized. Much remains to be done chemically, before anything approaching a full understanding of the structure and function of individual nucleic acids will be realized, but the increasing attention being paid to them certainly holds out considerable hope for the future.

The production of synthetic macromolecular materials—plastics, synethetic fibers, resins, and rubbers—is one of the fastest growing sectors of organic chemical industry. It had its beginnings in the production of synthetic resins like bakelite and in the efforts made, notably in Germany, to produce satisfactory substitutes for natural rubber by polymerizing butadiene and other conjugated dienes, and it has since undergone enormous development. The reason for this development is easily understood, since by applying polymerization or polycondensation methods to a variety of small organic molecules one can obtain materials analogously constituted to the great classes of natural macromolecules and so produce fibers, elastomers, and plastic materials which may in many cases be more suited to a particular use than naturally occurring materials (c.f., for example, nylon, wool, and silk). In this field the most striking recent advances have been perhaps in the field of olefine polymerization (notably, ethylene and propylene) at low pressures with organometallic catalysts, and the production of isotactic polymers in which the monomer units are arranged in a stereochemically regular manner. This regularity, which is always found in the natural macromolecules, opens the way to synthetic polymers with properties markedly different from the randomly arranged polymers produced by older processes.

POINTERS TO FUTURE

In these various fields there are visible a number of trends which, I believe, point to likely directions of future research and industrial development. On the academic side natural-product chemistry has been slowly changing in emphasis in recent years. Methods of analysis and synthesis have been brought to a high stage of perfection and, partly because of this, since the midthirties interest has been turning slowly from molecular structure as such to the study of structure in relation to function and to the mechanism of biosynthesis of natural products—an area of research which has received major stimulus from the availability of radioactive isotopes with which biosynthetic intermediates can be "labeled" and their ultimate location in the final products determined. A brilliant contribution in the field of biosynthesis has been the elucidation of the method used by living organisms to make steroids, terpenoids, and carotenoids, the raw material in every case being acetic acid. Examples of work in which structure and function are related are to be found in the study of chemical reactions in living systems where transfer of energy and oxidation are simultaneously effected using organic phosphates, and on the joining together of complex molecules by oxidation. These trends suggest that organic chemistry is likely to move deeper into the biological field and that academically its main growing points are likely to be in the study of the course of biochemical processes and in the investigation of the natural macromolecules and their functions in the cell. It seems likely, too, that theoretical organic chemistry will turn also in the direction of biological processes and so make a major contribution in the same general fields of advance. This is likely to be the case not only in the study of reaction mechanisms but also in the further development of dynamic stereochemistry which has sprung into prominence in many important fields of research—for example, in the search for new drugs related to cortisone.

All this does not mean that the broad field which I earlier described as synthetic organic chemistry is likely to wither. On the contrary, since it is an essential component of progress in organic chemical industry, it is likely to continue in vigorous growth searching for new and more economical methods of production, and for an ever-increasing array of new products each with some special property or combination of properties. On the industrial side the way ahead for the pharmaceutical industry is clear but it may find itself devoting more of its synthetic effort to the macromolecular substances as virus diseases become an increasing preoccupation. For the rest, plastics and polymers are likely to continue as a major growing point. Here, as indeed also in general synthetic chemistry, the trend to the study of compounds containing, in addition to carbon, other elements such as fluorine, silicon, and boron is likely to become increasingly evident.

Already polymers based on tetrafluoroethylene are being marketed and silicon-containing polymers (silicones) are well known. The introduction of other elements into carbon compounds opens up new fields of endeavor, since the products so formed often have quite different properties (such as thermal stability, behavior under extremes of temperature and pressure) from those met with in ordinary organic chemicals. It is likely, too, that synthetic polymers and polycondensates will find increasing use as structural materials in their own right. This will not only stimulate increased research in the field but it will lead to enormously greater production and to a number of plastics still regarded as "chemicals" becoming everyday structural materials and being used like wood and steel; such a change may considerably influence the structure of the industry producing them.

It is, of course, impossible to review adequately the present situation of organic chemistry either in the academic or industrial field within the compass of a short article. Developments in recent years have been so rapid and so multifarious that it is difficult to single out the really important advances or to see the whole in perspective. For this reason it is rash to prophesy; all that one can do is to make a personal estimate of current trends and where they may lead. But one thing is certain—organic chemistry is still in a period of vigorous growth and in the future the industry based on it will be an increasingly important factor in the national economy.

The New Age of the Sea [1]

By PHILIP B. YEAGER [2]

Member Professional Staff, Committee on Science and Astronautics
U.S. House of Representatives

[With 3 plates]

IF, IN the past few years, there has been doubt that the world is plunging into unprecedented social and technological revolutions, the doubt is swiftly fading. Too much is happening too fast in both areas. It is almost as if someone had pulled keystones from a mountainside and started twin avalanches—one a rapid acceleration of social problems (including economic, political, and military ones), and the other a tumbling series of brilliant technological advances.

But there is a curious phenomenon connected with all this. It is a phenomenon growing more pronounced with each passing day. It consists of the fact that insofar as the world's rising social difficulties may find their answer in science, each is likely to do so by a route leading directly through the sea. That is, nearly all the major challenges of the future which are now discernible seem to point like magnetized needles toward the oceans—indicating that an important part of their respective solutions lies somehow in deep water.

It is doubtful if there is any parallel for this situation in the history of mankind. Of course the sea has been a powerful influence on the affairs of men for thousands of years, particularly since the age of discovery and exploration spanning the 15th, 16th, and 17th centuries. Most of us are accustomed to the thought that the sea came into its own when venturesome, visionary men like Magellan, Cabot, Columbus, and Vespucci proved its utility as a medium of global transport. Some of us would set the date as early as the time of Eric the Red and his son Leif, or of the Mediterranean fleets of Carthage and Rome.

When the naval frigate and the 80-gun ship-of-the-line materialized, to be followed quickly by the American clipper and the steam

---

[1] Reprinted by permission from the United States Naval Institute Proceedings, vol. 87, No. 6, June 1961.

[2] The opinions or assertions in this article are the author's personal ones and are not to be construed as official or as the views of the House Committee on Science and Astronautics.

voyage of *Savannah*, the age of the sea appeared to have reached full maturity; it had become a primary area for both commerce and conflict. And such, magnified many times, it remains. Yet a careful look ahead shows that, influential as it has been in the past and is today, the true significance of the sea for civilization is only beginning to become apparent.

Those who have heard the scientific testimony presented to the committees of Congress in recent years are especially conscious of this. The inquiries of these groups have ranged from biological warfare to the political issues of exploring outer space, from the need for language computers to the potential uses of rocket engines, from geodetic myths and fallacies to the shifting curricula of American education. Through these and other technological surveys, there has been revealed not only the capabilities, wants, and expectations of the scientific fraternity, including anthropologists, but also those of the economist, the industrialist, the conservationist, the engineer, the government official, the teacher, the student, the soldier, and the sailor.

In addition to providing a factual base for current legislation, the inquiries have been designed to give public officials a preview of the issues they will be called upon to face in the decades ahead—issues so sweeping in scope that they must be anticipated and planned for well in advance if they are to be met at all.

It is from the analysis of the vast amount of information poured into Congress by the country's most knowledgeable men and women that the image of the sea has emerged, almost startlingly, as a potent force which spreads across the entire spectrum of future human affairs.

The direction in which we turn seems to make little difference. Regardless of the social complex or problem under study, if we trace its predictable convolutions far enough ahead, we discover that sooner or later the trail encounters some aspect of the expanding influence of the oceans.

The most competent forecasts available today indicate strongly that the remainder of the 20th century will find Americans—and, indeed, people everywhere—forced to concentrate upon seven great quests. These are: the search for Security, for Living Room, for Water, for Climate, for Resources, for Industry, and for Knowledge itself.

In every one of these areas, the sea is proving a crucial element—so crucial that it is difficult to escape the conclusion that the new age into which we are moving is not only the age of the atom, the electron, and space: it is also a new age of the sea.

THE SEARCH FOR SECURITY

Nuclear weapons, the rising tide of nationalism throughout the world, and the rapidly growing East-West battle for the mind of man are putting an unprecedented premium on national security. At the same time, it is apparent that today, more than ever, strength is crucial from a psychological as well as from a physical standpoint.

Since the channel to security through international comity and negotiation cannot be depended upon, either now or in the foreseeable future, a strong military posture is the alternative. There is very little disagreement about this. What is strange is the fact that our technological revolution, while introducing radical new concepts of weapons and weapon systems, actually tends to accentuate the ancient role of the sea as a theater of military activity.

One does not need to be a military expert to see that this is so. In fact, not being an expert has its advantages. For if one is not, it is possible to evaluate the meaning of our new technology without being overly influenced by tradition, pride, ambition, or economic security.

To the nonmilitary expert, who is, however, familiar with the various military and civilian views concerning the employment of modern science in national defense, it is clear that current technology is underlining the necessity for mobility and secrecy of operational bases. And this is where the finger of logic points squarely to the sea.

No doubt it is true, as many of our military men assert, that we are moving inevitably into a time of astropower. But it is equally true that for many years to come the most efficient operational bases for asserting such power will be located on earth. And even when bases in space become possible, their vulnerability from the standpoint of mobility and secrecy will scarcely be less than bases functioning on or below the surface of the sea. Paradoxically, the missile-space era itself seems destined to emphasize this salt-water utility.

Since the refinement of the missile, target accuracy has become uncomfortably high. With the addition of the nuclear warhead, its threat obviously is a devastating one. As soon as geodetic surveys have been perfected and geographical locations are precisely known, as soon as missile production and servicing become simplified and reliable, the risks we face will prove less and less tolerable and land bases more and more vulnerable. Even the so-called "hard" launching sites—those constructed underground—may find their effectiveness partially canceled, particularly if the enemy is capable of contaminating the surrounding area with a hovering lid of deadly radiation or destructive chemical or biological agents.

Mobility and secrecy, at this point in time, will cease to be marginal necessities. They will be absolute ones. They may be obtainable on land by such schemes as the mobile-transport Minuteman. They will also be easily and efficiently attained at sea.

It appears likely, then, that an increasing percentage of U.S. deterrent power will shift to the sea. This may include more than the submarine-Polaris-missile concept, which, for all its virtues, has certain limitations as to communications, timing, and attack potential. It will almost certainly have to include a new concept of an extremely fast surface fleet capable of firing missiles accurately, shifting its base materially at a moment's notice, and capable of utilizing any patch of water as a launching site for any type of missile needed. The idea, which conceives of firing the missile from the surface of the water itself, requires pinpoint navigation and new missile technology rather than radical approaches to naval shipbuilding. In other words, it is new weapon handling technique that will be essential, not revolutionary types of ships.

When viewed through political and economic eyes, this extra reliance on the sea assumes doubled import. Government officials and others well versed in international affairs and the economic facts of life are aware that the United States is not likely to keep military bases throughout the world forever. At the same time, such bases are an added liability (in the sense of being targets) when placed on American soil.

They may be kept partially in the air or, someday, in space. But the sea is also looming as a likely locale, since it will have virtually all the advantages of foreign or sky-based launch sites, few of the disadvantages, and seems to offer a more practical and generally cheaper way of doing the job.

Thus it appears that the role of the Navy in the security picture, far from diminishing with the revolutions of our times, may become more comprehensive and conclusive than it has ever been—despite the many innovations and changes in seagoing missions, methods, and machines.

SEARCH FOR LIVING ROOM

Recognition of the growing population problem is now fairly widespread. During the 1950's, its warning was sounded frequently enough and the evidence became concrete enough to initiate serious thinking on the consequences of overpopulation.

Still, and in spite of dire warnings from the sociologists, most of us tend to toss off the matter as something we cannot do anything about. Or else we persist in treating it as too remote to warrant doing something about right now.

Both attitudes seem fallacious. Certainly the second one is. To determine how much so, one need only glance at the United States. It required 300 years for the American population to reach the 1910 level of 90 million persons. Yet in the past 50 years that number has doubled. It will double again before the turn of the century, unless the birth rate slackens or some disaster wipes out great segments of the population.

One of the most important aspects of the population explosion is the problem of living space—of sufficient room to move around in with some semblance of freedom and privacy.

Interestingly enough, the evidence is that long before food or housing shortages become really serious, the difficulties arising from cramped living will have reached a critical peak, a peak demanding dramatic measures for a solution.

We have already begun to see the signs which are at once physical and psychological. Witness the mushrooming suburbs with their postage-stamp lots; the crowded expressways; the new traffic bottlenecks that materialize faster than old ones are dissolved; the smog blights; the polluted rivers; the disappearing trees and forest lands; the crowded classrooms; the accelerating noise level; the increasing crime rates; the high incidence of mental illness; the diminishing art of neighborliness; the self-enforced isolation of apartment dwellers; the periodic adult fetish for "getting away from it all"; the year-round emphasis on keeping children organized; the climbing divorce statistics; the courtroom dockets that are jammed with petty civil suits; and so on.

All these symptoms, in one way or another, stem at least in part from too many people living too close together. At the moment, the pressures creating the symptoms may not be sufficient to cause boiling. But imagine a doubling of the pressures. What then?

The social scientists believe that if our heterogeneous civilization is to remain reasonably healthy, in body, mind, and spirit, it cannot afford to let itself be forced to live like ants. Men need space. This means that the population must somehow spread out as it grows instead of concentrating more and more.

When a national park is forced to close its gates to 7,000 would-be campers during a single holiday weekend, when Congress must consider legislation to prohibit commercialization of the remaining 2 percent of American wilderness land in order to preserve at least a small part of the country in its natural state—the imminence of the problem begins to sink in.

Serious as is the situation, however, scientists do not believe solutions are impossible. They are depending on the sea and sea-related techniques to help find them.

The prognosticated picture is for gradually accelerating migration from heavily populated countries to lightly populated ones. The influx will be toward Australia, New Zealand, Canada, Alaska, and South America. In fact, the move has already begun. And it is receiving its greatest push, at the moment, from nations whose people historically have been strongly attached to their native lands—the English, the Dutch, the Danes, the French, the Belgians, even Americans.   Despite political obstacles to free migration, it is believed that such trends will quadruple before the turn of the century.   Our shrinking globe and the resultant style of international living, marrying, and working is bound to create a reciprocity of movement which would be quite unbelievable to the citizen of 1920 or even 1950.   If Western culture should rub off on the Soviets faster than the reverse, so that Russian barriers to general intercourse are lowered, this trend may also find its way into northern Eurasia.

An equal, and perhaps earlier, phenomenon arising from the press of population along the world's seaboards will be the jump to island living.   Presently there are thousands of coastal islands which are deserted or only sparsely inhabited.   They offer an attractive alternative to crowded mainland living, and the forecasters are convinced that in the decades ahead these islands will turn into much sought-after real estate.

A third result of the spreading out of the population is expected to be a migration into land areas within the boundaries of the homeland which at present are only marginally desirable or convenient. This movement should be made feasible by technological innovations already in process and on the verge of practical utilization.

The effect of these trends on sea-related activities, and vice versa, will be marked.

With the swift surge toward world travel which is expected to be crucial within 25 years, comes the need for additional sources of rapid, long-range transportation.   Air travel has expanded to meet this requirement, but air lanes are by no means likely to be able to handle the needs of the future.   Relatively speaking, the air is already more crowded than the sea and its problems of adequate termini are more difficult.

This means a much revitalized demand for ocean travel and for new types of fast, oceangoing transports, and there is little doubt that when the demand is great enough such craft will be made available. We cannot see exactly how tomorrow's sailors will navigate, but we can guess that the naval architects and oceanographers will have hydrofoil craft sailing accurately predicted currents at speeds heretofore reserved for land vehicles.   As the techniques grow, they will, in turn, stimulate their own use.

Potential island dwellers who are currently discouraged by the inaccessibility of remote coastal areas will find that smaller versions of these same craft would make an island home feasible and commuting easy.   Or the air-cushion vehicle, which rides a few inches or feet above the surface of the water, may be used.   Some of the latter are presently in ferry service between English Channel ports.   With refinement and simplification, this vehicle, too, has significance for extensive salt-water transportation, especially to and from coastal islands or bay and inlet areas, and upon the world's rivers.

In company with the fast-developing fuel cell, which may permit a reliable source of localized, domestic power, and with the conversion of salt water to fresh water, these oncoming sea-transport methods will make island living not only reasonable but highly desirable.

The need for removing large parts of the presently urbanized population into the hinterlands likewise depends upon independent power sources, fresh water, and a transportation system which does not require expensive (and soil destructive) highways. Here again the sea promises a large part of the solution—the fresh-water, and a land adaptation of the hovercraft, or ground-effect machine, evolved from techniques developed through use on ocean areas.

The search for living room thus conjures up a future network of ocean-current corridors, seagoing traffic, and sea-dependent facets of living which the most confirmed old sea dogs of yesterday could scarcely have visualized.

THE SEARCH FOR WATER

The years 1954–57 were particularly notable as hurricane years for the east and gulf coasts of the United States. There were many such disturbances, and the American public was presented with distressing facts and figures based on damage caused by such wayward whirlwinds as Hurricanes Connie, Hazel, and Carol.

Notwithstanding the tragedy and damage caused by these and similar storms, they were accompanied by a completely unpublicized but highly valuable asset—namely, relieving the water crisis of a large and parched section of the Nation.

This is one blessing, at least, inherent in the hurricane during earth's current dry cycle, 1951–62. As far as the United States is concerned, the torrential rains produced by the hurricane which moves inland have recently rescued more crops than they have destroyed and, while in the process of tearing down beach resorts and causing floods, they have nonetheless granted reprieves to thirsty agricultural industries and well-dry communities from Miami to Bangor.

The situation illustrates the growing fresh-water shortage which, in a few short years, promises to become acute not only in traditionally arid lands but also in such water-blessed areas as the United States, Europe, and western Russia.

More than 200 major communities of the United States face water shortages, and all but a handful of States are experiencing a serious water problem in one form or another. The Middle East, Holland, Spain, Italy, South Africa, Israel, the West Indies, and a number of South American countries are worse off.

Thus the stage is set for an acute shortage of man's most precious commodity. The precariousness of the situation is being augmented, of course, by the increasing population, the many new domestic uses to which water is being put, the rising use of irrigation and industrial water, the pollution of fresh-water streams and rivers, and a general failure to conserve water.

Very likely the world will get by the present 11-year dry cycle, which is scheduled to merge into a wet decade this year (1961), without too much suffering. And since the wet cycle may run as much as 7 to 12 percent above normal rainfall, the evolution of fresh-water problems from 1962 to 1973 may be somewhat retarded. But beginning with the dry cycle of 1973, when the needs of a much larger population will have to be met, the availability and use of fresh water is expected to take its place among the world's crucial issues—or so the water engineers predict—unless substantial new sources of fresh water are uncovered.

Education of water users, conservation, and rigidly enforced anti-pollution laws will aid a great deal in alleviating the situation. Assuming, however, that standards of living will not be allowed to slip and that the population will continue to increase, the experts prophesy that nothing offers a permanent solution to future shortages except large new sources of water. This means the conversion of sea water to fresh water.

Conversion, of course, is nothing new to sailormen who have been doing it aboard ship for many decades. (Large aircraft carriers today convert salt water at a rate of 200,000 gallons per day.) But it is quite another matter to convert salt water to fresh water when the method used must be made to serve the world's millions.

Progress is being made by a number of methods, mainly through a variety of distillation techniques, solar energy, electrodialysis, and freezing, chemical, and electrical conversion. At present the largest plants converting saline water are located in South Africa, the Persian Gulf, the West Indies, Venezuela, Argentina, Ecuador, Greenland, Italy, and, in the United States, California and Pennsylvania. They convert anywhere from 100,000 gallons per day to 3.5 million gallons per day, at a cost of from $1.74 to $4 per thousand gallons. This compares with American municipal water rates which range from 25 to 40 cents per thousand gallons—but which do not reflect the rising costs of developing *new* sources of fresh water by conventional means.

When conversion costs drop to around 35 cents per thousand gallons, ocean or bay water will become a major source of the world's fresh-water supply. The Dutch are already operating electrodialysis-membrane plants which come close to 50 cents when brackish water (less than a third the salinity of sea water) is used. It is interesting that this is the price paid by Dallas, Tex., residents for a single gallon of extra fresh water during the drought of 1957—twice what they paid for gasoline.

The U.S. Government, through the Interior Department's Office of Saline Water, is subsidizing research in this area at a rate of between $1 and $3 million a year. Seven States—California, New Mexico, Arizona, Texas, Florida, North Carolina, and South Dakota—are also spending tax money for the purpose. Compared to other government endeavors, however, the total amount is negligible—so far.

The average American family uses 550 gallons of fresh water a day, the average apartment building 50,000 gallons a day, hospitals 50,000 to 100,000 gallons per day, large office buildings 120,000 gallons and up. Total water use in the United States has increased from 40 billion gallons a day in 1900 to 323 billion gallons in 1960, and will go to 597 billion gallons by 1980. Moreover, when we consider that the maximum dependable supply of natural fresh water in the United States, if it were all captured, is 515 billion gallons daily—then we begin to see the urgent need for new water resources.

As the water engineers point out, we must look once again to the sea.

THE SEARCH FOR CLIMATE

The slight knowledge which humans have of weather forces can be seen from the fact that at present we do not even know exactly how rain begins. Learning to predict weather with great accuracy and to modify it is something which geological forecasters take to be a "must" in the years ahead. In this way we may be able to slow down the soil erosion of arable land—that "geological inevitability which man can only hasten or postpone." Like the fresh-water situation, increased human demands upon the soil are creating real difficulties.

The Russian steppes of Kazakhstan are providing the world with a great contemporary dust bowl, reminiscent of that of the middle 1930's, when dust from the Great Plains stretched from Texas to Saskatchewan. Poor land-cultivation policies, drought, and strong easterly winds have combined to produce the trials of southern Russia. So great is the extent of this disturbance that the dust cloud has been identified in photographs taken by American weather satellites at altitudes of 400 miles.

Of course, wind erosion is only one of the processes whereby the earth's arable land is diminishing and the deserts increasing; erosion by water also sweeps away the soil. But insofar as the dust bowl of the Soviet steppes has diminished food resources at a time when the number of mouths to feed is increasing rapidly, it is a rather ominous indication of more serious troubles to come.

How long, the geologists inquire, can the world afford floods and dust bowls? The answer, obviously, is not much longer. Not, at least, if we expect to avoid famine, pestilence, and the threat of an exhausted soil at a time when we can least afford it.

Doing something about understanding and controlling (to a degree) the climate is apt to prove a far more difficult task than easing the shortage of fresh water. It will involve a tremendous amount of research. But again that research apparently begins and ends with the sea.

Meteorologists know that the sea is the breeding ground for the two great forces which contribute most to soil erosion—wind and rainfall. But they do not yet have enough understanding of the interplay of all the various elements contributing to weather to know why the earth's climate is as it is—or even to predict the long-range trends our climate may be taking. Until they do have a very good understanding of how and why the forces of climate behave, man seems destined to remain relatively ineffective in his efforts to slow down the present all too rapid erosion of his fertile world.

No doubt there is much that can be done with the land itself. The development of contour farming, for instance, has proved greatly beneficial. Crop rotation, soil chemistry, reforestation, flood control and the like are all highly useful practices. But even they have limitations for the long haul and can scarcely be compared to the benefits which might arise from an ability to create or to modify climate.

While some scientists have grave doubts that such ability will ever exist, others who combine meteorology with oceanography are now inclined to believe that these doubts themselves stem from an insufficient concept of how much information remains to be uncovered—how little we really know of the character and forces of the sea and how inclusive the influence of the sea is upon climate. They believe that the two sciences cannot be separated and that the true understanding of climate must wait upon a true understanding of the sea, which handles the greater part of earth's total "heat budget."

Research into the mysteries of the ocean and its operation is by no means proceeding fast enough to suit the world's oceanographers, but it has picked up startlingly in the past few years and gives promise of accelerating still more. The United States has some 1,600 scientists now pursuing this endeavor, and its annual Federal expenditures of about $25 million are expected to be stepped up to $85 million during the 1960's. Other countries, notably England, Norway, Italy, Denmark, and the Soviet Union, are similarly increasing their sea study efforts.

Not all of this effort, nor even the major part of it, is being undertaken with the benefits of climatology in mind. Nevertheless, those benefits may be the greatest by far to come out of the seagoing laboratories now plying the oceans of the world.

LAUNCHING SOLID PROPELLANT ROCKETS FROM THE SEA

Handling and logistics requirements for such rockets are simple and inexpensive, and mobility is unlimited over the surfaces of the oceans. Furthermore, the launching pad environment costs nothing, cannot be destroyed, and hides the missile firing apparatus from would-be attackers.

1. Will Future Island Dwellers Commute in Hydrofoils?

These speedy craft would make living in presently isolated insular regions feasible. With a cheap, local supply of power and fresh water, islands would become highly desirable residential areas.

2. A Russian Hydrofoil, the 150-Passenger River Boat *Meteor*

Recognizing the need for improved water transportation systems, the Soviets already have fast passenger hydrofoils in operation on their lakes and rivers.

1. PILOT PLANT FOR CONVERTING SEA WATER TO FRESH

Assembled for sea site testing at Wrightsville Beach, N.C., this plant uses the vacuum-freezing method.   Its capacity is 15,000 gallons per day.

2. PROGRESS IN OCEANOGRAPHY HAS BEEN MADE; IT MUST BE INCREASED

The bathyscaph *Trieste* is shown preparing to dive off the Island of Panza in the Tyrrhenian Sea.   She was purchased by the U.S. Navy, and made a record dive of 35,800 feet off Guam in 1960.

THE SEARCH FOR RESOURCES

Running parallel with the patent needs for fresh water and productive soil is the less obvious but worldwide demand for new supplies of all resources. Among the most needed for the future, according to conservation engineers, are biological, mineral, and energy resources. In each category the sea offers particular hope for efficient capture and use. Moreover, the sea has as yet hardly been tapped as a supplier.

Biologically, the sea could be made to yield a limitless amount of protein enrichment for the human diet. Dr. Edward Wenk, a marine scientist who serves as executive secretary to the Federal Council for Science and Technology, points out that the sea "is filled with rich fauna and flora drifting at the surface, or in layers at intermediate depths; there are meadows of plants and swarms of large and small animals grazing or preying upon one another." He adds that only a very few of the 20,000 species of fish are caught and fewer still used, that little is actually known about fishing stocks, rhythmical seasonal changes and their sporadic fluctuation, but that the advent of such information will put a new face upon fishing. Fishing will then lose its hunting characteristics and assume those of cultivation. Development of important plants with life-stimulating properties may be handled the same way.

As far as minerals are concerned, the ocean floors have recently been found to contain high concentrations of manganese, cobalt, nickel, iron, and copper. But the potentially greater source of mineral supply rests in the sea water itself. Ordinary sea water is now known to contain 41 elements. Many of these (aside from chlorine and sodium) are in relatively large quantities—such as magnesium, sulfur, calcium, potassium, bromine, boron, carbon, strontium, silicon, and fluorine. Others, far less abundant, nevertheless are minerals which are becoming critical for modern scientific purposes—cesium (for plasma engines), uranium (for atomic energy), molybdenum (for heat-resistant alloys), and the like.

To date we have learned to extract only bromine and magnesium from sea water on a practical basis. But we know that plants extract potassium from the sea and animals like the octopus extract a copper compound for use in their blood as an oxygen carrier. So the processes for "mining" the sea undoubtedly exist. When they are uncovered, the world should have an unexcelled new natural supply of vital mineral resources.

Perhaps the most attractive side of the sea from a resources standpoint, however, is its potential as a source of energy—energy which can be tapped without depleting some limited type of fuel resource such as coal or oil.

A July 1, 1960, report of the House Committee on Science and Astronautics states:

The greatest source of energy in the sea lies in the water itself. Hydrogen, one of the elements in water and thus in enormous abundance in the oceans, may be considered the fuel from which energy may be someday derived, imitating the natural process of nuclear fusion that occurs on the sun. Should current research efforts succeed, man would have a virtually inexhaustible store of energy, but the quest is long and arduous.

Still another possible source of energy from the sea has been proposed by taking advantage of the difference in surface and bottom temperature. It has been said that almost 35,000 times the existing annual energy consumption of the world is delivered annually to the earth in the form of solar radiation and since most of the earth's surface is covered by ocean, a major portion of solar energy is absorbed by the sea. The temperature at depths below which sunlight does not penetrate, on the order of 1,200 feet, is ordinarily around 40° F. In the tropics, surface temperatures of 80° to 90° are common. Theoretically, this temperature difference could be utilized to drive a properly designed turbine, but it would operate at low thermal efficiency because the temperature differences are low. Quite obviously the amounts of energy so extracted are unlimited. The major question is whether such systems are economically attractive.

Finally, there is the possibility of extraction of power from the twice daily rise and fall of the tides—such as has been proposed many years ago for Passamaquoddy. It is natural that man should look for means of harnessing some of the power of the tides for his own benefit, and small tide mills have been operated in a few suitable localities for centuries. Many plans for tidal power stations such as the Severn Barrage scheme have been drawn up, but only one project has so far reached the construction stage. This is the French scheme for the Rance Estuary in the Bay of St. Malo which is designed to have a capacity of 340 megawatts and is due to be completed in 1960. The main difficulty in the development of tidal power is that, even with large tidal ranges, the hydraulic head available is comparatively small and large areas of tidal water would have to be enclosed at high capital cost.

While it should be noted that each possibility is accompanied by some reservation, it should also be noted that technological problems just about as difficult and expensive have been solved cleanly in the past 10 or 15 years. When the need becomes great enough—and that time is not far away—there seems little doubt that ways will be found to pull out and transmit the sea's restless, endless energy in the form of useful work.

THE SEARCH FOR INDUSTRY

For the American system of private enterprise, the need for new industry in the years ahead assumes marked importance, not only in order to maintain a high level of consumer goods and a growing economy, but as a means of employment for the rising population.

Exploitation of the oceans rates far up on the list of genuine new industrial possibilities. A recent issue of Dun's Review, for example, has cited the oceans as "industry's next frontier" and comments:

As flights into space become routine in the next decade, the nation may turn in another direction for the next great research frontier—and new multi-billion-dollar marketing opportunities. Close at hand, but still largely out of reach, the depths of earth's oceans are in many ways more a mystery than outer space. The coming drive to plumb the ocean's secrets will mean a great new source of profits for industry. As the navies of the world slowly submerge, demand for equipment that can function under water will burgeon. As the industrial nations exhaust many of the natural resources of the land surface, submarine miners will increasingly exploit the incredible mineral wealth of the oceans, and as the world's population expands beyond the capacity of arable land to feed it, the sea will become a critically important source of edible flora and fauna. . . . Although the objective of the oceanographers is more scientific knowledge of the ocean and the ocean floor, commercial benefits are sure to follow. Here is one example : leading oceanographers are convinced that underwater telephone cable breaks are the result of ocean bottom landslides. If and when oceanographers are able to predict where such displacements of bottom soil will take place, the telephone companies will be able to avoid multi-million-dollar repair bills by laying cables elsewhere or by other methods. . . . When all the current activity connected with the oceans is evaluated, the dimensions of present and potential market opportunities look really impressive.

But the industrial outlook for the sea encompasses far more territory than that suggested above. Besides a trend to improved and more efficient cable laying, a series of other submarine activities are beginning to take place—undersea pipelines, such as the projected crossing of the Mediterranean from North Africa to Spain for pumping gas and oil; undersea tunnels, such as the 32-mile Dover-to-Calais project beneath the English Channel; offshore mining, such as the new sulphur operations in the Gulf of Mexico; the development of robot equipment for undersea operations, such as the Remote Underwater Manipulator which can act as the hand of man on the ocean floor through a 5-mile coaxial cable.

Then there is the ultimate usefulness of the oceans and coastal areas as places of storage. The seas have been used for generations, of course, as a dumping ground for continental wastes. But the storage demands of the future will be far more sophisticated. One already showing urgency is the storage of unwanted radioactive byproducts of atomic energy. Low-level wastes are presently being dispersed in the sea. High-level wastes cannot be stored there, at least not until much more is known about the inner workings of the sea itself and ways are found to contain the material in a manner which permits radioactive dissipation over long periods of time without contaminating the water.

These very developments, however, as they crystallize, promise a revolutionary shift to sea storage for other commodities and purposes—especially for those which need to be maintained in cool, stable temperatures and/or unexposed to oxygen. As land becomes ever more scarce and the costs of using it for storage less feasible, it will not be surprising if government and commerce alike begin charting off segments of ocean area for this purpose.

Other potential industrial uses allied to the sea can be identified even now. Hydroponic farming—growing plants and vegetables in water containing the essential mineral nutrient salts, rather than in soil—is in its infancy. But there are those who foresee that this endeavor will necessarily become a very large one and that research into the qualitative transformation and manipulation of sea water will make it possible. Another important industry is evolving, based on supplying equipment needed by the world's one million skin divers, plus that of the salvage industry which has been tremendously stimulated by new skin-diving techniques. This, too, is a trend likely to accelerate on both business and pleasure bases.

Of one thing we can be sure. As research into the sea and sea-related activities increases, industrial uses will be found for it which today we cannot visualize. And new professions, unconjectured as of now, are bound to grow with these new industries.

THE SEARCH FOR KNOWLEDGE

When the United States inaugurated its space exploration program in March 1958, the President's science advisers issued a statement in which they observed:

Scientific research has never been amendable to rigorous cost accounting in advance. Nor, for that matter, has exploration of any sort. But if we have learned one lesson, it is that research and exploration have a remarkable way of paying off—quite apart from the fact that they demonstrate that man is alive and insatiably curious. And we all feel richer for knowing what explorers and scientists have learned about the universe in which we live.

Moreover, as technology continues to take over and the hours of the world's working day shorten, people must have purposeful and creative things to do. The burgeoning quest for knowledge is expected to fill a large part of this inchoate vacuum.

Perhaps the most immediate target of the knowledge seekers will be earth itself, about which so much remains to be learned. A true understanding of our own planet, its origin, composition, and what makes it tick, will be one of the first big steps toward understanding the universe. This, at least, is the allegation of the scientists, who add that the key to better smformation about the earth very probably lies with the sea.

"Yet the sea," says the House Committee on Science and Astronautics, "which represents 71 percent of the earth's surface, is mostly unexplored. Scientific information is meager concerning the physical and chemical properties of oceans and their currents, the biological and mineral resources of, in, and under the sea, the relationship of the oceans to weather and climate.   Even knowledge about the origins of the oceans themselves, their evolution and the changes which may be expected are little known and understood."

A long-held desire of geologists all over the world has been access to earth's interior—to that area below the crust.   The U.S.-proposed Project Mohole,[3] which contemplates ocean drilling, may provide it. This program gets its name from the Mohorovicic discontinuity which represents the interface between the familiar crust and the as yet unseen mantle.   Because what lies beneath the earth's crust, 7 to 15 miles from the surface, is of such vital importance to the understanding of the origin and geophysical processes of the earth, Project Mohole is designed to drill through the crust into the mantle.

The reason for the approach through the sea is simple.   Thus far the deepest successful drilling [for oil] has been limited to about 26,000 feet, far short of the 100,000 feet at which discontinuity is estimated to lie below the surface of continental masses.   In the oceans, however, the discontinuity rises to within 15,000 feet of the ocean bed.   It is thus proposed to undertake the drilling at sea so as to reduce by a significant amount the depth of hole required.

The answers to come from these and other phases of the growing drive toward ocean sciences will possibly provide us with the first basically accurate understanding of the globe on which we live.   What such understanding will mean in terms of material and economic effect, or in terms of mental and physical effect, can only be surmised. It will not be insignificant.

Each of the searches discussed in the foregoing contributes to the others and each, in some degree, is dependent on the others.   Taken as a group, however, and in light of their common denominator, they would seem to herald a coming Age of the Sea second to none in earth's history.

---

[3] See the following article in this Report.—EDITOR.

Drilling Beneath the Deep Sea[1]

By WILLIAM E. BENSON

Program Director for Earth Sciences
National Science Foundation

[With 4 plates]

Two miles below the surface of the Pacific Ocean off the west coast of Mexico, a drill bit studded with diamonds was gently eased inch by inch into the bottom ooze. Jets of water coming down the drill pipe then began to wash the bit farther into the mud. One of the most notable modern experiments in oceanography and geophysics was underway.

The experiment, part of Project Mohole, achieved important results through a combination of two factors—a scientific impetus bordering on the visionary, and imaginative engineering concepts that pushed to its limits today's technology.

Attached to 11,700 feet of pipe dangling from a drilling derrick mounted on a ship, the bit was the tip of an 85-ton probe wielded by scientists intent on unlocking some of the history that is recorded in the sediment that has been collecting on the bottom of the oceans for millions of years.

At the base of the steel tower, scientists and veteran petroleum drillers anxiously watched gages and recording pens trace the shakes and twists of the pipe as, in high winds and heavy seas, the drilling ship *CUSS I* held its position with steering motors.

For the scientists, the drilling operation was part of the first attempt to retrieve samples of the earth's crust at appreciable depths beneath the floor of the ocean basin. Their success has added a completely new technique to the study of the oceans of the world.

For the engineers and drilling personnel who had assembled the longest drilling pipe ever suspended from a ship, the operation was the world's first deep-sea drilling expedition. Furthermore, a drilling crew was working for the first time aboard an unmoored ship, and in water 40 times deeper than in the usual offshore operation.

---

[1] Reprinted by permission from Sperryscope, Sperry Rand Corp., vol. 15, No. 10, 1961.

As they watched the uncoiling ink lines and the quivering gages, the drillers were learning what takes place when more than 2 miles of pipe is hung in water, what effects the ship's pitch and roll produce, and how much vibration is set up by ocean currents and pipe rotation. As one remarked, "This is like hanging a piece of spaghetti from a 12th-floor window to the sidewalk, and then trying to drill a hole with it."

The drilling was the first at-sea experiment for Project Mohole, a 5- to 10-year nationally funded effort to drill through the earth's crust to sample its interior, the largest and least-known area on earth. Mohole is supported by the National Science Foundation and is a combined effort of the Nation's leading scientists and engineers working through the AMSOC Committee, organized in 1958, and the National Academy of Sciences-National Research Council.

The project takes its name from Andrija Mohorovicic, a seismologist born in Croatia in 1857, who determined from earthquake waves the existence of a seismic discontinuity. This discontinuity was later shown to be worldwide and has been accepted by most geologists as the boundary between the crust of the earth and its denser interior mantle. The discontinuity was named after its discoverer and, as is the wont of Americans, is commonly abbreviated to "Moho."

Drilling in the deep ocean long was regarded as impossible because of the fundamental limitations of existing methods and materials. It was only with the comparatively recent development and use of drilling ships by the petroleum industry, in coastal waters off California, that deep-water drilling could be considered seriously.

Of all ships developed for offshore work, the most suitable to the purposes of deep-water experimental drilling was the *CUSS I*, a 260-foot converted Navy freight barge, owned by the Global Marine Exploration Co., Los Angeles. Deriving its name from its original joint owners, the Continental, Union, Superior, and Shell oil companies, the ship represented a multimillion dollar technological development by the petroleum industry.

The 3-year theoretical work of the AMSOC Committee on the problem of deep-sea drilling represented a bold attack. By late 1960, the work had reached the point at which it was necessary to test their concepts at sea. These concepts were based on existing drilling technology but depended upon the solution of new problems such as keeping an unanchored vessel stationary over the drill site, enabling the ship's pilot to determine accurately the ship's position in relation to the hole, and drilling with an extremely long drill string without casing.

The first problem, that of positioning the ship, was solved by employing four outboard motors, powered by 200-horsepower diesel

CUSS I, deep-sea drilling ship, which participated in National Academy of Sciences experimental drilling program during March 1961 near Guadalupe Island, off the coast of Mexico. The project was undertaken as part of Project Mohole to obtain engineering data and deep-sea drilling experience, and to provide scientific data on the composition of the earth's crust beneath the ocean.

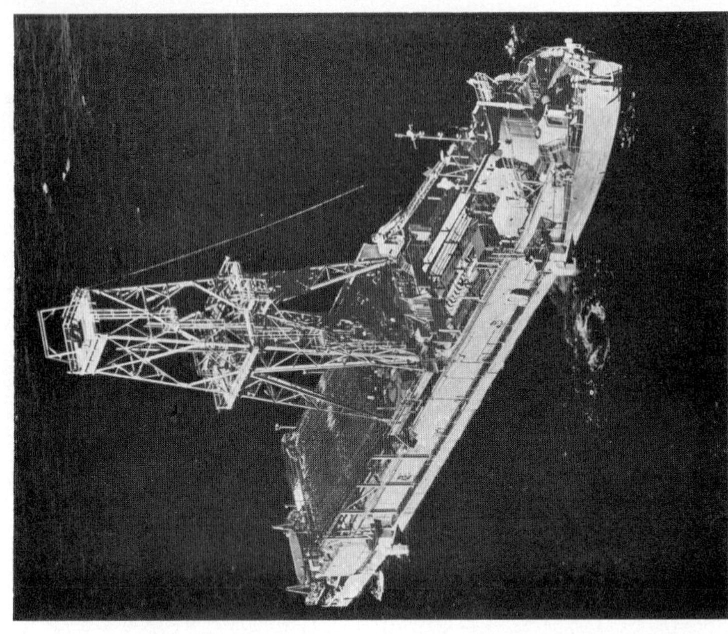

2. Aerial view of *CUSS I* in position off San Diego, Calif., at the start of the world's first deep-sea drilling. Note full pipe racks aft, and water turbulence created by the forward starboard steering engine.

1. One of four 200-horsepower diesel outboard engines used to power drilling ship *CUSS I* on experimental drilling project off Guadalupe Island, sponsored by the National Science Foundation as part of Project Mohole.

1. Controls of integrated steering system for *CUSS I*. System was designed by AMSOC engineer Robert Taggart. It permitted four outboard engines to be operated simultaneously, regulating their speed and direction of thrust from single "joystick" on console.

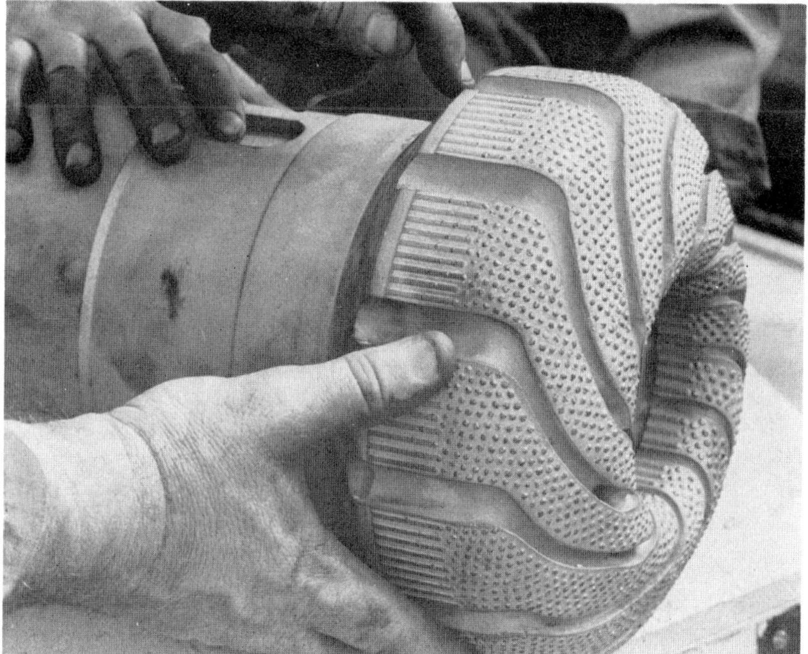

2. The 8½-inch, $8,000 diamond drill bit used in the experimental drilling program for Project Mohole shown aboard the *CUSS I*.

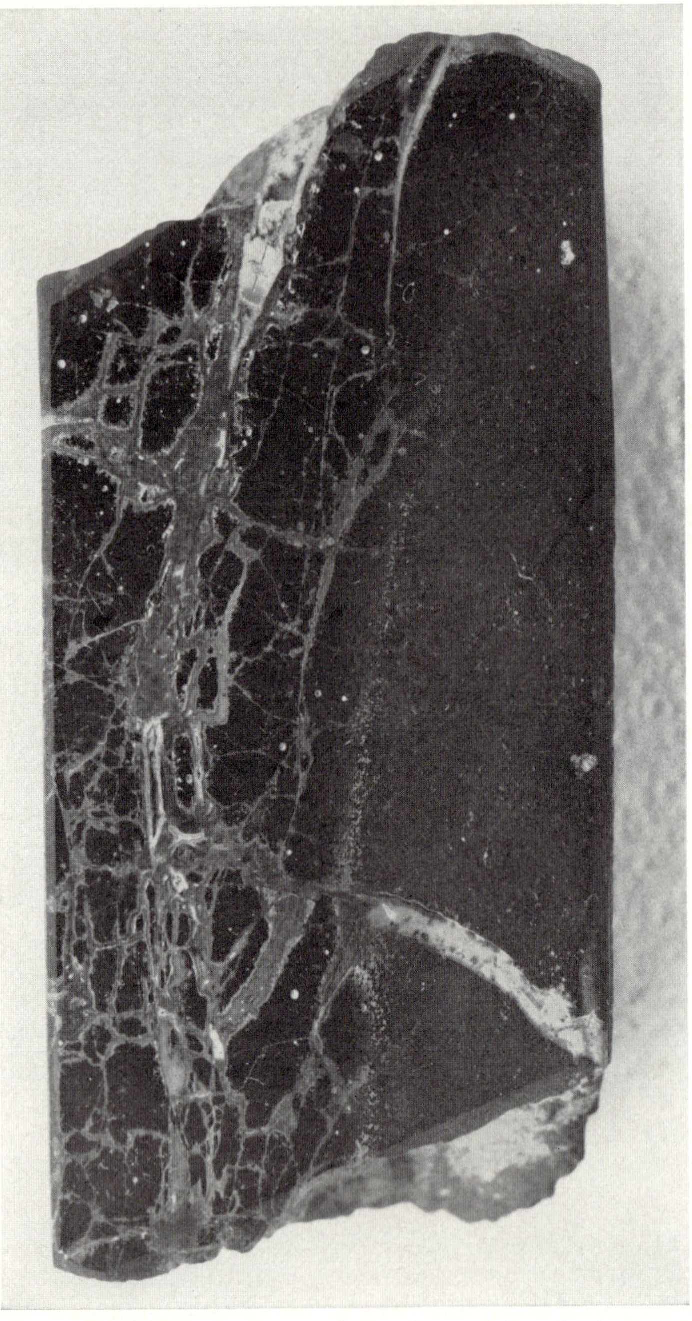

Enlarged view of cut and polished section of a 1-inch core of glassy basalt recovered from near the top of the second layer of the oceanic crust, about 575 feet below the ocean floor under 11,700 feet of water, off Guadalupe Island, April 1961. (Photograph by U.S. Geological Survey.)

engines, and capable of delivering thrust in any direction. These units, known as "Harbormasters," were mounted fore and aft and on both sides of the ship. The amount and direction of thrust of each engine were controlled at the pilot's console with a single lever resembling an aircraft joystick. The engines and steering system proved capable of holding the ship within its own length of a position in 12-foot waves and a 25-knot wind.

The second problem, that of determining the ship's position relative to the hole, was overcome by using a unique taut-line, deep-moored buoy system, together with sonar and radar, and a Sperry Mark 14 Gyro-Compass.

The AMSOC staff evolved the design of the 6-foot aluminum buoys in the shape of an oblate spheroid (elliptical viewed from the side, round viewed from above). These were placed about the drill site, anchored to the bottom, with the buoys about 100 feet below the surface of the water. Their special shape reduced their resistance to ocean currents and enabled them to remain moored almost directly over their anchors. Mounted on the buoys were sonar transponders that, when triggered on another frequency from the ship, sent back a signal, giving a sonar screen picture of the buoy pattern relative to the ship. Radar also scanned surface buoys that were secured to the deep-moored buoys. These devices, together with visual sightings of the surface buoys, gave the pilot his relative bearings. The ship's heading was maintained by reference to the Sperry Gyro-Compass repeaters on the bridge.

The third problem, that of the forces at work on the drill pipe, was worked out on paper for a variety of conditions by using a model. On the basis of the calculations, two sets of specially tapered drill pipes were ordered. One was a spare in the event that the other was dropped, or, if the doubters proved to be right, the pipe wound itself up like a corkscrew and snapped. In the course of the actual operation, the drill string proved to be the least troublesome component of the system.

WHY MOHOLE?

With all the attendant problems, why drill a Mohole at sea? The answer is simple.

Beneath continents, the average depth to the Moho—the thickness of the crust—is about 20 miles; beneath the ocean, only about 5 miles.[2] A hole drilled from land, therefore, would have to extend about 20 miles in order to reach the Moho, and the deepest hole yet drilled goes down only about 5 miles. But in some places in the ocean the crust is

---

[2] Geologists regard the continents as thick blocks of relatively light, or granitic, rock, "floating" upon the far denser supporting rock of the mantle. The rock of the oceanic crust, however, is relatively thin and dense.

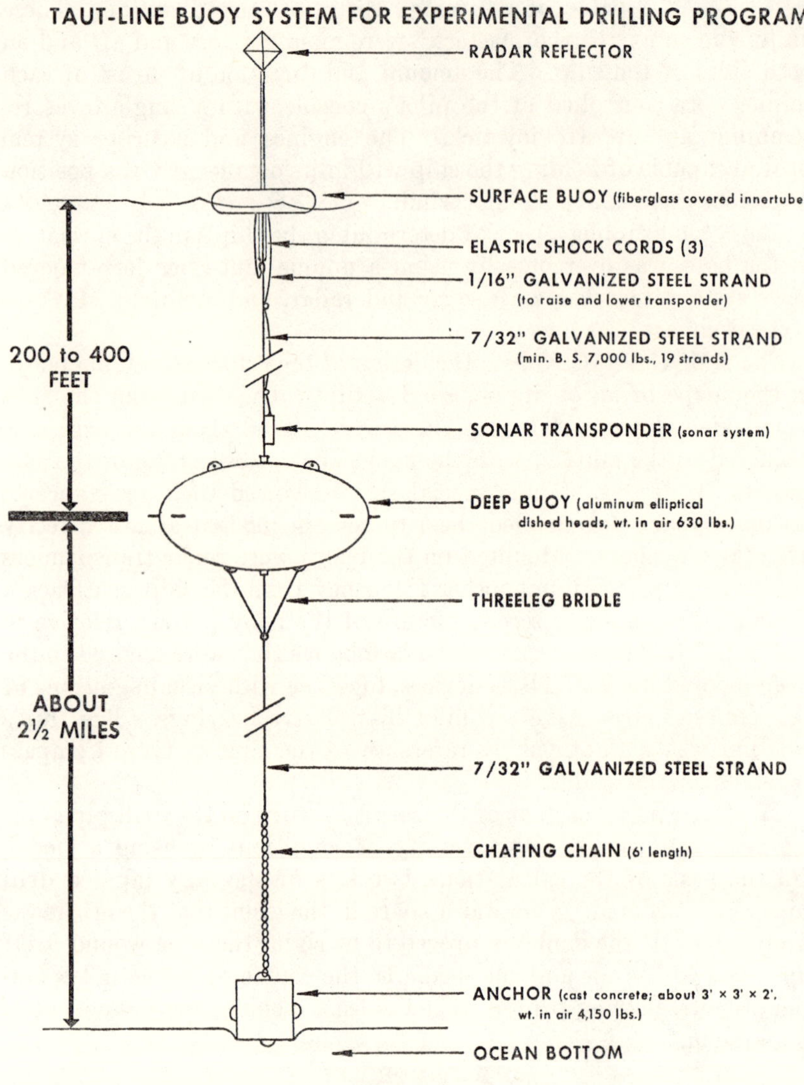

FIGURE 1.

thinner than its average 5 miles, and the total distance from the surface to the Moho is only about 6 miles, 3 miles of which is water. If a drill string could be made 20 percent longer than that of the record hole on land, and if the drilling could be accomplished from a ship, the eventual Mohole seems possible at sea. The 20-mile depth, of course, ruled out a boring on land.

Before an experimental drilling program at La Jolla, Calif., in 3,000 feet of water that preceded the deep-water experiment, oceanographers had reached no farther than 75 feet below the bottom of the sea, using the standard piston coring apparatus lowered on a wire line. Not only did the new drilling technique produce the first deep cores, or cylindrical samples, of the deep ocean bottom, but it also sampled the mysterious "second layer" of the oceanic crust, hitherto studied only by seismic means. Findings proved that at least the top of the layer at the site of the drilling was basalt, a hard rock formed by the solidification of lava.

The significance of this discovery has only begun to be debated by the geophysicists and marine geologists. They are, for example, puzzled by the fact that the sediment layer is not deep enough for the amount of sediment estimated to have been deposited from the beginning of the oceans. The discovery that the top of the second layer is basalt could mean that the basalt, at 560 feet at the site, underlies only part of the total depth of sediment and that earlier sediment records lie still deeper. Conversely, it is argued that since the layer is basalt, it could be the beginning of a very deep layer of hard rock. This would mean that the hoped-for earlier sediments, with their evidences of the formation of the oceans, somehow have been lost.

WHAT CAN BE LEARNED?

What can be learned from the oceanic sediments? Today, at more than a dozen laboratories around the country, scientists are analyzing the bits and pieces of evidence resulting from the operation. First, there are the geophysical logs, the records obtained by lowering instruments down the various holes. Then, there are the cores themselves, the sections of ooze and rock bitten out of the hole by a specially designed coring apparatus. From these and from subsequent tests will come facts that will be worked into existing hypotheses that try to explain what the ocean basins are like, how they were formed, and how old they are. New facts may force a revision of some hypotheses, or their rejection. In other cases, the evidence may link with other facts, clarify concepts, or point new directions. In addition, there is always the potential of any basic research—discovery of the unexpected.

Within the sedimentary layers will be found many new pages of the history of the earth and the oceans. Mohole scientists at sea reported finding fossil evidence of a flowering of sea life roughly 25 million years ago in the Guadalupe Island area. More than 100 feet of nearly continuous core of the deep ocean ooze showed that sea life in the area was prolific for about seven million years; by comparison the area is now an oceanic desert. The upper 500 feet of sediment was determined to be of late Miocene Age in the geologic time scale by correlating fossils with similar ones of known age found in continental rocks.

The geophysical logging hole reached a total depth of 576 feet, and penetrated to 20 feet within the basaltic layer. Geophones and seismic wave detectors were lowered into the hole to measure the velocity of sound in the deep rocks and to redetermine the thickness of the various layers beneath the reach of the drill. Preliminary analysis of the reading indicates that sound waves penetrate the soft sediment at a rate of 1.59 kilometers per second, a rate considerably less than the value generally assumed by seismologists. If this low velocity generally exists, oceanographic sediments could be thinner than has heretofore been supposed.

The geophysical logs also measured the heat flow coming through the layers of the earth beneath the ocean. These measurements provided improved scientific estimates of the earth's internal temperature. Readings off Guadalupe Island at 500 feet below the ocean floor showed a somewhat higher heat flow than was expected on the basis of earlier bottom measurements. The significance of this is not yet understood, but it is interesting in view of the fact that, while the heat flow through the ocean floor is less than that measured on land, it is still far too high to satisfy some theoretical considerations. According to present theories, heat flow through the oceans should be less than has been observed.

Most of the continental heat flow from within the earth derives from radioactive elements in granitic rocks. But the rocks thought to compose the oceanic crusts are supposedly low in radioactive material. Scientists believe, therefore, that there must be a suboceanic heat source other than the crust. There are many suggested explanations including an unsuspected radioactive heat source high in the mantle, or convection currents within the mantle.

A more exact understanding of suboceanic heat flow will also provide new information that can be fitted to current theories of the earth's origin and to the conjectures of whether the earth is heating or cooling. It may also be possible to determine how much of the suboceanic heat is primordial and how much derives from radioactivity.

What may be the first fixed-position current measurements in the deep ocean were reported by the Mohole scientists. A velocity of 0.2 knot was observed at 1,500 feet in measurements for as long as 9.5 hours with a rotor-type meter suspended between the drilling ship and one of the deep-moored buoys. This velocity was considerably less than estimates used in designing the drilling string.

ONLY A BEGINNING

Present scientific and engineering results are only the beginning. Project Mohole, born as a purely scientific concept, has led to the development of equipment and techniques with the potential of opening the oceans to commercial activity. The theoretical work on the experimental drilling operation could speed the day of ocean-floor mining, deep-sea oil drilling, and practical construction techniques. It definitely has paved the way for more scientific exploration.

Meanwhile, the Mohole scientists are currently pushing ahead with surveys to determine the site for the eventual Mohole, seeking ways to improve the speed of drilling in hard rock, and experimenting with a host of new instruments and techniques, all aimed at the next immediate objective—a drilling program, perhaps within a year, to sample the third layer of the oceanic crust, and to prove out new methods for the eventual drill to the Moho.

Reprints of the various articles in this Report may be obtained, as long as the supply lasts, on request addressed to the Editorial and Publications Division, Smithsonian Institution, Washington 25, D.C.

A Natural History of Trilobites[1]

By H. B. WHITTINGTON

Museum of Comparative Zoology, Harvard College

[With 8 plates]

TRILOBITES are arthropods, one class of a phylum of invertebrate, segmented animals with jointed legs that contains among its living representatives such diverse forms as insects, spiders, centipedes, crabs, and lobsters. They are found in the oldest rocks of the Paleozoic era, at the beginning of the Cambrian period, some 600 million years ago. These animals, abundant in the early part of the Paleozoic era, decreased during the middle part of that era, and were even fewer in its younger rocks. The last survivors are found toward the end of the Paleozoic, about 250 million years ago. Trilobite fossils occur in a wide variety of sediments—sands, silts, muds, and limestones. The other types of fossils found with them suggest that these sediments were laid down in relatively shallow, marine waters.

In the process of preservation, the original mineral matter in the trilobite's shell may be preserved, or there may be some addition to— or replacement of—this matter. Or the original material may be dissolved away altogether after burial and consolidation of the rock, leaving only an impression or mold of the shell (pl. 5, fig. 1). Study of the well-preserved shells of trilobites shows that the animal's body comprised a head region, followed by a thorax (a series of segments that articulated with each other), and a tail. The tail region is formed by the fusion of several segments like those in the thorax; it may be smaller, equal in size, or larger than the head. The shell covered the back of the body, and, on the underside, extended inward only a short distance from the margin. Since it is outside the body, it is called an exoskeleton.

The trilobite's body was bilaterally symmetrical; it had a raised region extending lengthwise down the middle and was flattened or

---

[1] Reprinted by permission from Natural History, vol. 70, No. 7, August–September 1961.

downcurved on each side. It is this three-lobed form that prompted the name Trilobita for these animals. The raised middle region of the head was prominent in some species and bore deep, transverse grooves reflecting the segmentation. On each side of the head were raised eye lobes. Across these eye lobes and around the front of the head ran an impressed line, the suture line, along which the shell split at the time when the animal molted.

Some trilobites are preserved with the body stretched out horizontally; in others, it is rolled up so that the tail is tucked tightly in beneath the head (pl. 4). There were articulating devices between the movable parts of the exoskeleton, and the outer parts of the thoracic segments were beveled and could slide over one another. The animal could only roll or unroll in the vertical plane, however. Its raised middle region and the horizontal adjacent parts of the segments make it evident that no side-to-side curving of the body in the horizontal plane was possible.

Complete exoskeletons are the exception in fossil finds. It is more common to find only parts such as heads, individual thoracic segments, and tails, disarticulated from each other. The head itself is often separated into parts along the suture line.

Among the best-preserved trilobite shells known are some remarkable ones from Virginia (pl. 1). After burial in lime mud (which later became limestone), these shells were replaced by minutely granular quartz in a manner that preserved all the details with extraordinary fidelity. When blocks of these limestones—they are Ordovician in age—are placed in dilute hydrochloric acid, the limestone is dissolved, but the replaced trilobite shells are unaffected and so can be freed from the enclosing rock without damage. The shells of any one species are not all of similar size, but form a graduated series. This series gives a record of the animals' shell growth—which took place by periodic molting—from that first formed, which was less than 1 millimeter in length, onward. Articulated skeletons, like that of *Remopleurides*, are extremely rare in these particular limestones, presumably because almost all the shells were dismembered as the dead animals drifted about on the sea bottom. Thus, size series are usually available only for individual parts of the exoskeleton; for example, the part of the head between the suture lines. Such a series exhibits the changes that took place in outline and convexity, as well as the reduction in relative size of the spines.

In the process of a trilobite's growth, new segments of the thorax were developed in the tail portion. As they became fully formed at the front edge, they were released to become freely jointed between the head and tail. The number of segments thus formed is characteristic for each trilobite species. Exoskeletons that include size

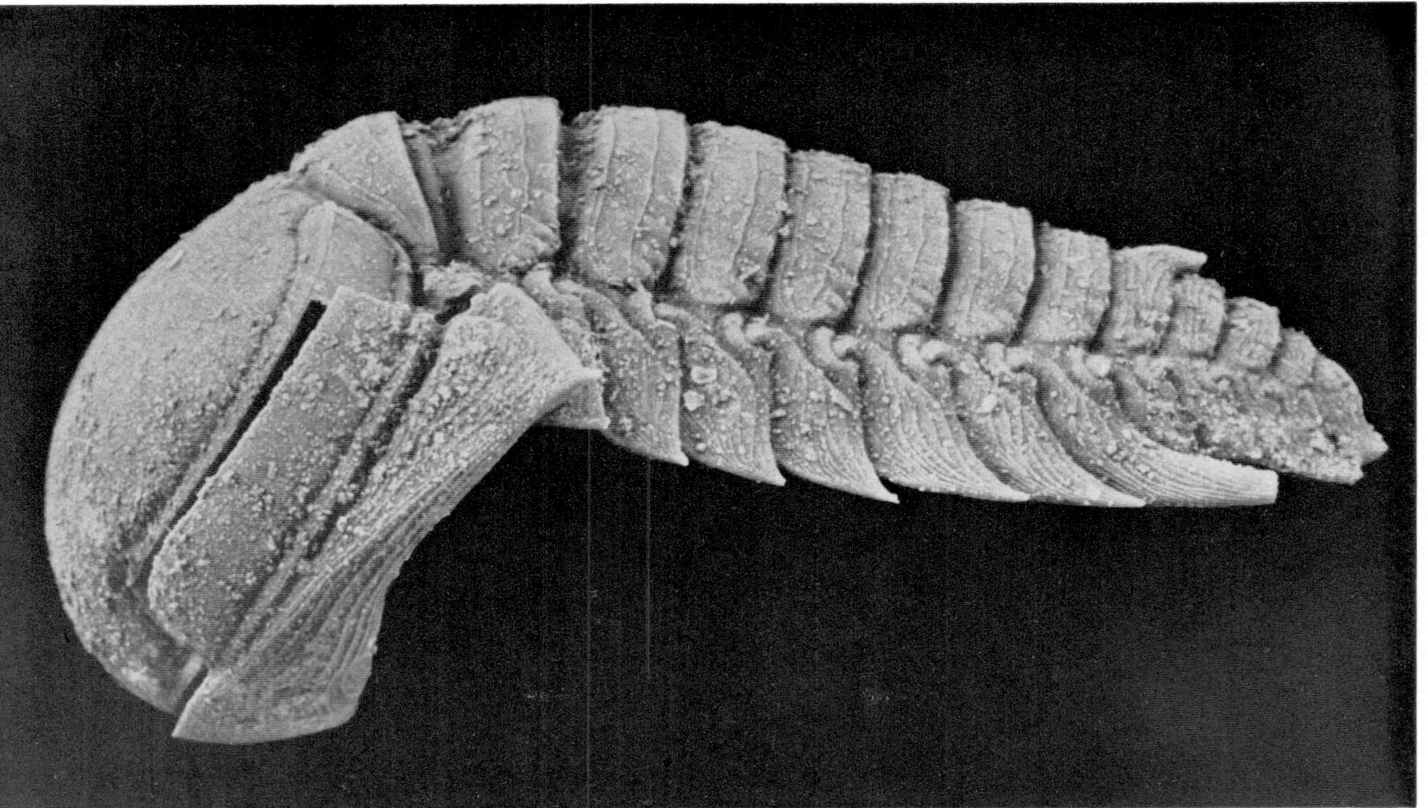

A rarity among silicified material from Ordovician limestones in Virginia is this still-articulated exoskeleton of *Remopleurides*, a 45-million-year-old animal. ×9.

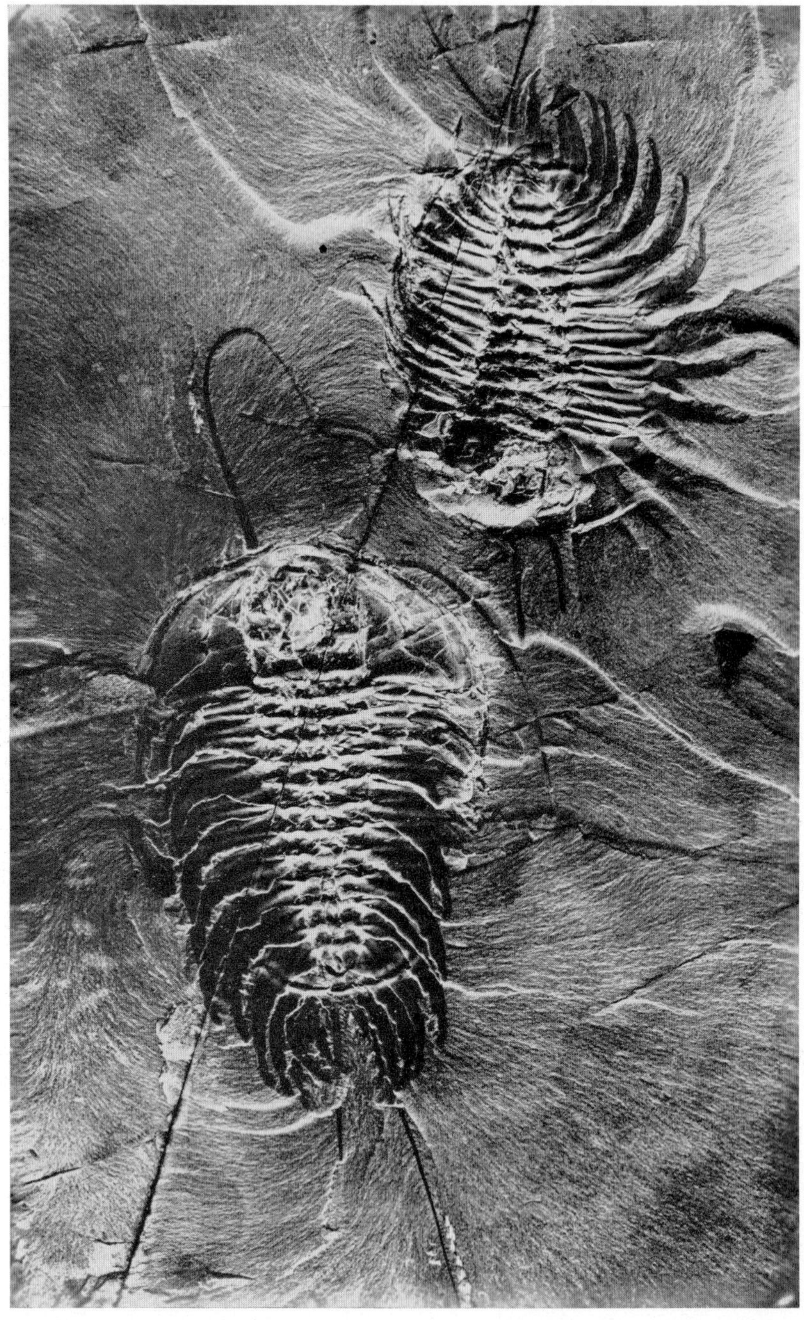

Trilobites such as this *Olenoides* pair, with appendages visible as a thin film extending beyond the body, come from the Burgess Shale of British Columbia. ×0.7. (From Walcott, 1918.)

1. The spinose exoskeleton of *Miraspis* from Silurian rocks of Czechoslovakia. Approx. ×4.

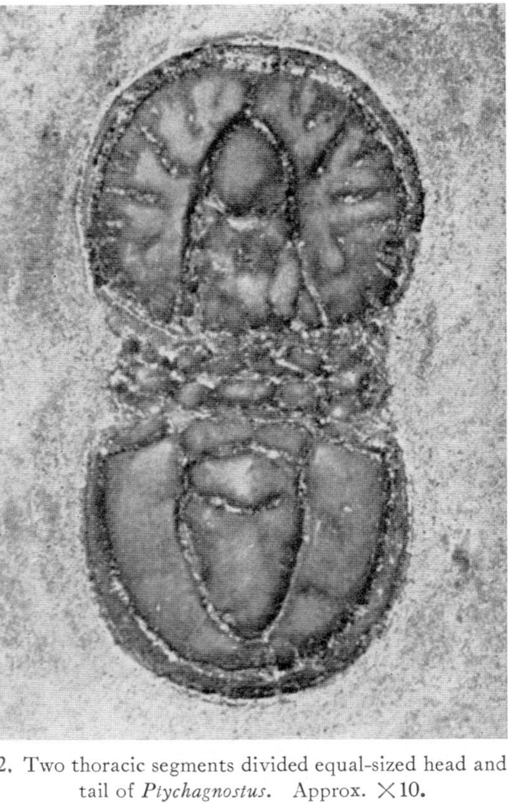

2. Two thoracic segments divided equal-sized head and tail of *Ptychagnostus*. Approx. ×10.

1. Enrolled exoskeleton of Ordovician genus *Flexicalymene* is seen from the side. Cup-shaped structure at top is eye, with suture line running to side. ×3.5.

2. From front, *Flexicalymene* shows the three-lobed form that prompted the name "Trilobita" for these animals. The shell splits on suture line at molting. ×3.5.

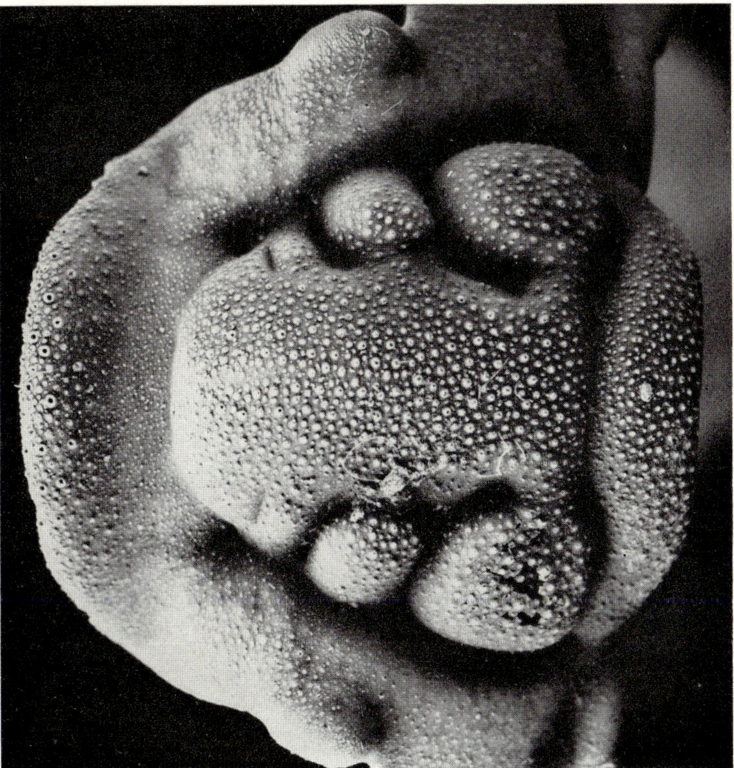

2. Midsection of this *Flexicalymene* head shows black spots on tops of tubercles. These are the openings of canals that once were occupied by sensory hairs. ×9.

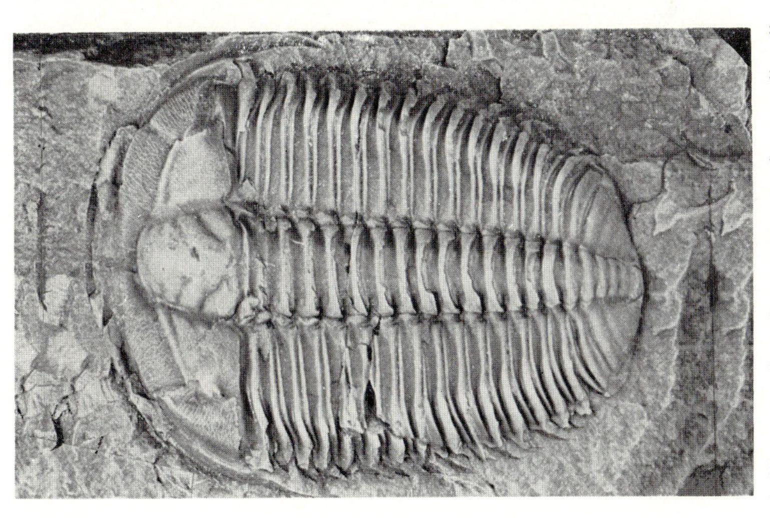

1. Fourteen thoracic segments and a small tail characterized *Ptychoparia*. ×1.3.

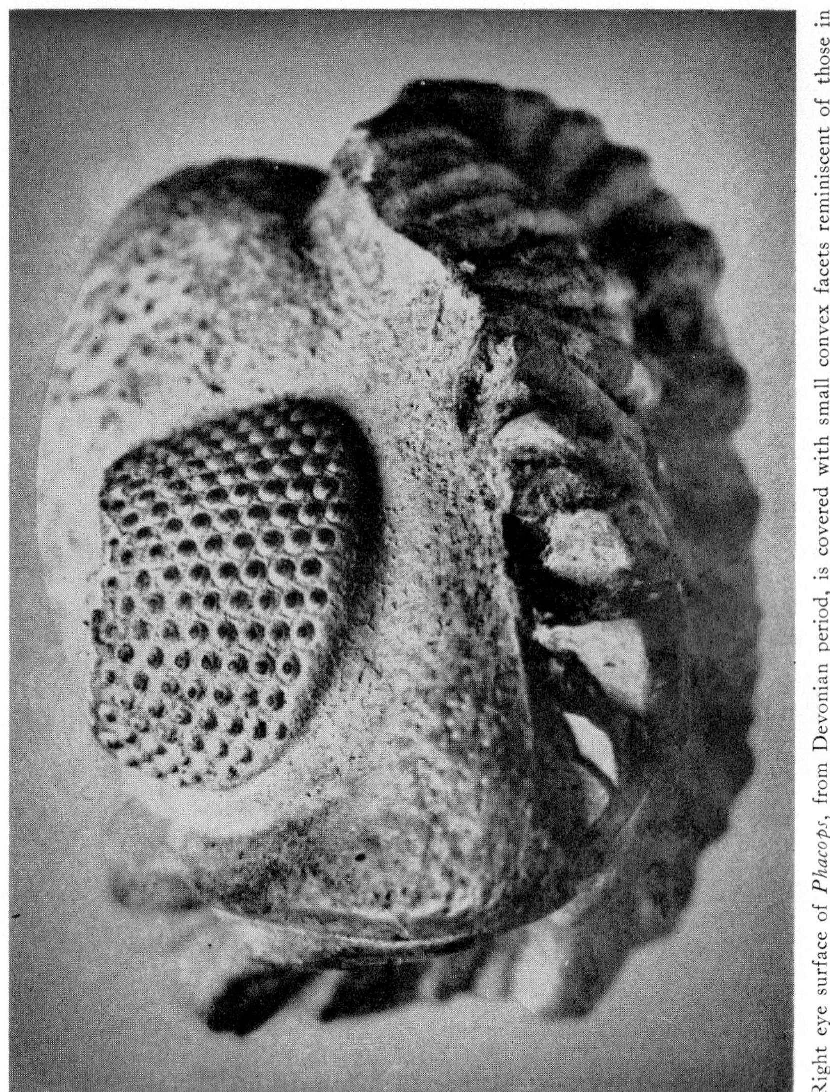

Right eye surface of *Phacops*, from Devonian period, is covered with small convex facets reminiscent of those in contemporary crustaceans and insects. Approx. ×5.

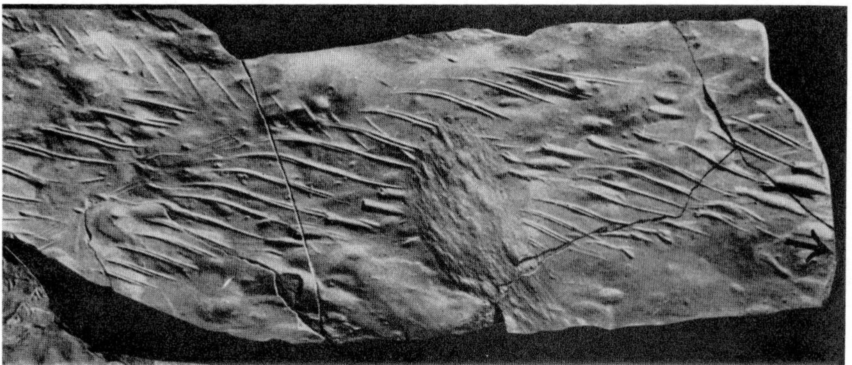

1. Fossil tracks, called *Dimorphichnus*, probably were made by trilobite. Tracks may have been made in the manner pictured below (figure 2). View is from beneath. ×0.4. (From A. Seilacher, 1955.)

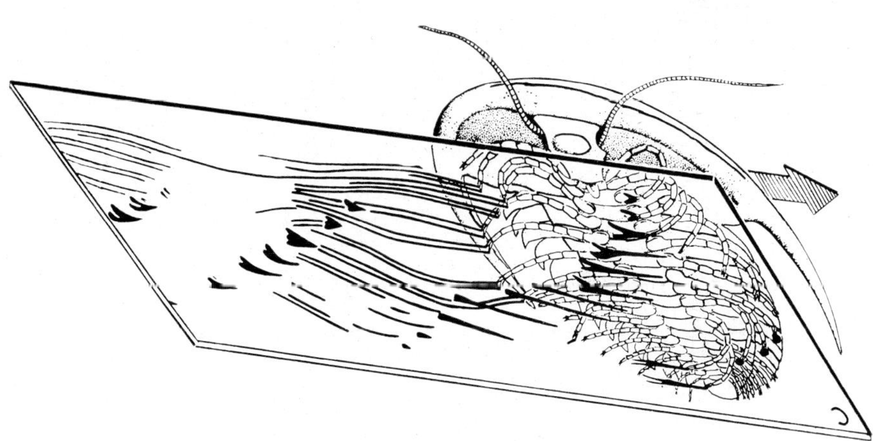

2.

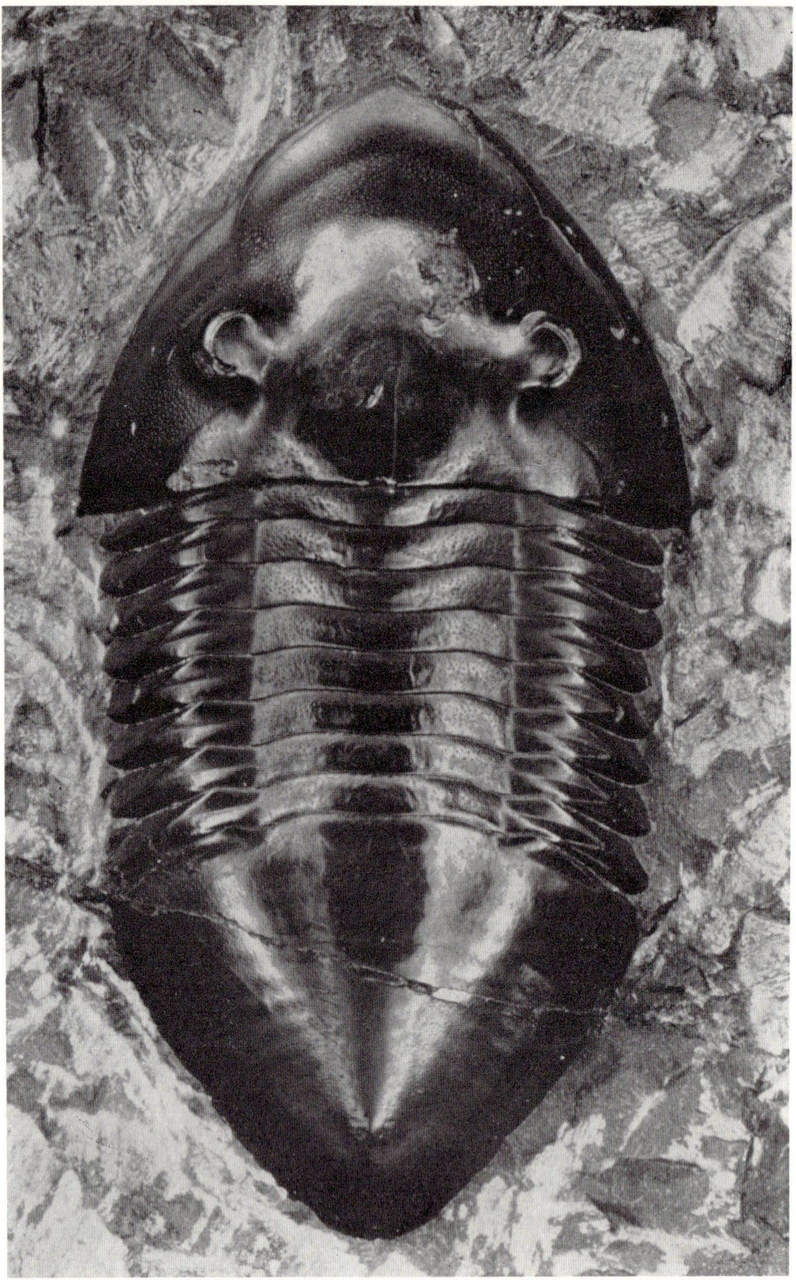

Isotelus, one of the first trilobites described from the New World, in 1824. A specimen discovered in New York State by Walcott. ×4.5.

series have also been obtained from limestones in Utah and Nevada, where they are preserved also by silicification. From other areas and countries, in shales and siltstones, have come size series of articulated exoskeletons, a notable example being those described from Czechoslovakia more than a hundred years ago by J. Barrande.

It is extremely rare to find parts of a trilobite preserved other than the exoskeleton. This is presumably because the exoskeleton was strengthened by secretion of mineral matter, but the covering of the antennules and other appendages was not so reinforced. From a few localities, the most important being in North America, remains of appendages are known. An early discovery, announced in 1876, was made by Charles D. Walcott (later the Secretary of the Smithsonian Institution) in a limestone bed near Trenton Falls, N.Y. Spurred on by his memory of the enthusiasm of Louis Agassiz, Walcott obtained over 3,500 entire trilobites, in a few of which the appendages were preserved. Walcott cut thin sections of these specimens, and demonstrated clearly that trilobites possessed jointed appendages.

A few years later, W. S. Valiant, then curator of the museum at Rutgers College, picked up a loose piece of rock near Rome, N.Y., which contained a trilobite with appendages preserved by having been infilled with pyrite. A patient 8-year search resulted in the discovery in 1892 of the dark shale layer, less than 1 centimeter thick, from which Valiant's loose specimen had come. The formation contained hundreds of similar specimens. Delicate excavations of these fossils were made by Prof. C. E. Beecher of Yale University, but he died while still working on a drawing of one of his remarkable preparations. His student, Percy E. Raymond, took up the work and wrote an epic monograph concerned with the nature of trilobite appendages.

Long before this monograph was completed, Walcott had made another sensational discovery, this time in the Burgess Shale—a formation of Middle Cambrian age—near Field, British Columbia. A great variety of arthropods are preserved in these shales, including trilobites with the appendages actually visible as a thin silvery film extending out beyond the margins of the exoskeleton (pl. 2).

No finds of comparable richness have been made since these early days, and advances in our knowledge have come from the application of more refined techniques. An example of such an investigation is that made by Prof. Leif Størmer of the University of Oslo, who came to the United States in 1931 and worked with fragments of Walcott's original material from Trenton Falls. Størmer ground a series of sections, parallel to each other and a small distance apart, through an enrolled specimen. An enlarged drawing of each section was made, and each drawing was traced on a sheet of wax. The thickness of the wax sheets was proportional to the enlargement of the

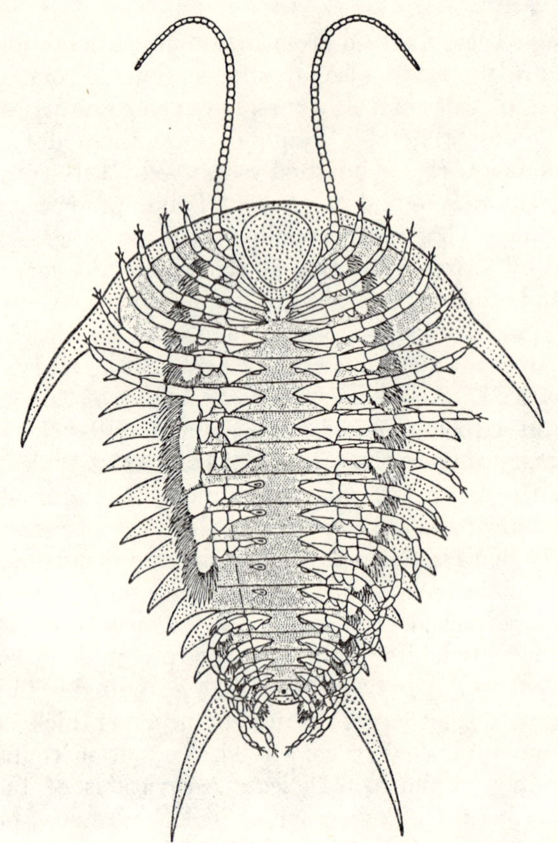

FIGURE 1.—Partial pattern of the way in which the appendages are attached to trilobite's body is shown in view of the animal's underside from restoration by Størmer.   Approx. x 2.

drawing and to the distance between successive sections. Each outlined wax sheet was then cut out and the sheets put together to form an enlarged model of the original specimen. The reconstruction (fig. 1) based on these models gives an idea of the great amount of detailed information provided by Størmer's work. This new knowledge, combined with a restudy of all previously discovered material, has resulted in a major advance in our understanding of trilobites.

The reconstruction of the underside of the body shows the large plate (or hypostome) which lay underneath the middle region of the head. On the head, beside and behind the hypostome, are shown four pairs of appendages; in front of them are the long, jointed antennules. Most students of trilobites today believe that the animal's mouth lay just inside the posterior edge of the hypostome, and that the stomach and other organs were enclosed in the capsule formed by the hypostome and the middle part of the head. The alimentary canal

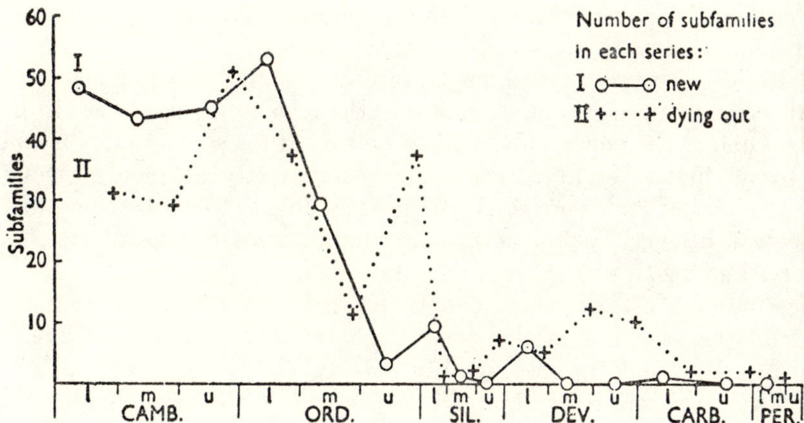

FIGURE 2.—Evolutionary history of trilobites portrayed in the rise and fall of subfamily groups in time.   (From C. J. Stubblefield, 1959.)

then extended back beneath the middle part of the body, terminating in an anus at the posterior tip.   Størmer's reconstruction of the underside of the body shows an enclosing membrane and a pair of similar appendages on each segment.   Each appendage consists of a jointed walking leg with bristles at the tip.   From near the base of the appendage rises a jointed branch that bears many fine filaments.

All investigations have shown that the trilobite's appendages were similar on each segment, and that none bore a claw or pincer for grasping and tearing food and passing it to the mouth.   Trilobites probably fed, therefore, on minute organic particles suspended in the water or enclosed in the sediment of the sea bottom, this material being brought to the mouth by currents of water.   The filament-bearing branches of the appendages may have been the main instruments in producing these currents.   They probably also functioned as gills, and constant movement of the branches would have kept the gills bathed with fresh water.

The trilobite's appendages were attached by muscles to the convex middle region of the exoskeleton.   Deep furrows in this region on the head, thorax, and tail formed projections on the inside of the shell for such attachments.   Trilobites with smooth shells may show dark patches, which are believed to be corresponding areas of muscle attachment.   The animal must also have possessed longitudinal muscles to effect its characteristic enrollment: these were probably situated in the middle region of the body.

It had been argued that trilobites like *Isotelus* (pl. 8), with its wide middle region and its relatively large tail, may have used a downward and forward stroke of the tail in swimming, as does the modern lobster.   The bodies of these two animals are not comparable, however:

the space for powerful muscles in the thorax and tail of this species of trilobite was not so great as that in the lobster tail.

Rigidity and strength must have been important requirements of the trilobite exoskeleton, since it was the framework upon which the muscular system operated.   On the outside of the shell are ridges and grooves, pits, tubercles, and raised lines, incorrectly called "ornament." These served to make the shell rigid, as do sheet-iron corrugations. In well-preserved specimens, many minute openings have been observed at the tips of short spines and tubercles (pl. 5, fig. 2).   These are the ends of exoskeletal canals that led to sensory hairs or from glands beneath the exoskeleton.   Such canals are also to be found disposed around the margins of the exoskeleton.

The main supply of the organic particles on which trilobites fed must have been close to the surface of, or within, the sediments of the sea bottom.   We may reasonably conclude, then, that trilobites lived largely in this bottom region, swimming by means of to-and-fro movements of their appendages, and also walking on, and digging or raking in, the bottom sediments.   The antennules extended forward, exploring the region immediately ahead, and the eyes, with their many small facets (pl. 6), were well adapted to detecting movements in such surroundings.

Gradually, then, a picture of the life of these animals begins to emerge from a study of their anatomy.   Trilobites must have made impressions in the soft mud of the ancient sea bottom as they searched for food.   If such impressions were later filled in by sand or silt, they might be preserved as fossil casts, projecting from the underside of a layer of silt or sand, now converted into rock.   Just such tracks and trails are found in Paleozoic rocks: one sort of trail, called *Rusophycus*, is known from many continents.   It is bilobed, with a prominent median longitudinal ridge.   On each lobe are obliquely directed ridges and grooves.   In one example, clear impressions are believed to be those of an animal's jointed appendages.

These trails are commensurate with trilobites.   They may be shallow, or deep and pocketlike, or more or less continuous.   Inward and backward movements of the walking limbs of the animal could have scraped out the hollows, pushing out the material in the midline behind them.   Impressions in the sides of some of the deep hollows are believed to have been made by the edges of the trilobite head and by spines on its thoracic segments.   The trails are thus interpreted as shallow excavations, or perhaps even tunnels, made by trilobites in the bottom sediment as they passed through it in search of food. Some of the deep pockets have been thought of as excavations made for the deposit of eggs, such as the horseshoe crab *Limulus* makes today.

One might expect that, occasionally, a dead individual trilobite would be found associated with such a trail—the remains of an animal that had died, or of one that was overwhelmed by a sudden inrush of sediments or some other catastrophe. Yet, so far, no such dramatic proof of this scientific detection seems to have been found. Thus, the interpretation of these trails, although reasonable, is not positive. In almost all cases, fossils are the remains of animals that possessed hard parts (skeletons impregnated with mineral matter) that could be preserved. Yet in these ancient seas there were, in all probability, many inhabitants that lacked such hard parts. Conceivably, some of these fossil trails are the enigmatic traces of just such soft and now vanished animals.

A different type of track, from Lower Cambrian rocks of Pakistan, has recently been described by Dr. A. Seilacher, University of Göttingen, Germany. This track, *Dimorphichnus*, is abundant on the surfaces of the sandstone layers in which the remains of trilobite shells are rare. Nevertheless, the size and nature of the track make it probable that it was made by the tips of the appendages of a trilobite (pl. 7). Dr. Seilacher considers that the animal held itself diagonally to its direction of progression, and that it dug in the walking legs on one side to make deep, short scars, while raking over the surface with the legs on the other side to form longer scraping marks.

Thus, compilation of all available knowledge of the trilobite body, combined with interpretations of the tracks and trails, affords a picture of how some trilobites may have lived. Those like *Isotelus*, smoothshelled, and with the tail similar to the head in size, or like *Diploura*, which had a narrower body and more thoracic segments, are presumed—because of their smooth, elongate form—to have burrowed into the sediments. There does not seem to be any obvious correlation between the type of exoskeleton and the habit of raking the surface of the sediments or making shallow excavations in it. Such a mode of life seems reasonable for such different trilobites as *Ptychoparia*, *Flexicalymene*, *Cryptolithus*, or *Cordania*. The broad, pitted fringe around the head of *Cryptolithus* and the long, backwardly directed spines may have served to prop the animal up on the sea floor with its thorax extended above it, so that its appendages could have stirred up the mud. The broad border around and behind the head of *Cordania* may have supported the animal in a similar way. Despite this possible similarity in habit, *Cordania*, which had eyes, facial sutures, and many more thoracic segments, can be only very distantly related to *Cryptolithus*.

Such spinose trilobites as *Ceratocephala* (fig. 3) and *Miraspis* (pl. 3, fig. 1) can hardly have burrowed or dug into the sea bottom. They may, however, have rested the level front and side edges of the head on the surface of the sediment, with thorax stretched out and limbs stirring up the mud in search of food.

The large head plate—hypostome—of many trilobites was firmly braced against the remainder of the head, thus affording both protection for the main organs and points of attachment for muscles. The posterior edge of the hypostome was sharply folded, and in some species it bore spines, so that these trilobites could have dug in the mud with their hypostomes by walking backward. However, evidences of this behavior, in the form of trails produced by such activity, have not yet been recognized by paleontologists.

Trilobites of a particular body form, or of an otherwise related group, are in most cases not found exclusively in any one type of sedimentary rock. Smooth-shelled forms like *Isotelus*, for example, are found in reef limestone, shale, siltstone, and sandstone, but so is the spiny *Ceratocephala*. Some of these occurrences may result from the burial of the animal's shell in a sediment that was laid down in an environment quite different from the one in which the living animal resided. If the trilobite exoskeleton is not disarticulated and is well preserved, however, we may presume that it probably was buried close to where it lived.

Thus, clues to the ancient environment may properly be sought from the enclosing rock. Many cases in which this procedure has been followed suggest that particular species of trilobites possessed a wide tolerance for such environmental variables as depth of water, amount of light, temperature, and type of bottom sediment. Other species or groups of species seem to have favored one environment, although they were not confined to it. The Upper Cambrian ancestors of *Triarthrus*, for example, are abundant in dark shales, deposited in stagnant waters that were probably deficient in oxygen. Again, *Dipleura* and its close relatives are found commonly, but not exclusively, in sandy sediments in which they probably dug.

Trilobite remains are abundant in Middle Paleozoic reef rocks, and it has been claimed that one smooth-shelled form inhabited the rough-water zone of a particular reef, clinging to rock surfaces like a modern chiton. Other examples are known of related but distinct species that are abundant in reef rocks of different ages and wide geographic separation.

Thus there is evidence that certain trilobites were adapted to life in particular ecological niches in the ancient seas, but little evidence that most were adapted to a restricted environment. The possession of large eyes (in *Remopleurides*, for example) or absence of eyes (in *Cryptolithus*) has been held to suggest a life spent in muddy or deep, dimly lighted waters. Analogy with living arthropods, however, does not point to any positive conclusions.

The nature of the rocks that contain trilobite fossils suggests deposition in waters not more than a few hundred feet deep. Thus we have no direct evidence that trilobites inhabited deep oceanic waters. Yet, extremely similar genera (*Ptychagnostus* (pl. 3, fig. 2) and *Dicranurus*, for example) have been shown to have a worldwide distribution. Does this mean that these and other kinds of trilobites inhabited the surface waters of the oceans, feeding on the microscopic floating plants or animals that constituted the Paleozoic plankton? Did they browse amid floating mats of seaweed, like those of the Sargasso today? If we assume this mode of life, the molts and dead bodies of such animals might have come to rest in widely separated localities, and have been included, in consequence, in very different types of sediments.

We know, however, that newly hatched trilobites formed their first shells when they were half a millimeter or so in length. These tiny creatures probably floated, like the larvae of today's crustaceans. The young may have existed in this stage for days or weeks and, in that time, could have drifted far from the point where the eggs were laid. At a size of less than 1 centimeter in length in most species, trilobites became bottom dwellers in shallow water, and probably spent the remainder of their lives within a limited area. Thus, the wide geographical dispersion of particular trilobites may be explained as taking place during the larval stages, the adults dwelling on the sea bottom—not drifting in the ocean's surface water.

It has been said that spiny trilobites like *Ceratocephala* and *Miraspis* were floating forms even in the adult stage, the spines inhibiting their sinking. However, we know nothing of the appendages of these trilobites and, as mentioned, the possession of a spiny exoskeleton does not preclude the possibility of bottom dwelling.

Some modern arthropod species exhibit sexual dimorphism—that is, male and female forms that differ in size or in other characters. More than a hundred years ago, Barrande (in that great study of trilobites from Czechoslovakia already mentioned) observed a broad and a narrow form in certain species. Today, we consider these differences to be the result of distortion that the fossils suffered when the rocks enclosing them were subjected to various stresses. Other such examples among fossils are well known. Not all the cases of two closely similar forms coming from the same rocks can be so explained, however, and it may be that sexual dimorphism did occur in trilobites. If so, however, it was not universal: the cases are equivocal.

Although during the 100-million-year period of the Cambrian, trilobites were the dominant animals of the shallow seas in kinds, numbers, and sizes, they did not have these seas to themselves. There were other aquatic arthropods in existence—types that, unlike the trilobites, were armed with pincers. However, the rarity of these arthropods as fossils

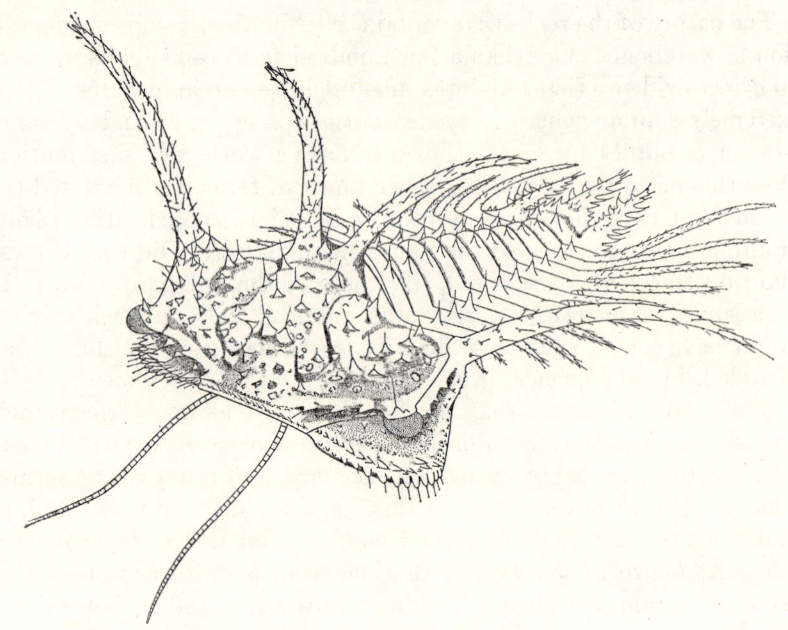

FIGURE 3.—*Ceratocephala*, an Ordovician to Devonian trilobite, restored to show the antennules and sensory hairs. x 4. (From Whittington and Evitt, 1954.)

suggests that they were not formidable enemies of the trilobites. From the earliest Cambrian onward, a succession of new genera and families of trilobites appeared, though the rate of extinction of trilobite groups was also high (fig. 2).

On balance, the picture is one of great evolutionary activity, of adaptation to a great variety of environments, expressed in a multiplicity of genera and species. At the end of the Cambrian and during the Ordovician period, this picture begins to change. New kinds of animals appeared. Previously existing ones became more numerous, and these animals must have competed with the trilobites for the food supply on and in the sea floor. Among these forms were the bivalved brachiopods and clams, and the snails. The nautiloids, molluscan ancestors of the modern *Nautilus*, were not only numerous and larger than trilobites, but probably had grasping tentacles and a powerful jaw. Such predators could have seized and eaten trilobites. But the capacity for enrollment may have afforded the trilobites some protection, and their spines must have made them an awkward mouthful. They may have lain partly buried in the bottom sediment, the projecting or stalked eyes of some species enabling them to detect nearby movement. Vegetation, clusters of marine animals such as sea lilies or corals, and crannies in reefs would also have afforded the trilobites places of concealment.

The evolution of many new kinds of trilobites in the Ordovician perhaps reflects adaptation to new environments in response to changing conditions. Yet it may be seen (fig. 2) that, toward the end of this period, the rate of extinction became greater than the rate of evolution of new forms. This is a pattern that continued through the animals' remaining history. Only a single group persisted through the Carboniferous and into the Permian. This decline—and the ultimate total extinction of trilobites—cannot readily be explained.

One of the mysteries of the evolutionary process is why such a fate should overtake a group of animals that, for millions of years, were well adapted to their surroundings and continued to evolve new species until near the close of the Paleozoic era. Phrases that imply "over-specialization" or "the senescence of the trilobite race" are neither apt nor meaningful. *Ceratocephala* has been regarded as a highly "specialized" trilobite, yet its exoskeleton is known from rocks ranging from Ordovician to Devonian age—a period of some 100 million years. This is clear evidence that types of animals well adapted to a particular environment may exist for an extremely long time without significant morphological change.

The competition with other groups for food may have played a part in the trilobites' demise. In addition, the Devonian fishes—among which jaws evolved for the first time—may have become trilobite predators. At present, however, there is no acceptable theory that explains the reasons for extinction of the trilobites.

New kinds of trilobites are constantly being found on all continents (although new information on trails and on appendages collects much more slowly). As the store of knowledge from new discoveries and improved techniques of investigation accumulates, we should be able to outline more precisely the natural history of these remarkable arthropods. For the present, we may agree with the late Prof. Percy Raymond that perhaps the greatest contribution that trilobites have made to our world "is the aesthetic pleasure the contemplation of their elegant shells has given to countless collectors and students of fossils." But paleontology is a science that does more than enjoy its raw material: it also tries to bring extinct animals back to life. To me, it is far more exciting to try to visualize these "elegant shells" as parts of living animals, inhabiting their particular niche in nature at a time so long ago that the vertebrate animals had yet to evolve.

Chromosomes and the Theory of Heredity[1]

By C. D. DARLINGTON, F.R.S.
Botany School, Oxford University, Oxford, England

MORGAN'S DISCOVERY

THE crisis of the struggle in the scientific world over the chromosome theory of heredity was reached in the 1920's when T. H. Morgan's views became the subject of dispute. Morgan, with his collaborators at Columbia University, had carried out breeding experiments with the fly *Drosophila* [1].[2] He claimed that by these experiments he could show that heredity, as long suspected, was indeed carried entirely by the chromosomes. It followed that these minute bodies in the cell nucleus were to be held responsible for the whole character of every living thing, plant or animal, man or microbe; and the course of evolution from the beginning had been determined by changes in these chromosomes. It was a complete scheme of determinism on Omar Khayyam lines.

This theory aroused misgiving and contradiction in many countries, especially among older men who might know the fly but certainly did not know its chromosomes. Before we look at their arguments, let us see what Morgan, and Mendel before him, had done.

Mendel had found that if he crossed two races of peas differing in two respects, as it might be $AB \times ab$, the hybrid gave germ cells of four kinds in equal numbers: AB, Ab, aB, and ab. Free assortment, random recombination, independent segregation were the explanations given for this behavior. Assortment of what? Assortment of certain "elements" carried in all cells and passed to the germ cells. Morgan, however, beginning in 1910, found that in the fly often less than half the germ cells were of the new types, Ab and aB. The proportion was characteristic of the particular pair of elements. Assortment was not free. The elements were linked; and, if the hybrid fly happened to be a male, the linkage was complete: the elements were held together in one block.

---

[1] Substance of a Royal Society Tercentenary Lecture delivered on July 20, 1960. Reprinted by permission from Nature, vol. 187, No. 4741, pp. 892–895, Sept. 10, 1960.
[2] Numbers in brackets refer to list of references at end of article.

At this point Morgan recalled that the previous year the cytologist Janssens [2] at Louvain had made a general proposal about chromosome behavior. He had noticed that after the pairing of maternal and paternal chromosomes in germ cell formation they fell apart but remained touching or attached at various points which he called "chiasmata." At these points, Janssens suggested, the mating chromosomes might exchange parts by breakage and reunion. Such behavior would give a statistical association or linkage of elements in the same chromosome of a kind already to be suspected from Bateson's breeding experiments. Conversely it would lead to the formation of new chromosomes by a recombination of parts.

Taking Janssens's hint, Morgan and his collaborators proceeded to make crosses between pairs of flies differing in many pairs of respects. They found that hundreds of elements could on this assumption be fitted into the four observed pairs of chromosomes of *Drosophila*. Moreover, if the proportion of regrouping or crossing-over was itself assumed to be related to the distance apart of the elements along each chromosome, they found that the whole assembly fitted into fixed linear orders. Thus the elements of heredity, or, using Janssens's word, the genes, could be put on a map which, like other maps, showed one how to find one's way about.

It soon seemed reasonable to advance from these direct inferences to more general principles. Morgan argued that all heredity in all organisms was carried by chromosomes as it was in *Drosophila*. Further, all chromosomes were composed of units of crossing-over or mutation which might be known as genes. Hence, he appeared to argue, the genes would add up to give the whole of heredity; and the differences between them would add up to give the whole of variation and of evolution.

THE OPPOSITION

Morgan's "Theory of the Gene" appeared in 1926; its reception in England could scarcely have been more unfavorable. Seven men might have been willing to assert their belief in the chromosome theory and give their reasons for it. But against this view there were seven hundred who held a contrary opinion. The supporters felt liberated by the new theory, its opponents felt confined and oppressed by it. The grounds they gave for their opposition were both general and specific [3].

The general objections were that the theory was naïve and mechanical and yet self-contradictory. For it was both statistical and deterministic. It left too much room to chance yet no room to free will. In evolution, moreover, its hard particulate basis shut out the hope of any soft Lamarckian adaptation. The Lamarckian principle, we must remember, was at that time generally maintained by naturalists and physiologists and assumed by medical and social scientists. Even philosophers had their opinions, and they were on the Lamarckian side. Yet there was no room in this picture for the Lamarckian emblems, the giraffe, the salamander, or the midwife toad.

The more specific objections to the chromosome theory were also very various. The assumption that the chromosomes were alone responsible for heredity left a gap in our theory of development. Is not heredity merely a repetition of development? Yet this theory of heredity almost ignored development, and it was based on a single organism— a fly with a most disorderly development of its own. The chromosome theory also left a gap where the cytoplasm should be—where indeed European workers had found evidence of determination. Loeb, with his unfortunate idea that the cytoplasm carried the solid basis of heredity while the nucleus bore only a few frills, provided a line of defense for weaker opponents of the chromosome theory.

Again it was pointed out, quite rightly, that the gene mutations of *Drosophila* could not be representative of natural variation for they were in their effects both disadvantageous and discontinuous. In the first respect they contradicted the helpful mutations of the evening primrose, *Oenothera*. In the second respect they failed to explain the universal property of continuous variation. As for the chromosomes themselves, did they not at the end of every cell division dissolve and disappear into that bag of fluid, the nucleus? As for crossing-over, the foundation of Morgan's interpretation, it was supposed to happen only in one sex and not in the other. But who had ever seen it happen anywhere? Crossing-over, like the genes themselves, was a stroke of fancy, a mathematical artifact invented to salvage a broken hypothesis.

With regard to these chromosomes, it was true, there were a variety of accounts of what they did [4]. The two cell divisions known as meiosis, when the germ cells were formed, were especially disputable. Some believed that there were general rules; others that there were many kinds of meiosis in different groups of plants and animals. Most believed that, if there was a rule, it was that the corresponding chromosomes from the two parents paired as threads side-by-side. But a few stoutly maintained that chromosomes in the nucleus were in an endless chain which split up crosswise into segments to give $2x$ single chromosomes at mitosis, x double chromosomes at meiosis, and, by a freak of nature, $4x$ chromosomes at mitosis making a new tetraploid [5]. Clearly this view was of no help to those who believed that the chromosomes made heredity and were differentiated in linear structure; but it was a help to those who did not think anything of the kind. Such differences of opinion—which were described in textbooks, taught in universities, and expounded in theses—created a verbal and literary jungle which had to be cleared before any general theory could be discussed.

Finally, there was one specific objection which no one seemed to make. It was that genes were inferred to exist from breeding experiments with "characters"; or more precisely, from studying the inheritance of differences of character when different parents were crossed. Yet the whole of heredity, of the genotype, was supposed to be made up of genes added together. There was a concealed gap between the analytical or differential gene and the integral genotype. In looking at the chromosomes one could see that they added up to make the nucleus. But their differences, their variations, were visibly of many kinds and degrees. The gap was revealed. How could it be bridged? Not, as it seemed to me, by pretending that it did not exist. It was necessary to work out a system of understanding life in terms of chromosomes, a system independent of experimental breeding, a system which would stand on its own feet. In this view I was strengthened by one man's opinion. "Cytology," Karl Belar said to me in 1928, "should not be the *ancilla* of genetics." That was just what I thought.

CROSSING-OVER AND THE CHIASMA

Belar had shown that mitosis and the chromosomes themselves had a universal character, a character which must underlie the uniformity of development of plants and animals and protista [6]. Here was a great and necessary step forward. In genetics, as in geology a century earlier, uniformity was bound up with evolution. Cytologists and geneticists too, so far as they took the chromosomes seriously, therefore liked to think that the same such universal character was true also of meiosis and underlay some uniformity in heredity. But *Drosophila* itself, with crossing-over at meiosis in the female but not in the male, faced us with the gravest objection to this view. It was possible to evade the issue for the time being. It was possible to begin with the simplest material offering experimental tests by purely chromosome criteria. For this purpose polyploid plants with large chromosomes, tulips and hyacinths, were admirably fitted. They revealed several unexpected principles. The important ones, in the present connection, concern the chiasma [7].

At a certain stage in the beginning or "prophase" of meiosis, like chromosomes come together as threads side-by-side in pairs. The association is limited to likes: it is chemically specific; and it was, I found, limited to pairs even when there are three or four of a kind. At a later stage the paired chromosomes reproduce, forming double threads, and at the same time fall apart.   But when they do so they stick at certain points, as Janssens had said, the chiasmata.

Why do they fall apart, in one sense, and stick together, in another? Their structure gave the answer.   Contrary to Janssens's view, the chiasmata always had the same structure: they were exchanges of partner between half-chromosome threads, chromatids as we call them. Further, these exchanges could be shown, on internal, cellular, microscopic, evidence to be invariably connected with a previous crossing-over between chromatids of the partner chromosomes.   On the simplest assumption, therefore, chiasmata were determined by such crossing-over.   The arrangement of four chromatids could be shown in a diagram that was at once genetic and cytological in its implications.   With capital and small letters in sequence for the pairing chromosomes, an asterisk for the mechanical center, and dots for the points of breakage, the diagram would be as follows:

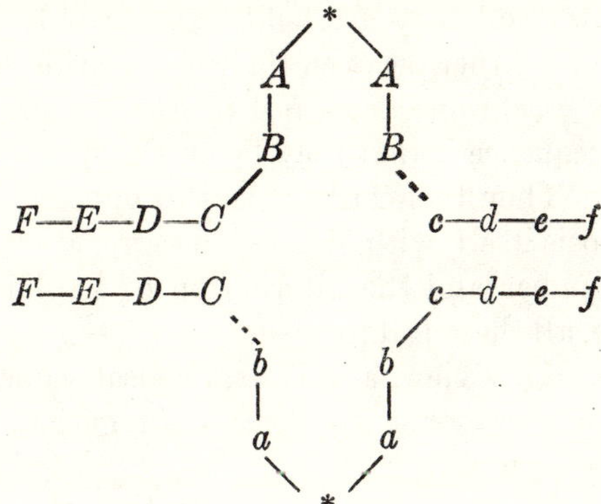

Thus from two chromosomes, *ABCDEF* and *abcdef*, two new chromatids, *ABcdef* and *abCDEF*, had been formed, and the four chromatids would pass as chromosomes into the four germ cells formed by meiosis.   The existence of these four cells would, as Janssens had put it, be justified by each of them being a unique combination of available genes different from the rest.

One could not of course prove that this principle was universally true (in those days most biologists believed that propositions ought to be "proved"); one could merely hope to render it increasingly probable.   This hope was gradually realized.   The critical configurations of several chromosomes united by, or interlocked with, successive chiasmata, the comparisons of frequencies and distributions of chiasmata and crossing-over in different organisms, in polyploids, in hybrids, with inversions and interchanges of segments of chromosome, in plants with defects of chromosome pairing and of sexual reproduction, these all helped to carry conviction. Even in *Oenothera* the occurrence of chiasmata, the inference of crossing-over, could be used to explain the modes of inheritance and the origins and kinds of mutations [8].

The solution of the problem of crossing-over was, however, obstructed by another, to me, unexpected but inseparable development. The study I had made of meiosis, and my interpretation of what a hundred others had seen in a great variety of plants and animals, made it clear that the chiasma had consequences which were as important as its causes [9]. People had supposed that the chromosomes were paired at the first metaphase of meiosis because they were, in a mysterious sense, attracted to one another. This was, they thought, the climax of the sexual process. What could be more natural? But I had found that, after pairing as single threads, the chromosomes fall apart as double threads. They do not attract, they repel one another after they become double; and they are held together only by chiasmata, by the exchanges of partner between their chromatids, after crossing-over. When pairs of chromosomes fail to form chiasmata, whatever the cause, the consequence is that they lie on the spindle, unconnected and unorientated. They then fail to pass to opposite poles. Without chiasmata meiosis itself, with Mendelian segregation, the reduction of chromosome number and the alternation of haploid and diploid in the sexual cycle, all these fail to ensue.

Thus there was, in my view, a universal causal sequence: crossing-over→chiasmata→chromosome pairing→segregation and reduction→sexual reproduction.

This reversal of the mechanical interpretation of meiosis made it possible to describe meiosis in the same physicochemical terms as mitosis. But what mattered first were its genetic implications. The new principle seemed to be true of all plants and animals (except male *Drosophila*). It therefore meant that meiosis and crossing-over had come in together, at one step. Crossing-over from its origin must have been coextensive with sexual reproduction. What Morgan had hoped to imply I was now forced to assert. The reason why the chromosomes were divisible into units or genes was that everywhere their division into such units was a condition of meiosis and hence of sexual reproduction. This, of course, made sense in terms of selection, adaptation, and the evolution of sexual reproduction itself. For if the chromosome were not divisible into genes, if it were not capable of crossing-over, it would be inherited as a block and no genes could be revealed either to the geneticist by his experiments or to nature by her selection. The original system would never have survived.

EVOLUTION AND THE CELL

It will be seen here that an evolutionary point of view was beginning to force itself into my argument.

There were several reasons why this should have happened to the student of chromosomes, by no stretch of the imagination but by hard necessity. While the experimental breeder could sort out linkage in one species, the chromosomes could reveal chiasmata in a hundred species and in every group of plants and animals. While the experimental breeder himself decided how his plants or animals should breed, the chromosome man had to pick up his cells and discover how nature had bred them, and why, and with what effect. These were two reasons. But a third was even larger. It was that through the chromosomes there is continuity between successive generations. To the naturalist and to the experimental breeder the organism is an independent discontinuous entity. To the cytologist it is part of a continuous process. Cell division is always a step between the past and future: it is always adapted to meet conditions which do not yet exist, to produce progeny which are irrelevant to their parent's success.

Oenothera first brought this home to me. In its evolution there had been interchanges between different chromosomes, each of which succeeded by virtue of its selective advantage over its predecessors. But success depended on whether plants were inbred or outbred. Thus the hereditary mechanism and the sexual mechanism, the means of distributing and recombining differences and the means of bringing them together, must be bound up together in one system, a genetic system. In a genetic system crossing-over of chromosomes is no good without crossing of germ cells, without outbreeding. The two processes must be adjusted to one another. They must also be adjusted to the needs, not of the individual, but of the breeding group and, more particularly, of its posterity.

A second example was in the male *Drosophila*, with its suppression of crossing-over. In these flies the male, I found, had contrived an anomalous kind of meiosis without crossing-over [10]. The chromosomes paired and separated without needing to form chiasmata. The breeding and the chromosome observations thus agreed. But how had an otherwise universal rule come to break down—and break down in the very species of organism in which the rule was first brought to light?

The reason is obvious as soon as it is pointed out. In the vertebrates or flowering plants the genes in the chromosomes are recombined once in every sexual generation. This may be once in 10 months or 10 years. But in the short-lived flies it happens once in 10 days. That is why from the whole animal kingdom Morgan chose to work with them. But to recombine genes so often does not give any combination a chance of being properly tested. Far better to let the genes recombine in one sex and pass unrecombined through the other sex, down the other line. It is an admirable solution: new things can be made, but good things can be kept.

In the evolution of the flies it was not therefore surprising that a new type of meiosis had been developed in one sex—it had to be the heterozygous sex—in which crossing-over was suppressed. The genetic system would benefit from this modification. The original type of meiosis, on the other hand, was the common ancestral type still found in all species of plants, animals, and protista, a type of nuclear division which had arisen at the origin of sexual reproduction, a type with a uniform physicochemical character.

At the time this speculative conclusion seemed to be rash. Today, however, we can clearly go further. The brilliant work that is now being used to reveal the genetic structure of fungi, bacteria, bacteriophages, and other viruses makes it indeed necessary to go further. We have to say now that crossing-over of gene sequences, or nucleotide sequences, is the original property of all systems capable of evolution; and we may add that sexual reproduction, as we ordinarily understand it, is the structure built around crossing-over which has made the higher organisms possible [11].

This view turned genetics upside down. In the short term one could still see fertilization as the focus of life's processes. For it is at this moment in the higher plants and animals that the individual is created. But in the long term the focus was shifted to the act of crossing-over and the origin of the chiasma. For this is the moment when, we may say, the gene is created. On this event all the processes of evolution converge and from it they all diverge.

DETERMINATION AND UNCERTAINTY

At an early stage in the discussion of crossing-over, the opponents of the chromosome theory objected that there was no visual or direct evidence that chromosomes did or could cross over at meiosis. When this evidence was provided they objected that there was no reason why it should happen. Fortunately the mechanical reasons were by this time only too evident. Chromosomes which pair as threads always coil around one another. Just as pairs of textile fibers spun under torsion release a part of their torsion by coiling around one another, so do the chromosomes. The part of their torsion released is in equilibrium with the rest which is stored; it is available to break the chromatids and to untwist them to a position where their broken ends can recombine in new combinations. The specificity in pairing of genes and of parts of chromosomes and the observed release of torsion at the chiasma provide for the time, place, and action of the event inferred in *Drosophila* and of the result seen in the chiasma [12].

Experiments with nucleic acid starvation later indicated that the nucleic acid component of the chromosomes was the means of developing their torsion. I therefore assumed it to have the structure not of a straight column but of a spiral staircase [13], an assumption which has been vindicated with beautiful precision by Watson and Crick [14]. How the molecular spiral works in detail, however, is a question we must ask later, when we have a more elaborate molecular model of the paired chromosomes.

What must be discussed now is the fact that this breakage, this crossing-over, can occur at hundreds or thousands of different places along the chromosome—indeed by one definition between any pair of genes in the whole sequence. But in a particular pair in a particular cell it occurs at only a few points, from one to a dozen; and there are conditions, even in *Drosophila* itself, where it seems to be almost fixed.

This situation, in our experience of the statistics of causal relations, seemed to be unique and significant. Its mere mechanics was easily understood. The frequency and distribution of crossing-over are characteristic of the organism. It can be regulated by the organism, by its heredity. If the chromosomes that are going to pair are regularly placed side by side in the nucleus, which sometimes happens, the amount of twisting they develop is regularly distributed and hence the crossing-over. If the chromosomes are irregularly placed, as they usually are, the crossing-over will be irregular and uncertain, as it usually is.

Thus the irregularity of crossing-over, which gives the characteristic variety of progeny in sexually reproducing organisms, is something controlled. Like the weather it shows uncertainty. But, like the weather also, we can predict it so far as we can expect to predict it. Its failure, as well as its normal conditions, show that it is a determined uncertainty. Indeed in asexual reproduction all uncertainty can be removed, and frequently is removed. Its general survival throughout the plant and animal world therefore shows that the uncertainty of crossing-over is original, is organized, and is of adaptive value. Through it, indeed, meiosis acts as a means of generating uncertainty [15].

To put the matter in another way: it is a paradox that the gene which is an organ of determinacy in life exists by virtue of a process of apparent indeterminacy. But when we examine it we find that the indeterminacy is spurious. It has been put there (if I may diverge from the present argument) by natural selection and for natural selection. It has been put there as a necessary complement of the uncertainty of the gene's mutation; together they produce adaptive variation.

The discovery of how crossing-over happens had long-range consequences beyond the previous limits of genetics, for it enabled us to split up the processes of life into two parts.   First there are those concerned with determining the character of individuals.   These are processes of physiology in which the greatest certainty of determination, the strictest predictability in reaction with the environment, a chemical determinism, is achieved; and second there are the processes of meiosis.   These, reinforced by the chances of fertilization which are derived from them, determine the differences in character of individuals.   They are the processes of classical genetics in which the greatest uncertainty of determination is organized and achieved.

This contrast, as I believe, between two kinds of process—the one deterministic, the other spuriously nondeterministic—also provides one of the several ways of splitting genetics into two.   It means that instead of speaking of the laws of heredity, as the early Mendelians were fond of doing (making biology echo the physics of the time), we should speak rather of the "paradoxes" of genetics.   For heredity is a relation between parent and offspring which is variably compounded of the certain and the uncertain elements, according to how like the parents or grandparents may have been; indeed, according to the effects of their system of breeding.

THE CONTINUING ISSUE

I have given an eye-witness account of a battle.   I believe it is a battle that we won.   The pursuit of the enemy has, to be sure, taken us far away from the original site of the conflict; and it could have taken us much farther with the elasticity of the gene, the organization of the chromosome, or the physiology of the nucleus.   But the site of the struggle matters less than its purpose.   The enemy, although defeated and dispersed, has not been destroyed.   They will, in my opinion, have to be fought many times again.   For mankind, if it happens to take note of the argument, will not willingly admit that its destiny can be revealed by the breeding of flies or the counting of chiasmata.

REFERENCES

1. Morgan, T. H. Random segregation versus coupling in Mendelian inheritance. Science, n.s., vol. 34, p. 384, 1911.
   Morgan, T. H. The theory of the gene. New Haven, 1926.
2. Janssens, F. A. La théorie de la chiasmatypie. Cellule, vol. 25, pp. 387–411, 1909.
3. MacBride, E. W., et al. The relation of chromosomes to heredity. Nature, vol. 96, pp. 424–425, 1915.
   MacBride, E. W. The present position of the Darwinian theory. Science Progress, vol. 18, pp. 76–96, 1923.

MacBride, E. W. Further evidence for the Lamarckian theory. Nature, vol. 143, p. 205, 1939.

MacBride, E. W. Prof. E. B. Wilson: obituray notice. Nature, vol. 143, p. 547, 1939.

4. Wilson, E. B. The cell in development and heredity (3d ed.). New York, 1925.

5. Farmer, J. B., and Digby, L. On the dimensions of chromosomes considered in relation to phylogeny. Philos. Trans. Roy. Soc., vol. 205, 1914.

6. Belar, K. Der Formwechsel der Protistenkerne. Jena, 1926.

7. Darlington, C. D. Polyploids and polyploidy. Nature, vol. 124, pp. 62–64, 98–100, 1929.

8. Darlington, C. D. The cytological theory of inheritance in *Oenothera*. Journ. Genet., vol. 24, pp. 405–474, 1931.

9. Darlington, C. D. Meiosis. Biol. Rev., vol. 6, pp. 221–264, 1931.

10. Darlington, C. D. Anomalous chromosome pairing in the male *Drosophila pseudoobscura*. Genetics, vol. 19, pp. 95–118, 1934.

11. Darlington, C. D. The evolution of genetic systems. Cambridge, 1939. 2d ed., Edinburgh, 1958.

12. Darlington, C. D. The time, place and action of crossing-over. Journ. Genet., vol. 31, pp. 185–212, 1935. (In Russian, Uspexi sovremennoi Biologii, vol. 5, pp. 848–870.)

13. Darlington, C. D. The chemical basis of heredity and development. Discovery, vol. 6, pp. 79–86, 1945.

14. Watson, J. D., and Crick, F. H. C. The structure of DNA. C.S.H. Symp. Quant. Biol., vol. 18, pp. 123–131, 1953.

15. Darlington, C. D. The facts of life. London and New York, 1953.

Tropical Climates and Biology[1]

By G. S. CARTER

Department of Zoology, University of Cambridge, Cambridge, England

[With 4 plates]

FORTY years ago, when I was young, our elders often told us that a zoologist's education was not complete until he had visited the Tropics and worked on a tropical fauna. The richness and variety of animal life in the Tropics are so great that they felt that a man who had not experienced tropical zoology could have no more than a very incomplete idea of the animal world and its distribution. It is my thesis in this address that work in the Tropics is still of great value to zoologists, though not for exactly the reasons that led our predecessors to think so.

Today, zoologists are not interested so much in describing new forms and recording their morphology and distribution; most of us are more interested in the general biology of animals—in trying to understand the interactions between animals and their environments, physical and biological, how they manage to live in face of the often antagonistic conditions of their environments, what controls their distribution and evolution, and so on. If we do not go outside temperate climates such as our own, we tend to think that the conditions we find here are general, or at any rate normal, for animal life, and to neglect the fact that elsewhere in the world animals live in very different conditions. More than this, the range of conditions in a temperate climate is midway between the extremes of heat and cold to which life is exposed in other countries, and knowledge of the means by which animals survive in conditions nearer the extremes of the viable range often helps toward understanding their life in our own climate. In some ways study of arctic faunas shares these advantages with tropical biology, but in cold regions the fauna is so restricted, and investigation is so difficult, that I cannot believe that arctic biology can ever rival that of the Tropics in value to the biologist.

---

[1] Address delivered to Section D (Zoology) on Sept. 1, 1960, at the Cardiff Meeting of the British Association for the Advancement of Science. Reprinted by permission from The Advancement of Science (London), September 1960.

I shall give some examples in which work in the Tropics has given results that seem to me of interest to the general biologist, choosing examples in which the results are not such as might be expected from knowledge of the biology of temperate climates. I shall not deal with the economic importance of tropical biology, which is being discussed elsewhere at this meeting. Any economic use of a fauna or flora must be based on knowledge of the general biology; we need not fear, I think, that our results will be valueless even from the economic point of view.

Before I go on to my examples of tropical biology I must summarize the climatic conditions in which tropical and temperate environments differ, insofar as they seem to be biologically important, for it is necessary to realize the nature of these differences if we are to discuss their effects on the animals. I shall speak only of terrestrial and fresh-water environments, saying nothing of the sea where the differences are of kinds other than those I shall be describing. They would need a separate discussion.

Ultimately, most of the climatic differences between tropical and temperate regions derive from the greater altitude of the sun at midday in the Tropics and from the world distribution of temperature and pressure, which is itself due partly to differences of solar heat at different latitudes and partly to rotational effects. How these ultimate causes produce their effects is the concern of meteorology and we need not go into it; we need only to know what the effects are.

On the Equator the altitude of the sun at midday is never more than $23\frac{1}{2}°$ from the vertical. It declines to this angle at the solstices in June and December, and is vertical at the equinoxes. In the equatorial region, therefore, any seasonal change there may be is double, as the sun passes north and south from the vertical. In temperature, however, the seasonal changes are very small, since, with the sun never far from the vertical, the amount of solar heat received does not vary by more than 8 percent, and the variation in the length of the day is insignificant. At the Tropics ($23\frac{1}{2}°$ N. and S.) the seasonal changes are greater, for the sun at the winter solstice is at a height of only 43°, giving a variation of solar heat of about 27 percent, and the length of day varies by about 2 hours. In our country [England] sunlight is about twice as powerful in June as in December, and the difference in heat received is greatly increased by the much longer daylight in summer.

As the result of these conditions, the seasonal change in mean temperature on the Equator is not usually greater than 1° to 2° C. and is much less than the diurnal range which is often 10° C. In equatorial regions, however, temperatures are never very high. The annual mean is usually between 25° and 30° C., being prevented from rising higher by the humidity, cloudiness, and other conditions. Extremes of heat are characteristic not of the equatorial regions but of the deserts in subtropical latitudes.

Though in fact the sun passes north and south of the vertical everywhere within the Tropics, the double seasonal change is practically restricted to latitudes within 10° of the Equator. Farther from the Equator than this, the sun does not pass far enough from the vertical at the summer solstice to produce a noticeable effect. But the range of seasonal temperature change increases as we pass away from the Equator and may be as high as 8° C. at the Tropics. It is, however, still less than in our latitude, where it may be as much as 15° C.

Rainfall is more important than the temperature in determining the differences between tropical environments. Equatorial regions are in general characterized by fairly high rainfall, because they lie where, between the north and south trade winds, rising currents of air are cooled and their moisture precipitated—the region known at sea as the doldrums, also a region of relatively high rainfall. As the sun passes north and south, this area of high rainfall follows it, and near the Equator the rainfall decreases. The result is that, although the seasonal change on the Equator is small in temperature, in rainfall it is considerable. It is unusual in an equatorial climate for any month to be entirely without rain, but the difference between the driest and wettest months may be great. Baker and Harrisson [1] [2] compared tropical climates in this respect and find that the rain of the wettest month is more than 2.5 times that of the driest in all but 3 percent. The farther we go from the Equator the difference increases, the dry season following the sun with a lag of 1 to 2 months. Total rainfall also becomes less, especially beyond 15° N. and S. where the subtropical dry belt is approached.

The character of the rain as well as its amount is very important in controlling environmental conditions in the Tropics. All over the Tropics cyclones with large variations of atmospheric pressure, such as we know here, do not normally occur. The rain is almost always convectional—owing to upward movement of currents of air—but its frequency is very different from one region to another. In the rain forests there is often rain on almost every day—there are on the average 249 rainy days a year at Pará near the mouth of the Amazon— and the rain usually falls as a storm of an hour or two's length, often with thunder. In some deserts the intervals between storms may be more than a year on the average.

It is the frequency of rain more than any other feature of the climate that controls the nature of environments in the Tropics. Where rain is frequent, the environment is unable to dry between storms,

---

[2] Figures in brackets refer to list of references at end of article.

and the relative humidity is high. It is usually above 90 percent in rain forests where fog is frequent at dawn. Much of the water flows off the land into the large rivers that are characteristic of rain-forest regions. In doing so it leaches the land and the surface soil becomes denuded of salts. Forest waters are for this reason among the softest in the world; they may have a salt content only two or three times that of rainwater.

More accurately, it may be said that the nature of the environment is controlled by the proportion (l/g) of the gain of water to the environment in rain to its loss, not only in evaporation from open water surfaces but in transpiration from the vegetation and percolation into the soil. Where the rain is less than would be lost in these ways if the water were there, the environment will be a dry one and no water will flow off the land; where the gain is more than the loss, the environment will be humid. In the rain forests the value of l/g is of the order of 0.2, so that much water flows off the land and the environment is humid. In deserts l/g may be as high as 200, and in tropical grassland and savannas it is probably often near unity.

Many other conditions in tropical environments are controlled by the value of l/g. Small diurnal and annual ranges of temperature are characteristic of humid environments, that is to say of those with a low l/g, not only in equatorial regions but generally in the Tropics; in deserts the annual range may be as high as 40° to 50° C. and the diurnal range 25° or 30° C. Ultraviolet light is less in the more humid environments, cloudiness is greater, and the hours of sunshine less (5 to 6 hours a day in rain forests).

This account of tropical climates is very summary and incomplete; the few data I have given are almost wholly confined to the two extremes of climate, the rainforests and the deserts. But I hope that it will serve to bring out some of the biologically important differences between tropical and temperate climates. The clearest of these are, besides the obvious difference in temperature, the much smaller seasonal differences in tropical and especially equatorial climates, and the greater part that water supply plays in controlling the environmental conditions. It is in fact true that in many tropical environments the effective rhythmical change of climate is not that of the seasons but that between rainstorms. I have myself found this to be clearly true in a country, the Paraguayan Chaco, where rain fell at intervals of about a fortnight. Pools and other small bodies of water would fill when the rain fell and dry before the next rain. Much of the smaller fauna of these pools—such, for instance, as the branchiopod Crustacea, e.g., *Estheria*—passed through their whole life history in the few days that the pools were full, hatching at the time of rain and laying eggs before the pool dried.

Between the two extremes of climate that I have discussed there is, of course, a very wide range of intermediate tropical environments. These extend from woodland of many types to grassland and savanna, and to arid scrub where desert conditions are approached. In their general distribution this series of environments follows the reduction of rainfall as one goes north or south from the Equator, but everywhere conditions are greatly modified by the local geography. Near the sea, and especially where trade winds blow onto the land, rain is more plentiful than farther inland; the monsoon modifies climate in some countries; mountains may precipitate rain on their windward sides and produce deserts in their lee; and many still more local features of the geography, such as the nature of the subsoil and the amount of percolation it allows, or the efficiency of the surface drainage, will modify the environment in smaller areas.

As a first example of work on tropical biology that has given results not to be expected from our knowledge of the biology of temperate regions, I will take work on the conditions of life in shallow and stagnant fresh waters. Such environments are very widely distributed in the Tropics. Mangrove swamps are found near the banks of many of the rivers, and papyrus swamps are widespread in Africa not only bordering the rivers and lakes but also filling shallow valleys far from the lakes. (In parts of Uganda 30 percent of the land is said to be under papyrus.) In rainforests large areas may be permanently flooded along the banks of the rivers, stretching many miles into the forest, and, besides all these, swamps of many kinds are found in open country.

Some of the features of these swamps are common to most of them. Almost always the water lies under thick growths of aerial vegetation—trees in the mangrove swamps and forest, papyrus which may grow to 12 to 15 feet high, and in the swamps of open country, grasses and other plants almost equally high. The water is often highly colored—it may have the color of weak tea—and is almost or quite stagnant even in the mangrove and papyrus swamps on the borders of rivers and lakes. In temperate countries undisturbed by man swamps may be equally widespread, but the conditions of life in their water are, as we shall see, very different from those in tropical swamps.

(My own interest in these environments has centered in the fact that they are of great interest for the study of evolution. It was almost certainly from swamps of this kind that vertebrates and probably many other terrestrial animals emerged from the water. But I shall not have space to discuss these matters in this paper.)

I take as a first example of tropical swamps some in the Paraguayan Chaco in South America, in which Professor Beadle and I worked [2].

These lie in the almost flat grassy plains to the west of the Paraguay River, which are in fact an extension northward of the pampas. Their latitude is near the southern Tropic and the climate is therefore subtropical rather than typically tropical; it has a seasonal change of mean temperature of 8° C. (27° to 19° C.). But in the hotter weather the characters of the environment are typical of those in true tropical swamps. The climate is moderately humid with an annual mean rainfall of 55 inches. The rain falls at intervals of about a fortnight, more frequently in the hot season. Between the storms the temperature gradually rises until the next storm comes.

The swamps occupy depressions in the plains only a few feet below the general level. They drain very slowly toward the river so that their water is for all practical purposes stagnant though its level varies in dry and wet periods by 2 feet or more. In the deepest parts of the swamp, which hardly ever dry, the water is at most 5 or 6 feet deep. The substratum is a black mud full of marsh gas (methane), consolidating in its deeper layers and passing gradually downward into a stiff and impervious clay.

The shallower parts of the swamp (pl. 1, fig. 1) near its edges are occasionally dry, and the water is covered by a floating blanket of aerial plants of many species, among which the swamp-lettuce (*Pistia*) and the swamp-hyacinth (*Eichhornia*) are dominant. Between these plants the blanket is completed by the smaller fronds of the water-ferns *Salvinia* and *Azolla* (pl. 1, fig. 2). There may also be open pools where the blanket is missing. The more central parts of the swamp are filled with large clumps of a flowering plant (*Thalia*) reaching 10 feet or so above the water and of the bulrush (*Typha*). Between these clumps the water is clear without vegetation and highly colored (pl. 2, fig. 1).

Investigation of the conditions in the waters of these swamps shows first that the content of nutrient salts is high. Phosphates, for instance, are present in concentrations of 2 to 4 mg. per liter, whereas in temperate waters concentrations around 0.1 mg. per liter are usual. Many other conditions such as the pH (6.2–6.8) and the bicarbonate content are suitable for the growth of phytoplankton, which we should therefore at first sight expect to be plentiful. In fact, in all parts of the swamp the water contains only a sparse plankton, both animal and plant, and in the central part there is almost none.

One probable explanation of this anomaly lies in the heavy shading of the water by the vegetation above its surface and the shallow penetration of the light into the highly colored water even if it is not shaded. In other similar tropical waters it has been found that the amount of light in the water may be below the compensation point for plants within a few inches of the surface. This is so in spite of the strength of the tropical sunlight.

Measurement of the dissolved oxygen content of the water shows an even more striking contrast with the conditions in similar waters in temperate countries. In the tropical swamps the oxygen is everywhere far from saturation even within an inch of the surface. It is in fact astonishing that in these and similar tropical waters one can often take a sample as close to the surface as is practicable—within at the most an inch—and find in it no measurable quantity of dissolved oxygen. In the central parts of the Chaco swamps even the surface water hardly ever in hot weather contained a measurable quantity of oxygen, and certainly less than 5 percent saturation. In the outer region under the floating blanket the water was also almost always without measurable oxygen. Pools free of the floating blanket sometimes contained at midday 2 to 3 cc. of oxygen per liter (about 50 percent saturation) at the surface, but the lower water, even here, was often without oxygen continuously for many days in hot weather.

How is this lack of oxygen in the swamp waters brought about? I believe that it is the result of several conditions which are all present in these waters and not normally present in otherwise similar temperate waters. Oxygen can be introduced into a body of water by diffusion from the air, and produced in it by photosynthesis. It will be removed by the respiration of plants and animals and by the chemical and biological oxidations of decay. In the tropical swamps little oxygen is produced by photosynthesis owing to the weak lighting of the water, and decay, rapid at the high temperature, will actively remove any oxygen that gets into the water. Oxygen can reach the water only by diffusion from the air above it.

Entry of oxygen from the air must always take place, but in liquids diffusion, though rapid over a distance of a small fraction of a millimeter, is negligibly slow over greater distances. A thin oxygenated film at the surface will always be produced, but practically no oxygen can reach the lower layers of the water by unaided diffusion. It can reach the lower layers only if it is carried down by vortical disturbance, which may be due either to wind and current—and in the flowing water of rivers and streams all layers of the water are usually well oxygenated—or to convection due to the surface being sufficiently cooled at night to cause overturn of the layers of the water. These waters are stagnant, and the thick vegetation above them prevents any disturbance in them by wind. Thus, overturn is the only means by which oxygen could reach the lower water. But in these tropical waters, exposed to hot sunlight during the day, there is set up at midday a very steep gradient of temperature from the surface downward (often 8° to 10° C. in a column of water 12 or 18 inches high), and in most nights no overturn occurs, so that the water is permanently stratified and the lower layers receive no oxygen. That this is the correct explanation is confirmed by the observation that in open pools in the outer parts of the Chaco swamps some oxygen—up to 20 percent saturation—was present in the lower water after unusually cool and rainy days or cold nights.

The deoxygenation of the water was paralleled by a high content of free carbon dioxide—up to 40 cc. per liter in the water of the outer parts and 70 cc. per liter in the central parts. This was clearly due to its inability to escape to the air by diffusion.

For animals breathing aquatically by gills these waters are therefore a very difficult environment, and this of itself is enough to explain the poverty of the zooplankton, even though, as was shown to be the case, the plankton is adapted to live at a low concentration of oxygen (5 percent saturation). All the fauna shows adaptation to life in a deoxygenated habitat. These swamps are a well-known habitat of the air-breathing lungfish *Lepidosiren*, and many of the teleost fishes have evolved accessory air-breathing organs. Some of the smaller fishes, however, do not breathe air. They succeed in maintaining their aquatic respiration by living near the surface and using the thin oxygenated surface film, nibbling at it but not breaking the surface. The invertebrates also show many adaptations. A small oligochaete (*Aulophorus*) lives in the surface film of the outer region of the swamp. Being an oligochaete it needs a tube, and this it makes for itself from the spores of the waterferns. It carries this tube about with it. Another oligochaete (*Drilocrius*) lives in very shallow water at the edge of the swamp making burrows in the mud. From time to time it extends from its burrow to the surface of the water where it captures a bubble of air in a modified part of its tail which is specialized for respiration. With this it retreats into its burrow. The large aquatic snail *Ampullaria* has a lung for air-breathing and lays its eggs in masses on the stalks of plants above the water. Some of the fishes make nests which float at the surface of the water and have below them a foam of air bubbles which the young use for their respiration. Others lay their eggs in the mud of the outer part of the swamp, but during the wet season when the lower water may contain some oxygen. *Lepidosiren* lays its eggs in an L-shaped burrow in the mud guarded by the male, which is said to aerate the nest with air brought from the surface and excreted from the vascular filaments which it bears on its pelvic fins during the breeding season.

I have worked on similar stagnant waters in two other parts of the Tropics—in the forests of British Guiana and in Uganda [3, 4]. In the Guiana forests the swamps (pl. 2, fig. 2) were shaded and protected from the wind by the trees above them. They were often as completely deoxygenated as the Chaco swamps but in them complete deoxygenation did not usually last for more than a few days at a time whereas in the Chaco swamps it might be unbroken for weeks. I believe that the reason for this difference is the greater frequency of rain in Guiana and the less heating of the surface by day. The African swamps (pls. 3 and 4) were thickly covered with papyrus and the deoxygenation in them was again extreme. Everywhere, except in lakeside swamps near the open water of the lake, even the surface water contained no measurable oxygen and the content of carbon dioxide was high. In these swamps the plankton was as sparse as in the Chaco swamps and the larger fauna mostly air-breathing. The African lungfish *Protopterus* and several air-breathing teleost fishes live in these swamps.

Thus, it appears that deoxygenation is a general condition in shallow and stagnant tropical waters, and this is borne out by the fact that air-breathing adaptations are found in the teleost fishes of similar habitats in many other tropical regions. In temperate countries deoxygenation does occur in shallow and stagnant waters occasionally during long periods of hot summer weather, but it is unusual. In the lake of the botanic gardens at Cambridge all the fish died some years ago in a hot spell; I believe that they were killed by stratification and consequent deoxygenation of the water, which is muddy and nearly stagnant. Normally in temperate climates, heating of the surface in the daytime is not strong enough to prevent overturn at night. But we have very few examples of work on such waters even in temperate countries, and still fewer on tropical waters. It seems to me that more accurate knowledge of the conditions in which overturn occurs in natural waters would be valuable. It might be expected that at high altitudes in the Tropics, where the temperature is lower, conditions more like those in temperate waters would be found, and Beadle [5] has found that in some papyrus swamps on the shore of Lake Naivasha in Kenya at about 6,000 feet the water was 50 percent saturated with oxygen. On the other hand, I have found in an open pool at Kigezi in Uganda at a similar altitude (5,579 feet) apparently permanent stratification and complete deoxygenation of the lower water. The reason for the difference is not apparent. Clearly more work is needed, and this should be both theoretical and in the field.

Equally unexpected results have been given by work on the sulfur content of tropical fresh waters in Africa. Beauchamp [6] pointed out that the sulfur content of many African fresh waters is very low; in several lakes it is not above 3 parts per million (mg. per liter). He suggested that lack of sulfur is a limiting factor in the growth of the aquatic fauna. The subject was further investigated by Hesse [7], working on Lake Victoria. He found that the lake water contained 0.5 to 2 p.p.m. total sulfur and less than 0.5 p.p.m. sulfate. In contrast the aquatic vegetation contained a normal sulfur content (average

0.1 percent), so that sulfur can be a limiting factor only for the plankton-feeding and not for plant-eating fish.

When Hesse analyzed the mud from the bottom of the lake, astonishing results were obtained. The sulfur content of the mud was extremely high at all depths down to 13 meters below its surface, but in all the samples far the greater part of the sulfur—in most samples more than 90 percent—was in organic form. Inorganic sulfur is present but in relatively low concentration, sulfides often below the limit for estimation.

Clearly, the sulfur is not held in the mud by precipitation as sulfide, and this is confirmed by the fact that the water over the mud is often well oxygenated and the mud itself not in a highly reducing state. What apparently happens is that the sulfur is absorbed from the water of the lake by the planktonic fauna and flora and carried down to the mud in their dead bodies, so that the water becomes denuded of sulfur. In the mud the organic sulfur compounds in the bodies of the planktonic organisms are preserved without breakdown even for the several thousand years required for the deposition of 10 to 15 meters of mud. Plants growing in the water, if their roots penetrate the mud, are able to absorb sulfur from this store, and this is apparently the only means by which the sulfur can be carried back from the mud to the water.

Soils around the lake were also found to have a low sulfur content except where they were covered with forest, being leached by water draining toward the lake. The same shortage of sulfur is found in many soils in other parts of Uganda, and Simpson and Butters [8] have found experimentally that addition of lake mud to such soil improves the growth of plants growing on the soil. The organic sulfur compounds in the mud break down if the mud is dried, boiled, or autoclaved. After being so treated it has been found to improve the fertility of fish ponds.

I now turn from work on fresh waters to a quite different branch of tropical biology, investigation of the control of seasonal rhythms of reproduction and migration in tropical animals. This again raises problems different from those met in temperate regions. In many tropical environments, especially in regions at considerable distances from the Equator, there may be, as we have seen, fairly large seasonal changes in the environment, and there is then no difficulty in showing that seasonal changes in the behavior of the fauna are controlled by the environmental changes, as they usually are in temperate countries. In the Paraguayan Chaco, for instance, many of the amphibians and fishes breed after the first heavy rains of the summer season and it is easy to show that the stimulus for breeding is in at least some

1. View of the Chaco swamps from the outer edge.

2. The floating blanket of the outer part of the Chaco swamps. The larger plants are *Pistia*, and the smaller frons between them *Salvinia* and *Azolla*.

1. The vegetation of the central part of a Chaco swamp from its outer edge.

2. Swamp vegetation in the Guiana forest. The ground is covered with 1 to 2 feet of stagnant water, but this is hardly evident in this photograph, since it is filled with decaying vegetation.

1. Aerial photograph of papyrus swamps on the shore of Lake Victoria.

2. A valley in Uganda filled with papyrus swamp, down the center of which a stream flows.

Vegetation of a papyrus swamp seen from its edge.

species cooling of the water by the rain. In the laboratory the easiest way to induce many of the frogs and fishes to lay eggs is to sprinkle the aquarium with cool water.

It is far less easy to see how biological rhythms are controlled in parts of the Tropics where seasonal changes of the climate are slight. We have seen that in equatorial regions the only large seasonal change is in rainfall, but it does not seem likely that variations in rainfall are the effective control of the rhythms, for there is rain in every month of the year, the humidity is always high and not significantly variable, and, though food may for some animals differ from month to month, it is always plentiful. Yet the fact is that most species have well-defined seasonal rhythms even in these environments, though a few breed all the year round and some others have double breeding seasons associated with the double seasonal change. Baker and his coworkers found [9], for instance, that in the rain forests at Noumea in the New Hebrides, a highly invariable climate though the latitude is 15° S., all the species he worked on were seasonal in their breeding, the birds and mammals at least as markedly seasonal as in temperate countries. A lizard (*Emoia* sp.) had a less clearly defined breeding season, though even it showed a seasonal rhythm of gonad growth. A bat (*Miniopterus* sp.), which spent the day in caves where the climate was even more invariable than in the forest outside the caves, was the most markedly seasonal of all, breeding on only a few days at the beginning of September. The breeding seasons were often not the same as those general in temperate regions, and in the case of a passerine bird, *Pachycephala pectoralis*, differed from its breeding times in places at the same latitude in Australia. He had evidence that the times of breeding persisted at the same dates from year to year. He was not able to find any seasonal climatic change that could control the periodicity of the animals. Owing to the latitude the length of day at Noumea varies by 1¾ hours, but he concluded that this was not the effective cause.

A large majority of species are seasonal in other invariable environments both in breeding and migration. Marshall and Williams found [10] that at Entebbe in Uganda on the Equator the yellow wagtail (*Motacilla flava*), which "winters" in Africa and spends the summer in Europe, was seasonal in the development of its gonad during its time in Uganda (December to April). They were unable to find any climatic change during this time to account for the periodicity. It is certainly not controlled by the length of day, for this does not vary significantly at Entebbe between December and April.

For some species details of their habits and biology provide the answer. Birds that nest on islands in rivers, or on river banks near the water, may be able to breed only in the drier months when their breeding sites are uncovered; and Marshall and Roberts [11], find that the cormorants (*Phalacrocorax* spp.) on Lake Victoria at 0°20′ N. are seasonal, breeding from May to December, and they come to the conclusion that the determining cause is the greater frequency of high winds between January and April, which destroy their flimsy nests.

Such reasons will not account for the general occurrence of periodicity in equatorial animals. If no explanation can be found in environmental changes, it may be suggested that the control lies in the animals themselves, in endogenous rhythms. But, if the breeding or migration is at the same date from year to year—and it seems to be so in most species—it is hardly possible, as Baker points out, for the control to be wholly by endogenous rhythm, for the period of the rhythm would have to agree very exactly with the annual cycle; any difference, however small, would mean that the time of breeding or migration altered from year to year. I know of only one instance in which the periodicity of a tropical animal is wholly due to an endogenous rhythm. This is the case of the wide-awake or sooty tern (*Sterna fuscata*), which nests on Ascension Island (8° S.). In this bird the interval between nesting times is not a year but 9 to 10 months [12]. No environmental stimulus could give this result.

Though the whole cause of the periodicity cannot be endogenous, this does not mean that endogenous rhythms play no part in its causation. It may be that in many species the rhythm is at base endogenous and is kept adjusted to the annual cycle by some external stimulus of which we are at present ignorant. Such a stimulus might be of almost any kind; it would probably differ from species to species and need not always be physical. Marshall and Williams, for instance, suggest that the northward migration of the yellow wagtails in Uganda is stimulated by the passage of birds of the same species from farther south where they have been stimulated to migrate by environmental stimuli. The rhythm of gonad growth in Uganda would be endogenous and the birds would only respond to the stimulation when the gonads were in the appropriate condition. Another explanation of this example would seem to be that their migration southward is determined by environmental stimulation in Europe and the time of the northward migration by an endogenous rhythm of gonad growth starting from the time of their arrival in Africa.

In the many species that live all the year round in apparently invariable environments but yet are seasonal, it seems that there *must* be some environmental stimulus, physical or other, that controls their periodicity. For almost all of them we cannot say what the stimulus is and we can only admit our ignorance. Clearly this is a subject on which further work is needed.

Lastly, I will take an example from physiology, and from an environment very different from the swamps and equatorial regions we have so far considered. My example is the problem how small mammals are able to satisfy their needs for water in desert conditions. This has been studied by B. and K. Schmidt-Neilsen [13].

It has always been difficult to understand how such animals as jerboas and desert rats can survive without drinking in deserts where the temperature may rise to 130° F. (54° C.) at midday. There are, however, some characters of the desert environment and the animals' biology that go part of the way to help us to understand their ability to do so.

First, the most striking characteristic of a desert climate is the large diurnal range of temperature, very hot at midday but cool and even near the freezing point at dawn. Dew is frequent in many desert climates, and Buxton [14] showed that grass blowing about on the surface of a desert and apparently entirely dry contained water to 50 percent of its weight at midday, presumably derived from the dew of the previous morning. Secondly, these animals are largely nocturnal; they avoid the extremes of midday heat in burrows.

They may obtain some water by eating the grass or from dew and may reduce their water loss by sheltering, but it seems unlikely that they can wholly maintain their water balance in these ways. The only other supply of water available to them is the metabolic water formed in the oxidation of their food; 1 g. fat yields 1.07 g. water in its oxidation, 1 g. carbohydrate 0.56 g., and 1 g. protein 0.40 g. Schmidt-Neilsen set out to determine whether this was a sufficient supply.

It should be noted that, as we should expect, desert animals are adapted in several ways to economy of water. They do not control their body temperature by sweating. Their sweat glands are reduced, and control of temperature by sweat is in fact impossible for small animals in desert conditions, for the amount of water loss required is far too large in proportion to their body weight. Schmidt-Neilsen finds that for a man of 70 kg. in the temperatures of a desert in daytime 1.47 percent of his body weight must be evaporated per hour, for the kangaroo rat (*Dipodomys*, 0.1 kg.) 12.8 percent, and for a mouse (0.02 kg.) 21.5 percent.

Then, again, their urine is more concentrated than that of other mammals. Comparable results are given in the following table.

	Concentration in urine	
	Electrolytes N.	*Urea M.*
Man	0.37 (2.2%)	1.0 (6%)
Rat (*R. norvegicus*)	0.6 (3.5%)	2.5 (15%)
Dipodomys	1.2 (7%)	3.5 (23%)

Also, very little water is lost in the feces. The feces of *Dipodomys* have a water content only one-quarter of that of the rat's feces.

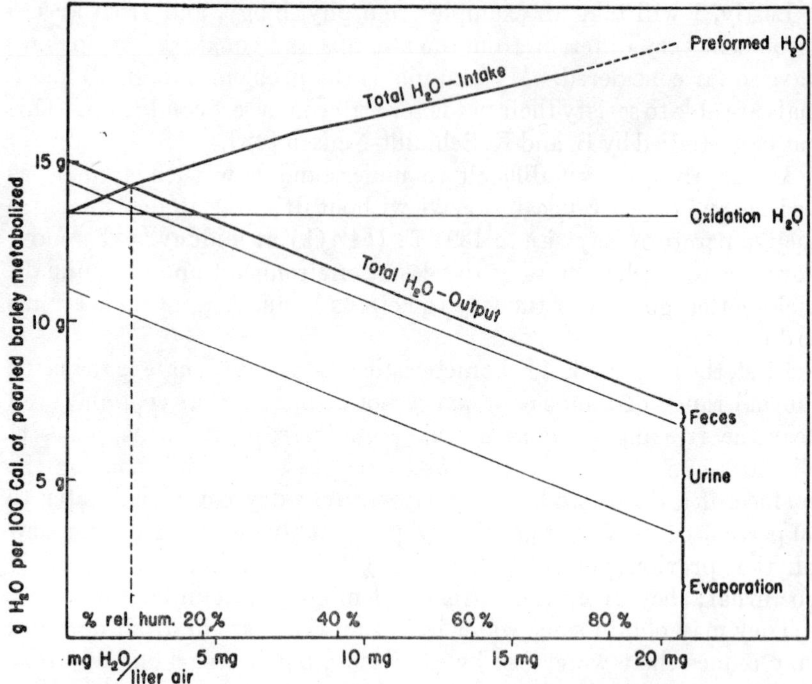

FIGURE 1.—The water balance of *Dipodomys*.   (After B. and K. Schmidt-Neilsen.)

Putting these facts together Schmidt-Neilsen draws the diagram given in figure 1 for the water balance of *Dipodomys* eating pearl barley without any supply of water beyond that present in the barley as preformed water and that produced in the metabolism (oxidation water). It shows that the water balance is positive at all relative humidities greater than 10 percent. Remembering that the animals spend most of the daytime in burrows, we may conclude that they are sufficiently adapted to live permanently in a desert climate without drinking. The rat is not quite in balance at a relative humidity of 100 percent. It is of interest to note that a similar balance was worked out by Krogh [15] for the seal (*Phoca*) living in the sea, which is for a mammal a "dry" environment since the osmotic pressure of sea water is greater than that of mammalian tissues and water must leave the body by diffusion. Krogh found that the seal was also in balance, but in neither case is any allowance made for water loss by the female when she is giving milk.

I hope that these examples will have shown that tropical biology offers us many problems that repay investigation, and that the results are often not those that we should expect from our knowledge of temperate biology. There are many advantages besides these for the zoologist in tropical work, especially for the young zoologist. Perhaps the most important is that tropical biology is at a much less advanced stage than that of temperate countries. It is much easier in the Tropics to find promising lines of work, and less likely to find that the work one is doing is in competition with that of others, or has already been done—the field, in fact, is much less crowded. It is also true that one lives closer to nature in the Tropics, and has greater opportunities to study animals in their natural lives. I know that it is for most of us impossible to get to the Tropics for a visit of a year or longer— and a shorter stay is hardly likely to lead to worthwhile results—but the fact is also true that when posts in tropical laboratories are advertised it is not by any means always easy to find people to fill them. I think that one reason for this is that the advantages of work in the Tropics are not sufficiently realized.

REFERENCES

1. BAKER, J. R., and HARRISSON, T. H.   Journ. Linn. Soc. (Zool.), vol. 39, p. 443, 1936.
2. CARTER, G. S., and BEADLE, L. C.   Journ. Linn. Soc. (Zool.), vol. 37, pp. 197, 327, 1930–31.
3. CARTER, G. S.   Journ. Linn. Soc. (Zool.), vol. 39, pp. 147–219, 1934–35.
4. CARTER, G. S.   The papyrus swamps of Uganda.   1955.
5. BEADLE, L. C.   Journ. Linn. Soc. (Zool.), vol. 38, p. 135, 1932.
6. BEAUCHAMP, R. S. A.   Nature, vol. 171, p. 769, 1953.
7. HESSE, P. R.   Hydrobiologia, vol. 11, p. 1, 1957.
8. SIMPSON, J. R., and BUTTERS, B.   East African Fish. Res. Org. Ann. Rep., p. 43, 1958.
9. BAKER, J. R., ET AL.   Journ. Linn. Soc. (Zool.), vol. 39, p. 507; vol. 40, pp. 123, 143; vol. 41, pp. 50, 243, 248.
10. MARSHALL, A. J., and WILLIAMS, M. C.   Proc. Zool. Soc. London, vol. 132, p. 313, 1959.
11. MARSHALL, A. J., and ROBERTS, J. D.   Proc. Zool. Soc. London, vol. 132, p. 617, 1959.
12. CHAPIN, J. P.   Auk, vol. 71, p. 1, 1954.
13. SCHMIDT-NEILSEN, B. and K.   Biology of deserts, pp. 173, 182.   Institute of Biology, London, 1954.
14. BUXTON, P. A.   Animal life in deserts.   London, 1923.
15. KROGH, A.   Osmotic regulation in aquatic animals.   Cambridge, 1939.

Outdoor Aerobiology[1]

By P. H. GREGORY

Head, Department of Plant Pathology
Rothamsted Experimental Station
Harpenden, England

[With 2 plates]

To THE sufferer from hay fever there will be nothing novel in the idea that outdoor air contains the pollen of many different kinds of flowering plants. But the air also contains many other particles of biological origin, such as the spores of cryptogams, fungi, bacteria, and yeasts, and also protozoan cysts, some of which may also cause allergies. Some species in all the major taxonomic groups of plants have evolved means of introducing their spores into the turbulent layers of the atmosphere [6].[2] Other organisms, however, are adapted to other dispersal routes, such as water or animal transport, and their spores seldom get into the air.

The systematic study of the microbiology of the atmosphere started about a century ago, in the expectation of finding the source of epidemic diseases such as cholera and typhoid. It is now clear, however, that outdoor air is not a serious source of human infection and it has been acquitted of complicity in the worst human and animal diseases, though recent American work shows that the agents of histoplasmosis and other fungus diseases of man are windborne. Outdoor air also conveys pollen, a major nuisance to hay-fever victims, and also infective spores of many important crop pathogens, such as the rusts and smuts of cereals.

In effect, aerobiology began at the Observatoire Montsouris in Paris with the work of the bacteriologist Pierre Miquel (1850–1922), who elaborated techniques that enabled him, throughout the last quarter of the 19th century, to analyze daily the microbial content of outdoor air. However, the first to attempt consciously to develop aerobiology as an individual branch of science was a plant pathologist, Fred C. Meier (1893–1938). Unfortunately he was lost on a flight over the Pacific after publishing no more than a few preliminary papers; these

<hr>

[1] Reprinted by permission from Endeavour, vol. 19, No. 76, October 1960.
[2] Numbers in brackets indicate references at end of text.

papers served, however, to kindle an interest in the subject in the United States. Also noteworthy in the history of aerobiology was a thesis published in 1935 by K. M. Stepanov of Leningrad [9]. From research based on the work of these and others during three generations it is possible—though our information is still meager—to picture the circulation of plant spores and other microbes in the atmosphere, and to assess its bearing on medicine, agriculture, and the biological sciences [4].

TECHNIQUES OF AEROBIOLOGY

Much has been learned about the microbial flora of the atmosphere (here termed the "air-spora" and taken to include the pollen of flowering plants) by examining deposits on sticky-surface traps exposed to the wind. But results obtained by this method are difficult to interpret quantitatively, because the catches depend on factors that vary greatly. For quantitative information about the air-spora it is necessary to use apparatus that removes spores efficiently from a measured volume of air. Such apparatus requires a means of drawing a measured volume of air through a filter, or of accelerating the air so that particles carried in it adhere to a sticky surface or are trapped in liquid.

Suction to draw a measured volume of air through the filter medium is required by sampling devices such as Pasteur's aspirated plug filter and the newer membrane filters. Another series of devices act by forcing the air through a narrow jet and directing it toward a sticky surface. The General Electric electrostatic air sampler applies the dust-collection principle worked out by Oliver Lodge. Each of these sampling devices has its virtues and limitations, but can give quantitative data if properly used. In outdoor work, high accuracy is not usually required at present, as results already obtained show that the spore content of the air differs enormously with place and time.

The results of sampling by different methods are difficult to compare. Some samplers deposit particles directly onto a microscope slide, where totals of the larger spores and pollen grains can be counted visually and classified. Others allow bacterial and yeast colonies, fungus mycelia, or whole moss plants to develop in culture, and identification of the cultivable fraction of the air-spora can then be more precise. This gain in precision of identification over the visual method is, however, balanced by loss of information about the total number of organisms, some of which may not be viable. A few workers have used both kinds of sampler simultaneously.

THE AIR-SPORA NEAR GROUND LEVEL

Most abundant in numbers near ground level are bacteria and fungus spores. When some abundant species of plant is in flower,

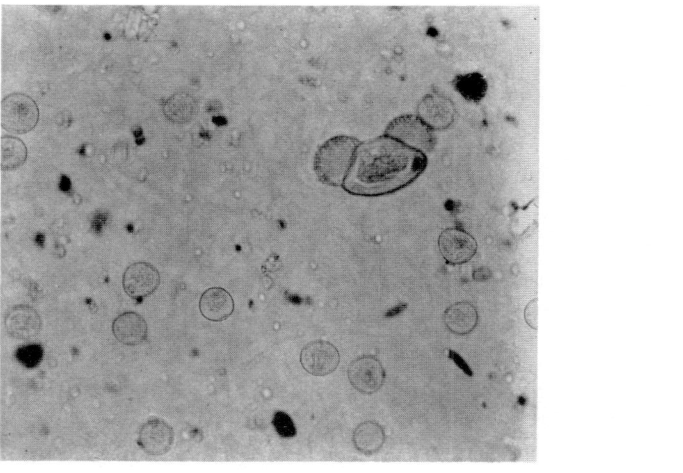

1.

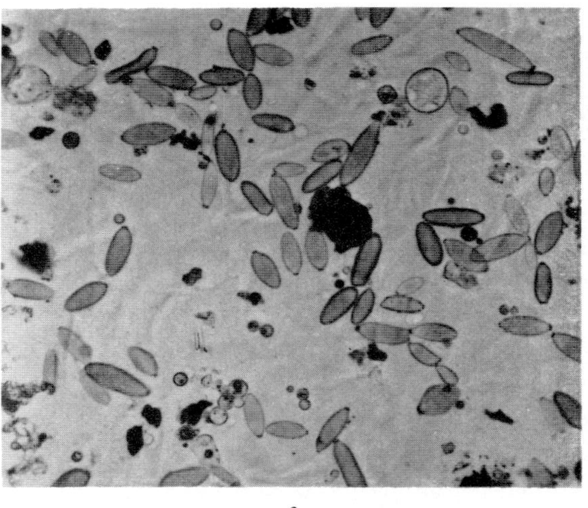

2.

Photomicrographs illustrating pollen and fungus spores in air at 0.5 meter above ground level, beside a stream, at Imperial College Field Station, Sunninghill, Berkshire, summer of 1958.   1, June 15, 17.00 hours, pollen of pine (with two air sacs) and grasses.   ×230. 2, June 16, 10.00 hours, spores of the mold *Cladosporium*.   ×450.

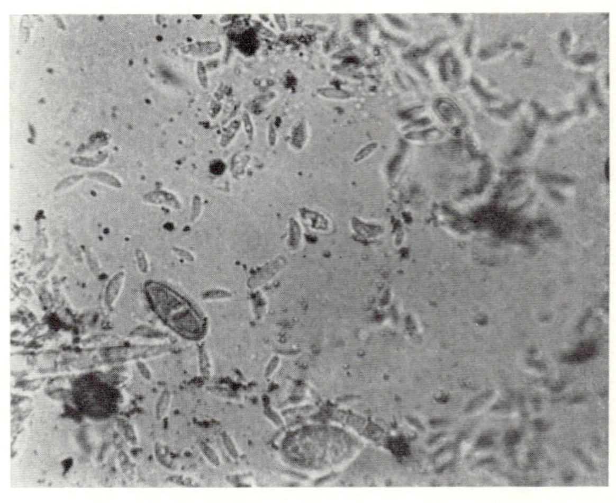

1.

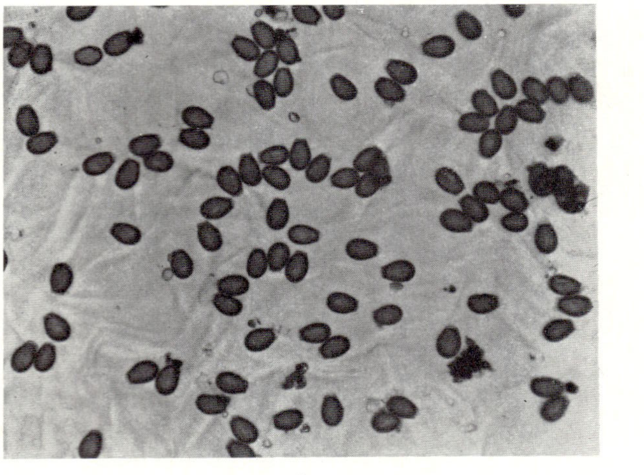

2.

Photomicrographs illustrating pollen and fungus spores in air at 0.5 meter above ground level, beside a stream, at Imperial College Field Station, Sunninghill, Berkshire, summer of 1958.   1, June 18, 02.30 hours, spores of the bracket fungus *Ganoderma applanatum.*   ×450. 2, June 19, 04.00 hours, spores of the mirror yeast *Sporobolomyces.*   ×1,000.

pollen may overshadow bacteria and fungi for a time in mass, but even then not usually in number of particles. About 90 percent of the species of flowering plants are usually insect-pollinated, but only about 10 percent are adapted for wind pollination and habitually shed their pollen into the air. However, these wind-pollinated species are numerically exceedingly abundant and in the aggregate shed large quantities of pollen, with the result that the unfortunate sufferer from hay fever who is allergic to certain species of pollen finds his respiratory tract a reliable indicator of flowering dates. In temperate countries there are three main seasons for airborne pollen. The "tree pollens" in spring begin with the opening of the catkins of deciduous trees and end with the conifers; fortunately, sensitivity to tree pollen, and especially to pine, is rare. In early summer the grass-pollen season brings the greatest number of hay-fever victims. Late summer brings a mixture generally grouped as "weed pollens." These include nettle in Europe and the highly potent pollen of ragweed (*Ambrosia* spp.) in North America; freedom from airborne ragweed pollen may be as valuable to an American health resort as a high figure for sunshine is in Britain.

Airborne bacteria can be enumerated only by cultural methods, and because of the technical problems of culture we have no idea how many such bacteria elude detection. It is therefore impossible accurately to compare total numbers of bacteria and fungi in the air. However, it is clear that the numbers of cultivable molds usually much exceed the numbers of bacteria, and Miquel was clearly embarrassed by the immense numbers of airborne molds. His early work suggested 700 bacteria and 30,000 mold spores per cubic meter; his long-term averages of about 300 bacteria and 200 mold spores per cubic meter at the Observatoire Montsouris were obtained only after he changed over to using sugar-free culture media so as to discourage mold growth, a practice that has been followed by many later workers. The bacteria of the air include many micrococci and bacilli, but also a surprisingly large proportion of kinds that do not form spores.

Visual examination of the fungus spores deposited on a microscope slide during continuous sampling with the Hirst trap in an arable field at Rothamsted Experimental Station [5] shows that the predominant organisms in outdoor air during the day in the warmer months are spores of *Cladosporium*, a genus of saprophytic molds found on decaying vegetation; the average was 5,800 per cubic meter of air near ground level during June to October 1952. This dominance of *Cladosporium* is also true of many other parts of the world, and it is fully confirmed by cultural methods and examination of dust deposits. More study is needed to find out how *Cladosporium* becomes airborne. Second most abundant in the air-spora at Rothamsted were spores of the type known as ballistospores. The sources of these include the mirror yeasts (sporobolomycetes) that flourish on the surfaces of living and aging leaves, mushrooms, and toadstools, averaging 4,400 per cubic meter and predominating at night. Recognition of ballisto-spores as numerically important components of the air-spora was long delayed by two causes. First, these very small spores were inefficiently collected by the sticky-surface traps used in much early aerobiological work, and, second, most microbiologists were not familiar with the spores of the higher fungi. Spores of various plant-pathogenic fungi such as the rusts, smuts, and mildews are often present in the air in large numbers, but their occurrence, like that of the pollen of flower-ing plants, is highly seasonal.

The figures given above are for average frequencies over a period of many weeks of continuous recording. Hourly means are often much higher or lower; for example, *Cladosporium* may reach 100,000 and *Sporobolomyces* about 1 million per cubic meter. There is evidence that shorter-term fluctuation may be still greater: ragweed pollen in spot tests lasting a couple of minutes has given concentrations of over 10 million per cubic meter [2].

Protozoan "eggs" in the air were estimated by Miquel at 0.1 per cubic meter, but later work by Puschkarew, based on fewer tests, suggests 10 times that figure. Blue and blue-green algae may average 1 to 10 per cubic meter, but spores of myxomycetes are probably less abundant. Spores of ferns and mosses are sometimes plentiful for short periods.

Concentrations of the few organisms that have been studied in detail fluctuate with a characteristic diurnal periodicity, as also does grass pollen. Miquel found two maxima and two minima in the daily cycle of bacterial numbers when sampling hourly at Montsouris for over a year. Nothing similar has been attempted with bacteria since 1884, however, and the work needs extending and repeating.

Spores of fungi show various diurnal periodicities, but normally any one type has only a single daily maximum and minimum. For example, in England spores of *Phytophthora infestans*, the fungus causing potato blight, are most abundant shortly before noon, whereas the numbers of spores of *Cladosporium* and of some rust fungi reach a maximum in the afternoon. Spores of *Sporobolomyces*, and basidio-spores of mushrooms, toadstools, and bracket fungi are all most abundant during the night. Little is yet known about differences in these cycles in various parts of the world. These diurnal cycles are clearly determined largely by the effect of meteorological factors on spore liberation and dispersal in ways understood for only a few species of fungi. Some, such as two important crop pathogens, *Ophiobolus graminis* and *Venturia inaequalis* (causing take-all of wheat and apple scab respectively), depend for spore liberation on the wetting of the substrate by rain or dew; they occur in the air in large numbers only after rain.

THE ORIGIN OF THE AIR-SPORA

Despite claims to the contrary, there is little doubt that most of the air-spora comes from ground sources on the surface, such as plants and vegetable debris, rather than from the soil itself. Only the sources of the protozoa, bacteria, and yeasts (other than the "mirror yeasts") remain in doubt. The air-spora is not rich in typical soil inhabitants but represents mainly organisms growing above the surface. Soil and surface dust raised by wind may possibly be the source of most atmospheric bacteria and yeasts, and the seasonal maximum numbers of bacteria in the air of temperate regions seems to be associated with the tilling of bare ground in spring or with strong winds. Splash droplets from marine and fresh water, and from wet soil, evidently help to make surface organisms airborne.

THE AIR-SPORA OVER THE OCEAN

Samples taken on ships show that, with an offshore wind, the influence of the land-spora often extends to several hundred miles from shore, but that in midocean the air is nearly free from microbial contamination. The proportion of airborne bacteria requiring sodium chloride for growth is stated to increase in proximity to the ocean. Pollen can sometimes be found in quantity for some miles out to sea, but its concentration usually decreases faster as the land recedes than does the concentration of molds or bacteria. However, even in midocean, on the coasts of Greenland, and on remote oceanic islands, tree pollen falls regularly in small but measurable quantities after being transported for hundreds or thousands of miles by the wind.

THE UPPER TROPOSPHERE

The presence of pollen and microbes in air layers above ground has been confirmed by catches on kites, balloons, and airplanes. Theoretical considerations suggest that spore concentration should decrease logarithmically with height, on the assumption that spores coming into suspension from the ground reach an equilibrium resulting from the rival actions of stirring up by atmospheric turbulence and sedimentation under gravity. In practice, concentration does at first usually decrease with height above ground level. On some occasions, and more often when several occasions are averaged, the decrease follows approximately the logarithmic law up to a height of several thousands of meters. However, a decrease in concentration according to the logarithmic law is an ideal condition seldom attained in the atmosphere, and in practice a zone of increased concentration often occurs at a height of perhaps 2,000 or 3,000 meters. This fact has led to speculation about a so-called "biotic zone" in the upper air, but the explanation probably lies partly in the different histories of air masses at different heights, and partly in the washing of the lower layers of air by rain. Microbial concentration is sometimes high in the bases of clouds, and spores may perhaps become concentrated there by being collected in droplets poised on ascending convection currents in cumulus clouds. The effect of these processes would be particularly noticeable over the ocean, where the air-spora is not constantly being renewed from the surface.

Systematic measurements of spore concentrations at different heights over the oceans have still to be made, but observations made by different methods on ships and from aircraft suggest that the gradient may be the reverse of that over land. Far out to sea, the surface air appears to contain exceptionally few microbes, whereas several thousand meters up, the concentrations of bacteria, fungus spores, and pollens may be considerably greater. Studies by S. M. Pady and coworkers [7, 8], for example, indicate fungus-spore and pollen concentrations of tens to hundreds per cubic meter at 3,000 meters above the North Atlantic, whereas G. Erdtmann [3], sampling on board ship, found values only a tenth or a hundredth of these. We thus have a picture of air masses carrying over the ocean the spore load they acquired during passage over land, and of the lower layers of air being gradually cleared in passage over the sea both by deposition and by scrubbing by rain showers.

It is remarkable that the microbial content of the atmosphere above the troposphere still remains almost uninvestigated. Samples were taken in the stratosphere by the balloon *Explorer II* in 1935, but there seem to have been no later attempts to sample the stratosphere.

CHARACTERISTICS OF THE AERIAL DISTRIBUTION PROCESS

The atmospheric concentrations reported in earlier paragraphs result from many spore sources. We must now turn to consider the problem of spatial distribution of spores liberated into the air from a single source. Common experience leads us to expect a decrease in contamination of air or of the ground as the horizontal distance from the source increases. This expectation is abundantly borne out in practice [10] and is a phenomenon exploited widely in isolating healthy from diseased crops, hay-fever patients from pollen sources, and seed crops from foreign windborne pollen which could cause genetic contamination. Plotted on a linear scale, a graph of the decrease of contamination downwind from a point source of spores at ground level typically gives an exponential-type curve. The mechanisms underlying this characteristic "infection gradient" are probably, in order of importance: (1) turbulent three-dimensional dilution of the spore- or pollen-laden air mass by spore-free air as the impure air travels downwind; (2) appreciable loss of particles from the spore cloud by deposition on the ground, vegetation, or other surfaces, especially in the early stages of travel when the cloud is concentrated near ground level; and (3) loss of viability, which may or may not affect the result. In reality, the source is not a point, and its magnitude and shape also affect the dispersal gradient; concentration is higher, and falls off less rapidly, if the source is a sizable area rather than a point. As would also be expected, raising the source above ground decreases loss from deposition near the origin.

Prediction of the concentration of the spore cloud after a given distance of travel presupposes both an adequate theoretical treatment of the very difficult problems of atmospheric turbulence and also an adequate quantitative theory of deposition. Different theories now current predict different concentrations at a given distance, but agree generally with observation and experiment in predicting a rapid decrease in concentration with increasing distance from source. For instance, there is evidence that 90 percent of spores of the wheat bunt fungus *Tilletia tritici* and the clubmoss *Lycopodium*, when liberated just above ground level, are deposited within 100 meters of the source. Theory suggests that smaller particles than these would be deposited less rapidly, but there is little experimental evidence to support this.

A paradox is apparent here. With such a high rate of deposition near the source, the effect of a point source at distances greater than a few hundred meters must be negligible, yet in spite of this the concentration of micro-organisms in the upper air and for some distance out to sea is substantial. The paradox is probably to be explained by the fact that although the distant tail of the distribution from a single point source is indeed negligible, the quantity in the upper air over the ocean is the sum of the tails of the distributions of all the point sources present on the continent from which the wind has traveled.

The pattern of windborne dispersal differs from a Gaussian frequency distribution around a point source by having increased concentrations both very close to the origin and at great distances, balanced by smaller concentrations at intermediate distances [1].

TERMINATION OF THE DISPERSAL PROCESS

Infection gradients of some plant pathogens have been traced over distances of tens or hundreds of kilometers. Spores of some of the cereal-rust fungi migrate annually for many hundreds of miles in India and in the Soviet Union, and over the North American Continent a northward migration of wheat-rust spores in early summer is followed by a return migration in autumn. Yet the distribution of the species and races of the rust fungi is not worldwide: oceans and large tracts of mountain and desert seem to present almost uncrossable barriers.

Apart from death by desiccation or irradiation while airborne, the flight of a microbe ends either by dry deposition on the ground or by washing out of the air by rain, snow, or hail. The phenomenon of washout has never been systematically investigated, and sound techniques have still to be worked out. Results from examining hail are particularly unambiguous, because the surfaces of hailstones can be sterilized to eliminate possible contamination from the ground. Falling raindrops sweep up a substantial proportion of the suspended microbes in their path, and all precipitated water brings down from the sky a rich flora of bacteria, algae, spores of fungi and mosses, and pollen. Precipitated water is not sterile, whether collected over the land, the ocean, or the polar regions. Although a spore is most likely to be deposited dry by sedimentation to ground or by impact with a surface within a few hundred meters of takeoff, most spores that escape into the free air probably have their flight ended by rain.

Conditions in outer space beyond our atmosphere, as far as they are known, would appear to offer a highly uncongenial environment to unprotected micro-organisms. If attempts are made to detect viable spores in interplanetary space, special techniques will be required that owe little to the methods of aerobiology. However, experience gained in sampling our own atmosphere can be applied to some of the problems of sampling in the atmospheres of other planets. Conventional methods of sampling aerosols of single bacterial cells indoors are defective when applied to taking samples of large spores from moving air, and we need to develop better sampling methods, especially for continuous sampling in culture.

The glimpses we now have of the circulation of minute organisms in the atmosphere of our planet with all the implications in agriculture, medicine, and theoretical biology tantalize us by their incompleteness. It is unfortunate that exploration of our atmosphere has scarcely begun, and that we are not yet adequately equipped with technical methods for the task, at a time when the opportunity of probing the atmospheres of other planets is hastening upon us.

REFERENCES

1. BATEMAN, A. J. Heredity, vol. 4, p. 353, 1950.
2. DURHAM, O. C. Journ. Allergy, vol. 18, p. 231, 1947.
3. ERDTMANN, G. An introduction of pollen analysis. Chronica Botanica, Waltham, Mass., 1943.

4. GREGORY, P. H. The microbiology of the atmosphere. London and New York, 1961.
5. GREGORY, P. H., and HIRST, J. M.   Journ. Gen. Microbiol., vol. 17, p. 135, 1957.
6. INGOLD, C. T. Endeavour, vol. 16, p. 78, 1957.
7. PADY, S. M., and KAPICA, L. Mycologia, vol. 47, p. 35, 1955.
8. PADY, S. M., and KELLY, C. D. Canadian Journ. Bot., vol. 32, p. 202, 1954.
9. STEPANOV, К. М. Труд. Защ. Раст. Ленинград (Сер. 2, Фитопат.), vol. 8, p. 1, 1935.
10. WOLFENBARGER, D. O. Lloydia, vol. 22, p. 1, 1959.

The Detection and Evasion of Bats by Moths[1]

By KENNETH D. ROEDER

Tufts University

and

ASHER E. TREAT

City College of New York

[With 6 plates]

A CENTRAL objective of a large segment of biological and psychological research is to provide a physiological basis for behavior. The first step toward this objective is analytic, and consists of determining the structure and function of neural components after they have been isolated from their connections with the rest of the nervous system. There has been much progress in this direction, and it is now possible to describe in terms of input and output performance the operation of many isolated sense cells, neurons, and muscle fibers, even though the principles of their internal operation are mostly not understood.

The next step, the synthetic process of assembling this information on isolated neural components and relating it to the behavior of the intact animal, is hampered by two kinds of difficulty. The first appears to be methodological, but is somewhat hard to define. When one regards the evergrowing literature on the unit performance of sense cells, nerve cells, and muscle fibers, it is to experience that sense of dismay first encountered at a tender age when the springs, gears, and screws of one's first watch were strewn upon the table. The modus operandi of analysis or taking apart seems to come naturally, and the problems encountered are essentially technical in nature. Synthesis or the derivation of a system from its components seems to lack the a priori logic of analysis.

The second general difficulty is technical, and stems from the fact that even the simplest behavior of the higher animals and man is ac-

[1] Reprinted from American Scientist, vol. 49, No. 2, June 1961. Copyrighted 1961, by The Society of the Sigma Xi and reprinted by permission of the copyright owner. Much of the experimental work reported in this paper was made possible by Grant E–947 from the U.S. Public Health Service.

companied by the simultaneous activity of millions of sense cells, nerve cells, muscle fibers, and glands. Even if it were possible to register the traffic of nervous and chemical information generated and received by each and all of these neural elements during the behavior, it is doubtful whether the record would provide a meaningful description of the action.

Even though these problems cannot be solved directly at the present time, they become less formidable if the behavior selected for study is simple and stereotyped, and only a small number of nerve cells are concerned in its execution. These conditions are partly fulfilled by the sensory mechanisms whereby certain nocturnal moths detect the approach of insectivorous bats.

ECHOLOCATION AND COUNTERMEASURE

Bats detect obstacles in complete darkness by emitting a sequence of high-pitched cries or chirps and locating the source of the echoes. As Griffin (1958) and others have shown, this form of sonar is unbelievably precise. By means of it, insectivorous bats locate and track flying moths, mosquitoes, and small flies (Griffin et al., 1960). North American bats, such as *Myotis lucifugus* and *Eptesicus fuscus*, emit chirps about 10 times a second when they are cruising in the open. Each chirp lasts from 10 to 15 milliseconds (msec.) with an initial frequency of 80 kilocycles (kc.) dropping about one octave in pitch toward its end (see pl. 3, fig. 2).

The frequencies in these chirps are ultrasonic, that is, inaudible to human ears, which cannot detect tones much above 15 to 18 kc. The higher frequencies used by bats make possible more discrete echoes from smaller objects. The chirps can be rendered audible by detecting them with a special microphone and rectifying the ultrasonic component. They then can be heard through headphones as a series of clicks. These clicks fuse into what Griffin has called a "buzz" when the bat is chasing an insect or avoiding an obstacle.

Several families of moths (in particular the owlet moths or Noctuidae) have evolved countermeasures enabling them to detect the chirps of bats. A pair of ultrasonic ears is found near the "waist" of the moth between thorax and abdomen (pl. 1, fig. 1). An extremely thin eardrum or tympanic membrane is directed obliquely backward and outward into the recess (dark area) found at this point (pl. 1, fig. 2).

Internal to the eardrum is an air-filled cavity that is spanned by a thin strand of tissue running from the center of the eardrum to a skeletal support (pl. 2, fig. 1). This tissue contains the sound-detecting apparatus, consisting of two acoustic sense cells (A cells). A single nerve fiber arises from each A cell and passes close to the skeletal support, where the pair is joined by a third nerve fiber arising from a large cell (B cell) in the membranes covering the support. The three fibers continue their course to the central nervous system of the moth as the tympanic nerve.

The traffic of nerve impulses passing over the three fibers from A cells and B cell to the nervous system of the moth can be followed if a fine metal electrode is placed under the tympanic nerve. Another electrode is placed in inactive tissue nearby. As each impulse passes the site of the active electrode it can be detected as a small action potential lasting about 1 msec. Since the tympanic nerve contains only three nerve fibers, it is not difficult to distinguish and to read out the respective reports to the nervous system from the pair of A cells and the B cell. A similar experiment in a mammal is practically meaningless since the auditory nerve contains about 50,000 nerve fibers.

This method of detection shows that the A cells transmit organized patterns of impulses over their fibers only when the ear is exposed to sound (Roeder and Treat, 1957). The B cell transmits a regular and continuous succession of impulses that can usually be distinguished from the A impulses by their greater height. The B impulses are completely unaffected by acoustic stimulation, and change in frequency only when the skeletal framework and membranes lining the ear are subjected to steady mechanical distortion (Treat and Roeder, 1959). The B cell behaves in a manner similar to receptors found in other parts of the body that convey information about mechanical stress on joints, muscles, and skeleton. The role of such a receptor in the ear of a moth is unknown.

In the absence of sound, the A cells discharge irregularly spaced and relatively infrequent impulses (pl. 2, fig. 2, A). A continuous pure tone of low intensity elicits a more regular succession of more frequent impulses in one of the A fibers (pl. 2, fig. 2, B). The other fiber is not yet affected. Any slight increase in the intensity of the tone causes a corresponding increase in the impulse frequency of the active fiber. When the intensity of the tone is increased to about tenfold that producing a detectable response in the more sensitive A fiber, the second A fiber begins to respond in like manner. Its action potentials are superimposed on those of the first (pl. 2, fig. 2, C and D) by the method of recording, but actually reach the central nervous system over their own pathway. This experiment reveals two of the ways in which the moth ear codes sound intensity. It is like an instrument having a graded fine adjustment (the intensity-frequency relation) and a coarse adjustment of two steps (the pair of A cells). Other ways of coding intensity will appear later.

The moth ear responds in this manner to tones from 3 kc. to well over 100 kc., but there is no evidence that it is capable of discriminating between tones of different frequency. It is most sensitive near the middle of its range, that is, to frequencies such as those contained in bat chirps.

In plate 2, figure 2, it will be noticed that, in each of the recordings, the intervals between the successive impulses increase as the pure tone stimulus continues. In terms of the nerve code outlined above, the A cells report that the sound is declining in intensity with time, although in fact it was kept constant. This adaptation to a constant stimulus occurs in most receptors registering changes in the outside world. In terms of our own experience, the impact of our surroundings would be shocking and unbearable if it were not distorted in this manner by sense organs. The brilliance of a lighted room entered after dark would continue to be blinding and the noise of a jet engine would remain unbearable. However, the A cells of the moth's ear adapt very rapidly to a continuous tone, and their full effectiveness as pulse detectors is revealed only when they are exposed to short tone pulses similar to bat chirps.

In the experiment illustrated in plate 3, figure 1, a tone pulse of 3 msec. duration was generated at regular intervals. It is similar to a bat chirp except for its regularity and the absence of frequency modulation. A microphone (upper trace) and moth ear (lower trace) were placed within range, and the intensity of the stimulus pulse was adjusted so that it just produced a detectable response in the most sensitive A fiber (0 db). The intensity was then increased by 5 decibel [2] (db) steps as each recording was made. It will be seen that the microphone begins to detect the sound pulse when it is about 10 db above the threshold of the most sensitive A cell in the moth's ear. As before, the increase in frequency of A impulses is evident if the 5 and 10 db records are compared, and a response of the less sensitive A cell appears first in the 25 db record where the extra peaks of its action potentials overlap those of the more sensitive A unit. In addition to these two ways of coding intensity, two more can now be recognized. If the interval between detection of the sound by the microphone and by the moth ear is compared at different sound intensities, it will be noticed that the tympanic nerve response occurs earlier and earlier on the horizontal time axis. In other words, the latency of the response decreases with increasing loudness. Also, the sense cells are seen to discharge impulses for some time after the sound has ceased, and this after-discharge becomes longer with increasing sound intensity.

---

[2] The decibel (db) notation expresses relative sound pressures. An intensity of 20 db is tenfold that of the reference level (0 db), a 40-db sound is a hundredfold the reference level.

THE DETECTION OF BATS

These experiments with artificial sounds suggest how the moth ear might be expected to respond to a bat cry. A few laboratory observations were made with captured bats. In one of these experiments, in collaboration with Dr. Fred Webster, the cries of a flying bat were picked up simultaneously by a moth ear and a microphone, and recorded on high-speed magnetic tape (pl. 3, fig. 2). Interesting though they were, these experiments served mainly to show that the full potentialities of the moth ear as a bat detector could not be realized within the confines of a laboratory, and efforts were made to transport the necessary equipment to a spot where bats were flying and feeding under natural conditions.

Finally, about 300 pounds of equipment was uprooted from the laboratory and reassembled at dusk of a July evening on a quiet hillside in the Berkshires of western Massachusetts. Moths attracted to a light provided experimental material. The insect subject was pinned on cork so that one of its ears had an unrestricted sound field, and with the help of a microscope its tympanic nerve was exposed and placed on electrodes. After amplification, the action potentials were displayed on an oscilloscope. They were made audible as a series of clicks by means of headphones connected to the amplifier and were stored on magnetic tape for later study.

It was dark before all was ready, but bats immediately revealed their presence to the moth ear by short trains of nerve impulses that recurred about 10 times a second (pl. 4, A). The approach of a cruising bat from maximum range was coded as a progressive increase in the number and frequency of impulses in each train, first from one and then from both A fibers. It was not long before we learned to read something of the movements of the bats from these neural signals. Long trains, sometimes with two frequency peaks, suggested the chirps of nearby bats that echoed from the wall of a neighboring house (pl. 4, B). An increase in the repetition rate of the trains coupled with a decrease in the number of impulses in each train signified a "buzz" as the bat attacked some flying insect in the darkness (pl. 4, C).

All this was inaudible and invisible to our unaided senses. With a powerful floodlight near the nerve preparation we were able to see bats flying within a radius of 20 feet, and some attacks on flying insects could then be both seen and also "heard" through the "buzz" as coded by the moth's tympanic nerve. However, most of the sounds detected by the moth ear were made by bats maneuvering well out of range of the light. A rough measure of the sensitivity of the moth ear to bat chirps was obtained at dusk on another occasion when the bats could still be seen. The A cells first detected an approaching bat flying at an altitude of more than 20 feet and at a horizontal distance of over 100 feet from the moth—a performance that betters that of the most sensitive microphones.

DIRECTION

Since differences in sound intensity are coded by the tympanic nerve in at least four different ways, the horizontal bearing of a bat might be derived from a comparison of the nerve responses to the same chirp in the right and left ears. A difference in right and left responses might be expected only if each ear had directional properties, that is, a lower threshold to sounds coming from a particular direction relative to the moth's axis.

Directional sensitivity was measured in an open area where echoes were minimal. A source of clicks of constant intensity was placed on radii to the moth at 45° intervals. The source was moved in and out on each radius until a standard tympanic nerve response was obtained, and the distance from the moth noted. Horizontal distances along eight radii were combined to make a polar plot of sensitivity (Roeder and Treat, 1961). The plot showed that, although there was little difference in sensitivity fore and aft, a click on the side nearest the ear at about 90° relative to the moth's longitudinal axis was audible at about twice the distance of a similarly placed click on the far side.

This led to further field experiments in the presence of flying bats. The tympanic nerve responses from both ears of a moth were recorded simultaneously on separate tracks of a stereophonic magnetic tape. The tape was subsequently replayed into a two-channel oscilloscope and the traces photographed (pl. 5). In the upper record (A) the increase in number of impulses in each succeeding train suggests the approach of a bat. When the signals from right and left ears are compared, it is evident that the greatest difference exists when the signal is faintest, the first response of the series occurring in one ear only. When both ears respond, the differential nature of the binaural response can be seen first as a difference in the number of spikes generated in right and left ears, second in the differential spike frequency, and third in the latency of the response, which is greater on that side generating fewer spikes. It is also evident that, as the sound intensity increases (presumably due to the approach of the bat), the differential becomes less until the responses of right and left ears become almost identical. In another experiment, it was found that the tympanic nerve response saturates, i.e., becomes maximal, when the sound intensity is about 40 db (hundredfold) above threshold. From this it can be concluded that the moth's nervous system receives information that would enable it to determine whether a distant bat was to the right or left, but if the bat was at close quarters this information would not be available. In plate 5, C, the "buzz" was picked up by one ear only, presumably because during this part of its performance the chirps of a bat are much less intense.

It is tempting to estimate just how close the bat must be before the moth fails to get information on its location. If it is assumed that a bat is first detected at 100 feet and approaches on a straight path at right angles to the moth's course while making chirps of constant loudness, the differential tympanic nerve response would diminish throughout the approach and disappear completely when the bat was 15 to 20 feet away. However, we have not yet determined how much of the information that we are able to read out of its auditory mechanism is actually utilized by the moth in its normal behavior.

THE EVASIVE BEHAVIOR OF MOTHS

Although the evasive behavior of moths in the presence of bats must have been witnessed hundreds of times, it is hard to find an adequate account of the maneuvers of either party. The contest normally takes place in darkness, and, even when it is illuminated by a floodlight, the action is too fast and complex to be appreciated by the eye. The flight path of the bat and its ability to intercept and capture its prey have been studied by Griffin (1958) and his students. More recently, Webster (in press) has shown by means of high-speed sound motion pictures that bats become adept at using echoes to plot an interception course with an object moving in a simple ballistic trajectory. Many people have noted the seemingly erratic dives and turns made by moths when bats are near, and similar behavior has been described when moths are exposed to artificial sources of ultrasound (Schaller and Timm, 1950; Treat, 1955).

In an effort to learn more about the behavior of moths under field conditions their flight was tracked photographically as they reacted to a series of ultrasonic pulses simulating bat cries. The sounds were generated by the equipment used in the experiment shown in plate 3, figure 1. The pulses were similar in form to those shown, although longer in duration (6 msec.). Each pulse ranged from 50 to 70 kc. with a rise and fall time of about 1 msec. Pulse sequences up to 50 per second could be released on closure of a switch. The sounds were emitted by a plane-surfaced condenser loudspeaker mounted so as to project a fairly directional beam over an open area of lawn and shrubs illuminated by a 250-watt floodlight.

The observer sat behind the sound generator and floodlight, holding in one hand the cable release of a 35 mm. camera set on "bulb," and in the other the switch controlling the onset of the sound-pulse sequence. Many moths and other insects flew out of the darkness into this floodlight arena. A number were attracted directly to the light and were disregarded. Many others moved across the arena at various angles but without marked deviation toward the light. When one of these appeared to be in line with the loudspeaker the camera shutter was opened and the sound pulses turned on.

Some of the tracks registered by the camera as the illuminated moths moved against the night sky are shown in plate 6. Many insects, including some moths, showed no change in flight pattern when they encountered the sound. In others, the changes in flight path were dramatic in their abruptness and bewildering in their variety. The simplest, and also one of the commonest reactions was a sharp power dive into the grass (pl. 6, A, B). Sometimes the dive was not completed and the insect flew off at high speed close to the ground. Almost as frequently the dive was prefaced or combined with a series of tight turns, climbs, and loops (pl. 6, C, D).

It is not known whether these maneuvers are selected in some random manner from the repertoire of individual moths, or whether they are characteristics of different species. However, Webster (in press) has shown that bats soon learn to plot an interception course with food propelled through the air in a simple ballistic trajectory. The random behavior elicited by simulated bat cries in the natural moth population seems to be a natural answer to this predictive ability in bats, while the sharpness of the turns must certainly tax the maneuverability of the heavier predator.

The reacting moths shown in plate 6 were mostly within 25 feet of the camera and sound source, and were exposed to an unknown but probably high sound intensity. Under these circumstances, the evasive behavior appeared to be completely unorientated relative to the sound source, as might be predicted from the binaural tympanic nerve recordings. In some instances, moths flying at a greater distance or only on the edge of the sound beam appeared to turn away from the area and fly off at high speed. This must be checked in future experiments.

THE SURVIVAL VALUE OF EVASION

In spite of the evidence that the moth ear is an excellent bat detector, and that acoustic stimulation releases erratic flight patterns, one may well ask whether this behavior really protects moths from attack by bats.

This question has been answered (Roeder and Treat, in press) by observing with a floodlight 402 field encounters between moths and feeding bats. In each encounter we recorded the presence or absence of evasive maneuvers by the moth, and the outcome, that is, whether it was captured by the bat or managed to escape. From the pooled data we determined the ratio of the percentage of nonreactors surviving attack to the ratio of reactors surviving attack. Thus computed, the

1. External opening of the right ear in *Agrotis ypsilon*. The external surface of the tympanic membrane faces obliquely backward and outward into the cavity below arrow. The body of the moth is about ¾ inch in length.

2. Close-up of the tympanic membrane of *Drasteria* sp. The tissue containing the A cells is attached at the black spot in the center of the white area, and is visible as a white thread through the transparent eardrum.

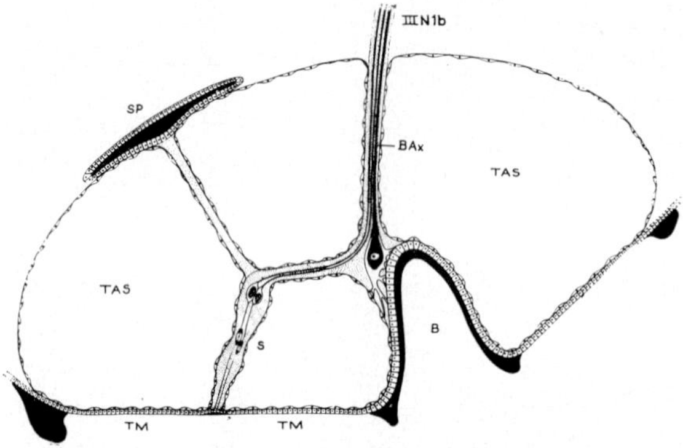

1. Diagram of the tympanic organ of a noctuid moth. The sensillum (*S*) contains the pair of acoustic receptors or A cells. The A nerve fibers are joined by that of the B cell (*BAx*) to form the tympanic nerve (*IIIN1b*). *TAS*, tympanic air sac; *B* and *SP*, skeletal supports; *TM*, tympanic membrane. (After Treat and Roeder, 1959.)

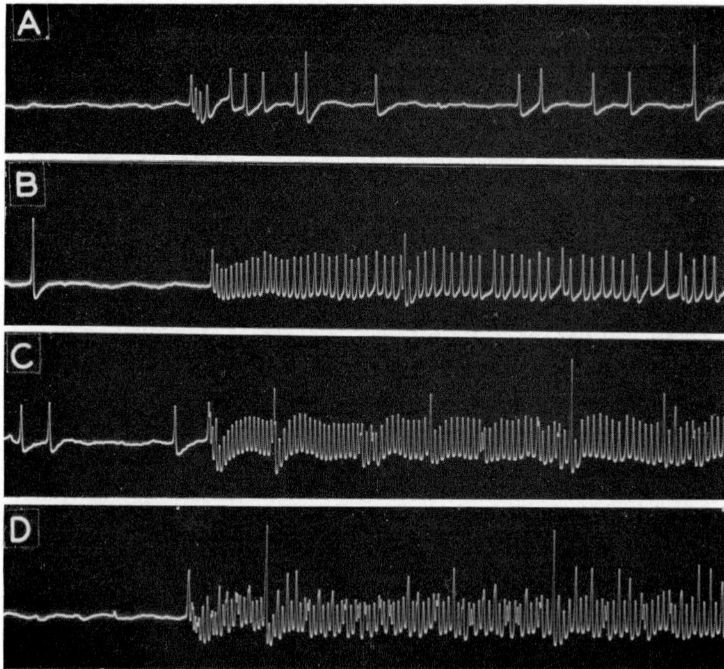

2. Tympanic nerve response in *Prodenia eridania* to a pure tone of 40 kc. The occasional large spikes originate in the B cell. (*A*) Response to a sound intensity close to the threshold of the sensitive A cell. (*B*) Intensity 7 db above that in (*A*). (*C*) Intensity 15 db above that in (*A*). (*D*) Intensity 23 db above that in (*A*). The less sensitive A cell discharges occasionally in (*C*), and frequently in (*D*), as indicated by the double peaks. Time line 100 msec. (From Roeder, 1959.)

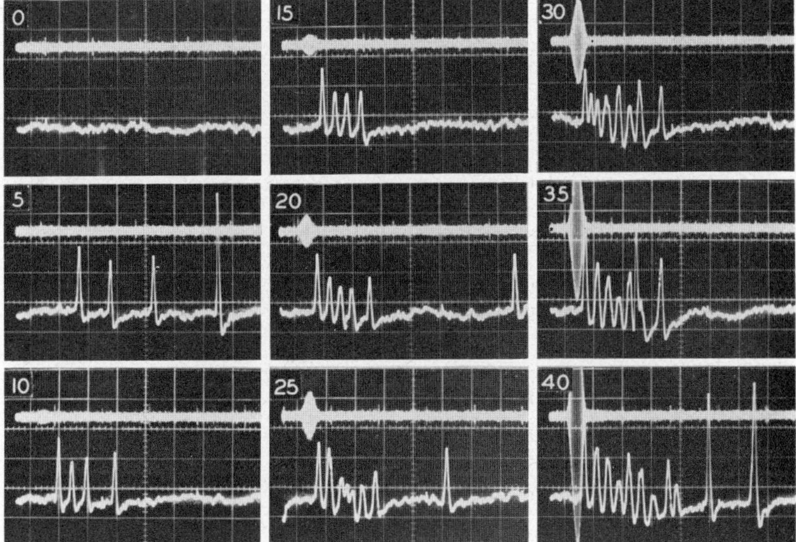

1. Tympanic nerve responses (lower traces) of *Noctua* (=*Amathes*) *c-nigrum* to a 70-kc. sound pulse recorded simultaneously by a Granith microphone (upper traces). The numbers indicate the intensity of the sound pulse in decibels above a reference level (0). The threshold of the sensitive A cell lies between 0 and 5 db. The large spikes appearing in some of the records are from the B cell. The less sensitive A cell responds in the 25 db recording. Vertical lines, 4 msec. apart.

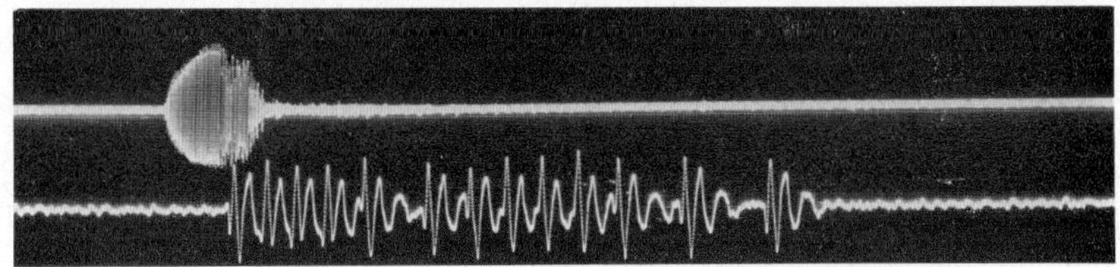

2. The cry of a flying bat (*Myotis*) recorded by a Granith microphone (upper trace) and the A cells (lower trace) of a noctuid moth (*Agroperina dubitans*). The A spikes shown in the lower trace have been distorted in form by the recording technique. Time line, 10 msec. Made in collaboration with Dr. Fred Webster in his laboratory.

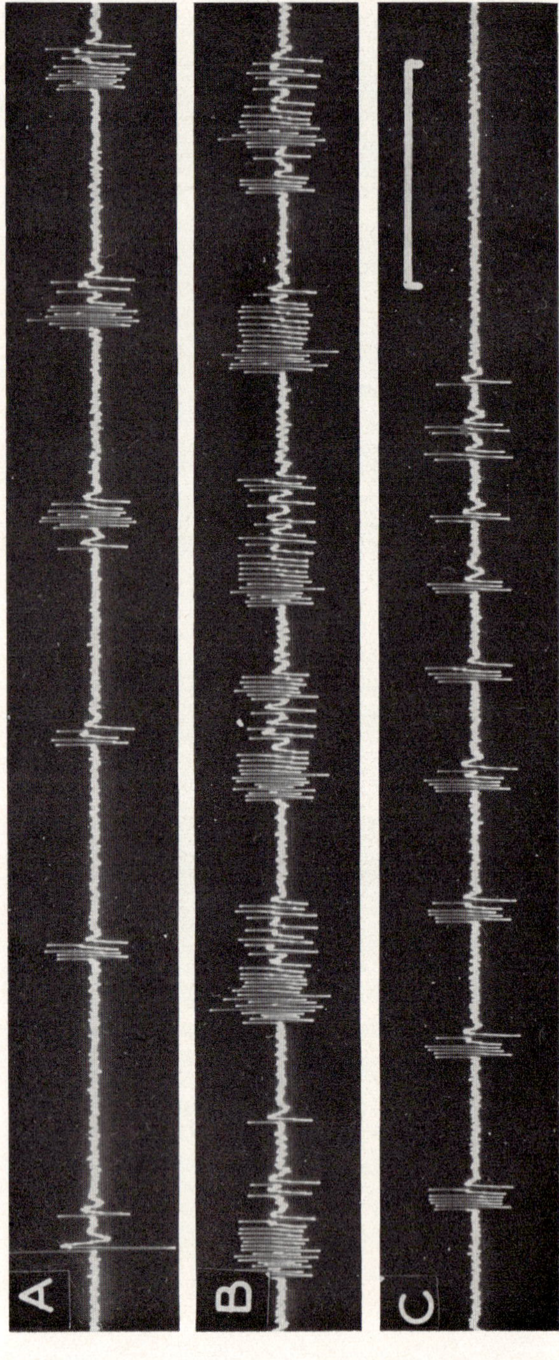

Tympanic responses of *Noctua* (=*Amathes*) *c-nigrum* to the cries of bats flying in the field. (*A*) The approach of a cruising bat emitting pulses at about 10 per second. (*B*) Tympanic response to the original cry and its echo made by a bat cruising nearby. (*C*) A "buzz." Time line, 100 msec. (From Roeder and Treat, 1961.)

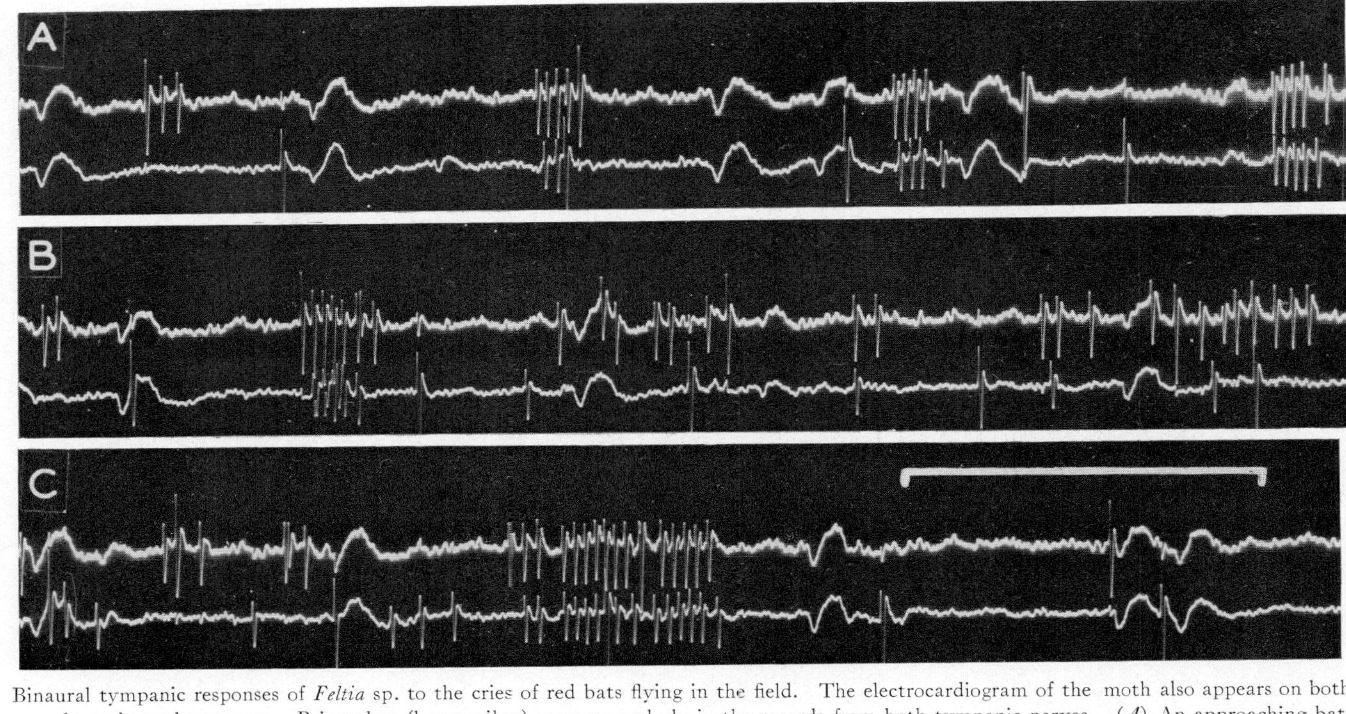

Binaural tympanic responses of *Feltia* sp. to the cries of red bats flying in the field. The electrocardiogram of the moth also appears on both channels as slow waves. B impulses (large spikes) appear regularly in the records from both tympanic nerves. (*A*) An approaching bat. Differential response is marked at first (response latency, number of spikes) but has practically disappeared in the final train. (*B*) A "buzz" registered mainly by one ear. (*C*) A "buzz" registered by both ears. Time line, 100 msec.

Flight tracks registered by various moths just before, and immediately following, exposure to a series of simulated bat cries. The dotted appearance of the tracks is due to the individual wingbeats of the moth. The beginning of each track appears in each photograph, and the moth finally flies out of the field.

selective advantage of evasive action was 40 percent, meaning that for every 100 reacting moths that survived, there were only 60 surviving nonreactors.

This figure is very high when compared with similar estimates of survival value for other biological characteristics. It seems more than adequate to account for the evolution of the moth's ear through natural selection even if the detection of bats turns out to be its only function.

CONCLUSION

As with most investigations, this work raises more questions than it has answered. The role of the B cell remains completely obscure. There is no evidence to connect it with the auditory function even though it is located in the ear, and its regular impulse discharge is a characteristic feature of the tympanic nerve activity of many species of moth (Treat and Roeder, 1959. See also pl. 5). The manner in which the A cells transduce sound waves recurring 100,000 times a second into the much slower succession of nerve impulses remains a mystery, and the synaptic mechanisms whereby information from the A fibers is translated into action by the nervous system of the moth, await investigation.

During the field experiments it was noticed that many other natural sounds initiated impulses in the A fibers. These included the rustling of leaves, the chirp of tree and field crickets, and, in one instance, ultrasonic components in the wingbeat sounds made by another moth. Occasionally, the A fibers discharged regularly as if detecting a rhythmic sound, though none was audible to the observers and its source (if any) remains a mystery. There is no evidence that these identified and unidentified sounds are important in the life of a moth, yet it must be said that a moth can detect them, and a careful study of moth behavior in their presence would be of value.

Several families of moths lack ears and show no response to ultrasonic stimuli. Some of these, such as the sphinx or hawk moths and the larger saturniid moths, are probably too much of a mouthful for the average bat, and might find no survival advantage in a warning device. Others are of the same size and general habits as the noctuids and might be expected to suffer attacks by bats. Included in this group are some common pests such as the tent caterpillar. It will be interesting to learn whether these forms owe their success in survival to some structural or behavioral countermeasure that compensates for the lack of a tympanic organ.

In spite of these unanswered questions, we believe that some progress has been made in putting together the sensory information received by an animal, and relating this to what the animal does. That this has been possible in moths is only because of the small number of channels

through which acoustic information reaches the nervous system in
these insects.   Further examples of this favorable situation have been
described in other insects, and still others are waiting to be explored.

REFERENCES

GRIFFIN, DONALD R.
1958. Listening in the dark.   Yale University Press, New Haven.
GRIFFIN, D. R.; WEBSTER, F. A.; and MICHAEL, C. R.
1960. The echolocation of flying insects by bats.   Animal Behaviour, vol. 8,
pp. 141–154.
ROEDER, K. D.
1959. A physiological approach to the relation between prey and predator.
In Studies in Invertebrate Morphology, Smithsonian Misc. Coll.,
vol. 137, pp. 287–306.
ROEDER, K. D., and TREAT, A. E.
1957. Ultrasonic reception by the tympanic organ of noctuid moths.   Journ.
Exp. Zool., vol. 134, pp. 127–158.
1961. The detection of bat cries by moths.   *In* Sensory Communication, ed.
by W. Rosenblith.   M.I.T. Technology Press, Cambridge, Mass.
—— The acoustic detection of bats by moths.   Proc. XI (1960) Internat.
Entomol. Congr.   (In press.)
SCHALLER, F., and TIMM, C.
1950. Das Hörvermögen der Nachtschmetterlinge.   Zeitschr. Vergl. Physiol.,
vol. 32, pp. 468–481.
TREAT, A. E.
1955. The response to sound of certain Lepidoptera.   Ann. Entomol. Soc.
America, vol. 48, pp. 272–284.
TREAT, A. E., and ROEDER, K. D.
1959. A nervous element of unknown function in the tympanic organs of
moths.   Journ. Insect Physiol., vol. 3, pp. 262–270.

The Honey Bee[1]

By JAMES I. HAMBLETON

Collaborator, U.S. Department of Agriculture

[With 4 plates]

OF ALL the insects in the world probably no one species is more widely distributed than the honey bee. Its present habitat includes the whole of the earth wherever flowering plants occur—from the polar regions to the Equator. Honey bees are not indigenous to all continents of the world, but they have become introduced and established essentially in all parts occupied by man.

If the statement seems too strong that the honey bee is more widely distributed than any other of our common insects, it can be said conservatively that the product of the bee is the most widely produced of man's food. Even such common foods as wheat and milk are not so universally known.

Honey bees were busily engaged in making honey and beeswax before the advent of man. Honey and wax of the bee were waiting in readiness for our earliest ancestors at the beginning of their evolutionary climb. In time they learned of the sweetness of honey and that wax could be employed for many purposes. For centuries honey was the only sweet, and it and beeswax were regarded so highly by the ancients that they wove into their religious ceremonies in one way or another frequent references to honey, wax, and bees. Symbols representing various phases of bee husbandry are found in the earliest recorded histories. Man throughout his existence has been closely associated with the honey bee.

Honey and beeswax were used in the payment of taxes and as indemnity. Conquered tribes and peoples paid off reparations in the form of honey and wax. To the present day beeswax plays an important part in the rites of the church. A beehive forms the central motive of the great seal of the State of Utah.

---

[1] This article in its original form, under the title "The Indispensable Honeybee," first appeared in the Smithsonian Annual Report for 1945, pp. 293–304, illus. In the intervening years the paper has proved so popular and useful that Mr. Hambleton welcomed the opportunity to bring it up to date, expand it along certain lines, and provide fresh illustrations, for a new generation of readers. The present version is the result.—EDITOR.

In spite of this close association, which goes back untold centuries, the honey bee has not acquiesced to man's influence in the same manner as have the domestic animals of our present day. In truthfulness it can be said that there are no domesticated honey bees. The life and the habits of the honey bee are the same today as when man first discovered that the product of these well-armed insects was worth risking life and limb. The social life of the bee with its complex division of labor and its various sexual forms have largely defied all effort to change its nature better to adapt it to man's use. The free nature of the bee and its insistence on mating in the wide open spaces have been the chief stumbling blocks in efforts to improve or to domesticate the honey bee. The sexual development and mating habits of bees are different from those of domestic animals. As an illustration of this difference, the male bees, the drones, are produced parthenogenetically; that is, the drone has no father but he can boast of a grandfather. Unmated queens can lay eggs that produce male bees and, even when they are mated, the mating has no effect on the male offspring.

Following many attempts to control mating, it is now possible to report that important progress in this direction is being made. Bee scientists, through the use of anesthesia and delicate instruments, can impregnate a virgin queen with the semen from a given drone. The parentage of the resulting offspring is thus definitely known. Inasmuch as colonies or strains of bees vary widely in temperament, color, ability to store honey, and to pollinate flowers, hardiness, and resistance to disease, controlled mating and careful selection should result in the development of superior bee stock.

Research workers have delved into the early records of man and written volumes on the antiquity of beekeeping; but, since the intent of this article is to acquaint readers with some facts of man's current dependence on bees and how they are handled, it will be necessary to leave the romantic past in favor of the equally romantic true story of today.

There is more to beekeeping than meets the eye. To the average person it has to do with the production of honey and beeswax. Other than those who have had actual experience in keeping bees, most persons have little conception of how they can be handled and made to work for their owners. There is little mystery about the production of most of our common foods. There is no mystery about the source of milk, butter, and eggs, and the production of fruits and vegetables and their route to the ultimate consumer are matters of everyday knowledge. On the other hand how can bees—wild, undomesticated insects—be directed to produce honey and beeswax? How are these products taken from the bees? Is it necessary to put honey through a manufacturing process before it is ready for consumption?

There was a time when beekeeping was thought of simply in terms of honey produced, but times have changed. Beekeeping now has a much more important part to play. The value of bees as agents of cross-pollination far outweighs the monetary value of the annual output of honey and beeswax.

Why do we hear so much about pollination these days? Is it a new fad or fancy, or is there some basic reason for emphasizing this subject? In grandfather's day and before his time this subject was seldom mentioned. The land was rich; there was little soil erosion, and for the most part the production of farm crops was satisfactory. As demands for agricultural products increased, farming operations enlarged, and with this came many new problems, one of which was pollination.

Sex plays as important a part in the plant kingdom as it does in the animal kingdom, but in a less obvious manner. Many plants contain both the male and the female elements on the same plant. This is true of all the grasses. Corn, wheat, barley, rye, oats, Kentucky bluegrass, and other grasses all belong to the great grass family. Pollen from the male part of the plant must come in contact with the female element if seed is to result. The corn tassel bears the male element which is the source of millions of tiny pollen grains. The long fine silks which protrude from the ends of an ear of corn are a part of the female element, one silk being attached to each newly formed grain. For this to develop to full size it is essential that a grain of pollen come in contact with the end of each silk. When this happens, the pollen germinates and sends a long tube down throughout the length of the silk through which the male germ migrates and eventually unites with the female cell. Without this union the ear of corn would be abortive and produce only a misshapen naked cob.

Because of the extraordinary number of pollen grains, it has been estimated that an acre of corn will produce in the neighborhood of 300 pounds of pollen. There is more than enough to go around, so that each strand of silk is assured its grain of pollen. Grass pollen is light in weight, easily blown about and carried by wind currents. All grasses are wind pollinated.

Let us look at another kind of plant—one with a more conspicuous flower than is usually found in the grasses—an apple tree for example. Each apple blossom contains both the male and the female element. For an apple to become fully developed and symmetrical in shape, enough pollen grains must be deposited on the stigmas of the flower to ensure the normal growth of the full complement of embryonic seeds. When insect damage is not a factor, insufficient pollination results in a misshapen and lopsided fruit. Most varieties of apple, however, like many other flowering plants, will not produce seed or fruit with its own pollen. The blossom of a Jonathan apple must receive pollen from an entirely different variety of apple. This introduces an interesting complication. Apple pollen is heavy and sticky; it cannot be carried by the wind. How then is pollen from one tree brought to another which may be many yards away? There is only one answer—through the medium of insects which live on nectar and pollen. One has only to look into the branches of an apple tree at full bloom to realize that honey bees are the predominating flower visitors and are the agents that put on a set of fruit.

The mode of reproduction, that is, seed or fruit formation, is slightly different from that of the apple in plants belonging to the cucumber family. Plants such as watermelon, cantaloupe, pumpkin, and cucumber, instead of having both sexual elements in the same blossom, contain two kinds of blossoms; one is all female and the other is all male. Here again pollen must be carried from the male flower to the female.

A small number of hermaphroditic flowers also occur in this family of plants. Here again, since pollen from these plants is sticky and not wind-borne, the indispensable service of pollen-carrying insects is apparent. Crooked cucumbers and flat-sided melons are the result of insufficient pollen coming in contact with the female flowers. A pollen grain is needed for the development of each seed. A well-formed cantaloupe may contain up to 600 seeds, the more seeds the larger and sweeter the melon. How many of us credit the honey bee when we cut into a luscious breakfast melon?

There are still other types of plants in which a single plant produces only male flowers, while another plant of the same species bears only female flowers. The wild persimmon and holly are good illustrations of this type. Since the wind cannot be depended upon to disperse the pollen adequately, insects again come into the picture.

There are approximately 50 cultivated crops grown in the United States that require insect pollination. In addition to those already mentioned, there are many other important plants—for example, alfalfa, sweetclover, red clover, alsike clover, white Dutch clover—which must have each tiny flower visited by an insect in order to produce seed and thus perpetuate themselves. Pollinating insects are either essential or highly desirable in the production of seeds of many vegetables, such as carrot, onion, cabbage, cauliflower, and brussels sprouts, to name only a few.

Insect pollination is a "must" in our present-day agriculture, but why is it more important today than it was 30 or 40 years ago?

There was a time in the history of agriculture, and not so many years ago either, when it was not uncommon to hull 6 to 10 bushels of red clover or alfalfa seed per acre. It is only rarely that such production is experienced today—in fact, the average yield of both these crops for the United States is slightly under 1 bushel per acre. Yet alfalfa and red clover grow just as well and blossom as profusely as in bygone days. But why has seed production fallen so low? Could inadequate pollination be one of the contributing factors?

There was at one time in this country an adequate population of native insects to take care of all pollination needs. These are insects that maintain themselves and raise their young largely on pollen and nectar. Their whole livelihood depends upon their flower-visiting habits. As farming operations expanded, the nesting sites of many of these insects were destroyed. Where the population of native insects could adequately pollinate a 10-acre field of clover or alfalfa, the same number of insects fall woefully short when the acreage jumped to several hundred acres. Since most plants have blooming periods of short duration, it is only logical that the numbers of pollinating insects be stepped up in proportion to the increase in acreage if seed yields are to be adequate and profitable. We have gone ahead increasing acreages manyfold but have made no effort to provide a proportionate increase in the number of pollinators.

Many factors have contributed to the decline of native pollinating insects. The plowing and clean cultivation of large tracts of land deprive these insects, many of which build their nests in the ground, of their natural nesting sites. Rail fences which were so difficult to keep clean of vegetation, afforded ideal places for these insects to nest. The picturesque rail fences have been replaced largely by well-kept wire fences, thus driving the pollinating insects farther and farther away from the crops which the farmer can grow profitably only when these insects are within flying range of his fields. Forest and brush fires have further decimated our population of beneficial insects. The tremendous increase in the use of pesticides is taking a huge toll of native bees. Honey bees are also subject to destruction by these chemicals. No way is known to conserve or to encourage the propagation of many of our native pollinators, while honey bees, in the hand of man, can be given some degree of protection from poisoning. Honey bees are the only pollinators that can be moved from crop to crop in the numbers required for the pollination of these crops.

The honey bee, the most numerous of all pollinating insects, is not native to the United States. It was brought to this country by the early settlers and became known to the Indians as the "white man's fly." It is now thoroughly at home in its new habitat. Swarms that escape from commercial apiaries make their way very nicely in the protection of a hollow tree or in the hollow pillars of our front porches, a place, incidentally, where they are not always welcome.

The honey bee, being exclusively a flower-visiting insect, does its share in pollination. It is estimated that honey bees are responsible for over 80 percent of all pollination effected. When swarms of bees escape and go to the woods they are subject to the same hazards as the native bees. Consequently their population in a wild or native state is not building up. This leaves the only stable source of pollinating insects in the hands of beekeepers.

The decline in seed and fruit production has been a matter of much concern in those crops that require insect pollination. Utah at one time was our leading alfalfa-seed-growing State. In its best year, 1925, Utah produced close to 25 million pounds of alfalfa seed. Over the years this figure fell to a low of less than 4 million pounds. There has been, however, an upward trend in production in recent years. Can it be that the grower of alfalfa seed is beginning to realize that Providence does not always bless the land with a sufficient number of pollinators? The grower must make a conscious effort to provide pollinators, usually colonies of honey bees, if he is to realize maximum seed possibilities.

What value can be placed on the honey bee's contribution to agriculture, over and above the bee industry's production of honey and beeswax? The agricultural statistics for 1959 give a total farm value of over $500 million for the following crops, all of which depend heavily on honey-bee pollination for seed and fruit: apples, pears, plums, sweet cherries, almonds, cucumbers, watermelons, cantaloupes, as well as seed of alfalfa, alsike, and white clover. In addition to these, there are many others to which bees contribute their service as pollinators.

The growing of seed and fruit involves many operations. To name only a few—use of viable seed and high producing varieties, cultivation, control of insect pests and diseases, pruning, soil enrichment and, of course, pollination. Even if all the crops listed above were given perfect growing conditions, there would be no production if pollinators were excluded. In some areas, particularly in the Pacific Northwest and places in the Intermountain States, certain species of native bees are highly efficient pollinators. Bee for bee they can outperform the honey bee. However, their numbers are too small to affect significantly the pollination picture. Taking the country as a whole, honey bees account for 80 percent or more of all insect pollination.

Only 11 of the primary insect-pollinated crops with a farm value of over $500 million are mentioned. Altogether, some 50 crops are benefited by bee visitation. Through the legerdemain of statistics we could say that honey bees, since they account for about 80 percent of all insect pollination, enrich agriculture to the extent of $400 million (80 percent of $500 million) annually not to mention the millions they add to other crops. To go a step further, since bees are a "must" in alfalfa and clover seed production and since the production of meat,

1. The worker honey bee. Gathering pollen to feed the brood is facilitated by the many finely branched hairs which cover her body. The same hairs serve as a brush to transfer pollen from flower to flower.

2. The apiarist examines a frame of comb taken from the center of the brood nest. It contains brood in various stages of development, honey, pollen, and adhering bees.

1. Worker bee on alfalfa blossom. This bee has "tripped" the flower for the purpose of collecting pollen. Note the pellet of pollen on the hind leg.

2. Bee on apple blossom. In working over the sexual organs of a flower a bee may gather nectar or pollen or both and at the same time transfer pollen to effect fertilization.

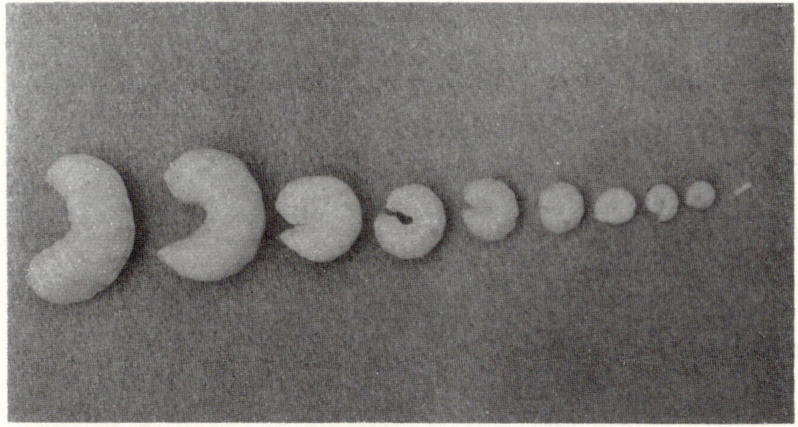

1. Stages of worker bee from egg to full-grown larva. In a period of five days the newly hatched larva increases in weight 1,500 times.

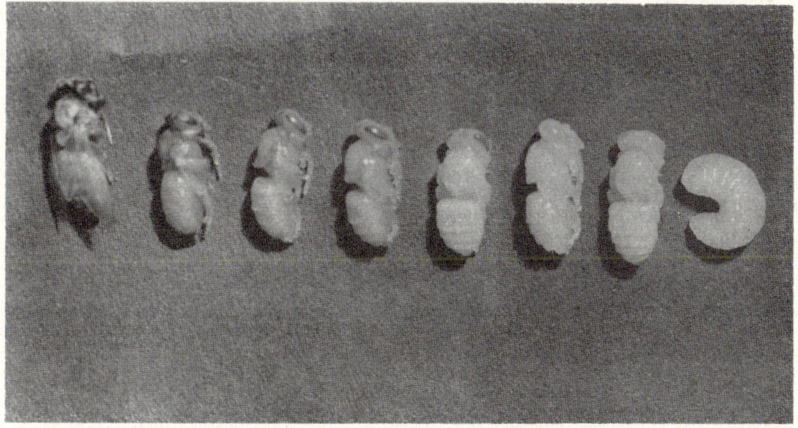

2. Stages of worker bee from full-grown larva to adult. Twenty-one days are required from the time an egg is laid until the new adult emerges from the cell.

1. An apiary of a commercial breeder of queen bees. Small hives are utilized for this purpose. A newly emerged queen bee remains in the hive for a few days. At the proper age she flies forth to mate with a drone. The queen bee is then ready to be mailed to a customer.

2. The installation of a new apiary. Package bees, as they are known in the trade, consist of two or three pounds of worker bees and a mated queen bee. Such packages are sufficient to start a new colony.

milk, butter, and eggs depends heavily on clover-rich pastures and alfalfa, we might give some credit to the bees for these commodities. Further, we should not lose sight of the many indigenous, insect-pollinated plants that play such an important part in soil and water conservation. However, it is evident that a prejudiced person could place an absurd value on honey bees. It is equally apparent how difficult it would be to arrive at a monetary evaluation of their worth to agriculture. It may suffice to say that without honey bees American agriculture would be in a sad way to the extent, certainly, of several times the value of the annual crop of honey and beeswax.

Pollinating insects have certain human characteristics. They will not fly farther for food than they have to and always select the richest and most easily obtainable. Sweetclover is a favorite source of nectar and pollen for honey bees and for many other pollinating insects. In the case of most flowers, bees readily and, of course, accidentally transfer pollen to the stigmas irrespective of whether the primary purpose of the visit is to obtain nectar or pollen. An alfalfa flower is an exception to this general rule in that the pollen is not exposed until a pollen-seeking bee "trips" the flower. When alfalfa and sweetclover, to name only two plants competing for bee visitation, are growing within the flight range of honey bees, the preference of the latter for sweetclover is conspicuous. Under such circumstances the chances for a crop of alfalfa seed are slim. The alfalfa flower not only has to be tripped by insects—it also has to receive pollen from another alfalfa plant.

By and large, insect pollination has been taken as a matter of course—something that nature ordinarily provides. In the event of crop failure it is seldom that insufficient insect activity is thought of as a reason. Neither farmers nor agricultural experts have paid much attention to how the proximity of one crop affects the pollination of another. When the natural flora is more attractive to bees than the planted crops, meager seed and fruit production can be expected.

As fields of single crops grow larger, adequate pollination becomes more and more critical. In our modern agriculture, pollination must be consciously provided. Since for most localities the number of pollinators is limited, attention should be given to the sequence in planting crops that compete for the visitation of pollinating insects. Plant breeders could well incorporate factors such as copious nectar secretion to make plants more attractive to pollinators. Protective nesting sites will encourage the propagation of wild pollinating insects. Growers can maintain apiaries of their own or better still they can encourage beekeepers to establish permanent apiaries within flight range of their fields.

The State of Washington enjoys the highest average per-acre production of alfalfa seed, often exceeding 400 pounds per acre. There are 200,000 alfalfa seeds per pound. At this rate 1 acre produces 80 million seeds. What a tremendous pollination job to obtain this! With thousands of acres devoted to alfalfa seed it is not strange that there are not enough wild bees to take care of this one crop alone. If a pollinator fails to feed at an alfalfa flower, the blossom holds on hopefully for about 10 days then, barren, it withers and falls off the plant.

Much the same story applies to red clover and other legumes. A good stand of red clover has enough blossoms to produce 10 or 11 bushels of seed per acre. The average annual per-acre yield is around 1 bushel. To what extent is inadequate pollination responsible for this low yield?

Bumble bees are among the most efficient of all pollinating insects. With their long tongues, considerably longer than those of honey bees, they are especially valuable in the pollination of red clover, which has a deep corolla from which honey bees can obtain nectar only with difficulty. Bumble bees are not so plentiful as they once were. The use of insecticides and other farming practices threatens to extinguish these useful insects. It is still the favorite sport of farm boys to fight bumble bees and rob their nests of a few thimblefuls of hard-earned honey. Why must the farmer continue to destroy one of his best allies—one which can contribute so significantly to bumper crops of clover seed, fruit, and melons?

The most immediate remedy for inadequate pollination is through intelligent use of honey bees. This is the only pollinating insect that can be moved from place to place and installed in fields when and where they are needed. Unfortunately, most farmers do not want hives of bees on their premises. Once in a while a farm animal or hired hand is stung or the owner himself may be the victim, with the consequence that bees are ordered off the place. What a sad state of affairs it is that beekeepers actually have to pay rental to farmers for small out-of-the-way pieces of land upon which to place their beehives. This is one reason why apiaries are not a common sight as one drives through the country. The beekeeper has to place his hives far from the farm buildings and from good roads. In such locations the hives are subject to pilfering, and it is costly for the beekeeper to manage them properly. If farmers understood the part that bees play in more bountiful fruit and seed crops, surely they would welcome beekeepers with open arms. That day must come!

At the moment the important agricultural job of providing pollination, inadequate though it may be, is dependent on the market price of honey. Queer relationship indeed! In volume of business done the production of honey cannot compare in importance with most branches of agriculture. Beekeeping is widely scattered. Almost every county numbers a few beekeepers. Because of the cost of transportation over so wide a territory, it is difficult to concentrate large quantities of honey for commercial distribution. The color, flavor, and consistency of honey vary depending upon where and from what it is produced. Buckwheat honey of our Eastern States has a strong flavor and is almost black; that from fireweed in the Pacific Northwest is water-white and mild in flavor. This great variation imposes a problem to food packers who like to maintain uniform and standard packs of whatever they merchandise. As a consequence, much honey—30 to 40 percent of the crop—is sold by producers directly to local consumers. Another reason why commercial processors of food may not be interested in honey is that it requires little or no processing. Honey can be made no better than it is when it comes from the beehive. For these and other reasons, this very delicious food is not advertised nationally. The price of honey is not stabilized or backed by large financial corporations. The vagaries of the market seem always to hound the beekeeper, and on top of it all his product has to compete with highly advertised manufactured foods, such as jams, jellies, and sirups. Whenever the price of honey falls, there is a lag in enthusiasm for beekeeping and the number of colonies is reduced. While this results in less honey per capita, perhaps not too serious a matter, what is more important is that fewer honey bees are available for pollination. Consequently, the production of many crops seemingly far removed from beekeeping is adversely affected.

Growers of orchard fruits have learned that bees are necessary for a full set of fruits, and many of them rent colonies from beekeepers to place in the orchard during blossoming. One would suppose that such an arrangement was as beneficial to the beekeeper as to the fruit grower, but this is not necessarily the case. Apple-blossom honey is almost unheard of. Colonies of honey bees shortly out of winter quarters are not populous enough early in the spring to make honey from apple blossoms. Colonies have to be strong and populous before they can make more honey than the bees require for their immediate needs. Fruit blossom is good for the bees to build up on, but they seldom if ever make honey from it. Also many bees are poisoned through spraying operations and so more and more beekeepers are reluctant to move bees to the orchards even when paid for it.

Growers of seed crops such as onion, carrot, and the various legumes are just beginning to realize that colonies of bees placed close to such crops pay big dividends. The bee industry as a whole receives relatively little rental for bees. For the most part, the services of the honey bee as a pollinator is free to those who most benefit from it.

This free service to agriculture is possible mainly for two reasons: (1) Bee culture is a fascinating study and many persons keep bees as a hobby or part-time activity, and (2) consumers of honey maintain the commercial beekeeper, precarious though his livelihood may be. The pollination of various crops is thus a distinct gamble and one which may persist pending the time the public develops a greater taste than it now has for honey. Better honey markets and better returns to the beekeeper will be good insurance toward having dependable insect pollination year after year.

Although no accurate counts have been made of persons keeping bees, it is estimated that some 500,000 persons consider themselves as keepers of the bees. Of this number, not over 3,000 depend on beekeeping as a principal means of livelihood. An apiary of 500 colonies is considered about the maximum number for a full-time, one-man outfit. Larger operations may involve 10,000 or more colonies.

The bulk of the fraternity are amateurs, backlot enthusiasts who keep from one or two to several hundred colonies. The production in 1960 from the 5,430,000 colonies estimated to be in the United States by the Department of Agriculture was 260,128,000 pounds of honey and 4,728,000 pounds of beeswax, with a total value of over $48 million.

Almost every State has an active beekeepers' association, and in many places the beekeepers are organized on a county basis. In addition, there are numerous bee clubs of one kind or another. A wide-awake group of city beekeepers meets monthly in the heart of New York City. A beginner will find many kindred spirits and persons with whom to compare notes.

To be successful with bees, one must like to work with them; capital and equipment alone are not sufficient to insure success. Partnerships in which one party furnishes the finances and the other the knowledge are rarely successful. Beekeeping on a commercial scale is mostly a one-owner business.

A successful, full-time beekeeper is a person to be envied. He is his own boss. During summer he works as hard as anyone, but after the harvest he can relax. Even at the height of the active season it is possible for him to attend a beekeepers meeting or go fishing. The bees do not require the daily attention that other types of livestock demand.

The per-colony production of honey in the United States averages between 40 and 50 pounds. For individual operators, a hundred pounds per colony is not at all unusual. In favored localities and under good management, 200 to 400 pounds is possible. On the less rosy side, there can be complete failure in the honey crops, a failure so serious as to require feeding the bees sugar sirup to keep them alive.

It is essential that the colonies be kept in proximity to an abundant source of nectar. This may be one-quarter mile to 1 mile away from where the colonies are actually situated. Acres of nectar-secreting flora should be within the flight range of the bees. It is mostly a waste to plant a crop for your own bees. Bees from neighboring apiaries will help themselves and they may outnumber and outwork your own bees.

While there may be literally hundreds of species of flowers upon which the bees work for nectar or pollen or both, in any given locality there are usually not more than two or three plant sources from which the bees can make more honey than they require for their own keep. Thus there are in the United States, perhaps, some three dozen or so species from which 90 percent of the commercial honey is derived. The clovers, including alfalfa, stand high in the list of principal honey plants. Red clover is an exception in that it seldom furnishes the beekeeper with extra honey. Other important sources are orange, tupelo, buckwheat, basswood, cotton, fireweed, star-thistle, sourwood, gallberry, and mesquite. Within limited areas, there may be other plant sources of a local nature that enable the beekeeper to obtain a surplus of honey.

Since beekeeping is so unlike gardening or taking care of livestock with which most of us at one time or another have had limited experience, a person who contemplates a career as a beekeeper, on either a large or a small scale, should start with not more than two or three colonies. This will keep the investment in bees and equipment low and still gives the beginner plenty of experience.

There are some 250 beekeepers scattered through the Southern States and California who specialize in furnishing bees to beginners or to established beekeepers who wish to enlarge their operations. Two or three pounds of bees and a queen are shipped by express or mail in wire-screen cages. The cost for a 3-pound package with a laying queen is approximately $5 to $6, and contains sufficient bees, from 11,000 to 12,000, to constitute a nucleus of a colony. If the new unit is established early, that is during fruit bloom, it may develop into a sufficiently strong colony to produce a worthwhile crop of honey the first season. The beginner, however, should feel satisfied if he gets his new pets in shape to produce a crop the second year.

The hive equipment will run from $15 to $25 per colony, depending upon the type of hive and the amount of extra equipment purchased. A study of the catalogs of manufacturers of bee supplies will help in making a proper selection.

The beginner should wear a veil when learning to handle bees. A timid or nervous person will find assurance in a pair of bee gloves. It is seldom that bees sting through clothing and so no special equipment is needed to protect the body. It is advisable to tie string around the trouser legs, and a lady might feel greater freedom from fear if she wears slacks. The beginner should take precautions to avoid stings until he becomes familiar with the behavior of his bees and how to handle them. Within a few weeks, and no doubt after a few stings, he will become so fascinated by their behavior, industry, and social organization that the occasional sting will not even dampen his enthusiasm. Even so the veil should always be worn.

All beekeepers, no matter how skillful they are in handling bees, receive occasional stings. To the inexperienced, the reaction may at first be rather severe with considerable swelling and itching, but a season's work with bees usually results in the development of some immunity against the venom.

In a short time one should learn to handle bees with confidence and seldom receive a sting. The beginner soon learns that bees are cross and irritable on cold and cloudy days, and that it is best to open the hive when the weather is warm and the bees are busily engaged in the fields.

Each colony has its own individuality. One may be quiet and gentle, while its next-door neighbor may be of a hot temperament. The gentlest bees are not always best for honey production, but on the other hand there is little pleasure in working with a colony that is ever ready to sting—no matter how much honey it produces.

It must be kept in mind that bees are wild and untamed. The average life of a worker bee during the active season of flight is only about 6 weeks, so that little or nothing can be done to train them to do what their owner wishes. By the same token there is no chance for the bees to learn who their master is. An expert beekeeper can go into a strange apiary and handle the bees with as much assurance and confidence and as good results as can the owner himself. It is essential, therefore, to learn a few of the fundamental principles that govern the reaction of bees. There are books and magazines galore devoted exclusively to the subject of helping the beekeeper master the principal manipulations.

Beekeeping is not all sweetness and honey. Like other types of livestock bees are subject to several kinds of diseases. Some of these are confined to brood (the young unemerged bees), and there are other diseases that affect only the adult bees. Since some of the diseases are contagious, careful check should always be kept of the colonies to see that they are healthy.

Each colony contains but one queen—the mother of all the bees; her importance to the welfare of the colony cannot be overemphasized. If the queen should fail because of old age—and a queen may live 2 or 3 years—or because of illness, the population of the colony goes down rapidly and may become so weak as to perish. The same persons who sell bees also sell queens, so that a new queen may be obtained in short order to replace a failing one.

The greatest mistake that beginners make is in not giving the bees sufficient hive space in which to work. Often the beginner, in an effort to keep his investment low, will try to maintain the bees in a single-story hive. A good queen that can lay 1,500 eggs a day and maintain this rate for days at a time requires at least two hive bodies. These should be considered the sacred property of the bees themselves from which the beekeeper is not to remove any honey. During rainy spells and periods when it is too cold for the bees to fly, they still must have their daily food. Large reserves of honey should be on hand at all times. Honey that the bees make in addition to that stored in the two hive bodies the beekeeper can claim for himself.

The nectar as brought by the bees into the hive may contain upward of 80 percent water, whereas honey contains only about 18 percent. This excess water has to be removed by the bees. For this purpose, comb space is required, so that the watery nectar may be spread over as large a surface as possible to hasten evaporation; thus more combs are necessary to make the crop than are required to hold the ripened, finished honey.

A colony of bees should never be allowed to fill the hive completely while the honey crop is being made. Shortly before every comb is filled with brood, pollen, or honey, a colony, sensing the end of its job, makes preparation to swarm. In this preparation there is a decided let-down in the storage of honey. Swarming is objectionable from this standpoint.

Reproduction, the natural dividing of a colony into two or more parts, is one of the involvements in the complex phenomenon of swarming. Perhaps the most obvious cause for a colony to swarm is that its living quarters are overly crowded. The colony has finished its job—part of the bees move on to new and more commodious quarters. Another colony is born. The old queen and the majority of bees old enough to fly leave the hive. If the swarm is not captured, the bees light off to the woods, find a hollow tree or a cavity in the wall of a dwelling and build a new home. In the parent hive will be left all the young bees, brood, and a number of queen cells from which one or more new queens will emerge. One of these will eventually head the newly formed colony.

The bees that fly to the fields for nectar and pollen do not deposit the nectar in the cells of the hive. They turn the nectar over to young house bees—bees too young to fly—and it is these house bees that do all the work from that point on in converting the nectar into full mellow-ripe honey. The combination of the young and old bees is essential to produce a crop of honey. When a colony swarms, this very essential teamwork is destroyed. For best honey production every effort should be made to control swarming.

There are other pitfalls in beekeeping beside diseases and swarming. A weakened colony of bees, like a weakened animal, is preyed on by enemies. A colony that is not strong enough to keep its house clean becomes infested with wax moths which, if not tended to, will destroy the combs. A colony too weak effectively to guard its entrance to the hive is subject to attack by bees from stronger colonies. Not only will the robbers carry away the honey, but they will leave in their wake many bees killed in the last defense of their home. Colonies are often weak because they lack sufficient food. Honey bees do not hibernate as do most other insects. They are in a semiactive state within the hive throughout the long winter, and food in the form of honey must be available to them at all times.

In spite of these drawbacks, there is much on the credit side of the ledger. It is not necessary to give bees daily attention. There are periods of weeks or months at a time when they require no looking after. Three or four hours to a colony throughout the year is ample to do all the work necessary. In the spring, and when the honey crop is in the making, a few minutes at the right time does more good than working with the colony for hours at the wrong time. This applies especially to heading off preparations for swarming.

Beekeeping is a challenge to one's ingenuity as well as nerve. Colonies are individualistic, and this has to be taken into consideration in managing them. A person who keeps bees always has an eye to the weather, knowing how sensitive these creatures are to changes in temperature, sunshine, and wind velocity. One's interest in the plant world is immediately stimulated by watching the blossoms upon which bees work.

Taking honey from the hive is not the least joy of working with the bees. No honey tastes so good as that produced by one's own effort. There is also the satisfaction in knowing that through your efforts and patience the fruit trees of your neighbors bear more bountifully and that as the busy bees wing their way to surrounding pastures, gardens, fields, and orchards they are enriching the entire countryside. They provide a function for which there is no substitute and give their keeper a food which man with all his skills has not been able to duplicate.

Australopithecines and the Origin of Man[1]

By J. T. ROBINSON

Transvaal Museum
Pretoria, South Africa

INTRODUCTION

THE FIRST australopithecine specimen came into scientific hands 37 years ago—the story of this and later discoveries has been told often and will not be repeated here.[2] For roughly 30 of those years, considerable controversy existed as to the nature of these creatures. In the last few years fairly general agreement has been reached that the australopithecines truly belong with the family of man and not with that of the apes. Emphasis has now shifted to attempts to evaluate the nature of the relationship with true man, and from the early majority view that they were nothing but apes, the pendulum has now swung almost to the other extreme with the rapidly growing tendency to regard them as the earliest true men. The view here presented is less extreme than either of these.

THE MAJOR PREHOMININE FEATURES

The australopithecines are roughly intermediate in grade of organization between the small-brained pongids and the large-brained, bipedal homines. They were erect walking, but had small brains. Well over 300 specimens, representing nearly a hundred individuals, are now known from South Africa. A small amount of material is known from East Africa and the Far East. Paleontologically speaking, this is a good sample and has provided much information about variation and other population characteristics. This is important since it is not individuals that evolve, but populations, and it is the business of the paleontologist to try to get back from the bits of individuals that comprise his material to the characteristics of the populations to which those individuals belonged.

---

[1] Reprinted, in expanded form, by permission from the South African Journal of Science, January 1961.

[2] For an account of the South African discoveries pertaining to ancient man, see the article by Raymond A. Dart entitled "Cultural Status of the South African Man-apes" in the Smithsonian Report for 1955, p. 317.

The evidence for erect posture in the prehominines is good. The pelvis is known from one almost complete specimen as well as a number of incomplete ones, and it differs markedly, in structure and function, from the pongid or monkey type but only insignificantly from the hominine type. The lumbar region of the spinal column, the proximal and distal ends of the femur, and the nature and orientation of the occiput all add to the evidence which shows that the australopithecines were structurally and functionally well adapted to erect posture and locomotion.

The dentition provides considerable evidence of hominid affinity. The anterior teeth are small, compact, and built closely on the hominine pattern. Even the canines are within the size range of hominines. Other teeth that are especially diagnostic are the first lower premolar (P_3), first lower deciduous molar (dm_1), and lower deciduous canine (dc). In pongids the first two are semisectorial teeth usually having one prominent cusp, though a second may be partially developed. In the prehominines and hominines P_3 is bicuspid and dm_1 well molarized, having five cusps as in the permanent molars. Sophisticated statistical analysis of the lower deciduous canines has shown that the prehominine teeth are easily and sharply distinguished from the pongid form while they closely resemble, and in some cases are indistinguishable from, the modern hominine form (Bronowski and Long, 1952).

These and other telling morphological features clearly indicate close affinity with hominines, but the small brain indicates a more primitive condition. The endocranial volume appears to be about 500 cm.[3] only—I know of no sound evidence at present indicating a brain significantly larger than this. The range was evidently about 450 to 550 cm.[3] and therefore well below the pongid maximum of 750 cm.[3] found by Schultz. The early hominines appear to have had endocranial volumes averaging about 900 to 1,100 cm.[3], although estimated volumes as low as 755 cm.[3] have been given.

Along with this small endocranial volume in the prehominines, the braincase is relatively small and the face relatively prognathous. It is therefore evident that an important feature of hominines—the enlarged brain and the modifications of skull architecture consequent upon this—was not yet significantly developed in the known prehominines.

TAXONOMIC DIFFERENTIATION WITHIN THE PREHOMININES

The prehominines are at present commonly regarded as comprising a morphologically variable group without any significant taxonomic differentiation within it (e.g., Le Gros Clark, 1955). A considerable volume of evidence exists which shows that this is not the case—so much in fact that it is my opinion that there is a far more fundamental split within the australopithecine group than there is between one of these subgroups (*Australopithecus*) and the hominines. That is to say, that if one has to divide the known hominids into two groups only, there is a good case for putting part of the australopithecine group (*Australopithecus*) with the hominines as one group and leaving the other australopithecine subgroup (*Paranthropus*) as the second group.

Two different forms of australopithecine are known in South Africa at present. *Australopithecus* occurs at Taung, Sterkfontein, and Makapansgat Limeworks, while *Paranthropus* has been found at Kromdraai and Swartkrans. It is important to realize that the largest *Paranthropus* sample (160 specimens from Swartkrans) occurs less than a mile from Sterkfontein, which yielded the largest sample of *Australopithecus* (108 specimens). Geographic variation can therefore be disregarded as an explanation of differences between the groups. Apparently the time difference between these two sites is not great, and since *Paranthropus* apparently occurs both much earlier and later in time without any significant difference in its morphology, one can virtually eliminate the effect of time differences as well as of geographical differences. One is thus in an exceptionally favorable position to assess the nature of the differences between the two population samples.

Australopithecus has a dolichocephalic skull with a good hominine shape. A distinct low forehead is present, and the vertex rises well above the level of the brow ridges. The latter are poorly developed, and the postorbital constriction is moderately developed. The face is fairly wide, the nasal region is slightly raised above the surrounding level of the face, which is distinctly prognathous. The skull is gracile without any heavy bone or strong development of ridges or crests. The mandible is robust with a moderately high ramus and an almost vertical chin region. The dentition is morphologically very similar to that of the early hominines. Molars and premolars are very well developed, and the canines are fairly large but do not protrude because they are recessed into the jaw to a greater extent than the other teeth. The proportions along the tooth row are typical of early hominines.

Paranthropus is very different. Although the endocranial volume appears to differ insignificantly from that of *Australopithecus*, the skull architecture is markedly dissimilar. The skull is brachycephalic with no trace of a forehead; the frontal passes straight back from the well-developed supraorbital torus in a manner reminiscent of the condition in the gorilla. The vertex rises very little above the upper level of the orbits. Le Gros Clark (1955) devised an index to measure

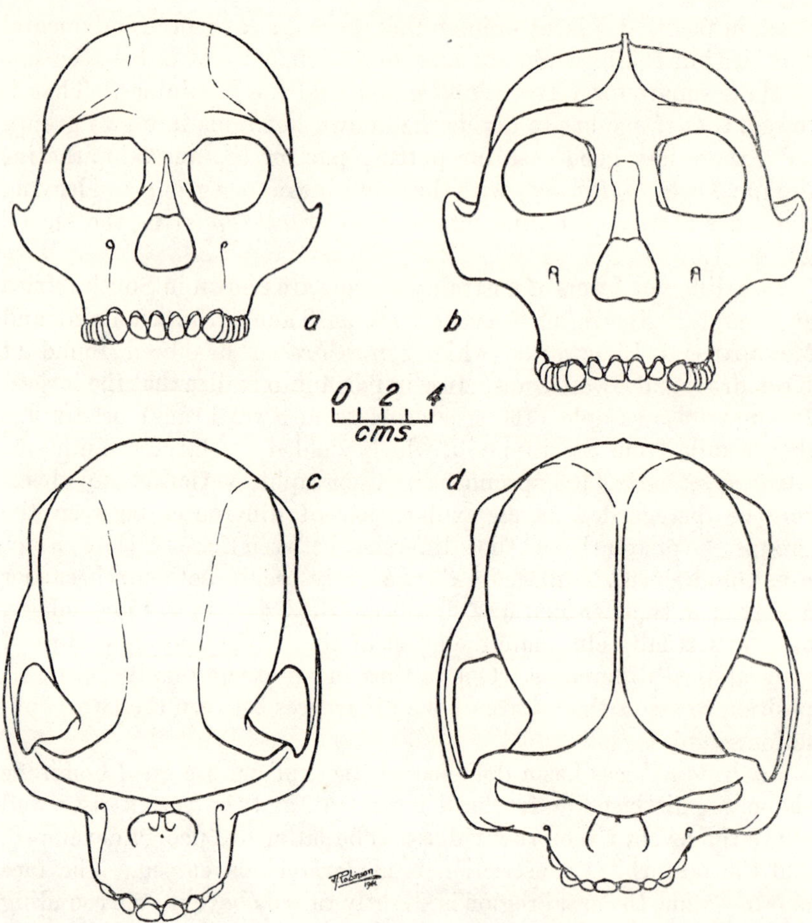

FIGURE 1.—Facial and top views of female skulls of *Australopithecus* (left) and *Paranthropus* (right). The former is represented by Sts. 5 from Sterkfontein while the *Paranthropus* illustrations are based mainly on Sk. 48 from Swartkrans.

this feature in primate skulls; it places *Paranthropus* right in the middle of the pongid range while *Australopithecus* is well outside this position and very near to that of modern man. In all known adults with the appropriate area preserved, a sagittal crest is present occupying roughly the middle third of the distance from glabella to inion. The degree of postorbital construction is relatively greater than in *Australopithecus*, and the zygomatic arches stand out well away from the braincase. The face is massive and wide. The enormously robust cheek bones actually project farther forward than does the nose, which is completely flat. The face is appreciably less prognathous than that of *Australopithecus*. The mandible is very massive with a very high and vertical ramus. A most unusual situ-

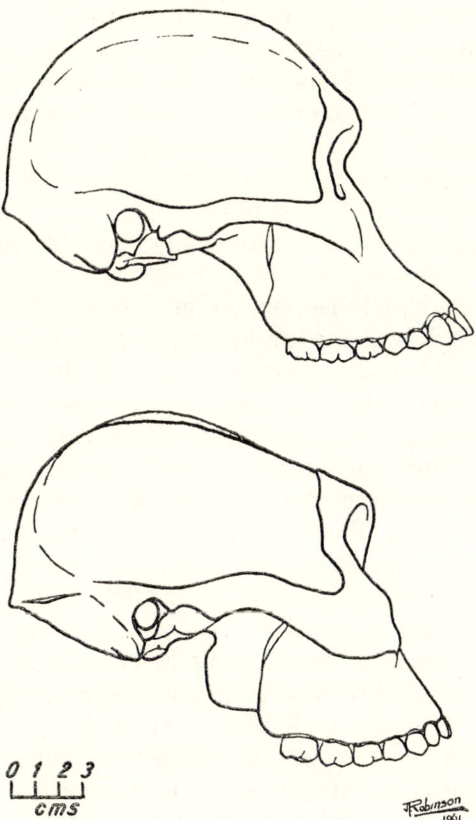

FIGURE 2.—Side views of skulls of *Australopithecus* (top) and *Paranthropus* (bottom).

ation exists in the dentition; the postcanine teeth are massive, being distinctly more robust than those of *Australopithecus*, but the canines and incisors are distinctly smaller than in the latter form. There is consequently a sharp change in proportion between the anterior and the postcanine teeth—a unique feature in hominoids.

Paranthropus thus has a very robust skull with strong development of bone and a curiously spheroidal braincase with strong development of rugosities and crests, a wide, dished face, and a dentition specialized quite differently from that of *Australopithecus*. These descriptions are based on female skulls in both cases, but sexual dimorphism does appear to be well developed. *Paranthropus* was a heavily built, muscular animal which probably stood over 5 feet in height and weighed a few hundred pounds. *Australopithecus* clearly was very small and slenderly built; females apparently were no more than about 4 feet in height and weighed some 40 to 50 pounds.

Besides these differences, which are obvious enough, there are other important dental differences. The first deciduous lower molar in

Australopithecus is of the same type as is found in all known hominines, having a characteristic specialization of the anterior half of the crown. *Paranthropus* is unique in the primates in having a completely molarized deciduous first lower molar without any trace of the specialization seen in *Australopithecus* and all hominines. The deciduous lower canines also differ considerably in the two forms.

The differences in skull architecture can be explained primarily in terms of differences of dental and dietary specialization. *Paranthropus* has very heavy crushing and grinding cheek teeth, but the anterior teeth were clearly less important since they not only are much reduced in size, but also wear less rapidly than the cheek teeth in spite of their smaller size. Strong reliance on crushing and grinding implies a vegetarian diet in which considerable bulk is required to provide the necessary nutritive value. Much chewing is necessary to comminute the often tough plant material. Enlargement of the cheek teeth with specialization for crushing and grinding are common features of creatures adapted to vegetarian diet. *Paranthropus* apparently also ate roots and bulbs, since there is clear evidence of grit in the diet, in the form of small chips and flakes of enamel which have broken off from the occlusal margins of the crowns through strong pressure being applied over a small area. The powerful chewing forces which must have been generated in this robust masticatory mechanism have resulted in substantial thickening of the bone in which the cheek teeth are set and along the avenues through which the chewing forces are dissipated. These include the palate, cheek bones and jugal arches, lateral parts of the supraorbital tori, and the pterygoids. The heavy jaws needed powerful muscles; hence there is further robustness in such areas as the origin and insertion of the masseter and pterygoid muscles. The relation of large temporal muscles to relatively small braincase was such that even females apparently normally had a sagittal crest. On the other hand, the very small anterior teeth resulted in a face which did not protrude forward at all markedly.

Australopithecus, on the other hand, has none of these extreme modifications. Both skull shape and structure and especially dental morphology, are closely comparable to the early hominine condition. It therefore seems reasonable to conclude that the diet of this form was basically the same as that of early hominines; i.e., they were omnivores eating both flesh and vegetable matter. This was probably the sort of diet still found in hunters and food gatherers of today.

The adaptive difference between these two forms is thus considerable. Their ecological requirements and direction of evolution were quite different. The degree of difference between them in these respects was of a distinctly greater order than between any two of

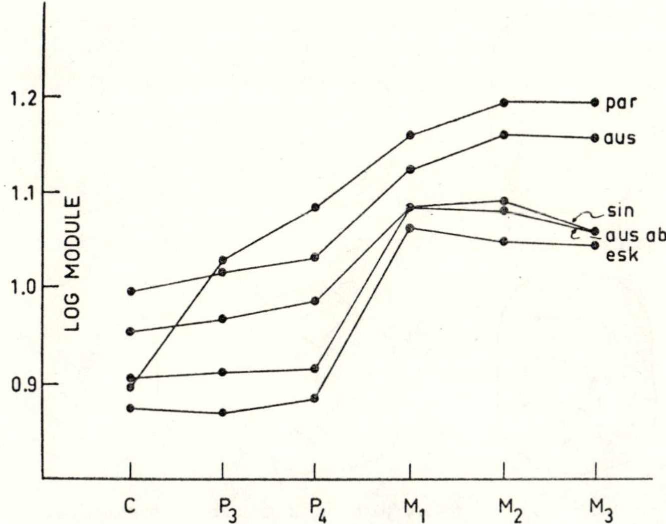

FIGURE 3.—Size comparison of some mandibular teeth in five hominids.   par, *Paranthropus;* aus, *Australopithecus;* sin, Pekin man; aus ab, Australian aborigine; and esk, Eskimo (East Greenland).   This demonstrates very clearly the aberrant nature of the *Paranthropus* dentition in which a marked change in proportion between the anterior and post-canine teeth occurs between the canine and P3.

the living pongids. This is precisely the sort of difference that modern mammalian systematists regard as excellent grounds for generic separation. It is interesting to note that good evidence exists indicating that the vegetarian *Paranthropus* was present in the Sterkfontein Valley in times when the climate was apparently significantly wetter than when the more carnivorous *Australopithecus* lived there.

In 1959 Leakey found a fine australopithecine skull in Bed I at Olduvai, Tanganyika, and gave it the new generic name "Zinjanthropus" (Leakey, 1959). He regarded it as being more advanced than either of the australopithecines already dealt with. However, it is very clear that while some differences may be found between it and *Paranthropus* from South Africa, the pattern of structure and function already described for the latter is very clearly developed. The same sort of modification of the skull architecture as a consequence of a specialized vegetarian diet is very obvious. No valid grounds appear to exist for regarding this form as anything other than a typical *Paranthropus* (Robinson, 1960).

Some mandibular fragments from Sangiran in Java, which have been called "Meganthropus" and regarded as members of the "Pithecanthropus" group (e.g., Le Gros Clark, 1955), seem to me manifestly to belong also to the genus *Paranthropus* (Robinson, 1953, 1955, and 1961). They agree very closely with the equivalent parts of *Paran-*

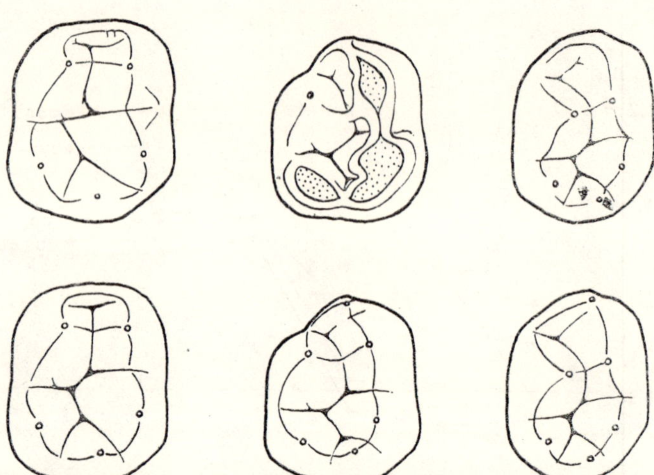

FIGURE 4.—Basic cusp and fissure patterns in mandibular first deciduous molars of *Paranthropus*, *Australopithecus*, and modern Bush (from left to right). Upper row illustrates actual specimens drawn under a camera lucida to the same scale; lower row illustrates diagrammatically the basic cusp and fissure patterns of the teeth in the upper row. The anterior half of the crown in *Australopithecus* and modern man is highly asymmetric but quite symmetric in *Paranthropus*.

thropus from South Africa. In almost every feature the morphology is identical with that of the latter form, up to and including the greatly reduced anterior teeth coupled with very large cheek teeth.

Paranthropus therefore appears to have been spread across the width of the Old World with little modification. If the new potassium-argon dates for parts of Olduvai (Leakey, Evernden, and Curtis, 1961) turn out to be valid, it will mean that the timespan represented by the various *Paranthropus* specimens is rather more than a million years in length. In other words, this genus would be one with a wide geographical range and a long history.

Australopithecus is not as yet known from quite so far afield. It is known from East Africa near Lake Eyassi (Remane, 1951; Robinson, 1953 and 1955), and the juvenile jaw from Bed I, Olduvai, a little below the "Zinjanthropus" level (Leakey, 1961a and 1961b) certainly does not belong to the latter type but bears a close resemblance to *Australopithecus*. Some apparently large parietal bones were associated with the jaw, which may mean either that *Australopithecus* and another larger-brained hominid were contemporaneously present, or perhaps that the form to which the jaw belonged had a larger brain than had *Australopithecus* and therefore represents a more progressive member of the same stock. The evidence is not yet clear, and more finds are needed to clarify the situation.

"TELANTHROPUS"

From among the large number of *Paranthropus* remains which have come from Swartkrans, I found a fragmentary upper and lower jaw, apparently of the same individual, another almost complete mandible along with a few other fragments of what is clearly a different type of hominid. Later an incomplete metacarpal came to light which probably belongs to the same form (Napier, 1959). This form was called *Telanthropus capensis* (Broom and Robinson, 1949), but subsequently this name was sunk in favor of *Homo erectus* (Robinson, 1961).

The teeth are distinctly smaller than those of either australopithecine and agree very closely in size with those of the hominine from Java and Pekin now generally known as *Pithecanthropus*. From the space available in the mandible and maxilla, it would seem that the canine crowns must have been of about the size of those of *Paranthropus*, but the roots were reduced compared to those of either of the australopithecines. Besides these there are some important characters found only among hominines but not among australopithecines. These are: (1) the structure of the nasal cavity floor and the subnasal surface of the maxilla, (2) the wide U-shape of the internal mandib-

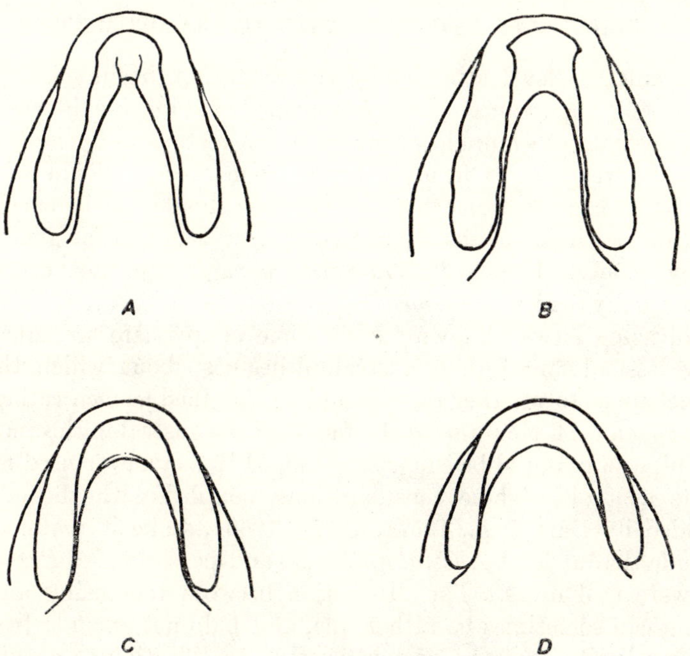

FIGURE 5.—Mandibular body contours in A, *Australopithecus;* B, *Paranthropus;* C, "Telanthropus"; and D, *Homo sapiens* (American white). Both australopithecines have narrow interramal distance anteriorly; "Telanthropus" has the hominine condition in this respect.

ular contour with wide interramal distance, (3) the small distance between the occlusal plane and the mandibular articulation with the skull, and (4) the slender construction of the mandible. None of these features can be matched in the australopithecines. In some respects "Telanthropus" is actually more advanced in the direction of modern man than is Pekin man. On the other hand, in no known feature is "Telanthropus" less advanced than either of the australopithecines. If the science of comparative morphology means anything, then surely "Telanthropus" must be classed with that group with which it shows closest and most fundamental resemblance. On the basis of the available evidence, that group is clearly the hominines.

"Telanthropus" is often passed over lightly on the grounds that so few specimens are known that its affinities cannot be determined. It should be remembered, however, that these few specimens occur right among the two largest australopithecine samples known and therefore in the best possible situation for determining whether this form is an australopithecine or not. Here again geographic differences do not enter into the matter and time differences are in one case entirely absent and in the other at worst very slight. Furthermore, although not much is known about variation in "Telanthropus," a great deal is known about that of both australopithecines *from that locality*.

STONE TOOLS ASSOCIATED WITH AUSTRALOPITHECINES

The cultural level attained by the australopithecines is of great interest and importance. Dart has argued that much evidence points to the australopithecines having used bones, teeth, and horns as implements and weapons. One may, it seems to me, accept this in principle, but with the reservations that (*a*) the case should not be carried beyond the legitimate evidence, and (*b*) the evidence so far available is largely concerned with *Australopithecus* and does not necessarily apply equally to *Paranthropus*.

Tool using is well known among some nonprimate animals manifestly less advanced than australopithecines about which there is now debate as to whether they should be classified as men rather than as near-men. In view also of the fact that the australopithecines were erect bipeds, it would be surprising indeed if they never used natural objects as tools. These considerations, coupled with the evidence provided by Dart (e.g., 1957a, 1957b, 1960), make it reasonable to conclude that at least *Australopithecus*, and possibly also *Paranthropus*, were tool users. The distinction between tool using and tool making can sometimes be rather fine, and I do not exclude from the former a limited amount of constructive modification to natural objects used as tools. If such modification is a regular and normal part of the situation, then one is dealing with toolmaking.

In 1956 Brain found evidence of a stone industry in breccia lying loose on the surface at Sterkfontein, and in 1957 and 1958, in two seasons of excavation in that site, I was able to demonstrate for the first time the direct association of an australopithecine (*Australopithecus*) and a true stone industry. As a consequence most students accepted the idea that *Australopithecus* must have been a stone-tool maker. The discovery by Dr. and Mrs. Leakey of a stone industry with the Olduvai *Paranthropus* seems to have clinched the matter in the minds of most workers, who are now convinced that the australopithecines were stone-tool makers and say so without reservation.

However, it seems to me, as I have pointed out elsewhere (Robinson, 1958, and in Robinson and Mason, 1957), that this is far too facile a view of the situation. At Sterkfontein there is a considerable depth of deposit, which has yielded a hundred specimens of *Australopithecus* and not a trace of stone artifacts or even unworked foreign stone. Unconformably overlying this is breccia which is demonstrably more recent by both faunal and lithological evidence. This breccia still contains *Australopithecus* but also a genuine stone industry, chiefly consisting of rock foreign to the immediate neighborhood of the excavation. This industry, it should be noted, is not of extreme primitiveness; it is not the very beginnings of toolmaking. In the opinion of Dr. R. Mason, of the Archeological Survey, Johannesburg, the industry belongs to the early levels of the Chelles-Acheul culture (Robinson and Mason, 1957; Mason, 1961). Even if the most conservative estimate is employed, it must be regarded as late Oldowan; perhaps it is most reasonable to regard the industry as being more or less transitional between Oldowan and Chelles-Acheul. This means that at Sterkfontein a large deposit of breccia has yielded the largest known sample of *Australopithecus* but no evidence of a stone industry, while a breccia immediately overlying it, and only a little later in time, has yielded a well-established stone industry. This time gap appears to correspond closely in age with the *Australopithecus* deposit at Makapan Limeworks, where tons of breccia have so far yielded no such stone industry as that at Sterkfontein. That is to say, roughly 96 percent of the known South African material of *Australopithecus* is not associated with a stone industry, but suddenly a stone industry representing a stage near the beginnings of the Chelles-Acheul culture appears in reasonable quantity toward the end of Sterkfontein time. Where did it come from? The only reasonable conclusion seems to be that a toolmaker invaded the Sterkfontein Valley during the time represented by the unconformity—and that invader could not have been *Australopithecus* as he had already been there for a long time.

It seems anything but coincidence that the stone industry appears

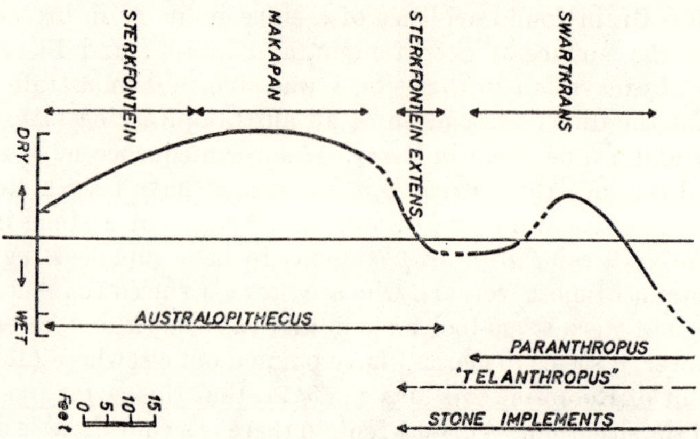

FIGURE 6.—Climatic curve for Sterkfontein, Makapan (Limeworks), Sterkfontein Extension and Swartkrans sites, modified after Brain. The curve is based on porosity, reflecting degree of rounding of the sand grains in the breccia from these sites. Central line indicates present rainfall conditions. The distribution of *Australopithecus*, *Paranthropus*, and "Telanthropus" is shown along with that of stone implements.

in the Sterkfontein Valley at just about the time that the remains of "Telanthropus" also appear there. As has been pointed out, "Telanthropus" has some major features which can be matched only among toolmaking hominines but not among the australopithecines. What could be more logical than that it was the invading toolmaker? It is of interest to note that at Sangiran in Java the hominine "Pithecanthropus" occurs side by side with *Paranthropus* (in the form of "Meganthropus") and, apparently, over quite a long period of time (Robinson, 1962). At Swartkrans the hominine "Telanthropus" occurs side by side with *Paranthropus*. In North Africa at Ternifine, "Atlanthropus," evidently a member of the "Pithecanthropus" group, occurs along with a slightly more advanced form of the same sort of culture as that found at Sterkfontein. This is the opinion of Dr. Mason, who has examined both industries.

What then of the Olduvai *Paranthropus* and the stone artifacts found with it? The most favorable migration route south into South Africa is down the eastern side of the continent. Olduvai and East Africa in general—evidently an important area in primate evolution—lie almost directly north of the Sterkfontein Valley and right on the route. It is therefore difficult to conceive of "Telanthropus" at Sterkfontein without its having been present at some stage in East Africa also. If this was not so, then "Telanthropus" must represent an independent evolutionary development of a hominine in South Africa and this is unlikely.

The newer Olduvai finds just below the *Paranthropus* level may have very direct relevance here. The mandible is quite clearly not of

Paranthropus type (Leakey, 1961a and 1961b). This I can confirm after having examined the originals through the kind courtesy of Dr. and Mrs. Leakey. In the opinion of Leakey, it is also not of *Australopithecus* type, but to me it appears to bear very close resemblance to the latter. The two parietal bones are of considerable interest in that they appear to be too large for either *Paranthropus* or *Australopithecus*. If this is in fact the case, then the implication is that a hominid with a larger braincase than that of either form of australopithecine was present at the site. If the parietals and the mandible belong to the same type of creature, then this would be a form closely related to *Australopithecus*. It has long been my opinion (e.g., Robinson, 1956, p. 171) that "Telanthropus" is a more advanced descendant of an earlier level of *Australopithecus* than that at present known. Therefore an early *Australopithecus*-like form with a relatively large brain could easily represent an early form of "Telanthropus"—on the new K–A dating of Olduvai (Leakey, Evernden, and Curtis, 1961) the Bed I form would appear to be approximately half a million years earlier than "Telanthropus" from the Sterkfontein Valley. However, these are very tentative ideas which must await confirmation of (*a*) the presence of a relatively large-brained hominid in the lower levels of Bed I, and (*b*) the fact that the creature represented by the parietals and that by the mandible are the same. A stone industry is present with these specimens, and this has led Leakey (1961b) to entertain the possibility that it, as well as the whole Oldowan industry of Bed I, were made by this form, including also the industry associated with "Zinjanthropus." It is manifest that these tentative conclusions emerging from the newer finds at Olduvai are strictly consistent with the conclusions reached above from the Sterkfontein finds.

If either of the australopithecines was to be a toolmaker, it is far more likely to have been *Australopithecus*. If it was not, as the Sterkfontein evidence seems to indicate, then it is very improbable that the vegetarian *Paranthropus* would be. Australopithecines, it will also be recalled, had brains well within the pongid size range. Finally, a characteristic feature of the earlier levels of the stone age culture sequence is the exasperating fact that remains of the makers of the tools are so exceedingly rare. Why then, if the australopithecines were toolmakers, should their remains be so common and stone tools rare when the normal experience is exactly the reverse? This seems a further argument against any of the australopithecines being toolmakers. "Telanthropus" remains, on the other hand, are very rare.

I submit, therefore, that there is no good evidence in support of the thesis that australopithecines were stone-tool makers but that there is very pertinent evidence against it, favoring the idea that this group consisted essentially of tool users. Even the Olduvai evidence, which at first appeared to support the idea that australopithecines made stone tools, is now beginning to appear to oppose such a conclusion.

ORIGIN OF THE AUSTRALOPITHECINES

The available australopithecine material makes it clear that erect bipedal posture developed before the brain enlarged beyond the size found in the larger pongids. Some of the more obvious differences between pongid and australopithecine skulls are closely related to erect posture. For example, the altered orientation, reduced size and separation of the occiput into a portion above and one below the inion, are apparently directly due to the acquisition of erect posture. These occipital changes result in the isolation of the sagittal crest from the superior nuchal line and the absence of a true nuchal crest on that line, in a form like *Paranthropus*, where muscular development is relatively great for the size of the braincase (Robinson, 1958). Also reduced canine size and the compactness of the anterior teeth and hence the nearly vertical chin region, are doubtless to some extent at least due to erect posture, even if indirectly. One may therefore conclude that the essential factor in the origin of australopithecines was their becoming erect bipeds. This has been discussed elsewhere (Robinson, 1962), and the conclusion reached that the process occurred in two stages. During the first, pelvic changes were proceeding under the control of selection which was not concerned with erect posture but which resulted in shortening of the innominate bone and broadening of the posterior portion of the iliac blade. This rendered the pelvis preadaptive for erect posture and allowed the second phase, adaptive for erect posture, to proceed. Animals with the altered pelvis would find when standing erect, as primates commonly do, that *gluteus maximus* no longer functioned as an abductor but as an extensor of the thigh. Thus movement in this position would be more efficient and would also allow the mobile, grasping hands to be put to much better use than had previously been possible when they were primarily concerned with locomotion. These advantages would result in rapid readaptation of the animals under the quite altered selection pressures now operating and would have opened up quite new evolutionary possibilities.

Higher primates are vegetarians with very few exceptions. It is highly probable therefore that whatever form was ancestral to the australopithecines will have been vegetarian. *Paranthropus* was a vegetarian, but *Australopithecus* was an omnivore. As has been shown, the former is less advanced in the direction of man than the latter and retains more primitive features. It would thus appear possible that *Paranthropus* is a comparatively little-modified descendant of the original australopithecine stock. Evidence thus far shows that *Paranthropus* occurs under at least reasonably wet conditions, whether in the Sterkfontein Valley, Olduvai, or Java. This, and its dietary specialization, probably indicates that it lived in fairly well-wooded country. However, there certainly will not have been true dense forest over the whole of the Sterkfontein area. It is likely that their habitat consisted of broken forest country with grassland.

ADAPTIVE RADIATION IN THE AUSTRALOPITHECINES

There is no obvious reason why *Paranthropus* should have altered its way of life significantly as long as it was able to continue living in the sort of habitat in which it had originated. It was adapted to a vegetarian diet, and as long as its needs in this direction were met there is no reason why it should have changed. Nor does this way of life bring challenges which would tend to promote evolutionary change, as can be seen in the modern pongids. For example, the capabilities of the chimpanzee in the direction of tool using and even primitive toolmaking find little outlet in its natural habitat and way of life. If the new Olduvai dating is correct, then *Paranthropus* is known in essentially the same form over considerably more than a million years across the width of the Old World. During this time considerable change occurred in the hominine line.

But clearly adaptive radiation did occur within the hominid group after *Paranthropus* came into existence and a very good reason for this seems to be present during the latter half of the Tertiary (Robinson, 1962). This was the very considerable desiccation undergone by a large part of the African continent. In the early Tertiary the relatively moist conditions resulted in the expansion of the forests and therefore in spread over much of the continent south of the Sahara of conditions suitable for a form such as *Paranthropus*. But with the onset of desiccation the forests contracted, grass savanna spread, and by the end of the Tertiary, Kalahari conditions existed over a large part of southern Africa, extending at least into the Congo Basin. At this time areas suitable for *Paranthropus* will have been very much scarcer.

It is not difficult, then, to visualize the steady but slow progress of the desiccation process. After a while australopithecine groups would begin to find it less easy to survive the critical time of the year—the latter end of the dry season—because of food shortage. Under these circumstances they will almost certainly have supplemented their diet with insects, birds, reptiles, and small mammals such as rodents. As aridity increased they will have had to rely on this supplement to their diet more and more. In some areas the populations will probably have died out entirely, but it is not unreasonable, in view of known evidence of primate dietary adaptability, to suppose that some groups will have succeeded in surviving on their modified diet.

However, these changed conditions will also have modified the selection pressures operating on the population. It would seem obvious that intelligence would be at a premium since some ingenuity would be required to get enough to eat, whereas this is much less so in the case of a vegetarian living under reasonably wet conditions. The more intelligent ones would therefore be able to adapt better to the changing conditions and are likely to have been the parents of the majority of the next generation. Also, whereas the simplest tools suffice for a vegetarian and in almost all cases none at all are needed, tools would obviously be of great use to the population adapting to more arid conditions. Implements for digging animals out of holes, snares for catching prey, implements for bashing or opening up animals, would all enable far more efficient adaptation.

The onset of drier conditions would therefore seem to lead inevitably to strong selection pressure in favor of tool using and improved intelligence in an early australopithecine population remaining in the areas affected. Other adaptive features might also be the retention of relatively large (for hominids) canines, or the increase in their size. Also smaller body size will have had adaptive value if the ancestral *Paranthropus* was as large and robust as the known ones. Where food scarcity combines with the need to be agile to get enough to eat, litheness and moderate size are advantageous. This is especially true when the adaptive process has reached a point where meat eating involves killing antelope and other mammals larger than the small creatures eaten in the earlier stages of adaptation.

In this manner it is easy to explain the origin of *Australopithecus*. But once this process had reached the point of producing such a creature, there is no reason at all why it should stop there. Improved intelligence and improved facility with tools would continue to improve adaptation and it would appear that sooner or later—and probably relatively soon—a stage would be reached when conceptual thought would begin to appear and tool using would improve to tool making as well. This point, of which toolmaking is, as it were, a symptom, seems a logical place to regard as that at which true man emerged. It was here that the fundamental feature of man, culture, became established. The tool-using phase was essential to its full establishment, but that was a transitional phase. Naturally there is no sharp division between the one and the other, but from our present position in time the point of separation between australopithecine and man is sufficiently defined to be useful.

On this view it is clear that *Paranthropus* belonged to a relatively slow-rate line which did not alter in essentials after it had come into existence and was still extant after *Australopithecus* had become extinct.   Progressive desiccation forced some early australopithecines to become meat eaters to some extent; not pure carnivores, but omnivores depending on both vegetable food and meat.   The altered selection pressures directly due to this resulted eventually in increased brain size and toolmaking and thus in the emergence of man.

ECOLOGICAL COMPETITION

From the fact that *Paranthropus* appears to be well adapted to a vegetarian diet and is found in periods which are at least moderately moist, it seems that its ecological requirements differed significantly from those of *Australopithecus*.   The latter appears to have been a typically hominid omnivore and is usually found under climatic conditions noticeably drier than those for *Paranthropus*.   It is probably not valid to conclude that *Australopithecus* lived only under conditions of appreciable aridity; its food requirements were apparently such that there is no reason to suppose that wetter conditions would adversely affect its way of life.   However, *Paranthropus*, being a vegetarian but not a grazer, would find the sort of semiarid conditions easily endured by *Australopithecus* unsuited to its way of life.   It is quite probable that neither would have found wet, dense forest conditions congenial.

What deductions can be made about the ecology of these two forms are in agreement with, and closely related to, the morphological evidence which indicates that *Paranthropus* is an aberrant hominid, while *Australopithecus* fits very well as an early hominid with characteristics which are basically just like those of the more advanced hominids but less well developed.   "Telanthropus" would appear to be one of these more advanced hominids with characters basically like those of *Australopithecus* but more advanced.   "Telanthropus," as I have attempted to show, appears to have been a toolmaker and presumably had a larger brain than *Australopithecus*.   The ecological requirements of these two forms are therefore likely to have been very similar, and if they simultaneously came to occupy the same territory they would find themselves in competition unless there was an overabundance of their necessities for life.   But since the ecological requirements of *Paranthropus* were different, it could coexist quite well with either of the other forms.

The evidence from the Sterkfontein Valley seems to support these conclusions.   *Australopithecus* lived in the valley for quite a long period of time when conditions were relatively dry.   If my interpretation of the evidence is correct, "Telanthropus" then moved into the valley when the dry conditions began to ameliorate. But by a relatively short time later, when wetter conditions allowed *Paranthropus* to move into the area, "Telanthropus" was still there but *Australopithecus* was no longer present—as could be predicted from the similarity of their ecology. The latter had either moved out of the region or suffered local extinction. Naturally, from the nature of the evidence, it is not known how long *Paranthropus* and "Telanthropus" were synchronously present in the valley. But evidence is available elsewhere. "Pithecanthropus" remains at Sangiran, according to von Koenigswald, came from both the Putjangan black clay and the later Kabuh conglomerate, while "Meganthropus" came from the former. But the 1953 mandible of the latter from that site, according to Marks (1953), was found loose in a lump of conglomerate. Therefore these two, a hominine and a *Paranthropus*, evidently occurred together in this area over a considerable period of time.

If "Telanthropus" is ignored in the Sterkfontein Valley, then it is not obvious why *Australopithecus* is not present at either Swartkrans or Kromdraai, because the differences of ecology between it and *Paranthropus* would not result in the one displacing the other.

The continued existence of *Paranthropus* long after *Australopithecus* is also perfectly reasonable on this interpretation of ecological differences. The rise of hominines would be disastrous for *Australopithecus*, who would survive only so long as he remained in areas not occupied or invaded by hominines. Inevitably this australopithecine would be exterminated. But since this does not apply to *Paranthropus*, its extinction would take longer and would not have depended on direct ecological competition.

TELANTHROPUS AND THE HOMININES

We have seen that *Paranthropus* and *Australopithecus* are very different creatures, ecologically quite differently adapted and morphologically quite distinct. "Telanthropus" must be classed with the hominines on morphological grounds, not the australopithecines. While this form clearly does not belong with either of the australopithecines, the question remains whether it is also a distinct form among the hominines. Answering that question requires a reconsideration of the whole hominid group, and to do that thoroughly would require a paper to itself.

Making the type of distinction that is so clear in the australopithecine group within the hominines seems to me out of the question. There is no evidence of which I am aware which suggests that any major adaptational differences existed that could be of generic quality and magnitude. The morphological differences are of a low order.

Probably the chief variable is brain size, the early "Pithecanthropus" forms being relatively small brained and hence with a slightly differently shaped braincase. But the known range in brain size of the earliest hominines can be accommodated entirely within the observed range of modern man. The dentition was also relatively robust in the early forms, hence the face was fairly robust and prognathous. But the dental and facial changes appear to be part of a continuous sequence of modification of no great magnitude. There is no evidence to show that there were several lines in which quite different things were happening. From the amount of probable fragmentation of the early human population of the Old World, it is to be expected that there were now and then, if not all the time, different streams of evolution in which the changes were not identical or proceeding at the same rate. But what was happening in these various lines of very low phyletic valence was essentially the same thing, so that the characteristics of all the groups still overlapped to a very marked degree.

The nature of these differences and the lack of any significant divergence of ecological requirements fit well into the picture of species differences within a well-defined genus among modern vertebrates. Furthermore, it seems clear that once the hominines were well launched on their path of cultural development, the character of their evolutionary mechanism would have been modified. As Mayr (1950) has pointed out, man occupies a wider range of environments than any other animal. This would clearly seem to be a result of his capacity for artificial adaptation. He can adapt himself to arctic or to tropical conditions without significant change in his morphology or physiology—in contrast to what occurs in other animals in such cases. This is not to suggest that natural selection does not operate on culture-bearing man—merely that its effects are modified by artificial adaptation.

This capacity for artificial adaptation reduces his capacity to speciate. Natural adaptation, under the control of natural selection, to different environmental conditions is the normal basis of speciation and hence also of the achievement of greater levels of taxonomic distinction. Reduced rate of speciation and the more recent tendency to interbreed increasingly over a wide area, have reduced very considerably the possibilities of significant adaptive radiation within the hominines.

For these reasons, it seems to me that the hominines must all be included within a single genus, *Homo*. This was suggested a decade ago by Mayr (1950) as part of a taxonomic scheme which included other aspects which do not appear to me to be valid. "Pithecanthropus" should therefore be reduced simply to a species of *Homo: H.*

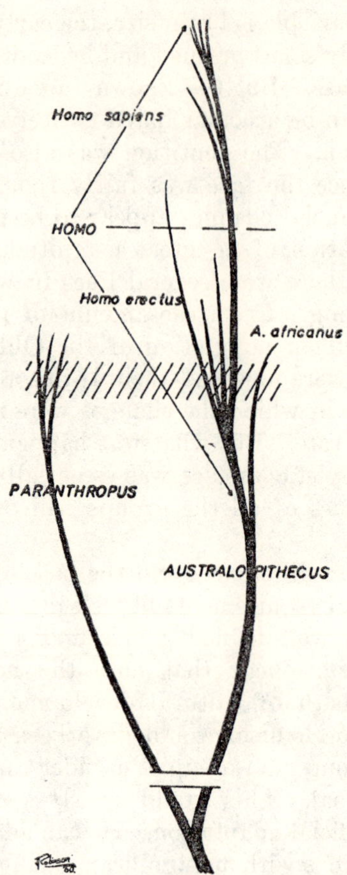

FIGURE 7.—Schematic representation of relationship between *Paranthropus*, *Australopithecus*, and *Homo*. The hatched zone represents approximately the time period from which the australopithecines and "Telanthropus" are known.

erectus. *H. sapiens* appears to be the only other valid species, which includes Neanderthal man as no more than a subspecies. Space shortage precludes further discussion of this topic save only to say that in this scheme "Telanthropus" becomes *H. erectus*. For this reason the genus *Telanthropus* (originally created by Broom and me in 1949) was sunk (Robinson, 1961).

This scheme reduces the contents of the whole family Hominidae to three genera only: *Paranthropus*, *Australopithecus*, and *Homo*. But it should be clearly recognized that these genera are not of the same sort or of equal magnitude. *Paranthropus* and *Australopithecus* are validly distinct on any grounds. They were divergent, adaptively well separated stocks which represented an adaptive radiation within the prehominines and could have occupied the same territory successfully for a long time. Both did in fact exist synchronously in Africa over a substantial period of time, though at present they are not known to have been sympatric. But *Australopithecus* and *Homo* are much more closely related and are probably two phases of the same phyletic sequence, though evidently one species of *Australopithecus* was contemporaneous for a short time with an early *H. erectus* in the Sterkfontein Valley. This overlap in time appears to have been short; the ecological similarity between the two makes it unlikely that it could have been long anywhere. But there is no sharp discontinuity between *Australopithecus* and *Homo*—except in brain size in the known specimens. But clearly there must have been at least one line in which this gap also was bridged. So, while it is clearly convenient to keep a generic distinction between the two groups, it should be recognized that this is not a distinction of the same type as that between *Paranthropus* and *Australopithecus* or *Paranthropus* and *Homo*. This is just another of the numerous examples where the conventional Linnean taxonomic approach breaks down. This "vertical" type of arbitrary taxonomic distinction—as opposed to the "horizontal" taxonomy of contemporaneous forms—is one of the troublesome things which the paleontologist has learned to live with but which does not trouble the neozoologist.

REFERENCES

Bronowski, J., and Long, W. M.
>   1952. Statistics of discrimination in anthropology. Amer. Journ. Phys. Anthrop., vol. 10, p. 385.

Broom, R., and Robinson, J. T.
>   1949. A new type of fossil man. Nature, vol. 164, p. 322.

Dart, R.
>   1957a. The osteodontokeratic culture of australopithecines . Transvaal Mus. Mem. 10.
>   1957b. The Makapansgat australopithecine osteodontokeratic culture. Proc. 3d Pan. African Congr. Prehist., Livingstone, 1955, p. 161.
>   1960.   The bone-tool manufacturing ability of *Australopithecus prometheus*. Amer. Anthrop., vol. 62, p. 134.

Leakey, L. S. B.
>   1959.   A new fossil skull from Olduvai. Nature, vol. 184, p. 491.
>   1961a. New finds at Olduvai Gorge. Nature, vol, 189, p. 649.
>   1961b. The juvenile mandible from Olduvai. Nature, vol. 191, p. 417.

Leakey, L. S. B.; Evernden, J. F.; and Curtis, G. H.
>   1961. Age of Bed I, Olduvai Gorge, Tanganyika. Nature, vol. 191, p. 478.

Le Gros Clark, W. E.
>   1955. The fossil evidence for human evolution. University of Chicago Press.

Marks, P.
>   1953. Preliminary note on the discovery of a new jaw of *Meganthropus* von Koeningswald in the Lower Middle Pleistocene of Sangiran, Central Java. Indonesian Journ. Nat. Sci., Nos. 1, 2, and 3.

MASON, R.
1961. The earliest tool-makers in South Africa. South African Journ. Sci., vol. 57, p. 13.

MAYR, E.
1950. Taxonomic categories in fossil hominids. Cold Spring Harbor Symposium on Quant. Biol., vol. 15, p. 109.

NAPIER, J. R.
1959. Fossil metacarpals from Swartkrans. British Mus. (Nat. Hist.): Fossil Mammals of Africa, No. 17.

REMANE, A.
1951. Die Zähne des *Meganthropus africanus*. Zeitschr. Morphol. Anthrop., vol. 42, p. 311.

ROBINSON, J. T.
1953. *Meganthropus*, australopithecines and hominids. Amer. Journ. Phys. Anthrop., vol. 11, p. 1.
1955. Further remarks on the relationship between *Meganthropus* and australopithecines. Amer. Journ. Phys. Anthrop., vol. 13, p. 429.
1956. The dentition of the Australopithecinae. Transvaal Mus. Mem. 9.
1958. Cranial cresting patterns and their significance in the Hominoidea. Amer. Journ. Phys. Anthrop., vol. 16, p. 397.
1960. The affinities of the new Olduvai australopithecine. Nature, vol. 186, p. 456.
1961. The australopithecines and their bearing on the origin of man and of stone tool-making. South African Journ. Sci., vol. 57, p. 3.
1962. The origin and adaptive radiation of the australopithecines. *In* Evolution and Hominisation, ed. G. Kurth, Gustav Fischer Verlag, p. 120.

ROBINSON, J. T., and MASON, R.
1957. Occurrence of stone artifacts with *Australopithecus* at Sterkfontein. Nature, vol. 180, p. 521.

Evolution, Genetics, and Anthropology[1]

By A. E. MOURANT

The Lister Institute
London

THE BEGINNINGS OF ANTHROPOLOGY

THE ABILITY to distinguish members of other species from those of one's own is, throughout most of the animal kingdom, a vital necessity for purposes of reproduction. The power of distinguishing members of other races or communities within the species is much less widespread, and seems to be most fully developed, apart from man, in that other great social and warlike group, the Hymenoptera. Somewhat ironically, we find that among the bees the basis of distinction, and of violent adverse discrimination, is not an inherited or in any way permanent set of characteristics, but the ephemeral flower perfume shared at any one time by the occupants of a given hive.

Among the primates we know little of any recognition or discrimination below the species level, but we can be certain that recognition of alien species as such has always existed, and that from the beginning human beings were aware of differences between themselves and the other primates. They did not, however, necessarily become aware immediately of the differences arising between human communities as one race diverged from another, for, as with most other animal species, spatial or ecological separation was undoubtedly necessary before physical differentiation could become established. Certainly, however, from the beginning of history as recorded in writing and pictures, we find descriptions and representations of those features, both of body and dress, which characterize different races and nations, at first usually in the form of records of conquered peoples, upon monuments of victory set up by their conquerors.

For thousands of years, however, the criteria used for describing, and distinguishing between, human populations lacked precision, and little attempt was made to distinguish between inherited and acquired

---

[1] The Huxley Memorial Lecture, delivered in the rooms of the Royal Society, Burlington House, on Friday, November 24, 1961. Reprinted by permission from the Journal of the Royal Anthropological Institute of Great Britain and Ireland, vol. 91, pt. 2, July–December 1961.

characteristics. Only in the last two centuries do we find any attempt at precise descriptions of racial characteristics. The science of physical anthropology can, it is true, in one sense, be traced back to the Renaissance, for it has its roots in the precise anatomical representations and descriptions of Vesalius. He, however, was not, as far as we know, interested in differentiating races, but was concerned, rather, in establishing those anatomical characteristics which all or nearly all human beings have in common.

At about the time of the Renaissance, too, the period of the great explorations began, during which most of the surface of the earth became known to, and much of it was conquered by, the peoples of Europe. Thus Europeans, within a relatively short space of time, became aware of the existence of a much greater range of human types, and incidentally of human cultures, than had ever been known to them before. Indeed, in the previous thousand years almost their only new contacts had been with invading armies from Asia.

An important step in the direction of precise differentiation of human individuals and populations was taken by Camper (1782), when he introduced the measurement of the "facial angle." With Blumenbach (1795) we are suddenly in the presence of a fully scientific investigator who, if it were possible for him to be present, would surely feel at home in a modern gathering of physical anthropologists. He proposed a classification of mankind, regarded as a single biological species, into five principal varieties, Caucasian, Mongolian, Ethiopian, American, and Malay, of which he gave qualitative but nevertheless precise anatomical specifications. He stressed, however, the variation which occurred within each variety. Cuvier (1854) reduced the varieties to the three, Caucasian, Mongolian, and Negro, which have since remained traditional.

In 1842 came one of the most important advances in the methods of anthropology, the introduction by Retzius of the concept of the "cranial index," expressing the breadth of the skull as a percentage of its length. This technical device, important in itself, became a sort of nucleus around which crystallized most of the observations made in physical anthropology during the subsequent hundred years.

EVOLUTION, NATURAL SELECTION, AND HEREDITY

In the whole of biological science, however, the middle years of the 19th century were a time not only of great advances in knowledge but of fundamental changes in views, affecting anthropology perhaps more than any other part of biology. Following the publication by Darwin in 1859 of *The Origin of Species*, he, and Huxley who took the major part in disseminating the new theory, became the unquestioned leaders of the biological world. Among their chief preoccupations were man's origin and his place in nature; in 1862 Huxley published *Man's Place in Nature* and in 1871 Darwin's *Descent of Man* appeared.

These two men, friends and close colleagues though they were, differed considerably in outlook, and this is instanced in particular by their views upon the nature of inheritable variations in living beings in general. These views had a particular bearing upon the nature of interspecific differences and upon the question, perpetually stressed by Huxley, of whether natural selection alone, acting upon a single species, could bring about a separation into two mutually infertile species.

Both men were almost certainly completely unaware of the contemporary work of Mendel who showed that, in the cases which he investigated, inheritable differences were finite and discontinuous. Darwin, though of course aware of isolated examples of discontinuous variation, appears, to the end of his life, to have regarded selection as operating essentially upon a continuous series of quantitative variations.

Huxley seems to have been much more actively interested than Darwin in the question of how hereditary variation took place, and more fully conscious of the existing lack of knowledge of these mechanisms, and of the need for further research. In 1861, four years before the publication of Mendel's classical work, he wrote to Sir Joseph Hooker asking "Why does not somebody go to work experimentally, and get at the law of variation for some one species of plant?"—a task upon which Mendel was probably even then at work. It would be possible to point to a number of statements by Huxley which show an intuitive anticipation of modern genetical theory, of which two may be quoted:

the important fact . . . that the tendency to vary, in a given organism, may have nothing to do with the external conditions to which the individual organism is exposed, but may depend wholly upon internal conditions. (Huxley, 1869.)

Hence it is conceivable, and indeed probable, that every part of the adult contains molecules, derived both from the male and from the female parent. . . . The primitive male and female molecules may . . . mould the assimilated nutriment, each according to its own type, into innumerable new molecules. (Huxley, 1878.)

It would, however, be wrong to assume that Huxley anticipated in any complete sense the modern genetical view that the heritable basis of all variation is discontinuous. Certainly in the science of physical anthropology, which Huxley did so much to foster, and which was growing so rapidly at this time, the stress was on the precise measurement of parameters regarded as forming continuous series.

In the hundred years which followed Retzius's introduction of the cranial index, the subject matter of physical anthropology consisted almost exclusively of measurements of the various parts of the body, and observations, with more or less precise measurements, of the color of certain tissues. The total amount of information amassed was prodigious. With the shift of stress from individual to population, and the development of appropriate statistical methods by Pearson, Fisher, and others, the material served to yield a fairly complete classification of mankind, and to throw much light on prehistory.

Throughout the period which we are considering the underlying object of investigators, even if it was not always expressed, was undoubtedly to define separately, and to measure, those features of the bodily constitution which were inherited, as distinct from those acquired during the life of the individual. But in the absence of any adequate theory of the inheritance of these features the channels of information tended in the course of time to become clogged by a vast mass of rather indigestible data.

GENETICS AND NATURAL SELECTION

In 1900 two discoveries were announced which were to have a very great influence on anthropology. One of these, and by far the more important, was the rediscovery, independently by De Vries, by Correns, and by Tschermak, of those principles of genetics which had already been described by Mendel in 1865 and which had been not simply forgotten, but completely disregarded by the main body of biologists. The other discovery, at first sight completely unrelated, was that by Landsteiner of the human blood groups.

The essence of the Mendelian revolution was the discovery that the inherited characters, which taken together constitute the differences between individuals, are indeed separated from one another by finite differences. In sexually reproducing species, any given character results from the action of a pair of genes, one inherited from the father and one from the mother or, perhaps more commonly, of several such pairs. When the individual reproduces, a replica of one of each pair of genes is present in each of the reproductive cells and is passed on to each of the offspring. The further discoveries that the genes are located on microscopically visible structures known as chromosomes, and that the latter consist chemically of chains built up from desoxyribonucleic acid molecules, need not concern us at present.

It was not at first obvious that the new genetical theories were relevant to the evolutionary process, to the theory of natural selection, or to anthropology. The characters which were studied in the early days of genetical science appeared to many biologists to be somewhat superficial, and little connected with the great differences which interested taxonomists. In man the few known genetically segregating characters were either relatively insignificant, or pathological. It is therefore not surprising that the statistical approach of the biometricians seemed to mark a much more promising line of advance, both in explaining evolution as a whole and in classifying and explaining the differences between human individuals and populations.

To three genetical statisticians, Fisher and Haldane in Britain, and Sewall Wright in America, is due the credit for the next major development in biological thought, the explanation of natural selection in terms of genetics. The most complete treatment of the subject is found in Fisher's *The Genetical Theory of Natural Selection* (1930) which is one of the most important works on biology to appear since *The Origin of Species*. Following the work done by Huxley in establishing the validity of the theory of natural selection, Fisher took the next logically essential step and showed, in terms of the by then well-established mechanisms of heredity, how selection had operated. In genetical language, Darwin and Huxley studied phenotypes; Fisher, genes and genotypes. Fisher, indeed, showed that the "atomic" nature of heredity was implicit in the work of Darwin: granted that evolution by natural selection took place, he showed that it could happen in no other way.

There could now be no doubt that the external and measurable body characters which provided the data of physical anthropology were genetically determined; Fisher and Gray (1937) in a concise paper brought together all that was known regarding the inheritance of stature in man and interpreted it in terms of genetical theory. The inheritance of these characters, however, did not prove readily amenable to genetical analysis, and has not even now proved to be so. Thus, while the object of physical anthropology was (and is) to isolate the inherited components in the measurements, and to use them for purposes of classification and the tracing of ancestral relationships, the observational methods perforce remained exclusively those of direct measurement, and the methods of statistical analysis to which the measurements were subjected took no cognizance of genetical theory.

The field was now clear, however, for the exploitation, largely fostered by Fisher himself, of blood groups and other genetically relatively simple characters as genetical, and ultimately as anthropological, markers.

Despite Huxley's efforts to give medical students a broad background of biological knowledge, medical research at the time of his death remained divided into a number of very distinct compartments. The highly active field of bacteriology and the investigation of the response of animals and human beings to bacterial infection was scarcely seen to have any connection with the great advances in biology initiated by Darwin and Huxley. It was, however, in the course of work in this field that Landsteiner in 1900 discovered the human blood groups.

BLOOD GROUPS AND ANTHROPOLOGY

While investigating possible reactions between the red corpuscles of the blood, or red cells, of certain persons and the blood serum of others, Landsteiner showed that the red cells of any given person may carry either of two substances known as A and B, or they may carry neither of them. Subsequent work showed that the red cells of some persons carry both substances. These substances, because of the reactions described below, and of other properties subsequently elucidated, are classified biochemically as antigens. Their chemical constitution is now fairly fully known but they could then be characterized only by the use, as reagents, of certain human sera containing proteins known as antibodies, specifically related to the A and B antigens and hence known as anti-A and anti-B. When a serum containing anti-A is added to red cells carrying the A antigen, the latter combines with the antibody and the red cells are thereby caused to agglutinate, or stick together in clumps. Similarly anti-B causes cells carrying the B antigen to agglutinate.

From a time soon after their first discovery, the main practical importance of the investigation of the blood groups has always lain in ensuring the compatibility of blood transfusions, millions of which are now given annually throughout the world. This has perforce led to the blood groups being studied in great detail, and they have as a result been shown to possess an interest and importance far transcending their immediate practical application.

It was clear from the beginning that the blood group of an individual was a more or less permanent attribute of his bodily constitution; it must soon have become clear that it was something inborn and in some sense inherited. The first suggestion that the blood groups were determined by Mendelian genes seems to have been made in 1908 by Epstein and Ottenberg, and in 1910 Von Dungern and Hirszfeld clearly showed that the possession of the A or B antigen was a well-defined genetical character, though the precise mode of inheritance was only determined by Bernstein in 1924. Meanwhile, in 1919, Professor and Mrs. Hirszfeld, who had been pioneers in many other aspects of blood-group study, were the first to apply them to anthropology. At the end of the First World War they were working at Salonika, a great crossroads for the movement both of troops and of refugees, and they were able to test the blood of large numbers of persons from many lands and most of the continents. They were thus able to show that, while most populations possessed all the four blood groups, the proportions in which they occurred differed widely from one population to another.

This investigation was of importance not simply as marking the discovery of one particular anthropological character, but as being the first application to anthropology of a totally new method, the study of gene distributions: since there was no necessary distinction between the individuals of one population and of another, the populations themselves became the units of study, and statistical methods, which could still perhaps be regarded as an extra embellishment in classical anthropometric work, became an essential feature of the new type of investigation.

The blood groups have certain other advantages as anthropological characters. They are fixed for life, at the moment of conception, by the genetical constitution of the individual. Also, unlike such features as the size of various parts of the body, they are unaffected by the subsequent history of the individual (apart from very rare cases, amounting to no more than a few per million of the population, who change their apparent blood group as a result of severe malignant disease). Moreover, while the visible characteristics of the body, and especially the color of the skin, have become associated in some quarters with racial prejudice, and allegations of inferiority and superiority, the blood groups have hitherto gathered no such unscientific accretions.

The medical importance of the blood groups, and the intrinsic interest of a new method of studying human populations, rapidly led to the publication of large bodies of blood-group frequency data, and in 1939 Boyd, who had himself performed large numbers of tests, was able to extract from the literature, and to compile and publish in the form of tables, the results of testing about one million individuals.

Until the year 1927 only the blood groups O, A, B, and AB were known. To these we shall now refer as belonging to the ABO system. In that year Landsteiner and Levine announced the discovery of three new blood groups, M, N, and P. The methods which they used, and which are used for the determination of all the blood groups, are technically similar, though the reagents are different, but when their mode of inheritance is examined the blood groups are found to fall into a number of genetical systems, those already named forming the ABO, MN, and P systems, the second of which has since been expanded to form the MNSs system. While the groups of the different systems may resemble one another biochemically, those of one system are as distinct and separate from those of another in their inheritance as are, for instance, hair color and head shape. In a given population there may indeed be a preponderance of people with some particular combination of hair color and head shape (each admittedly more complex genetically than the blood groups) but when we study the mode of inheritance within the population, we find that these two types of character are independently inherited. Similarly a particular combination of blood groups of different systems may be common, but again a study of their inheritance will show that those of each system are independently inherited. It ought, however, perhaps to be said that the phenomenon of linkage, which occurs when the genes for two sets of characters are at different places on the same chromosome, may affect the independence of the characters when studied in individual families, but, unless the linkage is extremely close, it will not affect their independence as anthropological markers.

In 1940 the very important Rh or Rhesus blood-group system was added to the three already known, and in the succeeding years a further seven have been discovered which are of anthropological interest, in addition to a number of rare blood groups which have each been found only in a very few individuals or families throughout the world.

OTHER HUMAN GENETICAL CHARACTERS

Until about 1950, the genetical characters known in man nearly all fell into two classes, the rare congenital diseases, of little anthropological interest, and the blood groups. Already a few other genetically determined biochemical characters had been discovered, such as the ability to secrete blood-group substances in the saliva, or to perceive a bitter taste in the simple organic compound, phenylthiocarbamide. Since then, however, the number of known biochemical characters under genetical control has multiplied greatly and many of the systems involved have proved to be of considerable anthropological interest.

Without doubt the most remarkable and instructive example is that of the hemoglobins. Since their population genetics are simpler and more fully worked out than those of the blood groups, we shall consider them somewhat fully, as a possible guide to the situations which may be expected to arise in the study of the much more complex blood groups, and of the other more recently discovered biochemical factors.

By the year 1949 it had long been known that certain Negroes have red blood cells which, when examined on a microscope slide under a cover-slip, do not remain round but become crescentic or sickle shaped. It had also been established for many years that some of these persons suffer from a severe and intractable hemolytic or blood-destructive anemia, and that the condition tends to be familial. In that year Pauling, Itano, Singer, and Wells showed that the cells which tend to form sickle shapes, or sickle-cells, carry an abnormal type of hemoglobin molecule, with a higher positive electrical charge than normal adult hemoglobin, and with a lower solubility in body fluids in the unoxygenated state. In the healthy persons with sickle-cells this type is present together with normal hemoglobin while in the anemic ones it occurs by itself. It gradually became clear that, apart from cases where other abnormal genes complicate the picture, the anemic persons with sickle-cells are homozygous for a gene determining the synthesis of the abnormal sickle-cell hemoglobin, that is to say, they have received such a gene from both parents, while the healthy sicklers, who have a mixture of abnormal and normal hemoglobin, are heterozygous for the same gene, having received an abnormal gene from one parent and a normal one from the other. Since under African conditions virtually all homozygous sicklers die without producing offspring, the frequency of their abnormal gene might be expected to diminish appreciably with every generation. Nevertheless there are numerous tribes in Africa with total frequencies of sicklers, mainly heterozygous, as high as 40 percent. It was a simple matter of genetical calculation to show that, in these tribes, about 4 percent of the babies conceived, and indeed of those born alive, since the condition is not lethal *in utero*, must be homozygous sicklers, almost inevitably destined to an early death. The question therefore arose as to how such high frequencies of sicklers could exist, and presumably persist from generation to generation.

One suggested explanation was that mutation, or spontaneous change from the normal gene responsible for producing normal hemoglobin to the abnormal one causing the production of the sickle-cell variety, was taking place with sufficient frequency to balance the loss of abnormal genes through deaths from anemia. This, however, implied a frequency of change thousands of times higher than for almost any other known case of mutation, and so seemed most unlikely to be the true explanation. The only alternative appeared to be that the abnormal heterozygote, under African conditions, enjoyed a selective advantage, not only over the abnormal homozygote, but also over the normal homozygote. This is a situation well known to geneticists, and is called balanced polymorphism, in which the supply of both genes is replenished from the pool represented by the favored heterozygote, so that the balance between them tends to remain stable from one generation to another. Several workers suggested that the advantage enjoyed by the heterozygotes might be that they were more resistant than normal persons to malaria; that this was so was first clearly demonstrated by Allison (1954) who also showed that the variety of malaria involved was the malignant tertian type. The relative resistance of heterozygotes to malaria was confirmed by Raper (1956) who worked out more fully how this resistance operated. The complete solution of this primarily medical problem took many years to reach, and was achieved only because the clinical investigators had the close collaboration of biochemists, geneticists, and anthropologists. Such a situation is at the moment unique but it may become not infrequent as the conquest of the environmental diseases brings into prominence, and exposes to investigation, the hard and therapeutically intractable residue of the congenital abnormalities.

It should be mentioned that, largely as a result of the attention paid to the sickling problem, several dozen other abnormal hemoglobins are now known, a number of which are sufficiently common in particular regions of the world to serve as valuable anthropological markers. Their frequencies are probably also maintained in a state of balanced polymorphism, but the mechanisms have not been worked out. The chemical constitution of normal adult hemoglobin has now been worked out almost completely, and that of many of the abnormal varieties nearly or quite as fully. The chemical abnormalities consist in the substitution of one amino-acid residue for another in the molecule of this protein. The molecule is composed of two parts (or rather, two pairs of identical parts), and substitution in each part is controlled by a separate set of allelomorphic (or alternative) genes.

HEMOGLOBINS AND NATURAL SELECTION

In the relationship between normal and sickle-cell hemoglobins we have the clearest example yet worked out of natural selection acting upon the human species, but the fact that we are within reach of being able to measure directly the effects of the selective process implies that the frequencies of the genes concerned are labile, and they can scarcely be used as long-term anthropological markers. While, however, high frequencies of the abnormal or sickle-cell hemoglobin gene are liable to rapid change from generation to generation, low frequencies may persist for a very long time, as indicators that a modern population is descended, at least in part, from an ancestral one which possessed it and which was probably exposed to endemic infection with malignant tertian malaria. In most cases this certainly means African ancestry, but the distribution of the sickling condition in southern Asia and Europe as well as in Africa has led Lehmann to suggest that its original center of dispersion lay in southwest Asia. An alternative possibility is that mutation from the normal to the sickle-cell hemoglobin gene has taken place independently in a number of places, the new gene persisting and spreading wherever malignant tertian malaria has been endemic.

We are bound to assume the existence of selective forces favoring the spread of other hemoglobins, especially hemoglobin C in West Africa, and hemoglobin E in southeast Asia; we do not know whether these forces have operated as rapidly as that involving sickle-cell hemoglobin, but the indications are that the gene for hemoglobin E, at any rate, is a fairly stable part of the genetical picture of southeast Asia. The gene or genes for thalassaemia are found in the Mediterranean area as well as parts of Africa and Asia, and among New World populations of Mediterranean and African ancestry. It is not known whether they belong to either of the genetical systems mentioned above, which determine the production of particular abnormal types of hemoglobin, but they cause a disturbance of normal hemoglobin production broadly similar to that produced by the sickle-cell hemoglobin gene, the heterozygotes being clinically almost normal and the homozygotes suffering from a severe hemolytic anemia. Here again it is thought that the heterozygotes have an advantage over normal persons in being more resistant to malaria, but the process is less fully understood than in the case of the sickle-cell condition. Anthropologically, thalassaemia is of similar value in classifying populations to the more specific hemoglobin abnormalities.

GENETICAL CHARACTERS IN ANTHROPOLOGY

Bearing in mind the relatively simple model provided by the hemoglobins we are now in a position to consider more fully and critically the contribution to anthropology which has been made, and that which can in the future be made, by the study of the blood groups and other genetically simple biochemical characters.

All the 11 major blood-group systems have contributed to anthropological knowledge, but three of them, the original ABO system of Landsteiner and the MNSs and Rh systems, have made by far the greatest contributions. Because of their earlier discovery, their medical importance, and the ready availability of the testing reagents, far more information is available about the distribution of the ABO groups (Mourant et al., 1958) than of the others (Mourant, 1954). On the basis of blood-group frequencies as a whole the world can be divided into about six major regions differing markedly in frequencies for nearly all systems. Within each region the frequencies of the MNSs and Rh groups show highly characteristic patterns with relatively little fluctuation, whereas those of the ABO groups vary considerably even within comparatively small areas such as Great Britain. The ABO groups appear to have been subject to more intense and rapid differential processes of natural selection than those of the other systems. The comparative constancy of the frequencies of the MNSs and Rh groups may be due to the relative absence of selection, or to balance of selective effects, but the existence of an absolutely higher selection pressure on the ABO groups is in agreement with what we know more directly about the relationship of blood groups to diseases.

The best known example of association between blood groups and disease is that shown by hemolytic disease of the newborn, which is the result of blood-group incompatibility between mother and foetus, most frequently with respect to the Rh system (Levine, Katzin, and

Burnham, 1941). Other systems, including the ABO system, are sometimes involved. The problem of natural selection due to this disease is interesting and important but a full discussion of it would lead us too far from our main topic. It has however been shown mathematically (Li, 1953) that it should not lead to the establishment of a balanced polymorphism such as we discussed in the case of the hemoglobins. Apart from hemolytic disease of the newborn, some half-dozen diseases have been shown to have an association with particular blood groups, groups in all cases belonging to the ABO system; the most marked example is the association between duodenal ulcer and group O. There is, however, no evidence that, in the case of any of the diseases studied, blood-group heterozygotes are relatively favored as are the hemoglobin heterozygotes by malaria. Moreover, none of the diseases proved to have a connection with blood groups has an incidence sufficiently early in life to affect appreciably the blood-group composition of the next generation. On the anthropological side too, it is (fortunately for practical applications) true to say that resemblances between populations known to be related but long separated suggest that ABO frequencies are relatively stable for periods of the order of 2,000 years.

It would be unsafe, however, to accept the ABO blood groups, even for periods of under 2,000 years, as completely stable population markers. One possible cause of sudden large frequency changes is epidemic disease. If the blood groups show a differential survival among sufferers from any of the diseases responsible for major epidemics, frequencies may perhaps remain stable for periods of centuries and then suffer sudden very large changes as a result of an outbreak of one of these diseases, or of a series of outbreaks. That this is a possibility is suggested by the recent work of Vogel, Pettenkofer, and Helmbold (1960), who have examined the micro-organisms responsible for plague and smallpox for the presence of antigens resembling the blood-group substances. They find an antigen like that of blood-group A in the smallpox virus, and in the plague bacillus an antigen resembling the blood-group substance H which is most abundant in group O cells. Basing their argument upon the hypothesis that an individual will have difficulty in elaborating a protective antibody to an organism antigenically resembling any of his own blood-group substances, they suggest that group-A persons are particularly susceptible to smallpox and group-O persons to plague. They compare the world distribution of the ABO blood groups and of smallpox and plague epidemics: these correspond sufficiently well to suggest the desirability of further investigation of the hypothesis that such epidemics have played a major part in determining blood-group distribution.

While, however, natural selection has almost certainly been the preponderant influence in determining blood-group frequencies in different populations, accidental fluctuations have undoubtedly affected the frequencies found in small isolated communities, and in some cases such accidentally determined frequencies may have become stabilized when, in an improved but still isolated environment, the numbers of a population have undergone a large increase. The extent to which such a process may have affected the blood-group frequencies now found in large population groups is difficult to estimate. For light upon this problem we must look on the one hand to experimental studies of animal population genetics, and on the other to such work as that initiated by Vogel, Pettenkofer, and Helmbold, and to the examination of many more small and intermediate human population groups.

It is tempting to regard the various genetical systems which have been discussed as providing us with a series of probes reaching varying distances into the past, the hemoglobins some hundreds of years, the ABO blood groups one or two thousand years, the Rh and MNSs blood groups and perhaps most of the others several thousand years. If this situation represents the truth, then we are even better provided with information than if all genetical frequencies were highly stable, for then we should have no genetical clues to events taking place within any of the major population groups since conditions became stable.

Empirically, by calling written history to witness, we can show that the temporal hierarchy of genetical systems just suggested does at least in part account for the present genetical constitution of populations. However, until far more is known than at present of the conditions determining the frequencies of the genes we are studying, we must be content to feel our way gradually from one established fact to the next. For instance, though blood-group frequencies, including ABO frequencies, are similar in populations known to be closely related, this may be the result not, as we have tended to suppose, of the absence of selective influences since separation, but of the presence of a number of strong selective forces causing gene frequencies to remain balanced at particular levels, levels determined by some condition, whether wholly external like climate, or cultural like food preferences, which the two populations, though separated, have continued to share. Alternatively, even in the absence of any continuing similarities in the external conditions responsible for natural selection, the frequencies of a particular set of allelomorphic genes may have been maintained at or near particular levels by the stabilizing influence of the gene pool as a whole controlling the operation of natural selection.

In the last 10 years many more biochemical systems under simple genetical control have been found in man. Most conveniently for practical purposes, the majority of them are expressed in some way in the blood, and so they can be investigated by using portions of specimens obtained for blood grouping. The number of known systems of this kind is rapidly increasing. Those who discover them are usually aware immediately of their possible anthropological significance and soon carry out surveys of a number of different populations, between which, as a rule, significant differences in gene frequency are found. Many of the substances involved have known physiological functions: among these are the haptoglobins and the transferrins, classes of plasma proteins involved in different stages of iron metabolism. Genetically determined variations in the control mechanisms of such important vital processes are likely to be subject to intense natural selection, and hence perhaps to be relatively short-term population markers, but the details of the mechanisms of selection are in most cases not yet known.

One system where something is known of the selective mechanism is that involving a genetically determined deficiency of the enzyme glucose-6-phosphate dehydrogenase (sometimes called G6PD). The normal biochemistry of this enzyme has long since been well established, and empirically, though the chain of biochemical events is not entirely clear, a deficiency of it is found to cause a liability to hemolytic or blood-destructive anemia following the consumption of certain drugs or of the common broad bean, *Vicia faba*, leading in the latter case to favism, a condition long familiar in Mediterranean populations. The gene involved is unique, or nearly so, among those known to give rise to human polymorphisms, in being sex-linked, or carried on the female-determining X chromosome. Thus the male, with only one X chromosome, either has the condition fully developed or not at all. Unlike some other sex-linked genes, such as those for hemophilia and color blindness, this one is readily recognizable in female heterozygotes, but there is a quantitative overlap with homozygotes. Thus surveys of gene frequency can be reliably carried out only on males. Rather surprisingly, population studies leave little doubt that this apparently harmful gene is, like those for sickle-cell hemoglobin and for thalassaemia, in some way protective against malaria. It may be that the protected persons are the female heterozygotes.

This large and growing class of known genetical systems with a biochemical expression will thus almost certainly prove to include some with gene frequencies fluctuating readily in response to changes in external conditions, but it may be expected, like the blood-group class, also to include others with gene frequencies stable over very long periods.

GENETICS, ANTHROPOMETRY, AND THE FUTURE OF PHYSICAL ANTHROPOLOGY

It may be that few new blood-group systems remain to be discovered, but biochemical systems are likely to multiply considerably in number in the near future. As all the methods of testing involved become fully applied to anthropological material, then, even if classical anthropometric methods are also fully applied, the amount of information available about the inherited features of any population will become preponderantly serological and biochemical, and remain only in relatively small degree morphological.

This does not mean, however, that it will then be permissible to neglect morphological observation, or to disregard the results of past morphological measurements. There are many weighty reasons for this. For one thing, apart from the results of ABO blood-group tests on a small number of bodies and skeletons, the only means of comparing living populations with those of the past is by means of skeletal measurements. A further reason is that the vast bulk of our existing information about living or recently living populations consists of body measurements. We must continue to make it possible to compare the peoples of the present day, and indeed of the future, with archeological material, and with living populations examined during the past century, but possibly now inextricably intermarried with others. Quite apart from these considerations, it would clearly be wrong for anthropologists to neglect just those characteristics of individuals and populations by which they are identified in everyday life.

But an understanding of the physical nature of man, and his relation to the rest of nature, demands more than a comparison of individuals or populations with one another as they exist at the time when the observations are made. Man has been evolving, however slowly, during recent millennia, and he will continue to evolve in the future. The study of the processes of natural selection and evolution is, therefore, an essential part of the investigation, not only of ancient skeletal material, but of living human populations.

Already, as we have seen, some of the serological and biochemical characters are being studied with regard to the liability of their possessors to suffer from certain diseases. The results of such studies must ultimately be interpretable, at least in part, in terms of natural selection related to features of the environment. Similarly the external characters of the body must have evolved and must, indeed, still be evolving, in response to the nature of the environment. This process of evolution may be slow, and the genetics involved almost inextricably complex, but the major morphological features of the body, being the ultimate results of the selective process, may be expected to show, and have indeed in many cases been found to show, a close relationship to certain features of the environment.

In the almost complete absence of analytical methods related, in the Mendelian sense, to the genetical content of the data, much effort has been devoted, with great effect, toward increasing the efficiency of more empirical methods of statistical analysis, that is to say, analysis in terms of phenotypes. The whole accepted edifice of physical classification of human populations depends, in fact, upon the results of such analysis.

The genetical analysis of the blood groups and biochemical characters has enabled populations to be compared much more effectively than could have been done on the basis of the observed characters (or phenotypes) alone. A knowledge of the genetics involved has also, in some cases, made possible a fairly full analysis of the mechanism by which these characters, through natural selection, become adapted to the environment. A full analysis of the modes of inheritance of the external body characters might be expected to have similar consequences for these characters. However, it is now clear that continuously varying characters such as skin color and stature are each under the control of a large number of genes, known as polygenes. Generalized methods of analysis of observations on such characters have been devised by Darlington and Mather (1949), but a full analysis in terms of individual genes is not at present in sight.

In view of the greatly increased discriminatory power which genetically based methods would almost certainly confer, much further effort is needed, but few geneticists appear to be aware of the need, and very few indeed have contributed at all substantially to the subject. In the case of stature, Fisher and Gray, as we have seen, many years ago extracted virtually all possible genetical information from the data then available; since then Tanner and Healy (Tanner, 1954; Tanner and Healy, 1956) have extended such analysis to some more recent data, but no other work of importance has been done. In the case of skin color, however, a considerable amount of work has been done recently, especially by G. A. Harrison (Harrison, 1957; Harrison and Owen, 1956–57) with promising results.

I believe that a more fundamental genetical analysis of mammalian and human morphological characters is possible than has so far been achieved, and I would commend this difficult problem to any younger geneticists who may hear or read this lecture. Such an analysis would, I hope, lead in time to much more efficient methods of dealing with the raw data of morphological anthropology. Hitherto the data themselves have proved intractable genetically: not only this, but also their sheer volume, even that of the reliable and well-standardized data alone, has discouraged any attempt at a systematic comprehensive analysis. If only methods for their analysis could be devised which were genetically sound, statistically efficient, and practically convenient, then the modern availability of electronic calculators, capable of dealing both with the complexity of the genetical situation and with the vast extent of the data, would, I predict, release from the treasure houses of the past an abounding harvest of priceless information.

Such developments are, however, not to be expected immediately, and we must now consider further the relation between the two main methods of human classification available at the present time. When blood-group observations began to be applied to anthropology there was a tendency on both sides to place emphasis on the discrepancies between the results of the new methods and those of classical anthropometry, and to claim that one method or the other was the more reliable. It is indeed not surprising that a classification based on a single genetical system, that of the ABO blood groups, failed to agree at all fully with one based on morphological characters representing the integrated effects of scores, if not hundreds, of sets of allelomorphic genes. Few physical anthropologists would now deny the classificatory value of the blood groups and biochemical characters, and most serologists and geneticists who apply their results to anthropology appreciate the importance of the morphological characters, despite the lack of any means of analyzing them genetically. The time is past, however, if it ever existed, for the two classes of information to be contrasted to the detriment of either. Morphological observations have now as great a value as they ever possessed, but they can be supplemented by information derived from a rapidly growing range of serological and biochemical investigations. Those who have attempted fully to use both methods, such as Beckman (1959) in Sweden, have found not only that there is a high degree of agreement between the classifications of populations based on the two methods, but that the most complete picture of hereditary connections between populations can be obtained only by combining all the available information of both kinds.

To Huxley more perhaps than to any other man we owe the existence, at the present time, of a fully scientific discipline of biology as a whole. To the scientific status of anthropology too, in particular, he made a very great contribution, but he did not live to see it achieve the objectiveness of, for instance, the remainder of zoology. Even at the present time anthropology still suffers both from a pseudo-scientific racialism which lingers in a few quarters, and from a failure to use to the full all the methods of investigation which are now available. Only by calling upon the full resources of paleontology, anatomy, physiology, biochemistry, genetics, ecology, and psychology, that is to say, on the whole available power of biological analysis, will irrational prejudices be overthrown and a science of physical anthropology arise which is both fully objective, and adequate in its compass and its achievement to the great subject of its investigations.

ACKNOWLEDGMENTS

I should like to thank Miss D. T. Cox and Drs. K. L. G. Goldsmith, G. A. Harrison, Dorothy Parkin, and P. M. Sheppard for their kindness in reading and criticizing drafts of this lecture; also Mrs. K. Domaniewska-Sobczak for assistance with the bibliography. I am indebted to Dr. Cyril Bibby for tracing and transcribing passages on heredity from little-known works of Huxley. I have since consulted those which were reprinted in the *Collected Essays*.

REFERENCES

ALLISON, A. C.
  1954. Protection offered by sickle-cell trait against subtertian malarial infection. British Med. Journ., vol. 1, pp. 290–294.
BECKMAN, L.
  1959. A contribution to the physical anthropology and population genetics of Sweden. Doctorate thesis, Lund. Hereditas, vol. 45.
BERNSTEIN, F.
  1924. Ergebnisse einer biostatistischen zusammenfassenden Betrachtung über die erbliche Blutstrukturen des Menschen. Klin. Wochschr., vol. 3, pp. 1495–1497.
BLUMENBACH, J. F.
  1795. Generis humani varietate nativa, ed. tertia, Göttingen. (*See* The anthropological treatises of Johann Friedrich Blumenbach, trans. and ed. by Thomas Bendyshe. London, 1865.)
BOYD, W. C.
  1939. Blood groups. Tabul. Biol., Hague, vol. 17, pp. 113–240.
CAMPER, P.
  *1782. Natuurkundige Verhandelingen. Amsterdam.
CORRENS, C.
  1900. G. Mendels Regel über das Verhalten der Nachkommenschaft der Rassenbastarde. Ber. Deutsch. Bot. Ges., vol. 18, pp. 232–239.
CUVIER, G.
  1854. The animal kingdom. New ed. (trans.) by W. B. Carpenter and J. O. Westwood. London.
DARLINGTON, C. D., and MATHER, K.
  1949. The elements of genetics. London.
DARWIN, C. R.
  1859. On the origin of species by means of natural selection, or the preservation of favoured races in the struggle for life. London.
  1871. The descent of man, and selection in relation to sex. 2 vols. London.
DUNGERN, E. VON, and HIRSZFELD, L.
  1910. Ueber Vererbung gruppenspezifischer Strukturen des Blutes. Zeitschr. Immun. Forsch., vol. 6, pp. 284–292.
EPSTEIN, A. A., and OTTENBERG, R.
  1908. Simple method of performing serum reactions. Proc. New York Path. Soc., vol. 8, pp. 117–123.
FISHER, R. A.
  1930. The genetical theory of natural selection. Oxford.

---

*This is the earliest work of Camper available in London, but the concept of the "facial angle" may have been introduced in one of his earlier works.

FISHER, R. A., and GRAY, H.
   1937. Inheritance in man: Boas's data studied by the method of analysis of variance. Ann. Eugen., London, vol. 8, pp. 74–93.
HARRIS, H.
   1959. Human biochemical genetics. Cambridge.
HARRISON, G. A.
   1957. The measurement and inheritance of skin colour in man. Eugen. Rev., vol. 49, pp. 73–76.
HARRISON, G. A., and OWEN, J. J. T.
   1956–57. The application of spectrophotometry to the study of skin colour inheritance. Acta Genet., vol. 6, pp. 481–484.
HIRSZFELD, L., and HIRSZFELD, HANNA.
   1919. Serological differences between the blood of different races. The result of researches on the Macedonian front. Lancet, vol. 2, pp. 675–679.
HUXLEY, T. H.
   1862. Evidence as to man's place in nature. London.
   1869. The genealogy of animals. Rev. of Natürliche Schöpfungs Geschichte *in* The Academy, 1869. Reprinted in Collected Essays, vol. 2.
   1878. Evolution in biology. Encycl. Britannica, 9th ed., vol. 8. Reprinted in Collected Essays, vol. 2.
LANDSTEINER, K.
   1900. Zur Kenntnis der antifermentativen, lytischen und agglutinierenden Wirkungen des Blutserums und der Lymphe. Zentralbl. Bakt., vol. 27, pp. 357–362.
LANDSTEINER, K., and LEVINE, P.
   1927a. A new agglutinable factor differentiating individual human bloods. Proc. Soc. Exp. Biol., New York, vol. 24, pp. 600–602.
   1927b. Further observations on individual differences of human blood. Proc. Soc. Exp. Biol., New York, vol. 24, pp. 941–942.
LANDSTEINER K., and WIENER, A. S.
   1940. An agglutinable factor in human blood recognized by immune sera for rhesus blood. Proc. Soc. Exp. Biol., New York, vol. 43, p. 223.
LEVINE, P.; KATZIN, E. M.; and BURNHAM, L.
   1941. Isoimmunization in pregnancy, its possible bearing on etiology of erythroblastosis fetalis. Journ. Amer. Med. Assoc., vol. 116, pp. 825–827.
LI, C. C.
   1953. Is Rh facing a crossroad? A critique of the compensation effect. Amer. Nat., vol. 87, pp. 257–261.
MENDEL, G.
   1865. Versuche über Pflanzen-Hybriden. Verh. Naturf. Ver. Brünn, vol. 4, pp. 3–47. (Publ. 1866.)
MOURANT, A. E.
   1954. The distribution of the human blood groups. Oxford.
MOURANT, A. E.; KOPEĆ, ADA C., and DOMANIEWSKA-SOBCZAK, KAZIMIERA.
   1958. The ABO blood groups: Comprehensive tables and maps of world distribution. Oxford.
PAULING, L.; ITANO, H. A.; SINGER, S. J.; and WELLS, I. C.
   1949. Sickle-cell anemia, a molecular disease. Science, vol. 110, pp. 543–548.
RAPER, A. B.
   1956. Sickling in relation to morbidity from malaria and other diseases. British Med. Journ., vol. 1, pp. 965–966.

RETZIUS, G.
    1842.   Über die Schädelformen der Nordbewohner.   Stockholm.
TANNER, J. M.
    1954.   Lack of sex linkage and dominance in genes controlling human
            stature.   Proc. 9th Int. Congr. Genet., pp. 933–934.
TANNER, J. M., and HEALY, M. J. R.
    1956.   The genetics of human morphological characters.   Adv. Sci., London,
            vol. 13, pp. 192–194.
TSCHERMAK, E.
    1900.   Über künstliche Kreuzung bei *Pisum sativum*.   Ber. Deutsch. Bot
            Ges., vol. 18, pp. 158–168.
VOGEL, F.; PETTENKOFER, H. J.; and HELMBOLD, W.
    1960.   Über die Populationsgenetik der ABO-Blutgruppen.   Acta Genet.
            Statist. Med., vol. 10, pp. 267–294.
VRIES, H. DE.
    1900.   Sur la loi de disjonction des hybrides.   C. R. Acad. Sci. Paris, vol.
            130, pp. 845–847.

The Skull of Shanidar II[1]

By T. D. STEWART

Head Curator of Anthropology
Smithsonian Institution

[With 9 plates]

WHEN I restored the first adult Neanderthal skull from Shanidar cave, northern Iraq, during the late months of 1957 (Stewart, 1958), another skull of an adult, designated as "Shanidar II" (Solecki, 1957, 1960a and b), had already been worked on in the laboratory of the Iraq Museum, Baghdad. The attention it had received from the laboratory technicians had consisted of the careful removal of the earth (it had been brought to Baghdad in a block of earth) and of the consolidation of all surfaces and loose fragments by means of a plastic cement. This procedure served to reveal the skull in the picturesque condition in which it was recovered; that is, broken into many pieces, flattened from side to side, the lower jaw still in articulation but with the mouth somewhat agape, and the upper half of the spinal column adherent to, and curving around, the base from pterygoids to occiput.

All this is shown in the three photographs, plates 1, 2, and plate 3, figure 1, which were taken in 1957 by Antran Evan. Otherwise the only records made earlier on this specimen are some radiographs of the teeth taken in the Radiological Institute, Baghdad. These radiographs will be considered in due course.

Although I left Baghdad early in 1958 with the impression that the skull of Shanidar II could not be restored, in the sense that the first skull had been, eventually I decided that any restorational effort must yield information of scientific value. Furthermore, I decided that the information thus obtained would be more useful than simply keeping the specimen in its original form for exhibition purposes. Thus, when Dr. Solecki made plans for the Fourth Shanidar Expedition and applied to the National Science Foundation for a grant, further work on the second skull was included in the schedule, along with the recovery from the cave of the remaining postcranial bones of the skeleton.

---

[1] Reprinted, with minor changes, by permission from Sumer, vol. 17, 1961.

I saw the skull for the second time in early June 1960, when the expedition arrived in Baghdad, and, with the gracious consent of the museum authorities, worked on it almost daily from then until the middle of July. The first step was to detach and reassemble the lower jaw. Next, the vertebrae were detached, separated, and individually reassembled.[2] At this stage it became apparent that the posterior part of the left side of the skull was very little more than adherent left scapula (pl. 3, fig. 2).[3] This, too, was detached, but left for later study. Nothing now remained except the skull proper and it was taken apart first in the right rear, then at the left top, and finally in the front midline. Only at this stage, when so many facial parts, including the upper front teeth, were seen to be missing, did I suspect that a collection of loose pieces was preserved separately in the museum. This turned out to be the case, and their inclusion in the study increased the information obtained.

I was right in my original impression about the restorational possibilities of the skull. Many parts were missing; others were broken into such small pieces that they could not be reassembled, especially since usually the inner and outer tables had separated through the diploë. Most discouraging of all, however, was the tenacity of the plastic cement which locked together the whole broken mass, including remnants of earth and bone meal. By contrast, the loose fragments stored separately, being in their original state, required almost no cleaning and could be fitted together rapidly. At times I thought that areas of the skull had warped, but what seems like warping may be an irreducible cement-preserved set of the fragments. In trying to correct these malpositioned parts it was discouraging, after soaking off a piece of bone with acetone, to find it still encased in a sticky envelope of cement and then in the course of brushing off the remaining cement to have the bone crumble into little pieces. Under these circumstances it seemed better to leave undisturbed the areas where fragments fit reasonably well together. Also, of course, I had to assume when I could not prove otherwise that the pieces belonged where I found them. To some extent, therefore, I attribute my failure in satisfactorily restoring this specimen to the presence of the cement. This statement is not intended as criticism of the preparatorial work on this specimen. Probably any other method of handling would have yielded much less information.

Before considering the findings, it may be helpful to explain the curious position of the skull in relation to the vertebrae and left scapula. I would judge that sometime after death the skull rolled or

---

[2] A description of the cervical vertebrae appears in the volume honoring Adolph H. Schultz (Stewart, 1962).

[3] This and subsequent photographs were made by Antran Evan in 1960, using a lens of shorter focal length.

was forced backward on the thorax and came to rest on its right side with the occiput between the spinous processes of the upper thoracic vertebrae and the inner side of the left scapula.   In the course of this unnatural movement the atlas became detached from the foramen magnum and, still alined with the other vertebrae, came to rest against the pterygoids and between the ascending rami of the lower jaw. Since with the skull in this position the face was toward the excavation, it is understandable why the latter was the part first encountered and hence why it was damaged.

I spent the last 2 weeks of July 1960 at the cave helping to recover the rest of the postcranial skeleton of Shanidar II.   Unfortunately, only a few more vertebrae—three thoracic and four lumbar—parts of three ribs, and the left tibia and fibula were found.   Obviously, therefore, this was a partial or disturbed burial.

As the pictures show, the right side of the skull and lower jaw is better preserved than the left side.   The same is true of the skull and lower jaw of Shanidar I.   For this reason most of the comparisons will be made from this point of view.

LOWER JAW

Plate 5 and plate 6, figure 1, and the corresponding interpretative drawings made on a stereograph (pl. 4 and pl. 6, fig. 2) show the form of the lower jaw as reconstructed.   From these it is evident that no connection remained between the right and left halves in the symphyseal region.   In orienting the two halves, the amount of space needed for the missing central incisors was estimated and the preserved bottom midpoint of the symphysis was oriented in relation to the midpoint of the tooth row.[4]   Also, there was no clear connection between the left horizontal and ascending rami, and these parts had to be oriented visually.   In trying to achieve a symmetrical-looking jaw, reasonable dimensions were sacrificed, with the result that probably the posterior part of the dental arch is too wide and the condyles too far apart, mainly because the sides of the jaw are a little too much inclined outward at the top (or inclined inward at the bottom).   It should be added that almost the whole inner left side and the forepart of the inner right side were missing and had to be reconstructed with a filler compound (Savogran), either by reference to the intact side or by reference to the jaw of Shanidar I.   No accuracy is claimed for the result.   Note, too, that although both coronoid processes are intact, the tops and foreparts of both condyles have had to be reconstructed.   The resulting shapes are only approximate.   In spite of such deficiencies, I believe the lateral views of the jaw cannot be far wrong.

---

[4] A fragment of the lower left central incisor turned up in the loose fragments after the reconstruction of the lower jaw was finished and the illustrations completed.

In plate 4, figure 1, and plate 6, figure 2, outline drawings of the corresponding views of Shanidar I have been added for comparison. In both lateral and superior aspects, as these drawings show, the two jaws are remarkably similar, discounting the differences in tooth wear due to age differentials.[5] Shanidar II has a sturdier right coronoid process, but then Shanidar I has an almost equally sturdy process on the left side. Shanidar II also has a somewhat more prominent gonial angle (with a little more lateral flare that does not show in the illustrations) and a shallower sigmoid notch. The difference in angulation of the condyles is especially noteworthy, as is the difference in thickness of the rami. Actually, Shanidar II is slightly larger and heavier throughout the rami.

Plate 6, figure 2, should be compared with the similarly constructed figure 164 in McCown and Keith (1939), here reproduced as figure 1.

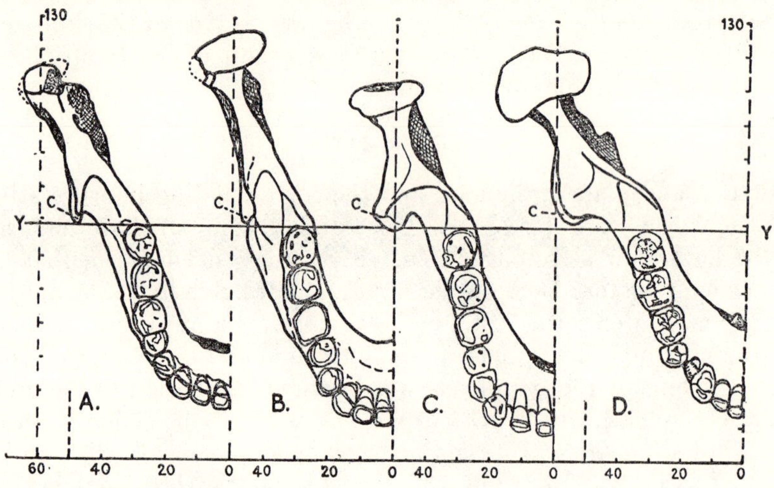

FIGURE 1.—McCown and Keith's (1939) figure 164 showing the superior aspect of the lower jaws of Tabūn I (A), Tabūn II (B), Skhūl V (C), and Krapina J after Kramberger (D). Y–Y, postmolar transverse axis; c, tip of coronoid process. (Reproduced by permission.)

In the latter figure all the Mount Carmel specimens have their coronoid processes touching the postmolar transverse axis, indicating a much more forward tilt to the processes in those specimens. Also, the anterior tooth-carrying portion is relatively longer than the posterior muscular portion in the Mount Carmel specimens, whereas the two portions are about equal in the Shanidar specimens.

The following figures (in millimeters) give some idea of how the Shanidar jaws compare in size with each other and with other

---

[5] Judging from tooth wear and arthritis, Shanidar II could not have been over 30 years of age; Shanidar I was probably at least 40 years of age. Both are thought to be males.

Neanderthals as reported by McCown and Keith (1939, pp. 211, 229–230):

	Shanidar		Tabūn	Skhūl			La Chapelle
	I	II	II	IV	V	VI	
Bicondylar width	144. 0	(156. 0)	(130. 0)	(132. 0)	(132. 0)	----	147. 0
M₂–M₂ width	70. 2	(72. 5)	66. 2	-----	-----	----	------
Minimum width of ascending ramus	[a] 40. 0	44. 0	40. 0	(42. 5)	36. 2	(42. 0)	43. 0
Height of symphysis	37. 0	37. 0	(42. 0)	42. 5	36. 5	----	36. 0
Height of ramus at M₂	[b] 34. 0	[b] 34. 0	38. 5	35. 5	34. 5	----	------

[a] On left; 42.0 on right.
[b] On right; 35.0 on left.

Plate 7, figures 1 and 2, show the inner side of the lower jaws of Shanidar II and I, respectively. Obviously, the basic morphological pattern is the same for both specimens. All the elements that Keith stressed in connection with the Mount Carmel jaws (McCown and Keith, 1939, p. 226, fig. 161) are well developed here, and especially what he called the lingual supramarginal sulcus. In Shanidar I this sulcus is so deep that the external surface of the ascending ramus becomes convex. The contrary is the case in Shanidar II.

Visible in these views also is the form of the mylohyoid canal. Although it is open in Shanidar I and is visible for a distance of 23 mm. below the mandibular foramen, in Shanidar II it enters a 5-mm.-long tunnel about 11 mm. below the foramen. Whether in Shanidar II this canal was symmetrical on the two sides, as in Shanidar I, cannot, of course, be determined. The differing shapes of the lingula, the bone flange shielding the medial side of the mandibular foramen, is also apparent.

Just as important as the differences between these lower jaws are the differences between their two sides; in other words, their asymmetries. Lacking numerous specimens from the same stratigraphic level for comparison, we gain some insight into individual variation from whatever asymmetries exist. From what remains of the jaw of Shanidar II, and this means mainly external surfaces, it seems clear that the ascending rami were fairly symmetrical, the main difference between the two sides being a greater external concavity on the right. The coronoid processes and sigmoid notches are very much alike in this specimen. By contrast, the jaw of Shanidar I is quite asymmetrical posteriorly. The supramarginal sulcus noted on the inner side of the right ramus as being extraordinarily deep is represented on the left side by one that is shallow. Correspondingly, whereas the external surface of the ascending ramus is convex on the right, it is concave on the left. Perhaps these morphological differences explain the far greater development of marginal tubercles in this area on the right side, as compared with the left. The differences in the coronoid processes have already been mentioned.

Several features cannot be compared in detail owing to the location of breakage in Shanidar II. For instance, almost complete loss of bone in the symphyseal area makes it impossible to determine whether the same cross-sectional shape existed as in Shanidar I (fig. 2).

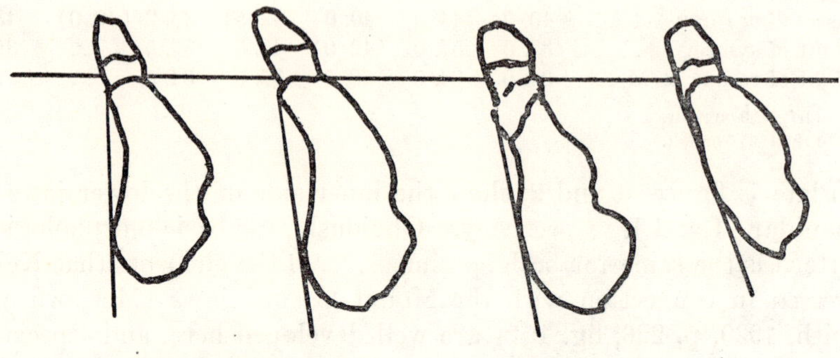

FIGURE 2.—Outline of sagittal section through mandibular symphysis of Shanidar I compared with the same section of three other specimens supplied by McCown and Keith (1939, figs. 143, 144, 148).

However, the small piece of symphyseal base that is preserved shows sculpturing (digastric fossa) comparable to that of Shanidar I. Nor is it certain that lateral infracondylar tubercles existed in Shanidar II, although the conformation of the remaining part of the right condyle would suggest it. On the other hand, breakage has just spared most, if not all, of the mental foramina. It is positive, therefore, that whereas Shanidar I has a single large foramen on each side, Shanidar II, like many Neanderthalers, has multiple foramina: at least two on the right and three on the left.

UPPER FACE

Damage to the midline of the face at the time of discovery, as already explained, together with the crushing that took place in ancient times, greatly restricted the possibilities of reconstruction in this area. Nevertheless, very fortunately it has been possible to learn a great deal about the original form. In general, there can be little doubt that it was a Neanderthal face like that of Shanidar I, but with certain differences. From several unconnected pieces of the supraorbital ridges, these structures appear to be every bit as heavy as those of Shanidar I, and likely of much the same form.

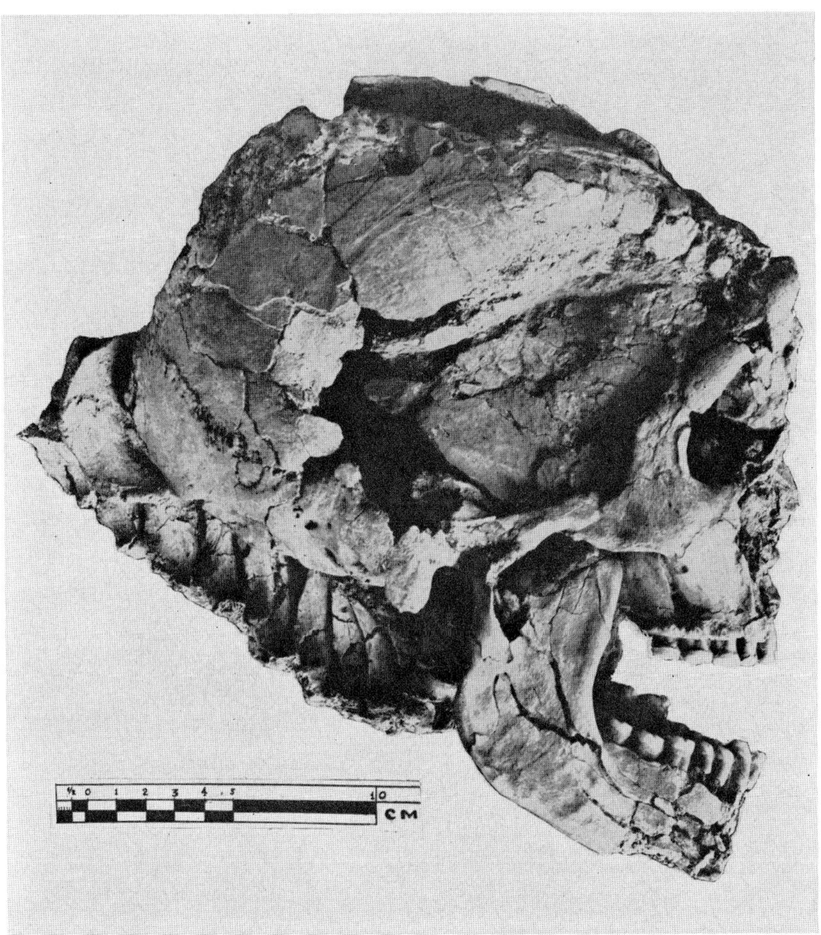

Right side of skull of Shanidar II after initial cleaning in 1957. Note cervical and upper thoracic vertebrae extending along base and at occiput meeting left scapula protruding from left side.

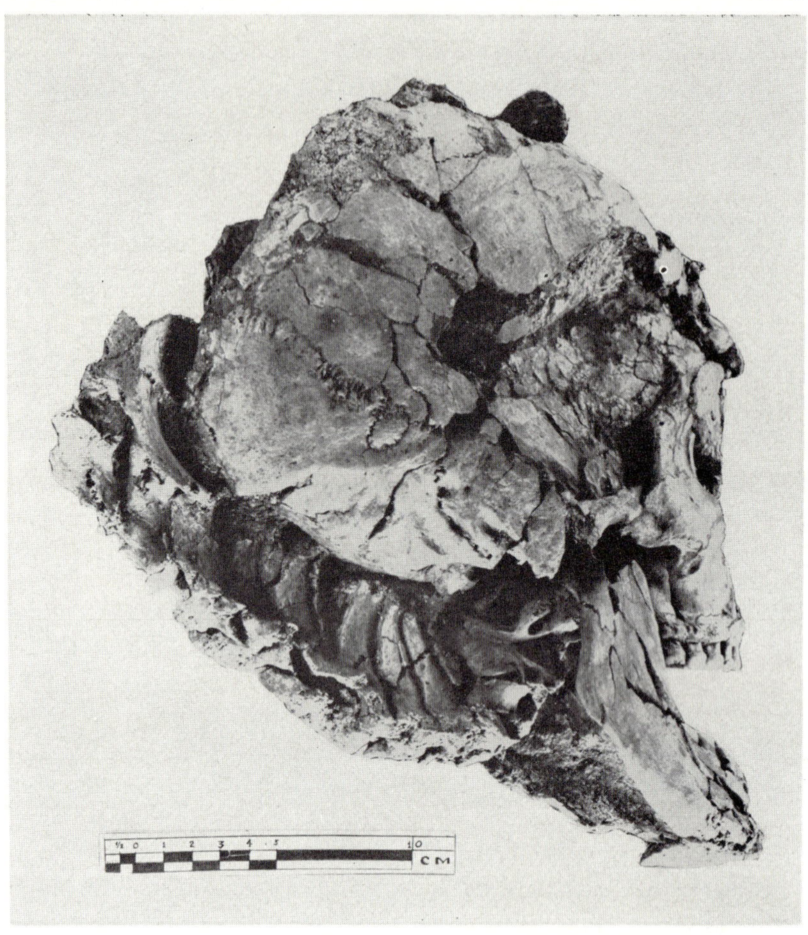

Right side of occiput of the Shanidar II skull after initial cleaning in 1957.

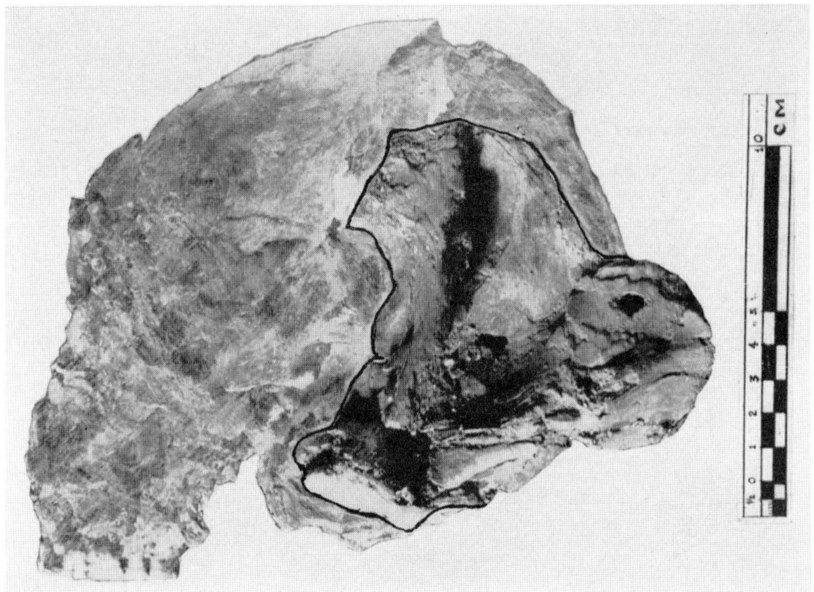

2. Appearance of scapula attached to left rear of the Shanidar II skull after removal of vertebrae in 1960.

1. Left side of face of the Shanidar II skull after initial cleaning in 1957. Note that scapula is not apparent.

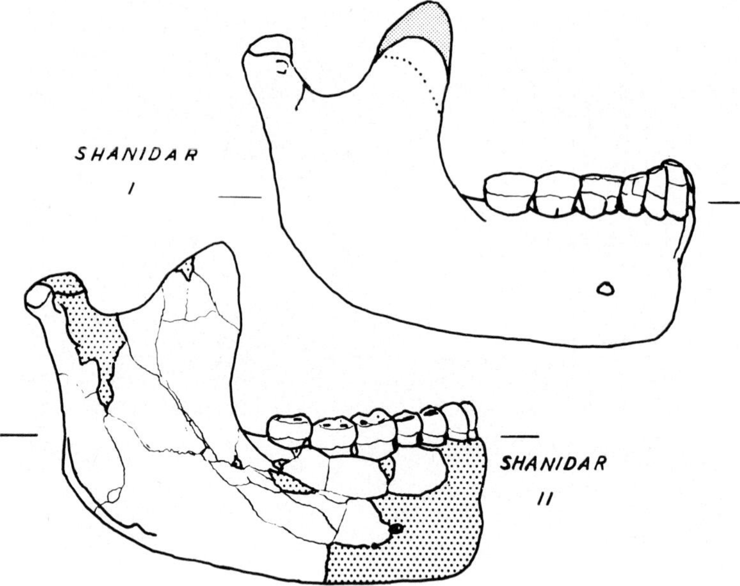

1. Stereographic drawings of the right side of the lower jaws of Shanidar I (simplified) and Shanidar II.   In the case of Shanidar I the coronoid process is shown as restored originally (immediately above dotted line) and as restored to match that of Shanidar II (fine stippling).   Coarse stippling indicates missing bone.

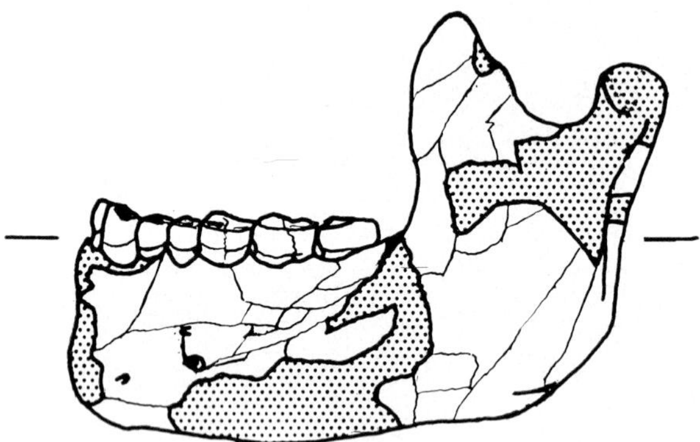

2. Stereographic drawing of the left side of the lower jaw of Shanidar II.   Stippling indicates missing bone.

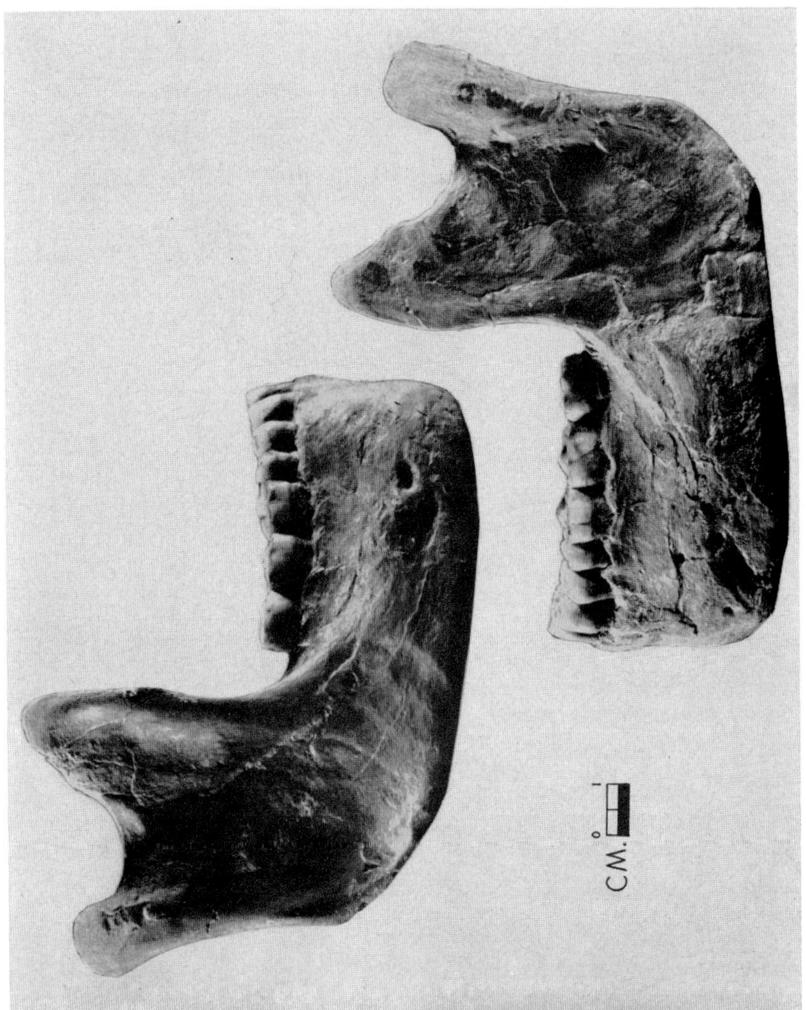

Upper left: right side of the restored lower jaw of Shanidar II; *lower right:* left side of same jaw.

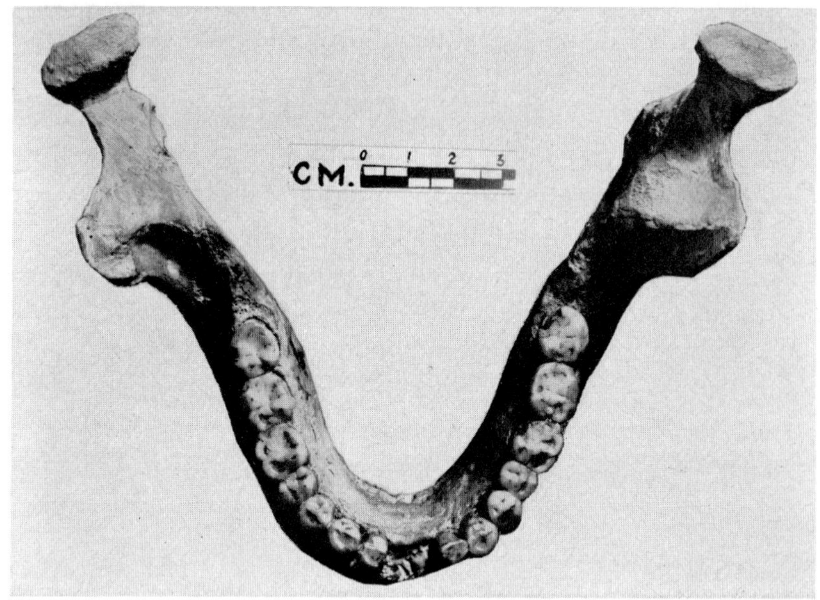

1. Superior aspect of the restored lower jaw of Shanidar II.

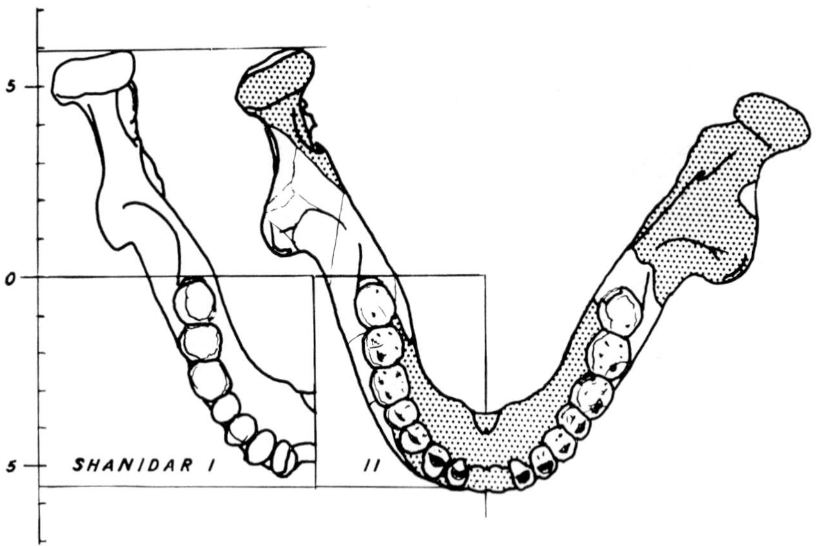

2. Stereographic drawings of the superior aspect of the lower jaws of Shanidar I (right half simplified) and Shanidar II, arranged according to the scheme of McCown and Keith (1939, fig. 164). Stippling indicates missing bone. Note that drawing of Shanidar II has been adjusted to improve on the actual restoration.

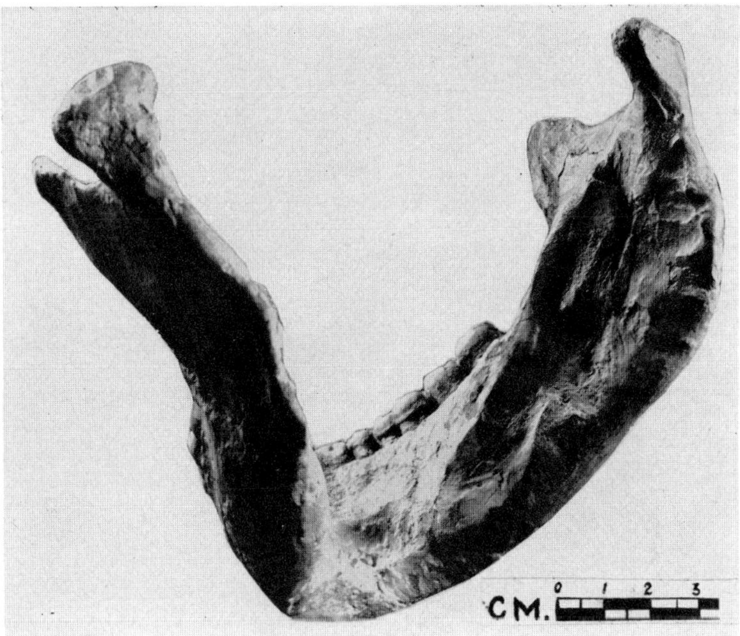

1. Inner aspect of right side of restored lower jaw of Shanidar II.

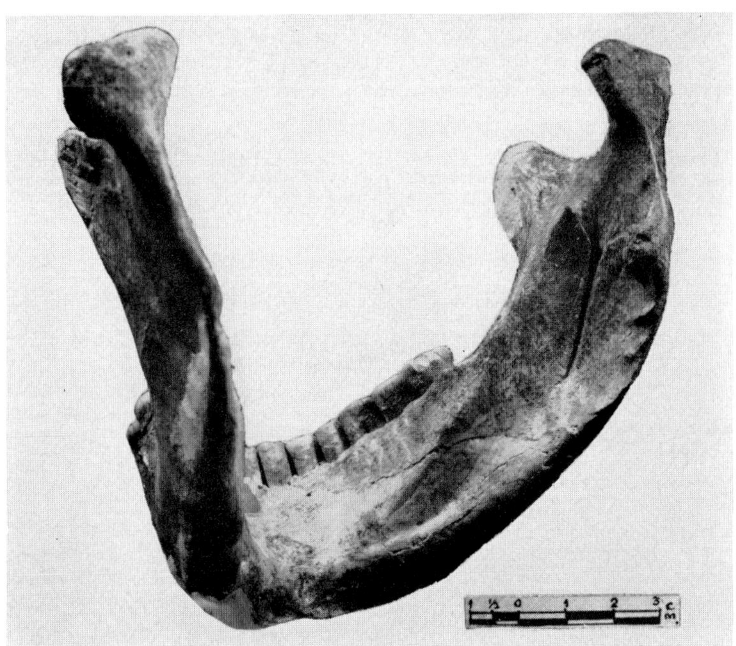

2. Inner aspect of right side of restored lower jaw of Shanidar I.

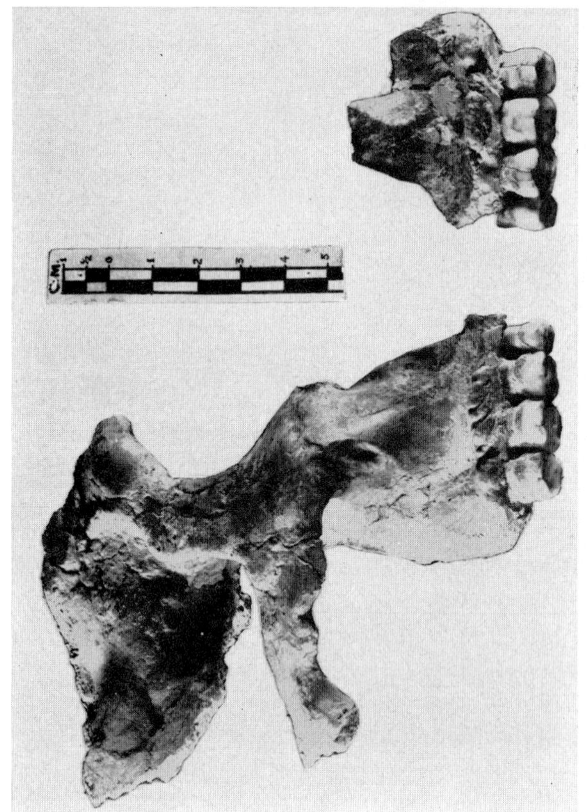

2. View of exostoses along upper alveolar margin above the molar teeth of both sides. Shanidar II.

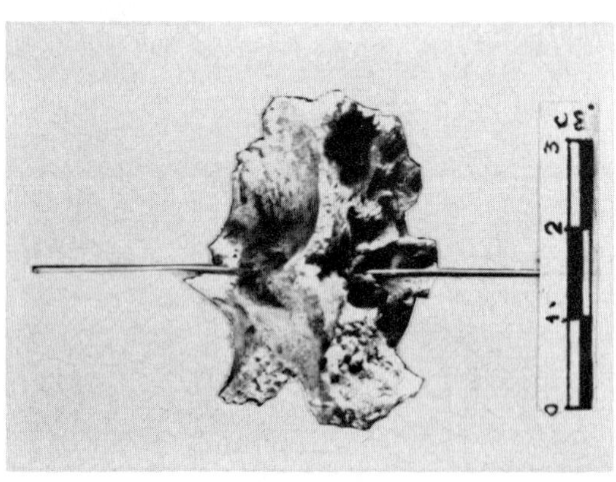

1. Rear view of the lower anterior portion of the nasal cavity (above) and of the anterior portion of the palate (below) in Shanidar II. Wire has been passed through the incisive canal. Note that the nasal floor declines back of the nasal aperture.

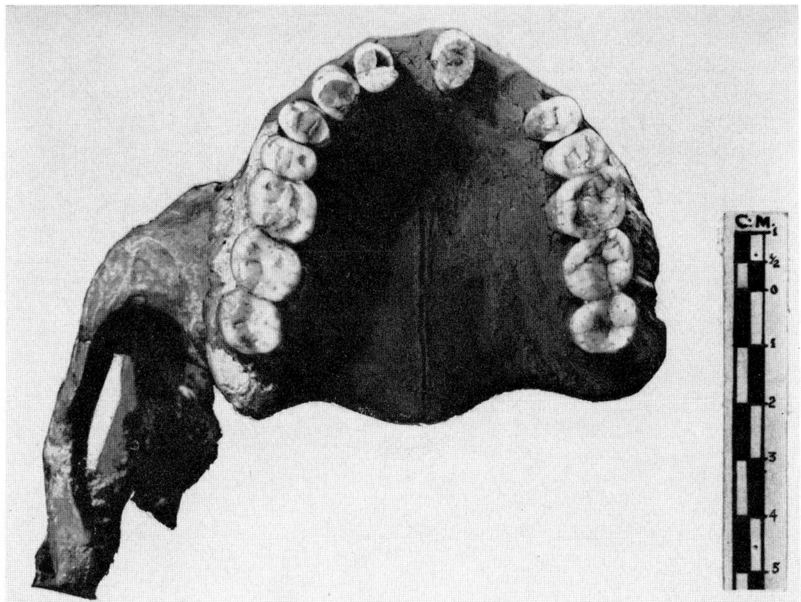

1. View of a temporary restoration of the upper jaw of Shanidar II showing tentative identification of damaged anterior teeth.

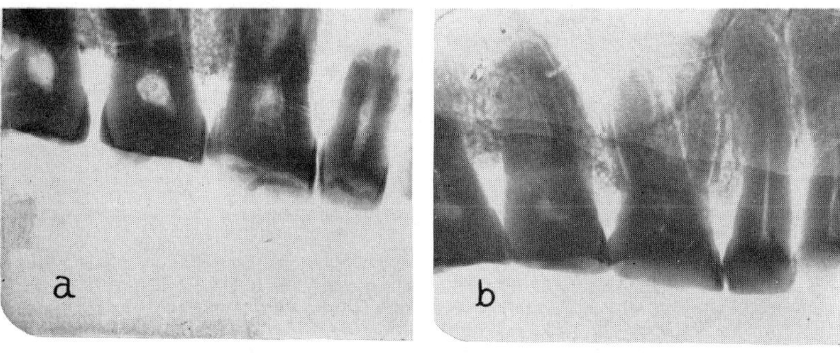

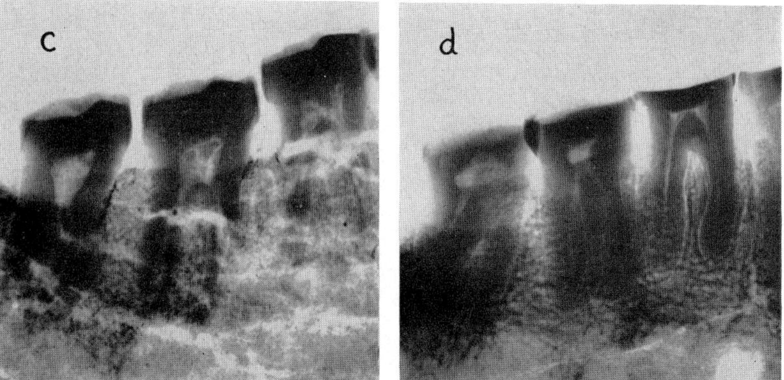

2. *a*, Radiograph of right upper molar teeth of Shanidar II made in 1957. *b*, Same for Shanidar I. *c*, Radiograph of the right lower molar teeth of Shanidar II made in 1957. *d*, Same for Shanidar I. (Courtesy of Radiological Institute, Baghdad.)

Orbital shape and size are indicated from the preserved lateral border on the right (fig. 3) and the medial border on the left (fig. 4). In both areas the likeness to Shanidar I is strong.

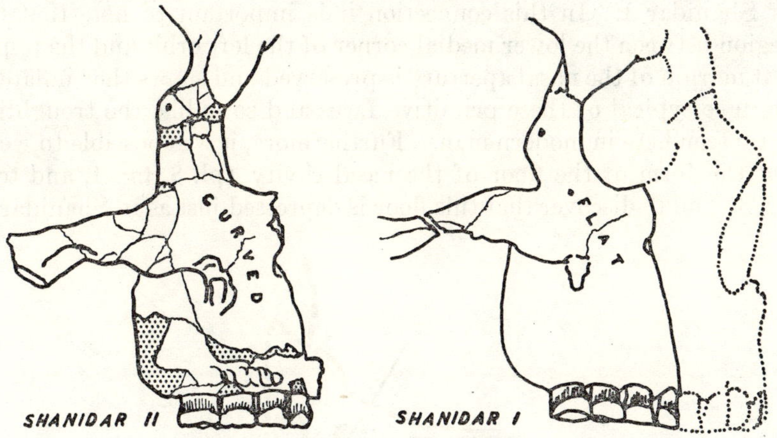

FIGURE 3.—Stereographic drawing of a fragment of the right side of the face of Shanidar II compared with a stereographic drawing of the same area in Shanidar I.

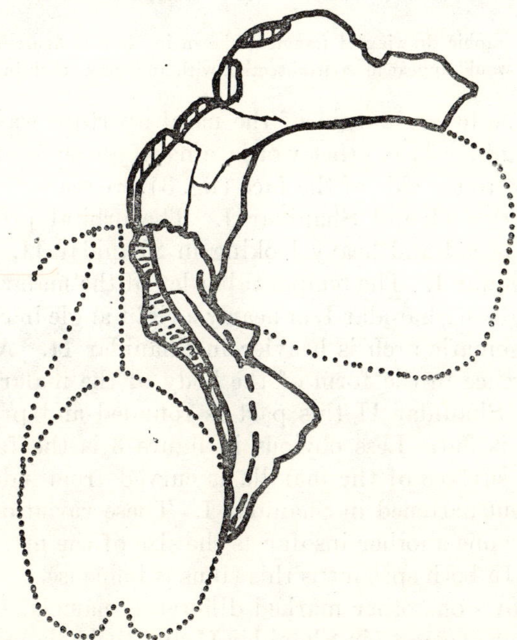

FIGURE 4.—Stereographic drawing of a fragment of the midface of Shanidar II. Note "inflation" of area between orbit and nose indicated by line of dashes. This line is the shortest surface distance between its terminal points. By laying the fragment on its side this line can be made to coincide with the horizontal plane.

Nasal shape and size are indicated by a fragment of the left side extending from the nasofrontal suture to the midportion of the nasal aperture (fig. 4). A convincing orientation of this fragment can be made around a nasal aperture of the same size and shape as that of Shanidar I. In this connection it is important to note that the region between the lower medial corner of the left orbit and the upper left margin of the nasal aperture is preserved and shows the "inflated" form so typical of these primitive faces and so unlike the troughlike form seen here in modern man. Furthermore, it was possible to work out the form of the floor of the nasal cavity (pl. 8, fig. 1, and text fig. 5) and to discover that this floor is depressed just as in Shanidar I.

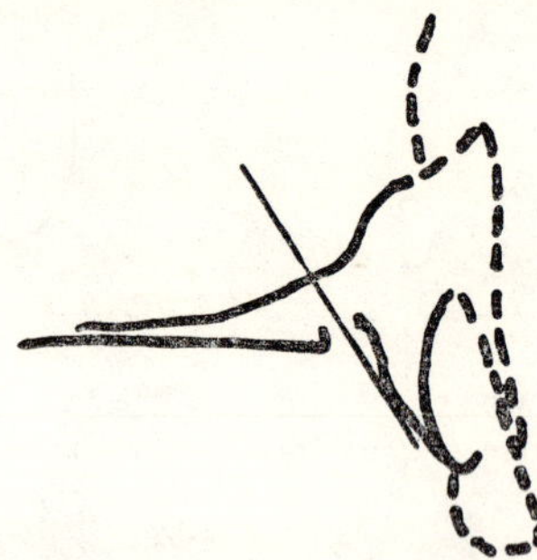

Figure 5.—Stereographic drawing of fragment shown in plate 8, figure 1, showing how the latter would appear in sagittal section with an incisor tooth in place.

Likely, also, the lower margin of the nasal aperture was fairly distinct as in Shanidar I; in other words, a nasal gutter is absent.

Turning now to the side of the face (fig. 3), we see some differences between Shanidar II and Shanidar I. The orbital process of the malar bone is broad and heavy looking in Shanidar II, slender and gracile in Shanidar I. The temporal border of the malar is indented at an acute angle in Shanidar I, at nearly a right angle in Shanidar II. The whole zygomatic arch is heavier in Shanidar II. Added to all this is a difference in the form of the body of the malar in the two specimens: In Shanidar II this part is rounded and prominent, in Shanidar I it is flat. Less obvious in figure 3 is the fact that the infratemporal surface of the maxilla is curved from side to side in Shanidar II, but flattened in Shanidar I. These variations probably compensate for one another insofar as the size of the maxillary sinus is concerned. In both specimens this sinus is immense.

Figure 3 shows one other marked difference, namely, the presence of large alveolar exostoses in Shanidar II and their absence in Shanidar I. Plate 8, figure 2, shows how symmetrical the exostoses are on the two sides. It would seem that such exostoses bear no relationship to the process of mastication, since the teeth of Shanidar II are much less worn than those of Shanidar I and the latter lacks exostoses of this sort. In any case, as far as I know at present, this is the earliest example of alveolar exostoses to come to light.

DENTITION

As explained at the beginning, all the lower teeth with the exception of the right central incisor were recovered. Three of the upper teeth are missing: a canine (left?), a lateral incisor (left?), and a central incisor (right?).[6] The uncertainty about the position of these upper teeth is due to the difficulty of identifying some of the front teeth that were recovered. The damage to the midface at the time of discovery reduced some of the teeth to fragments and all the pieces were not recovered. Plate 9, figure 1, shows the occlusal surfaces of the upper teeth according to the best identification that could be made under the circumstances. By comparison with the corresponding view of the lower teeth (pl. 6, fig. 1) it is evident that in both jaws tooth wear increases from the third molars forward to the incisors. Also, in the upper jaw wear is greatest on the lingual cusps, whereas in the lower jaw it is greatest on the buccal cusps. The teeth of the two sides appear to be worn about equally.

The teeth of Shanidar II can be compared with those of Shanidar I only in a general way, because of the difference in wear. So worn are all the teeth of Shanidar I that the exposure of dentine is complete in all cases and in a few (first molars, canines, incisors) little or no enamel remains. A notable fact, however, is the rather uniform size of the lower molars in both specimens. The upper molars are shorter and broader, and the upper third molars have undergone slight reduction in the proximo-distal diameter. This is shown by the following measurements (in millimeters) of the Shanidar II molars:

	Proximo-distal diameter				*Bucco-lingual diameter*		
M^3	{ R 10.0 { L 10.0	M_3	{ R 11.0 { L 12.0	M^3	{ R 12.0 { L 12.0	M_3	{ R 10.7 { L 11.0
M^2	{ R 10.5 { L 10.5	M_2	{ R 11.0 { L 12.2	M^2	{ R 12.5 { L 12.5	M_2	{ R 11.2 { L 11.2
M^1	{ R 10.5 { L 10.5	M_1	{ R 11.0 { L 11.3	M^1	{ R 12.0 { L 12.0	M_1	{ R 11.0 { L 11.0?

Even more remarkable is the size of the lower incisors in both Shanidar specimens; they are very large bucco-lingually as compared with corresponding modern teeth. The lower lateral incisors of Shanidar

---

[6] After this paper was completed, I accidentally discovered three loose upper anterior teeth among some postcranial fragments of Shanidar I. It seems likely that these are the missing teeth of Shanidar II, but more study is needed to settle this point.

II have their greatest bucco-lingual diameter below the enamel and it amounts to 9 mm. The figure is only a little less in the case of Shanidar I (8.0–8.2 mm.).

A selection of the radiographs made in 1957 are given in plate 9, figure 2, *a–d*. These show moderately large pulp cavities in the only slightly worn molars of Shanidar II and greatly reduced pulp cavities in the much worn molars of Shanidar I. Neanderthals are no longer regarded as being unusual in their tendency to taurodontism (large pulp cavities).

<h3 style="text-align:center">SKULL VAULT</h3>

Relative to size the skull vault yielded less information than the lower jaw and face. This was to be expected, because so little of the vault is characterized by surface relief. Fortunately, the one area that does have surface relief, the occiput, is preserved in its right half. The intact fragment (fig. 6) includes, among other things, half of the lambdoid suture, the mastoid process, and half of the foramen magnum. Viewed from the outside, the moderately intricate pattern of the lambdoid suture stands out boldly, showing no signs of closure; but on the inside there is no such pattern, only a fissure, or more likely a postmortem crack. I conclude, therefore, that endocranial suture closure has taken place in this area. As so often is the case, the external part of this suture is made up of serrations of bone from the occipital overlapping the parietal elements. It is noteworthy, also, that the suture takes a fairly direct course from the midline to the point of juncture with the temporal bone. This is very different from the curving course of the suture in Shanidar I (fig. 6) and may denote more dolichocrany.

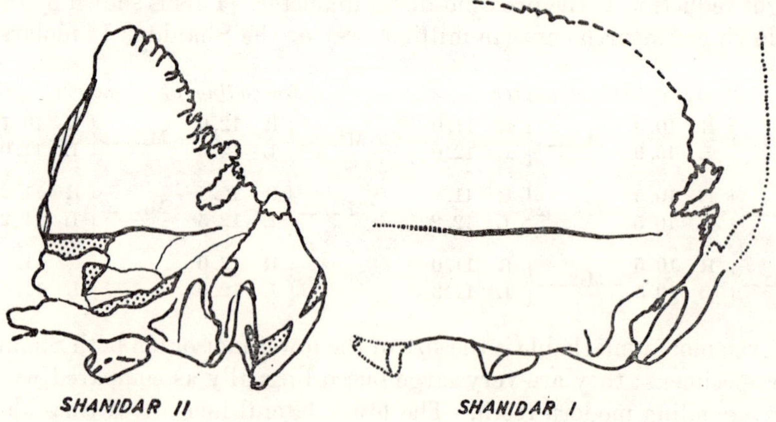

FIGURE 6.—Stereographic drawing of right occipitotemporal fragment of Shanidar II compared with a stereographic drawing of the same area in Shanidar I. Both specimens oriented with the sagittal axis of the foramen magnum horizontal.

The mastoid process of Shanidar II is much larger than that of Shanidar I; indeed the tip of the process extends lower than that of the occipitomastoid crest, which is the reverse of the situation in Shanidar I. Such a large mastoid process is unusual in Neanderthals. However, the occipitomastoid crest still is larger than in modern man. (Cf. Stewart, 1961). The occipitomastoid suture is still open.

The foramen magnum must have had a long oval shape just as in Shanidar I. Probably in both cases the length was around 41 to 42 mm. and the width around 26 to 28 mm. The right occipital condyle of Shanidar II and both condyles of Shanidar I impress me as being small in proportion to the size of the foramen. The posterior border of the right condyle of Shanidar II is not well defined owing to the presence here of an arthritic area. This is the reason for the question mark in the following list of measurements of the occipital condyles:

		Shanidar	
		I	II
Maximum length (mm.)	R	23.5	25.0?
	L	22.0	----
Maximum width (mm.)	R	11.0	13.0
	L	13.0	----

The occipital torus has about equal prominence in the two specimens, but is shorter in Shanidar II in conformity with the generally narrowed upper part of the occipital squama in this specimen.

As for the rest of the vault, only a few additional facts could be gleaned. The sagittal suture is gone entirely. A good part of the area of the left half of the coronal suture is present. Unlike the external lambdoid suture, the external coronal does not stand out boldly and has disappeared lateral to the temporal line. Loss of inner table here makes it impossible to determine the status of the suture internally.

The original thickness of the skull vault could not be investigated in many places, but it was noted that the midright parietal reached a maximum thickness of 11 mm. at one point. The surrounding area did not exceed 8 to 9 mm. in thickness. Much the same thing was observed in Shanidar I. Thus, these skulls would not be considered primitive on the basis of vault thickness.

In view of the fact that Shanidar I has ear exostoses, the remains of the right auditory meatus of Shanidar II were explored and a loose nodule of bone resembling an exostosis recovered. This finding obviously contains the elements of wishful thinking and therefore does not deserve to be accepted as proof of the existence of ear exostoses in this case.

DISCUSSION

The reason for comparing the second skull found in Shanidar cave mainly with the first skull is their differing antiquity. Shanidar II was found 8½ feet lower in the cave deposit than Shanidar I (and some distance to the west) and on this basis is judged to be 10,000 to 15,000 years older (Solecki, 1960a and b). One no longer expects to discover an evolutionary change in skull form in such a short period of time, so interest now centers on learning more about individual variability in those ancient times (in this case up to about 60,000 years ago). The roughly contemporaneous Mount Carmel Neanderthals of Palestine were found by McCown and Keith (1939) to be so variable that these authors considered them to be in "the throes of evolutionary change." The writer, on the other hand, has argued (1960) that the Mount Carmel remains represent two very different isolates, one of which was present at Shanidar. This is based mostly on a peculiarity of the pubic bone, a part unfortunately not recovered in the case of Shanidar II. In view of these diverse opinions, and considering that Shanidar cave is located in a mountainous area (virtually a refuge area), it is of current interest to know whether or not Shanidar presents a parallel to Mount Carmel in individual variability.

The results of my present investigation lead me to conclude that the first two Shanidar skulls are remarkably alike in features unaffected by age changes. Both appear to be almost classic Neanderthals; also, both possess a curious feature—depression of the nasal floor—which thus far appears to be unique to the inhabitants of this cave. I am immensely impressed that this unique feature occurs in two skulls from the same place but so widely separated in time. I am much less impressed by the accompanying variations in such things as mastoid size, face flatness, etc. Variations of the latter sort, like differences in stature, occur in every population and are too often given undue emphasis when observed in isolated ancient specimens.

The Fourth Shanidar Expedition discovered remains of other Neanderthals from both levels before this report was completed. This new material should add more to our knowledge of the variability of the local population at each time period. Unfortunately, however, experience shows that much time and effort will have to be expended on restoration and study before the information from this source will be forthcoming. For the present, therefore, the evidence indicates that the Shanidar Neanderthals retained an almost classic skull form from about 60,000 years ago until about 45,000 years ago, when the Mousterian cultural period ended and, as far as we know, the type disappeared.

LITERATURE CITED

McCown, Theodore D., and Keith, Sir Arthur.
    1939. The stone age of Mount Carmel. The fossil human remains from the Lavalloiso-Mousterian, vol. 2, xxiv+390 pp., pls. 1–28, Oxford.

SOLECKI, RALPH S.
  1957. Shanidar cave. Sci. Amer., vol. 197, No. 5, pp. 58–64.
  1960a. Neanderthal men in the heart-land of human evolution: Discoveries
        at Shanidar cave, in northern Iraq. Illus. London News, May 7,
        pp. 772–775.
  1960b. Three adult Neanderthal skeletons from Shanidar cave, northern
        Iraq. Ann. Rep. Smithsonian Inst. for 1959, pp. 603–635.
STEWART, T. D.
  1958. First views of the restored Shanidar I skull. Sumer, vol. 14, Nos. 1
        and 2, pp. 90–95. Reprinted in Ann. Rep. Smithsonian Inst. for
        1958, pp. 473–480, 1959.
  1960. Form of the pubic bone in Neanderthal man. Science, vol. 131, May
        13, pp. 1437–1438.
  1961. A neglected primitive feature of the Swanscombe skull. *In* Homenaje
        a Pablo Martínez del Río en el xxv aniversario de la edición de Los
        Orígenes Americanos, pp. 207–217. Mexico.
  1962. Neanderthal cervical vertebrae, with special attention to the Shanidar
        Neanderthals from Iraq. Bibl. Primat, vol. 1 (Adolph H. Schultz
        anniversary volume).

Heyerdahl's Kon-Tiki Theory and Its Relation to Ethnobotany

By F. P. JONKER

Professor of Special Botany
University of Utrecht, Netherlands

IT IS well known that in the year 1947 an expedition conducted by the Norwegian biologist and ethnologist Thor Heyerdahl crossed the eastern Pacific by balsa raft. The voyage started in Peru and after 101 days reached the Polynesian island of Raroia. Inspiring this voyage was Heyerdahl's theory that the Polynesian islands had been populated not from a western direction, i.e., from the Malaysian area by way of Micronesia or Melanesia, but that Polynesia had been reached by two successive waves of immigrants from America. According to this concept, the first immigrants reached Polynesia by balsa raft about A.D. 500 from South America; the second wave arrived more than 500 years later by double canoes, perhaps from Asia but using British Columbia as a temporary steppingstone. This theory, consequently, assumes that the first wave of immigrants, identified by Heyerdahl with a pre-Inca population of Peru, crossed the eastern Pacific. To support this concept, he utilized arguments from mythology, language, and culture, referring especially to buildings and to such monoliths (megaliths) as statues representing human figures.

The principal objection originally expressed against this theory was that these Peruvian Indians were no navigators. They possessed boats made of totora reed (*Scirpus totara* (Nees et Meyen) Kunth), in which they sailed on Lake Titicaca, and rafts of the very light balsa wood, *Ochroma lagopus* Sw., by which they navigated the coasts. It was commonly believed, however, that these rafts would

---

[1] Slightly modified and translated by the author from his "Heyerdahl's Kon-Tiki Theorie en de Ethnobotanie," delivered as his inaugural address as professor of special botany at the University of Utrecht, Netherlands, on Nov. 21, 1960; the original Dutch version was separately printed in Amsterdam as of that date.

not be seaworthy and that they would by no means be suitable craft on which to cross the ocean. Heyerdahl then decided to make a faithful copy of an old Peruvian balsa raft, and on this, with five companions, he attempted to cross the eastern Pacific driven by wind and by currents. As mentioned above, this daring voyage succeeded and the raft and its passengers arrived in good condition on the reef of Raroia in the Tuamotu Islands. The raft was equipped as it might have been 1,500 years ago with the exception of a wireless set and certain other modern inventions. In addition to fruits and tubers which they took along, the travelers obtained from the sea sufficient food for the voyage. Such a journey had great appeal to the general public, and Heyerdahl's popular account became a bestseller and was translated into many languages. But when we ask ourselves what was proved by this adventurous expedition, we must answer that the voyage established only that it is possible to cross this part of the Pacific Ocean from east to west by means of a balsa raft provided with sails. The trip did not prove that the pre-Incas or any other South American inhabitants left Peru in that way and formed the original population of Polynesia. To be fair to Heyerdahl, one must add that he never made such a claim. The popular book describing this voyage, "The Kon-Tiki Expedition" (1948), provided its author with enough income so that he was able to fit out another expedition, this time to Easter Island, where he collected more data to support his theory.

In 1952 Heyerdahl published a detailed voluminous work, "American Indians in the Pacific," in which he collected all the arguments in favor of his theory. In the present review I omit the arguments borrowed from language, cultures, mythology, anthropology, zoology, and other disciplines. I wish only to remark here that the author gives evidence of his wide knowledge of both western South America and Polynesia, but on the other hand he appears to be not very familiar with Indonesia. In the following pages I restrict myself to a discussion of his botanical documentation, especially in the field of ethnobotany. Such documentation we find assembled in a special chapter of his book.

Before Heyerdahl's study appeared, the occurrence and use of the sweet potato, *Ipomoea batatas* (L.) Lam., in Polynesia had already been amply discussed in the ethnobotanical literature. In a publication by Dixon (1932, p. 40), we find the problem summarized in the following words:

If we accept the present conclusions of the botanists that the sweet potato is a plant of undoubted Central or South American origin, then the fact of its widespread occurence in Polynesia in the eighteenth century, as reported by the

great explorers of the period, can be explained only in one of three ways. Either
the plant had been introduced by the Spanish from South America in the six-
teenth and seventeenth centuries when the earliest European discoveries in the
Pacific were being made, or it was of pre-Columbian introduction accomplished
either by Polynesians who visited South America and brought the new food plant
back with them, or by Peruvian or other American Indian navigators who carried
it with them in exploring voyages to the west.

The first possibility may be rejected for sound historical reasons:
the first European travelers reported the occurrence of extensive plan-
tations of sweet potatoes in the islands visited.   The second possibility
is frequently accepted.   The third alternative is the one emphasized
by Heyerdahl, who argued that the crop is known in Polynesia by
its Peruvian name "kumara," and also that, according to old myths,
the ancestors of the Polynesians originated from the country where
the "kumara" grew.   Riesenfeld (1951), on the other hand, states
that according to old Polynesian myths the native country of the
Polynesians was situated somewhere in the west.   Also, Sir Peter H.
Buck, the distinguished former director of the Bernice P. Bishop
Museum in Honolulu and a recognized authority in the field of Polynesian myths and legends, nowhere in his most readable book "Vikings
of the Sunrise" (1937) mentions tales to the effect that the Polynesians
came from the east.   It was Buck's belief that a Polynesian canoe
expedition in pre-Columbian times left the Marquesas and, sailing
in an easterly direction, reached Peru.   After disembarking on the
continent, the travelers returned after a short stay in fear of conflicts
with the natives, first laying in a supply of sweet potatoes, perhaps
among other foods.   Harold St. John (1953, 1954), an authority on
the vegetation of Polynesia, considered Buck's theory the most likely
explanation of the early occurrence of *Ipomoea batatas* in the Polynesian archipelago.   E. D. Merrill, a leading student of the Aus-
tralasian tropical flora and a decided opponent of Heyerdahl's theory,
at first (1937) considered the sweet potato of American origin and
the single American plant among the species mentioned by Heyerdahl.
However, in one of his last publications (1954) Merrill stated that
it is now admitted that *I. batatas* may have originated outside of
America, possibly in Africa, by hybridization.   In that case it could
have been carried across the Atlantic to America a few centuries before
Columbus reached the West Indies, and perhaps even earlier by way
of Madagascar and the Mascarene Islands to Malaysia, Papuasia, and
Polynesia, and even to the west coast of South America.   Certainly
an investigation of the African species of *Ipomoea* is needed in order
to clarify this hypothesis, and such an investigation may give the problem quite another aspect.   According to Merrill, moreover, it is also

possible that the vernacular name "kumara" is of Polynesian origin and reached Peru together with the plant.[2]

A second plant grown in pre-Columbian times both on the American Continent and in the Pacific islands is the bottle gourd, *Lagenaria siceraria* (Mol.) Standl. As a food crop this species was unimportant, but as a supplier of containers for water and other liquids it was and still is an extremely significant plant in tropical countries. Without doubt this species is of African origin. It was found in the Egyptian royal graves dating from 3000 B.C., and Captain Cook reported it as grown in Polynesia on his first voyage in 1769. The use of the bottle gourd spread from Africa over the Old World, and Eames and St. John (1943) believed that the distribution both on the American mainland and in the Pacific could be explained, as in the case of the sweet potato, by a hypothetical canoe expedition from Polynesia to Peru as suggested by Buck (1937). The Polynesian travelers would have taken the bottle gourd to South America with them and on the return voyage they would have brought back the sweet potato. However, more recently discovered data have made this hypothesis untenable, because archeological investigations in Peru have indicated that bottle gourd remains were, according to radiocarbon dating, 3,000 to 5,000 years old. This means that the species had been used in Peru long before the Polynesians lived in the Pacific islands. It is of course possible that Polynesian canoe expeditions fetched bottle gourds from Peru rather than having introduced them into that country. Heyerdahl believes that the bottle gourd reached South America at that early date through navigators from Africa, and that from Peru, together with the sweet potato, it reached Polynesia when those islands were populated by Peruvian pre-Incas.

Therefore the history of the distribution of the bottle gourd all over the Tropics is still unknown. In addition to the distribution by migrating pre-Incas, as suggested by Heyerdahl, the possibilities exist either that the gourd was taken home by a Polynesian canoe expedition that visited South America, or that it was introduced into Poly-

----

[2] For a discussion of the sweet potato problem, see also Hornell (1946). Very interesting comments on the sweet potato were made at the recent 10th Pacific Science Congress, in Honolulu, at a symposium entitled "Plants and the Migrations of Pacific Peoples," convened by Dr. Jacques Barrau on Aug. 28, 1961. At this symposium Dr. Douglas E. Yen expressed the opinion that *Ipomoea batatas,* a hexaploid and heterozygous species, was of hybrid origin in America, where the greatest morphological variability of the cultivated plant is seen. He pointed out that the species frequently produces seeds, each of which has the potential of developing into a distinct race, and that transportation could conceivably have been by nonhuman agencies. Dr. Ichizo Nishiyama indicated the probability that *I. batatas* was derived from the American *Ipomoea trifida* (H.B.K.) Don, also a hexaploid. In the same symposium Dr. Harold C. Conklin presented linguistic evidence to indicate that the sweet potato in Africa, Indonesia, and adjacent regions was almost certainly a European introduction. This symposium, which one hopes may be published in full, reached no conclusion as to the identity of the humans who may have first transported the sweet potato across the eastern Pacific.

nesia from Melanesia or from Micronesia—to say nothing of the possibility that the Polynesians reached their present living area by one of these latter routes. The oldest known finds in southeastern Asia indicate the occurrence of the bottle gourd in China sometime before the beginning of our era. For the sake of completeness, I must also add that Heyerdahl further adduces evidence that both in Peru and in some Polynesian islands gourds were used to make flutes.

Merrill (1954) believed it most probable that bottle gourds reached the South American coast from Africa in a floating state. He mentioned floating experiments showing that these gourds could stand floating in salt water for nearly 2 years and still contain viable seeds. He also was unable to provide any other explanation.

A third very important crop occurring already in pre-Columbian times both on the American mainland and on the Pacific islands, and in fact in nearly all tropical regions, is the coconut, *Cocos nucifera* L. Formerly this distribution was ascribed to the ability of the coconut to float for a long period. However, floating experiments have shown that coconuts drifting in sea water rather quickly lose their powers of germination, and that fruits floating more than 110 days are no longer viable. Heyerdahl's voyage on the Kon-Tiki raft supplied an important contribution, as the crossing lasted 101 days; but of course smaller objects drift somewhat more slowly. It seems out of the question, consequently, that drifting coconuts can cross this part of the Pacific within the critical period of 110 days. Moreover, the coconuts that floated on the raft in sea water decayed, and then the pelagic fauna rapidly completed their deterioration. However, the other coconuts on the raft that were not subjected to the sea water maintained their viability. I agree with Heyerdahl in concluding that the distribution of *Cocos* in pre-Columbian times was possible only with the help of man.

But there is no unanimity among botanists concerning the region of the origin of the species. A number of botanists regard South America as such, and especially either Colombia or Panama, since related genera and species occur in those countries. Also, old travel stories reported rich coconut vegetation in regions not previously visited by European travelers. Other competent botanists, e.g., Merrill (1937, 1954), are convinced, following Alphonse de Candolle (1883), that the species originated in the Old World Tropics. It is not necessary in this paper to review Merrill's arguments, but I shall only remark that his mention of fossil species, probably belonging to the genus *Cocos*, in both New Zealand and in India, in my opinion is irrelevant. Distribution by man must be connected with the recent area of distribution of the species. A large number of genera and species in Tertiary times occupied an area covering two or three continents, whereas these same groups in recent times are restricted to a part of one continent only. We must conclude that the distribution of *Cocos nucifera* does not establish anything in favor of Heyerdahl's theories, since no certainty exists as to its original area. Heyerdahl also agrees with this conclusion. Buck (1937) cited a Polynesian myth in which the coconut is said to have originated from the head of the demigod Tuna after he was beaten and killed; the nut still shows the mouth and eyes of Tuna. This story of course does not cast any light on the situation. Riesenfeld (1951) has called attention to the fact that archeological investigations in Peru have never brought to light the remains of coconuts.

Up to the present, only the three useful plants discussed above can cast doubt upon the final conclusions of Alphonse de Candolle (1883) in his classical work "Origine des plantes cultivées." De Candolle, in that work (English translation of 1885, pp. 461, 462) wrote: "In the history of cultivated plants I did not find any indication as to contact between the populations of the Old World and of the New World before the discovery of America by Columbus." And he added, "Between America and Asia perhaps two transports of useful plants took place: one by man [sweetpotato], the other either by man or by currents [coconut]."

Much dependence is placed upon cotton by Heyerdahl. In Polynesia some wild species occur (*Gossypium taitense* Parl. and *G. tomentosum* Nutt.), and Heyerdahl here refers to the investigations of J. B. Hutchinson, R. A. Silow, and S. G. Stephens (1947). These investigators found that the Old World species of cotton possess a haploid number of 13 large chromosomes, the wild American species of cotton have 13 small chromosomes, and the cultivated American cotton has 26 chromosomes: i.e., 13 large and 13 small ones. This means, according to them, that the cultivated American cotton is allopolyploid and originated by hybridization of Asiatic and American cotton. Since the cultivated cotton was known in America in pre-Columbian times, they assumed that the old, civilized, American populations introduced cotton on their voyages from Old World countries, and then developed the hybrids. Heyerdahl agrees with this conclusion and thinks it probable that this cotton reached America by the southern Atlantic. Hutchinson, Silow, and Stephens, moreover, stated that the wild Polynesian *Gossypium* species, considered to be endemics, had 26 chromosomes as in the American-cultivated cotton, and they also argued that *Gossypium taitense* was not a distinct species but a mere form of the American *G. hirsutum* var. *punctatum* (Schum.) J. B. Hutchinson et al. According to Heyerdahl we can thus arrive at only one conclusion: the migrating Peruvian population brought with them, from Peru, the cultivated cotton. In Polynesia, later on, the custom of cotton spinning was lost and the Polynesians took up the use of bark for cloth. The distribution of cotton, in his opinion, is a still more obvious proof of his theory than that of the sweet potato and the bottle gourd. These plants, he believes, must have been taken to Polynesia by migrating South American Indians and not introduced by Polynesians from a return voyage to Peru. Why should Polynesians introduce cotton? They were unaware of its use and did not know how to spin.

In the tetraploid cotton theory of Hutchinson, Silow, and Stephens, however, one weak point exists. Their theory is based on the direct introduction by man of Asiatic cotton into America followed by its hybridization with some native American cotton. This hybridization happened only there. But these facts have never been proved and it is doubtful if they can be proved. Therefore, it is quite understandable that there are different opinions to explain such a situation. Harland (1935, 1939) believes that the tetraploid cotton species originated in Polynesia during Cretaceous or early Tertiary times. According to him, Asiatic and American diploid species could have come into contact by a land bridge over a portion of the Pacific of which the Polynesian Islands formed a part. Stebbins (1947) agrees with this theory as to the age, but rejects the land-bridge hypothesis. According to him, the subtropical Eocene flora of North America consisted of a mixture of Asiatic and American elements and here the allopolyploids originated. From this center of origin they spread to South America and Polynesia, and after the deterioration of the climate they disappeared from North America. Merrill (1954) strongly disagreed with the theory of Hutchinson, Silow, and Stephens. To him a rather recent introduction of Asiatic species of *Gossypium* into tropical America seemed more reasonable. He rejected the idea that civilized inhabitants of India traveled to America and took with them only cotton, remarking (p. 338) : "In claiming and inferring that early civilized man did introduce an Asiatic cotton species to America, the simple fact that not a single Asiatic cultivated food plant made the journey is overlooked; and food was infinitely more important 2,000 to 3,000 years ago than cotton!" Merrill also disagreed with the concept that the central Polynesian species *Gossypium taitense* could be identical with the American *G. hirsutum* var. *punctatum*.

Carica papaya L. is another cultivated plant mentioned by Heyerdahl, and according to him introduced into Polynesia before the arrival of the Europeans. Its fruits are eaten by man and its juice is used to heal wounds. Consequently, it is a species that could support Heyerdahl's theory. In connection with this, Heyerdahl is quoting from F. B. H. Brown (1935), asserted by him to be a leading authority. On the other hand, Merrill (1954), in reference to Brown's work states: "What he claims is, in general, most acceptable to those who argue for American origins, but unfortunately, his claims are almost all without foundation. . . . I note so many extraordinary conclusions in his Flora of S.E. Polynesia that I think it is regrettable that no critical review of his work has ever appeared" (p. 250). Merrill points out that almost certainly *Carica papaya* was not established in Polynesia previous to the arrival of the Europeans.

What is said of the papaya here is also true of the pineapple. Again Heyerdahl cites F. B. H. Brown (1935) in claiming the occurrence of *Ananas comosus* (L.) Merr. in Polynesia before the arrival of the European navigators. These navigators, however, thoroughly recorded which plants they imported into the islands visited. And according to Merrill (1954), the earliest Polynesian record indicates that Captain Cook planted pineapple seeds in Tahiti in 1769. If Quiros, who sailed in 1595 from Peru to Polynesia, introduced either pineapples or papayas into the Marquesas Islands, he did not record this fact and we do not possess any statement of their occurrence there.

Furthermore, Heyerdahl published a list of American plants, for the greater part weeds, which according to him occurred in early times in Hawaii. This list is borrowed from G. F. Carter, whose publication (1950) is called by Merrill (1954, p. 252) an "extraordinary paper," which he further states contains many gross and inexcusable errors. Carter's list indeed is a strange one. It contains species related only to American species and even a number which are not American at all but of European origin. Heyerdahl, not professing to be a botanist, here uncritically accepts botanical assertions from a paper written by one who also is not a professional botanist, since they support his theory.

Finally I wish to mention two species of plants which also are highly valued by Heyerdahl. The first of these is a species of the well-known genus *Argemone*, of which the best-known species, *A. mexicana* L., was introduced long ago from its native region, Mexico, into other tropical countries and also into Europe, especially as an ornamental. The species of this genus all occur in America except one, *Argemone glauca* (Nutt. ex Prain) Degener, which is endemic in Hawaii and which was collected there as early as the second voyage of Captain Cook in 1779. Heyerdahl refers to works by Fedde and Prain, who stated that *A. glauca* is only a variety of the North American *A. alba* Lestib., and who considered its proper name to be *A. alba* var. *glauca* Nutt. ex Prain. In Fedde's opinion, the plant is probably a hybrid of *A. alba* and *A. mexicana*. Since Heyerdahl holds the view that seeds of *Argemone* cannot cross the ocean without human help, he concurs with Carter's opinion (1950) that the natives introduced this plant into Polynesia because of its medicinal properties, together with the sweet potato and the tetraploid cotton. Merrill

(1954, pp. 220, 259), on the other hand, states that still unpublished morphological and cytogenetic studies show that *A. glauca* is not related either to *A. mexicana* or *A. alba*. In his opinion, it is a Hawaiian endemic and an American element in the Hawaiian flora, not man introduced and not identical with any American representative of the genus. He states (p. 259): ". . . the American progenitor of this Hawaiian species reached Hawaii by natural means long before man appeared," and: "How long a period of isolation is required to develop specific differentiation within this genus we do not know."

The other species deserving some attention is *Heliconia bihai* L. (Musaceae), a well-known component of the tropical American primeval and secondary forest. In pre-Columbian times the leaves of this plant were already used as roofing, to make walls, hats, mats, and for basket weaving. Here Heyerdahl refers to O. F. Cook (1904), who was of the opinion that the species for this reason was introduced into Polynesia in prehistoric times. It maintained itself in the mountains of Samoa and in some other islands, and became extinct elsewhere in the region as its use by man died out, perhaps because *Pandanus* leaves appeared to be more serviceable. Merrill (1954), on the other hand, is of the opinion that the genus *Heliconia* has an originally Antarctic distribution. As a matter of fact, the Heliconiae occurring in the Moluccas, New Guinea, and some of the Polynesian islands do not, as indicated by Schumann (1900) in his monograph of the family, belong to *H. bihai*. They represent other species as recorded by Backer, Bakhuizen van den Brink, Sr., and other botanists working in the former Dutch East Indies. Moreover, as Merrill (1954, p. 306) states: "*Heliconia* [*bihai*], once introduced and established in the tropics, is one of those groups of plants that simply do not 'die out,' unless there be a very radical change in climatic conditions." As a matter of fact, the group that has been passing as *H. bihai* in botanical literature is actually composed of numerous species, some of them very narrow endemics. Furthermore the leaves of these species are frequently utilized by the natives of Polynesia and Melanesia in their construction of temporary shelters.

An ethnobotanical argument which Heyerdahl does not discuss in his chapter on botany, but rather in his historical observations on old navigators, is based on stories indicating that these early navigators knew of a plant of which the leaves when chewed had the power to quench thirst and to make sea water potable. This property might point to cocaine, and it is known that the early Peruvian Indians chewed the leaves of coca (*Erythroxylum coca* Lam.) against weariness, thirst, and hunger. The old Polynesian legends also speak of the addition of lime, and this might point to a parallel with the chewing of sirih (*Piper betle* L.) as well. But the use of *Piper betle* would indicate an introduction of the practice from a direction contrary to that hypothesized by Heyerdahl.[3]

Another habit mentioned by Heyerdahl is the drinking of kava on special occasions in Polynesia. The drink in early days was made by women, who chewed the roots of *Piper methysticum* Forst. f. for that purpose. This practice Heyerdahl compares with the preparation and drinking of chicha in Andean South America. This latter drink originally was made only by women, who chewed corn; molasses is added to the mixture and is followed by fermentation of the juice. The result is a vile-smelling, milky suspension which is drunk to excess by certain classes of the population. In my opinion, the parallel between kava and kasiri drinking, such as takes place among the Indians in the interior of Surinam, where the drink is made from fermented chewed cassava (*Manihot esculenta* Crantz), is still stronger. Here also the chewing is usually done by women. But this custom, which occurs not only in Surinam but in many parts of the Amazon Basin, is apparently not known to Heyerdahl. Merrill does not mention Heyerdahl's arguments based on cocaine and kava. Apparently these items escaped him since they are not found in the botanical chapter of Heyerdahl's voluminous work.

Having discussed the plant species regarded by a number of authors as introduced into Polynesia from America and for that reason mentioned by Heyerdahl in support of his theory, we should now concern ourselves with the absence of certain American-cultivated plants in the Polynesian area. It would have been very strange if the migrating pre-Incas had brought of their crops only sweet potatoes and perhaps coconuts, and not corn (*Zea mays* L.), the most important food plant of pre-Columbian America. That this species originated in America has been adequately demonstrated by the investigations of Mangelsdorf and his collaborators. The hypothesis of Stonor and Anderson (1949) to the effect that corn was cultivated in India before the arrival of Europeans is rejected by Mangelsdorf and Oliver (1951), who stated that there is no proof of the use of corn in Asia in pre-Columbian times. As to its use and popularity, they compare maize in Asia with potatoes in Ireland. Merrill (1950, 1954) is convinced that corn reached India by the Portuguese trade route from Brazil to Goa by way of the Cape of Good Hope. Heyerdahl, also convinced of the American origin of maize, has accordingly some difficulties in explaining the established lack of corn in Polynesia before the arrival of Europeans. He suggests the possibilities that either the stock of corn was lost during the disembarkation of the

---

[3] Actually, *Piper betle* is nowhere used in Polynesia by the Polynesians themselves. Its use extends from India east to the Solomons. The only Polynesians who use it are the Polynesian "outliers" within Melanesia.

immigrating Peruvian Indians, or that the growing of the imported maize failed. At least he does not permit the absence of maize to upset his theory, illustrating the point with the following parallel: If a burglar had somewhere lost his gloves with incriminating finger-prints, he cannot very well be excused on the basis that he did not also leave his coat, hat, and shoes behind him.

In my opinion the absence of maize in Polynesia may also be adduced as evidence against the canoe expedition by Polynesians to Peru as suggested by Buck, St. John, and others; it is assumed that they carried home the sweet potato, which they also used as food during the voyage. Similarly, corn is easy to carry along and to put under cultivation, and the same also holds for the originally American beans belonging to the genus *Phaseolus*. It is known, however, that Spanish missionaries from Peru grew beans in Tahiti soon after Captain Cook's first voyage. These beans, however, were not accepted as a popular food by the natives. In Merrill's opinion (1950, 1954), the explanation lies in the probability that the Polynesians in those days were not a seed- or grain-eating people. For that reason, according to Buck's concept, they did bring back sweetpotatoes from their expeditions to Peru but neither corn nor beans.

From the discussions above, it appears that Heyerdahl's arguments borrowed from the botanical evidence are not particularly strong. When we except the coconut, which, because of its early pantropical distribution and the fact that its area of origin is unknown, must be regarded as unsuitable evidence, only a single food plant remains— that is, the sweet potato. And even if this is to be considered an originally American plant, a hypothesis that is open to doubt, it is merely an indication of a pre-Columbian contact between South America and Polynesia. This plant does not offer any conclusive proof as to the direction in which the contact took place.

The bottle gourd may have reached Polynesia in pre-Columbian times by quite another route and consequently its present distribution does not support Heyerdahl's theories. The Polynesian species of cotton appear to be autochthonous and endemic. Other botanical arguments brought forward by Heyerdahl are based on the opinions of a comparatively small number of authors, occasionally by a single author. These opinions are not shared by specialists in the field of tropical American or Polynesian vegetation and ethnobotany. Sometimes these opinions have been founded on incorrect or doubtful data. Consequently, we must conclude that Heyerdahl's botanical evidence can hardly stand. It does not offer his theory any real support. In particular, the absence of nearly all the originally South American food plants in Polynesia before the arrival of the European navigators is significant. The food plants observed during the first voyage of

Captain Cook in 1769, with the exception of the sweet potato, were all Malaysian and therefore presumably introduced from the west. Among such plants may be mentioned the taro (*Colocasia esculenta* (L.) Schott) as well as the related *Alocasia macrorrhiza* (L.) Schott and some other aroids, three species of yam (*Dioscorea*), some bananas (species of *Musa*), and the breadfruit (*Artocarpus altilis* (Parkins.) Fosb.). Accordingly it is not surprising that two well-known specialists on the flora of Polynesia, Merrill and St. John, were outspoken opponents of Heyerdahl's theory.

Similarly in ethnological circles the Kon-Tiki theory has been criticized and censured. I may briefly mention here the critical review by de Josselin de Jong (1953), professor of ethnology at the University of Leiden, the Netherlands. De Josselin de Jong wisely did not comment too strongly on Heyerdahl's ethnobotanical ideas, but he definitely rejected the manner in which Heyerdahl in his botanical chapter adduced arguments in support of his theory.

I also wish to mention here a critical review by the Viennese ethnologist Heine-Geldern (1952), who similarly concluded that Heyerdahl failed to prove the American origin of the Polynesians. He pointed out, however, that we must not lose sight of Heyerdahl's real contribution, because he proved that a voyage—for instance a voyage homeward of Polynesians who had managed to reach the South American coast—might be possible even if their food supply had become exhausted. Heine-Geldern amply reviewed Heyerdahl's botanical chapter. Of the mentioned species of plants, he discussed the coconut, rejecting an American origin for this plant; he stated that as early as a century before our era, coconuts were grown in India. The sweet potato, in his opinion, was brought to Polynesia from America by Polynesians. Finally he gives a detailed review of the cotton problem. He is firmly convinced that American cotton has been introduced into Polynesia, basing this conclusion upon the chromosome pattern of the American species. As to why this introduction was made, Heine-Geldern cites Miss Teuira Henry ("Ancient Tahiti," Bishop Mus. Press), who stated that in Tahiti cotton was formerly cultivated and was used to embalm the dead. By this expression we may presumably understand that the body was filled with raw cotton. A somewhat similar custom occurred in Peru, but the practice may have been imported from Peru by Polynesians and not necessarily carried to Polynesia by Americans. Heine-Geldern's hypothesis is that the originally imported species of cotton became extinct, and afterward another species was brought into Polynesia which did become a sub-spontaneous weed, whereas the practice of "embalming" died out. However, every trace of proof is lacking. Heyerdahl (1951–1952), countering Heine-Geldern's critical review, stated that it referred to his popular account and was published before the appearance of his principal work, "American Indians in the Pacific." This counterargument, however, did not disclose any new aspects.

In 1955 a doctor's thesis of the University of Amsterdam, the Netherlands, appeared, in which the author, Mrs. Heeren-Palm, tried to prove that the origin of Polynesian civilization was principally Indonesian. She dated the migration of the Polynesians out of Indonesia before the introduction of textile art and rice-growing in that region, and also before the influence of metal-working was noticeable. According to her, by the time the first European navigators reached Polynesia, relations and connections with the Indonesian countries were no longer maintained. Mrs. Heeren also paid attention to the cultivated plants. She included a list of 30 such plants grown in Polynesia before the arrival of the Europeans. The greater part (14 species) of this list was borrowed from Forster (1777), and of the 30, only 3, according to Mrs. Heeren, are of American origin. As such she regarded the sweet potato (*Ipomoea batatas*), the cotton (two species of *Gossypium*), and the so-called large gourd. The last, however, was identified by Eames and St. John (1943) as a true gourd, i.e., a form of *Lagenaria siceraria* (Mol.) Standl., and not as a squash, *Cucurbita maxima* Duch., as had been previously believed by Mrs. Heeren, among others. All the known species of *Cucurbita* are American, but, as discussed above, the genus *Lagenaria* in all probability is of African origin and was widely distributed in the Tropics of both hemispheres as early as pre-Columbian times. The large gourd is an extreme form presumably developed by the Hawaiians.

Mrs. Heeren amply discussed the plant species that she listed and showed their tropical Asiatic origin, but unfortunately a discussion of the sweet-potato problem is missing. She thinks it possible, because of Heyerdahl's Kon-Tiki voyage and excavations in the Galápagos Islands, that American Indians reached Polynesia on their balsa rafts, but she absolutely rejects the hypothesis of an American origin of the Polynesians.

In 1955 and 1956 Heyerdahl visited Easter Island, and in his popular account of this trip, "Aku-Aku, the Secret of Easter Island" (1958), he adds two botanical arguments to his Kon-Tiki theory—the occurrence of both the sweet potato and the totora reed (*Scirpus totara*) before the arrival of the first explorers. The former has been discussed above. The latter species is also found in large quantities in Lake Titicaca in Peru and Bolivia. It is there used as a material for building houses and other shelters, and also for rafts and boats which are called "balsas," in which the natives have sailed on the lake from pre-Columbian times until the present. Easter Island, however, is considerably nearer the coast of South America than the other Polynesian islands. In connection with the distribution of this plant, I consider it wiser to wait until the scientific report of the investigations of Heyerdahl and his collaborators on Easter Island is published. At that time we shall know what conclusions he draws from the distribution of this particular plant. It is my surmise that this problem also is more complicated than it appears to be at first sight, since the occurrence of *Scirpus totara* is not restricted to Peru and Easter Island only. Merrill (1954) was, in my opinion, often too outspoken in opposing Heyerdahl's views, but nevertheless one must agree with him that these views were not entirely justified, perhaps because Heyerdahl too frequently depended upon the works of specialists who were not entirely qualified to express detailed opinions in such an area. One must agree with Merrill's statement that "One can see little or no basis for the Heyerdahl claims that the Polynesians came from America, or that the American Indians ever peopled Polynesia proper." Merrill continues: "There seems to be no doubt that they did reach the Galápagos Islands, but these islands are not Polynesian, and they may accidentally have reached certain Pacific islands nearest to the west coast of America."

REFERENCES

BROWN, F. B. H.
:   1935. Flora of southeastern Polynesia III. Dicotyledons. Bernice P. Bishop Mus. Bull. 130, pp. 1–386.

BUCK, P. H. [TE RANGI HIROA].
:   1937. Vikings of the sunrise. 335 pp. New York.

CANDOLLE, ALPHONSE DE.
:   1883. Origine des plantes cultivées. 377 pp. Paris.

CARTER, G. F.
:   1950. Plant evidence of early contacts with America. Southwest. Journ. Anthrop., vol. 6, pp. 161–182.

COOK, O. F.
:   1904. Food plants of ancient America. Ann. Rep. Smithsonian Inst. for 1903, pp. 481–497.

DIXON, R. B.
:   1932. The problem of the sweet potato in Polynesia. Amer. Anthropologist, n.s., vol. 34, pp. 40–66.

EAMES, A. J., and ST. JOHN, H.
:   1943. The botanical identity of the Hawaiian Ipu Nui or large gourd. Amer. Journ. Bot., vol. 30, pp. 255–259.

FORSTER, J. R.
:   1777. A voyage round the world in H.M.S. *Resolution*, commanded by Capt. Cook during . . . 1772–1775. London. (Also translated into German: Reise um die Welt. 1778–1783. Berlin.)

HARLAND, S. C.
:   1935. The genetics of cotton. XII. Homologous genes for anthocyanin pigmentation in New and Old World cottons. Journ. Genetics, vol. 30, pp. 465–476.
:   1939. The genetics of cotton. 193 pp. London.

HEEREN-PALM, C. H. M.
1955. Polynesische Migraties. Thesis, Univ. Amsterdam, 189 pp.

HEINE-GELDERN, R.
1952. Some problems of migration in the Pacific. Kultur and Sprache. Wiener Beiträge zur Kulturgeschichte und Linguistik, vol. 9, pp. 311–362.

HEYERDAHL, TH.
1948. The Kon-Tiki Expedition. London, Chicago.
1951–1952. Some problems of aboriginal migration in the Pacific. Beiheft 1 zu Archiv. f. Völkerkunde. vols. 6/7, pp. 1–8.
1952. American Indians in the Pacific. The theory behind the Kon-Tiki Expedition. 820 pp. Stockholm, London, Oslo.
1958. Aku-Aku, the secret of Easter Island. (Originally published in Norwegian.)

HORNELL, J.
1946. How did the sweet potato reach Polynesia? Journ. Linn. Soc. Bot., vol. 53, pp. 41–62.

HUTCHINSON, J. B.; SILOW, R. A.; and STEPHENS, S. G.
1947. The evolution of *Gossypium* and the differentiation of cultivated cottons. 160 pp. Oxford University Press. London, New York, Toronto.

JOSSELIN DE JONG, P. E. DE.
1953. The "Kontiki" theory of Pacific migrations. Bijdr. tot de Taal-, Land- en volkenkunde, vol. 109, pp. 1–22.

MANGELSDORF, P. C., and OLIVER, D. L.
1951. Whence came maize to Asia? Bot. Mus. Leafl. Harvard Univ., vol. 14, No. 10, pp. 263–291.

MERRILL, E. D.
1937. On the significance of certain oriental plant names in relation to introduced species: the coconut. Proc. Amer. Philos. Soc., vol. 78, pp. 112–146. (Reprinted *in* Merrilliana. A selection from the general writings of Elmer Drew Merrill. Chronica Botanica, vol. 10, No. 3/4, pp. 295–315, 1946.)
1941. Man's influence on the vegetation of Polynesia, with special reference to introduced species. Proc. 6th Pacific Sci. Congr. (1940), vol. 4, pp. 629–639. (Reprinted *in* Merrilliana. A selection from the general writings of Elmer Drew Merrill. Chronica Botanica, vol. 10, No. 3/4, pp. 334–345, 1946.)
1950. Observations on cultivated plants with reference to certain American problems. Ceiba, vol. 1, pp. 3–36.
1954. The botany of Cook's voyages. Chronica Botanica, vol. 14, No. 5/6, pp. 161–384.

RIESENFELD, A.
1951. Kon-Tiki and Pacific migration. Natural History, vol. 60, pp. 50, 96. Amer. Mus. Nat. Hist., New York.

ST. JOHN, H.
1953. Origin of the sustenance plants of the Polynesians. Proc. 7th Int. Bot. Congr., Stockholm, 1950, pp. 152–154.
1954. The vegetation of Hawaii at the time of Capt. James Cook in 1778–79 and a comparison with its present status. Huitième Congrès Int. Botanique, Paris, 1954. Rapp. et Comm., aux sect. 21 à 27, pp. 176–177. And Compt. Rend. des Séances et Rapp. et Comm. déposés lors du Congr. dans les sect. 21 à 27, pp. 125–126.

SCHUMANN, K.
1900. Musaceae. *In* A. Engler, Das Pflanzenreich IV, vol. 45, p. 36.
STEBBINS, G. L.
1947. Evidences on rates of evolution from the distribution of existing and fossil plant species. Ecol. Monogr., vol. 17, pp. 149–158.
STONOR, C. R., and ANDERSON, E.
1949. Maize among the hill peoples of Assam. Ann. Missouri Bot. Garden, vol. 36, pp. 355–404.

Minerals in Art and Archeology

By Rutherford J. Gettens

Head Curator, Freer Gallery Laboratory
Freer Gallery of Art
Smithsonian Institution

[With 8 plates]

"From earth come stones, including the more precious kinds, and also the types of earth that are unusual because of their color, smoothness, density, or any other quality." Thus wrote Theophrastus in the fourth century B.C. at the beginning of his treatise "On Stones." The Greek philosopher realized the full importance to man of the mineral products of the earth. Since the dawn of civilization, man has tried to create useful and beautiful things for his living and creature comfort; he has sought unusual materials for personal adornment, for ceremonial and religious purposes, and for the expression of ideas, both concrete and abstract.

Man and art have developed side by side. The materials for art and invention have had to come from the three grand divisions into which formerly all natural objects were classified: animal, vegetable, and mineral. We might debate which of the three classes is the most important, but there is little doubt that the art materials chosen from the mineral kingdom are the most durable over long periods of time; hence, from them we have learned indirectly most of what we know about the art and ideas of antiquity. Let us, therefore, take a special look at products of the mineral kingdom which have long served the artist well and will continue to serve him in the future.

In this article we will use the term "mineral" in its narrower meaning to indicate natural inorganic species of earth substance of more or less constant composition; we will not deal with "rocks," which are heterogeneous aggregates of two or more mineral species. Many mineral substances have been employed by the artist and artisan directly as they came from the earth, and with little preparation or manipulation, except for shaping and modeling as in sculpture, or by grinding to a powder for use as paint pigments. There are other minerals, however, which only indirectly and after a considerable amount of modification, either physical or chemical, can serve the artist's needs. A few of these occur widely and plentifully, hence are inexpensive, while others are rare and are sought for in distant places, hence are costly and precious.

MINERALS IN SCULPTURE

Several of the massive minerals have long been used to produce sculpture, including statuary and elements for the ornamentation of buildings, tombs, and monuments. The first among these is marble, which is the crystalline metamorphosed form of limestone, or calcium carbonate. Marble is more extensively used today by sculptors than is any other form of stone. It is softer than granite and similar igneous rocks. Because it is denser and not so porous, it is more durable than limestone and other sedimentary formations [1].[1] The important role played by marble in the plastic arts of Greece and Rome is well known. White marble from the quarries of Mount Pentelicus served the great artist Phidias for the ornamentation of the Parthenon; the Greek island of Paros produced a coarser grained but pure-white marble of incomparable beauty, which was modeled by many of the famous Greek sculptors. The white marble of the quarries at Carrara in Italy was the favorite sculpture medium of Michelangelo, who carved it into figures of beauty and dignity such as the *Madonna and Child* in the Church of Notre Dame in Bruges (pl. 1, fig. 1). Variegated marbles have been widely used for table-tops and fireplaces and interior paneling. Polished black marble, especially "Belgian black," is highly regarded by modern sculptors.

Alabaster is a mineral name with a double meaning. It is probably derived from the Greek word *alabastron* (L. *alabastrum*), which is the name for the small stone flasks or vases used by the Egyptians for oils, ointments, and perfumes, having a flattened top with narrow orifice and a body usually rounded at the bottom, and without handle. Many are artistically conceived. Those alabastrums made in Egypt are usually cut from a hard compact form of calcite, somewhat trans-lucent and sometimes quite beautifully banded, which is nearly iden-tical with onyx (onyxlike) marble. The Egyptians also used calcite alabaster for making those strange "canopic jars" in which they pre-served the viscera of the deceased, usually for burial with the mummy. They bear on their covers carved heads, representative of the four genii of the dead called Amenti. Among objects in the exhibition of "Tutankhamun Treasures" recently circulated among American museums are several that are made from creamy alabaster. An especially fine piece is an alabaster lid from one of the compartments of the "canopic" chest which is in the form of the king's head [2]. To Egyptologists the term "alabaster" always refers to calcite.

---

[1] Numbers in brackets indicate references at end of text.

The close relationship of calcite alabaster to onyx marble has been mentioned. Onyx marble is a banded calcite from shelf deposits formed about the orifices of hot springs. It is often beautifully tinted by metallic impurities and, because of its translucency and color, was used by the pre-Columbian inhabitants of Mexico for carving masks for religious purposes. A fine example of a pale green onyx marble mask is shown as frontispiece in the catalog of the Robert Woods Bliss collection of pre-Columbian art [3].

In Europe including England alabaster is the name given to a massive and compact form of gypsum, calcium sulphate dihydrate ($CaSO_4 \cdot 2H_2O$), of fine texture which is usually white and translucent. It is nearly as soft and as easy to work as soapstone and has been used especially in Italy since Roman times for carving vases and statuary. It is too soft and too easily weathered for general sculpture purposes, but was used extensively in England for the carving of tomb figures and for interior architectural ornamentation [4]. The gypsum was quarried in the Middle Ages near Tutbury in Staffordshire and near Derby. Many of the English alabaster sculptures were painted and gilded; a fine example is the painted alabaster figure of *Saint George and the Dragon* in the National Gallery of Art, Washington (pl. 1, fig. 2). The Hildburgh collection of English alabasters at the Victoria and Albert Museum, London, has many religious images and narrative panels in gypsum alabaster [5]. The so-called "Mosul Marble" used by the Assyrians is gypsum grading into anhydrite. Good examples are the winged human-headed lions from the palace of Sargon II at Khorsabad which now stand in the entrance to the Assyrian Galleries in the British Museum [6]. Gypsum has long been employed in Italy and in other areas for the production of ornamental vases, statuettes, and small stele for indoor use.

The anhydrous form of calcium sulphate called anhydrite ($CaSO_4$), although plentiful, had more limited use as a sculpture medium, but at both the Metropolitan Museum of Art and the Brooklyn Museum (pl. 2, fig. 1), one can see attractive bowls, vases, and figurines cut by the ancient Egyptians from a pale bluish variety of anhydrite. Both gypsum and anhydrite had another important use in art, which was for making plaster for wall construction and for casting purposes, but those uses will be discussed later.

The sedimentary rocks, limestone, sandstone, and slate, and the igneous rocks of composite minerals like granite, porphyry, and diorite have been transformed into beautiful and transportable objects by the sculptor's hammer, but these more common and massive forms of mineral and rock are not within the scope of this essay. We think of them mainly as architectural media.

There is a group of minerals, however, sometimes called semiprecious stones, which have been used since prehistoric times for miniature sculptures, ornamental inlays, and jewelry. Most of them have special appeal because they are hard and have a pleasing appearance, luster, and color. Many of these stones are inherently beautiful and require no modeling—only polishing—to bring out their artistic qualities. Perhaps first among these are two minerals which are collectively known as jade. One of them is a hard mineral made of the sodium aluminum silicate, a member of the pyroxene group now called by its scientific name "jadeite." It was employed by the aborigines of Guatemala and other parts of Central America for carving and ornamental purposes. The Spanish conquistadores called it *piedra de ijada*, or "stone of the side," because when worn on the loins it was supposed to cure kidney ailments. In the collection of the Honorable Robert Woods Bliss, now on loan to the National Gallery of Art in Washington, one can see many fine examples of worked jadeite from Central America, including small images, ceremonial weapons, and inlays which vary in color from yellowish green to gray to black [7]. Perhaps the most familiar type of jadeite is that which comes mainly from Burma and is colored or mottled a bright emerald green from impurities of chromium. A selected variety of green jadeite called "imperial jade" is highly prized in the lapidary trade.

The name "jade" is also given, by modern lapidarists, to a tough, hard stone which was valued by the ancient Chinese who called it *yü*. It is nephrite, a variety of amphibole or calcium magnesium silicate which is translucent white when pure, but there are colored varieties ranging through pale green, spinach green, and yellowish brown to black. Quantities of exquisitely worked nephrite have come from Chinese tombs of the first and second millenniums B.C. These are mostly ceremonial objects, small ornaments, figurines, and inlays [8]. The Freer Gallery of Art has a collection of nearly 500 nephrite objects from early Chinese tombs, among them many masterpieces of fine and delicate workmanship. It is believed that the main source of this nephrite was Chinese Turkestan in innermost Asia, where the jade was found in boulders in beds of streams which flowed out of the K'un-lun Mountains in the vicinity of Khotan. A Russian writer, Kretchetova, says that nephrite was a matter of particular importance in the trade from Khotan to China. By order of the Chinese rulers, unwrought pieces of jade by thousands of pounds were brought to China over the great "silk roads" from the west. He adds that the Imperial treasury consisted to a considerable extent of jade and jasper; the lack of it meant that the treasury was exhausted [9]. Dark green or "spinach jade" came mostly from the Lake Baikal region of Siberia. Many extraordinary pieces of nephrite carving have come out of ancient royal tombs in China dating from the first millennium B.C. Some exceptional nephrite ceremonial axes and blades about 30 inches long, 8 inches wide, and only about a quarter of an inch thick are on exhibition in the Freer Gallery of Art (pl. 2, fig. 2). A number of good examples of "tomb jade" are pictured, many in color, in a recently published work on "Chinese Art" by Daisy Lion-Goldschmidt of Paris [10]. Many of these pieces were obviously made for religious and symbolic purposes, but over the centuries the meaning of the symbols has been lost.

In the late 18th century in China, especially under the patronage of the Emperors K'ang-hsi and Ch'ien Lung, jade cutting was revived and many fine artisans were brought into the service of the Imperial Court. A new style was developed, entirely different in artistic conception from the style of earlier times, which resulted in the production of large and flamboyantly worked vessels, plates, cups, ornamental pieces, and small screens. Many of them were in the shape and style of archaic bronzes. There are many fine examples of this kind of jade in the Vetlesen collection [11] adjoining the gem room in the Mineral Hall in the Museum of Natural History of the Smithsonian Institution (pl. 3, fig. 1); also in the Bishop collection of the Metropolitan Museum of Art and in the Dane collection in the Fogg Museum of Art, Harvard University. Jades of this period, because of their striking form and color, are often shown in catalogs and picture books on Chinese art [12]. Recently from Russia has come a splendidly illustrated book [9] showing unique pieces of Chinese carved stone including much jade of the 17th and 18th centuries in the famous Hermitage Museum in Leningrad. Many of the pieces were collected by the former czars and nobles of Russia.

For a long time it was not realized by either Europeans or Chinese that the two kinds of minerals, jadeite and nephrite, are of different composition until this was demonstrated by Damour in 1863. When pure, both varieties are white. Jadeite is an aggregate of small grains and has, when polished, a sort of vitreous luster. Nephrite, on the other hand, is built up of interlocking fibers, and has an oily luster; hence, white nephrite is appropriately called "mutton fat" jade. Jadeite has a hardness of $6\frac{3}{4}$ on Mohs scale of 1 to 10; nephrite is slightly less hard—$6\frac{1}{2}$—but has a peculiar toughness which gives it greater resistance to lapidary tools and to breakage. Neither can be scratched with the point of a pocketknife, whereas some other minerals used to imitate jade, such as serpentine, prophyllite, and steatite, can be. The two minerals can easily be distinguished and told from imitations by X-ray diffraction analysis. Nevertheless, both varieties of mineral will continue to be called "jade."

Rock crystal or transparent crystalline quartz (silicon dioxide, SiO_2) has been almost as important to art as jade. (Pl. 3, fig. 2.) The stonecutters of the Chinese Imperial Court work it much like jade and converted long, stout crystals of clear quartz into vases, jars, and statuettes. The Philadelphia Museum of Art possesses some marvelous examples of Chinese rock crystal. The production of flawless crystal spheres for crystal gazing was a tour de force enjoyed by Chinese lapidarists. The crystal ball in the U.S. National Museum, which is 12⅞ inches in diameter and weighs 106¾ pounds, is the largest known flawless sphere of this kind in the world. The quartz came from Burma and required 18 months labor in China for the cutting and polishing. Two fine crystal bowls of 17th-century Italian workmanship are shown in the Morgan Library, New York, and there are many notable rock crystal pieces in European collections [13]. Amethyst, which is a violet-tinted variety of crystal, was occasionally cut into small vases and dishes, but mostly it was used in antiquity for gems and beads.

The hard cryptocrystalline forms of quartz like chalcedony, agate, carnelian, prase, and jasper have also been widely used by lapidarists for carving small figures, ornamental vases, and seals. They differ only in the fineness of their crystalline structure and translucency and in their color, which is caused by impurities—chiefly oxides and silicates of iron and manganese.

Carnelian was a favorite medium of the cylinder seal makers of Babylon and Assyria. A. Lucas tells us that it occurs abundantly in the eastern desert of Egypt and was much used from predynastic times onward for inlay in jewelry, furniture, and coffins [14]. It was so highly valued that in later times an imitation carnelian consisting of translucent quartz set in red cement was often employed to supplement the genuine article as inlay. There are some striking white agate dishes ornamented with orange-red carnelian flowers cut from a single stone in the Bishop collection of the Metropolitan Museum of Art. Carnelian and amethyst were sought after in ancient Egypt for making bead necklaces, although drilling of the holes in the beads must have required nearly inexhaustible patience.

Agate, especially banded agate, is another excellent lapidary material, and even the purely functional agate mortar found in most present-day analytical chemical laboratories can be a work of art. One of the most notable ancient objects in agate is the carved vase once owned by the great painter Peter Paul Rubens, which is now one of the showpieces of the Walters Art Gallery in Baltimore (pl. 4, fig. 1). According to Marvin Chauncey Ross, "It is a vessel over seven inches high carved from a single mass of agate, shading from a warm honey color to a milky white. The ornamentation is carved in very high solid relief thus adding some strength to the walls of the vase, which are worked to the thinness and translucence of porcelain." [15.] Rubens strongly admired the vase which Ross believes dates from the fourth or early fifth century A.D. and is Byzantine in origin. An engraving of it in the Berlin Print Cabinet is made after a drawing in Rubens' own sketchbook.

Flint is another cryptocrystalline variety of quartz and is allied to chalcedony, but it is opaque, usually in gray, brown, or even smoky tones. It was of prime importance to primitive man for tool and implement making because it could so easily be worked by flaking. Because of its dull color it was not much used for art forms, even for small sculpture, but many will agree that a finely worked flint knife or spear point is an artistic creation. Agatized or petrified wood is still another variety of quartz, and when well banded and streaked with red from iron oxide, it can be worked like onyx into attractive book ends and other sculptural forms.

Some copper minerals, because of the bright colors, have been employed for small sculptures and inlays. Perhaps the best known is banded malachite or green basic copper carbonate, which the Russians got in considerable quantities from the Ural Mountains and worked into all sorts of shapes. A remarkable pair of large bronze vases clad with Russian malachite and ornamented with gilt bronze fittings is shown mounted on pedestals at the Natural History Building of the U.S. National Museum. They came from the collection of Prince Demidoff and Princess Mathilde Bonaparte, his wife. Visitors to the Hermitage and museums of Moscow speak of the extraordinary amount of malachite lapidary and inlay work that can be seen there. The banding of alternate layers of dark green and light green seen in botryoidal masses of malachite produces interesting designs in inlay and mosaic.

The use of turquoise, which is basic hydrous aluminum phosphate tinted with copper, as a lapidary mineral is well known to those who are familiar with the Indian-made silver jewelry of the American Southwest. An outstanding example is the pre-Columbian turquoise necklace and eardrops found by the Pueblo Bonito expedition in New Mexico now on display at the National Geographic Society in Washington [16]. Turquoise was also employed effectively by Chinese silversmiths and goldsmiths for embellishing elaborately worked brooches and bracelets [17]. The Chinese gold and turquoise scepter in the Freer Gallery collection has been rightfully termed a "royal piece." Large pieces of carved turquoise are rare, but a Buddha carved from turquoise exhibited in the Harvard University collection of minerals and another in the Natural History Building of the U.S. National Museum are several inches high. A half-dozen bronze ceremonial dagger-axes at the Freer Gallery of Art are lavishly inlaid with small square-cut turquoise chips like the tessarae used in mosaic (pl. 4, fig. 2).

Even some of the rarer minerals are used for lapidary purposes. A figure of the Chinese god of longevity, Shou-lao-hsien, carved in an altered form of yellow and black crocidolite called "tiger eye," was recently added to the mineral collection of the U.S. National Museum.

A carved disk of bright red cinnabar in matrix of quartz and agalmatolite is a curiosity in the Freer Gallery collection. In a private collection in New York an unusual and attractive piece is a small, elegantly carved Chinese mask of the translucent green mineral prehnite. A prehnite pendant is shown in the Robert Woods Bliss collection of pre-Columbia art [3]. Dr. Foshag says, in the catalog of that collection, that in Mexico carvings in this stone are rare, but beads of prehnite are not uncommon. Bluish and greenish tinted varieties of feldspar were used by the Egyptians for jewelry and small sculptures. An amulet of green feldspar set in gold which represents the funerary god Anubis was found in the mummy wrappings of Tutankhamun [2]. The dark purple massive variety of fluorite or fluorspar known as "Blue John" is found only in Derbyshire, England. Various ornamental vases of this unique kind of fluorite (calcium fluoride) are shown at the Geological Museum in London. There must be many more carved mineral oddities like these hidden away in collections all over the world.

Objects carved from lapis lazuli (ML *lazulus* from Per. *lazhuward;* in modern mineralogy, lazurite) are not uncommon. Lapis lazuli is a complex sodium aluminum silicate of the zeolite type, which owes its blue color to loosely attached sodium polysulphide. Some notable examples of lapis carving are cited by Miss Miner and Miss Edelstein of the Walters Art Gallery [18] in their scholarly description of a late Roman lapis-lazuli spread eagle, which was found some years ago near Naples (pl. 5, fig. 1). It probably once served as the finial for a scepter used by a Roman consul as insigne of office. Perhaps one of the most distinguished examples of the use of this mineral is the lapis and gold "Ram in a Thicket" found by the late Charles Leonard Woolley at Ur, and now shown among the many treasure items of the University Museum in Philadelphia. A small bust of a Median lion strangler in carved lapis lazuli (7¾ inches high) is pictured in color on the cover of the February 1961 issue of the Cleveland Museum of Art bulletin [19]. It perhaps represents the hero protecting the sacred flocks of the goddess of fertility.

Amber, although organic in origin, is classed as a mineral, and Baltic amber is called succinite. It is fossil resin from a species of fir tree which became extinct millions of years ago. Amber was one of the first substances used by man for carving. In Europe especially it has been employed for making ornaments, crucifixes, and small votive images, and in England it has been in almost continuous use for beadmaking since the Bronze Age. An outstanding collection of examples of the judgment and craftsmanship of Chinese amber workers of the past two centuries was made by Mary Hooper Packard and is shown at the Museum of Fine Arts in Boston [20]. Mrs. Packard's chief interest was amber ornaments made in the Far East, and her discrimination was exercised in the field of color and quality of the substance rather than in variety of use or method of working. Pendants and strings of beads form the major part of the collection.

Although steatite, or soapstone (hydrous magnesium silicate) (pl. 5, fig. 2), is not regarded as a great art medium, its softness (No. 1 on Mohs hardness scale) and ease of carving have caused it to be used widely by the Chinese, but, unfortunately, in this century mostly for cheap export ware. A soapstone Hellenistic head of fine quality is exhibited in the Egyptian galleries of the Brooklyn Museum. In the same collection are several other well-modeled Egyptian steatite heads with inlaid eyes.

A hard variety of serpentine (Mohs scale 4–5), which is related to steatite, was sometimes employed by the Chinese as a substitute for jade. In fact it is sometimes difficult to distinguish this mineral from jade. Serpentine has waxlike luster and color and can be variegated, showing mottling in lighter or darker tones of green. A handsome mask of serpentine from Mexico is shown in the Robert Woods Bliss collection already mentioned [3]. Some of the finest accomplishments of Olmec artists are in this stone.

The native metals are also minerals, and since they were easy to recognize and to work, they were prized by primitive artists and craftsmen. Chief among these, of course, is gold, which was widely employed by primitive peoples for all kinds of art and ornamental purposes. They fashioned objects by hammering gold nuggets directly into wire, beads, and thin sheets. It was melted and cast in simple molds to form images and ceremonial objects. The Robert Woods Bliss collection has many unusual examples of Middle and South American gold masks, figurines, and ornaments showing all techniques (pl. 6, fig. 1). In Colombia, the aboriginal Americans learned to make an alloy of gold and copper called *tumbaga*, which they cast into images and other objects by the lost-wax process. Native silver, and even copper, also served the early peoples of Europe and America for making beads, amulets, and hair ornaments.

Nearly all the precious gem stones, including diamonds, have been sculptured or engraved. Sapphire heads of Presidents Washington, Jefferson, Lincoln, and Eisenhower are owned by the Kazanjian Foundation of Los Angeles. The original stone for the Lincoln head (pl. 7, fig. 1), which was shown several years ago at the Smithsonian Institution, was obtained after a year of negotiations with a rancher in Queensland, Australia, where it had been kept for 15 years. The deep blue stone was sculptured by the artist Norman Maness, counseled by Merrill Gage, professor of sculpture at the University of Southern California, and the job required almost 2 years. Because of the hardness of the sapphire stone, only diamonds could be used to cut it. The weight is 1,318 carats, approximately 8½ ounces.

A set of small bowls of American gem stones was recently installed in the Natural History Building of the U.S. National Museum, and there are many small pieces of sculpture made from rare minerals in that collection including chrysocolla, idocrase, rhodonite, variscite, amethyst, and others. A visit to newly installed collections of gems and minerals in the Natural History Building is an unforgettable experience.

One thinks of hematite (Fe_2O_3) principally as an iron ore, but this hard, dense mineral with metallic luster was a favorite medium for cutting cylinder seals in Babylonian and Assyrian times. In the Egyptian collection of the Brooklyn Museum there is a splendid small gold inlaid head of a hippopotamus carved in hematite (pl. 6, fig. 2).

Banded and layered minerals have lent themselves to the making of fine cameos. A cameo is a precious or semiprecious stone or shell carved in low relief on layers of different colors; the figure is cut in one layer and another layer serves as background. In Roman and medieval times in Europe, banded agate and other hard stones were used for cameo cutting, especially black and white banded agate (onyx), because it permitted a white figure to be projected against a black background. Outstanding examples of cameo working are illustrated in catalogs of the Bibliothèque National [21] in Paris and at the Kunsthistorisches Museum in Vienna [22]. In these catalogs the majority of cameos are indicated as being carved from "sardonyx," but a number of varieties of quartz and other minerals are also listed.

In former days when war was a sport engaged in by nobles and their attendants, personal arms were lavishly decorated and embellished. Some fine examples of carved and modeled semiprecious stones can be seen in the hilts of swords and daggers in the Arms and Armor collection of the Metropolitan Museum of Art. A Persian dagger of the 19th century has a hilt in the shape of a horse's head carved from nephrite, and other daggers have rock-crystal hilts. A state scimitar of Murad V, Sultan of Turkey (1876–78), has a jade hilt, and the mountings of gold and silver are set with diamonds and emeralds; a tassel of strung pearls adds to the sumptuousness of the weapon.

One of the finest exhibits of sculptured mineral is shown at the Virginia Museum of Fine Arts in Richmond. It is a collection of Russian jewels and objets d'art from the atelier of Peter Carl Fabergé, jeweler and goldsmith to the Imperial Russian Court in the early part of this century. The objects were collected between 1933 and 1946 by Lillian Thomas Pratt, who willed them in 1947 to the Virginia Museum. In the handbook of the Lillian Thomas Pratt collection, recently published [23], are shown numerous objects: animals, Easter eggs, flowers, picture frames, parasol handles, and miscellaneous items in which a variety of semiprecious stones, including agate, jade, aventurine, chalcedony, jasper, rhodonite, and others were carved into thin and cunningly wrought shapes and then combined in patterns and colors to make precious objects to be used by their imperial patrons as gifts, room decorations, and religious symbols. Among the superb items in the collection is an orange blossom with emerald center and buds of chalcedony; the leaves are made of Siberian nephrite, and the gold stem is set in a rock-crystal vase cut to appear half filled with water.

"Easter Eggs" were the central theme of an exhibit of master works of Carl Fabergé shown in the spring of 1961 at the Corcoran Gallery of Art in Washington [24]. These eggs, made of enamel and semiprecious stones and mounted in gold, were used as Easter gifts by members of the Russian Imperial Court. Some of the eggs opened up to give the favored one a surprise such as a vase of spring flowers or a golden hen. One striking object in the collection is a polar bear of frosted rock crystal, standing on a floating cake of clear rock-crystal ice. One feels after seeing these collections of bibelots that Fabergé and his school could really "make magic" with minerals.

Frequent mention has been made of cylinder seals used by the Sumerians as well as the later Babylonians and Assyrians. These are small cylinders generally from about 1 to 2 inches in length with a lengthwise center hole. Around the cylindrical surface was cut a device or inscription in intaglio, which was in effect the signature of the owner who rolled it with the aid of a spindle and handle onto a damp clay tablet. Some show ritual scenes, others hunting scenes, heroic actions, and scenes from farming and agriculture. The seals were made from almost any hard material such as stone, shell, faience, glass, or ivory. Many Sumerian seals discovered by Sir Leonard Woolley at Ur were made from lapis lazuli. Many hundreds, probably thousands, of these seals are in existence. There is a notable collection of them in the Morgan Library in New York [25] and a somewhat smaller one in the Smithsonian Institution. The interesting thing is that a collection of cylinder seals presents about as wide a variety of minerals as any art form, and many of them are true works of art.

MINERALS IN PAINTING

Since prehistoric times, minerals ground to a fine powder have been used as paint pigments. Only a handful of mineral substances, however, have the necessary properties, namely: high color intensity when ground to a fine powder; refractive index sufficiently high to provide hiding power and opacity; and permanence to light and atmosphere. The iron- and manganese-bearing earth pigments which contain hematite, limonite, and pyrolusite, mixed in various proportions with silicate minerals, have enjoyed an important place on the artist's palette going back to the prehistoric cave paintings of France and Spain. They are plentiful and cheap. The Egyptians, employing earth pigments, decorated tombs with incredibly fine and realistic paintings, as did the pre-Columbian Indians who painted designs on the walls of their *kivas* in the American Southwest. If one observes carefully the flesh tone of figures done in tempera technique by the Italian masters of the Middle Ages he will see that they are underpainted with a greenish pigment. This is a native earth appropriately called *terra verde* (green earth). It is made up principally of glauconite (also called celadonite), a complex mineral composed principally of potassium, iron, and aluminum silicates. These earth greens serve well in the tempera medium of the Italian masters, but they are too low in refractive index to be used in oil.

In the early times, bright blue pigments were rare and highly valued, sending painters' suppliers to the remotest parts of the then known world to find sources of lapis lazuli (lazurite) and azurite, the only two blue minerals which had the necessary properties to make them good paint pigments. Only one important source of lapis lazuli was known in antiquity, and that was in a distant and remote valley in Asia near the source of the Oxus River in the mountains of the Hindu Kush [26]. Here in the northeast province of Afghanistan, called Badakshan, are the lapis lazuli mines that were visited by Marco Polo on one of his trips to China, and there is good reason to believe that these mines were worked long before the Christian Era. The Sumerians in the third millennium B.C. used lapis lazuli to ornament gold, and it has already been mentioned that their successors, the Babylonians and Assyrians, used it for cylinder seals. It was known very early that lapis lazuli, when ground to a powder, yielded a deep bright blue pigment suitable for making paint. In the West, lapis lazuli apparently first began to be used as a pigment in Byzantium in the early Middle Ages. At this time, the blue stone was carried across Central Asia over the "silk routes" to the Levantine port of Acre and thence by sea to Venice. A method was invented which permitted the separation of blue particles in impure ground lazurite from colorless gangue materials in a way which is similar to modern flotation processes for the beneficiation of metallic ores. The medieval Italians called the blue pigment "ultramarine," because its source was from "beyond the sea." The Renaissance painters employed it to paint the Virgin's robe and to represent distant mountain landscapes and the vault of heaven. Ultramarine, along with gold, was specifically named in contracts given by patrons to painters, and early account books speak of its costliness and special worth. About

1830, a method for artificial production of ultramarine was invented, and following that, natural ultramarine nearly disappeared from the artist's palette, although it can still be bought from an artists' colorman in London.

Azurite, the blue basic carbonate of copper, was probably used in greater quantities by early European painters than lapis blue. Sources of azurite in Europe are little known, but probably much of it came from Hungary from copper mines that were long ago completely worked out. The early medieval writers called it *azzurum citramarinum* to distinguish it from *azzurum ultramarinum*. In the Far East, ground malachite (green) enjoyed the same wide use as azurite, but for some obscure reason it was sparsely used in medieval European painting. This is strange because malachite and azurite generally occur together in secondary copper ore deposits, with malachite in greater abundance. Both malachite and azurite pigment were used plentifully in Chinese paintings on mud walls, on silk, and on paper, going back to an early date. In China and Japan, the powdered mineral was sieved to produce three tones of blue—dark, medium, and light. The dark blue azurite on some Japanese screens in the Freer Gallery of Art is so coarse that it feels like sandpaper. An especially striking example of the lavish use of these two pigments is on a pair of Japanese screens in the Metropolitan Museum of Art (pl. 8, fig. 1); the subject attributed to Korin (1661–1716) is "Iris and Bridge." The blue iris flowers are painted with azurite pigment, the leaves are malachite, and both color and texture are superb. Occasionally a bright green pigment on ancient paintings turns out to be chrysocolla (copper silicate), not malachite. These two minerals are so similar in outward appearance it is not likely that they were known apart.

The only stable bright yellow pigment available to the ancients was the jonquil yellow sulphide of arsenic called orpiment. Although poisonous and difficult to grind because of its platy nature, orpiment was used in Persian and Indian miniature paintings of former centuries. It is encountered occasionally on early European paintings, especially on illuminated writings on parchment. The Egyptians, and later the Copts, also used it. A probable early source was Macedonia from which supplies are still obtained. Orange-red realgar, the other arsenic sulphide mineral, was also used, but apparently to a much lesser extent.

It was inevitable that cinnabar (mercuric sulphide), with its rich vermilion red color and high opacity, should find early use as a paint pigment. Cinnabar was well known to the Greeks and Romans, who got it mainly from the Almaden mines of Spain, which are still the world's most important producers of mercury. Pliny called it *minium*, a name which in later centuries became fixed to red lead, an adulterant and poor substitute for cinnabar.   Cinnabar has often been identified on Pompeian and Roman wall paintings.   It was perhaps known even earlier in China, where it was used for strewing graves, and for filling the incised characters written on animal bones, now called "oracle bones," which were used in Shang times for divining purposes.   Sometime about the beginning of the Christian Era, the Chinese discovered a way to make cinnabar artificially, simply by recombining mercury and sulphur, the elements of cinnabar, and subliming the product to get the red modification of the sulphide. This product, now called "vermilion," is purer and brighter than natural cinnabar.   The Chinese have used it since Han times for making the red ink which is so often seen in the red seals stamped on Chinese silk and scroll paintings, as well as for general paint purposes.

A number of important inorganic paint pigments that have no counterpart in nature are derived from metallic ore and mineral sources.   In some instances, the natural substance is known, but is too rare or too impure for commercial use.   It is rather strange that no usable chromium pigment is found naturally, although the mineral chromite is the starting material for making several chromium pigments including viridian (hydrous chromic oxide) and chrome yellow (lead chromate) which came into use after 1800.   No cobalt minerals are directly useful as pigments, but the cobalt minerals smaltite, erythrite, and asbolite have been used since prehistoric times to color glass and ceramic glaze deep blue.   The blue color is developed when cobalt combines with complex silicates in the glaze at the high temperatures attained in the pottery kiln.   The skilled makers of glazed porcelain of the Sung and later dynasties in China brought cobalt minerals from as far away as Persia to decorate their beautiful blue-and-white porcelain.   In the Middle Ages, smalt, a kind of glass colored with cobalt, was added to the painter's palette, and in the 19th century three more cobalt pigments—cobalt blue (cobalt aluminate), cobalt green (cobalt zincate), and cobalt yellow (cobalt potassium nitrite), all derived from cobalt minerals by chemical processes—filled it out.

Natural cadmium sulphide, greenockite, is a rare mineral of no pigment importance, but artificial cadmium sulphide made from cadmium-bearing zinc ores is a rich and opaque stable yellow and is now a mainstay of the artist's palette.

The importance of the copper minerals malachite and azurite has been mentioned.   Artificial copper pigments made directly from copper minerals also had their special uses.   In Mesopotamia, as early as the second millennium B.C., a way was discovered to make an artificial blue frit by calcining a mixture of lime, silica, and a copper mineral, either malachite or cuprite. The product, bright blue crystalline copper calcium silicate, is called "Egyptian blue." It was the most widely used blue pigment of Classical times, and it is found on ancient paintings from Mesopotamia in the East to Roman sites in Scandinavia in the West. It is strange that this product seems to have no counterpart in nature, although several copper silicate minerals are well known.

The lead minerals, cerussite (lead carbonate) and hydrocerussite (basic lead carbonate), are not uncommon and were known to the ancients, but they apparently never served as pigments. White lead, the artificial counterpart of hydrocerussite, has been made artificially probably since it was known how to win lead metal from galena. Likewise, zinc oxide and titanium oxide, both widely used by artists, are made artificially, the former mostly from sphalerite and the latter from ilmenite.

Like the sculptor, the painter has had to go to the earth for the materials of his craft. The painter can bring together on a single panel or canvas the minerals and mineral-derived products of several countries and climes. In order to express fully his ideas it may be necessary for him to assemble on his palette minerals and chemical compounds that represent as many as three dozen of the chemical elements. In addition to paint pigments, the painter has other mineral needs.

NONMETALLIC MINERALS IN ART

There is still another class of minerals which has always played an important if less glamorous role in the creation of art. Among paint manufacturers they are called "inert pigments," but others call them nonmetallic minerals. They are mostly white, or nearly white, bulk minerals with low refractive index and include such familiar minerals as gypsum and anhydrite, chalk, China clay, and others.

In Italy, gypsum and anhydrite were abundant, and in addition to their use in sculpture they were employed to make gesso (It. = gypsum) which was used with glue binder to undercoat wood panels, picture frames, and furniture to ready them for painting and gilding. Raw gypsum, which is calcium sulphate dihydrate, requires heating to a temperature only slightly above the boiling point of water to dehydrate it and permit it to be ground easily to a fine powder. The product, calcium sulphate hemihydrate (plaster of paris), can be used directly for casting purposes, and for mortars and plaster finishes. Some of it is especially refined to make *gesso a oro*, or gilding base for use on the wood of furniture or picture frames. Microscopic examination of the gesso undercoating or ground of most Tuscan paintings shows that it rontains mostly fine particles of anhydrite. Apparently an impure gypsum-anhydrite mixture was the raw material used for making gesso in that region. Gypsum has always been a key material in the craft of the Italian painters.

In the northern countries—England, France, and the Low Countries—calcite in the form of chalk served the same purpose as gypsum did in Italy. Lump chalk needed only grinding and bolting to produce the white inert for the multiple-layer ground coat of artists' panels and canvases. When examined at high magnification, a sample of the white underlayer of a Flemish or Dutch painting often shows presence of coccoliths, the calcareous skeletons of ancient minute marine organisms which formed the layers of chalk in some bygone geological age. In this way natural chalk can easily be distinguished from precipitated chalk.

The Chinese mural painters employed kaolin for the same purpose. The Japanese, however, used mostly a lime white from burnt shells for both undercoat and white pigment purposes.

All these white inert pigments have been employed as the substrates or carriers of vegetable and animal dyes in the production of organic pigments, especially those with high tinctorial power, to give the dye pigment body and some opacity. In modern paints, ground barite is frequently used as an extender and bulking agent. Diatomaceous earth, chalk, mica, talc, and even ground silica have special uses in both artists' and commercial paints.

A wide variety of minerals are used in making and coloring ceramics, which are among the finest expressions of art ever conceived. All the minerals of ceramics, however, are much modified in the ceramic furnace, and in the finished product they appear as entirely new inorganic species. Kaolin, feldspar, and quartz, when strongly heated, are changed into compounds which correspond to sillimanite, cristobalite, mullite, and others. These are minerals which in nature are produced in contact zones by chemical reactions and physical changes like those which take place in the potter's kiln.

Mosaic is a form of art which employs minerals in a quite different way. The design is executed in small cubes or tessarae of mineral, stone, or glass and fixed in a setting bed of plaster. Various colored marbles and semiprecious stones are used to produce shading and brilliance. Small tessarae of malachite and azurite have been seen on Russian and Byzantine icons done in fine mosaic (pl. 7, fig. 2).

MINERAL ALTERATION PRODUCTS ON ANCIENT METALS

Collectors of ancient bronzes admire those pieces which have acquired a fine green or blue "patina." Patina is made of mineral alteration products formed by reaction of copper in the alloy with corrosive agencies of air or earth (pl. 8, fig. 2). The most admired bronze patinas are the adherent crusts of malachite or azurite inter-

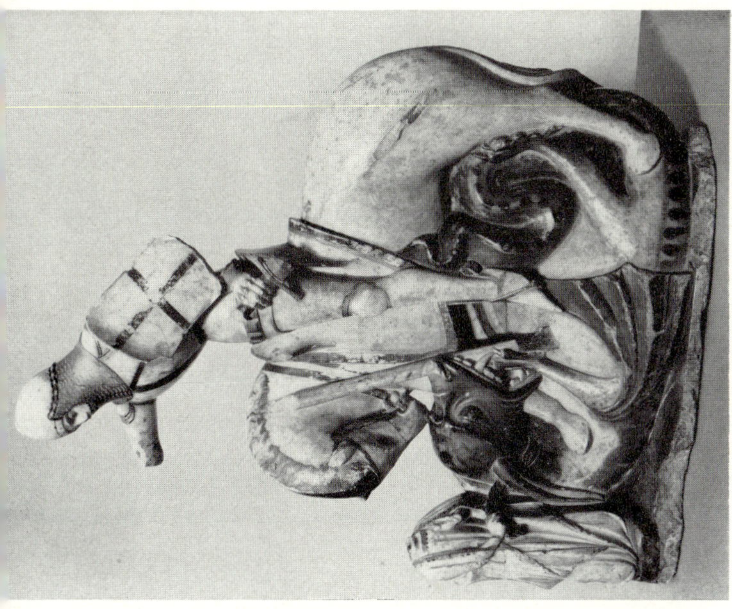

2. This painted figure of *Saint George and the Dragon* in gypsum alabaster is attributed to the English school, early 15th century. Height 81.2 cm. (Courtesy Kress Collection, National Gallery of Art, Washington D.C.)

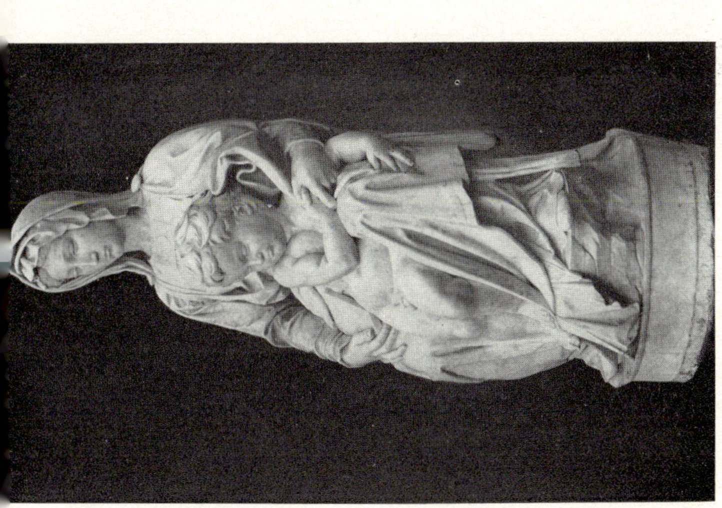

1. The potentialities of marble as a sculpture medium were thoroughly exploited by Michelangelo in this figure of the *Madonna and Child* in the church of Notre Dame in Bruges, Belgium. The original figure is nearly life size. (Copyright A.C.L. Bruxelles.)

1. Anhydrite bowl, Egyptian, XII Dynasty; in the Brooklyn Museum. Diameter 11.5 cm. (Courtesy Brooklyn Museum.)

2. Nephrite ceremonial ax, Ching dynasty (Chien-Lung), China. Note the elaborate carving and the precise engraving done in one of the "toughest" of stones. Height 6⁹⁄₁₆ in., width 5⅞ in. Freer 19.40.

1. One of a pair of quadrangular jadeite vases with cover in the Vetlesen collection (No. 30) in the Hall of Gems and Minerals, Museum of Natural History, Washington. It was carved in China in the Chien Lung period (18th century) from jadeite which probably came from Burma. Height 36.6 cm.

2. Rock crystal or clear crystalline quartz was widely used in Asia and in Europe for making vase forms like this 10th-century Egyptian piece in the Freer collection. The crystal vases were often mounted in gold. Height with mounting 15.2 cm. Freer 49.14.

1. The great Flemish painter Peter Paul Rubens owned and admired this elaborately carved vase of honey-colored agate. It is in the collection of the Walters Art Gallery in Baltimore. It is probably Byzantine in origin and dates about A.D. 400. Height 7½ in.   (Courtesy Walters Art Gallery, Baltimore, Md.)

2. A mosaic made of small squares (tessarae) of turquoise decorates the bronze handle of this Chinese ceremonial implement of the Shang period. The blade is of polished nephrite. Overall length 21.3 cm. Freer 41.4.

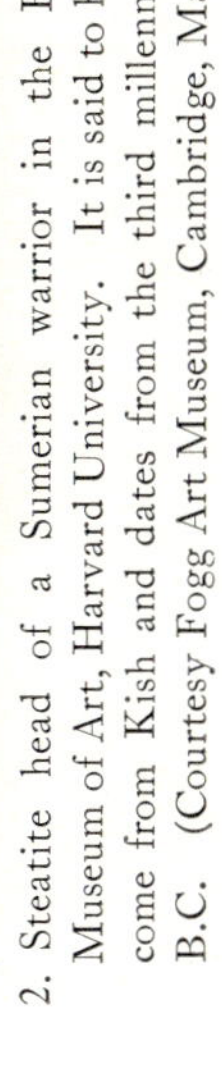

2. Steatite head of a Sumerian warrior in the Fogg Museum of Art, Harvard University. It is said to have come from Kish and dates from the third millennium B.C. (Courtesy Fogg Art Museum, Cambridge, Mass.)

1. This spread-eagle of lapis lazuli probably once served as the finial of a scepter used by a Roman consul as insigne of office. It was found near Naples and now belongs in the collection of the Walters Art Gallery, Baltimore. The eagle stands about 3 in. high. (Courtesy Walters Art Gallery, Baltimore, Md.)

1. The pre-Columbian Indians of Central and South America fashioned native gold into jewelry and ornaments by hammering and casting. This pert-looking bird of cast gold in the Robert Woods Bliss Collection is from Colombia. (Courtesy National Gallery of Art.)

2. One of the most unusual sculpture materials is hematite which was used as the medium for this finely sculptured head of a hippopotamus made in Egypt about the XXVI Dynasty. Height 2.4 cm. (Courtesy Brooklyn Museum.)

1. This head of Abraham Lincoln carved in dark blue sapphire was the first of the series of four Presidents cut in this exceptionally hard mineral. The sculptor, Norman Maness, spent about 14 months carving the stone with diamond tools. Height 2½ in. (Courtesy Kazanjian Foundation, Los Angeles, Calif.)

2. Mosaic is an ancient art form in which the design was made by setting small cubes (tessarae) of stone of different tones and colors into fresh plaster or other bonding agent. The miniature Byzantine mosaic represents St. John Chrysostome. Height 27.7 cm., width 13.2 cm. (Courtesy Dumbarton Oaks Collection, Washington D.C.)

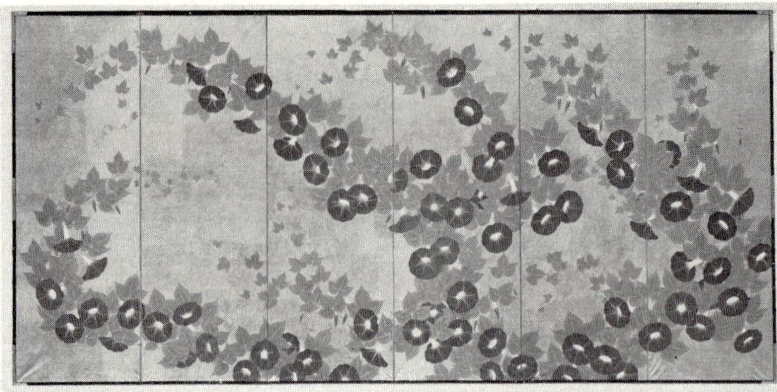

1. This Japanese six-fold screen by Kiitsu Susuki (1796–1858) of *Morning Glories and Leaves* is a splendid example of the use of copper mineral pigments. The deep blue of the flowers is painted with coarsely ground azurite; the bright green of the leaves with malachite. (Courtesy Metropolitan Museum of Art, Seymour Fund, 1954.)

2. Mineral corrosion products of copper add brilliant colors to this Chinese bronze ceremonia vessel of the type *hu* which dates from the second millennium B.C. Dark green areas are malachite; smooth, pale green surface is a thin layer of tin oxide stained with copper; blue is azurite and the red is cuprite. Freer 48.1.

spersed with patches of red cuprous oxide or cuprite. Equally color-ful, but less wanted, is the crystalline green atacamite or basic copper chloride frequently seen on bronzes which have been in contact with the saline soils of desert regions like Egypt and Mesopotamia. Ata-camite-encrusted bronzes sometimes cause alarm in museums because underlying the atacamite and cuprite and next to the metal core is a layer of colorless nantokite or cuprous chloride; nantokite is un-stable, and if the object is exposed for extended periods to humid atmosphere, it is transformed by hydration and oxidation to the end product, atacamite. This behavior is called "bronze disease" and is sometimes troublesome for museum curators since bronzes afflicted with it have to be kept in a dry atmosphere. Most other mineral alteration products on ancient metal objects are ugly and undesirable, including limonite and goethite which form on iron, cerargyrite on silver, and cerussite on lead. Tin in ancient bronzes is transformed by corrosion into a product similar to but not identical with cassiter-ite. The smooth gray-green patina on ancient high-tin Chinese bronzes is mainly this hydrous form of tin oxide stained green with copper impurities.

Occasionally on ancient bronzes one finds deposits of minerals that are quite rare. Some years ago, Prof. Clifford Frondel of the Har-vard Mineralogical Museum observed a peculiar blue-green mineral alteration product on the inside of an Egyptian bronze figurine of a cat-headed deity known as Bast. By X-ray diffraction methods he identified the product as botallackite, a basic copper chloride which many years ago was first found in the Botallack Mine in Cornwall, England. The type specimen in the British Museum was the only other specimen of the mineral known to exist. The present writer and Professor Frondel found on other Egyptian bronze objects a bluish-green double salt of copper and sodium carbonate hitherto unobserved. Since it was formed by natural processes, they gave it the name "chalconatronite" and published its properties and its chemi-cal formula which is $CuCO_3 \cdot Na_2CO_3 \cdot 3H_2O$ [27]. Other rare copper and lead minerals such as cumengite, $Pb_4Cu_4Cl_8(OH)_8 \cdot H_2O$, and phosgenite, $PbCl_2 \cdot PbCO_3$, have been reported as occurring on cor-roded bronzes. The mineral alteration products in ancient metal objects is an interesting field of study in which there is still much to learn.

We have recorded many examples of the importance of minerals to art and have demonstrated that plastic and pictorial art requires a great variety of earthy materials as media of expression. This leads to the thought that a new kind of art exhibit, "Minerals in Art and Art in Minerals," would be a challenging and most interesting innovation.

REFERENCES

1. RICH, JACK C.
     1947. The materials and methods of sculpture. New York.
2. AMERICAN ASSOCIATION OF MUSEUMS.
     1961–63. Tutankhamun treasures. Catalogue of a loan exhibition from
          The Department of Antiquities of the United Arab Republic.
          34 figs.
3. LOTHROP, S. K.; FOSHAG, W. F.; and MAHLER, JOY.
     1957. Catalogue of the Robert Woods Bliss collection of Pre-Columbian
          Art. Text and critical analysis. New York.
4. HOPE, W. H. ST. JOHN.
     1904. On the early working of alabaster in England. Archaeol.
          Journ., vol. 61, pp. 221–240.
5. VICTORIA AND ALBERT MUSEUM.
     1956. English alabasters. 28 plates. London.
6. MIDDLEMISS, F. A.; MOSS, A. A.; and CLARINGBULL, G. F.
     1953. The stone of the ancient Assyrian monumental carvings. Geo-
          logical Magazine, vol. 90, No. 2, p. 141.
7. FOSHAG, WILLIAM F.
     1957. Mineralogical studies on Guatemalan jade. Smithsonian Misc.
          Coll., vol. 135, No. 5.
8. HANSFORD, HOWARD.
     1950. Chinese jade carving. London.
9. KRETCHETOVA, M. N.
     1960. Carved stone of China at the Hermitage Museum. Leningrad.
10. LION-GOLDSCHMIDT, DAISY, and MOREAU-GOBARD, JEAN-CLAUDE.
     1960. Chinese art: Bronze—jade—sculpture—ceramics. New York.
11. VETLESEN, MAUDE M.
     1939–40. Chinese jade carvings of the XVth to the XIXth century in
          the collection of Mrs. George Vetlesen. An illustrated descrip-
          tive record compiled by Stanley Charles Nott. 3 vols. London.
          (Produced for private circulation only.)
12. GORER, EDGAR, and BLACKER, J. F.
     1911. Chinese porcelain and hard stones. 2 vols., 254 color ills. of Chi-
          nese ceramic and glyptic art.   London.
13. LAMM, CARL JAHON.
     1920. Mittelalterliche Gläser und Steinschnittarbeiten aus dem Nahen
          Osten. 2 vols. Berlin.
14. LUCAS, A.
     1948. Ancient Egyptian materials and industries. London.
15. ROSS, MARVIN CHAUNCEY.
     1943. The Reubens vase: its history and date. Journ. Walters Art Gal-
          lery, vol. 6, pp. 9–39.
16. JUDD, NEIL M.
     1954. The material culture of Pueblo Bonito. Smithsonian Misc. Coll.,
          vol. 124. (See pl. 19.)
17. LAUFER, BERTHOLD.
     1913. Notes on turquoise in the East. Field Museum of Natural History,
          Publ. 169, Anthrop. Ser., vol. 13, No. 1.
18. MINER, DOROTHY, and EDELSTEIN, EMMA J.
     1944–45. A carving in lapis lazuli. Journ. Walters Art Gallery, vols.
          7–8, pp. 83–103.

19. SHEPHERD, DOROTHY G.
    1961. An Achaemenid sculpture in lapis lazuli. Cleveland Museum of
        Art Bull. 48, No. 2, pp. 18–25.
20. KERSHAW, FRANCIS STEWART.
    1925. The Mary Hooper Packard collection of amber. Museum of Fine
        Arts, Boston, Bull. 23, pp. 36–37.
21. BABELON, ERNEST.
    1897. Catalogue des cameès antiques et modernes de la Bibliothèque
        Nationale. Paris.
22. EICHLER, FRITZ, and KRIS, ERNST.
    1927. Die Kameen im Kunsthistorisches Museum, Wien.
23. LESLEY, PARKER.
    1960. Handbook of the Lillian Thomas Pratt collection of Russian Im-
        perial jewels. Virginia Museum of Fine Arts, Richmond.
24. CORCORAN GALLERY OF ART.
    1961. Easter eggs and other precious objects by Carl Fabergé. (All
        ills. in color.) Washington, D.C.
25. PORADA, EDITH.
    1948. Corpus of ancient Near Eastern seals in North American collec-
        tions of the Pierpont Morgan Library. Bollingen Series XIV.
        Washington, D.C.   .
26. GETTENS, RUTHERFORD J.
    1950. Lapis lazuli and ultramarine in ancient times. Alumni (Brus-
        sels), vol. 19, pp. 342–357.
27. GETTENS, RUTHERFORD J., and FRONDEL, CLIFFORD.
    1955–56. Chalconatronite: an alteration product on some ancient Egyp-
        tian bronzes. Studies in Conservation, vol. 2, pp. 64–75.

INDEX

A

Abbot, C. G., x

Accessions, 20, 79, 110, 113, 114, 124, 126, 128, 133, 135, 193, 205
    Bureau of American Ethnology, 79
    Freer Gallery of Art, 110, 113, 114
    Library, 205
    National Air Museum, 124, 126, 128
    National Gallery of Art, 193
    National Museum, 20
    National Zoological Park, 133, 135

Adams, Cynthia L., vii

Adams, G. H., 174, 175

Aerobiology, Outdoor (P. H. Gregory), 445

Aero engines, Three famous early (Robert B. Meyer, Jr.), 357

Allen, Brooke, Maj. Gen., USAF, viii

Anderson, Clinton P., regent of the Institution, v, 17, 40, 46

Andrews, A. J., vi

Andronicos, Basil, 45

Anglim, John E., vi, 44

Anthropology, Evolution, genetics, and (A. E. Mourant), 501

Appropriations, 18, 52, 94, 163, 193, 235
    Astrophysical Observatory, 94
    National Gallery of Art, 193
    National Zoological Park, 18, 163, 235
    River Basin Surveys, 18, 52, 235

Art and archeology, Minerals in (Rutherford J. Gettens), 551

Astrophysical Observatory, vii, viii, 81
    Astrophysical Research, Division of, vii, 81
    Buildings and equipment, 94
    Funds available, 94
    Publications, 89, 216
    Radiation and Organisms, Division of, viii, 94
    Report, 81
    Staff, vii, viii, 93
    Table Mountain, Calif., field station, viii, 81

Australopithicines and the origin of man (J. T. Robinson), 479

B

Baker, Thomas G., 34, 42, 44

Bakos, Gustav A., vii, 85, 87

Bales, Richard, 203, 204

Barker, Bert J., 133, 174

Bass, William M., 49

Bassler, R. S., ix

Battison, E. A., vii

Bayer, Frederick M., vi, 33, 42

Beaubien, Paul L., 48

Becklund, W. W., 170

Beggs, Thomas M., Director, National Collection of Fine Arts, viii, 99, 107, 109

Belin, Ferdinand Lammot, viii, 192

Benjamin, C. R., ix

Bennett, Charles F., Jr., 181

Benson, William E. (Drilling beneath the deep sea), 397

Beville, Henry B., 204

Biebighauser, Ernest E., 216

Bishop, P. W., vii

Blake, Doris H., ix

Blake, J. B., vii

Blaker, Mrs. Margaret C., 74

Blanchard, Ruth E., librarian, v, 208

Blest, Andrew, 181

Bliss, Robert Woods, 99

Boardman, Richard S., vi, 35

Bory, Bela S., vii, 44

Bouton, Margaret, 201

Bow, Frank T., regent of the Institution, v, 17, 40

Bowman, T. E., vi

Boyd, Sylvia, 82

Boyle, W. E., vi

Bradley, James C., Assistant Secretary of the Institution, v, 99, 100

Bredin, J. Bruce, ix

Briggs, Robert E., vii, 83

Brink, C. E., 174